Communications in Computer and Information Science 3148

Series Editors

Rationale

The CCIS series is devoted to the publication of proceedings of computer science conferences. Its aim is to efficiently disseminate original research results in informatics in printed and electronic form. While the focus is on publication of peer-reviewed full papers presenting mature work, inclusion of reviewed short papers reporting on work in progress is welcome, too. Besides globally relevant meetings with internationally representative program committees guaranteeing a strict peer-reviewing and paper selection process, conferences run by societies or of high regional or national relevance are also considered for publication.

Topics

The topical scope of CCIS spans the entire spectrum of informatics ranging from foundational topics in the theory of computing to information and communications science and technology and a broad variety of interdisciplinary application fields.

Information for Volume Editors and Authors

Publication in CCIS is free of charge. No royalties are paid, however, we offer registered conference participants temporary free access to the online version of the conference proceedings on SpringerLink (http://link.springer.com) by means of an http referrer from the conference website and/or a number of complimentary printed copies, as specified in the official acceptance email of the event.

CCIS proceedings can be published in time for distribution at conferences or as post-proceedings, and delivered in the form of printed books and/or electronically as USBs and/or e-content licenses for accessing proceedings at SpringerLink. Furthermore, CCIS proceedings are included in the CCIS electronic book series hosted in the SpringerLink digital library at http://link.springer.com/bookseries/7899. Conferences publishing in CCIS are allowed to use our online conference service (Meteor) for managing the whole proceedings lifecycle (from submission and reviewing to preparing for publication) free of charge.

Publication process

The language of publication is exclusively English. Authors publishing in CCIS have to sign the Springer CCIS copyright transfer form, however, they are free to use their material published in CCIS for substantially changed, more elaborate subsequent publications elsewhere. For the preparation of the camera-ready papers/files, authors have to strictly adhere to the Springer CCIS Authors' Instructions and are strongly encouraged to use the CCIS LaTeX style files or templates.

Abstracting/Indexing

CCIS is abstracted/indexed in DBLP, Google Scholar, EI-Compendex, Mathematical Reviews, SCImago, Scopus. CCIS volumes are also submitted for the inclusion in ISI Proceedings.

How to start

To start the evaluation of your proposal for inclusion in the CCIS series, please send an e-mail to ccis@springer.com

Christoph Meinel · Tania Di Mascio ·
Benedict du Boulay · Edmundo Tovar
Editors

Computer Supported Education

17th International Conference, CSEDU 2025
Porto, Portugal, April 1–3, 2025
Revised Selected Papers, Part I

Springer

Editors
Christoph Meinel
German University of Digital Science
Potsdam, Germany

Tania Di Mascio
University of L'Aquila
L'Aquila, Italy

Benedict du Boulay
University of Sussex
Sussex, UK

Edmundo Tovar
Madrid Polytechnic University
Madrid, Spain

ISSN 1865-0929 ISSN 1865-0937 (electronic)
Communications in Computer and Information Science
ISBN 978-3-032-39102-5 ISBN 978-3-032-39103-2 (eBook)
https://doi.org/10.1007/978-3-032-39103-2

This Springer imprint is published by the registered company Springer Nature Switzerland AG
The registered company address is: Gewerbestrasse 11, 6330 Cham, Switzerland

Preface

The present book includes extended and revised versions of selected papers from the 17th International Conference on Computer Supported Education (CSEDU 2025), held in Porto, Portugal, from April 1st to 3rd, 2025, bringing together researchers, practitioners, educators, and innovators from around the world who share a passion for improving education through technology.

Over the years, CSEDU has become much more than a conference—it is a vibrant community where ideas, practices, and visions about the future of learning are exchanged and challenged. The event provides an opportunity to explore the role of digital technologies in education, from pedagogical innovation and adaptive systems to data analytics and AI-driven learning environments.

For the 2025 edition, 245 papers from 47 countries were submitted, reflecting the diversity and vitality of the field. After a thorough double-blind review process, 17% of the submissions were selected for presentation and later invited to submit extended and revised versions for inclusion in this post-proceedings volume. Each invited paper underwent further review and revision, with the requirement of introducing at least 30% of new and original material.

The chapters collected in this book offer a valuable overview of the most recent developments and research directions in Computer Supported Education. They cover a wide spectrum of topics, including Next Generation Teaching and Learning Environments, 21st Century Skills, Emerging Technologies in Education for Sustainable Development, AI Literacy, Adaptive Educational Systems, Engineering Education, Feedback and Learning Support, Active Learning, e-Learning Platforms and Portals, and Intelligent Learning and Teaching Systems.

In the area of Artificial Intelligence in Education, several contributions explore how generative AI—particularly Large Language Models (LLMs)—is reshaping learning and teaching practices. Other papers investigate well-established themes such as knowledge tracing and learning analytics, while a number of review papers reflect on the use of AI in higher education, small and rural schools, and problem-based learning settings.

We would like to express our heartfelt thanks to all authors for their dedication and insightful contributions, and to the reviewers and program committee members for their time, expertise, and commitment to maintaining the quality and integrity of the conference. We also wish to thank the participants who made CSEDU 2025 a lively and inspiring event, reaffirming once again the importance of collaboration in shaping the future of education.

April 2025

Christoph Meinel
Tania Di Mascio
Benedict du Boulay
Edmundo Tovar

Organization

Conference Chair

Christoph Meinel	German University of Digital Science, Germany

Program Co-chairs

Benedict du Boulay	University of Sussex, UK
Tania Di Mascio	University of L'Aquila, Italy
Edmundo Tovar	Technical University of Madrid, Spain

Program Committee

Jorge Acosta	Universidad Distrital Francisco José de Caldas, Colombia
Airil Haimi Mohd Adnan	Universiti Teknologi MARA, Malaysia
Dewan Ahmed	University of North Carolina at Charlotte, USA
Eleftheria Alexandri	Hellenic Open University, Greece
Giora Alexandron	Weizmann Institute of Science, Israel
Arif Altun	Independent Researcher, USA
Francisco Arcega	Universidad de Zaragoza, Spain
Ivon Arroyo	Worcester Polytechnic Institute, USA
Miguel Rodríguez Artacho	Universidad Nacional de Educación a Distancia, Spain
Juan Ignacio Asensio	University of Valladolid, Spain
Breno Azevedo	Instituto Federal de Educação, Ciência e Tecnologia Fluminense, Brazil
Jorge Baptista	Universidade do Algarve, Portugal
Jorge Barbosa	University of Vale do Rio dos Sinos, Brazil
João Barros	Polytechnic Institute of Beja, Portugal
Patrícia Bassani	Universidade Feevale, Brazil
Jesús Berrocoso	University of Extremadura, Spain
Roberto Bittencourt	University of Victoria, Canada
Peter Blanchfield	Nottingham Trent University, UK
Andreas Bollin	Klagenfurt University, Austria
Ivana Bosnic	University of Zagreb, Croatia

Federico Botella	Miguel Hernández University of Elche, Spain
Denis Bouhineau	Grenoble Alpes University, France
Karima Boussaha	University of Oum El Bouaghi, Algeria
Patrice Bouvier	LDLC VR Studio, France
Michael Brückner	Naresuan University, Thailand
Adriana Burlea-Schiopoiu	University of Craiova, Romania
Manuel Caeiro Rodríguez	University of Vigo, Spain
Renza Campagni	Università di Firenze, Italy
Pasquina Campanella	University of Bari "Aldo Moro", Italy
Sanja Candrlic	University of Rijeka, Croatia
Federica Caruso	University of L'Aquila, Italy
Amitava Chatterjee	Jadavpur University, India
António Coelho	Universidade do Porto/INESC TEC, Portugal
Miguel Ángel Conde González	University of León, Spain
Ana-Paula Correia	Ohio State University, USA
Gennaro Costagliola	Università di Salerno, Italy
Manuel Perez Cota	Universidade de Vigo, Spain
Rogério da Silva	University of Roehampton, UK
Francesca Dagnino	Italian National Research Council, Italy
Sergiu Dascalu	University of Nevada, USA
Umberto Dello Iacono	University of Campania "Vanvitelli", Italy
Nicoletta Di Blas	Politecnico di Milano, Italy
Yannis Dimitriadis	University of Valladolid, Spain
Amir Dirin	Metropolia University of Applied Sciences, Finland
Blaženka Divjak	University of Zagreb, Croatia
Toby Dragon	Ithaca College, USA
Gijsbert Erkens	Utrecht University, Netherlands
Larbi Esmahi	Athabasca University, Canada
Vanessa Esteve-Gonzalez	Universitat Rovira i Virgili, Spain
João Esteves	University of Minho, Portugal
Ramon Fabregat Gesa	Universitat de Girona, Spain
Si Fan	University of Tasmania, Australia
Laura Fedeli	University of Macerata, Italy
Richard Ferdig	Kent State University, USA
Márcia Fernandes	Federal University of Uberlândia, Brazil
Angela Fessl	Know Center GmbH, Austria
Cecilia Fissore	University of Turin, Italy
Vittorio Fuccella	Università di Salerno, Italy
Francisco García Peñalvo	University of Salamanca, Spain
Isabela Gasparini	Universidade do Estado de Santa Catarina, Brazil

Henrique Gil	Escola Superior de Educação do Instituto Politécnico de Castelo Branco, Portugal
Jean-Marie Gilliot	IMT Atlantique, CNRS, France
Apostolos Gkamas	University Ecclesiastical Academy of Vella, Greece
Anabela Gomes	Instituto Superior de Engenharia de Coimbra, Portugal
Maria João Gomes	Universidade do Minho, Portugal
Sergio Gómez	University of La Salle, Colombia
Ana González Marcos	Universidad de la Rioja, Spain
Christiane Gresse von Wangenheim	Federal University of Santa Catarina, Brazil
Ani Grubišć	University of Split, Croatia
Christian Gütl	Graz University of Technology, Austria
Yasemin Gülbahar	Ankara University, Türkiye
David Guralnick	Kaleidoscope Learning, USA
Roger Hadgraft	University of Technology Sydney, Australia
Jiangang Hao	Educational Testing Service, USA
Orit Hazzan	Technion Israel Institute of Technology, Israel
Martina Holenko Dlab	University of Rijeka, Croatia
Marcelo da Silva Hounsell	Santa Catarina State University, Brazil
Sébastien Iksal	University of Le Mans, France
Ulas Ilic	Pamukkale University, Türkiye
Dzintra Ilisko	Daugavpils University, Latvia
Tomayess Issa	Curtin University, Australia
Ivan Ivanov	SUNY Empire State University, USA
Malinka Ivanova	Technical University of Sofia, Bulgaria
M. J. C. S. Reis	University of Trás-os-Montes e Alto Douro, Portugal
Hannu-Matti Järvinen	Tampere University, Finland
Stéphanie Jean-Daubias	Université Claude Bernard Lyon 1, LIRIS, France
Yang Jiang	Educational Testing Service, USA
M.-Carmen Juan	Instituto Ai2, Universitat Politècnica de València, Spain
Katerina Kabassi	Ionian University, Greece
Charalampos Karagiannidis	University of Thessaly, Greece
Ilias Karasavvidis	University of Thessaly, Greece
Dragutin Kermek	University of Zagreb, Croatia
ChanMin Kim	Penn State University, USA
Siu Cheung Kong	Education University of Hong Kong, China
Marguerite Koole	College of Education, University of Saskatchewan, Canada
Vitomir Kovanovic	Adelaide University, Australia

Amruth Kumar	Ramapo College of New Jersey, USA
Lam-For Kwok	HKCT Institute of Higher Education, China
Myriam Lamolle	Centre de Génie Industriel, Université de Toulouse, IMT Albi, France
Eitel Lauría	Marist University, USA
Borislav Lazarov	Institute of Mathematics and Informatics, Bulgarian Academy of Sciences, Bulgaria
Chien-Sing Lee	Sunway University, Malaysia
Chul-Hwan Lee	Independent Researcher, USA
Marie Lefevre	University Claude Bernard Lyon 1, France
Andreas Lingnau	German University of Applied Sciences, Germany
Chee-Kit Looi	Education University of Hong Kong, China
Claudio Lucchiari	Università degli Studi di Milano, Italy
Luca Andrea Ludovico	Università degli Studi di Milano, Italy
Maria Marcelino	University of Coimbra, Portugal
Verónica Marín	University of Córdoba, Spain
Lindsay Marshall	Newcastle University, UK
Raúl Marticorena	University of Burgos, Spain
Alejandra Martíinez-Monés	Universidad de Valladolid, Spain
Scheila Martins	Independent Researcher, UK
Khairul Azhar Mat Daud	University Malaysia Kelantan, Malaysia
Bruce Maxim	University of Michigan-Dearborn, USA
Madeth May	Le Mans Université, France
Elvis Mazzoni	University of Bologna, Italy
Víctor Menéndez-Domínguez	Universidad Autónoma de Yucatán, Mexico
Agathe Merceron	Berlin University of Applied Sciences, Germany
Marco Mesiti	University of Milano, Italy
José Carlos Metrôlho	Instituto Politécnico de Castelo Branco, Portugal
Laurent Moccozet	University of Geneva, Switzerland
Andrea Molinari	University of Trento, Italy
Gyöngyvér Molnár	University of Szeged, Hungary
Rafael Morales Gamboa	University of Guadalajara, Mexico
Leonel Morgado	Universidade Aberta, Portugal
Jerzy Moscinski	Silesian University of Technology, Poland
Maria Moundridou	School of Pedagogical and Technological Education (ASPETE), Greece
Antao Moura	Federal University of Campina Grande, Brazil
Maxim Mozgovoy	University of Aizu, Japan
Pedro Mucharreira	University of Lisbon, Portugal
Pablo César Muñoz Carril	Universidad de Santiago de Compostela, Spain
Antoanela Naaji	Vasile Goldiş Western University of Arad, Romania

Minoru Nakayama	Meiji University, Japan
Rosa Navarrete	Escuela Politécnica Nacional, Ecuador
Mai Neo	Multimedia University, Malaysia
Maureen D. Neumann	University of Vermont, USA
Yoshifumi Nishida	Tokyo Institute of Technology, Japan
Omid Noroozi	Wageningen University and Research, Netherlands
Prasart Nuangchalerm	Mahasarakham University, Thailand
Dade Nurjanah	Telkom University, Indonesia
Francesco Orciuoli	University of Salerno, Italy
Ebba Ossiannilsson	Swedish Association for Distance Education, Sweden
Patricia Paderewski Rodríguez	University of Granada, Spain
Stamatios Papadakis	University of Crete, Greece
Kyparisia Papanikolaou	School of Educational and Technological Education (ASPETE), Greece
Marcello Passarelli	National Research Council of Italy, Italy
Paula Peres	ISCAP, Portugal
Donatella Persico	CNR - Italian National Research Council, Italy
Elvira Popescu	University of Craiova, Romania
Francesca Pozzi	CNR - Italian National Research Council, Italy
Andreas Prinz	University of Agder, Norway
Augustin Prodan	Iuliu Hațieganu University of Medicine and Pharmacy, Romania
Yannis Psaromiligkos	University of West Attica, Greece
João Quadros	Centro Federal de Educação Tecnológica Celso Suckow da Fonseca, Brazil
Araceli Queiruga Dios	University of Salamanca, Spain
Ramkumar Rajendran	Indian Institute of Technology Bombay, India
Liana Razmerita	Copenhagen Business School, Denmark
Fernando Ribeiro	Instituto Politécnico de Castelo Branco, Portugal
Leon Rothkrantz	Delft University of Technology, Netherlands
Razvan Rughinis	University "Politehnica" of Bucharest, Romania
Matteo Sacchet	University of Turin, Italy
Jesus Salinas	University of the Balearic Islands, Spain
Juan M. Santos	University of Vigo, Spain
Georg Schneider	Trier University of Applied Sciences, Germany
Wolfgang Schreiner	Johannes Kepler University Linz, Austria
Edgar Seemann	Furtwangen University, Germany
Sabine Seufert	University of St. Gallen, Switzerland
Ramesh C. Sharma	Dr. B. R. Ambedkar University Delhi, India
Pei Hwa Siew	Universiti Tunku Abdul Rahman, Malaysia

Pedro Silva	Independent Researcher, Portugal
Thomas Staubitz	German University of Digital Science, Germany
Krassen Stefanov	Sofia University "St. Kliment Ohridski", Bulgaria
Eliza Stefanova	Sofia University, Bulgaria
Claudia Steinberger	University of Klagenfurt, Austria
Michael Striewe	Trier University of Applied Sciences, Germany
Jun-Ming Su	National University of Tainan, Taiwan
Jaspal Subhlok	University of Houston, USA
Kelvin Sung	University of Washington, Bothell, USA
Irfan Sural	Eskisehir Osmangazi University, Türkiye
Katsuaki Suzuki	Kumamoto University, Japan
Nestori Syynimaa	University of Jyväskylä, Finland
Seng Chee Tan	National Institute of Education, Nanyang Technological University, Singapore
Dorith Tavor	Shamoon College of Engineering, Israel
Dirk Tempelaar	Maastricht University School of Business and Economics, Netherlands
Uwe Terton	Southern Cross University, Australia
Ralf Teusner	Hasso Plattner Institute, Germany
Georgi T. Tuparov	New Bulgarian University, Bulgaria
Marta Turcsányi-Szabó	Eötvös Loránd University, Hungary
Mireia Usart	Universitat Rovira i Virgili, Spain
Aristides Vagelatos	Computer Technology Institute, Greece
Leo van Moergestel	HU Utrecht University of Applied Sciences, Netherlands
Carlos Vaz de Carvalho	ISEP, Portugal
Charles Wallace	Michigan Technological University, USA
Alf Wang	Norwegian University of Science and Technology, Norway
Mary Webb	King's College London, UK
Fridolin Wild	Independent Researcher, UK
Iwan Wopereis	Open University of the Netherlands, Netherlands
Ahmed Mohamed Fahmy Yousef	Sultan Qaboos University, Oman
Thomas Zarouchas	Computer Technology Institute and Press "Diophantus", Greece
Meina Zhu	Wayne State University, USA

Additional Reviewers

Gabriel Badea	University of Craiova, Romania
Emanuele Cavalleri	University of Milan, Italy
Vinh Le	University of Nevada, Reno, USA

Invited Speakers

Carlos Delgado	Universidad Carlos III de Madrid, Spain
Mutlu Cukurova	University College London, UK
Fernando Moreira	Universidade Portucalense, Portugal

Contents

Contrasting Affective Sequence Patterns in Collaborative Problem-Solving: Insights from High- and Low-Performing Groups

Yaping Xu[1], Weitong Guo[1(✉)], Sen Bao[1], and Xiren Tang[2]

[1] School of Educational Technology, Northwest Normal University, Lanzhou, China
{guowt,baosen}@nwnu.edu.cn
[2] Faculty of Education, Beijing Normal University, Beijing, China
xirentang@mail.bnu.edu.cn

Abstract. Understanding how emotions evolve over time within collaborative learning groups is essential for fostering effective interaction and enhancing learning outcomes. This study investigates the affective dynamics of students engaged in online collaborative problem-solving by modelling their valence–arousal state sequences using Hidden Markov Models (HMMs). Specifically, facial behaviour data were collected from 18 student groups and processed through a machine learning pipeline to automatically detect individual emotional valence and arousal levels. Group-level emotional states were then derived using a voting strategy, and HMMs were applied to model the temporal patterns of emotional transitions. Building upon the general comparison between high- and low-performing groups, the study further selected one representative group from each category for case analysis, revealing detailed emotion characteristics. The findings contribute to a more nuanced understanding of emotional changes during collaborative learning and offer valuable guidance for designing adaptive support systems in technology-enhanced learning environments.

Keywords: Collaborative Problem-Solving · Affective Dynamics · Machine Learning · Hidden Markov Model · Case Analysis

1 Introduction

Collaborative problem solving (CPS), recognized as a key 21st-century skill, is a prevalent form of collaborative learning in higher education and plays a vital role in promoting active learning. It involves two or more students working together to share knowledge and skills in order to solve open-ended, ill-structured problems [1]. Increasingly, researchers acknowledge that students' affective states significantly influence the effectiveness of online CPS, interacting with cognitive processes to shape learning outcomes. For example, Mandler claims that students' emotional reactions and physiological experiences caused by challenges and obstacles are closely related to problem-solving [2]. According to Mayer [3], non-cognitive factors such as individual emotions and motivations, together with cognitive factors such as knowledge and strategies, influence the problem-solving process.

C. Meinel et al. (Eds.): CSEDU 2025, CCIS 3148, pp. 1–13, 2027.
https://doi.org/10.1007/978-3-032-39103-2_1

While the importance of affect in collaborative problem solving is well recognized, capturing learners' emotional states in real time—particularly in online settings—remains a significant challenge. Traditional approaches such as self-report questionnaires or manual observation are often limited by subjectivity, time delays, and lack of scalability. In response, recent advances in affective computing and learning analytics have enabled the automatic detection of emotions using non-intrusive methods such as facial expression analysis, voice signals, and physiological data. Among these, computer vision techniques based on facial behaviours recognition offer a promising, low-cost solution for identifying emotional state continuously and unobtrusively in CPS environments [4]. By leveraging the dimensional emotion model proposed by Russell [5], which posits that all emotions can be described along two dimensions—valence (ranging from negative to positive) and arousal (ranging from relaxed to excited)—researchers are able to trace affective trajectories over time and gain deeper insights into how emotions evolve and interact with cognitive and social processes during collaboration.

Our previous work leveraged machine learning techniques to achieve automatic recognition of students' emotions and applied Hidden Markov Models (HMMs) to reveal group-level affective sequence patterns derived from valence–arousal states in high- and low-performing CPS groups [6]. The use of these methods allowed us to model the temporal dynamics of emotional states and identify distinct transition patterns across performance levels. However, that study primarily focused on aggregated group-level data, potentially masking individual differences and intra-group emotional divergence during collaboration.

Therefore, the present study extends the original work by incorporating a case-based analysis of one high-performing and one low-performing group. In addition to modeling group-level affective sequences using HMMs, we further examine individual-level emotional state distributions. This extension not only enriches the understanding of affective dynamics in CPS, but also offers deeper insights into the emotional patterns exhibited by groups with different performance levels.

2 Literature Review

2.1 Emotions in Collaborative Problem-Solving Activities

CPS is a complex, multidimensional process in which learners work together to share perspectives and integrate their knowledge, skills, and efforts to find solutions [7, 8]. During this process, differing viewpoints often emerge, potentially leading to conflict. Consequently, participants may exhibit a wide range of emotional responses. Both individual and group-level emotional states play a critical role in shaping behaviours and interactions within the collaborative setting [9].

From the perspective of dimensional emotion theory, students participating in collaborative groups experience varying levels of valence and arousal, which in turn influence their learning processes and outcomes. Prior research has shown that valence is associated with cognitive flexibility, perceptual processing, and creative problem-solving [10], while arousal plays a key role in regulating attention and cognitive performance [11]. Since these two dimensions shape emotional responses and directly impact learning, it is essential to examine each component in depth to understand how they are expressed and how they affect educational experiences. In the context of collaborative learning, negative emotions have been linked to disengagement and social loafing, whereas deactivated positive emotions (e.g., calm) are positively associated with group interaction. In contrast, deactivated negative emotions (e.g., fatigue) tend to undermine group dynamics [12].

In conclusion, the emotions that consistently emerge during collaborative group interactions play a crucial role in shaping the learning process [13]. When individuals engage in group work, their affective states often become aligned, leading to shared and interactive emotional experiences. However, research on the dynamic evolution of group-level emotional patterns remains limited.

2.2 Facial Expression-Based Methods for Student Emotion Recognition

Owing to their ease of acquisition, non-invasiveness, and cost-effectiveness, facial expressions have been widely recognized as a primary source for automatically measuring emotions, as a substantial proportion of emotional and attitudinal information can be discerned through these expressions [14]. According to Lek and Teo, there are two main approaches for recognizing students' emotions based on facial expressions [15]: (1) training emotion recognition models using deep neural networks—for example, Savchenko et al. developed lightweight models based on convolutional neural network (CNN) architectures to extract emotional features from facial images [16]; and (2) constructing models using hand-crafted features—for instance, Zatarain Cabada et al. applied a geometric-based method to extract facial features, which were then fed into machine learning classifiers to detect and respond to students' emotional states [17].

The first approach has the advantage of directly using raw facial images or videos as model input, which often leads to high emotion recognition accuracy. However, it typically demands large-scale training datasets and offers limited interpretability. In contrast, the second approach—which emphasizes the design and extraction of facial features—generally requires fewer samples and allows for greater transparency in how predictions are made. Given the limited sample size available for training deep neural networks in this study, the feature-based method was considered more appropriate.

2.3 Analysis Methods for Sequence Data

Sequence analysis methods are increasingly employed to examine longitudinal data involving multiple independent subjects. In the field of education, various studies have applied sequence-based analytical techniques to uncover patterns within learning processes. For instance, lag sequential analysis has been widely used to investigate temporal patterns of group learning engagement [18, 19]. However, this method is limited in its ability to capture interconnections across multiple dimensions. In contrast, Hidden Markov Models (HMMs) offer the advantage of extracting simplified latent states and modeling their transition relationships, while also accommodating multi-channel data, making them a more powerful tool for analyzing complex emotional or behavioral sequences.

In a Hidden Markov Model, sequence data consist of observed states that are treated as probabilistic functions of underlying hidden states. These hidden states are not directly observable but can be inferred from the sequence of observed outputs. The transition probabilities between hidden states capture the temporal dynamics of the process. When applied to multi-channel data, HMM assumes a shared latent structure across all channels. Even in the presence of missing data in some channels, the model remains robust and can operate without requiring imputation. Given these strengths, HMM is particularly well-suited for analyzing two-channel valence–arousal data in this study. It offers the potential to capture the interplay between the two emotional dimensions and to model their evolution over time.

3 Methodology

3.1 Participants

This study involved 54 undergraduate students (46 females and 8 males), aged between 20 and 25, all from the same normal university in Beijing, China. The participants came from a range of academic disciplines, including educational technology, psychology, statistics, and physics. They were divided into 18 groups according to their respective majors.

3.2 Learning Activity and Procedure

Each group was instructed to complete an online collaborative problem-solving task themed "Migration of Migrant Workers", which involved predicting population trends while considering multiple influencing variables. Prior to the activity, all students were informed about the study's purpose, procedures, and their right to withdraw at any time. Additionally, the researchers assured participants that all collected data would be kept strictly confidential and used solely for research purposes.

The procedure of the activity is illustrated in Fig. 1. At the outset, the researcher introduced the objectives, steps, and requirements of the collaborative task. Each participant was instructed to install Open Broadcaster Software (OBS), a cross-platform, open-source tool commonly used for video recording. During the session, each group was allotted 120 min to complete the task in a designated Tencent Meeting room, where they collaboratively produced a written report of approximately 1,000 words outlining their proposed solutions. Simultaneously, participants were required to use OBS to record their facial behaviors throughout the activity. The video recordings were configured with a frame rate of 20 frames/s and a resolution of 512×288. Upon completion of the task, participants were asked to complete a post-test and annotate their recorded videos.

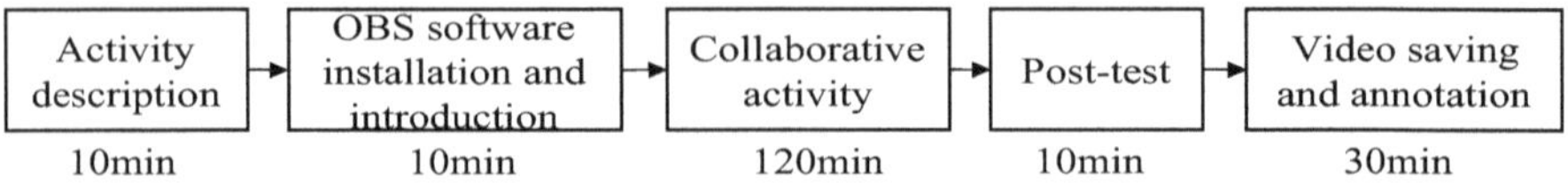

Fig. 1. The process of the collaborative problem-solving activity [6].

After completing the learning task, each group member was required to upload their recorded video to a designated cloud storage platform. The researchers then downloaded and trimmed the videos into 20-min segments, which were returned to the respective students for annotation. Using a dedicated annotation tool, students played their own video clips, during which a pop-up window appeared every 30 s, presenting valence and arousal items rated on a 5-point Likert scale (see Fig. 2). To ensure annotation reliability, students were instructed to rate each 30-s segment immediately, based on their emotional state at that moment. This real-time annotation approach was designed to minimize memory bias and improve rating accuracy. All timestamps and corresponding affective labels were automatically saved in a CSV file.

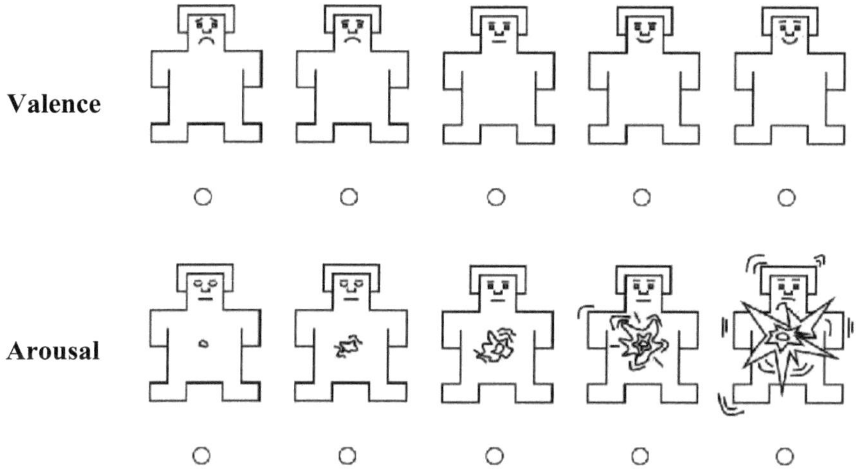

Fig. 2. A scale used to assess affective valence and arousal [20].

3.3 Data Collection and Preprocessing

Papers submitted were used to measure the group's performance. Each paper contained the group's solution to three experimental problems: (1) Based on the materials and data provided, a multiple regression model was constructed to predict the change of population in a city from 2023 to 2028; (2) The reasons for the result in (1) were given; (3) Put forward effective measures to attract the young people to the city. To measure the group performance, the researchers developed the scoring rubric according to the mathematical abilities [21]. Four components were included in the rubric: typography, model building, application, and testing. Each component was given a score ranging from 0 to 5, and the sum of all component scores determined the paper's final score. All papers were rated by two researchers who have acquired training in using a scoring rubric. Then, we ranked the groups from high to low based on the mean scores of their papers. In line with prior studies [22], groups that scored in the top 27% were divided into the high-performing (HP) groups (N = 5) and those that scored in the bottom 27% were low-performing (LP) groups (N = 5).

As previously noted, group members' facial behaviours were video-recorded during the collaborative task, and participants later annotated the valence and arousal levels of selected segments from their own recordings to train the machine learning model. A total of 53 students (with one participant withdrawing from the annotation task) provided 4,240 self-reports. These reports were aligned with the corresponding video segments using saved timestamps, and the recordings were divided into 30-s clips, resulting in 4,240 annotated segments—each labelled with both valence and arousal values.

Statistical analysis revealed that video clips with extremely low or high valence-arousal levels were infrequently observed. To achieve a more balanced label distribution, the original five-level ratings were consolidated into three categories: low/negative, medium/neutral, and high/positive. Figure 3 illustrates the distribution of valence and arousal labels after this reclassification. Despite the grouping, the data remained imbalanced, which could lead to biased predictions by machine learning models due to the underrepresentation of minority classes. To address this issue, the SMOTE-Tomek method was applied to mitigate the class imbalance [23].

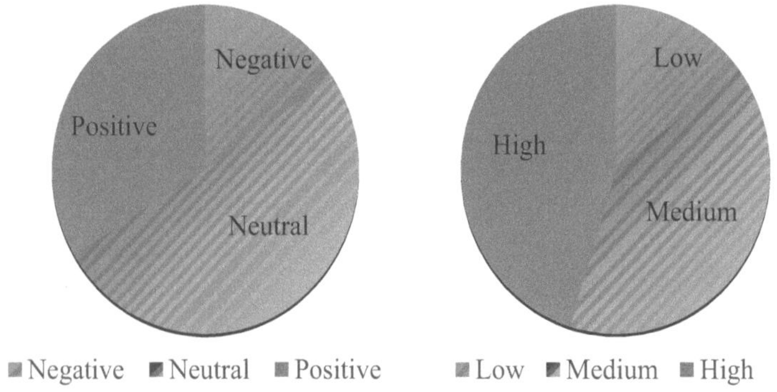

Fig. 3. The distribution of data with different labels in valence and arousal [6].

3.4 Emotion Modeling with Machine Learning

Following data preprocessing, a three-step pipeline—feature extraction, feature selection, and model training—was employed to develop the valence and arousal evaluation models. Facial features were first extracted from the students' video clips using the open-source tool OpenFace 2.0. Subsequently, a feature selection technique was applied to identify the optimal subset from the original feature set. Based on the selected features, six machine learning classification algorithms—k-nearest neighbor (KNN), decision tree (DT), naïve Bayes (NB), support vector machine (SVM), logistic regression (LR), and random forest (RF)—were used to train the valence and arousal detection models. The performance of these algorithms was evaluated using precision, recall, F1-score, and overall accuracy.

Once the best classification model is determined, it can be used to automatically detect each student's affective valence (i.e., positive, neutral, negative) and arousal level (i.e., high, medium, low) at each 30-s clip. The group's valence and arousal level were then measured at each 30-s clip through the use of a voting strategy. For instance, the group is high-level arousal if two or three members are. Note that the group's label is classified as medium level in cases where three members have inconsistent labels.

3.5 Hidden Markov Model

For each group, two separate sequences were ultimately obtained to represent the temporal dynamics of valence and arousal levels, respectively. These time-dependent processes were modeled using a Hidden Markov Model (HMM) within a statistical and probabilistic framework. The HMM approach was applied to describe a Markov chain with latent, unobserved parameters, uncover hidden emotional states embedded in the sequences, and capture the transition patterns between those states [24]. Compared to other sequence analysis techniques (e.g., lag sequential analysis), HMM is particularly effective in modeling multi-channel sequence data.

In this study, the seqHMM package in R [25] was employed to analyze the two-channel valence–arousal data and to construct separate HMMs for the HP and LP groups. The Expectation-Maximization (EM) algorithm, with 100 iterations, was used to fit and estimate the model parameters for both groups. The optimal number of hidden states in each HMM was determined using the Bayesian Information Criterion (BIC). Specifically, we tested models with a pre-defined number of hidden states ranging from 2 to 8, and selected the configuration with the lowest BIC value, indicating the best model fit. In addition, the seqHMM package was used to visualize the inferred latent structures and transition patterns for both groups through graphical representations of hidden states and their dynamics.

4 Results and Discussion

4.1 Performance Analysis of Machine Learning Models

For each 30-s video segment, a total of 62 facial features were extracted using OpenFace 2.0, encompassing three categories of facial behavior: facial action units, eye gaze, and head posture. Following feature selection, 19 features were retained for valence modeling and 20 for arousal modeling. To reduce the risk of overfitting, 80% of the data was randomly assigned to the training set, while the remaining 20% was reserved for validation. The training and validation sets were mutually exclusive to ensure evaluation integrity. Additionally, ten-fold cross-validation was employed during training to assess model performance more reliably.

The indicators calculated by different machine learning algorithms are shown in Table 1. It can be seen that RF (Random Forest) is superior to other algorithms in all metrics, with accuracy of 0.72 and 0.73 in the valence and arousal dimensions, respectively, indicating that the RF model is the best-performing model overall. The results of this study show that it is feasible and effective to use computer vision technology to automatically identify students' affective valence and arousal levels during collaborative learning. Therefore, the trained RF model was applied to measure the remaining video clips for subsequent analysis.

Table 1. Classification results of different models in valence and arousal dimension

Emotional Dimension	Model	Precision	Recall	F1-score	Accuracy
Valence	KNN	0.63	0.63	0.63	0.67
	LR	0.62	0.63	0.62	0.65
	NB	0.51	0.45	0.47	0.60
	DT	0.56	0.56	0.57	0.61
	SVM	0.69	0.61	0.63	0.69
	RF	**0.70**	**0.67**	**0.68**	**0.72**
Arousal	KNN	0.67	0.70	0.68	0.69
	LR	0.56	0.53	0.54	0.62
	NB	0.53	0.51	0.52	0.61
	DT	0.54	0.55	0.54	0.59
	SVM	0.69	0.59	0.62	0.66
	RF	**0.72**	**0.73**	**0.73**	**0.73**

4.2 Sequential Patterns of Affective Valence and Arousal Between the HP and LP Groups

The RF model was used to detect students' affective valence (positive, neutral, negative) and arousal level (high, medium, low) in 30-s steps. For each dimension, a 2-h learning activity was able to generate 240 values. With the video start time of group members aligned, a voting strategy was used to determine group-level valence and arousal levels in each 30-s clip based on members' emotional responses. In order to mine the hidden states and state transition patterns that cannot be observed in sequence data, HMM was used in this study. We set 2 to 8 states to fit the HMM models to the data and used the BIC to determine which model best fits the data, with lower values indicating better model fits (see Fig. 4). It was found that the 4-state model best fit the data for both HP (BIC 9537.63) and LP groups (BIC 10059.29).

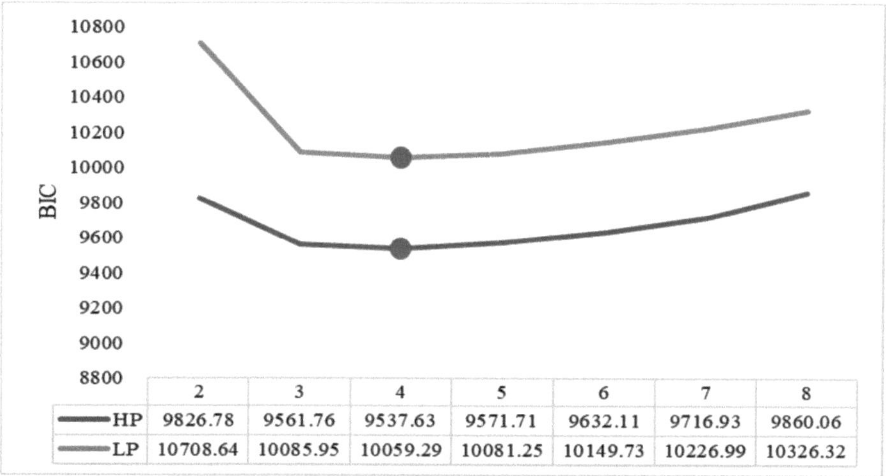

	2	3	4	5	6	7	8
HP	9826.78	9561.76	9537.63	9571.71	9632.11	9716.93	9860.06
LP	10708.64	10085.95	10059.29	10081.25	10149.73	10226.99	10326.32

Fig. 4. Model fit (BIC) for 2 through 8 states [6].

The structure of the best-fitting HMM was plotted in Fig. 5. The pies stand for the hidden states and the slices represent the probabilities of the observed states within each hidden state. The labels below represent codes observed from both dimensions at the same time (probability <0.05 not shown). The arrows between pies represent the transition direction and probabilities, the greater the arrow's thickness, the higher the probability. The results of the HMMs revealed different sequential patterns in learning emotions between the HP and LP groups. Specifically, while the initial state for both the HP and LP groups was neutral valence and medium-level arousal, the HP groups showed a greater possibility of transitioning to the second state, in which participants experienced a higher level of arousal. It was also easier for the HP groups to go from their last state to their third one. In other words, negative emotions with medium-level arousal of students from the HP groups were more easily transferred to positive emotions with high arousal. Moreover, the second state and the fourth state in the LP group had a greater probability of moving to each other.

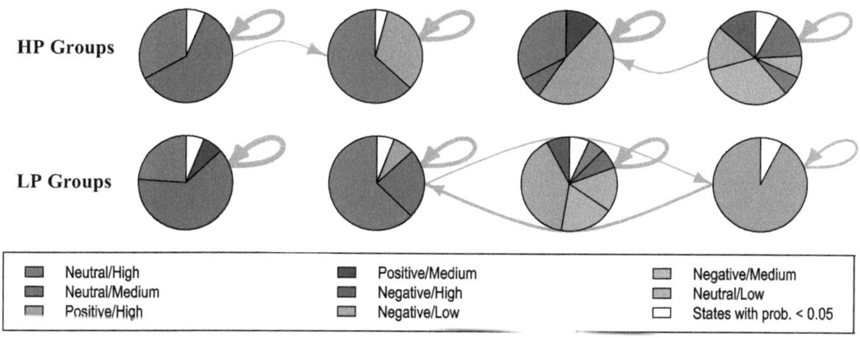

Fig. 5. The HMM results of HP and LP groups [6].

4.3 Case Study: Unpacking Affective Differences in Depth

To gain a deeper understanding of affective patterns beyond aggregate comparisons, we conducted a case study analysis of one HP group and one LP group. The focus was placed on the proportional distribution of affective valence (positive, neutral, negative) and arousal (high, medium, low) during their collaborative problem-solving sessions, the result is shown in Fig. 6.

For the HP group, the emotional landscape was largely dominated by neutral valence (74.0%), followed by positive valence (26.0%), with no negative valence observed. In terms of arousal, the HP group displayed a remarkably high proportion of high arousal states (72.9%), with the remainder falling into the medium arousal category (27.1%), and no instances of low arousal detected. This pattern suggests a group that maintained relatively stable emotional valence while sustaining high levels of engagement and activation throughout the task.

In contrast, the LP group exhibited a more diversified and less optimal affective profile. Neutral valence remained dominant (66.3%), but the proportion of positive valence was slightly lower (23.6%), and notably, negative valence appeared in 10.1% of the time slices. In the arousal dimension, although high arousal was still the most frequent state (56.2%), it was substantially lower than in the HP group. The LP group also demonstrated a higher percentage of medium arousal (36.7%) and a non-negligible proportion of low arousal (7.1%), indicating possible disengagement or lack of sustained cognitive effort during the task.

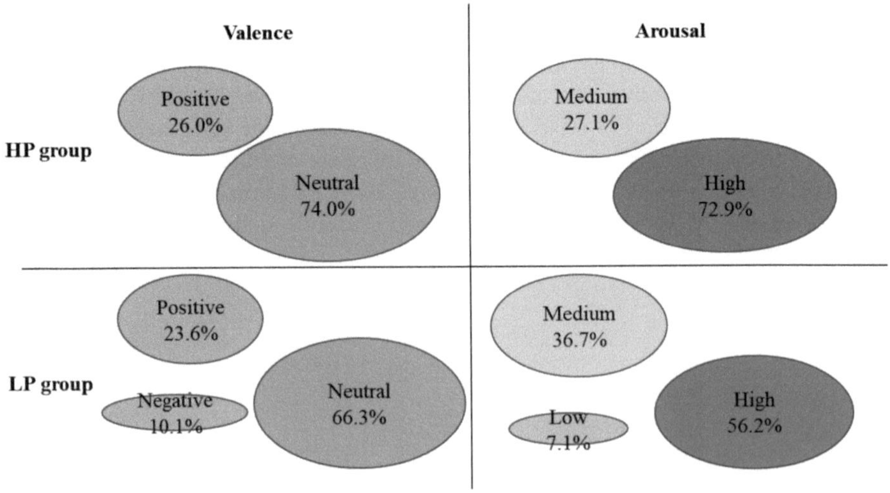

Fig. 6. Comparative affective profiles of HP and LP groups

Continuing the analysis at the individual level (see Fig. 7), members of the HP group exhibited consistent emotional patterns, characterized by high arousal and neutral-to-positive valence, with minimal emotional variation across students. In the LP group, however, students showed greater emotional divergence: some exhibited elevated negative valence or low arousal, while others maintained relatively positive states, reflecting weaker emotional alignment. This affective fragmentation likely disrupted collaborative focus and cohesion.

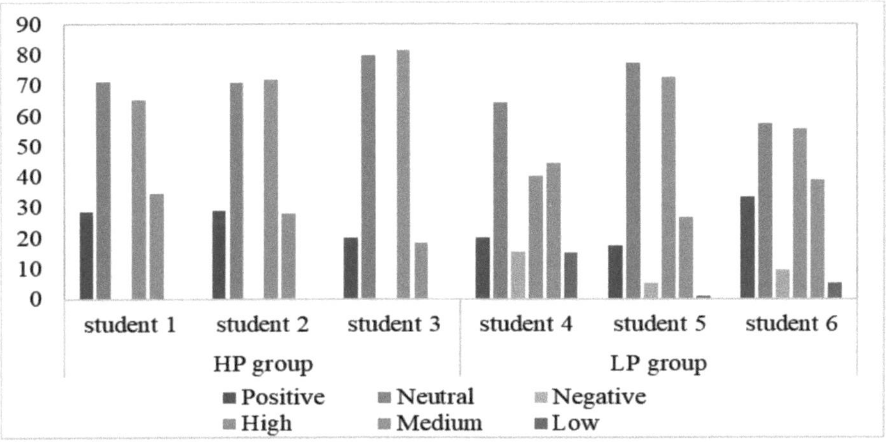

Fig. 7. Student-level valence and arousal distributions

5 Conclusion and Future Work

Learning emotions are closely tied to students' cognitive engagement and academic achievement, making them a central focus in educational research. However, the complexity of online learning environments and the limitations of traditional observation-based methods present challenges for accurately and non-invasively identifying learners' affective states. To address this issue, the present study employed computer vision techniques to automatically detect emotional valence and arousal from students' facial behaviours. In addition, we used HMMs to identify distinct affective sequence patterns between HP and LP groups: high-performing groups were more likely to transition into emotionally productive states, whereas low-performing groups exhibited greater emotional variability, including more frequent occurrences of low arousal and negative valence. To further interpret these differences, we conducted a case study comparing one HP and one LP group, analysing both group-level emotional distributions and the affective profiles of individual members. The HP group showed strong affective coherence, with members consistently maintaining high arousal and positive-to-neutral valence, while the LP group demonstrated emotional divergence and signs of misalignment that may have hindered effective collaboration. These findings highlight the effectiveness of facial-based affect recognition combined with temporal modeling in analyzing emotional dynamics during collaborative learning.

Despite these contributions, several limitations remain. First, the study relied solely on facial video data, which provides useful cues but does not represent the complete spectrum of emotional expression. Future research should incorporate multimodal data sources—such as voice, gesture, posture, and physiological signals—to improve model robustness and affect detection accuracy. Second, the models were trained and tested within a specific collaborative task context, which may limit generalizability. Expanding the scope to include varied learning tasks and environments will help validate and refine the approach. Additionally, further exploration of feedback mechanisms based on affective state detection could bridge the gap between emotion awareness and actionable pedagogical strategies.

Acknowledgments. This work was supported by the National Natural Science Foundation of China (Grant No: 62267008), the Science and Technology Plan Project of Gansu (Grant No: 23JRZA407).

References

1. Hmelo-Silver, C.E., DeSimone, C.: Problem-based learning: an instructional model of collaborative learning. In: The International Handbook of Collaborative Learning, pp. 370–385. Routledge (2013)
2. Mandler, G.: Affect and learning: causes and consequences of emotional interactions. In: Affect and Mathematical Problem Solving: A New Perspective, pp. 3–19. Springer, New York, NY (1989)
3. Mayer, R.E.: Cognitive, metacognitive, and motivational aspects of problem solving. Instr. Sci. **26**, 49–63 (1998). https://doi.org/10.1023/A:1003088013286
4. Hayashi, Y.: Detecting collaborative learning through emotions: an investigation using facial expression recognition. In: Intelligent Tutoring Systems: 15th International Conference, pp. 89–98. Springer International Publishing (2019). https://doi.org/10.1007/978-3-030-22244-4_12
5. Russell, J.A.: A circumplex model of affect. J. Pers. Soc. Psychol. **39**(6), 1161 (1980). https://doi.org/10.1037/h0077714
6. Xu, Y., et al.: Hidden Markov models to capture sequential patterns of valence-arousal in high- and low-performing collaborative problem-solving groups. In: Proceedings of the 17th International Conference on Computer Supported Education, pp. 173–179 (2025). https://doi.org/10.5220/0013038900003932
7. Hmelo-Silver, C.E.: Problem-based learning: what and how do students learn? Educ. Psychol. Rev. **16**, 235–266 (2004). https://doi.org/10.1023/B:EDPR.0000034022.16470.f3
8. Fiore, S.M., et al.: Collaborative Problem Solving: Considerations for the National Assessment of Educational Progress. National Center for Education Statistics, Alexandria, VA (2017)
9. Schunk, D.H., Zimmerman, B.J.: Motivation and Self-Regulated Learning: Theory, Research, and Applications. Routledge (2012)
10. Isen, A.M.: On the relationship between affect and creative problem solving. In: Affect, Creative Experience, and Psychological Adjustment, pp. 3–17. Routledge (2015)
11. Critchley, H.D., Eccles, J., Garfinkel, S.N.: Interaction between cognition, emotion, and the autonomic nervous system. In: Handbook of Clinical Neurology, vol. 117, pp. 59–77 (2013). https://doi.org/10.1016/B978-0-444-53491-0.00006-7
12. Linnenbrink-Garcia, L., Rogat, T.K., Koskey, K.L.: Affect and engagement during small group instruction. Contemp. Educ. Psychol. **36**(1), 13–24 (2011). https://doi.org/10.1016/j.cedpsych.2010.09.001

13. Baker, M., Andriessen, J., Järvelä, S.: Affective Learning Together: Social and Emotional Dimensions of Collaborative Learning. Routledge, Abingdon, England (2013)
14. Mehrabian, A., Russell, J.A.: An Approach to Environmental Psychology. The MIT Press (1974)
15. Lek, J.X.-Y., Teo, J.: Academic emotion classification using FER: a systematic review. Hum. Behav. Emerg. Technol. **2023**(1), 9790005 (2023). https://doi.org/10.1155/2023/9790005
16. Savchenko, A.V., Savchenko, L.V., Makarov, I.: Classifying emotions and engagement in online learning based on a single facial expression recognition neural network. IEEE Trans. Affect. Comput. **13**(4), 2132–2143 (2022). https://doi.org/10.1109/TAFFC.2022.3188390
17. Zatarain Cabada, R., Barrón Estrada, M.L., Ríos Félix, J.M., Alor Hernández, G.: A virtual environment for learning computer coding using gamification and emotion recognition. Interact. Learn. Environ. **28**(8), 1048–1063 (2020). https://doi.org/10.1080/10494820.2018.1558256
18. Hou, H.T., Sheng-Yi, W.: Analyzing the social knowledge construction behavioral patterns of an online synchronous collaborative discussion instructional activity using an instant messaging tool: a case study. Comput. Educ. **57**, 1459–1468 (2011). https://doi.org/10.1016/j.compedu.2011.02.012
19. Tao, Y., Zhang, M., Su, Y., Li, Y.: Exploring college English language learners' social knowledge construction and socio-emotional interactions during computer-supported collaborative writing activities. Asia Pac. Educ. Res. **31**, 613–622 (2022). https://doi.org/10.1007/s40299-021-00612-7
20. Bradley, M.M., Lang, P.J.: Measuring emotion: the self-assessment manikin and the semantic differential. J. Behav. Ther. Exp. Psychiatry. **25**(1), 49–59 (1994)
21. Medová, J., Bulková, K.O., Čeretková, S.: Relations between generalization, reasoning and combinatorial thinking in solving mathematical open-ended problems within mathematical contest. Mathematics. **8**(12), 2257 (2020). https://doi.org/10.3390/math8122257
22. Kelley, T.L.: The selection of upper and lower groups for the validation of test items. J. Educ. Psychol. **30**(1), 17 (1939). https://doi.org/10.1037/h0057123
23. Swana, E.F., Doorsamy, W., Bokoro, P.: Tomek link and SMOTE approaches for machine fault classification with an imbalanced dataset. Sensors. **22**(9), 3246 (2022). https://doi.org/10.3390/s22093246
24. Eddy, S.R.: Hidden Markov models. Curr. Opin. Struct. Biol. **6**(3), 361–365 (1996). https://doi.org/10.1016/S0959-440X(96)80056-X
25. Helske, S., Helske, J.: Mixture hidden Markov models for sequence data: the SeqHMM package in R. J. Stat. Softw. **88**(3), 1–32 (2019). https://doi.org/10.18637/jss.v088.i03

The Remote Virtual Computer Networks Labs: On the Concept and Development of a Browser-Based Software as a Service Computer Networks Lab

Henry-Norbert Cocos(✉), Christian Baun, Martin Kappes, Malte Koch, and Maurizio Petrozziello

Department of Computer Science and Engineering, Frankfurt University of Applied Sciences, Nibelungenplatz 1, Frankfurt am Main 60318, Germany
{cocos,christianbaun,kappes,maltekoch,petrozziello}@fra-uas.de

Abstract. This paper presents an innovative browser-based platform for virtual computer networking labs in higher education. The SKILL/VL platform enables even non-experts to flexibly and easily create and use complex IT infrastructures, which is especially beneficial for foundational courses such as computer networks, IT security, and distributed systems. The system is based entirely on open-source technologies, notably Proxmox VE and CEPH, and features an intuitive web-based user interface. The platform is highly scalable, easily accessible, and significantly reduces the setup and maintenance effort compared to traditional physical labs. Additionally, the paper introduces a concept for integrating and migrating workloads between physical and virtual environments to realize hybrid labs. The latest version of the user interface incorporates state-of-the-art accessibility standards. Practical use cases and evaluation results from university teaching demonstrate the platform's advantages and capabilities.

Keywords: Virtual Teaching · Proxmox VE · CEPH · Teaching Computer Science · Asynchronous Teaching · Hybrid Laboratories · Workload Migration · Accessible Web-UI

1 Introduction

The COVID-19 pandemic underscored the pressing need for digital transformation, especially in the field of education, where adaptable and high-quality teaching solutions have become indispensable. The combination of innovative classroom instruction and digital offerings depends on IT infrastructures that are both user-friendly and able to respond flexibly to evolving requirements.

Modern digital technologies are enhancing university-level teaching, for example by integrating online assessments and multimedia, which supplement traditional lecture-based approaches [11]. Various strategies now include digital

C. Meinel et al. (Eds.): CSEDU 2025, CCIS 3148, pp. 14–42, 2027.
https://doi.org/10.1007/978-3-032-39103-2_2

teaching formats and online courses [6], with important factors being the appropriateness of specific courses, thoughtful content selection, and the integration of digital components [12].

Although learning management systems such as Moodle proficiently handle administrative and organizational tasks, such as participant registration, they do not provide sufficient support for practical, location-independent laboratory work. There is an apparent demand for virtual teaching platforms that extend learning opportunities beyond physical classrooms, allowing for more flexible educational experiences. However, existing solutions offer only limited capabilities when it comes to the design and use of intricate IT infrastructures.

This paper responds to these challenges by presenting a platform designed for intuitive setup and management of complex IT environments using virtualization technologies. The described platform caters even to users with a minimal technical background. It details its architecture, features, scalability, and security aspects, while demonstrating its practical use in academic contexts and highlighting potential directions for future development.

2 Background and Related Works

Digital infrastructure projects in academia are not a new phenomenon. Significant initiatives like Fed4FIRE+ [19] and SLICES-RI [8] provide large-scale testbeds for research in networking and cloud-to-edge computing. Fed4FIRE+ established the world's largest federation of Next Generation Internet testbeds, offering open, reliable facilities for experimental research. At the same time, SLICES-RI focuses on creating a sustainable, pan-European infrastructure for advanced digital infrastructure research. However, both projects are primarily oriented toward research applications rather than addressing the specific needs of higher education teaching environments.

In the realm of network education, a variety of tools have become popular. Cisco's Packet Tracer [1] is widely used and recognized for its intuitive drag-and-drop interface for modeling network topologies in a virtual environment. However, it is inherently bound to Cisco hardware. Mininet [14], often used for software-defined network simulation and protocol analysis, provides a programmable environment for emulating real network traffic with scalability for hundreds of nodes, but lacks a user-friendly (graphic) interface, making it less approachable for some students. GNS3 [10] is another platform that combines real and virtual network devices, supporting complex, real-world networking labs. However, it is mainly confined to network-specific scenarios and is less extensible for broader computing applications.

Dietz's work [9] on a virtual lab for cyber security presented an innovative academic work exploring the use of cloud-based design tools, such as the IONOS Data Center Designer, for constructing virtual training labs with visual (drag-and-drop) configuration capabilities. However, implementations relying on external cloud service providers introduce disadvantages such as increased operational costs and limited control over the educational infrastructure. The

SKILL/VL platform was developed to directly address these issues by leveraging open-source components on institutional hardware, thus ensuring extensibility, cost-effectiveness, and complete in-house control over virtual lab environments.

3 Designing a Virtual Lab

The decision to design a virtual lab to simulate networking scenarios stems from the necessity of extending the physical lab for computer networks since the physical lab only has space for a maximum number of 24 students in a class. Another reason for designing such a virtual lab stems from the experiences during the COVID-19 pandemic. Asynchronous teaching methods using digital platforms were a pivotal element for teaching in higher education during that period and essential for successfully implementing courses without the need for face-to-face teaching. The use of a virtual teaching platform is beneficial out of logic reasons like:

The choice to develop a virtual lab for simulating networking scenarios was driven primarily by the limited capacity of the physical computer networks lab, which can accommodate only up to 24 students per class. Additionally, the experiences gained during the COVID-19 pandemic highlighted the critical role of asynchronous teaching methods supported by digital platforms in higher education. These methods proved essential for delivering courses effectively without requiring in-person attendance. The adoption of a virtual teaching platform offers several logical advantages, including:

- **Time and Location-Independent Offers:** Increasing housing costs in metropolitan areas make it difficult for students to live near their universities. Many students endure long commutes to attend their preferred institutions. Partial virtualization of courses helps mitigate these challenges by enabling access to education regardless of physical location.
- **Improving Collaboration Capabilities:** Virtualization enables collaboration scenarios that would be challenging otherwise, such as students from partner universities working together on joint projects. For example, in fields like computer science, lab environments can be virtually connected over large geographical distances, including across continents. This approach has shown promise in areas like IT security and the Internet of Things (IoT).
- **Virtual Sessions and Labs:** Offering virtual workspaces accessible from any location is a significant step toward balancing work and study commitments. It allows students to participate in courses and laboratory exercises at flexible times, including evenings, thereby broadening access and convenience.

Therefore, the focus was to implement a virtual lab that is flexible and powerful enough for the operation of networking courses. Table 1 presents characteristics demonstrating the benefits of using a virtual lab in higher education. However there are still limitations to the setup of virtual labs like the hazard of a lack of encouragement in communication and isolation of students. We have seen this issues in the COVID-19 pandemic and do not advocate to steer away from learning spaces in presence. However we advocate to extend the physical resources (in this work a computer networks lab) by virtual resources and extend the possibilities for location independent learning.

Table 1. Characteristics of physical and virtual labs [2,4].

Characteristics	Physical Lab	Virtual Lab
Realism	High	High
Content	Stable	Dynamic
Focus on study	Lecturer	Student
Form	Synchronous	Asynchronous
Number of students	Limited	No (physical) limits
Time	Scheduled	Anytime
Focus of course	Group	Individual
Accessibility	Low	High
Cost	Very high	Low
Maintenance effort	Very high	Low
Remote work	Impossible	Possible

Table 2. Comparison of SKILL/VL to exisitng solutions [4].

Criteria	SKILL/VL	Cisco Packet Tracer	Mininet	GNS3
Open Source	Yes	No	Yes	Yes
Simulator	Yes	Yes	No	Yes
Emulator	No	No	Yes	Yes
Scalability	Yes (by extending web service)	No	Limited (using more processes)	No
Automatic setup	Yes	No	No	No
Graphical User Interface	Yes	Yes	No	Yes
Extensible beyond networks	Yes	No	No	No

At the start of the project, open-source tools for simulating networking courses were evaluated. Three alternatives were introduced and compared based on key criteria: whether they are open source, serve as a simulator, and support automatic setup. These factors were critical in guiding the development of the platform, with open-source status being vital to ensure cost-effectiveness for higher education institutions. This evaluation helped shape the platform to meet the practical needs of teaching complex networking concepts while minimizing licensing and operational costs (Table 2).

- **Open Source:** Most inspected solutions, except Cisco, are free to use. This was crucial to avoid high licensing fees and maintain flexibility.

- **Simulator:** The platform needed to realistically represent real-world scenarios.
- **Automatic Setup:** Integration into the university's IT infrastructure was essential for seamless operation.

Among the evaluated tools, GNS3 distinguished itself by being open-source and providing a graphical user interface, making it accessible even to students with limited networking experience. However, its use is confined primarily to computer networking courses, restricting its applicability for broader educational purposes.

To address this limitation, the SKILL/VL platform (Strategic Competence Platform - Innovative Learning and Teaching/Virtualization of distributed environments for teaching) was developed as a more extensible and comprehensive solution. Unlike GNS3, SKILL/VL is not limited to computer networks but is designed to support a broader range of disciplines, including courses on distributed systems and software engineering.

Section 4 outlines the infrastructure developed for the platform, focusing on the selection of open-source components and a design optimized for reliability. Section 5 details the implementation of these components and their internal communication, while Sect. 6 showcases a practical use case of the platform and compares it to the traditional physical computer networks lab.

4 Infrastructure SKILL/VL

The virtualization platform operates on a cluster of 12 high-performance servers, designed to support virtual teaching across all disciplines and eventually serve the entire university. This demands high standards of usability, scalability, and security.

Exclusively built with open-source software, the platform ensures flexibility and avoids licensing challenges. It is developed as an on-premise cloud service [5] managed within the university's own infrastructure, though it can also be adapted for public cloud deployment. The core technology is Proxmox [3,7], running on Debian Linux with QEMU/KVM for virtualization. Proxmox supports clustering and offers extensive control tools, making it well-suited for professional-grade virtual machine operations. Network virtualization is enabled by the VXLAN protocol [15], which encapsulates virtual machines within isolated network enclosures, thus providing secure and flexible virtual network management.

A user-friendly web interface (see Fig. 1), developed using NextJS and ReactFlow [21], offers intuitive drag-and-drop capabilities for setting up virtual machines, networks, and entire learning environments. Predefined templates further simplify the creation and configuration of virtual labs, making the system accessible even to users with limited technical expertise.

Students, faculty, and teaching staff benefit from a straightforward system access, facilitating the rapid development and use of complex IT scenarios.

This setup also streamlines course design and modernizes existing modules by enabling remote engagement with practical content. At present, no comparable free platform offers these combined features.

The platform's underlying infrastructure is hyper-converged, meaning all necessary IT components are centrally managed and mapped to hardware through software-defined components, providing efficient and flexible resource management [17].

Figure 1 highlights key functionalities:

- Fig. 1a: A graphical room creator for designing networking scenarios using drag-and-drop.
- Fig. 1b: Real-time interaction with network components, showing IP and MAC addresses.
- Fig. 1c: Permission configuration for virtual resources using Keycloak.
- Fig. 1d: Virtual machine views integrated into a browser, eliminating the need for additional software.

The platform's goals are the exclusive use of open-source software and the creation of an intuitive virtual environment to enhance practical computer science education. Details of the implementation are in Sect. 5.

5 Implementation of Individual Components

The platform emphasizes the use of free software and incorporates established frameworks to ensure reliability. Figure 2 illustrates the infrastructure and interactions. At the core of its infrastructure is Keycloak, which manages user authentication by linking to the university's service, providing a centralized and expandable single sign-on (SSO) solution.

User interaction occurs through a NextJS-based web interface, allowing users to create and share templates for virtual learning environments. Resource sharing is managed via Keycloak using the User-Managed Access (UMA) [16] protocol, enhancing secure and flexible access control.

The platform's backend, implemented in Python with the FastAPI framework, interfaces with the Proxmox hypervisor and controls the automatic provisioning of virtual machines and VXLAN networks via a RESTful API.

Users can select from pre-configured operating system ISOs that include the QEMU-Guest-Agent pre-installed, enabling automated application of configurations such as static IP addresses. The backend enforces strict user permissions to control access to virtual machines, for example, restricting VNC access to designated VMs.

Designed with extensibility in mind, the backend architecture supports future integration with public cloud providers such as AWS, Google Cloud, or Azure, enabling hybrid or multi-cloud deployment scenarios.

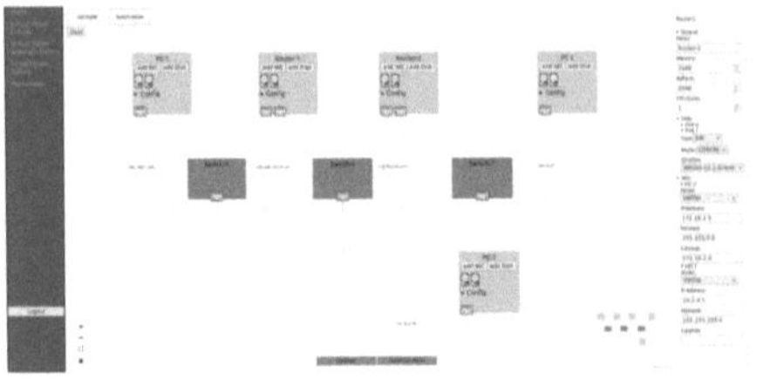

(a) Template for a learning room

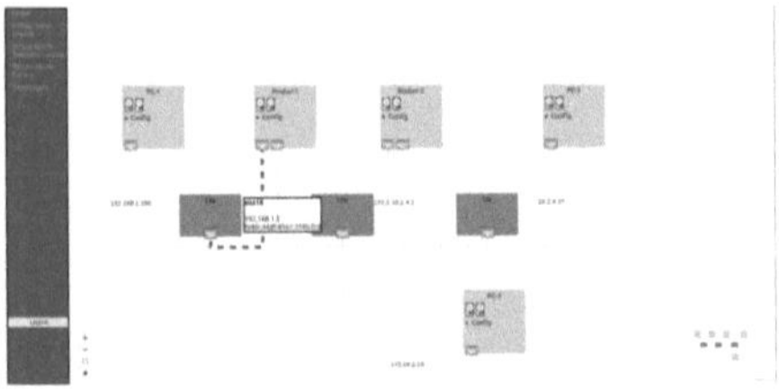

(b) Interactive selection of interfaces

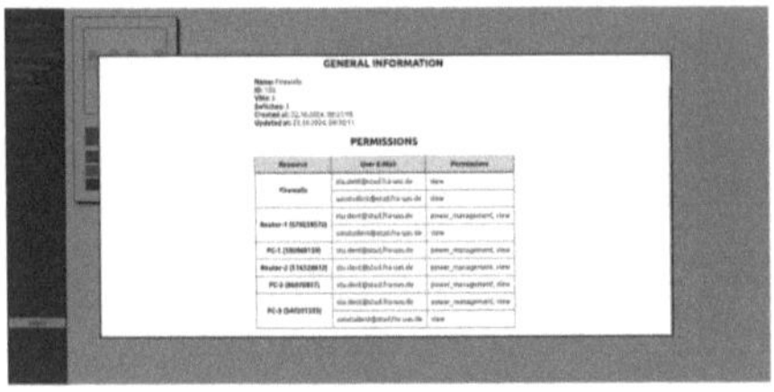

(c) Permission management for resources

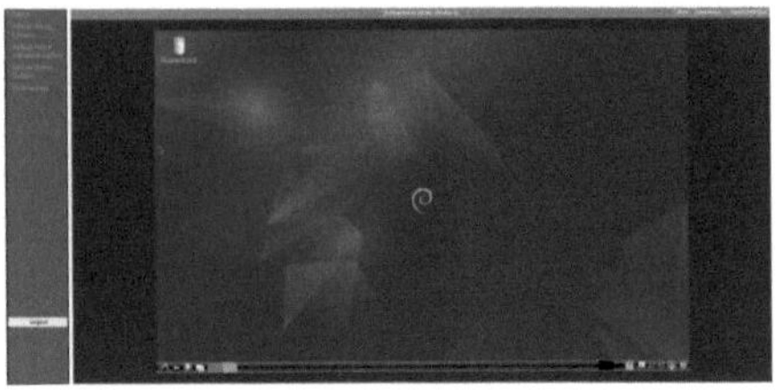

(d) Virtual machine running in browser

Fig. 1. The user web interface of the platform [4].

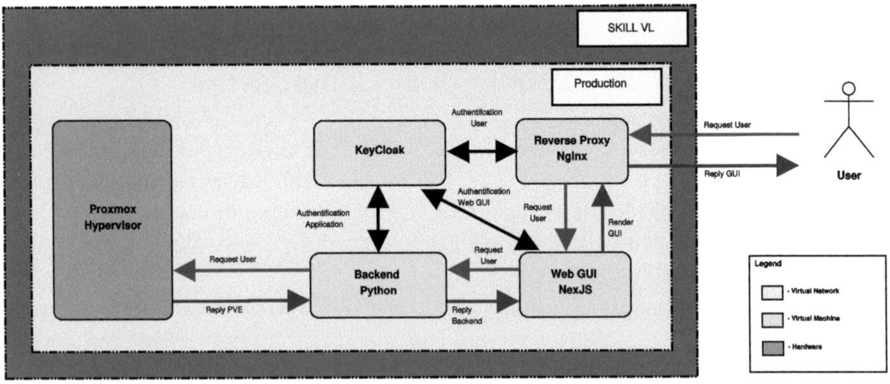

Fig. 2. Software components of the SKILL/VL infrastructure and interaction [4].

6 Practical Application in Laboratories

This section describes a practical application of the computer networks lab using a network setup consisting of four hosts: two workstations and two routers. The network topology, shown in Fig. 3, serves as a reference configuration for university labs focused on computer networks and IT security experiments. This topology simulates a basic real-world network scenario. It is used for comparative analysis between the traditional physical lab setup (illustrated in Fig. 4) and the virtual lab environment (depicted in Fig. 5).

6.1 Network Topology

The hosts in the institution network connect to the public network (172.16.2.0/24) through two routers. Institution A, with the subnet 192.168.1.0/24, connects via Router 1, while Institution B, with the subnet 10.2.4.0/24, connects via Router 2. After installing the Linux operating system on the hosts, students configure network parameters such as IP addresses, gateways, and router settings. A JavaScript-based web service runs on the machines, communicating with clients through browsers or the command-line tool `curl` via TCP sockets. Additionally, another host on the public network is designated for testing and monitoring purposes.

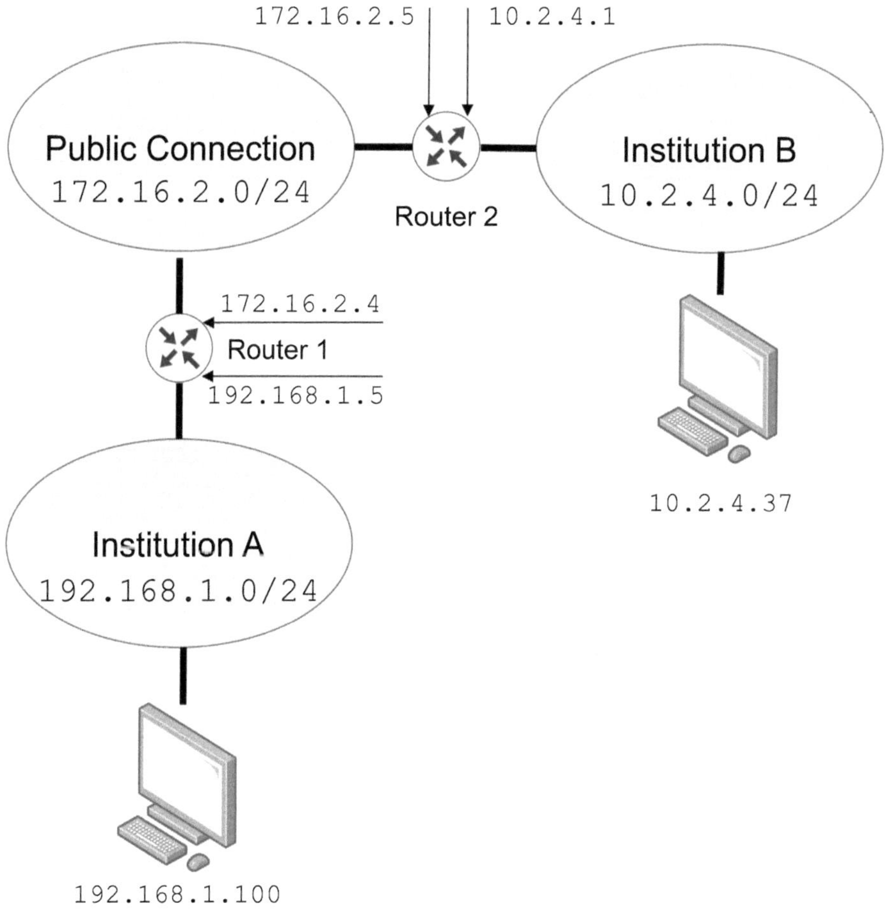

Fig. 3. Topology of IT-Security class [4,13].

6.2 Setup in Physical Lab

The physical computer networking lab consists of 24 workstations, each with five Ethernet interfaces, organized into groups of four. Each workstation is connected to a switch, with additional network components provided by teaching staff based on the experiment. Workstations are linked to a management server via DHCP for network parameter distribution.

The management server uses the open-source imaging software linux-muster [20], which provides different OS images, such as Linux or Windows, and automatically deploys images to workstations. Students or teachers select the appropriate image, which configures the host for the exercise, either automatically or manually. This functionality was adapted for the SKILL/VL platform, replicating the setup in a virtual form.

Fig. 4. Physical Lab for computer networks [4].

The network topology setup in the physical lab is a time-consuming process, typically requiring students an average of four hours to complete. Much of this time is spent on setting up the workstations and networking equipment, which distracts from focusing on the core tasks of machine configuration and routing.

Moreover, the physical lab has a capacity limit of 24 workstations, restricting the number of students who can work concurrently. This limitation reduces the depth of learning and increases the workload for teaching staff in managing the setup. The lab uses the imaging system linuxmuster to deploy different operating system images (e.g., Linux or Windows) to workstations. While robust, this system is also time-intensive, taking about 30 min to install an image on a single workstation and up to 6 h for the entire lab.

These factors make virtualization a more efficient alternative, particularly for handling multiple scenarios across different exercises, as discussed later in the comparison between physical and virtual labs.

6.3 Setup in Virtual Lab

In class, students implemented the network topology described in Sect. 6.1 in the virtual lab, completing the task in less time than in the physical lab. We also increased the complexity by adding a physical Raspberry Pi into the scenario. The hybrid approach of combining virtual hosts with a physical Raspberry Pi allowed us to extensively test the environment. SKILL/VL enables us to offer complex experiments to larger groups with minimal location restrictions, providing significant benefits to the students.

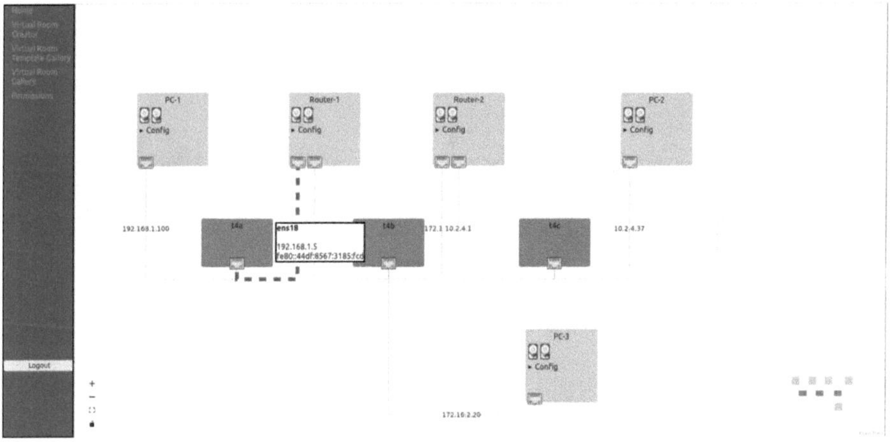

Fig. 5. Virtual representation of network topology from Fig. 3 [4].

The platform supports logical separation of project and student groups to enable independent work while still allowing connections through virtual switches and routers when necessary. This design facilitates the creation of sophisticated network scenarios for both teaching and research. The practical lab example using this platform was evaluated as part of a computer networks module.

Figure 6 shows how virtual learning rooms are implemented using VXLANs to achieve physical separation. Each virtual room is isolated with its own VXLAN bridge, enabling automatic and invisible network configuration, and providing individual address spaces for each user.

Compared to the physical lab, this infrastructure supports many more students simultaneously, reducing the operational overhead. It also simplifies simulating large corporate networks, useful for tasks such as troubleshooting and testing security mechanisms.

During the summer semester of 2023, a test run was conducted with computer science bachelor students who completed lab tasks via the platform, including analyzing network traffic between virtual machines using Wireshark.

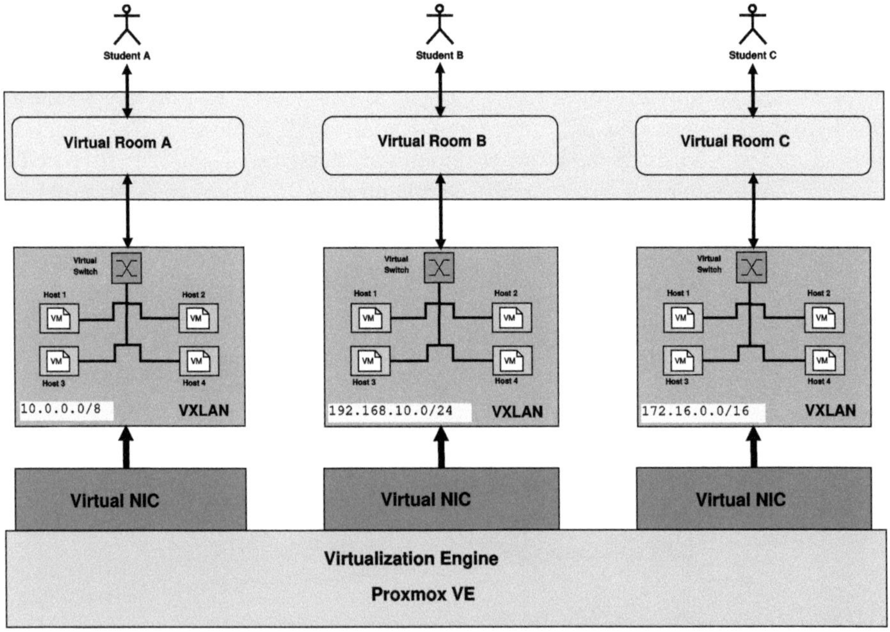

Fig. 6. Mapping virtual learning spaces to physical components [4].

The test run of the virtual lab platform provided valuable insights for its further development, particularly regarding user-friendliness, performance, and overall applicability. One notable challenge was that many students found adapting to virtual cabling difficult, as it requires a higher level of abstraction compared to physical cabling.

Some students also faced difficulties with the web interface, which was still in an experimental phase during the test. Additionally, delays or lags were observed when interacting with virtual machines through the noVNC client, which streams the graphical output to the browser.

Despite these challenges and relying mainly on subjective student feedback, the technical feasibility of the platform was confirmed. There were no major impediments to the user experience, and students were able to successfully complete networking tasks using the platform.

The SKILL/VL platform emphasizes extensibility, making it suitable for various computer science courses. This is a key advantage over other tools like Mininet and GNS3, which are limited to computer network classes. Section 9 discusses the platform's potential in different application scenarios.

6.4 Comparison Physical Vs Virtual Lab

The characteristics of the SKILL/VL platform make it very beneficial for use in the lab environments of the computer network classes. Table 3 shows the comparison of the different characteristics of the physical lab and the SKILL/VL platform and its benefits.

Table 3. Comparison of physical lab vs. virtual lab using SKILL/VL [4].

Characteristics	Physical Lab	SKILL/VL
Images	LINBO	QEMU/KVM
Rollout time for images	30 min	5 min
Rollout of scenario	Time dependent	Time independent
Rollout of multiple parallel scenarios	Impossible	Possible
Snapshots	Impossible	Possible
Time	Scheduled	Anytime
Logical separation of networks	Whole lab	Individual group or student
Separation on network layer	Layer 3 (IP)	Layer 2 (VXLAN)
Focus of course	Group	Individual
Accessibility	Low	High
Remote Work	Impossible	Over ordinary web browser
Maintenance effort	Very high	Low

One key advantage of the SKILL/VL platform is the significant reduction in setup time. While setting up an experiment in the physical lab typically takes over an hour, the SKILL/VL platform considerably shortens this time, allowing students to focus more on configuring networks and monitoring traffic. Furthermore, the platform supports the parallel rollout of multiple scenarios, such as introducing configuration errors or vulnerabilities, which the physical lab environment cannot accommodate.

The use of VXLAN in SKILL/VL provides logical separation of networks at layer 2 of the OSI stack, in contrast to the physical lab which separates networks at the physical layer. This logical separation prevents address collisions and offers greater flexibility in network configurations. An additional major benefit is the platform's accessibility through a web browser, enabling remote work for students and teachers alike.

Although a comprehensive scalability analysis is still pending, the current setup utilizes Proxmox and software-defined networking (SDN) on 12 high-performance servers, each equipped with 64 CPU cores and 1 TB of RAM. Based on available resources, a single server can theoretically host 32 virtual machines (VMs) considering CPU constraints or up to 256 VMs based on memory capacity. Equation 1 and 2 show the calculation for the assumptions. With 12 servers, the theoretical VM capacity ranges from 384 to 3,072 units. Realistically, applying a 2:1 CPU core overprovisioning ratio, reliable operation of up to 768 VMs is expected. This capacity supports more than 150 simultaneous experimental setups, compared to only 24 workstations in the physical lab, representing an increase in lab capacity by a factor of 6.25.

$$\frac{64\ physical\ CPU\ cores}{2\ vCPU\ cores\ per\ VM} = 32\ VMs\ per\ server \tag{1}$$

$$\frac{1024\ GB\ physical\ RAM}{4\ GB\ vRAM\ per\ VM} = 256\ VMs\ per\ server \tag{2}$$

However, VXLAN's limitation on the Maximum Transfer Unit (MTU) to 1450 bytes (compared to 1500 bytes in regular Ethernet networks) could impact performance in network benchmarks, though it does not affect configuration tasks.

7 Extending the Physical Lab Beyond Local Network Boundaries

In order to deal with the limited resources of the computer networks laboratory, extending the physical lab with resources from the SKILL/VL platform seems like a promising opportunity. Figure 7 schematically shows the idea behind this field experiment. The service (or parts) will be migrated to the end devices in the physical laboratory for computer networks.

This way, the server cluster's resources can be transferred via the campus network to the lab's computer network and used there. The platform uses a powerful hypervisor and virtual overlay networks based on the VXLAN protocol to realize encapsulated virtual learning spaces. Extending the overlay network and including the physical lab's network infrastructure results in a heterogeneous environment regarding hardware and network resources connected using virtualization to alleviate this heterogeneity. This way, the cloud platform's resources could be extended to the end devices in the lab environment, enabling the distribution of the service (or parts of it) to the laboratory and thus to end devices. The results of the lab experiments presented in Sect. 7.1 serve as a basis and ground truth for comparing service migration and as an indicator of further developments in the research.

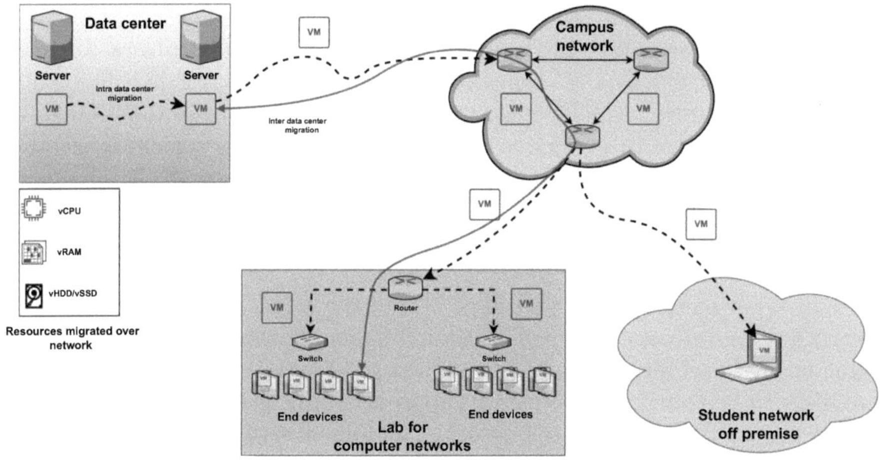

Fig. 7. Concept for extending the computer networks lab.

7.1 First Experiments on Virtual Machine Migration

To test the idea behind workload migration, VM migration is carried out as a fully controllable experiment under laboratory conditions. This allows the independent variables of the experiment, specifically the experimental variables such as operating system, CPU, RAM size, etc., to be controlled. The dependent variables, specifically downtime and performance, can thus be observed uniformly. The variable downtime describes the time during which a service running in a VM is unavailable. The basis for this is an experiment on VM migration in a "classic" setup in a local network environment, whereby the VM migration takes place between two identical machines. Figure 8 shows the schematic setup of the experiment.

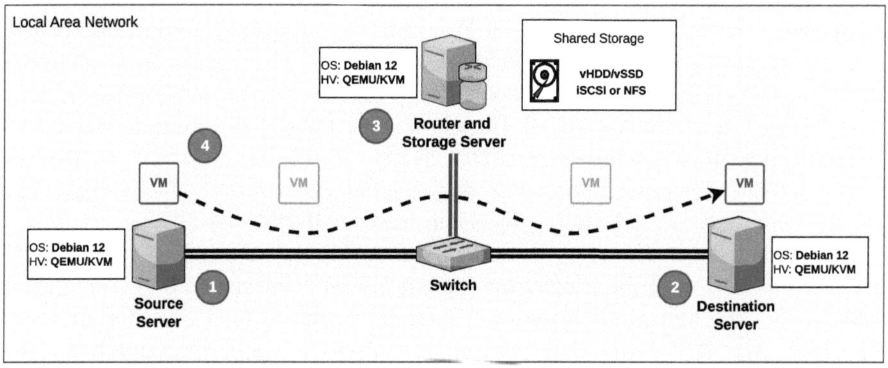

Fig. 8. Experimental setup for the virtual machine migration.

The operating system used for the server machines in the experiments is Debian 12 and is installed and configured on all servers (**numbers 1 to 3**). Debian 12 is selected as a reference operating system, since it is a free Linux distribution and serves as a basis for the Proxmox hypervisor in the SKILL/VL environment. The identical version of the Debian operating system is installed on all machines so that the framework conditions for this and all subsequent experiments remain the same. The same version of QEMU/KVM is also installed on these machines to create a uniform and thus comparable environment for the first experiment.

In all experiments, the virtual hard disk of the VMs (vHDD) is made available via a shared storage device. This setup further contributes to the laboratory character of the experiment and is intended to eliminate the variability of the hard disks to be transferred. With this approach, only the dynamic components of the VMs (vCPU, vRAM) are relevant. The influence of vHDDs on the migration of VMs over the network (especially over WAN) can be investigated in a subsequent series of experiments. After the setup has been configured, VMs are configured and migrated from a source server to a target server in a local area network (LAN) (**number 4**).

The first experiments are based on the hypothesis that the downtime of the services is very low, since migration takes place within a local network environment using live migration of the VM. This provides a comparative value under controlled conditions, which can be used as a reference for the following experiments. These values are the total migration time of VMs in a local network environment with two different bandwidth and latency parameters. For the first scenario, the measured bandwidth of the 1 Gbit/s interconnect in the computer networks lab was taken as a reference for the local network environment. The measurements were carried out with the `iperf3` tool. The results for bandwidth and latency were 938 Mbit/s and 0.724 milliseconds of latency. For the second scenario the assumption was that students have an internet connection with 100 Mbit/s bandwidth at home and that this has a maximum upload rate of 40% of the gross download rate. This results in a maximum upload speed of 40 Mbit/s. The measurements with `iperf3` confirm this assumption. The measured bandwidth from a home in the vicinity of Frankfurt using `iperf3` were a bandwidth of 37.21 Mbit/s and a latency of 36.784 milliseconds. This results in a difference of 25 times more bandwidth in scenario one compared to scenario two and a 50 times higher latency in scenario 2. Based on these values, the command-line tool `tc` was used with the parameters `netem delay 36.784ms` and `rate 37.21mbit` simulating the measured bandwidth in the local networking environment. The aim is to compare the effects of migration under different conditions.

The VMs used in the tests should be differentiated in terms of their vRAM size and application. Table 4 contains the parameters that are to be varied in this experiment. The test applications can initially generate load at different levels (e.g., 25%, 50%, 80%, 100%) for different system resources (CPU and RAM r/w). These resources can be generated using the `stress` tool. In a first step, 80 tests are generated for the parameters CPU load and RAM load of the VMs, which

Table 4. Variables in the virtual machines.

Virtual machine	unit
vRAM	2 GB
vRAM	4 GB
Application	`stress`, Monte Carlo π calculation
CPU load	idle, 25%, 50%, 80%, 100%
RAM load	idle, 25%, 50%, 80%

can be used as a reference for further experiments. The trials are conducted for all experiments with the parameters from Table 4. The downtime of the VMs can be measured by analyzing the migration time of the host (in the hypervisor) and the blackout time (the time during which the VM is unavailable) experienced by the VM during migration. For this test, a Python script was implemented, polling the application and detecting outages in the communication with the virtual machine.

Figure 9 shows the results of migration of the virtual machines with varying CPU load induced by the tool `stress`. Figures 9aand 9bdemonstrate that it took the virtual machines in both configurations (2 GB and 4 GB RAM) approximately. 12.5 to 12.8 s for a migration in a 1 Gbit/s network. Figure 9cand shows that it took the virtual machines between 531.846 and 533.719 s (roughly 8 min) to fully migrate between one server and the other, while Fig. 9dpresents that it took the machines between 870.852 and 942.933 s (between 14 and 15 and a half minutes) to migrate completely. We find that the bandwidth and latency have a significant impact on the migration time, whereas the CPU load does not significantly affect the total migration time.

Figure 10 shows the results of migration of the virtual machines with varying RAM load induced by the tool `stress`. Figure 10a shows that the migration of the virtual machine with 2 GB RAM in a 1 Gbit/s network took approximately 12.5 s for migration in idle mode and 65.971 s for a complete migration with 80% RAM load. In Fig. 10b, we see that the migration took between approximately 12.5 s in idle mode and 461.587 s with 80% RAM load. This first example already shows a significant impact of the RAM size on the total migration time. Compared to the migration time, the migration of the VM with 2 GB RAM took 6.99 times longer when the RAM load is at 80%. This factor stays constant for different RAM loads in the setting of 1 Gbit/s (see Fig. 11a). RAM loads of 100% were initially tested but resulted in an infinite migration time. This effect is discussed in more detail in Sect. 7.2.

The analysis of the migration time in a network setting with 37 Mbit/s demonstrates that it took the virtual machines in both configurations (2 GB and 4 GB RAM) significantly longer than in the 1 Gbit/s setting. Figure 10cpresents a migration time between 531.846 s in idle load and 1992.972 s (more than 31 min) with 80% RAM load and 2 GB of RAM, whereas in the case of 4GB of RAM and the same configuration for the bandwidth the results show that it took the

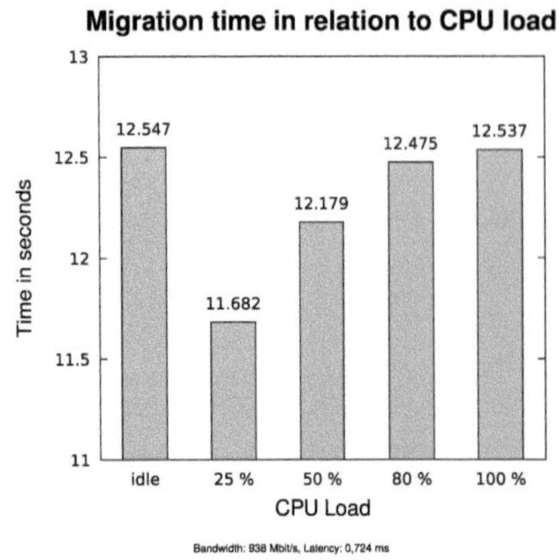

(a) Migration of VMs with 2 GB RAM in a 1 Gbit/s network

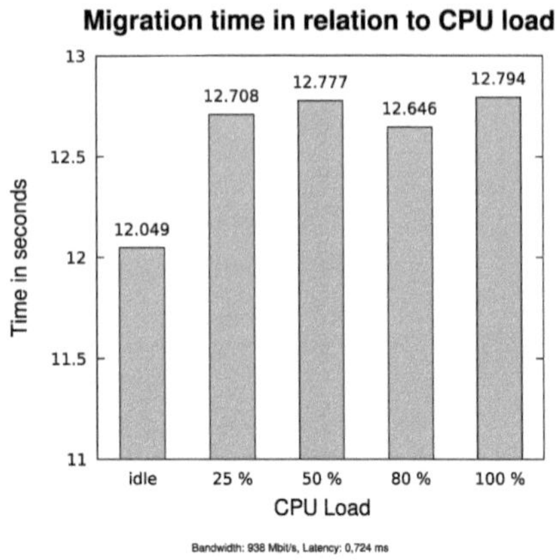

(b) Migration of VMs with 4 GB RAM in a 1 Gbit/s network

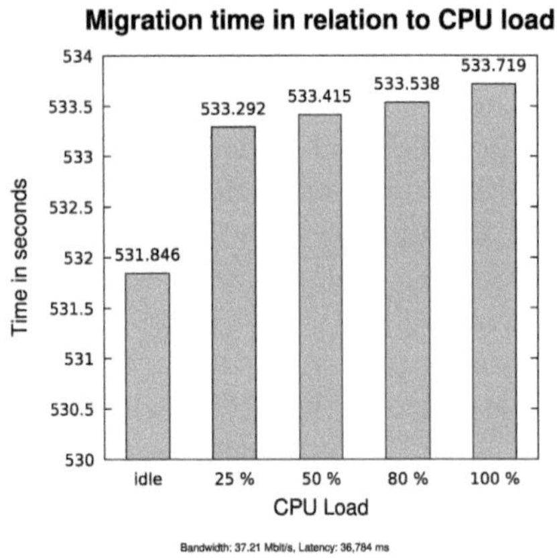

(c) Migration of VMs with 2 GB RAM in a 37 Mbit/s network

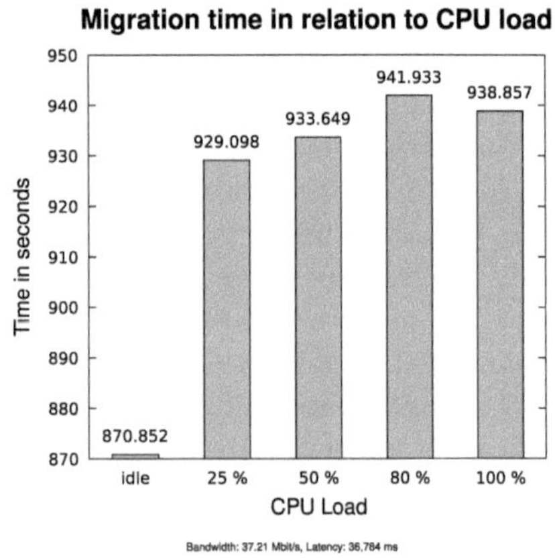

(d) Migration of VMs with 4 GB RAM in a 37 Mbit/s network

Fig. 9. Migration of virtual machines in two different networking scenarios (Fig. 9aand 9bwith 1 Gbit/s and Fig. 9cand 9dwith 37 Mbit/s) with varying CPU load.

virtual machines between 870.852 s (idle mode) and 2184.305 s (roughly 36 min) with 50% of RAM load to migrate between one server and the other entirely. Curiously, the migration of the virtual machine in the case of 80% RAM load took less time than in the case of 50% of RAM load (1760.850 compared to 2184.305 s). Figure 10dshows the results for the migration time. The influence of the RAM load on the migration time of the VMs is in the range of 1.4 to 1.6 for the idle mode and RAM loads between 25% and 50%. In the case of 80% we see that there is a smaller factor of 0.883. This can be explained by taking the Auto-convergence feature of the QEMU/KVM Hypervisor into

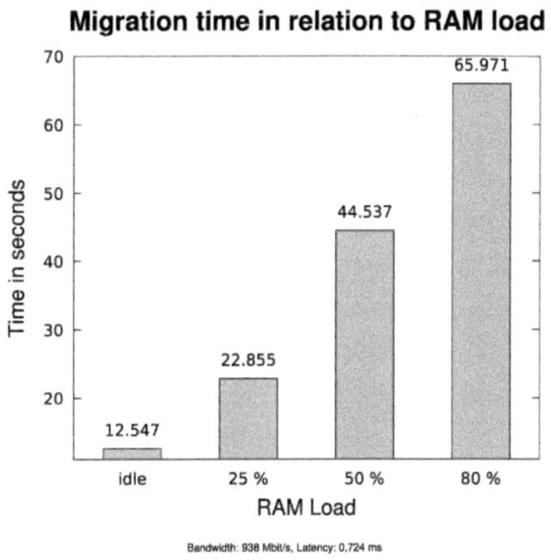

(a) Migration of VMs with 2 GB RAM in a 1 Gbit/s network

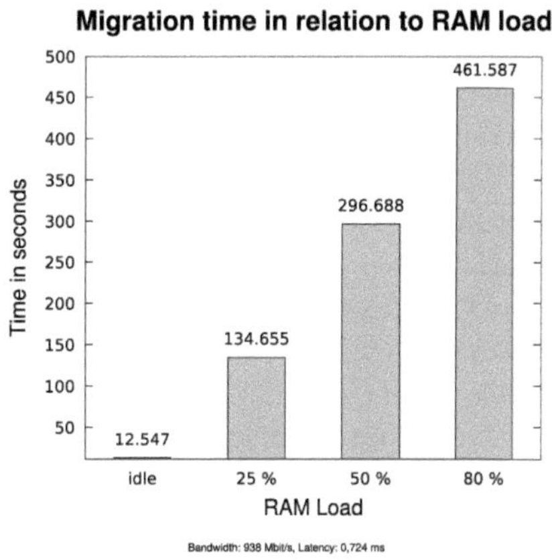

(b) Migration of VMs with 4 GB RAM in a 1 Gbit/s network

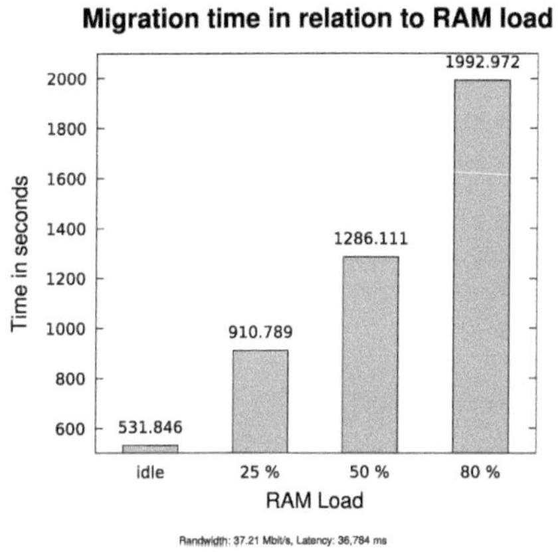

(c) Migration of VMs with 2 GB RAM in a 37 Mbit/s network

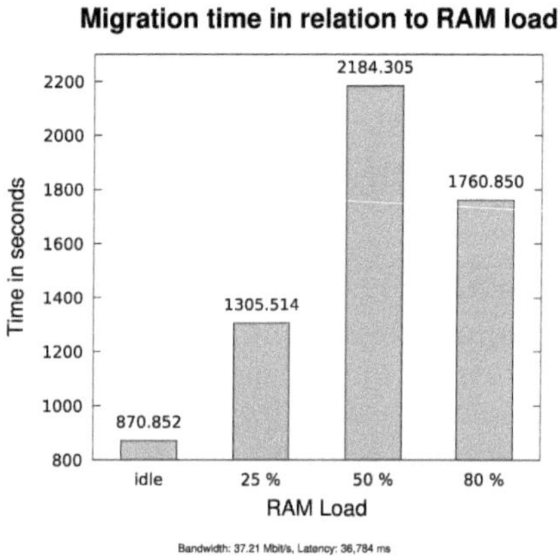

(d) Migration of VMs with 4 GB RAM in a 37 Mbit/s network

Fig. 10. Migration of virtual machines in two different networking scenarios (Fig. 10aand 10bwith 1 Gbit/s and Fig. 10cand 10dwith 37 Mbit/s) with varying RAM load.

account. The `auto-converge` parameter influences the behaviour of the migration process. The idea behind this parameter is to throttle the virtual CPU execution time and prevent the guest computer (the virtual machine) from polluting memory faster than memory can be transferred over the network. By default, QEMU/KVM throttles the vCPU by 20% and increases the throttling rate by 10% with each iteration. This guarantees that the guest computer will eventually migrate[1] inducing non-deterministic behaviour into the migration process. The details behind this behaviour are discussed in the following section.

The analysis of the downtime while migrating a virtual machine shows that at 1 Gbit/s, the downtime varies between 4.740 milliseconds and 2.743 milliseconds. The values show no real dispersion in the downtime of the virtual machines. The values vary along this range with these bandwidth parameters. For the configuration with 37 Mbit/s and 36 milliseconds of latency, the downtime varies for the CPU loads between 123.280 milliseconds for 25% CPU load and 198.840 milliseconds with 100% CPU load. Compared to the idle mode, this is a relative increase of between 3,075 times and 4,961 times. For the RAM load, the values vary similarly for loads between 25% and 80%. This demonstrates that the bandwidth and latency influence the downtime, as it increases this value by a factor of 10 for idle mode, and then has a linear relationship to the CPU and RAM load. The CPU and RAM load have a similar influence on the migration time, but not as drastic as on the migration time (Fig. 12).

The next thing that was inspected was the influence of migration on the performance of applications running in the virtual machine. To investigate the influence of the migration process, a client/server application for calculating a Monte Carlo estimation of the number π written in Python was developed and deployed in the virtual machine. Listing 1 demonstrates the algorithm implemented for the generation of the number π.

Algorithm 1. Estimate Pi using Monte Carlo method.

Input: Number of random points $N \leftarrow 1{,}000{,}000$
Output: Approximation of π as a string
$points\_inside \leftarrow 0$
for $i = 1$ **to** N **do**
  $x \leftarrow$ random number in $[0, 1]$
  $y \leftarrow$ random number in $[0, 1]$
  $distance \leftarrow \sqrt{x^2 + y^2}$
  if $distance \leq 1$ **then**
    $points\_inside \leftarrow points\_inside + 1$
  end if
end for
$\pi\_estimate \leftarrow 4 \times (points\_inside/N)$
$\pi\_rounded \leftarrow$ round $\pi\_estimate$ to 10 decimal places
return $\pi\_rounded$ as string

The algorithm is a simple program that generates one million random numbers and calculates the points inside the quarter of the circle. It then calculates the square root of the squared sum of these values, resulting in the distance of the points. The number of points inside the circle is then divided by the total

[1] More information: https://vlad-nikityuk.github.io/2016/08/10/qemu-live-migrations-post-copy-and-auto-converge-features/.

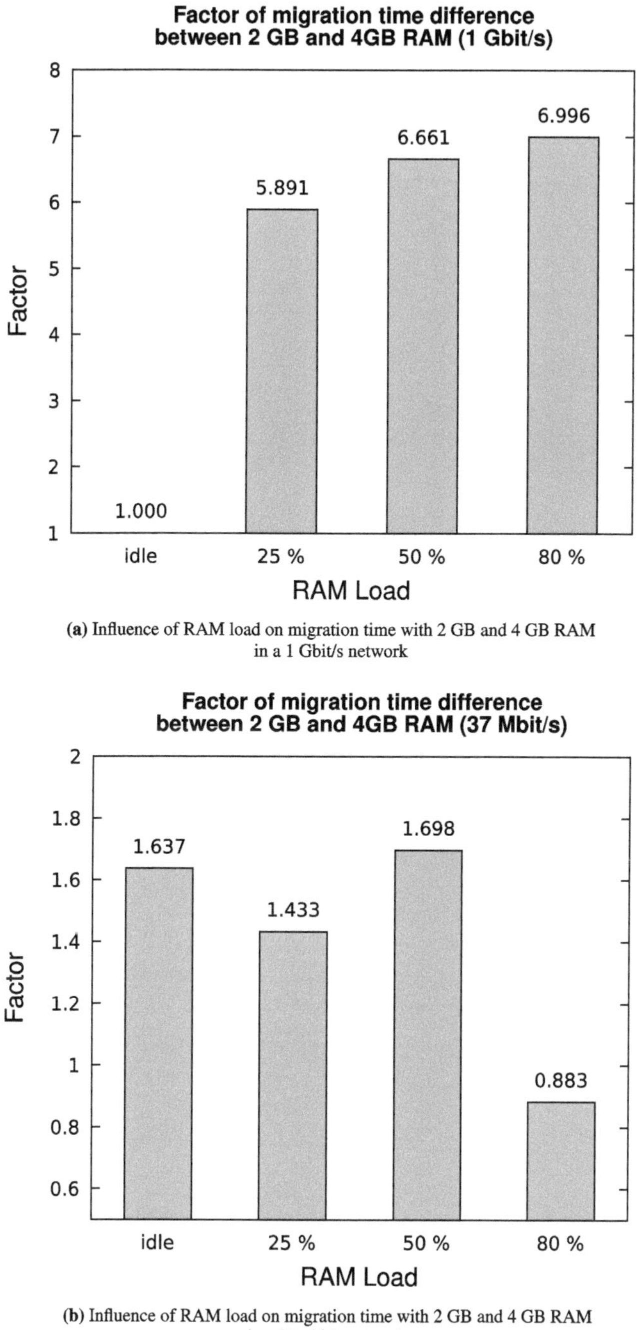

(a) Influence of RAM load on migration time with 2 GB and 4 GB RAM in a 1 Gbit/s network

(b) Influence of RAM load on migration time with 2 GB and 4 GB RAM in a 37mbit/s network

Fig. 11. Migration time increase factor of virtual machines in two different networking scenarios (Fig. 11awith 1 Gbit/s and 11bwith 37 Mbit/s) with varying RAM load.

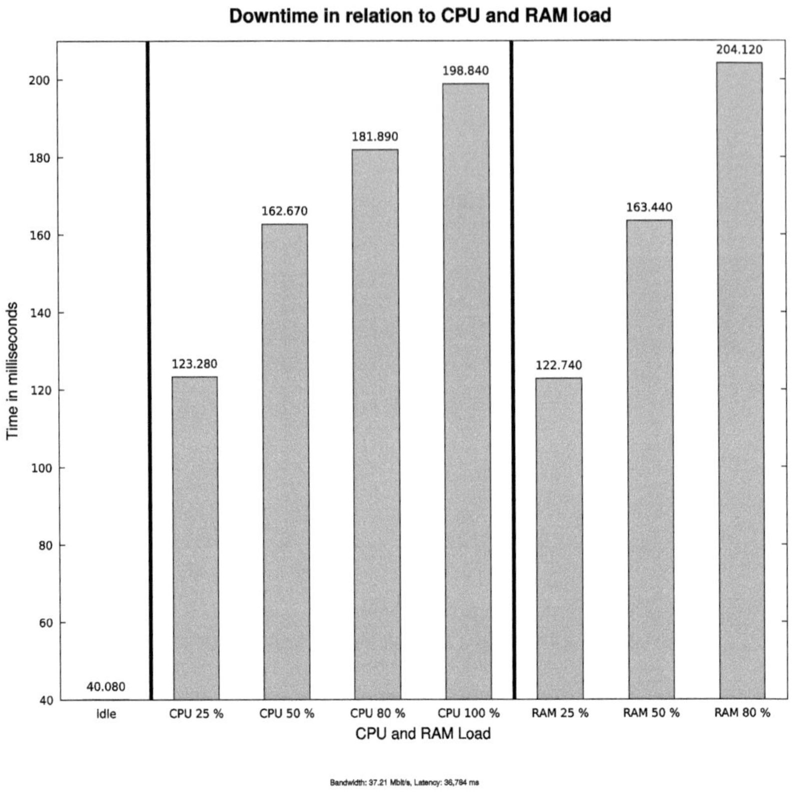

Fig. 12. Migration of virtual machines with 37 Mbit/s with varying CPU and RAM load.

number of points N and multiplied by 4 to calculate the area of a full circle. The rounded result of π is returned to the client, and the client calculates the time it takes for the request to be fulfilled. The Python application uses the `flask` package to implement a web application and serves a REST endpoint for the consumption of the service.

Figure 13 presents the results of the duration of requests. Figures 13aand 13bshow the duration for the requests in the scenario of 1 Gbit/s with and without migration of the virtual machine. The results show that the performance of the application is uniform across migration (mean of 362.637 vs. 347.945 milliseconds). The main difference lies in the number of outliers during the migration of the virtual machine.

The Figs. 13cand 13dshow the duration for the requests in the scenario of 37 Mbit/s with and without migration of the virtual machine. The results show that the performance of the application varies a lot across migration (mean of 450.969 vs. 940.093 milliseconds). The request times increased by 24.35% compared to

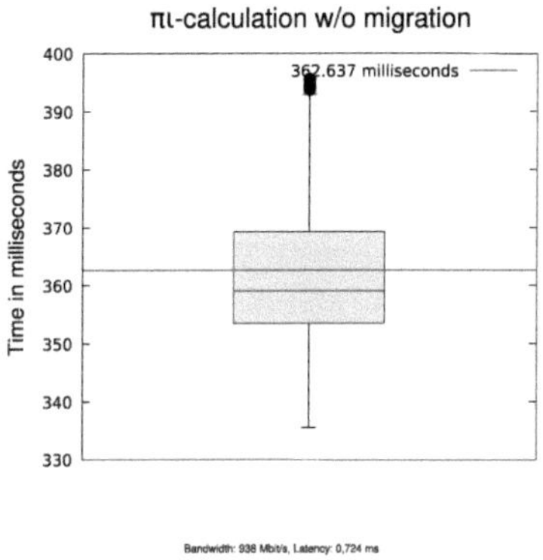

(a) Performance of VMs calculating π in a 1 Gbit/s network – no migration

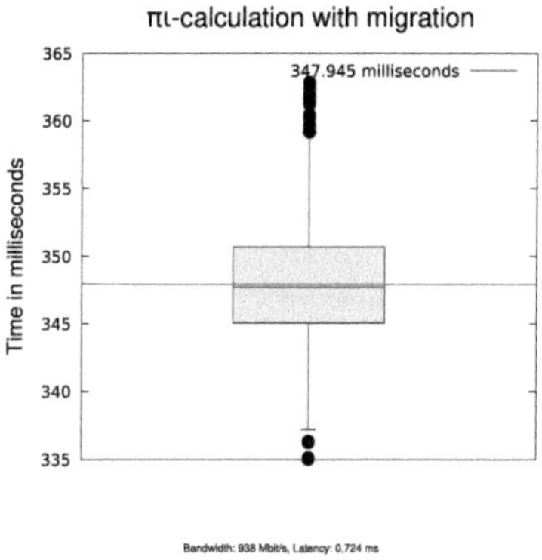

(b) Performance of VMs calculating π in a 1 Gbit/s network– with migration

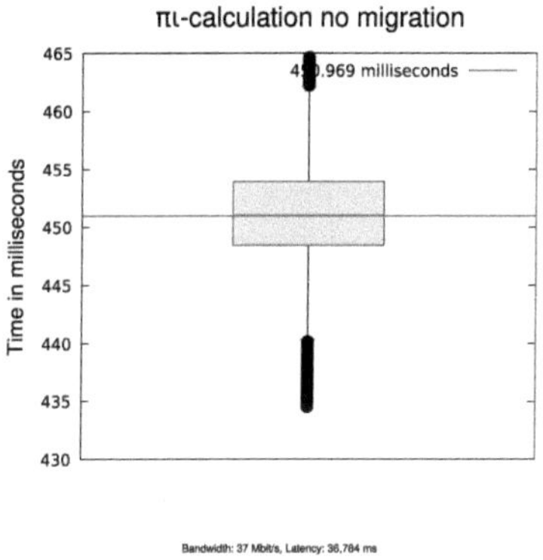

(c) Performance of VMs calculating π in a 37 Mbit/s network – no migration

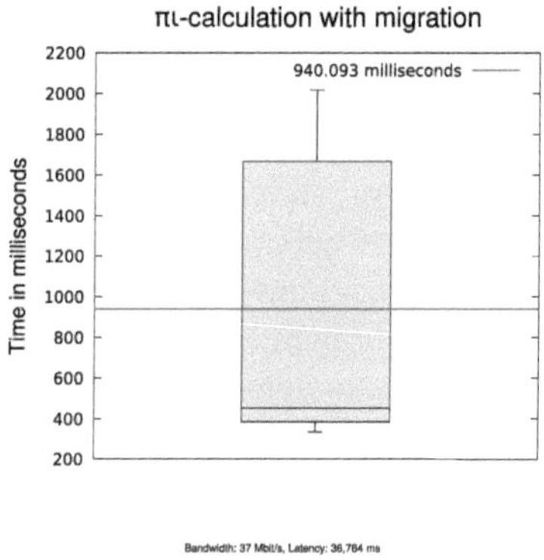

(d) Performance of VMs calculating π in a 37 Mbit/s network– with migration

Fig. 13. Performance of virtual machines calculating the number π (Fig. 13a, no migration in 1 Gbit/s network and 13b, with migration in 1 Gbit/s network) (Fig. 13c, no migration in 37 Mbit/s network and 13d, with migration in 37 Mbit/s network).

the same application in a 1 Gbit/s network setting. The requests while migrating increased by 270.18% in the case of a 37 Mbit/s network setting. On top of this, the standard deviation increased significantly (627.948 milliseconds vs. 4.960 milliseconds). Also, the quartile values increased drastically (1668.059 vs. 350.704 milliseconds). These results show that the reduced bandwidth has a significant impact on the request times of the application during migration, resulting in a highly fluctuating request time for the migration.

7.2 Conclusions of the Experiments

The first lab experiments show that it is possible and feasible to migrate virtual machines and workloads over a network. Even though the lab experiments represent a simplified and limited testing bed for the virtual extension of the physical lab, they deliver interesting insights. The first insight is that the downtime of the virtual machine stays constant over the migration within a 1 Gbit/s network, indicating that a migration of service parts from the SKILL/VL platform in the campus-wide network is possible. However, the migration over the WAN to the end devices, where the bandwidth is drastically smaller than within the campus network, results in a decrease in the performance of the application (270.18% increase in request time). The migration times also increase drastically (2184.305 s $\approx$ 36 min) while the downtime increased by a factor of 41,9 (4.740 compared to 198.840 milliseconds). This illustrates that a migration over the campus network is feasible, while moving parts of the lab to the users' end devices is not practical.

The migration experiments were carried out using the `auto-converge` parameter in the settings of the QEMU/KVM hypervisor. The parameter was important during migration, since memory-intensive workloads were executed. In the case of live migration, this can lead to an infinite migration, because the virtual machine will never complete the migration process. After all, the guest writes to memory faster than QEMU can transfer the memory changes to the targeted server. In this case, the migration would never have enough progress to stop the guest and proceed to the phase of transferring the remaining memory contents. `auto-converge` provides a method for slowing down guest execution speed, thus hopefully, also slowing down guest memory write speed. As time advances, `auto-cenverge` will continually increase the amount of guest CPU throttling until guest memory write speed slows enough to allow the guest to be stopped and migration to finish.

The experiments presented further limitations of the setup. Among other things, the servers performing the migration need to have the same CPU architecture. This is mandatory for the live migration of virtual machines because register entries and microcode optimizations are mirrored between servers. This is a considerable limitation of live migration in this setting, since it limits the possibilities of choosing the end device for the migration process. This limits the possibilities to choose a laptop for the end device in the migration process, since the CPU architecture between the server and the laptop is never the same, as well as the hypervisor setting. This limitation can be alleviated by using container virtualization for the migration process. Something that needs to be investigated in the future. Another limitation is the need for a shared persistent memory for the virtual HDD of the virtual machines. It is required that shared storage be available for the servers at all times, so that the servers can share the virtual HDD. This is not a problem inside a cluster network with very high bandwidths, but it becomes an issue over the WAN.

However, setting up an overlay network for migration seems promising in the case of migrating workloads within a campus network. The configuration of the campus network and the intermediate stations (switches, routers, and servers) can be controlled. Therefore, the necessary packages for this process are in place for rolling out the whole networking environment. Therefore, the following steps and future developments in extending the computer networks lab focus on extending the VXLAN campus-wide and including the physical networks lab.

8 Accessibility Improvements

Thanks to technological developments, people today can not only gather information, exchange ideas, and interact in the real world, but also network and perform tasks in the digital space – the more advanced the purpose, the more complex the information and applications. Digital content needs to be created with the user in mind. Even if it simulates complex processes, it should be presented in a way that is easy for the user to understand. In this context, multiple limitations in the sense of disabilities or impairments, e.g., visual impairments like red-green deficiency, need to be considered.

To address these limitations, on June 28, 2025, the Barrier-Free Accessibility Act (in German language *Barrierefreiheitsstärkungsgesetz (BFSG)*)[2] entered into force in Germany and implements the EU directive of the European Accessibility Act (EAA), ensuring that uniform rules on accessibility apply throughout Europe. The regulations are based on the European standard EN 301 549, which in turn is primarily based on the international guidelines for accessible web content (WCAG)[3]. Therefore, in response to the regulatory changes, a more accessible version of the graphical user interface introduced in Sect. 5 was developed. It is primarily based on the WCAG 2.1 standard and therefore implements the requirements posed in the BFSG.

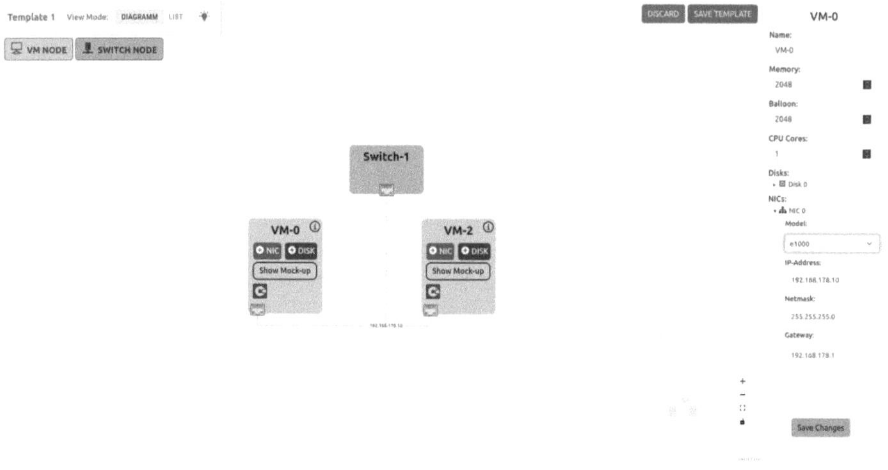

Fig. 14. Improved Accessibility on the new version of the GUI.

[2] Source in german language https://bfsg-gesetz.de/.
[3] https://www.w3.org/TR/WCAG21/#main.

Figure 14 presents the new improved version of the GUI. The improvement were based on the four standards defined by the WCAG 2.1, abbreviated as POUR:

- **P - Perceivable:** Information and user interface must be accessible to the user, including the provision of text content with visual content. The application and its content must be readable (sufficient contrast).
- **O - Operable:** The user must be able to control the elements of the user interface. The user must be able to perform actions using the keyboard, the application must allow the user sufficient time to respond. The navigation mechanism must be consistent and predictable.
- **U - Understandable:** The information and operation of the elements of the user interface should be understandable by the majority of users. Possible error, the application should display a clear message.
- **R - Robust:** The application should ensure support for assistive technologies, such as screen readers.

To achieve the standards required by the WCAG standard, WAVE[4] (Web Accessibility Evaluation) was used. WAVE is a tool that helps evaluate the accessibility of digital resources. It automatically scans websites and identifies accessibility issues. WAVE is available as a browser extension and is compatible with all popular browsers such as Chrome, Firefox, and Edge.

The evaluation of the old version of the GUI presented several accessibility issues, including contrast errors and missing control components for keyboard access. Especially, color-blind users cannot perceive information through color, but only through the contrast of the content. To make it easier for visually impaired users to access text information, the standard font of the application has been enlarged, and a uniform color system has been used. This is to ensure contrast between the text content and the background color. According to the results, the new version of the application has fully met the minimum contrast requirements. The evaluation shows that the ARIA results achieved in the new version have increased from 1 to 524. ARIA (Accessible Rich Internet Applications) is a W3C specification that provides additional information about the HTML element that conveys the role, state, and attributes of the corresponding element. This information helps tools such as screen readers to inform the user about the state of the UI element. In the new version of the application, the purpose of each button is also indicated by the ARIA label. This allows the assistive tool to inform the user about the functionality of the An interface element without relying on visual perception.

The new version of the application shows users more clearly where they are by displaying the page title, which was missing in the previous version. In addition, the current page in the menu bar has been designed to stand out from the other elements. If a virtual machine node (VM node) or network node (switch node) If it is added by mistake, the user can delete it without having to start the

[4] https://wave.webaim.org/.

network recovery process from scratch. One of the new features in the application is feedback to the user after each action, such as creating a new virtual space.

The new version of the virtual project environment eliminates the limitations of the old GUI and, at the same time, expands its functionality to make it more comprehensive and accessible to all users. Nevertheless, it cannot yet be said that the new version is ideal for all users. Based on WCAG 2.1, there are some points where the application does not meet the requirements. For example, the application is not ideal to control solely with the keyboard. There are actions in the application that must be performed by dragging and dropping, and this gesture cannot be performed with the keyboard alone. However, the improvements present a considerable improvement over the old version of the GUI, meeting the needs of people with visual impairments.

9 Future Work

The virtual environment presented in the platform shows strong potential not only for computer network courses but also for broader applications. For example, in distributed applications courses, it facilitates the design of various distributed architectures ranging from basic three-layer models to complex service-oriented architectures [18].

Another significant application is in creating a virtual Internet of Things (IoT) learning space, where physical sensors interact with virtual nodes. This setup allows students to rapidly build and test IoT applications, visualize cyber-physical systems (CPS) [22], and simulate Industry 4.0 scenarios through an intuitive graphical editor (see Fig. 1a).

The investigation into the migration process revealed limitations associated with virtual machines, highlighting the need to explore container virtualization in future research. Migrating containers to end devices appears promising because containers have a smaller resource footprint compared to virtual machines. Additionally, running a container engine on end devices such as laptops is simpler and more practical than operating a full hypervisor. This makes container virtualization a potentially more feasible option for workload migration to end devices.

Future work includes investigating container technologies for seamless migration between end devices and servers. Expanding the platform's capabilities will involve supporting various Linux distributions, prioritizing open-source components while considering the integration of Windows virtual machines. Additionally, refactoring the software toward a container-based architecture is expected to enhance efficiency and accelerate release cycles, leveraging a cloud-native approach.

10 Conclusion

The development and deployment of the SKILL/VL platform demonstrate that browser-based virtualization solutions can fundamentally transform practical computer science education. By leveraging exclusively open-source technologies and focusing on intuitive usability, the platform significantly lowers the technical and administrative barriers typically faced by both students and instructors. This fosters broader participation and enables scalable, remote laboratory experiences that were previously limited by physical resources.

The practical evaluations carried out in teaching environments highlight the platform's strong potential to deliver realistic network scenarios efficiently, while also identifying areas for further improvement—such as optimizing performance over lower-bandwidth networks and refining the user interface for accessibility. The lab experiments on migration of workloads in Sect. 7 present a possibility of extending the platform within campus networks and prove the technical feasibility for hybrid lab concepts, despite challenges such as CPU architecture compatibility and WAN performance, which remain for full end-device integration.

Looking ahead, SKILL/VL provides a robust foundation for integrating container technologies and expanding to broader use cases, including distributed systems and IoT applications. Ongoing user feedback and technical assessment will play a critical role in iteratively enhancing the platform, ensuring that it continues to meet the evolving needs of digital higher education and supports inclusive, hands-on learning experiences at scale.

Acknowledgments. The SKILL/VL project described in this paper is part of the SKILL project network (Strategic Competence Platform - Innovative Learning and Teaching), which is funded by the Initiative Hochschullehre durch Digitalisierung stärken der Stiftung Innovation in der Hochschullehre, at Frankfurt University of Applied Sciences.

Disclosure of Interests. The authors have no conflicts of interest to declare that are relevant to the content of this article.

References

1. Abdul Rashid, N.B., bin Othman, M.Z., bin Johan, R., bin Hj. Sidek, S.F.: Cisco packet tracer simulation as effective pedagogy in computer networking course. Int. J. Interact. Mob. Technol. (iJIM) **13**(10), 4–18 (2019). https://doi.org/10.3991/ijim.v13i10.11283, https://online-journals.org/index.php/i-jim/article/view/11283
2. Alam, A., Mohanty, A.: Discerning the application of virtual laboratory in curriculum transaction of software engineering lab course from the lens of critical pedagogy. In: Sentiment Analysis and Deep Learning, pp. 53–68. Springer, Singapore (2023)
3. Algarni, S.A., Ikbal, M.R., Alroobaea, R., Ghiduk, A.S., Nadeem, F.: Performance evaluation of xen, kvm, and proxmox hypervisors. Int. J. Open Source Softw. Process. **9**(2), 39–54 (2018). https://doi.org/10.4018/ijossp.2018040103
4. Baun, C., Kappes, M., Cocos, H., Koch, M., Petrozziello, M.: The virtual computer networks lab: on the design and implementation of a location independent networks laboratory in higher education. In: Proceedings of the 17th International Conference on Computer Supported Education - Volume 1: CSEDU, pp. 199–207. INSTICC, SciTePress (2025).https://doi.org/10.5220/0013199400003932

5. Baun, C., Kunze, M., Nimis, J., Tai, S.: Cloud computing - web-based dynamic IT services. Springer (2011). https://doi.org/10.1007/978-3-642-20917-8
6. Beckmann, A.: Digitalisierung in der hochschullehre: Erfahrungen mit dem mathedu digital-lehrkonzept und zur akzeptanz digitaler lehrelemente durch die studierenden. MedienPädagogik: Zeitschrift für Theorie und Praxis der Medienbildung, pp. 1–20 (2020). https://doi.org/10.21240/mpaed/00/2020.02.24.x
7. Chen, L., Huang, W., Sui, A., Chen, D., Sun, C.: The online education platform using proxmox and novnc technology based on laravel framework. In: 2017 IEEE/ACIS 16th International Conference on Computer and Information Science (ICIS), pp. 487–491 (2017). https://doi.org/10.1109/ICIS.2017.7960041
8. Demchenko, Y., Gallenmüller, S., Fdida, S., Rausch, T., Andreou, P., Saucez, D.: Slices data management infrastructure for reproducible experimental research on digital technologies. In: 2023 IEEE Globecom Workshops (GC Wkshps), pp. 1–6. (2023). https://doi.org/10.1109/GCWkshps58843.2023.10464944
9. Dietz, M.: The internet of digital twins: advances in hyperscaling virtual labs with hypervisor- and container-based virtualization. In: Auer, M.E., Pachatz, W., Rüütmann, T. (eds.) Learning in the Age of Digital and Green Transition, pp. 574–586. Springer International Publishing, Cham (2023)
10. Emiliano, R., Antunes, M.: Automatic network configuration in virtualized environment using gns3. In: 2015 10th International Conference on Computer Science & Education (ICCSE), pp. 25–30 (2015). https://doi.org/10.1109/ICCSE.2015.7250212
11. Erpenbeck, J., Sauter, W.: Handbuch Kompetenzentwicklung im Netz Bausteine einer neuen Lernwelt, 1st edn. Schäffer-Poeschel, Stuttgart, Germany (2017)
12. Handke, J.: Handbuch Hochschullehre Digital, 1st edn. Tectum Wissenschaftsverlag, Marburg an der Lahn, Germany (2015)
13. Kappes, M.: Netzwerk- und Datensicherheit, 3rd edn. Springer Vieweg, Wiesbaden, Germany (2023)
14. Lantz, B., Heller, B., McKeown, N.: A network in a laptop: rapid prototyping for software-defined networks. In: Proceedings of the 9th ACM SIGCOMM Workshop on Hot Topics in Networks. Hotnets-IX, Association for Computing Machinery, New York, NY, USA (2010). https://doi.org/10.1145/1868447.1868466
15. Mahalingam, M., et al.: Virtual eXtensible local area network (VXLAN): a framework for overlaying virtualized layer 2 networks over layer 3 networks. RFC 7348 (2014). https://doi.org/10.17487/RFC7348
16. Maler, E., Machulak, M., Richer, J., Hardjono, T.: Federated authorization for user-managed access (UMA) 2.0. Internet-Draft draft-maler-oauth-umafedauthz-00, Internet Engineering Task Force (2019). https://datatracker.ietf.org/doc/draft-maler-oauth-umafedauthz/00/, work in Progress
17. Meneses, S., Maya, E., Vasquez, C.: Network design defined by software on a hyper-converged infrastructure. case study: Northern technical university fica data center. In: Botto-Tobar, M., Zamora, W., Larrea Plúa, J., Bazurto Roldan, J., Santamaría Philco, A. (eds.) Systems and Information Sciences, pp. 272–280. Springer, Cham (2021)
18. Richards, M., Ford, N.: Fundamentals of Software Architecture. O'Reilly Media, Sebastopol, CA (2020)
19. Serrano, M., Isaris, N., Schaffers, H. (eds.): Building the Future Internet through FIRE. Taylor & Francis, London, England (2022)
20. Steffen Auer, A.F.S.E.: linuxmuster.net – documentation (2024). https://www.linuxmuster.net/en/documentation/, Accessed 08 Sep 2026, https://www.linuxmuster.net/en/documentation/

21. Thakkar, M.: Building React Apps with server-Side Rendering: Use React, redux, and Next to build full server-Side Rendering applications. APRESS, New York, NY (2020)
22. Wolf, W.: Cyber-physical systems. Computer **42**(3), 88–89 (2009). https://doi.org/10.1109/MC.2009.81

From Training to Teaching: Evaluating Pilot Educational Robots Regional Integration in Upper Austrian Primary and Secondary Education

Sara Hinterplattner[1(✉)] and Eva Schmidthaler[2]

[1] University of Education Upper Austria, Kaplanhofstr. 40, 4020 Linz, Austria
sara.hinterplattner@ph-ooe.at
[2] Johannes Kepler University Linz, Altenbergerstr. 69, Linz, Austria
eva.schmidthaler@jku.at

Abstract. This paper presents a research-based teacher training program designed to promote digital literacy and computational thinking through the use of educational robots in Austrian primary and secondary schools. The program was developed as part of the Steyr Digitalization Project, a localized initiative aimed at integrating digital tools into compulsory education. It follows a design-based research approach, combining findings from previous pilot projects with insights from the literature on effective teacher education. The training modules emphasize hands-on, inquiry-based learning, progressive skill development, and collaborative reflection, supported by over 650 pages of freely accessible, curriculum-aligned teaching materials. Quantitative data was obtained through a structured questionnaire study involving 65 teachers, of whom 46 fully completed the survey. The questionnaire, based on Davis' Technology Acceptance Model (TAM), evaluated perceived usefulness, ease of use, attitude toward using, behavioral intention to use, and actual system use. Key findings show that 87.0% of participants engaged in further training, and 71.74% conducted educational robot workshops in their classrooms. While 58.70% successfully used educational robots to teach programming basics, only 19.57% integrated them as a regular part of their teaching plans. The results highlight the potential of educational robots to enhance computational thinking and digital literacy, while also identifying challenges such as limited institutional support and long-term integration. This study provides evidence for the role of educational robotics in supporting digital competence and offers insights into the conditions necessary for scaling and sustaining technology-supported learning environments. The findings contribute to the broader discourse on digital education reform in Austria and inform the design of future professional development initiatives for educators.

Keywords: Educational Robots · Teacher Training · Digital Education · Technology Acceptance Model · Computational Thinking

C. Meinel et al. (Eds.): CSEDU 2025, CCIS 3148, pp. 43–71, 2027.
https://doi.org/10.1007/978-3-032-39103-2_3

1 Introduction

One of the central aims of education across all levels is to nurture a lifelong disposition toward learning. While young children often display an intrinsic curiosity about their surroundings, it is the responsibility of educational systems to provide structured, developmentally appropriate curricula that cultivate this curiosity and support cognitive growth. Research shows that during the earliest years of life, children form up to 700 neural connections per second, a rapid developmental phase that underscores the critical importance of early stimulation through exploration, interaction, and observation [5]. These formative years represent an ideal period to introduce fundamental STEM (Science, Technology, Engineering, and Mathematics) concepts, setting a foundation for later academic success [5,25]. Moreover, early engagement in STEM has been shown to help reduce gender-based stereotypes and address barriers to participation in STEM fields [8,26]. Effective STEM instruction requires more than content delivery - it must foster critical thinking, inquiry, and problem-solving skills [11]. However, despite the widespread recognition of its importance, many educators report lacking confidence and competence to implement such approaches. Research highlights that insufficient training and limited familiarity with STEM tools often cause teachers to feel overwhelmed and uncertain about how to facilitate these learning experiences [24]. Professional development programs based on inquiry, hands-on, and embedded in authentic teaching contexts have been shown to significantly improve teacher knowledge, self-efficacy, and attitudes toward STEM [7,28,36,42]. Teachers who undergo such training are better able to connect children's everyday experiences to scientific concepts and to engage them in meaningful, developmentally appropriate STEM activities. In response to the increasing demand for digital literacy, the Austrian education system has taken steps to integrate digital and STEM education into early schooling. Formal education in Austria begins at age six with four years of primary school. Students then progress through lower and upper secondary levels, with options ranging from general academic to vocational tracks (Fig. 1).

1.1 Digital Education in Austria

Since the 2018/19 school year, the subject "Digital Education"has been gradually introduced into Austrian schools [37]. Initially integrated into other subjects, it became a compulsory standalone subject for grades 5 to 8 in 2022, with one weekly lesson [16,22]. Prior to this, computer science education was only mandatory in the ninth grade and often treated as a specialization in vocational schools. In early childhood education centers, the national curriculum outlines several developmental domains, including "Nature and Technology"and "Language and Communication,"which embed early STEM and digital education elements [18]. However, there remains a discontinuity in progression: while kindergartens aim to introduce STEM through basic scientific exploration and media literacy, primary schools have not systematically continued these efforts [16]. This creates

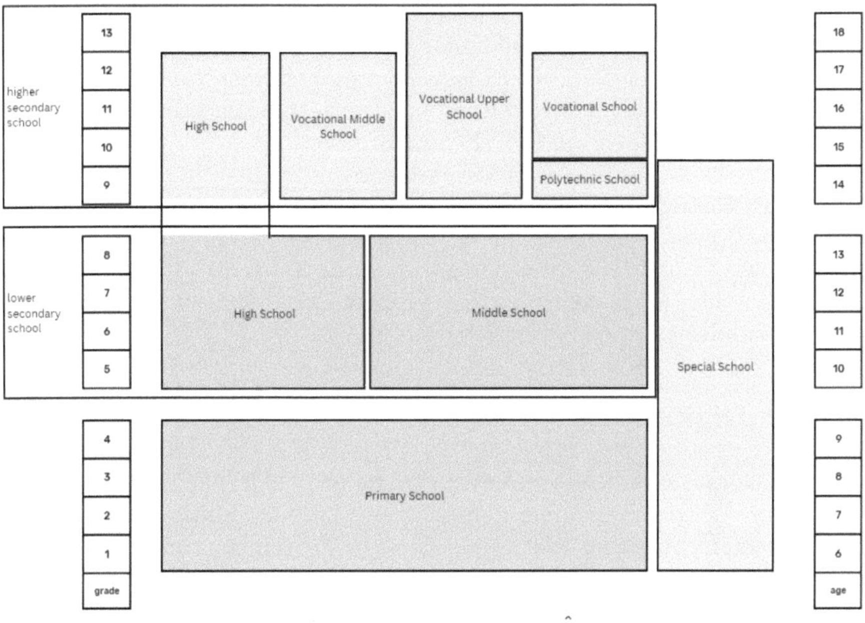

Fig. 1. Overview of the Austrian school system [19].

a missed opportunity during a sensitive developmental stage when children are most receptive to such learning experiences.

1.2 Programming and Robotics in Austrian STEM Lessons

As Austria continues to adapt its curriculum to meet the needs of a digitally connected society, educators face both new opportunities and significant challenges. Integrating creative tools such as robotics and programming into STEM education has been shown to foster computational thinking, motivation, creativity, and collaboration among students [16,18,41]. Case studies show the positive trends regarding educational robots fostering students' computational thinking - especially in creative interdisciplinary settings, and supporting first programming experiences [20,38,39,41]. These technologies not only support conceptual understanding but also enhance engagement and allow learners to connect theoretical content with real-world applications [14,32,33]. However, these benefits can only be realized when teachers are well-prepared and confident in using such tools. Teacher enthusiasm and instructional quality are strongly linked to student outcomes in STEM, making professional development a critical component of any educational reform [3,4,12]. Without sufficient support, educators may avoid STEM content altogether, inadvertently reinforcing gender stereotypes or limiting student access to essential twenty-first-century skills [3,24]. To support this transformation in Austrian schools, creative and scalable solutions are required that bridge the gap between traditional education and digital learning environments [1]. By combining inquiry-based teaching methods with robust professional development and technology-enhanced learning tools, teachers can help shape a future-ready generation equipped with the skills necessary to thrive in an increasingly complex world [7,17,18,41].

This study explores the role of targeted teacher training in fostering digital competencies through the use of educational robotics, specifically Ozobots, in Austrian classrooms. It seeks to understand how such training affects teachers' confidence, usage, and long-term integration of digital tools in STEM instruction, and identifies areas where further support may be needed to ensure the sustainable implementation of digital education at scale.

2 Steyr Digitalization Project

The Steyr Digitalization Project represents a unique model of educational transformation in Austria, combining digitalization, interdisciplinary learning, and teacher development within a city-wide strategy. Driven by a multi-stakeholder partnership between the city of Steyr, the private tech company Dynatrace, and Johannes Kepler University Linz (JKU), the project brought together public, private, and academic sectors to address one of the central challenges in 21st-century education: how to equip all students-not just a privileged few- with the skills and tools needed to thrive in a digitally driven world.

2.1 Project Context and Rationale

Steyr, a city in Austria with 16 public schools - including nine primary schools, six middle schools, and one polytechnical school - launched this initiative as a response to the increasing need for meaningful digital education at the compulsory school level. While many educational reforms in the digital field focus narrowly on providing hardware or software, Steyr's initiative set itself apart by emphasizing pedagogical integration, teacher readiness, and inclusive access. To achieve this, the city allocated a specific budget for acquiring digital tools. However, a key condition was that the funds must be used for non-obligatory equipment - devices and technologies the city was not otherwise required to provide by law. This caveat served a crucial function: it ensured that the funding would not be used to replace existing infrastructure or fulfill legal obligations but would instead support innovative, future-oriented educational technologies. It signaled a clear intention to go beyond minimum standards and to prioritize pedagogical transformation. The overarching vision of the pilot project was to reshape the educational landscape through digital inclusion, innovative teaching, and interdisciplinary approaches that extend across subject boundaries and school types, similar to other Austrian pilot initiatives such as *DigiCase* and *Technikbox* [6,27]. These two example projects promote computational thinking, creative problem-solving, and STEM competencies in primary education, with

DigiCase integrating algorithmic thinking into the curriculum and the *Technikbox* using a robotics module to introduce children to digital technologies in a playful way [6,27]. Importantly, the Steyr Digitalization Project was designed to be sustainable, inclusive, replicable, and scalable, offering a blueprint for other municipalities in Austria and beyond.

2.2 Goals and Educational Philosophy

At the core of the initiative were five strategic educational goals that guided its development and implementation. These goals reflect a holistic understanding of what digital education should achieve: First, the project aimed to promote digital literacy among students, ensuring they gain foundational knowledge of digital tools, coding, computational thinking, and media literacy. Second, the project sought to enhance student engagement through the use of interactive, hands-on tools that could motivate students and encourage active participation, especially in STEM subjects. Third, it emphasized the importance of collaboration, both at the classroom level - by enabling group work, peer tutoring, and shared learning experiences - and at the institutional level through partnerships between schools, universities, and the private sector. Fourth, it supported differentiated and inclusive instruction, using digital tools to address individual learning styles, prior knowledge, and pace. This approach helped ensure that digital education would not increase inequalities but actively reduce learning disparities. Finally, the project was built on the principle of equal access. By including all public compulsory schools in Steyr and focusing explicitly on accessibility, the initiative worked to prevent digital exclusion and to democratize educational opportunities for students from all backgrounds. An overview of the objectives can be seen in Fig. 2.

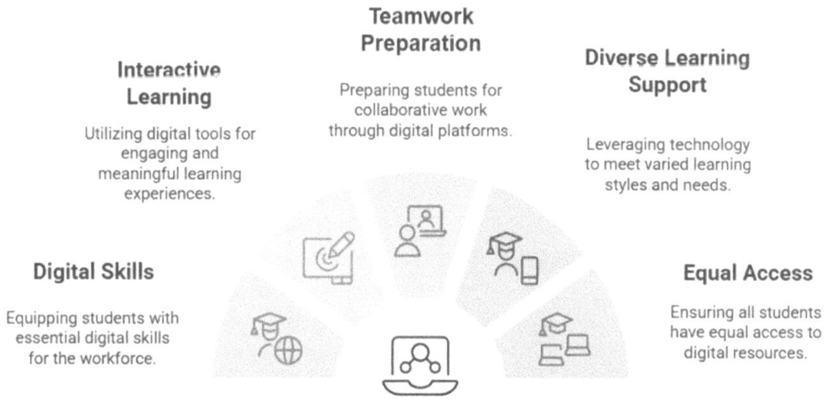

Fig. 2. Key objectives of the Digitalization Project in Steyr.

2.3 Project Leadership and Partnerships

To lead such a multi-layered initiative, the city appointed a STEM education researcher with expertise in teacher development and educational innovation. Under her leadership, the project formed a partnership between the City of Steyr, Dynatrace, and Johannes Kepler University Linz. The rationale for selecting the additional partners was twofold: both institutions had pre-existing programs in STEM outreach and had demonstrated a commitment to early STEM engagement, gender equality, and digital education. Their contributions were substantial: together, Dynatrace and JKU volunteered over 1,100 working hours, supporting the project without financial compensation. This collaboration exemplifies how public-private-academic alliances can be mobilized to support public education goals, while also aligning with each partner's mission of promoting innovation, equity, and technological literacy.

2.4 Project Structure and Implementation

The Steyr Digitalization Project was implemented in several interconnected phases, each designed to build on the previous steps and reinforce long-term impact. These phases included initial assessment, teacher training, school implementation and student workshops, teaching material development, and evaluation. An overview can be seen in Fig. 3.

Fig. 3. Overview of the project plan and its stages of the Digitalization Project in Steyr.

The first step involved a structured needs assessment, conducted through teacher questionnaires. These surveys explored existing STEM infrastructure, the availability of digital tools, teacher preparedness, and the presence of interdisciplinary or extracurricular STEM programs. The results offered an essential baseline and helped shape the scope and direction of subsequent phases [19]. Based on these findings, a two-module teacher training program was developed [21]. Participation was mandatory for at least two teachers per school, ensuring a minimal level of competence at each institution. Module 1 introduced teachers to Ozobots, small programmable robots used to teach foundational coding skills. Teachers learned how to program them using color codes, providing an accessible and visual introduction to algorithmic thinking. Module 2 expanded this by teaching block-based programming, deepening the teachers' technical skills and expanding their pedagogical toolbox. Optional extensions - such as in-school coaching and workshops - provided additional support in further developing their practice. In parallel, the project team began offering student workshops, delivered in cooperation with trained teachers. These workshops reached over 1,000 students, allowing them to explore robotics and coding in a creative, hands-on environment. All student workshops were developed according to the COOL Informatics Teaching Approach, a pedagogical framework grounded in neurodidactics and the Dalton Plan, emphasizing cooperation, freedom, individualized learning, and activity [20,29–31]. The workshops were designed around open learning principles and included role differentiation (such as peer tutors), task variation, and cross-curricular integration. One such workshop, introduced the educational robots using Storytelling [19,21]. It led young learners through five structured phases - from initial robot exploration to the creation and presentation of their digitally-augmented fairy tales. The structure encouraged both computational thinking and creative literacy, and the workshop was adaptable for children as young as three and as old as ten, depending on task complexity and teacher guidance. In total, more than 150 teachers were trained, and the project produced more than 650 pages of high-quality teaching materials, all of which are publicly accessible and free to use.

2.5 Teaching Materials

A cornerstone of the project was the development of teaching resources, created specifically to support the integration of Ozobots and other digital tools into everyday classroom practice. This includes 88 didactically differentiated workshops tailored to both primary and secondary levels. The materials are structured to address diverse learning goals, ranging from introductory coding concepts to interdisciplinary applications in mathematics, science, language, and geography. The worksheets are designed to be used flexibly - either as printed copies or in digital formats on tablets and computers. The interactive design allows for programming tasks to be performed directly on screen, which is particularly useful for remote learning or classroom settings with limited physical resources. Beyond the content itself, the materials are supported by tutorial videos, solution guides, and reflection questions, allowing teachers to reflect on student understanding and facilitate classroom discussions. Examples include tasks like –The

Very Hungry Caterpillar", where students use Ozobots to retell the story, integrating literacy, sequencing, and basic programming. By making these materials freely available online, the project ensured that its impact would extend beyond the original participants. Schools elsewhere in Austria - and potentially internationally - can benefit from tested, classroom-ready resources that combine digital education with inclusive pedagogy.

2.6 Research Design and Scientific Framework

The project followed a structured, three-phase research design to ensure that the development and implementation of the educational robotics program were both evidence-informed and scientifically evaluated. The process was iterative and responsive, with each phase building upon insights of the previous one. An overview of the project's research plan is shown in Fig. 4.

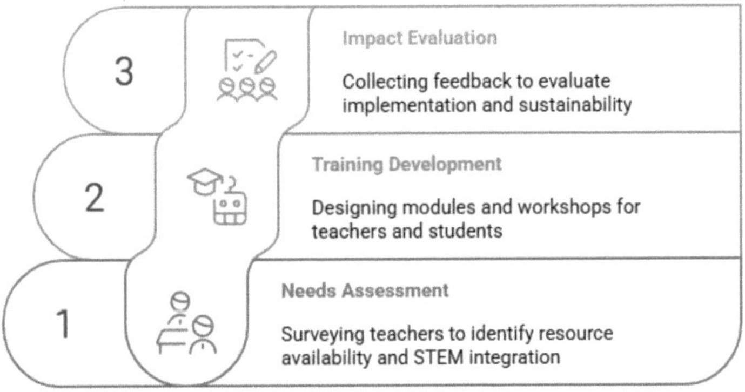

Fig. 4. Overview of the project's research plan.

The first phase focused on identifying the initial conditions for STEM and digital education in participating schools. A comprehensive questionnaire was distributed to teachers to assess the following core areas: Availability of STEM equipment and digital tools, Integration of STEM topics within the curriculum, Teachers' self-assessed skills, attitudes, and confidence in teaching STEM, Existing collaboration with STEM-related institutions or partners, and Opportunities for student engagement through interdisciplinary or project-based learning. These data formed the foundation for understanding the current landscape and identifying the support needs of teachers. In the second phase, the results of the initial study were combined with a systematic literature review to inform the design of the teacher training modules with a focus on: Enhancing teachers' digital literacy and STEM-related pedagogical strategies, Fostering hands-on, inquiry-based learning through the use of educational robotics (specifically Ozobots), and Promoting creativity, collaboration and curriculum integration.

This phase also addressed additional research objectives, such as: Teachers' satisfaction with the training, Development of STEM-related confidence and motivation, and Perceived relevance and transferability of Ozobot activities to real classroom settings. The third and current phase of the project involves evaluating the effectiveness and sustainability of the intervention. A follow-up questionnaire was used to capture teacher feedback related to: Implementation of Ozobot-based activities in lessons, Student engagement and interest in STEM, Challenges encountered in classroom implementation, and Ongoing support needs and conditions for long-term integration Across all three phases, the project pursued a broad set of research objectives, which are summarized in Fig. 5. These include both structural factors (e.g., equipment, collaborations) and personal-professional aspects (e.g., teacher motivation, training satisfaction, confidence).

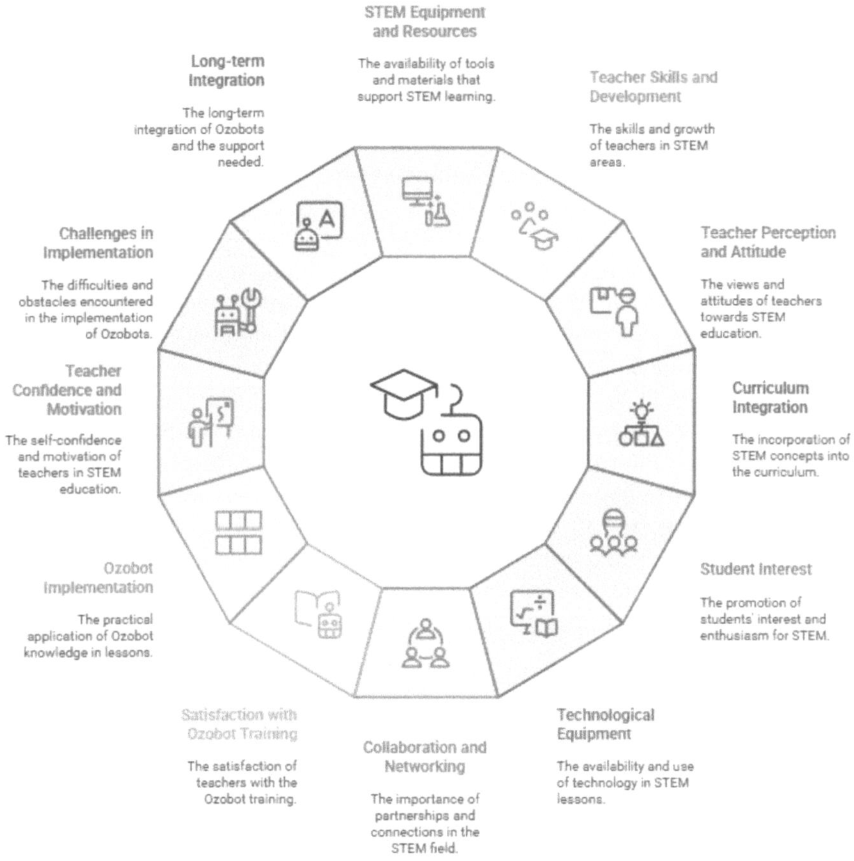

Fig. 5. Overview of the research project's objectives.

3 Findings from Previous Research

The Steyr Digitalization Project was accompanied by a multi-phase research framework that provided crucial empirical insights into the state of STEM education, teacher training needs, and the design of age-appropriate student workshops. These results, gathered through questionnaires, interviews, and qualitative analysis, laid the foundation for the project's pedagogical strategy and serve as a contribution to the academic discourse on digital transformation in compulsory education.

3.1 Initial Survey: Assessing STEM Readiness in Schools

The first phase of the research focused on evaluating the baseline conditions in the 16 participating schools. A comprehensive questionnaire was developed and distributed to educators prior to the project's implementation. Afterwards, the questionnaires were discussed in interviews with the participants. The findings highlighted substantial heterogeneity in the availability of digital resources and in teachers' preparedness for integrating STEM content into their curricula. While some schools already had access to digital tools and STEM-specific spaces, others were markedly under-equipped. In terms of teacher qualifications and professional development, the survey revealed that many educators had limited formal training in digital or STEM-specific pedagogy. Although motivation and general openness to innovation were high, respondents frequently expressed uncertainty about how to translate this into concrete instructional practices. Teachers also reported a lack of structured support systems and collaboration opportunities, which often led to isolated and sporadic engagement with STEM topics. The data further revealed that STEM was inconsistently embedded in school curricula. While isolated projects and thematic weeks were common, sustained interdisciplinary integration was rare. Moreover, only a few schools actively participated in STEM competitions or partnerships with external organizations, suggesting untapped potential for leveraging existing networks to enhance STEM learning opportunities. These results underscored the necessity of both targeted teacher training and structural support if STEM and digital education were to be sustainably embedded in daily teaching practice [19].

3.2 Literature-Informed Design of Teacher Training

The design of the teacher training modules was directly informed by findings from previous project phases as well as a focused review of relevant literature on professional development in STEM and digital education. The aim was to create an effective, evidence-based training structure that equips teachers with both the practical and pedagogical tools needed to integrate educational robotics, specifically Ozobots, into their classrooms in meaningful ways. Central to this approach were four core principles identified through the literature: hands-on,

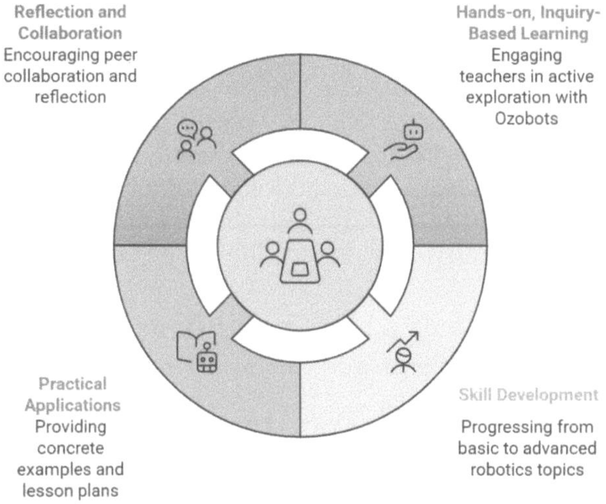

Fig. 6. Key Principles of Training Modules for Promoting Digital Literacy.

inquiry-based learning, progressive skill development, practical classroom application, and collaborative reflection. These principles were systematically implemented in the training modules and accompanying support formats (Fig. 6).

First, the workshops emphasized hands-on, inquiry-based learning by engaging participants in active exploration and experimentation with the Ozobots. This mirrors the kind of student-centered inquiry processes that teachers are expected to later facilitate in their own classrooms [12,23]. Teachers were encouraged to test code, explore challenges, and develop problem-solving strategies in an open-ended way, promoting both digital competence and confidence. Second, the training was structured to support progressive skill development. Module 1 introduced participants to foundational concepts such as color-coded programming and the basic functioning of the Ozobots. Building on this, Module 2 advanced into more complex applications, including block-based programming and interdisciplinary lesson planning. This progression ensured that teachers with varying prior knowledge could benefit from the training [7,32]. Third, a strong focus was placed on practical application. Participants received a broad range of ready-to-use lesson plans, worksheets, and classroom scenarios, all aligned with the national curriculum and adaptable to different school contexts [18]. These resources were designed to be low-threshold and inclusive, enabling usage even in schools with limited technical infrastructure. Fourth, the training embedded structured opportunities for collaboration and reflection, encouraging teachers to exchange ideas, adapt materials to their specific contexts, and form supportive peer communities. This element was informed by research on professional learning communities and their role in fostering sustained pedagogical innovation [42]. In recognition of the limitations of one-time interventions, the project also offered optional in-school workshops, follow-up modules, and access to a growing pool of open-access teaching materials. These extensions supported long-term implementation and addressed the need for ongoing support repeatedly emphasized in the literature. Feedback collected during the sessions indicated high levels of acceptance and engagement. Participants especially valued the structured yet flexible nature of the modules, the direct applicability of the teaching materials, and the opportunity to collaborate with colleagues from other institutions. These findings validate the literature-informed training design and suggest strong potential for scalability and transferability to broader educational contexts [21].

3.3 Workshop Development and Student-Centered Design

Parallel to the teacher training, the third phase of research focused on designing student workshops and teaching material. These were conceptualized based on both didactic principles and empirical findings from educational neuroscience and informatics education research. A key theoretical influence was the "COOL Informatics Teaching Approach,"which draws on Helen Parkhurst's Dalton Plan and incorporates elements of cooperative learning, open exploration, and structured self-regulation [20, 29–31]. The workshops were designed to foster computational thinking in children from preschool to lower secondary school. Emphasis was placed on active discovery, creativity, and autonomy. One workshop, "Storytelling with Ozobots,"served as a model: structured into five clearly defined phases - from exploration to implementation and presentation - it combined narrative thinking with algorithmic logic. The workshop was evaluated through both observation and feedback forms, and the results demonstrated high levels of student engagement and creativity. Children not only learned programming basics but also practiced teamwork, problem-solving, and digital storytelling in a playful and inclusive setting [20].

The workshops were intentionally designed to be scalable and adaptable, allowing differentiation based on age and ability. These qualities were crucial in ensuring that the workshops could be used across a wide range of school types and classroom settings.

4 Research Goals and Objectives

The current study builds upon the implementation of the Steyr Digitalization Project by evaluating the long-term impact of teacher training and digital toolkits on actual classroom practice. While the earlier phases of the project focused on development, piloting, and dissemination, this research phase seeks to examine whether and how the trained teachers are actively using the introduced technologies, particularly the Ozobots, and associated teaching materials, such as the GeoGebra book, in their daily teaching routines. This study is designed around a comprehensive questionnaire that explores multiple dimensions of teacher experience and perspective, guided by elements of the Technology Acceptance Model (TAM) [9]. The model provides a valuable framework for assessing teachers' perceptions toward technology, as well as the reception and application of the project's teaching materials. This approach leads to a multifaceted investigation of both subjective perceptions and real-world implementations. This research aims to answer the following central questions:

1. How do teachers perceive the usability and pedagogical potential of Ozobots as a tool for teaching programming and digital literacy? (RQ1)
2. To what extent have teachers integrated Ozobots into their classroom practice, and what patterns of actual use can be observed? (RQ2)
3. What factors influence teachers' intentions and attitudes toward the continued use of Ozobots, including the impact of professional development, external support, and teaching resources? (RQ3)

The first research question investigates how teachers perceive both the usability and pedagogical potential of educational robots. It covers aspects such as ease of use, clarity of instruction, intuitive design, and the effectiveness of Ozobots in conveying complex programming concepts in a playful, accessible way. This also includes teachers' evaluations of the accompanying teaching materials, especially the worksheets, in terms of their classroom applicability and didactic value. The second research question focuses on the actual integration of Ozobots into classroom practice. It explores whether and how frequently the robots are used following the professional development sessions, how many teaching units are dedicated to them, and the extent to which they have become part of regular lesson planning. It also captures differences in usage across grade levels and the level of teacher engagement during initial workshops. The third research question addresses the factors that influence teachers' intentions and attitudes toward the continued use of Ozobots. This includes not only enthusiasm for the tool and perceived educational benefit but also institutional and contextual conditions such as support from school leadership, availability of technical assistance, feedback from students and parents, and the impact of professional development. It also examines teachers' willingness to advocate for the tool within their professional community. Together, these three research questions form the foundation for the analysis of the survey data and allow for nuanced conclusions regarding the effectiveness, long-term sustainability, and broader transferability of the project's interventions. By connecting individual experiences with systemic conditions, this study provides deeper insight into how digital innovations can be successfully embedded into everyday teaching practice beyond initial pilot phases.

5 Methodology

To evaluate the long-term effects and perceived value of the Steyr Digitalization Project's teacher training modules and accompanying digital resources, a structured questionnaire was administered to teachers who had participated in the project. The goal of the survey was to collect systematic, empirical data on teachers' experiences with using Ozobots and the provided teaching materials in real classroom settings.

5.1 Participants and Sampling

The sampling method used was voluntary sampling. All compulsory schools in the city of Steyr were included, but teacher participation in the training, evaluation, and online questionnaire was entirely optional. A total of 64 participants started the survey using *LimeSurvey*, with 46 respondents fully completing the questionnaire. The analysis for this study is based on these 46 complete responses. Among these respondents, 40 teachers (87.0%) identified as female, five teachers (10.9%) as male, and one (2.2%) chose not to disclose their gender. In terms of age and educational background, the majority of participants were between 30 and 59 years old (84.8%) and held a bachelor's or master's degree in education (89.1%).

5.2 Prior Experience and Constituted Agreement to Participate

Of the primary and secondary school teachers from Steyr who participated in the project, 22 were already familiar with Ozobots prior to the trainings and workshops, while 21 (45.7%) had no prior knowledge of the tool. The survey was conducted in full compliance with data protection standards to ensure the privacy and confidentiality of all participants. Prior to participation, all respondents received a detailed explanation of the data collection process and the intended use of the findings. Informed consent was obtained through the completion of the questionnaire, which included a statement clarifying that submission constituted agreement to participate. No personal identifiers were collected, ensuring the anonymity and confidentiality of the participants' responses. Participation in the survey was voluntary, and respondents were informed about the purpose of the study, the anonymity of their responses, the handling of their data, and their right to withdraw at any time without providing a reason and without any negative consequences. Before participation, all respondents received a detailed explanation of the data collection process and the intended use of the findings. Informed consent was obtained through the completion of the questionnaire, which included a statement clarifying that submission constituted agreement to participate. No personal identifiers were collected, ensuring the anonymity and confidentiality of the participants' responses. Furthermore, the survey was approved by the *Educational Directorate of Upper Austria* (German: "Bildungsdirektion Oberösterreich"), which provided formal consent for its implementation. This approval ensured that the study adhered to ethical and institutional guidelines for research involving educators and schools.

5.3 Survey Instrument

The questionnaire used in this study was specifically developed based on the TAM by Davis (1985) (Fig. 7) [9,10]. It is structured into five thematic sections, each addressing a key construct of the TAM framework: Perceived Usefulness (U), Perceived Ease of Use (E), Attitude Toward Using (A), Behavioral Intention to Use (BI), and External Factors (EX) [9,10]. Additionally, questions on

Actual System Use (AU) were included to assess participants' real-world experiences with Ozobots. This model was chosen due to its widespread application in educational technology research and its suitability for evaluating the acceptance of digital tools and educational technology (EdTech) like Ozobots in classroom settings [15]. Furthermore, it was already successfully used by the authors in several previous case study evaluations on EdTech utilization in Austrian education [34,35]. The survey comprises both closed-ended questions and items designed to capture standardized and quantifiable responses. Most items are measured using a five-point Likert scale, ranging from "strongly disagree" to "strongly agree" or from "not at all" to "very much". Participants could also choose the option "no answer". This format allows for a detailed analysis of participants' perceptions, attitudes, and behaviors related to the use of Ozobots in educational contexts. The instrument was designed to ensure clarity, relevance, and alignment with the study's objectives, providing a comprehensive assessment of the factors influencing the acceptance and use of Ozobots. The online survey consists of 32 closed-ended questions divided into the following five sections:

1. Demographic Information (3 items)
2. Professional Development Participation in Training (2 items)
3. Classroom Experience with Educational Robots (5 items)
4. Technology Acceptance and System Use (18 items)
5. Evaluation of the Teaching Materials (GeoGebra book) (4 items)

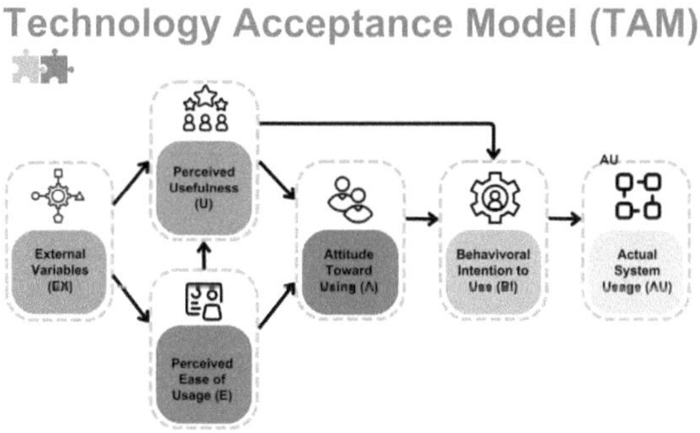

Fig. 7. Technology Acceptance Model (Davis, 1985).

5.4 Data Collection and Analysis

Data was collected between February 2025 and May 2025 using *Limesurvey* and analyzed using descriptive statistical methods to identify general trends and distributions in teacher responses. This includes calculating frequencies, means, and standard deviations across the different TAM dimensions and material evaluations.

6 Results

Findings show that 87.0% of all participants engaged in further teacher training sessions: 45.7% (21) attended one training or workshop, 37.0% (17) attended two, and 2.2% (1) participated in four sessions. Beyond the teacher training modules (Modules 1 and 2), participants reported involvement in 90 different student workshops for grades 1 through 8 (Fig. 8). Of these workshops, 81.1% were conducted at primary schools, while 18.9% took place at middle schools. Furthermore, the respondents answered the question, "Was an Ozobot workshop conducted with students in your classroom?" Here, "your classroom" refers to the class for which the respondent is the primary teacher or class leader (*German: Klassenlehrperson*). Of these, 33 participants (71.74%) responded "Yes", 12 (26.09%) responded "No", and 1 participant (2.17%) was "Not sure". In the following, the results classified according to the TAM model by Davis are presented [9,10].

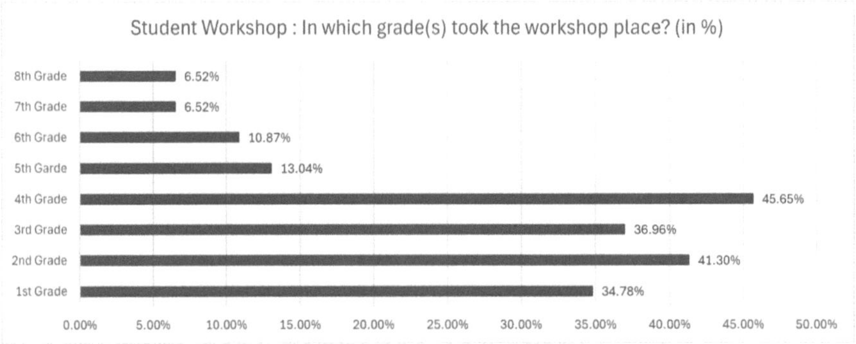

Fig. 8. Overview of the grade(s) the student workshops in Steyr took place (Data shown in %).

6.1 Perceived Usefulness

Perceived Usefulness (PU) in the Technology Acceptance Model (TAM) refers to the degree to which a user believes that using a particular technology will enhance their performance or achieve desired outcomes. In the context of Ozobots, this section evaluates how participants perceive the educational benefits of using Ozobots. The items in this section focus on whether Ozobots help playfully convey complex programming concepts, influence students' motivation to learn programming, and contribute to the development of students' technical problem-solving skills. These items assess the perceived impact of Ozobots on teaching effectiveness and student learning. The participating teachers were asked to evaluate statements regarding their experiences with Ozobots on a scale from 1 to 5 (1 = does not apply at all, 3 = neutral, 5 = fully applies; no answer). For the statement "Ozobots would help convey complex programming concepts in a playful way" the majority of participants expressed positive views. A total of 40.00% of respondents rated the statement with a 5 (fully applies), and 33.33% rated it with a 4. Neutral responses (3) accounted for 15.56%, while 11.11% rated it with a 2, and no participants selected 1 (does not apply at all). The arithmetic mean for this statement was 4.02, with a standard deviation of 1.01, indicating a strong overall agreement among participants. The statement "Students actively experimented with Ozobots and thereby improved their problem-solving skills" received mixed but generally positive. A total of 33.33% of participants rated the statement with a 4, and 17.78% rated it with a 5, indicating that 51.11% of respondents agreed. Neutral responses accounted for 28.89%, while 13.33% selected 2, and 6.67% selected 1. The arithmetic mean was 3.42, with a standard deviation of 1.14, suggesting moderate agreement with the statement (Fig. 9).

Perceived Usefulness of the GeoGebra Book. Regarding the use of the GeoGebra book, participants were asked "Do you regularly use the GeoGebra book in your teaching?" The majority (89.13%) responded "No", while only 8.70% answered "Yes", and 2.17% did not provide an answer. The perceived usefulness of the GeoGebra book was assessed with the question "How do you rate the usefulness of the GeoGebra book for lesson planning?" Responses were varied, with 41.30% selecting "Neutral", 13.04% finding it "Useful", and 4.35% rating it as "Very useful". On the other hand, 6.52% found it "Less useful", and 2.17% rated it as "Not useful at all". Notably, 32.61% of participants did not answer this question. Finally, participants were asked "Do you find the GeoGebra book user-friendly?" The majority of responses were neutral (47.83%), while 13.04% found it "Rather user-friendly," and 4.35% rated it as "Very user-friendly." Only 2.17% found it "Not user-friendly at all" and no participants selected "Rather not user-friendly". However, 32.61% of participants did not provide an answer (Fig. 10).

6.2 Perceived Ease of Use

Perceived Ease of Use (E) in TAM measures how effortless and intuitive users find a technology to operate [9,10]. For Ozobots, this section evaluates the simplicity of programming and using the devices. Answers concentrate on the ease of programming and using Ozobots, the quick and straightforward learning process for operating Ozobots, and lastly, the intuitiveness and user-friendliness of the Ozobot software interface. Regarding the claim "Learning to use Ozobots is quick and straightforward" responses were similarly positive. A total of 35.56% of participants rated the statement with a 5, and 33.33% rated it with a 4. Neutral responses accounted for 15.56%, while 15.56% rated it with a 2, and no participants selected 1. The arithmetic mean for this statement was 3.89, with a standard deviation of 1.07, suggesting that most participants found the learning process to be relatively simple. For the statement "The user interface

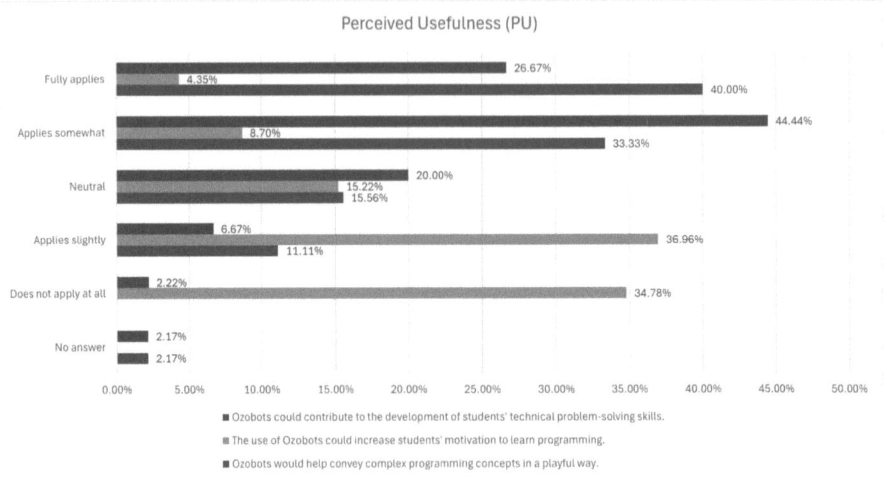

Fig. 9. This graphic illustrates participants' responses (N = 46) to three statements regarding the perceived usefulness of using Ozobots in programming education (in %). The responses were collected using a Likert scale ranging from "Does not apply at all" to "Fully applies," with an additional option for "No answer".

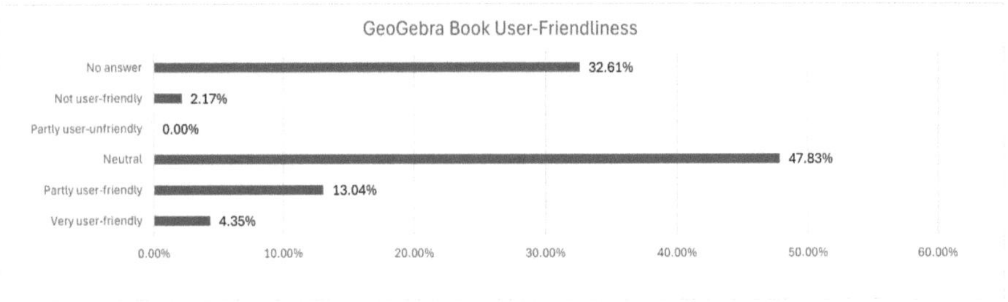

Fig. 10. This graphic presents participants' responses to statements evaluating the perceived user-friendliness of the GeoGebra Book (in %). The responses (N = 46) were collected using a Likert scale ranging from "Not user-friendly" to "very user-friendly," with an additional option for "No answer".

of the Ozobot software is intuitive and user-friendly" the majority of participants provided positive feedback. A total of 26.67% rated the statement with a 5 (fully applies), and 31.11% rated it with a 4. Neutral responses accounted for 28.89%, while 13.33% rated it with a 2, and no participants selected 1 (does not apply at all). The arithmetic mean was 3.71, with a standard deviation of 1.01, indicating that most participants found the interface to be user-friendly. Next, for the statement "I find Ozobots easy to program and use" 26.67% of the teachers rated it with a 5, and 40.00% rated it with a 4, showing that 66.67% of respondents agreed that Ozobots are easy to program and use. Neutral responses accounted for 20.00%, while 11.11% selected 2, and 2.22% selected

1. The arithmetic mean was 3.78, with a standard deviation of 1.04, indicating a strong overall agreement with this statement. Next, the negatively phrased statement "In my opinion, using Ozobots cannot increase students' motivation to learn programming" received strong disagreement from participants. A total of 34.78% rated the statement with a 1 (does not apply at all), and 36.96% rated it with a 2. Neutral responses accounted for 15.22%, while 8.70% selected 4, and 4.35% selected 5. The arithmetic mean was 2.11, with a standard deviation of 1.12, indicating that most participants believe Ozobots can indeed enhance students' motivation to learn programming. The statement "Ozobots could help students develop technical problem-solving skills" was rated positively by most participants. A total of 44.44% selected 4, and 26.67% selected 5, indicating that 71.11% of respondents agreed with the statement. Neutral responses accounted for 20.00%, while 6.67% selected 2, and only 2.22% selected 1. The arithmetic mean was 3.87, with a standard deviation of 0.97, suggesting a strong overall agreement (Fig. 11).

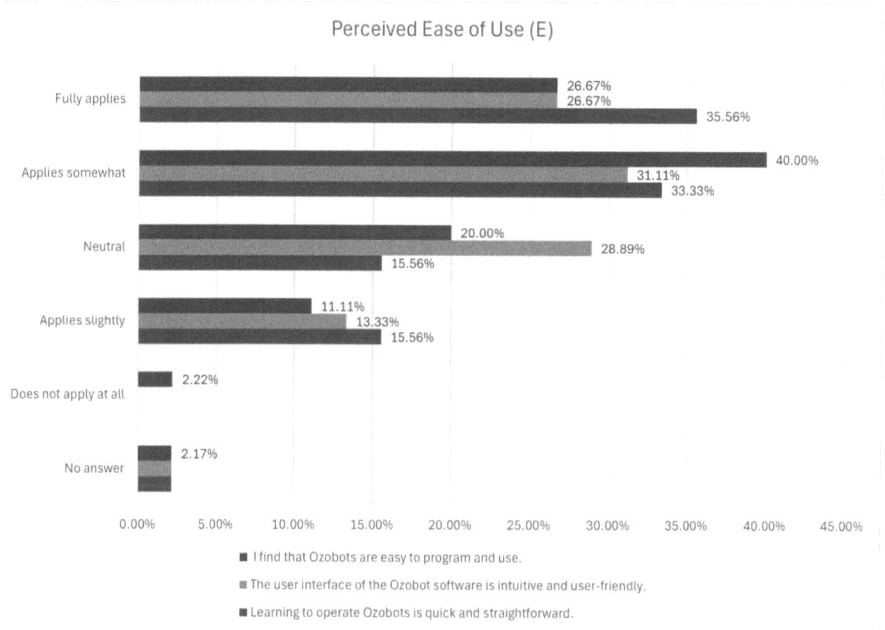

Fig. 11. This graphic illustrates participants' responses to three statements assessing the perceived ease of use of Ozobots (in %). The responses were collected using a Likert scale ranging from "Does not apply at all" to "Fully applies," with an additional option for "No answer."

6.3 Attitude Toward Using

Attitude Toward Using (A) reflects users' overall feelings and perceptions about adopting a technology [9,10]. In the case of Ozobots, this section explores participants' enthusiasm and positive outlook toward their use. The items address the belief that Ozobots contribute positively to students' education, the perception of Ozobots as an exciting way to make lessons more interactive, and lastly, the personal excitement about integrating Ozobots into teaching. Regarding excitement (Item: "The idea of using Ozobots in my teaching excites me") 26.09% of participants rated it with a 5 in the Likert scale, and 34.78% rated it with a 4, indicating that most participants were enthusiastic about using Ozobots in their teaching. Neutral responses accounted for 21.74%, while 10.87% selected 2, and 6.52% selected 1. The arithmetic mean was 3.63, with a standard deviation of 1.18, suggesting a generally positive attitude toward integrating Ozobots into teaching. When asked about the statement "I am convinced that Ozobots can make a positive contribution to students' education", the majority of participants agreed. Specifically, 28.26% rated the statement with a 5 (fully applies), and 36.96% rated it with a 4. Neutral responses accounted for 15.22%, while 13.04% selected 2, and 6.52% selected 1 (does not apply at all). The arithmetic mean was 3.67, with a standard deviation of 1.21, indicating that most participants believe Ozobots can positively impact students' education. A particularly high level of agreement was observed for the statement "I see the use of Ozobots as an exciting way to make lessons more interactive". Nearly half of the participants (47.83%) rated the statement with a 5, and 32.61% rated it with a 4, resulting in 80.43% of respondents expressing positive views. Neutral responses were minimal (8.70%), while 6.52% selected 2, and 4.35% selected 1. The arithmetic mean was 4.13, with a standard deviation of 1.11, indicating strong enthusiasm for the interactive potential of Ozobots (Fig. 12).

6.4 Behavioral Intention to Use

Behavioral Intention to Use (BI) captures users' plans and intentions to adopt a technology in their practices [9,10]. For Ozobots, this section examines participants' willingness to incorporate them into teaching. This includes plans to use Ozobots regularly to teach programming concepts, intentions to use Ozobots as a tool to foster students' digital competence, and further efforts to convince colleagues of the benefits of using Ozobots. The intention to use Ozobots regularly in teaching was explored through the statement "I plan to use Ozobots regularly in my teaching to convey programming concepts". Here, responses were more varied. While 8.70% of participants rated the statement with a 5 and 34.78% with a 4, a significant portion of respondents were neutral (26.09%) or disagreed, with 26.09% selecting 2 and 4.35% selecting 1. The arithmetic mean was 3.17, with a standard deviation of 1.06, suggesting moderate intentions to integrate Ozobots regularly into teaching. Regarding colleagues' recommendations (item: "I intend to convince colleagues of the benefits of using Ozobots"), responses were more varied. While 22.22% of participants rated the statement with a 5

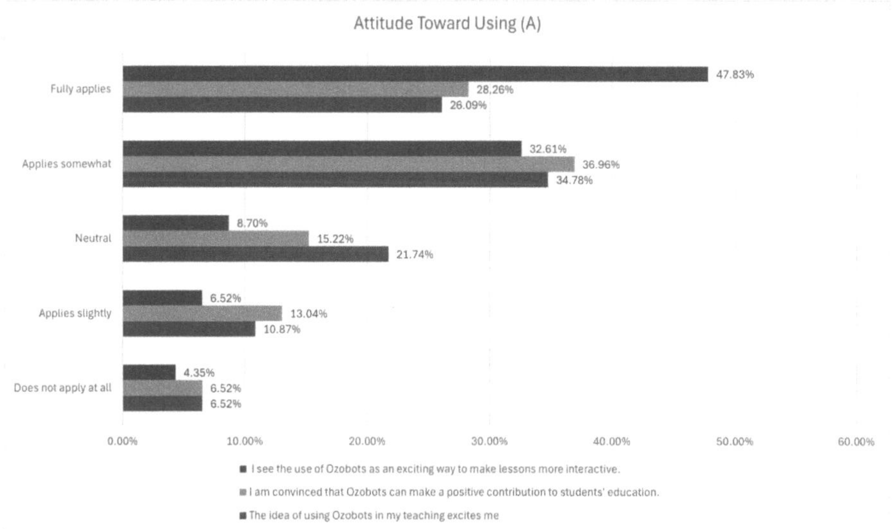

Fig. 12. This graphic presents participants' responses (N = 46) to three statements evaluating their attitudes toward using Ozobots in education (in %). The responses were collected using a Likert scale ranging from "Does not apply at all" to "Fully applies," with an additional option for "No answer". (No participant choose the option "no answer").

and 31.11% with a 4, a notable portion of respondents were neutral (17.78%) or disagreed, with 20.00% selecting 2 and 8.89% selecting 1. The arithmetic mean for this statement was 3.38, with a standard deviation of 1.28, indicating a more mixed level of agreement compared to the other statements. The intention to use Ozobots as a tool to promote students' digital competence was also highly rated. For the statement "It is my intention to use Ozobots as a tool to foster my students' digital competence", 33.33% of participants selected 5, and 46.67% selected 4, meaning 80.00% of respondents agreed with the statement. Neutral responses accounted for 6.67%, while 8.89% selected 2, and 4.44% selected 1. The arithmetic mean was 3.96, with a standard deviation of 1.09, reflecting a strong commitment to using Ozobots for this purpose (Fig. 13).

6.5 External Factors

External Factors (EX) assess the external influences that impact users' decisions to adopt an educational technology [9,10]. For Ozobots, this section evaluates the role of external support and feedback. The items focus on the importance of school administration support for using Ozobots, the influence of training opportunities and technical support on willingness to use Ozobots, and the role of feedback from parents and students in the decision to continue using Ozobots. Regarding "The availability of training opportunities and technical support influences my willingness to use Ozobots" 30.43% of participants rated it with a 5,

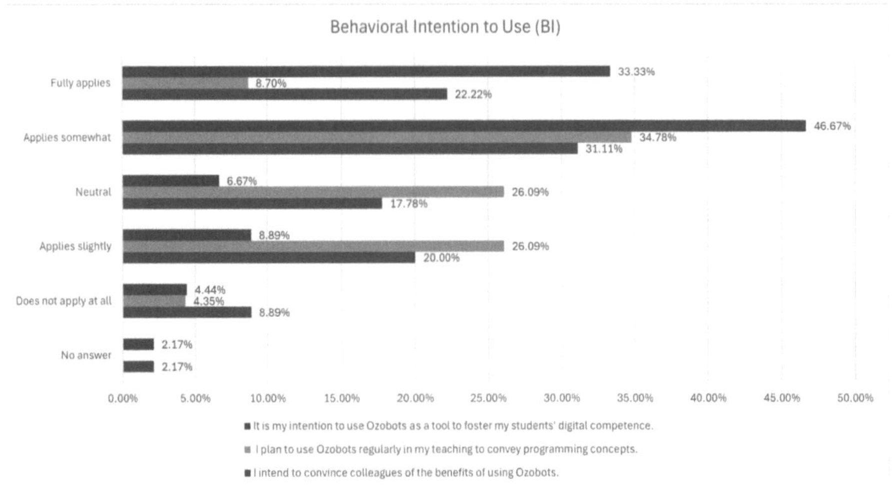

Fig. 13. This graphic illustrates participants' responses (N = 46) to three statements assessing their behavioral intention to use Ozobots in teaching (in %). The responses were collected using a Likert scale ranging from "Does not apply at all" to "Fully applies," with an additional option for "No answer".

and 36.96% rated it with a 4, showing that the majority (67.39%) agreed that training and support are essential factors. Neutral responses accounted for 8.70%, while 15.22% selected 2, and 8.70% selected 1. The arithmetic mean was 3.65, with a standard deviation of 1.30, reflecting a generally positive but slightly more varied response. The role of school administration support was addressed in the statement "Support from my school administration is crucial for my decision to use Ozobots in teaching". Opinions on this topic were mixed. While 17.78% of participants rated the statement with a 5 and 22.22% with a 4, a notable portion of respondents were neutral (22.22%) or disagreed, with 13.33% selecting 2 and 24.44% selecting 1. The arithmetic mean was 2.96, with a standard deviation of 1.45, indicating that while some participants value administrative support, others do not consider it a decisive (external) factor. In contrast, the statement "Feedback from parents and students about the use of Ozobots does NOT play a role in my decision to continue using them" received more mixed responses. While 33.33% of participants selected 3 (neutral), 17.78% strongly disagreed (1), and 15.56% disagreed (2). On the other hand, 22.22% selected 4, and 11.11% selected 5, indicating that for some participants, feedback does not influence their decision. The arithmetic mean was 2.93, with a standard deviation of 1.25, suggesting a more divided perspective on the importance of feedback (Fig. 14).

6.6 Actual System Use

Actual System Use (AU) measures the real-world application and integration of a technology [9,10]. For Ozobots, this section examines how partic-

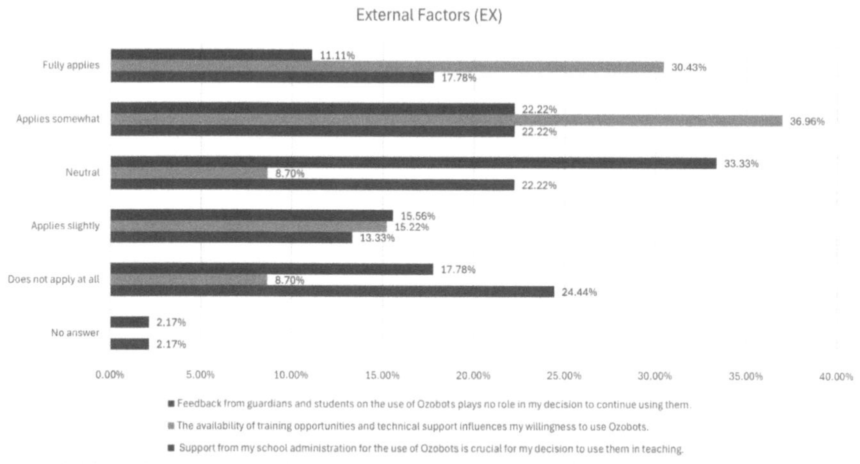

Fig. 14. This graphic illustrates participants' responses (N = 46) to three statements regarding the influence of external factors on their decision to use Ozobots in teaching (in %). The responses were collected using a Likert scale ranging from "Does not apply at all" to "Fully applies," with an additional option for "No answer".

ipants have already used them in teaching. The items include the successful use of Ozobots to teach programming basics, the students' active experimentation with Ozobots to improve problem-solving skills, and the integration of Ozobots as a regular part of the teaching plan. The integration of Ozobots into regular teaching was explored through the statement "Ozobots have become an integral part of my teaching plan and are used regularly." Here, responses were more critical. A significant portion of participants (36.96%) strongly disagreed (1), and 21.74% disagreed (2). Neutral responses accounted for 21.74%, while only 13.04% selected 4 in the Likert scale, and 6.52% selected 5. The arithmetic mean was 2.3, with a standard deviation of 1.28, indicating that Ozobots are not yet widely integrated into regular teaching plans. Participants were also asked about their prior experiences with Ozobots through the statement "I have already successfully used Ozobots to teach programming basics". A total of 28.26% of participants rated it with a 5, and 30.43% with a 4, indicating that 58.70% of respondents have had positive experiences using Ozobots for teaching programming. Neutral responses accounted for 8.70%, while 10.87% selected 2, and 21.74% selected 1. The arithmetic mean was 3.33, with a standard deviation of 1.54, reflecting a mix of experiences, with many participants reporting success (Fig. 15).

6.7 Summary Quantitative Data

The findings highlight significant engagement with Ozobots and their perceived educational value. A total of 87.0% of participants attended further teacher

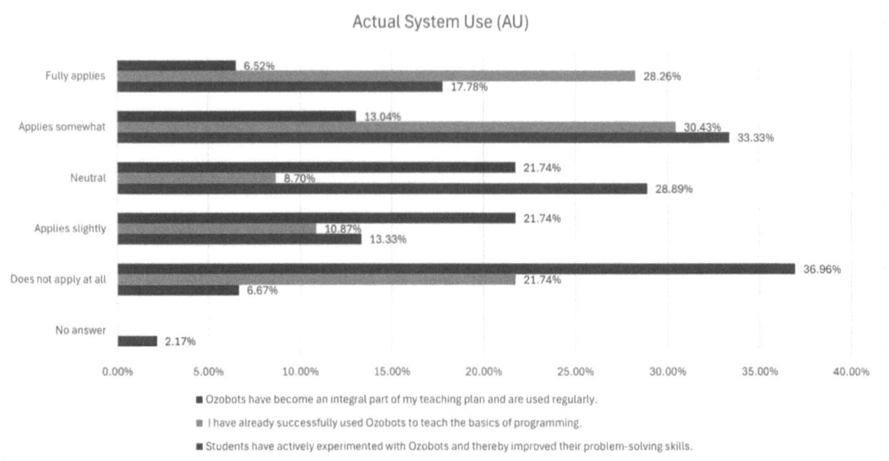

Fig. 15. This graphic illustrates participants' responses (N = 46) to three statements regarding their actual use of Ozobots in teaching (in %). The responses were collected using a Likert scale ranging from "Does not apply at all" to "Fully applies," with an additional option for "No answer".

training sessions, with 45.7% attending one session and 37.0% attending two. Participants also conducted 90 student workshops, primarily in primary schools (81.1%), with 71.74% of respondents confirming that they conducted an Ozobot workshop in their own classroom.

1. Perceived Usefulness: Teachers largely agreed that Ozobots help convey complex programming concepts (mean = 4.02) and improve students' problem-solving skills (mean = 3.42).
2. Perceived Ease of Use: Participants found Ozobots easy to program (mean = 3.78) and the software interface user-friendly (mean = 3.71).
3. Attitude Toward Using: Teachers expressed enthusiasm for using Ozobots, with 80.43% agreeing that they make lessons more interactive (mean = 4.13).
4. Behavioral Intention to Use: While 80.00% intended to use Ozobots to foster digital competence (mean = 3.96), intentions to use them regularly were more moderate (mean = 3.17).
5. External Factors: Training opportunities and technical support were seen as important (mean = 3.65), but opinions on the role of school administration support were mixed (mean = 2.96).
6. Actual System Use: Although 58.70% reported successfully using Ozobots to teach programming basics (mean = 3.33), only 19.57% indicated that Ozobots are a regular part of their teaching plan (mean = 2.3).

7 Discussion

The findings of this study provide valuable insights into the integration of educational robotics, specifically Ozobots, into Austrian primary and secondary education. The results demonstrate that teachers perceive Ozobots as a useful and engaging tool for teaching programming and fostering digital competencies. Similar findings are found using Ozobots for novice programmers indicate their potential of increasing programming and digital skills [39–41]. The high levels of agreement on statements related to perceived usefulness and ease of use suggest that Ozobots are well-suited for classroom applications, particularly in conveying complex programming concepts in a playful and accessible manner. Teachers also expressed enthusiasm for using Ozobots, with many highlighting their potential to make lessons more interactive and engaging, as shown in previous case studies and research [20,38,39,41].

Despite these positive perceptions, the study also reveals challenges in the regular integration of Ozobots into teaching practices. While 58.70% of participants reported successfully using Ozobots to teach programming basics, only 19.57% indicated that Ozobots are a regular part of their teaching plans. This gap between perceived usefulness and actual system use highlights the influence of external factors, such as institutional support and access to training opportunities. Mixed responses regarding the role of school administration support and feedback from parents and students further underscore the need for a supportive ecosystem to facilitate the sustainable adoption of educational robotics. The project was implemented exclusively in Steyr, encompassing all compulsory schools in the city, including primary, middle, and polytechnic schools. This localized approach allowed for a focused evaluation of the integration of Ozobots within a specific educational context. However, the findings also highlight the need to explore how such initiatives can be scaled to other regions and adapted to diverse educational settings. As Ertmer et al., this study emphasizes the importance of professional development in fostering teachers' confidence and competence in using digital tools [13]. The majority of participants attended at least one training session, and many conducted student workshops following the training. These results suggest that targeted teacher training programs, such as those implemented in the Steyr Digitalization Project, play a critical role in equipping educators with the skills and resources needed to integrate innovative technologies into their teaching. However, the study also highlights areas for improvement. For instance, while the GeoGebra book was included as part of the teaching materials, its perceived usefulness and user-friendliness received largely neutral ratings. This suggests a need for further refinement of resources to ensure they meet the practical needs of teachers and align with their classroom contexts.

7.1 Limitations

First, the quantitative data is based on self-reported data, which would lead to potential bias [2]. Furthermore, due to the limited sample size (N = 46), the study is not intended to deliver generalizable conclusions but rather to provide detailed, practice-oriented insights into the mid-term impact of the project and identify areas for further development and support. Second, the localized nature of the study (Steyr only) and the lack of long-term follow-up data should be addressed in future work. Furthermore, the pilot study relies heavily on quantitative data. While this is valuable, qualitative insights (e.g., teacher or student feedback) could provide a richer understanding of the challenges and successes of the project; therefore, future research will concentrate on qualitative perceptions.

8 Conclusion and Outlook

This Upper Austrian study demonstrates the potential of educational robotics, such as Ozobots, to enhance digital literacy and computational thinking in primary and secondary education. Teachers generally perceive Ozobots as useful, easy to use, and engaging, with many reporting successful implementation in their classrooms. However, the findings also reveal barriers to regular integration, including external factors and varying levels of institutional support. To address these challenges, future initiatives should focus on creating a supportive ecosystem that includes ongoing professional development, access to technical support, and collaboration between schools, policymakers, and private sector partners. Additionally, refining and expanding teaching materials, such as the GeoGebra book, could further enhance the usability and applicability of digital tools in diverse educational settings. Future work will further focus on other educational robot options as well. Building on the success of the Steyr Digitalization Project, future efforts will aim to scale the initiative to other regions, ensuring that the lessons learned can benefit a broader range of schools and educators. Furthermore, the project team plans to develop new training modules focused on text-based programming that support programming languages such as *Python*. This expansion will provide teachers and students with opportunities to engage in more advanced programming concepts, further bridging the gap between introductory coding and real-world applications - even for older students. The Steyr Digitalization Project serves as a promising model for integrating educational robotics into compulsory education, offering valuable lessons for scaling similar initiatives in other regions. By addressing the identified barriers and building on the strengths of the current approach, educational stakeholders can ensure that digital tools and educational robots become an integral part of everyday teaching, equipping students with the skills needed to thrive in a digitally connected world.

Disclosure of Interests. The authors have no competing interests to declare that are relevant to the content of this article

References

1. Adera, N.: Innovative learning spaces and blended learning: quest for 21st century competency teaching and learning approaches, pp. 139–174. IGI-Global (2025). https://doi.org/10.4018/979-8-3693-6930-2.ch006, www.igi-global.com/chapter/staff-development/253467?camid=4v1a

2. Anvari, F., Efendic, E., Olsen, J., Arslan, R.C., Elson, M., Schneider, I.K.: Bias in self-reports: an initial elevation phenomenon. Soc. Psychol. Pers. Sci. **14**(6), 727–737 (2023). https://doi.org/10.1177/19485506221129160
3. Beilock, S.L., Gunderson, E.A., Ramirez, G., Levine, S.C.: Female teachers' math anxiety affects girls' math achievement. In: Proceedings of the National Academy of Sciences of the United States of America, vol. 107, pp. 1860–1863 (2010). https://doi.org/10.1073/PNAS.0910967107
4. Brenneman, K., Stevenson-Boyd, J., Frede, E.C.: Mathematics and science in preschool: policy and practice (2009)
5. Buchter, J., Kucskar, M., Oh-Young, C., Welgarz-Ward, J., Gelfer, J.: Supporting STEM in early childhood education (2017). https://digitalscholarship.unlv.edu/co_educ_policy/2
6. Bundesministerium für Bildung (BMB), eEducation: Denken lernen - probleme loesen: Bmb-projekt digi.case (2025). https://dlpl.at/startseite, accessed: 2023-10-12
7. Chalufour, I.: Learning to teach science: strategies that support teacher practice. In: Collected Papers from the STEM in Early Education and Development (SEED) Conference (2010). https://ecrp.illinois.edu/beyond/seed/chalufour.html
8. Davidson, C.N.: Now you see it: how the brain science of attention will transform the way we live, work, and learn, Viking (2011)
9. Davis, F.D.: A technology acceptance model for empirically testing new end-user information systems: theory and results. Doctoral dissertation, Massachusetts Institute of Technology (1985)
10. Davis, F.D.: Perceived usefulness, perceived ease of use, and user acceptance of information technology. MIS Q. **13**(3), 319–340 (1989). https://doi.org/10.2307/249008
11. DeJarnette, N.K.: America's children: providing early exposure to STEM (science, technology, engineering and math) initiatives. Education **133**, 77–84 (2012). https://eric.ed.gov/?id=EJ996974
12. Duschl, R.A., Schweingruber, H.A., Shouse, A.W.: Taking Science to School: Learning and Teaching Science in Grades K-8. The National Academies Press (2007). http://www.nap.edu/catalog/11625.html
13. Ertmer, P.A., Ottenbreit-Leftwich, A.T.: Teacher technology change: how knowledge, confidence, beliefs, and culture intersect. J. Res. Technol. Educ. **42**(3), 255–284 (2010). https://www.iste.org/jrte
14. Frances, D., et al.: What works?: A study of effective early childhood mental health consultation programs. Technical Report, Georgetown University Center for Child and Human Development (2009)
15. Granić, A., Marangunić, N.: Technology acceptance model in educational context: a systematic literature review. Br. J. Educ. Technol. **50** (2019). https://doi.org/10.1111/bjet.12864
16. Hinterplattner, S., Rottenhofer, M., Groher, I., Sabitzer, B.: Exploring students' experiences and perceptions of computer science: a survey of austrian secondary schools. In: International Conference on Computer Supported Education, CSEDU - Proceedings, vol. 2, pp. 238–247 (2022). https://doi.org/10.5220/0011049000003182
17. Hinterplattner, S., Sabitzer, B., Skogø, J.S.: Working on interdisciplinary projects to strengthen creative computational thinking and to support talent development. Commun. Comput. Inf. Sci. **1473 CCIS**, 317–340 (2021). https://doi.org/10.1007/978-3-030-86439-2_17

18. Hinterplattner, S., Schalk, M., Leitner, S., Schwinghammer, M.: MINT-Begabungsförderung in der Elementarpädagogik: analyse und Chancen in der Ausbildung, pp. 279–291. Waxmann (2024)
19. Hinterplattner, S., Schmidthaler, E., Schwinghammer, M., Skogø, J., Hörmann, C.: The integration of digital education within an ozobot pilot project: Austrian teacher perspectives and practices. In: Proceedings of the 17th International Conference on Computer Supported Education - Volume 1: CSEDU, pp. 60–71. SciTePress (2025). https://doi.org/10.5220/0013211400003932
20. Hinterplattner, S., Schmidthaler, E., Skogø, J.S., Leitner, S., Sabitzer, B.: Once upon a time there was an ozobot: storytelling with educational robots. In: The 15th International Conference on Education Technology and Computers, pp. 120–126. ACM (2024). https://doi.org/10.1145/3629296.3629315
21. Hinterplattner, S., Schmidthaler, E., Skogø, J.S., Sabitzer, B.: Fostering digital literacy through creative learning approaches with educational robots. J. Educ. Pract. **16**, 65–74 (2025). https://doi.org/10.7176/JEP/16-5-07, https://www.iiste.org/Journals/index.php/JEP/article/view/63166
22. Hörmann, C., Schmidthaler, E., Kuka, L., Rottenhofer, M., Sabitzer, B.: From non-existent to mandatory in five years – the journey of digital education in the Austrian school system. In: The 15th International Conference on Informatics in Schools (2022)
23. Inan, H.Z., Inan, T.: 3hs education: examining hands-on, heads-on and hearts-on early childhood science education. Int. J. Sci. Educ. **37**, 1974–1991 (2015). https://doi.org/10.1080/09500693.2015.1060369
24. Jamil, F.M., Linder, S.M., Stegelin, D.A.: Early childhood teacher beliefs about STEAM education after a professional development conference. Early Childhood Educ. J. 2017 46:4 **46**, 409–417 (2017). https://doi.org/10.1007/S10643-017-0875-5, https://link.springer.com/article/10.1007/s10643-017-0875-5
25. Katz, L.G.: STEM in the early years (2010). http://ecrp.uiuc.edu
26. Kazakoff, E.R., Sullivan, A., Bers, M.U.: The effect of a classroom-based intensive robotics and programming workshop on sequencing ability in early childhood. Early Childhood Educ. J. **41**, 245–255 (2013). https://doi.org/10.1007/S10643-012-0554-5/FIGURES/4, https://link.springer.com/article/10.1007/s10643-012-0554-5
27. Land Oberösterreich: Von feuer bis coding – die mint-welt spielerisch entdecken: Land ooe startet pilotprojekt technikboxextended in 20 oberoesterreichischen volksschulen (2023). https://www.land-oberoesterreich.gv.at/, Accessed 01 Mar 2025
28. Nugent, G., Kunz, G., Rilett, L., Jones, E.: Extending engineering education to K-12. Technol. Teach. **69**, 14–19 (2010). https://eric.ed.gov/?id=EJ887811
29. Parkhurst, H.: Education on the Dalton Plan. E. P. Dutton & Company, New York (1922)
30. Sabitzer, B.: A neurodidactical approach to cross-curricular open learning. Cool informatics. Habilitation (2013)
31. Sabitzer, B.: A Neurodidactical Approach to Cooperative and Cross-curricular Open Learning: COOL Informatics. Alpen-Adria-Universität Klagenfurt (2014)
32. Schacter, J., Jo, B.: Improving preschoolers' mathematics achievement with tablets: a randomized controlled trial. Math. Educ. Res. J. **29**, 313–327 (2017). https://doi.org/10.1007/S13394-017-0203-9, https://link.springer.com/article/10.1007/s13394-017-0203-9
33. Schacter, J., et al.: Math shelf: a randomized trial of a prekindergarten tablet number sense curriculum. Early Educ. Dev. **27**, 74–88 (2016). https://doi.org/10.1080/10409289.2015.1057462

34. Schmidthaler, E., Hoermann, C., Hornsby, D., Fraser, A., Cápay, M., Sabitzer, B.: Easy coding in biology: combining block-based programming tasks with biological education to encourage computational thinking in girls. In: 16th International Conference on Informatics in Schools, ISSEP 2023, Local Proceedings (ISSEP2023). Lausanne, Switzerland (2023). https://doi.org/10.5281/zenodo.8431893
35. Schmidthaler, E., Staeter, R., Cápay, M., Ludwig, M., Lavicza, Z.: Easy coding in biology: pilot workshop design and experiences from block-based programming with colette in secondary education. J. Res. Sci. Math. Technol. Educ. **6**(SI), 177–206 (2023). https://doi.org/10.31756/jrsmte.619SI
36. Silverstein, S.C.: How teaching matters. **5**, 317 (017). https://doi.org/10.1187/CBE.06-09-0186, https://www.lifescied.org/doi/10.1187/cbe.06-09-0186
37. Swertz, C.: Digitale Grundbildung im Pilotversuch: Beobachtungen einer entstehenden praxis. Medienimpulse **56**(3) (2018). https://doi.org/10.21243/mi-03-18-11
38. Tangler, K.: Klein, kreativ, ozobot: Förderung von kreativität und informatischem denken durch spielerisches programmieren. R&E-SOURCE (2020). https://journal.ph-noe.ac.at/index.php/resource/article/view/825
39. Tengler, K., Kastner-Hauler, O., Sabitzer, B.: Enhancing computational thinking skills using robots and digital storytelling. In: Proceedings of the 13th International Conference on Computer Supported Education (CSEDU 2021), - vol. 1, pp. 157–164. SCITEPRESS – Science and Technology Publications, Lda (2021). https://doi.org/10.5220/0010477001570164
40. Tengler, K., Kastner-Hauler, O., Sabitzer, B.: A robotics-based learning environment supporting computational thinking skills — design and development. In: 2021 IEEE Frontiers in Education Conference (FIE), vol. 1, pp. 1–6 (2021). https://doi.org/10.1109/FIE49875.2021.9637351
41. Tengler, K., Sabitzer, B., Kastner-Hauler, O.: First programming with ozobots - a creative approach to early computer science in primary education. In: INTED2020 Proceedings, vol. 1, pp. 5156–5162 (2020). https://doi.org/10.21125/INTED.2020.1398
42. Wenglinsky, H., Silverstein, S.: The science training teachers need. Educ. Leadersh. **64**, 24–29 (2006)

From Ecological Intention to Digital Action: How Implementation Intention (SSBC) Influences the Acceptance of an e-Learning Platform

Lisa Michanol[1], Charles Aivar[2], and Jean-Christophe Sakdavong[1](✉)

[1] CLLE, University of Toulouse, Toulouse, France
jean-christophe.sakdavong@univ-tlse2.fr
[2] TP demain, Paris, France

Abstract. Facing the urgency of integrating the ecological transition into professional practices, this study provides an in-depth analysis of the psychological and social factors governing the acceptance of an e-learning platform for Public Works (PW) professionals. While digital tools are proliferating, their effective adoption remains a challenge. Drawing on data from 42 users of the "tpdemain" platform, this research distinguishes itself by combining two major theoretical frameworks: the Stage Model of Self-Regulated Behavioral Change (SSBC) and the Unified Theory of Acceptance and Use of Technology (UTAUT2), enhanced by the concept of Situated Acceptance. The objective is to examine in depth how specific psychological mechanisms, notably implementation intention, and contextual factors, such as social influence and the organizational dimension, affect the acceptability and effective use of educational resources.

Detailed statistical analyses reveal that implementation intention (the concrete planning of an action) is a powerful and statistically significant predictor of both the acceptability and acceptance of the platform. Furthermore, the study highlights a significant contextual chain of influence: the perception of organizational support for the ecological transition positively influences perceived social pressure, which in turn increases the tool's perceived acceptability. The rich and nuanced discussion explores the theoretical implications of successfully bridging environmental psychology and technology acceptance, as well as the practical outcomes for designing more effective training strategies. Ultimately, this research demonstrates that to maximize the adoption of green digital tools, it is more relevant to support action planning in already-engaged individuals than to limit efforts to general awareness campaigns.

Keywords: UTAUT2 · SSBC · Public Works · e-Learning · Ecological Transition · Technology Acceptance · Implementation Intention · Social Influence

C. Meinel et al. (Eds.): CSEDU 2025, CCIS 3148, pp. 72–81, 2027.
https://doi.org/10.1007/978-3-032-39103-2_4

1 Introduction

Climate change represents a systemic threat that impacts all infrastructures and human activities. The Public Works (PW) sector, by its very nature as a major consumer of energy, producer of waste, and contributor to soil sealing, is at the forefront of this mandatory transformation. In France, IPCC projections and analyses by the National Federation of Public Works (NFPW) highlight a growing vulnerability, with, for example, 75% of the road network exposed to extreme heat risks. Faced with this reality, the public sector and companies must not only adapt their infrastructures but also, crucially, evolve the skills of their workforce.

In this context, digital technologies offer unprecedented opportunities for continuous training. E-learning platforms, such as "tpdemain", initiated by the NFPW as part of the DEFFINUM project, have been specifically designed to provide educational resources on the ecological transition, accessible to all professionals in the sector. However, experience shows that the mere availability of a technology does not guarantee its appropriation and effective use by trainers and learners. The adoption of these tools is a complex process, influenced by a multitude of individual, social, and organizational factors.

A central challenge in both technology adoption and behavioral science is the well-documented gap between intention and action. Therefore, this study moves beyond measuring simple acceptability (the intention to use) to also assess effective acceptance as measured by self-reported effective use. This approach allows for a more complete picture of technology appropriation, differentiating factors that foster positive attitudes from those that trigger concrete action.

The scientific literature on technology acceptance (e.g., TAM, UTAUT models) is abundant, as is the literature on pro-environmental behaviors (e.g., TPB, NAM, VBN models). However, very few studies have attempted to bridge these two fields. It is this gap that our work aims to fill. Building on an initial study [1], this article provides an in-depth analysis of its most significant findings. The objective is to dissect the specific links between the advanced stages of ecological behavior change and the mechanisms of acceptance for a supporting technology in order to propose concrete and theoretically grounded levers for action.

2 Theoretical Framework

To adequately address the distinction between user attitude and actual behavior, our theoretical framework is built on a synergistic combination of models. We posit that predicting technology adoption requires understanding two distinct phases: first, the formation of user acceptability, which represents a state of psychological readiness and positive intention, and second, the transition to effective use, which constitutes a concrete action. To model this, we use the UTAUT2 model [6] as a foundation for acceptability, but we enrich it with the stage-based SSBC model [2] to explain the progression towards concrete action, and with the concept of Situated Acceptance [8] to ground the entire process in its professional context.

2.1 From Desire to Action: The SSBC Model

To model pro-environmental behavior change, we mobilized the Stage Model of Self-Regulated Behavioral Change (SSBC) by Bamberg [2]. Unlike static models such as the Theory of Planned Behavior (TPB) [3], the SSBC model views change as a dynamic process unfolding in four distinct stages, conceptually based on the Model of Action Phases (MAP) [4]. It also incorporates elements from the Norm-Activation Model (NAM) [5]. A visual description of this model is presented in Fig. 1 [2].

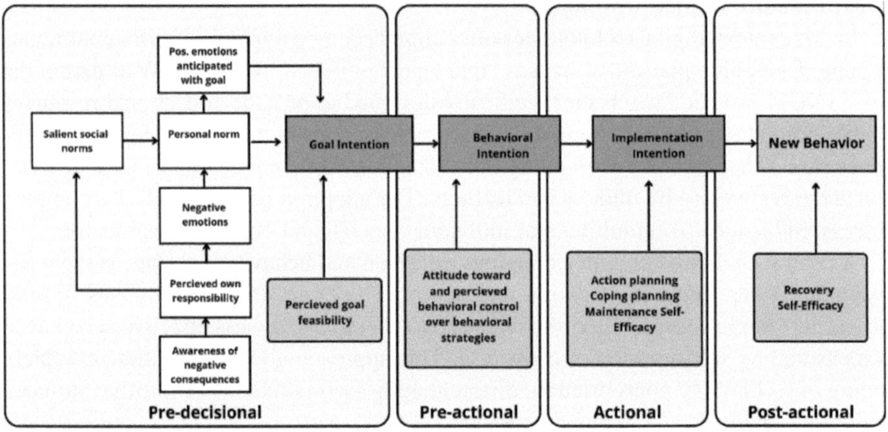

Fig. 1. SSBC Model from [2].

1. **The Pre-decisional Stage:** The individual becomes aware of the negative consequences of their current behavior and begins to feel personal responsibility. This awareness, influenced by social norms, gives rise to a "personal norm" and leads to the formation of a goal intention (e.g., "I want to adopt more sustainable practices").
2. **The Pre-actional Stage:** The goal intention is transformed into a more concrete **behavioral intention**. The individual evaluates different strategies, weighs the pros and cons, and assesses their perceived control over the new behavior.
3. **The Actional Stage:** This is the execution phase. This stage is critically dependent on **implementation intention**, a key concept for our study, which is defined by the precise planning of an action ("when, where, and how to act"). It turns a vague intention into a concrete action plan.
4. **The Post-actional Stage:** The individual evaluates the outcomes of their new behavior, strengthens their sense of self-efficacy, and works to maintain this behavior over the long term to prevent relapse.

2.2 From Tool to Use: Models of Acceptance

To analyze the adoption of the "tpdemain" platform, we rely on the Unified Theory of Acceptance and Use of Technology 2 (UTAUT2) by Venkatesh et al. [6]. While powerful, models like UTAUT2 primarily predict behavioral intention or acceptability. They are less equipped to explain the 'intention-action gap', the frequent disconnect between a user's positive attitude towards a technology and their actual, sustained use of it. To bridge this gap and understand what drives effective acceptance (or effective use), our framework integrates two complementary perspectives.

To ground the process in its real-world context, we integrate the concept of Situated Acceptance by Bobillier-Chaumon [8]. This approach emphasizes that a technology is only truly accepted when it is evaluated in its actual context of use. We specifically retain the organizational dimension from this model, which measures the individual's perception of their organization's support for both the technological tool and the values it embodies (here, the ecological transition).

2.3 Research Hypotheses

Our combined research model (Fig. 2) shows the interactions that we hypothesize between the elements of SSBC, UTAUT2, Situated Acceptance and Effective acceptance (gree)

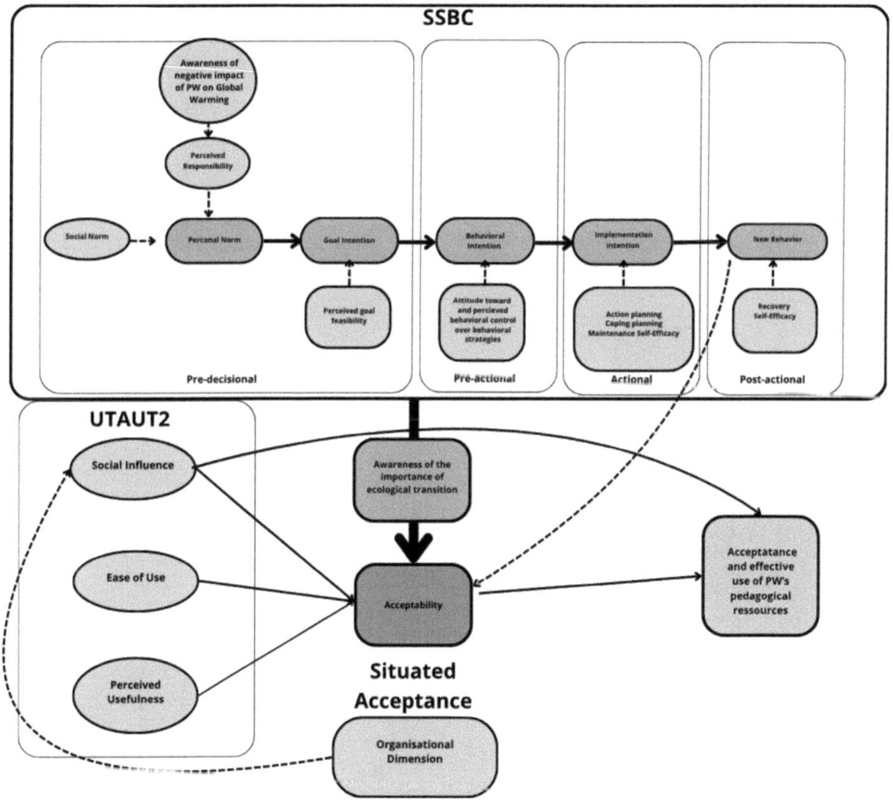

Fig. 2. Updated combined research model of SSBC, UTAUT2, Situated Acceptance and Effective Use from [1].

Based on this integrated framework, our hypotheses (see Fig. 3) are strategically designed to test the antecedents of both acceptability (H2c, H4b) and acceptance, defined as effective use (H2d). This design allows for a direct comparison of their respective drivers. Hypotheses H1, H2a, H2b and H4a were described and discussed in [1].

- **H2c.** The implementation intention (from SSBC) positively influences the acceptability of a PW e-learning platform.
- **H2d.** The implementation intention (from SSBC) positively influences the effective acceptance (effective use) of a PW e-learning platform.
- **H3.** The organizational dimension (from Situated Acceptance) has a positive influence on social influence (from UTAUT2).
- **H4b.** Social influence (from UTAUT2) has a positive influence on the acceptability of the resources from a PW e-learning platform.
- **H5.** The level of awareness (from SSBC) influences perceived usefulness (from UTAUT2).

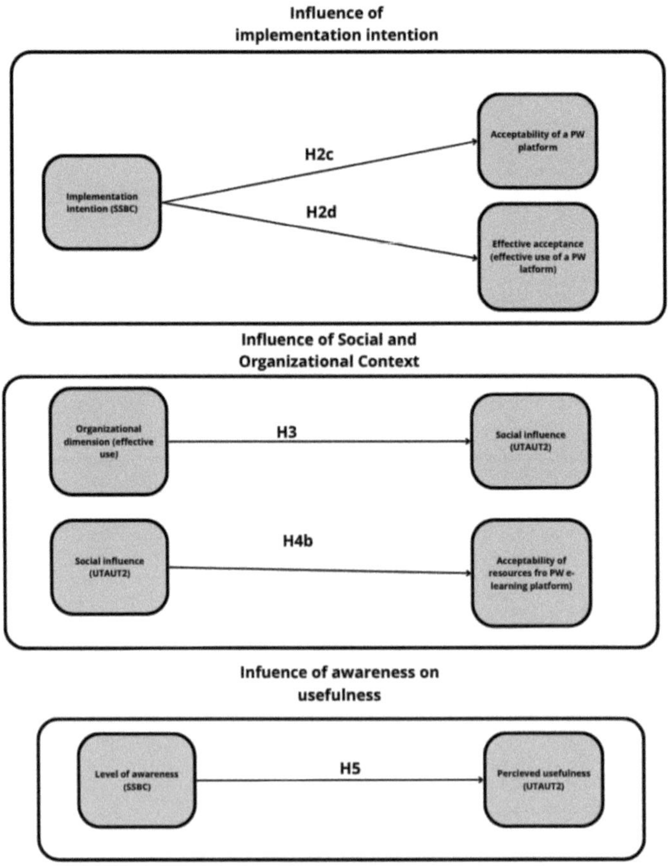

Fig. 3. Proposed hypotheses.

3 Methodology

The complete methodology is described in detail in our original publication [1]. The following sections outline its key components.

3.1 Participants and Procedure

The study targeted a community of Public Works instructors who had prior experience with the "tpdemain" e-learning platform. An online questionnaire was distributed to this community via social networks and remained accessible for approximately two months. An initial pool of 59 participants began the questionnaire. However, for the final analysis, we retained only the data from participants who had completed a sufficient portion of the survey. A total of 17 participants were excluded for providing insufficient data (less than 18% of the questionnaire completed), resulting in a final sample of N = 42 participants.

The final sample was composed mostly of men (n = 30), with a smaller number of women (n = 4). One participant did not specify their gender, and seven did not answer the question. The average age was 49.1 years for men, 45.5 years for women, and 53 years for the participant who did not specify their gender. The vast majority of participants (91.2%) confirmed having used the digital platform at least once.

3.2 Materials and Measures

The central technological artifact of this study is the "tpdemain" platform, an e-learning initiative created by the French National Federation of Public Works (NFPW). It was developed as part of the DEFFINUM project, a national plan for the transformation and digitalization of training. The platform offers a wide range of educational resources, including videos, texts, and complete courses produced with the French Learning Content Management System (LCMS) Storiz. These resources cover various PW jobs and have a strong focus on the ecological transition.

The data was collected via a questionnaire created on the Qualtrics platform, which was divided into five main blocks:

- **UTAUT2 Block:** This section contained thirty-four items designed to measure the core constructs of the UTAUT2 model, such as social influence and perceived usefulness.
- **Effective Acceptance Block:** This consisted of one question measuring how many teaching sessions were built with "tpdemain" resources.
- **SSBC Block:** This section included specific questions tailored to assess which of the four stages of pro-environmental behavior change each participant was in.
- **Organizational Responsibility Block:** This consisted of one question divided into five parts, aimed at measuring the participants' perception of their organization's awareness and responsibility regarding the environmental impact of PW activities.
- **Demographics Block:** This section collected basic information about the participants.

Crucially, the questionnaire was designed to differentiate between two key dependent variables. The first, acceptability, was captured through constructs reflecting user perceptions and attitudes (e.g., from UTAUT2 in block 1). The second, effective acceptance, was operationalized as the self-reported frequency and manner of the effective use of the platform's resources, thus measuring concrete past behavior (from block 2).

For each item, a five-point Likert scale was used.

3.3 Data Analysis

All collected data was centralized and statistically processed using the software Jamovi. The analyses included descriptive statistics, analyses of variance (ANOVA), and linear regressions to test the formulated hypotheses.

4 Results

Statistical analyses were conducted to test each of our hypotheses. A comprehensive description is available in [1].

4.1 Influence of Implementation Intention (H2c and H2d)

To assess the impact of implementation intention on acceptability (H2c) and effective acceptance (H2d), two analyses of variance (ANOVA) were conducted.

- **For H2c:** The ANOVA revealed a statistically significant effect of implementation intention on the perceived **acceptability** of the platform, $F(3.16) = 3.16$, $p = .017$. The effect size, measured by eta-squared, is large ($\eta^2 = .404$), suggesting that implementation intention explains approximately 40.4% of the variance in acceptability.
- **For H2d:** Similarly, the analysis confirmed a significant influence of implementation intention on **effective acceptance** (actual use), $F(3.62) = 3.62$, $p = .007$. The effect size is also large ($\eta^2 = .404$).

These results strongly confirm that an individual's concrete planning of pro-environmental actions is highly associated with a positive perception and actual use of the platform.

4.2 Influence of Social and Organizational Context (H3 and H4b)

- **For H3:** An ANOVA was used to test the influence of the organizational dimension on social influence. The result is highly significant, $F(3.88) = 3.88$, $p = .002$, with a very large effect size ($\eta^2 = .556$). This means that the perception of strong support from one's organization is a powerful predictor of the social pressure felt from peers and superiors to use the platform.
- **For H4b:** A simple linear regression was conducted to predict acceptability from social influence. The model was found to be significant, $F(1, 39) = 7.45$, $p = .009$. The R^2 of 0.161 indicates that social influence explains 16.1% of the variance in acceptability, with a positive regression coefficient ($B = 6.53$). Thus, the stronger the social influence, the higher the acceptability of the platform.

4.3 Influence of Awareness on Usefulness (H5)

To test whether the level of awareness of ecological issues influenced the perceived usefulness of the platform, an ANOVA was performed. The test revealed no statistically significant effect, $F(1, 38) = 0.0731, p = .930$. The initial level of awareness does not, therefore, appear to be directly linked to the perception of the tool's usefulness in our sample.

5 Discussion

5.1 The Power of Intention in Action (H2c and H2d)

The most striking result of this study is undoubtedly the confirmation of the central role of implementation intention. This finding provides a significant nuance to classic behavioral models such as the Theory of Planned Behavior [3], which positions behavioral intention as the primary antecedent of action. Our results suggest that for complex, pro-environmental behaviors, the quality of that intention, specifically its translation into a concrete plan as conceptualized in the volitional phases of Heckhausen & Gollwitzer's MAP [4] and later by Bamberg [2], is the more decisive factor. Users who derive the most value from the platform are those who have already moved past general intent and are actively planning the "how, when, and where" of their behavioral change. For these individuals, the platform becomes an indispensable tool for implementing their personal action plan.

5.2 Acceptance, a Matter of Context (H3 and H4b)

A primary contribution of this study lies in its distinct measurement of acceptability and effective use, which reveals a critical divergence in their antecedents. The validation of the H3 → H4b chain of influence provides valuable insight into the social context of acceptability. The strong influence of the organizational dimension on social influence echoes the importance of normative factors, a concept central to social psychology since the work of Schwartz on the activation of social and personal norms [5]. This confirms the robustness of the "Social Influence" construct, a cornerstone of the UTAUT framework since its inception [7], in predicting user attitudes. In short, a supportive organization creates a social climate where a tool is perceived as legitimate and desirable.

However, as noted in our initial analysis [1], this social influence was not sufficient to predict effective use. This highlights the intention-action gap: while the social environment makes a tool acceptable to approve of, it is the individual's planned implementation intention (H2d) that converts this passive approval into active, effective use. The distinction is therefore critical: one set of factors governs social approval, while another, more personal and concrete factor, governs actual use.

5.3 Interpretation of Non-significant Results (H5)

The lack of a link between the level of awareness and perceived usefulness (H5) may seem counter-intuitive, but it is actually very informative when considered in light of foundational pro-environmental models. While "Awareness of Consequences" is a critical starting point in frameworks like the NAM [5] and VBN theory [9], our results suggest that once an individual has progressed to later behavioral stages, the direct influence of this initial awareness on the perception of a specific tool may diminish. For our sample, composed of individuals already advanced in their pro-environmental journey, the "usefulness" of the platform is likely judged on more pragmatic grounds: its ability to solve concrete problems, rather than on its alignment with a state of awareness they have long since internalized.

5.4 Implications, Limitations, and Future Directions

Theoretically, this research demonstrates the feasibility and relevance of combining models from environmental psychology and technology acceptance to study sustainability-oriented technological objects. The limitations of our study, extensively discussed in [1], must be recalled. The small sample size ($n = 42$) limits the generalizability of our conclusions. Furthermore, the reliance on self-reported data is subject to social desirability biases. For the future, a longitudinal study would be particularly relevant to track individuals over time. It would also be wise to broaden the sample to include novices who are less familiar with the subject to test the validity of our conclusions on a wider audience.

6 Conclusion

At the end of this in-depth analysis, it is clear that the adoption of an e-learning technology for the ecological transition is a complex phenomenon, situated at the intersection of individual psychology and socio-organizational context. Our main contribution is to have empirically demonstrated that the most powerful driver of the acceptance and use of such a tool is not ecological awareness per se, but the concrete planning of action by the individual. The work environment plays an essential facilitating role, but ultimately, the decision to use and maintain that use seems to belong to the individual and their own dynamics of change. For training designers and managers, the message is clear: for digital tools for the ecological transition to be fully adopted, we must accompany people not only in their awareness, but above all in the transformation of their intentions into tangible action plans.

Acknowledgement. This research has been funded by TP D'AVENIR.

Use of AI The authors also wish to acknowledge that an artificial intelligence (AI) language model was utilized to improve the readability and linguistic style of the manuscript. The AI was not used for data analysis, interpretation of results, or the formulation of the core scientific arguments, which remain the sole work of the authors.

Disclosure of Interests The authors have no competing interests to declare that are relevant to the content of this article.

References

1. Michanol, L., Sakdavong, J.-C.: The influence of pro-environmental behavior stages on e-learning platform acceptance in public works. In: Proceedings of the 17th International Conference on Computer Supported Education - Volume 1: CSEDU, pp. 349–355, Porto, Portugal (2025). https://doi.org/10.5220/0013275900003932
2. Bamberg, S.: Changing environmentally harmful behaviors: a stage model of self-regulated behavioral change. J. Environ. Psychol. **34**, 151–159 (2013). https://doi.org/10.1016/j.jenvp.2013.01.002
3. Ajzen, I.: The theory of planned behavior. Organ. Behav. Hum. Decis. Process. **50**, 179–211 (1991). https://doi.org/10.1016/0749-5978(91)90020-T
4. Heckhausen, H., Gollwitzer, P.M.: Thought contents and cognitive functioning in motivational versus volitional states of mind. Motiv. Emot. **11**, 101–120 (1987). https://doi.org/10.1007/BF00992338
5. Schwartz, S.H.: Normative influences on altruism. Adv. Exp. Soc. Psychol. **10**, 221–279 (1977). https://doi.org/10.1016/S0065-2601(08)60358-5
6. Venkatesh, V., Thong, J.Y., Xu, X.: Consumer acceptance and use of information technology: extending the unified theory of acceptance and use of technology. MIS Q. **36**(1), 157–178 (2012). https://doi.org/10.2307/41410412
7. Venkatesh, V., Morris, M.G., Davis, G.B., Davis, F.D.: User acceptance of information technology: toward a unified view. MIS Q. **27**(3), 425–478 (2003). https://doi.org/10.2307/30036540
8. Bobillier-Chaumon, M.-E.: L'acceptation située des technologies dans et par l'activité: premiers étayages pour une clinique de l'usage. Psychologie du travail et des organisations. **22**(1) (2016). https://doi.org/10.1016/j.pto.2016.01.001
9. Stern, P.C.: Toward a coherent theory of environmentally significant behavior. J. Soc. Issues. **56**(3), 407–424 (2000). https://doi.org/10.1111/0022-4537.00175

Haptics in Cognition: Disruptor or Enabler of Memory?

Bibeg Limbu and Irene-Angelica Chounta(✉)

Department of Human-centered Computing and Cognitive Science, University of Duisburg-Essen, Duisburg, Germany
{bibeg.limbu,irene-angelica.chounta}@uni-due.de

Abstract. This exploratory pilot study investigates the impact of haptic perception—specifically tactile sensitivity (touch) and kinaesthetic intensity (movement)— on learning, operationalized as information retention (immediate recall) through handwriting. Participants (N = 20) were randomly assigned to one of four experimental groups in a 2×2 factorial design, manipulating touch (via glove use) and movement (via increased writing pressure). Information retention was measured using an immediate recall test, while mental effort (reaction time in a secondary task) and perceived workload (NASA-TLX) were examined as mediating variables. Bayesian binomial regression revealed moderate evidence that increased writing pressure negatively influenced recall (85–88% probability of negative effect), whereas glove use alone demonstrated no clear effect. Bayesian mediation analysis found no strong evidence that mental effort or perceived workload mediated these effects, as all 95% credible intervals included zero, indicating substantial uncertainty. These findings suggest that increased Kinaesthetic demands may slightly impair immediate recall, independent of perceived workload or mental effort. Importantly, the manipulation of touch alone does not appear to influence information retention. The study contributes to understanding the nuanced relationship between embodied interactions and cognitive outcomes, with implications for designing sensor-based multimodal learning environments.

Keywords: Handwriting · Haptic Senses · Multimodal Learning · Embodied Cognition · Sensors · Memory

1 Introduction

Haptic perception is typically understood as encompassing both tactile and kinaesthetic modalities [43]. The tactile modality, or simply touch, provides awareness of stimulation of the outer surface of the body, whereas the kinaesthetic sense, or simply movement, provides an awareness of static and dynamic body posture. Robert [29] draws attention to the ambiguous philosophical status of touch, a key aspect of Haptic perception alongside movement [43]. He notes that touch has occupied a paradoxical position, being alternately dismissed as

C. Meinel et al. (Eds.): CSEDU 2025, CCIS 3148, pp. 82–102, 2027.
https://doi.org/10.1007/978-3-032-39103-2_5

the most negligible but also revered as the fundamental of the senses. Thomas Aquinas—a 13th-century Italian philosopher and theologian—sought to reconcile Aristotle's hierarchical senses in which sight often held primacy, into a coherent model where all sensory inputs—including touch—play a vital role in shaping the understanding of reality. He argued for the precedence of touch based on its optimal performance in the process of gathering knowledge, as touch roots perception in the entire bodily system. Aligning with Aquinas's view, Geza Révész stressed that knowledge acquired through the sense of touch was more convincing and persuasive [57]. To form coherent mental models and/or cognitive representations through haptic senses, a vital process in encoding and storage of information in memory, and consequently learning, an agent must actively explore using both touch and movement [30].

According to [50], the acquisition of complex skills takes place in authentic real-world settings. Complex skills comprise a collection of cognitive and psychomotor skills with a collective goal, as is often the case in most real-life skills. For example, playing badminton often consists of knowing how to swing, move on the court, and having knowledge of the rules. Acquiring badminton skills requires playing badminton; that is, learning must be situated. Situated Cognition posits that learning is situated, goes hand in hand with doing, and is embedded in activities bound to social, cultural, and physical contexts [23]. Such learning, regardless of domain (for example, sports or mathematics), emerges through action [1], in which the human body acts as an actuator for the brain to act on the world and collects high-quality information through the haptic sense [57].

The body and the haptic senses play a vital role in learning and, by extension, to cognition as well. According to [71], (embodied) cognition is not the body influencing the mind, but that the body and environment are part of the cognitive system itself. Therefore, cognition can be viewed as a dynamic, distributed process that depends on embodied interactions across the brain, body, and environment. [71] posits cognition as situated and task-specific, arising from solving concrete, real-world problems (see "4E cognition"by [12]). At the same time, embodied cognition has been criticized for its lack of formalization and theoretical rigor, rendering many of its claims vague and unfalsifiable [12,25]. For example, it is unclear how bodily states translate into cognitive processes. Embodiment theories often reject classical cognitivist frameworks—such as internal representations and symbolic processing—without offering sufficient empirical justification [12]. [25] instead advocates combining embodied and classical cognitivist models, rather than treating them as mutually exclusive. In line with these perspectives, we explore the following research questions:

RQ1: How does the sensitivity of tactile perception affect Information Retention?
RQ2: How does the intensity of motor activity affect Information Retention?

As stated earlier, Haptic senses consist of tactile and Kinesthetic modalities [43]. We explore how the two dimensions of haptic sense impact cognition, specifically information processing in memory. First, we examine the impact of the sensitivity of tactile perception (touch) on mental effort and information retention (**RQ1**). As Tactile and Kinesthetic modality (movement) are tightly intertwined during an embodied learning activity, we secondly examine the impact of the intensity of motor activities during movement on mental effort and information retention (**RQ2**). Our work aims to contribute to our understanding of the cognitive mechanisms by which the bodily state impacts cognition and learning.

The rest of the paper is structured as follows: in Sect. 2, we provide the background necessary for the study, followed by the method of study (see Sect. 3). Then, we present the results of the data analysis in Sect. 4, followed by a discussion on the theoretical and practical implications and limitations of this work (Sect. 5).

2 Related Work

Information retention in memory is affected by the following four cognitive processes: encoding, consolidation, storage, and retrieval [10]. Encoding is a vital process for the acquisition of new information, which transforms new information into mental representations to be stored in memory for later recall. Embodied cognition suggests that sensorimotor experiences, such as with haptic senses, contribute significantly to the formation of cognitive representations during the encoding process (see Grounded Cognition by [5]). Integration of multiple senses has been found to improve task performance in complex skills, particularly in high-load conditions [46,61]. Successful recall of domain-specific information from memory is a requisite for demonstrating task performance in complex skills [58,67]. Moreover, practice in a familiar context in which the learner was situated or embedded during the learning phase can significantly improve recall of information from memory [26].

Although the use of multiple senses may enhance learning in specific scenarios, Vermeulen et al. [69], in contrast, also found that sensory overload often leads to higher mental effort. The encoding process, much like the other three cognitive processes, exerts mental effort and impacts the assimilation, retention, and retrieval of information in/from long-term memory (see Cognitive Load Theory [66]). Mental effort can be conceptualised as how hard a person tries to actively process incoming information in working memory [32]. Working memory holds a limited amount of information during encoding [4], and requiring a learner to hold more information can lead to cognitive overload, which is detrimental for learning. [4]'s model of working memory, as depicted in his 1990 book "Human Memory: Theory and Practice", ignored the role of haptic senses, only accounting for the verbal & auditory information, and the visual & spatial information. [3] later acknowledged the scarcity of tactile-working-memory research and emphasized the need for multimodal integration, which implies including haptic modalities in the working memory model. Other relevant works have alluded to haptic working memory being a limited-capacity system, similar to Baddeley's working memory model [35,60]. [51,60] found that performing two distinct tasks within the same sensory modality leads to significant interference due to limited modality-specific capacity, while performing tasks across different modalities (e.g., visual and haptic) also causes interference, though typically to a lesser extent. Their findings support the idea of a partially shared, capacity-limited working memory system with modality-specific buffers, similar to the visual and auditory buffers in working memory (see Dual-coding theory [13]). This suggests that high bodily involvement or physical activity—particularly when not directly related to the learning task—may impede learning by contributing to cognitive overload [63]. In embodied learning, as is often the case in situated learning and authentic practice, multiple senses and motor activities are involved. How the inclusion of additional haptic sense modalities during learning impacts mental effort and information retention remains unclear. To further explore this gap, in this study, we explored the association between haptic senses and memory through the context of handwriting.

2.1 Handwriting and Memory

Handwriting remains a prevalent motor activity in educational contexts and has proven beneficial for learning [55,62]. This highlights the importance of internalizing competent handwriting fluency and is a prerequisite for all further handwriting-related learning benefits. Several studies [21,52,72] found that students who took notes on laptops performed worse on conceptual questions than students who took handwritten notes. Similarly, other related research demonstrated that taking notes by hand – instead of typing – can lead to improved memory [9,64,70]. This may partly explain why handwritten note-taking continues to be widely practiced even within the academic community [28]. The authors argued that laptop note-takers tend to transcribe lectures verbatim, which is detrimental to learning. In contrast, handwriting necessitates processing information and reframing it in their own words, as handwriting is slower than typing, and learners need to condense the incoming information. This additional mental effort requires learners to cognitively engage with the material, leading to improved retention of information in memory.

Learning strategies referred to as "Desirable Difficulties"[7] often use handwriting to slow down the learner, forcing learners to expend more mental effort, leading to deeper levels of processing, and consequently better memory [14]. However, higher-level cognitive processes involved in handwriting may also lead to cognitive overload, and instead inhibit the storage of information [54]. Nonetheless, [53] found that handwriting induces theta-range synchronized activity in brain areas linked to memory and learning, which supports encoding of new information. Furthermore, handwriting resulted in increased activation in brain regions associated with language processing, working memory, and executive functions during handwriting tasks [70]. [42,64] argued that the brain receives multiple sensory stimuli during writing (visual, motor, and kinaesthetic), which typing does not do in the same manner. Typing may limit the embodied reinforcement needed for robust cognitive-symbolic representations during encoding, particularly in young learners [45].

2.2 Sensors in Handwriting

Sensors and actuators enhance authentic practice within situated learning environments by monitoring learners' multisensory experiences and, when necessary, engaging their perception through actuator-driven interventions [40,47,65]. Multimodal Immersive Learning Environments (MILEs), using sensors and actuators, embed the learner in (simulated) realistic contexts for complex skills training [17,34,38]. For example, [11,39,59] used virtual reality to embed the user in authentic contexts by simulating the contextual surroundings. MILEs are projected to play a key role in facilitating embodied learning and facilitating inquiry into (embodied) cognition theories [22].

In the context of handwriting, digital stylus/pen with tablets are increasingly used to train, analyse, and inquire into the phenomenon of handwriting learning [8,18]. [15] propose various forms of supplementary stimuli, in addition to the naturally present primary stimuli, which can be introduced during handwriting with the help of MILEs [15,31]. For example, [41,44] have used color gradients in their applications to provide supplementary visual information about pen pressure while writing. As previously established, handwriting benefits memory by activating multiple sensory pathways [42,64], the potential benefit of providing supplementary stimuli encourages MILEs designers to make use of haptic senses. However, it is essential to exercise caution, as [44] found that the supplementary information led to an increase in mental effort. In contrast, [36,41] found no significant difference in mental effort when supplementary stimuli was provided compared to not providing them. It should be noted that [36,41] had limited participants to make definite conclusions. [73] postulate a smaller memory capacity for haptic senses than for visual senses. A complex implementation of supplementary haptic stimuli can more easily create cognitive overload. While the advantages of handwriting on paper have been well studied, there is a lack of understanding of how those benefits will transfer to digital devices [31]. Consequently, sensors and MILEs are becoming indispensable for the study of embodied cognition theories, but the design of MILEs requires a nuanced understanding of the role of haptic senses and multisensory learning principles, to which this study seeks to contribute.

3 Methods

To investigate our research questions, we conducted a formative study in which we conceptualized haptic sense along two key dimensions: (a) the acuity of tactile perception (touch), and (b) the intensity of kinaesthetic engagement (movement). We compared learning performance across four groups—each defined by a unique combination of high or low levels of these two dimensions—using an immediate post-test. Quantitative data on participants' mental effort and perceived workload were also collected and analyzed as potential mediating variables.

3.1 Participants

Twenty (20) right-handed, German native-speaking university students participated in the study. We invited only right-handed students to control the variation that may arise from the dominant hand. Twelve (12) participants were female, and eight (8) were male. The mean age of the female participants was $M_{\text{female}} = 21.6$ (SD = 1.83), and the mean age of the male participants was $M_{\text{male}} = 23.1$ (SD = 2.23).

3.2 Experimental Design

This study investigated the effects of haptic senses on memory recall across two dimensions—tactile sensitivity and proprioceptive intensity—using a between-subjects 2×2 factorial design (see Table 1). The two treatment conditions were: (1) proprioceptive intensity, induced by increased handwriting pressure (P), and (2) reduced tactile sensitivity, achieved through the use of a glove (G). Participants in Group 1 applied additional handwriting pressure and wore a glove (P+G). Group 2 participants applied additional pressure without wearing a glove (P+¬G), while those in Group 3 wore a glove but did not apply additional pressure (¬P+G). The control group (Group 4) neither applied additional pressure nor wore a glove (¬P+¬G). Participants assigned to conditions requiring increased pressure received auditory feedback cues to maintain the required pressure level during the task. This feedback cue was acoustically distinct from the auditory stimuli used in the secondary task to avoid confusion (see Sect. 3.5).

Table 1. Experimental groups based on two factors: proprioceptive intensity (P) and tactile sensitivity (G) as seen in [36]

Group	Condition	N
1	P + G	5
2	P + ¬G	6
3	¬P + G	5
4	¬P + ¬G	4

3.3 Procedure

Upon arrival, participants were briefed on the study's objectives and the experimental task procedures. Participants were informed of their rights, including the right to withdraw at any time, and were asked to provide written informed consent. The participants were assigned a unique identifier code, which was used to anonymize participants' data. The study received ethical approval from the ethics committee of the Department of Human-centered Computing and Cognitive Science, University of Duisburg-Essen (Ethics Committee Opinion ID: *2407CMLB3526*).

Before the study began, the participants familiarised themselves with the apparatus. After that, they were randomly assigned to one of the study groups (Sect. 3.2). Participants were subsequently reminded of the primary task (copying the text displayed on the prompter) and the secondary task (responding to auditory stimuli by pressing a key on the keyboard). The text for the experimental task that the participants copied was displayed on the prompter sentence by sentence. Based on the treatment conditions/group allocation, participants were assigned to either wear a glove, write with extra pressure, do both, or write normally. Following the experimental task, participants responded to the questionnaires assessing their recall and perceived workload. The order of test administration was randomized to mitigate potential ordering effects, such as the influence of the recall task on workload ratings or vice versa. The entire procedure took approximately 30–45 min.

3.4 Apparatus

Fig. 1. Experimental setup with a teleprompter displaying text for participants to copy using a stylus.

Participants used a WACOM One^{TM}tablet and stylus to copy text from the teleprompter (Fig. 1). The tablet was connected to a laptop that ran a custom application to log data. The application also reminded the participants in the

"P"treatment group to exert more pressure when needed. The participants were instructed to press the spacebar key (secondary task) on the wireless keyboard placed next to them as quickly as possible in response to the auditory signal (Sect. 3.5). A gardening glove selected to exert minimal impact on the pen grip was used to reduce the tactile sensitivity for the groups with the "G" treatment.

3.5 Materials and Measures

Mental Effort. In this study, *Mental effort* was measured using the dual-task method. Mental effort is the cognitive capacity that is allocated to accommodate the demands imposed by the task [32]. The dual-task paradigm is a behavioural method used to assess mental effort over time by providing an additional secondary task (such as, reacting to auditory stimuli [36,41]) to measure decay in secondary task performance (or primary) [20]. As a secondary task, participants reacted to the auditory stimuli as fast as possible by pressing the spacebar key on a wireless keyboard. The reaction time was logged in milliseconds.

Perceived Workload. *Perceived workload* is the physical and mental effort invested and was measured using the NASA-TLX instrument [24]. The NASA-TLX is a subjective instrument that evaluates perceived workload across six dimensions: *mental demand, physical demand, temporal demand, performance, effort, and frustration.* Participants scored each dimension on a scale from 0 to 100, reflecting the perceived intensity of each factor. A pairwise comparison between the 15 pairs from 6 dimensions is then performed, in which the participant selects the most influential dimension from the two. Based on this, the individual weights for each dimension were calculated and then used to calculate the overall perceived workload.

Information Retention. Retention of learned information is defined as the storage of information in long-term memory such that it can be readily retrieved or recalled, for example, in response to standard prompts, and not merely in response to experiential cues [6]. *Information Retention* was measured using a multiple-choice knowledge test and was administered immediately after the experiment to assess the participant's ability to recall the information presented during the experiment. The knowledge test consisted of 10 questions related to the content presented during the experiment. For each question, there were four possible choices with only one correct answer. A control question was included to verify that responses were not given at random. Furthermore, participants were also instructed to skip the question if they did not know the answer rather than guessing.

4 Results

The data collected as part of this study is publicly accessible [37]. The R script used for the analysis of data can be found here[1]. We adopted the BARG

[1] https://github.com/bibeglimbu/Haptics_HWCompare_Bayes.git.

(Bayesian Analysis Reporting Guidelines) for reporting our results [33]. We opted for Bayesian analysis as it is more robust to smaller sample sizes and does not depend on the P-values.

Table 2. Mean and Standard Deviation for Immediate Recall, Perceived Workload, and Mental Effort.

Group	Information Retention (0–10)	Perceived Workload (0–100)	Mental Effort (sec) (2.74–14.88)
1	**7.20**, *1.64*	**57.2**, *21.0*	**5.42**, *1.18*
2	**7.17**, *1.72*	**46.8**, *16.2*	**4.55**, *1.12*
3	**8.40**, *1.52*	**40.2**, *14.2*	**8.77**, *4.07*
4	**8.25**, *1.71*	**52.0**, *13.6*	**4.77**, *2.09*

4.1 Information Retention

We fitted a Bayesian binomial regression model with a logit link function using the brms package[2] in R to examine group performance differences in Information Retention. Information Retention was measured as a post-test using a 10-item multiple-choice test. In the model, we initially included weakly informative priors: $normal(0,1)$ for group-level effects and $normal(0,5)$ for the intercept (control group/Group 4). Prior and posterior predictive checks were conducted to evaluate the plausibility of the initial priors (Fig. 2). We placed the intercept prior to $normal(1.5,1)$, reflecting the belief that most participants would perform moderately well ($\sim$ 80% correct) with moderate uncertainty.

We expected the group-level effects to be small, with most groups performing sufficiently well, as the text used for the study was not complicated and the only immediate recall was measured (Sect. 3). As previously discussed in Sect. 2, there is a mixed consensus on the true effect of handwriting on memory. However, there is a positive trend for the benefits of handwriting indicated by seminal papers such as [52] and, more recently, evidence from cognitive neuroscience studies [70]. Therefore, the new prior for the intercept is fitting, based on evidence and theoretical assumptions, as all groups used handwriting. In contrast, we have very little to no information on the effect of the groups. The updated prior yielded predictions that aligned well with plausible pre-data expectations and passed the prior predictive check. Four Markov Chain Monte Carlo (MCMC) chains were run with 4000 iterations each (2000 warm-up), yielding 8000 post-warmup samples. All $\hat{R}$ values were 1.00, indicating good convergence. After examining posterior means and 95% credible intervals (CI) for each group coefficient, we quantified directional evidence by computing the posterior probability that each effect was negative and the corresponding Bayes factors.

The intercept, representing the estimated log-odds of a correct answer for the reference group (Group 4), was 1.48 (95% CI: 0.84, 2.18), which corresponds to

[2] https://cran.r-project.org/web/packages/brms/index.html.

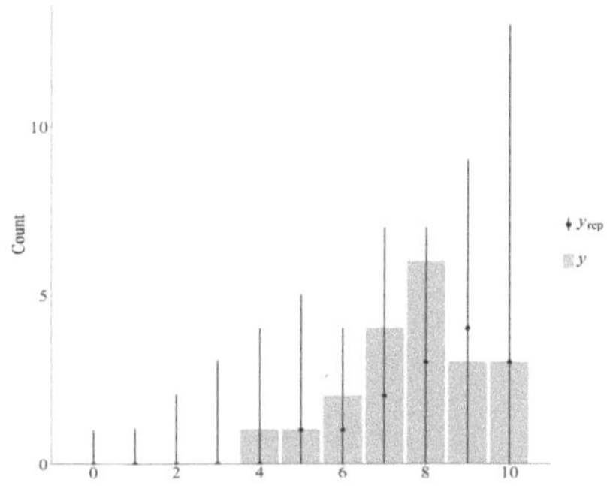

(a) Binomial Prior for IR

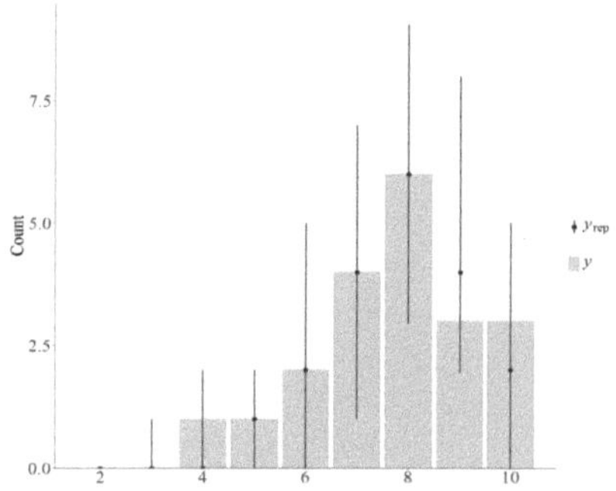

(b) Binomial Posterior for IR

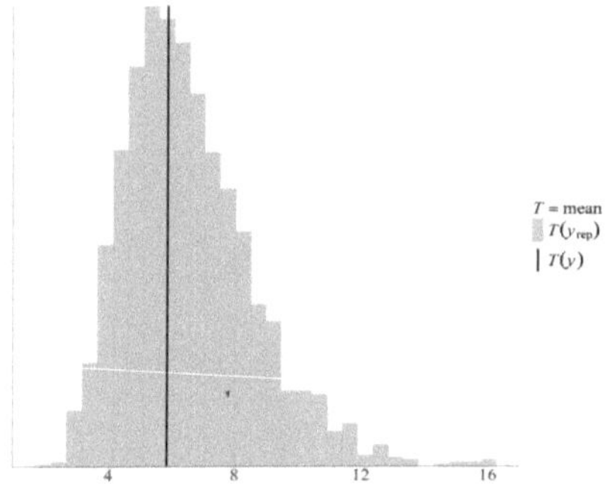

(c) Lognormal prior for ME

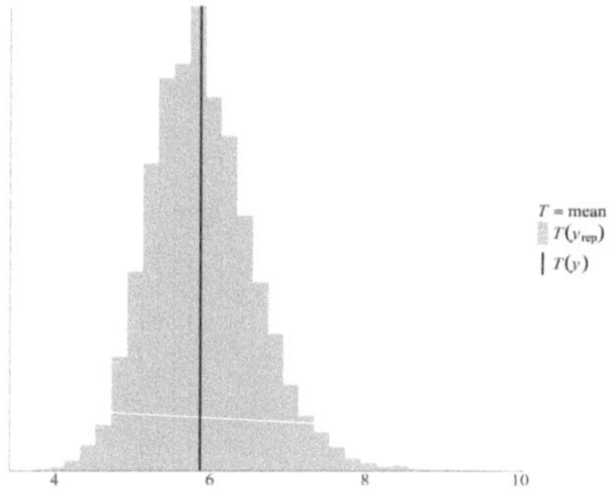

(d) Lognormal Posterior for ME

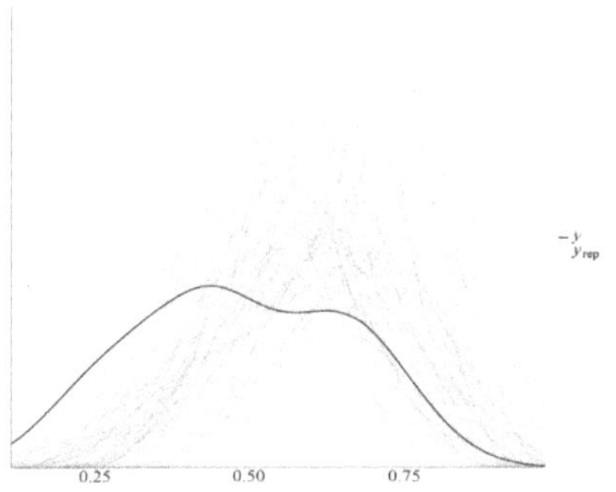

(e) Beta Prior for PW

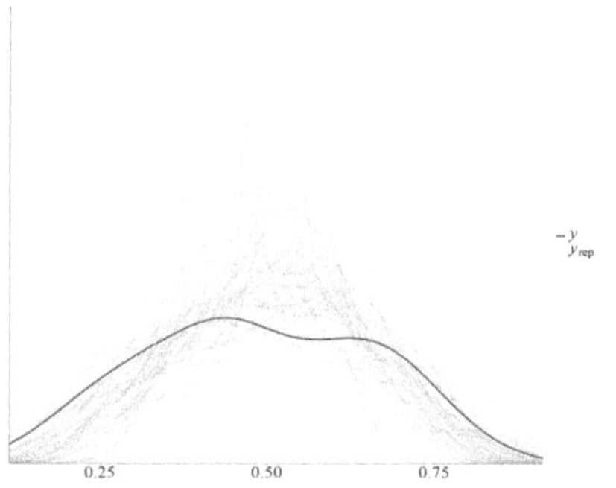

(f) Beta Posterior for PW

Fig. 2. Prior and Posterior distributions of Immediate Recall (IR), Mental Effort (ME), and Perceived Workload (PW) based on binomial, lognormal, and beta likelihoods, respectively.

an estimated probability of approximately 0.82 (95% CI: 0.70, 0.91) (see Fig. 3). For Group 1 (pressure + gloves), the estimated log-odds difference versus control was −0.46 (95% CI: −1.33 to 0.38), corresponding to about a 85% chance that the condition truly reduces recall. A Bayes factor of 5.83 indicates moderate

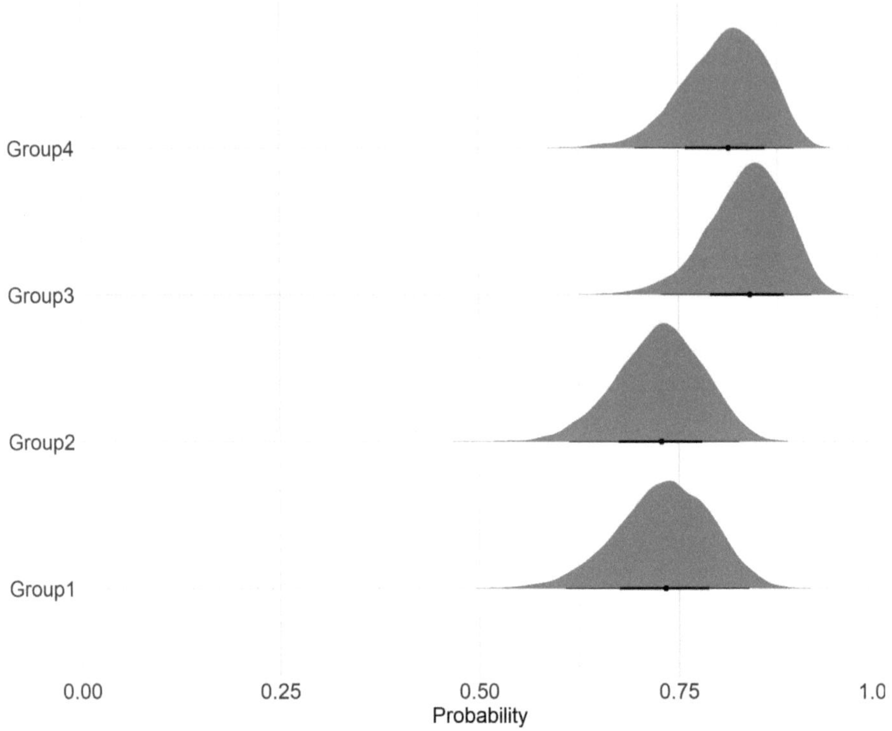

Fig. 3. Posterior distribution of Group Probabilities.

evidence in favor of a negative effect. Similarly, Group 2 (pressure only), the estimated log-odds difference against group 4 (control) is −0.49 (95% CI: −1.33 to 0.33), corresponding to about an 88% probability that the pressure alone reduces recall. A Bayes factor of 7.1 indicates moderate evidence in favor of a negative effect. For group 3 (glove only), the estimated log-odds difference for gloves only versus group 4 (control) indicated a small positive effect (0.21; 95% CI: −0.69 to 1.14) with very high uncertainty. There was a 33% probability that this small effect is negative (i.e., that gloves reduce recall), and the Bayes factor of 0.5 slightly favors a non-negative effect. Posterior predictive checks indicate our observed mean (7.8) lies at the center of the model's simulated means, demonstrating good fit (Bayesian $p \approx 0.5$).

4.2 Bayesian Mediation Analysis

A Bayesian multivariate model was used using the brms package in R to examine whether perceived workload (rescaled to the [0,1] interval) mediated the effect of pressure on information retention. The model included the two factors: pressure & gloves, and their interaction as predictors of both perceived workload and information retention. The perceived workload was modeled using a Beta distribution with the following priors: a normal prior of $normal(0.4, 0.3)$ for the intercept, reflecting moderate expected workload; weakly informative slope priors of $normal(0, 0.3)$; and a $Gamma(30, 2)$ prior for the precision parameter (phi), assiming a weak effect of pressure and gloves on information retention and perceived workload. The mental effort (raw reaction time in seconds) was modeled with a lognormal distribution with a $Normal(1.77, 0.3)$ prior on the intercept—reflecting an expected mean reaction time of ≈5 s—and weakly informative $Normal(0, 0.3)$ priors on the slopes for pressure, gloves, and their interaction. Finally, we used a half-Normal prior, $normal(0, 0.2)$, to encode modest trial-to-trial variability in log-RT. For the information retention, the priors from the previous Sect. 4.1 were used (see Fig. 2).

Prior predictive check was conducted for perceived workload and mental effort, confirming that the priors generated plausible simulated data consistent with our weak informative stance. The multivariate Bayesian model was estimated using four MCMC chains, each with 4000 iterations, including 2000 warm-up iterations, resulting in 8000 post-warmup samples. Convergence was assessed using the potential scale reduction factor $\hat{R}$, which was equal to 1.00 for all model parameters, indicating satisfactory convergence across chains. Furthermore, effective sample sizes (Bulk ESS and Tail ESS) for all parameters exceeded 6000, suggesting high precision and stability in the estimation of both central tendencies and tail distributions of the posterior.

The effect of pressure on perceived workload was 0.08 (95% CI: −0.32, 0.48), indicating a small, uncertain increase in perceived workload under pressure. The credible interval included zero, suggesting a lack of strong evidence for any effect. Similarly, Fig. 4 depicts neither indirect nor direct paths were statistically significant, indicating no evidence of mediation through perceived workload. The path from perceived workload to information retention was negative but uncertain, -1.09 (95% CI:−2.57, 0.38). Bayesian estimation indicated a 63% probability that perceived workload negatively mediates the effect of Pressure on Information Retention, and a 65% probability that it positively mediates the effect of Glove use. However, the 95% credible intervals include zero in both cases, suggesting limited and uncertain evidence for mediation. Overall, neither intervention showed a clear effect on retention via perceived workload.

The Pressure condition had a small negative, uncertain effect on mental effort −0.12 (95% CI: −0.44, 0.18). The credible interval included zero, suggesting a lack of strong evidence for any effect. Although the Glove condition significantly increased reported mental effort, Fig. 5 suggests neither indirect nor direct paths were statistically significant, indicating no evidence of mediation through mental effort. The path from mental effort to information retention was positive but uncertain, 0.52 (95% CI: −0.45, 1.48). There is a 70% probability that mental effort negatively mediates the effect of Pressure on Information Retention, and an 85% probability that it positively mediates the effect of Glove use. In both cases, however, the 95% credible intervals for the indirect effects include zero, suggesting substantial uncertainty in the mediation effects. Overall, neither intervention showed a clear effect on retention via mental effort.

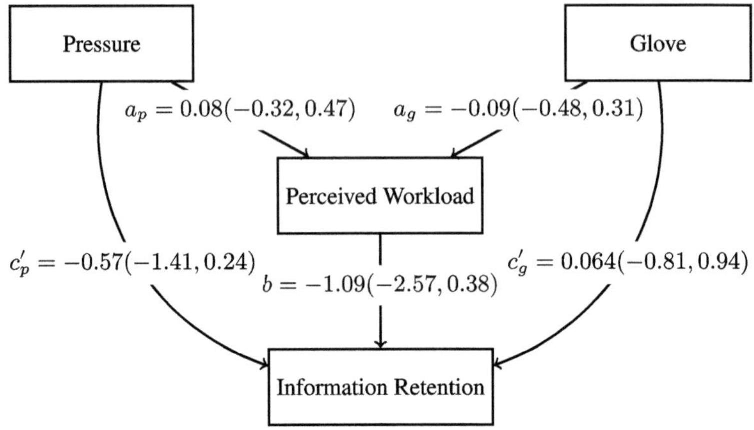

Fig. 4. Mediation diagram for perceived workload.

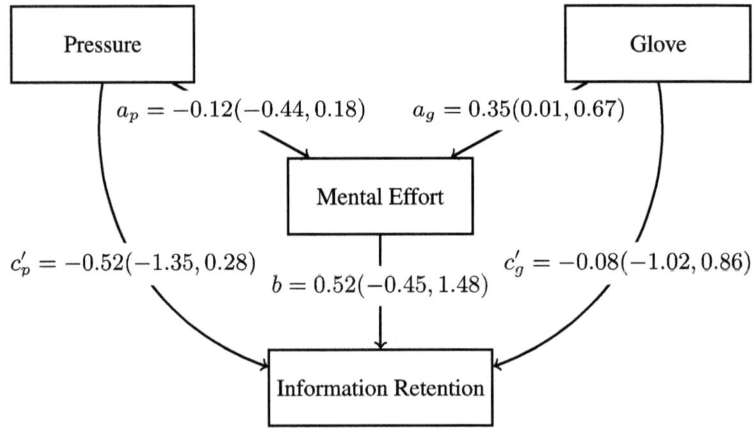

Fig. 5. Mediation diagram for mental effort.

5 Discussion

In this study, we explored the effect of haptic perception/senses (touch + movement) on information retention through mental effort and perceived workload as mediator variables. Touch sensitivity (as deprivation of tactile perception) was enforced by requiring participants to wear gloves during handwriting (**RQ1**). Movement (as the intensity of motor activity) was enforced by requiring participants to write with additional pressure (**RQ2**). The learning performance was measured by the participant's performance on the immediate recall test(10-item test). The mental effort and the perceived workload were recorded as the mediating variables. The mental effort was measured using reaction time in a secondary task using the dual task method. The perceived workload was measured with the Nasa-TLX taskload questionnaire.

We used a Bayesian binomial regression with a logit link to model information retention, applying weakly informative priors refined through prior predictive checks. The posterior for the control group suggested an 82% average correct response rate (95% CI: 70%–91%). Compared to control, group 1 with added pressure (movement) + wearing gloves (touch) and Group 2 with added pressure only, both showed moderate evidence of reduced recall, with posterior probabilities of 85% and 88% for negative effects and Bayes factors (BF) of 5.83 and 7.1, respectively. Gloves only (Group 3) showed a small, highly uncertain positive effect (33% probability of being negative; BF = 0.5). Posterior predictive checks indicated good model fit. Overall, there was moderate evidence suggesting that both pressure conditions (with or without gloves) negatively impacted information retention, whereas the glove-only condition showed no clear evidence of an effect. Furthermore, all groups performed relatively well in the information retention test. Since learning in the context of this study was purely cognitive, that is, assimilation and recall from memory, our results are in line with [55], who only found weak evidence for the effect of psychomotor aspects on cognitive learning. The memorization and conceptualization benefits of handwriting [21,52,72] were assumed to be the result of the cognitive engagement due to the time constraint, which required learners to actively process information to condense it. For example, [56] found that the drawing condition, which necessitates learners to physically and visually depict each word—a form of contextualized, multimodal activity—resulted in significantly better recall than handwriting or typing.

Using Bayesian multivariate analysis, we found no clear evidence that perceived workload or mental effort mediated the effect of pressure or gloves on information retention. Although small trends suggested potential negative mediation via workload (63% probability) and positive mediation via mental effort for gloves (85% probability), all Credible Intervals included zero, indicating substantial uncertainty and weak evidence for any mediation effects. Mental effort is generally considered to positively impact memory [7]; [54] cautions against the possibility of handwriting to cognitively overload learners. The small potential negative mediation via workload, which measures both mental and physical effort, potentially hints towards physical effort playing a negative role outside the mental effort constraints. However, the physical act of handwriting is contextually coupled with the mental processes involved in processing incoming information, and as most participants have already internalised handwriting, the treatments may not have had the intended effect. This aligns with the remarks of [15] and potentially hints towards the integration of haptic modality in the Modality principle in Multimedia Learning [49], which suggests that the use of multiple modalities results in efficient learning when the information is contextually coupled.

5.1 Theoretical and Practical Implications

Sensors are indispensable for the study of embodied learning and complex skills development through authentic practice. Paradoxically, the use of such sensors and actuators, which are added on top of the actual authentic settings, can impact learning. For example, [48] used smartphone sensors by attaching a smartphone to the learner's body, arguably affecting the learner's authentic performance. Thus, understanding the effect of such additions on learning is of utmost importance, not only for designing authentic learning environments but also for studying embodied learning theories in situated contexts.

The results of this study also suggest that wearing a glove and/or exerting additional pressure during handwriting does not affect recall, mental effort, or perceived workload. Such additions in the context of handwriting may not cognitive overload the learner. However, [69] found that sensory overload resulted in cognitive overload when additional stimuli were presented, but the increase in the intensity of existing primary stimuli seemed to have no impact. This potential to provide additional feedback and support during authentic practice may improve learning and acquisition of complex skills [15].

This may suggest that wearable sensors can potentially be safely used for learning handwriting. [19] found that the students' handwriting performance is continuously degrading, affecting their academic performance. While occupational therapy-based interventions have proven beneficial [27], they cannot address the issue at the required scale. Immersive learning technologies that support authentic practice can contribute towards solving this problem by automating educational aspects surrounding handwriting. For example, automated systems utilizing consumer tablets have been developed to diagnose handwriting difficulties such as dysgraphia [2].

Similarly, [18] developed a sensor-based application for training handwriting that provides real-time feedback on various handwriting attributes based on the teacher's expertise. Such attributes, like pen pressure and perceptual-motor abilities, directly impact handwriting itself [16], which further impacts academic performance. The potential to make use of (invasive) sensors, such as the SenseGlove^{TM}, potentially without adversely affecting learning, broadens the horizons for more inclusive multisensory and seamless learning design [65].

5.2 Limitations

The study is limited by the sample size (N=20). Despite the use of Bayesian analysis, which does not necessarily rely on a large number of participants, the posteriors remain uncertain, reflecting the limited data.

The study was constrained by the use of a structured text excerpt as the basis for the recall task. This contrasts with prior research employing lists of unrelated words to assess memory performance [9,70]. Structured text excerpts may not necessarily overload the working memory, especially in the presence of prior knowledge. Notably, no prior-test was conducted to assess participants' baseline knowledge. However, the text was deliberately selected from a geology textbook under the assumption—based on participants' enrollment in computer science programs—that prior familiarity with the content would be minimal. Using a text excerpt was a conscious choice to test the effects of handwriting in the absence of repetition.

The experimental treatment involved manipulating two modalities of the haptic sense, but each was only altered in one direction, even though opposite manipulations might also influence learning. For example, writing on paper is superior in terms of brain activation in comparison to writing on digital tablets [68], conceivably due to the increased friction provided by the paper's rough texture. In this study, the touch or tactile perception was reduced, and the writing pressure was increased. However, the corresponding reverse manipulations were not done due to logistical constraints.

Lastly, the NASA Task Load Index (NASA TLX) questionnaire used in the study consists of only 14 categories compared to its 15 categories. One category was removed as it was irrelevant to this study. This discrepancy can impact the reliability of the instrument.

6 Conclusion

In this exploratory pilot study, we experimentally investigated the effect of manipulating two attributes associated with haptic perception/sense, namely touch and movement, on learning. Learning is defined as the assimilation and recall of information from memory. Mental effort and perceived workload were observed as the mediating variables. Perceived workload is the combined mental and physical effort, which was included due to the emphasis on the haptic senses. The tactile perception or touch was manipulated by wearing a glove, while the movement was manipulated using software to enforce higher pressure while writing. Moderate evidence suggested that increased writing pressure negatively affected information retention, while glove use showed no clear effect. No evidence was found that perceived workload or mental effort mediated these effects, with all estimates remaining uncertain. The findings of this study may contribute to our understanding of the design of authentic learning environments with sensors and actuators. It may also contribute to future studies aiming to understand embodied theories and how the potentialities of our bodies and environments impact cognitive processes.

Acknowledgments. We want to thank the students at the University of Duisburg-Essen who helped execute the study in various roles. Namely, *Anna Luisa Färber*, *Bünyamin Yilmaz*, *Hannah Holland*, *Joshua Jung*, *Katarzyna Pogorzala*, *Van Hoang*, and *Zhang Xinyu*.

Disclosure of Interests. The authors have no competing interests to declare that are relevant to the content of this article

References

1. Abrahamson, D., Lindgren, R.: Embodiment and embodied design. In: Sawyer, R.K. (ed.) The Cambridge Handbook of the Learning Sciences, 2nd edn., pp. 358–376. Cambridge University Press, Cambridge (2014). https://doi.org/10.1017/CBO9781139519526.022
2. Asselborn, T., Chapatte, M., Dillenbourg, P.: Extending the spectrum of dysgraphia: a data driven strategy to estimate handwriting quality. Sci. Rep. 10, 3140 (2020). https://doi.org/10.1038/s41598-020-60011-8
3. Baddeley, A.: Working memory: looking back and looking forward. Nat. Rev. Neurosci. **4**(10), 829–839 (2003). https://doi.org/10.1038/nrn1201
4. Baddeley, A.D.: Human memory: Theory and practice. Allyn & Bacon, Needham Heights, MA (1990)
5. Barsalou, L.W.: Grounded cognition. Annu. Rev. Psychol. **59**, 617–645 (2008). https://doi.org/10.1146/annurev.psych.59.103006.093639
6. Bennett, A.G., Rebello, N.S.: Retention and learning. In: Seel, N.M. (ed.) Encyclopedia of the Sciences of Learning, pp. 2856–2859. Springer, Boston (2012). https://doi.org/10.1007/978-1-4419-1428-6_664
7. Bjork, E.L., Bjork, R.A.: Making things hard on yourself, but in a good way: creating desirable difficulties to enhance learning. In: Psychology and the Real World: Essays Illustrating Fundamental Contributions to Society, pp. 56–64. Worth Publishers, New York (2011)
8. Bonneton-Botté, N., Miramand, L., Bailly, R., Pons, C.: Teaching and rehabilitation of handwriting for children in the digital age: issues and challenges. Children **10**(7), 1096 (2023). https://doi.org/10.3390/children10071096, https://www.mdpi.com/2227-9067/10/7/1096
9. Bouriga, S., Olive, T.: Is typewriting more resources-demanding than handwriting in undergraduate students? Read. Writ. **34**(9), 2227–2255 (2021). https://doi.org/10.1007/s11145-021-10137-6
10. Brem, A.K., Ran, K., Pascual-Leone, A.: Learning and memory. Handb. Clin. Neurol. **116**, 693–737 (2013). https://doi.org/10.1016/B978-0-444-53497-2.00055-3, https://www.ncbi.nlm.nih.gov/pmc/articles/PMC4248571/
11. Cardenas Hernandez, F.P., Schneider, J., Di Mitri, D., Drachsler, H.: On-your marks, ready? Exploring the user experience of a VR application for runners with cognitive-behavioral influences. In: Proceedings of the 17th International Conference on Computer Supported Education - Volume 1: CSEDU, pp. 331–341. INSTICC, SciTePress (2025). https://doi.org/10.5220/0013271300003932
12. Carney, J.: Thinking avant la lettre: a review of 4E cognition. Evol. Stud. Imaginative Cult. **4**(1), 77–90 (2020). https://doi.org/10.26613/esic.4.1.172
13. Clark, J.M., Paivio, A.: Dual coding theory and education. Educ. Psychol. Rev. **3**(3), 149–210 (1991). https://doi.org/10.1007/BF01320076
14. Craik, F.I.M., Tulving, E.: Depth of processing and the retention of words in episodic memory. J. Exp. Psychol. Gen. **104**(3), 268–294 (1975). https://doi.org/10.1037/0096-3445.104.3.268
15. Danna, J., Velay, J.L.: Basic and sensory feedback in handwriting. Front. Psychol. **6**, 169 (2015). https://doi.org/10.3389/fpsyg.2015.00169
16. Dennis, J.L., Swinth, Y.: Pencil grasp and children's handwriting legibility during different-length writing tasks. Am. J. Occup. Ther. **55**(2), 175–183 (2001). https://doi.org/10.5014/ajot.55.2.175

17. Di Mitri, D., Schneider, J., Limbu, B., Mat Sanusi, K.A., Klemke, R.: Multimodal learning experience for deliberate practice. In: Giannakos, M., Spikol, D., Di Mitri, D., Sharma, K., Ochoa, X., Hammad, R. (eds.) The Multimodal Learning Analytics Handbook, pp. 183–204. Springer, Cham (2022). https://doi.org/10.1007/978-3-031-08076-0_8
18. Dikken, O., Limbu, B., Specht, M.: Deliberate practice of handwriting: supervision under the ghost of an expert. In: Hilliger, I., Muñoz-Merino, P.J., De Laet, T., Ortega-Arranz, A., Farrell, T. (eds.) Educating for a New Future: Making Sense of Technology-Enhanced Learning Adoption, pp. 434–440. Springer, Cham (2022). https://doi.org/10.1007/978-3-031-16290-9_33
19. Doug, R.: Handwriting: developing pupils' identity and cognitive skills. Int. J. Educ. Literacy Stud. **7**(2), 177–188 (2019). https://doi.org/10.7575/aiac.ijels.v.7n.2p.177, https://journals.aiac.org.au/index.php/IJELS/article/view/5367
20. Esmaeili Bijarsari, S.: A current view on dual-task paradigms and their limitations to capture cognitive load. Front. Psychol. **12** (2021). https://doi.org/10.3389/fpsyg.2021.648586
21. Flanigan, A.E., Wheeler, J., Colliot, T., Lu, J., Kiewra, K.A.: Typed versus handwritten lecture notes and college student achievement: a meta-analysis. Educ. Psychol. Rev. **36**(3), 78 (2024). https://doi.org/10.1007/s10648-024-09914-w
22. Giannakos, M., Cukurova, M.: The role of learning theory in multimodal learning analytics. Br. J. Edu. Technol. **54**(5), 1246–1267 (2023). https://doi.org/10.1111/bjet.13320
23. Greeno, J.G., Moore, J.L.: Situativity and symbols: response to vera and Simon. Cogn. Sci. **17**(1), 49–59 (1993). https://doi.org/10.1207/s15516709cog1701_3
24. Hart, S.G.: Nasa task load index (tlx) (1986). https://ntrs.nasa.gov/citations/20000021487
25. Hommel, B.: The theory of event coding (TEC) as embodied-cognition framework. Front. Psychol. **6** (2015). https://doi.org/10.3389/fpsyg.2015.01318
26. Horz, H.: Situated prompts in authentic learning environments. In: Seel, N.M. (ed.) Encyclopedia of the Sciences of Learning, pp. 3086–3088. Springer, Boston (2012). https://doi.org/10.1007/978-1-4419-1428-6_699
27. Hoy, M.M.P., Egan, M.Y., Feder, K.P.: A systematic review of interventions to improve handwriting. Can. J. Occup. Ther. **78**(1), 13–25 (2011). https://doi.org/10.2182/cjot.2011.78.1.3
28. Jäckel, Y., Schiffner, D., Schneider, J.: Our notes leave too much to say: investigating note-taking practices and technological tools in academia. In: Proceedings of the 17th International Conference on Computer Supported Education - Volume 2: CSEDU, pp. 493–503. INSTICC, SciTePress (2025). https://doi.org/10.5220/0013218600003932
29. Jütte, R.: Haptic perception: an historical approach. In: Grunwald, M. (ed.) Human Haptic Perception: Basics and Applications, pp. 3–13. Birkhäuser, Basel (2008). https://doi.org/10.1007/978-3-7643-7612-3_1
30. Kaas, A.L., Stoeckel, M.C., Goebel, R.: The neural bases of haptic working memory. In: Grunwald, M. (ed.) Human Haptic Perception: Basics and Applications, pp. 113–129. Birkhäuser, Basel (2008). https://doi.org/10.1007/978-3-7643-7612-3_9
31. Kiefer, M., Velay, J.L.: Writing in the digital age. Trends Neurosci. Educ. **5**(3), 77–81 (2016). https://doi.org/10.1016/j.tine.2016.07.008, https://linkinghub.elsevier.com/retrieve/pii/S2211949316300205
32. Kirschner, P.A., Kirschner, F.: Mental effort. In: Seel, N.M. (ed.) Encyclopedia of the Sciences of Learning, pp. 2182–2184. Springer, Boston (2012). https://doi.org/10.1007/978-1-4419-1428-6_226

33. Kruschke, J.K.: Bayesian analysis reporting guidelines. Nat. Hum. Behav. **5**(10), 1282–1291 (2021). https://doi.org/10.1038/s41562-021-01177-7
34. Lee, Y., Limbu, B., Rusak, Z., Specht, M.: Role of multimodal learning systems in technology-enhanced learning (tel): a scoping review. In: Viberg, O., Jivet, I., Muñoz-Merino, P., Perifanou, M., Papathoma, T. (eds.) Responsive and Sustainable Educational Futures, pp. 164–182. Springer, Cham (2023). https://doi.org/10.1007/978-3-031-42682-7_12
35. Lerch, R.A., Cui, H., Patwardhan, S., Visell, Y., Sims, C.R.: Exploring haptic working memory as a capacity-limited information channel. In: 2016 IEEE Haptics Symposium (HAPTICS), pp. 113–118 (2016). https://doi.org/10.1109/HAPTICS.2016.7463164, https://ieeexplore.ieee.org/abstract/document/7463164, iSSN: 2324-7355
36. Limbu, B., Chounta, I.A.: Can the mighty pen be mightier? Investigating the role of haptic senses in multimodal immersive learning environments. In: Proceedings of the 17th International Conference on Computer Supported Education, vol. 1, pp. 72–82 (2025). https://doi.org/10.5220/0013285600003932
37. Limbu, B., Chounta, I.A.: Dataset for the paper "can the mighty pen be mightier? investigating the role of haptic senses in multimodal immersive learning environments" (2025). https://doi.org/10.5281/zenodo.14639096
38. Limbu, B., Fominykh, M., Klemke, R., Specht, M.: A conceptual framework for supporting expertise development with augmented reality and wearable sensors. In: Buchem, I., Klamma, R., Wild, F. (eds.) Perspectives on Wearable Enhanced Learning (WELL), pp. 213–228. Springer, Cham (2019). https://doi.org/10.1007/978-3-319-64301-4_10
39. Limbu, B., van Roijen, R., Beerens, M., Specht, M.: Hololearn: towards a hologram mediated hybrid education. In: Dascalu, M., Mealha, Ó., Virkus, S. (eds.) Smart Learning Ecosystems as Engines of the Green and Digital Transition, pp. 117–132. Springer, Singapore (2023). https://doi.org/10.1007/978-981-99-5540-4_7
40. Limbu, B.H., Jarodzka, H., Klemke, R., Specht, M.: Using sensors and augmented reality to train apprentices using recorded expert performance: a systematic literature review. Educ. Res. Rev. **25**, 1–22 (2018). https://doi.org/10.1016/j.edurev.2018.07.001
41. Limbu, B.H., Jarodzka, H., Klemke, R., Specht, M.: Can you ink while you blink? Assessing mental effort in a sensor-based calligraphy trainer. Sensors **19**(14), 3244 (2019). https://doi.org/10.3390/s19143244
42. Longcamp, M., Zerbato-Poudou, M.T., Velay, J.L.: The influence of writing practice on letter recognition in preschool children: a comparison between handwriting and typing. Acta Physiol. (Oxf) **119**(1), 67–79 (2005). https://doi.org/10.1016/j.actpsy.2004.10.019, https://www.sciencedirect.com/science/article/pii/S0001691804001167
43. Loomis, J.M., Lederman, S.J.: Tactual perception. In: Boff, K.R., Kaufman, L., Thomas, J.P. (eds.) Handbook of Perception and Human Performance, vol. 2, chap. 31, pp. 1–41. John Wiley & Sons, New York (1986)
44. Loup-Escande, E., Frenoy, R., Poplimont, G., Thouvenin, I., Gapenne, O., Megalakaki, O.: Contributions of mixed reality in a calligraphy learning task: effects of visual feedback and expertise on cognitive load, user experience and gestural performance. Comput. Hum. Behav. **75**, 42–49 (2017). https://doi.org/10.1016/j.chb.2017.05.006, https://linkinghub.elsevier.com/retrieve/pii/S0747563217303187
45. Mangen, A., Balsvik, L.: Pen or keyboard in beginning writing instruction? Some perspectives from embodied cognition. Trends Neurosci. Educ. **5**(3), 99–106 (2016). https://doi.org/10.1016/j.tine.2016.06.003, https://www.sciencedirect.com/science/article/pii/S2211949316300114

46. Marucci, M., et al.: The impact of multisensory integration and perceptual load in virtual reality settings on performance, workload and presence. Sci. Rep. **11**(1), 4831 (2021). https://doi.org/10.1038/s41598-021-84196-8
47. Mat Sanusi, K.A., Iren, D., Fanchamps, N., Geisen, M., Klemke, R.: Virtual virtuoso: a systematic literature review of immersive learning environments for psychomotor skill development. Educ. Tech. Res. Dev. **73**(2), 909–949 (2025). https://doi.org/10.1007/s11423-025-10449-2
48. Mat Sanusi, K.A., Mitri, D.D., Limbu, B., Klemke, R.: Table tennis tutor: forehand strokes classification based on multimodal data and neural networks. Sensors **21**(9), 3121 (2021). https://doi.org/10.3390/s21093121, https://www.mdpi.com/1424-8220/21/9/3121
49. Mayer, R.E.: Cognitive theory of multimedia learning. In: Mayer, R.E. (ed.) The Cambridge Handbook of Multimedia Learning, pp. 31–48. Cambridge University Press, Cambridge (2005). https://doi.org/10.1017/CBO9780511816819.004
50. van Merriënboer, J.J.G., Kester, L.: The four-component instructional design model: multimedia principles in environments for complex learning. In: Mayer, R.E. (ed.) The Cambridge Handbook of Multimedia Learning, 2nd edn., pp. 104–148. Cambridge University Press, Cambridge (2014). https://doi.org/10.1017/CBO9781139547369.007
51. Morimoto, T.: The nature of haptic working memory capacity and its relation to visual working memory. Multisens. Res. **33**(8), 837–864 (2020). https://doi.org/10.1163/22134808-bja10007
52. Mueller, P.A., Oppenheimer, D.M.: The pen is mightier than the keyboard: advantages of longhand over laptop note taking. Psychol. Sci. **25**(6), 1159–1168 (2014). https://doi.org/10.1177/0956797614524581
53. Ose Askvik, E., van der Weel, F.R.R., van der Meer, A.L.H.: The importance of cursive handwriting over typewriting for learning in the classroom: a high-density eeg study of 12-year-old children and young adults. Front. Psychol. **11** (2020). https://doi.org/10.3389/fpsyg.2020.01810
54. Peverly, S.T.: The importance of handwriting speed in adult writing. Dev. Neuropsychol. **29**(1), 197–216 (2006). https://doi.org/10.1207/s15326942dn2901_10
55. Ray, K., Dally, K., Rowlandson, L., Tam, K.I., Lane, A.E.: The relationship of handwriting ability and literacy in kindergarten: a systematic review. Read. Writ. **35**, 1119–1155 (2022). https://doi.org/10.1007/s11145-021-10224-8
56. Richardson, L., Lacroix, G.: Which modality results in superior recall for students: Handwriting, typing, or drawing? J. Writ. Res. **15**(3), 519–540 (2024). https://doi.org/10.17239/jowr-2024.15.03.04, https://www.jowr.org/jowr/article/view/963
57. Révész, G.: Die menschliche Hand: Eine psychologische Studie. S. Karger, Basel and New York, 1st edn. (1944). mit 37 Abbildungen
58. Sawyer, K.: Zig Zag: The Surprising Path to Greater Creativity. Wiley (2013)
59. Schneider, J., Romano, G., Drachsler, H.: Beyond reality—extending a presentation trainer with an immersive VR module. Sensors **19**(16), 3457 (2019). https://doi.org/10.3390/s19163457, https://www.mdpi.com/1424-8220/19/16/3457
60. Sebastián, M., Mayas, J., Manso, A.J., Ballesteros, S.: Working memory for visual and haptic targets: a study using the interference paradigm. In: Ferre, M. (ed.) EuroHaptics 2008. LNCS, vol. 5024, pp. 395–399. Springer, Heidelberg (2008). https://doi.org/10.1007/978-3-540-69057-3_52
61. Siqueira Rodrigues, L., Schmidt, T.T., Israel, J.H., Zachow, S., Nyakatura, J., Kosch, T.: Comparing the effects of visual, haptic, and visuohaptic encoding on memory retention of digital objects in virtual reality. In: Proceedings of the 13th

Nordic Conference on Human-Computer Interaction. NordiCHI 2024, pp. 1–13. Association for Computing Machinery, New York (2024). https://doi.org/10.1145/3679318.3685349
62. Skar, G.B., Lei, P.W., Graham, S., Aasen, A.J., Johansen, M.B., Kvistad, A.H.: Handwriting fluency and the quality of primary grade students' writing. Read. Writ. **35**(2), 509–538 (2022). https://doi.org/10.1007/s11145-021-10185-y
63. Skulmowski, A., Rey, G.D.: Embodied learning: introducing a taxonomy based on bodily engagement and task integration. Cogn. Res. Principles Implications **3**(1), 6 (2018). https://doi.org/10.1186/s41235-018-0092-9
64. Smoker, T.J., Murphy, C.E., Rockwell, A.K.: Comparing memory for handwriting versus typing. In: Proceedings of the Human Factors and Ergonomics Society Annual Meeting, vol. 53, no. 22, pp. 1744–1747 (2009). https://doi.org/10.1177/154193120905302218
65. Specht, M., Limbu, B.H., Schneider, J.: Sensors for seamless learning. In: Looi, C.K., Wong, L.H., Glahn, C., Cai, S. (eds.) Seamless Learning: Perspectives, Challenges and Opportunities, pp. 141–152. Springer, Singapore (2019). https://doi.org/10.1007/978-981-13-3071-1_7
66. Sweller, J., Ayres, P., Kalyuga, S.: Cognitive Load Theory. Explorations in the Learning Sciences, Instructional Systems and Performance Technologies, Springer New York, NY, 1 edn. (2011). https://doi.org/10.1007/978-1-4419-8126-4
67. Tricot, A., Sweller, J.: Domain-specific knowledge and why teaching generic skills does not work. Educ. Psychol. Rev. **26**(2), 265–283 (2014). https://doi.org/10.1007/s10648-013-9243-1
68. Umejima, K., Ibaraki, T., Yamazaki, T., Sakai, K.L.: Paper notebooks vs. mobile devices: brain activation differences during memory retrieval. Front. Behav. Neurosci. **15** (2021). https://doi.org/10.3389/fnbeh.2021.634158
69. Vermeulen, N., Corneille, O., Niedenthal, P.M.: Sensory load incurs conceptual processing costs. Cognition **109**(2), 287–294 (2008). https://doi.org/10.1016/j.cognition.2008.09.004
70. Van der Weel, F.R.R., Van der Meer, A.L.H.: Handwriting but not typewriting leads to widespread brain connectivity: a high-density EEG study with implications for the classroom. Front. Psychol. **14** (2024). https://doi.org/10.3389/fpsyg.2023.1219945
71. Wilson, A.D., Golonka, S.: Embodied cognition is not what you think it is. Front. Psychol. **4** (2013). https://doi.org/10.3389/fpsyg.2013.00058
72. Wrigley, S.: Avoiding 'de-plagiarism': exploring the affordances of handwriting in the essay-writing process. Act. Learn. High. Educ. **20**(2), 167–179 (2019). https://doi.org/10.1177/1469787417735611
73. Yoshida, T., Yamaguchi, A., Tsutsui, H., Wake, T.: Tactile search for change has less memory than visual search for change. Attention, Percept. Psychophys. **77**(4), 1200–1211 (2015). https://doi.org/10.3758/s13414-014-0829-6

From Awareness to Action: Designing Targeted AI Training Modules Based on Faculty Needs in Higher Education

Britt Petjärv[1(✉)], Vitali Retsnoi[2], Anne Uukkivi[2], Monica Vilms[3], Kristiina Tuisk[4], Elena Safiulina[2], and Oksana Labanova[2]

[1] Centre for Humanities and Economics, TTK University of Applied Sciences, Pärnu mnt 62, Tallinn, Estonia
britt.petjarv@tktk.ee

[2] Centre for Sciences, TTK University of Applied Sciences, Pärnu mnt 62, Tallinn, Estonia
{vitali.retsnoi,anne.uukkivi,elena.safiulina, oksana.labanova}@tktk.ee

[3] Institute of Engineering and Circular Economy, TTK University of Applied Sciences, Pärnu mnt 62, Tallinn, Estonia
monica.vilms@tktk.ee

[4] Productory AI Agency, Educational and Strategic Consulting, Tallinn, Estonia
kristiina@productory.eu

Abstract. This article presents the design and implementation of a modular training programme in generative artificial intelligence (hereafter referred to as AI), developed for faculty at TTK University of Applied Sciences (TTK UAS). The programme emerged as a structured response to previously identified institutional needs, particularly the gap between general awareness of AI tools and their confident, ethical integration into teaching practice. Using a design-based research (DBR) approach, the development process emphasised stakeholder input, iterative refinement, and contextual alignment with faculty roles. Rather than offering new empirical data, the study documents how needs-driven insights were translated into an actionable training framework through participatory design. The resulting model comprises four modular tracks that address foundational knowledge, ethical considerations, creative media tools, and research applications. This practice-informed approach demonstrates how faculty development in AI can be rooted in institutional context while offering a potentially adaptable model for other higher education settings.

Keywords: Generative AI in Higher Education · Faculty Development · Modular Training · Design-Based Research · Pedagogical Integration

1 Introduction

Generative AI tools and large language models (LLMs) are making their way into everyday academic routines, reshaping how we teach, research, and manage information. While technologies like ChatGPT (a generative AI tool based on large language models)

C. Meinel et al. (Eds.): CSEDU 2025, CCIS 3148, pp. 103–120, 2027.
https://doi.org/10.1007/978-3-032-39103-2_6

offer considerable potential, they also raise complex ethical, pedagogical, and strategic challenges for institutions [1, 2]. Responding effectively requires not only individual awareness but also coordinated, context-sensitive capacity-building for faculty [3, 4].

In early 2024, a study at TTK UAS mapped faculty experiences, perceived risks, and training expectations related to AI [5]. Survey responses indicated that although faculty had begun integrating AI into tasks such as lesson planning and administration, significant concerns persisted regarding ethical use, misinformation, and pedagogical appropriateness. Most critically, the study identified a pronounced need for structured, modular professional development to bridge the gap between general familiarity and pedagogical confidence.

This article responds to that need. Whereas the original study offered a diagnostic baseline, the current paper presents an applied follow-up, grounded in a design-based research (DBR) orientation as outlined by the Design-Based Research Collective [6]. The training programme described here was developed through an iterative, collaborative process rooted in institutional context and faculty input. Instead of introducing new empirical data, the focus lies on how previously identified needs were translated into a structured, needs-driven training model. Such an approach reflects DBR principles of stakeholder engagement, contextual relevance, and the creation of usable, replicable solutions [7, 8].

Accordingly, the article builds on earlier research questions concerning faculty awareness, usage, risks, and training needs, and adds one further guiding question:

How can faculty's stated needs and expectations regarding AI be translated into meaningful training modules?

By addressing this question, the article contributes to the growing literature on AI in higher education and offers a practical institutional model for responding to rapid technological change in ways that are pedagogically grounded and ethically informed.

2 Background and Literature Review

As AI tools become embedded across higher education, the body of literature on their pedagogical, ethical, and institutional implications has expanded considerably. Generative AI is seen as a transformative force for teaching, learning, and academic productivity [1, 4, 9], yet also raises concerns around academic integrity, bias, misinformation, and the evolving role of educators [2, 10, 11]. Many of these issues are now widely acknowledged and reflected in recent global policy frameworks and ethics codes [12, 13].

While the rapid uptake of tools like ChatGPT has sparked curiosity and experimentation, studies confirm that educators often face uncertainty about how to implement AI in ways that are pedagogically sound and ethically responsible [10, 14–16]. Several sources emphasize that the challenge is not merely technical proficiency but rather developing pedagogical and critical AI literacy suited to specific disciplinary and institutional contexts [17–20].

Faculty surveys across regions consistently reveal both interest and anxiety: educators recognize AI's potential but express concerns over data security, bias, and loss of pedagogical control [3, 21, 22]. These findings are echoed in national and institutional research, including a 2024 study at TTK UAS [5], which identified high levels of awareness and initial use of generative AI tools, particularly for lesson planning and administrative support, while also revealing widespread uncertainty around responsible classroom integration. Faculty were open to training yet lacked clear pathways or trusted resources.

In response, researchers increasingly call for faculty development that goes beyond awareness-raising. Modular, context-specific and needs-responsive approaches are widely encouraged [14, 17, 23, 24]. This is reinforced by the 2025 Global AI Faculty Survey, where 64% of respondents called for AI-related training, 60% requested concrete implementation guidelines, and 50% asked for examples of best practice. These numbers underscore the strong interest in modular and actionable training formats, rather than generic orientation sessions [3]. Educators at different stages of their professional careers consistently express interest in training models that reflect their actual teaching contexts, ethical concerns, and institutional responsibilities [19, 23, 25].

Moreover, research in teacher development highlights the importance of participatory design, where faculty are actively involved in shaping training content and formats. Scholars such as Guskey [7] and Webster-Wright [8] argue that authentic and sustainable professional learning emerges when educators are treated not merely as recipients but as co-designers of the learning process, ensuring alignment with their beliefs, motivations, and daily teaching realities.

However, despite this growing consensus on what is needed, fewer studies offer concrete examples of how AI-related training can be designed, piloted, and implemented institutionally. According to the Digital Education Council (2025), only 4–6% of faculty members feel they have received sufficient training or resources to use AI responsibly in their teaching contexts [3]. Some comparative analyses [20, 26] identify fragmented efforts and a lack of alignment between training content and actual educator roles. Other research notes that while many universities now offer optional webinars or resources, structured, evaluated programmes remain rare [2, 15, 27].

Scholars have emphasized that effective professional development should include iterative co-design [6, 8], authentic learning tasks, and discipline-sensitive cases [5, 16, 17, 19]. More broadly, AI-related training must be viewed not as a one-off intervention, but as an evolving support system responsive to rapid technological change [28, 29].

In addition to needs-based and contextualised approaches, instructional design literature offers tested frameworks that can further inform faculty training models. Merrill's First Principles of Instruction emphasise task-centred learning that builds on prior knowledge, provides guided demonstration, facilitates application, and supports integration into professional contexts [30]. These principles underscore the value of aligning content with real-world tasks and enabling progressive competence development. The modular training structure described in this study reflects this orientation by offering hands-on exploration, contextual guidance, and peer exchange-key components for turning general awareness into actionable pedagogical skill.

Similar to TTK UAS, another Estonian higher education institution, the University of Tartu has adopted a long-term, multi-modal strategy to strengthen faculty AI competence, coordinated by a central working group. Between 2024 and 2025, iterative internal surveys revealed a marked reduction in uncertainty: in 2024, nearly half of non-users (125 of n = 396) reported not knowing how to use AI effectively, while by 2025, only 10 out of n = 278 respondents expressed the same concern [31]. This improvement coincided with regular workshops, peer discussion forums, and updated institutional guidelines demonstrating how structured, responsive training can foster measurable gains in confidence and pedagogical readiness. These practices align with the modular, participatory principles described in this study and underscore the role of institutional commitment in achieving meaningful professional development.

In summary, existing research highlights the need for:

- structured, modular AI training tailored to educators' actual work,
- ethical and pedagogical orientation, not just technical tutorials,
- alignment between institutional strategy and professional learning,
- and the co-creation of resources that are sensitive to local and disciplinary needs.

The present article responds to these gaps by documenting a four-module training programme developed at TTK UAS. It moves beyond mapping faculty needs, as established in the earlier study [5], toward an institutionally grounded intervention that seeks to translate those needs into meaningful learning design.

3 Methodology and Previous Results

The research methodology builds upon the findings of a previous study [5] and incorporates a comprehensive document analysis. The results presented in [5] are based on both qualitative and quantitative statistical methods, whereas the outcomes of the document analysis are discussed in the next section.

The findings of the previous study provide detailed insights into the use and perceptions of AI among faculty members at TTK UAS. These results are based on an empirical study in which data were collected through an online survey. In this section, we briefly introduce the results of the initial survey, along with a slightly more detailed explanation.

In the previous article [5], the following research questions were formulated:

1. What is the level of awareness and familiarity with GenAI tools among faculty at TTK UAS?
2. In which work fields are GenAI tools most commonly used?
3. What are the perceived potentials and concerns regarding GenAI across different fields at TTK UAS?
4. What AI-related training and guidance do faculty members need to ensure that the use of GenAI tools is both effective and aligned with academic ethical principles?

The survey among the academic staff was conducted in June 2024 to find answers to the research questions. The study group consisted of 81 lecturers who responded to the survey, resulting in a response rate of approximately 34.18%. Participants were categorized by discipline (engineering or social sciences/humanities), teaching experience, and AI training experience (those who had previously participated in AI training and those who had not).

Data were analysed using MS Excel and the statistical software R. Correlations between variables were examined using Spearman's rho coefficient. Differences between groups were assessed using the Wilcoxon rank-sum test and the Kruskal-Wallis rank-sum test. Significance was set at a minimum level of 0.05, with other significance levels (0.01 and 0.001) also reported.

To evaluate the overall impact of generative AI on higher education, a 5-point Likert scale was used (1 = Very Negative, 5 = Very Positive). The results indicated that participants perceived the overall impact of generative AI tools on higher education as slightly rather positive (M = 3.49, SD = 0.88). Specifically, 61.73% of participants rated the impact as rather or very positive, 20.99% as neutral, and 17.28% as rather or very negative. These findings pointed to a generally positive perception of generative AI in higher education, with room for improvement and dialogue. Stakeholders should support this positive trend while also understanding and addressing the concerns raised by a notable minority.

The survey comprised five distinct subscales, each focusing on different aspects of generative AI usage among lecturers. These include the Purpose of Using Generative AI, Capabilities of Using Generative AI Tools in Teaching, Risks Associated with Using Generative AI Tools in Teaching, Training Needs in AI, and Workload Dynamics of Academic Staff ([5, Table 3]).

The 'Purpose of Using Generative AI' subscale was an 8-item scale used to measure the extent to which lecturers use AI in the preparation and conduct of teaching, research, writing documentation, answering emails, etc., with all item means falling between 1.64 and 2.68 on a 4-point scale. The total score ranges from 2 to 27, with a higher score indicating more frequent use of generative AI. The results indicated that the most common use of generative AI tools was for preparing teaching materials. Other areas where AI showed potential, though not yet widely adopted, included conducting teaching activities in exercises and practical sessions, supporting research-related tasks, and assisting in writing project documentation. Usage was notably lower for student-related tasks, such as support for non-graded assignments and graded evaluations. Similarly, the use of AI for managing email correspondence was limited. The least frequent application was in guiding students and providing feedback.

The 'Capabilities of Using Generative AI tools in Teaching' subscale was an 8-item scale used to measure how useful generative AI can be in teaching from a lecturer's perspective, with all item means falling between 2.85 and 3.88 on a 5-point Likert scale ([5, Table 1]). The total score ranges from 13 to 38, with a higher score indicating that the lecturers see more opportunities for using generative AI tools in teaching. The results indicated that the highest-rated capability was the ability to complement traditional teaching methods, which suggests that AI is seen as an effective supplement, not a replacement. Respondents generally believed that AI tools provide additional opportunities to enrich learning, encourage experimentation with new pedagogical approaches, and promote creativity. There was a strong belief that generative AI can help students acquire skills relevant to future job markets. The respondents generally agreed that AI facilitates faster and customized content generation, and that it can enhance efficiency in assessment and feedback processes. The results indicated some skepticism regarding AI's role in fostering real-world, active learning experiences, as well as its capacity to enhance deep, structured thinking.

The ‘Risks Associated with Using Generative AI Tools in Teaching’ subscale was a 9-item scale used to measure how risky generative AI can be in teaching from a lecturer’s perspective, with all item means falling between 3.00 and 4.20 on a 5-point Likert scale ([5, Table 2]). The total score ranges from 14 to 45, with a higher score indicating that the lecturers see more risks associated with using AI tools in teaching. The results indicated strong agreement among participants that generative AI significantly increases the risk of academic fraud and that AI tools can produce unreliable or misleading content, which could compromise academic standards and distort students’ worldviews. Many respondents believed that reliance on AI could hinder students’ critical thinking and contribute to inequities in education, possibly due to unequal access, skills, or usage, although the higher standard deviations indicate greater variation in opinions. The results reflected moderate concern about privacy and data security, indicating that AI is perceived not only as an academic risk but also as a technological one. There was also concern that AI tools may blur ethical norms, potentially making academic misconduct harder to define or recognize. The respondents perceived a moderate risk that AI diminishes creative output, though responses were more divided. They were least convinced that AI has a direct negative effect on students’ mental health; this item had the lowest mean, indicating overall neutral views.

The ‘Workload Dynamic of Academic Staff’ subscale was a 6-item scale to assess how the use of generative AI has affected lecturers’ workload. The total score ranges from 0 to 18, with a higher score indicating that lecturers perceive an increase in workload due to the use of generative AI. The results indicated that the faculty did not perceive major shifts in workload due to AI. Most means cluster between 1.65 and 2.23 on a 4-point scale, suggesting stability or modest changes. Areas likc administrative duties and teaching preparation saw slight perceived decreases, indicating AI may be easing some burdens due to automation or better management tools powered by AI. The assessment of students’ work was the only area showing a slight increase in perceived workload. This might reflect faculty needing to adapt AI-generated student work or review it more critically for authenticity or quality, adding to the assessment burden. Note that the workload score tends to be higher when the lecturer’s field of activity is broader, rather than reflecting a genuine increase in workload.

In this extended version of the article, we provide a deeper analysis of the training expectations of academic staff and introduce the systematic training model developed at TTK UAS based on the results.

The survey collected information on which topics faculty believe should receive the most attention in training. Originally, the ‘Training Needs in AI’ scale consisted of 11 items ([5, Table 5]). The means of all items cluster between 3.98 and 4.49 on a 5-point Likert scale (1 = Strongly Disagree, 5 = Strongly Agree). Responses to the individual items were summed to calculate a total score, ranging from 31 to 55, with higher scores reflecting a greater interest in diverse training. To increase the reliability of the ‘Training Needs in AI’ scale, three out of eleven items were omitted. The summed scores of the remaining eight items ranged from 22 to 40, and the scale demonstrated more satisfactory internal consistency reliability (Cronbach’s alpha 0.85). Thus, the findings indicated that training for academic staff should focus on the eight topics listed below.

The highest-rated topics were practical recommendations for using text bots in planning and organizing teaching, including evaluation and feedback ($M = 4.49$, $SD = 0.63$), enhancing the effectiveness of teaching staff through AI tools ($M = 4.48$, $SD = 0.63$), and the use of text bots (including those that generate images, videos, and audio) in relation to academic fraud ($M = 4.46$, $SD = 0.78$). These indicate a clear demand for practical pedagogical applications of AI technologies, highlight interest in improving instructional performance, and reflect concerns about academic integrity.

Other highly rated areas included legal and ethical aspects of data protection and the use of text, image, video, and audio generators ($M = 4.43$, $SD = 0.79$), and learning methods in the age of AI ($M = 4.38$, $SD = 0.66$), both underscoring the importance of responsible and pedagogically appropriate integration of AI in the educational process.

Training needs related to broader contextual topics, such as the future of the labour market and the skills required of graduates ($M = 4.21$, $SD = 0.89$), as well as applications of text robots in research ($M = 4.26$, $SD = 0.92$) and project work ($M = 4.27$, $SD = 0.84$) were also considered important, although with slightly lower average scores.

Overall, the results suggest a comprehensive interest among academic staff of TTK UAS in both the practical implementation and broader implications of AI tools in teaching, learning, and research.

In this study, the main purpose of the adjusted 'Training Needs in AI' scale was to examine its correlations with other measured variables. There was a statistically significant moderate positive correlation between 'Training Needs in AI' and 'Capabilities of Using Generative AI' ($\rho = 0.39$, $p = 0.0003$; previously $\rho = 0.30$), as well as with the 'Overall Impact Rate of AI' ($\rho = 0.36$, $p = 0.0009$; previously $\rho = 0.26$) and the 'Purpose of Using AI' ($\rho = 0.40$, $p = 0.0002$; previously $\rho = 0.29$). This means that lecturers who are more interested in diverse training see more opportunities for using generative AI tools in teaching. They use AI more frequently for preparing and conducting teaching, research, writing documentation, answering emails, and other tasks, and overall, they have rated the impact of generative AI on higher education more positively.

The Wilcoxon rank-sum test and the Kruskal-Wallis rank-sum test were used to assess statistically significant differences between groups based on institution, teaching discipline (engineering or social sciences/humanities), teaching experience, and whether the individuals were AI trained or not. It was found that there were no statistically significant differences between the groups based on institution and teaching experience with respect to the 'Training Needs in AI' variable. The Wilcoxon rank sum test revealed that the total scores for 'Training Needs in AI' slightly differ according to the lecturers' teaching discipline ($W = 503$, $p = 0.084$). Specifically, the test result indicated that the total scores for 'Training Needs in AI' were higher for lecturers who teach social sciences or humanities (Median = 37) than for those who teach engineering disciplines (Median = 34).

3.1 Methodological Approach to Training Design

The development of the AI training programme followed a design-based research approach, building on earlier empirical insights while integrating new, context-sensitive design elements. DBR was selected as the methodological framework due to its suitability for educational innovations that evolve through iterative refinement in real-world settings.

Rather than relying on generic training templates, the process was grounded in participatory design principles, where academic staff acted not only as end-users but also as co-designers. Structured consultations with faculty members across all institutes were conducted by the university's AI working group, and the outcomes were systematically summarised. These consultations helped to bring out discipline-specific needs and highlight practical concerns such as access to tools and questions related to ethical use. The results formed the basis for a formal needs assessment and provided a qualitative complement to the original survey data, playing an instrumental role in prioritising training content.

To ensure cross-institutional relevance and coherence, an external expert was invited to conduct a comparative analysis, drawing on AI training initiatives in other Estonian higher education settings. This step allowed for benchmarking and contextual calibration, helping the TTK UAS model reflect both local priorities and broader national trends in digital competence development.

4 Development of the Training Modules

Building on the methodological approach outlined above, the development of the AI training modules at TTK UAS followed a four-phase cycle: (1) needs assessment, (2) stakeholder validation, (3) expert review, and (4) thematic clustering. Rather than adopting a pre-packaged training solution, the university applied a bottom-up approach that emphasized contextual relevance, practical usability, and faculty empowerment.

Needs Assessment. The starting point for the training module development was a comprehensive needs assessment, based on findings from the earlier empirical study [5].

The objective of this phase was to establish a grounded understanding of faculty needs across disciplines and levels of digital maturity. The results revealed a broad interest in modular and practice-oriented training, particularly in areas such as text bot integration, ethical frameworks, and the pedagogical use of media-generating AI tools. Respondents expressed confidence in AI's potential but also emphasized uncertainty about responsible implementation and institutional expectations. This phase provided the evidence base for the training design, allowing the development team to identify content priorities, training depth, and delivery preferences before engaging in further validation.

Stakeholder validation. To ensure the programme reflected authentic institutional priorities, aggregated survey themes were presented and validated in structured discussions with teaching staff and programme leads. These sessions served to contextualise the data, surface hidden assumptions, and prioritise topics based on both urgency and feasibility. In addition, targeted briefings and feedback consultations were held with institutional units during December 2024 and January 2025 to further align the training content with ongoing strategic developments.

In these sessions, the results of the AI survey and the preliminary structure of the training programme were presented and discussed with faculty representatives from all academic institutes and centres at TTK UAS. These discipline-specific consultations provided valuable insights and revealed additional training needs not fully captured by the initial survey.

At the Institute of Logistics, for example, there was a strong interest in practical applications of generative AI, while ethical topics were deemed less relevant. The Institute of Technology indicated that foundational AI skills were often acquired independently but expressed demand for advanced training and exposure to tools such as DeepSeek. Meanwhile, the Centre for Humanities and Economics emphasized the need for institution-wide guidance on AI use in teaching, especially in relation to academic integrity and acceptable tool use. At the Institute of Service Economy, there was high interest in participating across all modules, along with a request for access to paid tools. At the Institute of Engineering and Circular Economy, general interest in training was expressed, although fewer concrete suggestions were made, and difficulty identifying suitable trainers was noted.

These decentralized consultations helped to validate and refine the training content, allowing for prioritization based on disciplinary relevance and feasibility. They also supported institutional ownership by incorporating early-stage faculty input and identifying potential barriers to participation, such as access to tools or uncertainty about ethical standards.

Through this dialogue, the training initiative moved beyond surface-level interest and gained alignment with both grassroots needs and strategic institutional goals.

Expert review. Following internal validation, an external expert was engaged to conduct a content review. Drawing on nearly two years of experience designing and delivering AI training programmes across academic and professional settings, the expert brought an informed perspective to the evolving needs of higher education institutions. The expert compared the TTK UAS survey findings with previous training frameworks to identify alignment gaps and opportunities for adaptation. In addition to drawing on her own teaching experience and programmes, the expert integrated knowledge gathered through observing and collaborating with other AI educators, ensuring the modules reflected pedagogical approaches already in use within the Estonian higher education landscape. This phase helped confirm the feasibility of proposed module themes and informed refinements in both content scope and delivery format, ensuring that the programme remained practical, ethically grounded, and institutionally relevant.

Thematic clustering. Following validation, conceptually related topics were clustered into coherent thematic blocks. These blocks became the foundation for the four training modules. The goal was to balance breadth and depth: each module would offer comprehensive coverage of a specific domain while remaining accessible to participants with different levels of prior experience. The clustering process was grounded in two key considerations: faculty preferences and the current technological maturity of AI tools. While the initial survey and consultation sessions revealed diverse interests across disciplines, it became clear that text-based tools – particularly LLMs – offered the broadest pedagogical value and the most immediate usability across teaching, research, and administrative contexts. As a result, most of the final module themes were intentionally built around these capabilities.

4.1 Methodological Approach to Training Design

Each of the four modules (see Fig. 1) was designed to address a specific yet connected area of AI use in higher education. Together, they offer a clear learning pathway, progressing from basic understanding to more advanced application, while remaining flexible enough to support modular participation based on individual goals or institutional needs.

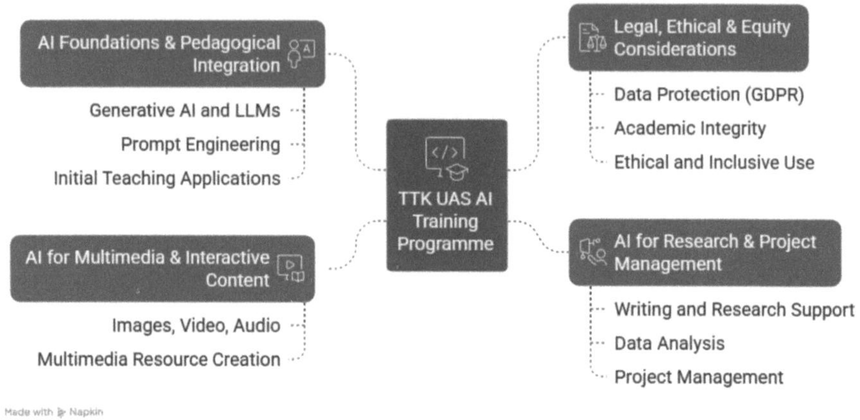

Fig. 1. Structure of the TTK UAS AI training programme, illustrating the modular design and core focus areas. This flowchart was created using Napkin, an AI-assisted visualisation tool. Reviewed and edited by the authors.

Module 1: AI Foundations and Pedagogical Integration. This entry-level module introduces participants to the core principles of generative AI, with a particular focus on LLMs and text-based tools. It reflects a dual objective: building baseline AI literacy across the academic staff and equipping educators with immediate applications for teaching and planning. The module covers key concepts such as prompt engineering, the limitations and risks of AI-generated content, and hands-on use of tools like ChatGPT, Gemini, and Copilot.

Its design was informed by survey results showing that while 83% of faculty were aware of generative AI, many lacked the foundational skills and confidence to use it pedagogically [5]. These findings were reinforced during consultations with academic units, where educators emphasised the need for introductory-level, hands-on training closely linked to everyday teaching tasks. In response, the module also explores how AI can support learning path personalisation, improve feedback efficiency, and enrich teaching materials, while placing strong emphasis on maintaining academic integrity when adopting these tools.

Module 2: Legal, Ethical, and Equity Considerations in AI Use. Informed by widespread faculty concerns about the ethical and legal risks of AI, this module focuses on responsible and inclusive AI adoption. It explores key issues such as academic misconduct, privacy and data protection under GDPR, and fairness and bias in algorithmic systems. Participants learn how to communicate acceptable AI use policies to students, design assignments that minimize the risk of misuse, and critically evaluate the limitations of AI-detection tools. The module also addresses broader questions of accessibility and equity, including how institutions can ensure inclusive AI use across cost, language, and disability-related barriers.

Both the initial survey and subsequent consultations with academic units confirmed that concerns about plagiarism, data privacy, and algorithmic bias were among the most pressing. Faculty also highlighted uncertainty around institutional policies and expectations, which led to the inclusion of concrete case examples, student-facing guidelines, and equity-focused design elements

Module 3: AI for Multimedia and Interactive Content Creation. This module responds to strong faculty interest in diversifying instructional approaches through the use of new media and creative tools. It introduces participants to AI platforms that generate and process visual, audio, and video content (e.g., DALL·E, Midjourney, ElevenLabs, and Sora). Through hands-on activities, educators practice designing infographics, converting lectures into podcasts or short-form videos, and enhancing accessibility through captions and visual aids. The emphasis is not only on technical proficiency, but also on content quality, ethical use, and pedagogical alignment.

This module was added in response to survey feedback indicating a need for more support in using AI to create engaging and diverse teaching materials [5]. These needs were echoed in departmental consultations, where participants emphasized the importance of connecting media-rich content to clearly defined learning goals.

Module 4: AI for Research, Academic Writing, and Project Management. This advanced module supports faculty in applying AI to research, academic writing, and organizational tasks. Participants are introduced to tools such as Elicit, Jenni.ai, and integrated AI assistants for conducting literature reviews, supporting data analysis, managing projects, and streamlining communication. The module also addresses the evolving boundary between human authorship and machine assistance, with a focus on maintaining scholarly standards and transparency. In addition, practical examples illustrate how AI can support academic project management, including tasks such as budgeting, scheduling, coordination, and dissemination. The module's focus reflects survey results that revealed high interest in using AI for academic productivity, particularly writing and planning support [5]. These findings were reinforced in discussions with academic staff, where researchers called for clearer guidance on responsible authorship practices and practical strategies for integrating AI into research workflows.

Together, these modules reflect the diverse and evolving needs of higher education professionals. By grounding each training element in both research evidence and validated practitioner feedback, the programme supports not only short-term skill acquisition but also long-term institutional capacity building.

4.2 Implementation and Delivery Strategy

To accommodate the diverse schedules and learning preferences of faculty, all training modules were designed for hybrid delivery. Each session is accessible both in person and online, with recordings available for asynchronous review. This flexible structure ensures broad participation and allows faculty to integrate new tools and practices gradually into their teaching, research, and administrative routines.

The programme prioritizes practical, hands-on learning. Each module is divided into multiple subtopics and instructional units that emphasize experimentation, peer exchange, and tool-based assignments. Participants are encouraged to apply new skills between sessions, with support available via internal knowledge-sharing platforms and follow-up sessions.

Training is delivered by a mix of internal and external experts. Internal trainers include TTK UAS faculty who already use AI tools in their daily work, offering relatable and context-specific guidance. External trainers – specialists in AI ethics, data protection, and generative media – add cross-disciplinary perspectives and bring in best practices from broader educational and industry ecosystems. Many modules are co-taught or split among instructors to ensure deep topical expertise.

Tool selection also reflects an accessibility-first approach. While some sessions demonstrate advanced AI platforms that require paid licenses, the programme prioritizes free or low-cost tools that can be used independently by both faculty and students. Decisions around tool adoption are made transparently, with attention to licensing, data privacy, and long-term institutional feasibility.

Evaluation and feedback mechanisms are integral to the programme. After each session, participants complete a feedback survey covering instructional clarity, content relevance, and practical applicability. This feedback is analysed and used to iteratively improve both module content and delivery methods. In addition, a longitudinal follow-up survey is planned to assess how faculty implement AI tools over time, what barriers persist, and how organizational learning can be further supported.

Finally, a dedicated online group for AI in education has been established on TTK UAS internal platform, functioning as a professional learning community. This channel enables participants to share success stories, ask implementation questions, and maintain engagement with peers and trainers beyond the training period.

4.3 Impact and Strategic Value of the Training Programme

In Estonia, both national and institutional strategies recognise the growing importance of artificial intelligence in education, research, and public sector development. The AI training programme at TTK UAS has been developed with the intention of supporting these broader goals. At the institutional level, the programme is closely aligned with the TTK UAS Development Plan 2021–2025 [32], with a focus on innovation, high-quality teaching, responsible technology use, and staff development. Each module supports these priorities by providing faculty with practical skills for everyday teaching and long-term professional growth. In doing so, the programme serves both as a response to the needs identified in the 2024 faculty survey and as a direct implementation of the university's strategic goals, enhancing the institution's capacity to deliver modern, ethical, and forward-looking education.

The AI training programme at TTK UAS is also closely aligned with Estonia's key national policy documents. Each of the four modules reflects priorities outlined in the White Paper on Data and AI 2024–2030 [33], Estonia 2035 [34], and the Education Sector Development Plan 2021–2035 [35].

The AI basics and teaching module introduces educators to core AI concepts and tools that enhance lesson planning, student engagement, and personalised learning. This supports the goals of the Education Sector Development Plan [35] related to modern, learner-centred teaching, contributes to the Estonia 2035 [34] vision of widespread digital competence and educational innovation, and addresses the White Paper's [33] call to enhance AI awareness and skills across various sectors.

The AI ethics and legal aspects module introduces academic staff to ethical AI use, covering topics like GDPR, fairness, and academic integrity. This supports the White Paper's [33] focus on responsible and human-centred AI, aligns with the Education Sector Development Plan's [35] emphasis on ethics and values in education, and reflects Estonia 2035's [34] priority of building a transparent, inclusive, and people-centred society.

The AI and multimedia tools module help educators create interactive, student-centred digital learning materials. This supports inclusive and engaging learning environments in line with the Education Sector Plan [35] and reinforces the Estonia 2035 [34] aim of smart digital solutions that improve the quality and accessibility of education.

The AI in research and project work module equips participants with skills for using AI in academic writing, data analysis, literature reviews, and project planning. This reflects the White Paper's [33] emphasis on applied research and innovation, aligns with the Education Sector Plan's [35] focus on supporting R&D competence in higher education, and contributes to Estonia 2035 [34] objectives for strengthening a competitive, knowledge-based economy.

Together, the four modules of the AI training programme bring national and institutional strategies into practice by supporting educators with the tools, knowledge, and values needed for innovation, quality, and responsibility in higher education.

5 Discussion

This extended study builds directly upon an earlier publication that analysed faculty awareness, practices, and perceived risks related to generative AI in higher education, using TTK UAS as a case study [5]. Whereas the previous article offered a diagnostic view, the current contribution addresses the gap highlighted both in the literature and in the earlier institutional study, namely the scarcity of actionable models that support educators in moving from AI awareness to responsible, discipline-sensitive practice. By documenting the design of a targeted training programme, the present findings demonstrate how such gaps can be bridged through institutionally grounded, need-driven development.

The earlier TTK UAS survey confirmed what many studies have shown: lecturers are generally aware of tools such as ChatGPT but lack confidence in applying them ethically and pedagogically. Ethical concerns, including academic honesty, bias, misinformation, and data protection, emerged as central themes in both the local data and recent reviews highlighting transparency and fairness challenges in AI-enhanced education [10, 11, 18]. These shared concerns underscored the need for structured professional development rather than ad-hoc experimentation.

Faculty were, however, open to receiving training, which aligns with evidence from comparative studies that highlight strong demand for context-specific guidance [3, 5].

Crucially, respondents already experimenting with AI perceived greater pedagogical potential and expressed higher motivation for structured learning. This observation aligns with global faculty surveys [36, 37], showing that familiarity increases interest in deeper competence building. It also highlighted a clear path forward: practical training should be closely connected to educators' existing interests and daily practices.

The present study offers such a connection through the practical realisation of a modular, needs driven training model. Although the research literature frequently calls for long term, contextualised faculty development [3, 14, 17, 36], [14] detailed design blueprints remain rare [2, 3, 15, 27]. The model described here emerged from direct consultation with faculty, who prioritised content and shaped delivery formats. Such participatory design aligns with established principles of effective professional development, which emphasise the importance of contextual relevance, active engagement, and reflective practice [7, 8]. This participatory approach contrasts with top-down initiatives that assume a uniform baseline of readiness. By involving educators in every stage, from the validation of survey findings to the refinement of module themes, the programme translated diagnostic knowledge into tangible learning opportunities. This approach also aligns with Merrill's instructional principles, which emphasise authentic tasks, guided practice, and progressive integration into professional routines [30].

Several programme features mirror best-practice recommendations. First, the modular structure allows flexible engagement in line with evidence that AI competence is uneven and often discipline-specific [22, 23]. Second, ethics and legal topics are introduced at the outset, answering calls for responsible, human-centred AI education [18, 33, 38]. Third, a balance between hands-on exploration and pedagogical integration reflects findings that confidence grows when tool use is explicitly tied to teaching methods and disciplinary cultures [23, 25]. Combined, these elements translate general guidelines into a practical institutional model that helps bridge the gap between theory and everyday application.

Faculty at TTK UAS expressed a clear preference for hybrid or in-person sessions that support peer interaction and guided exploration, reflecting findings from earlier studies that highlight educators' appreciation for collaborative and flexible learning environments [39]. This reinforces the importance of aligning training formats with both pedagogical goals and institutional culture, ensuring adaptability to local conditions.

The training model was developed in dialogue with Estonia's national strategies on digitalisation and education yet was driven primarily by articulated faculty needs. By translating policy ambitions into day-to-day academic practice, the programme demonstrates how strategic goals can be anchored in real institutional settings. This represents another step toward narrowing the gap between broad directives and practical classroom realities.

The experience further supports the view that technical knowhow alone is insufficient. Sustainable AI literacy depends on parallel investment in ethical frameworks, policy clarity, time allocation, and institutional trust [11, 13, 17]. Iterative feedback cycles [6], peer exchange [8], and continuous refinement were therefore integrated into the programme to foster lasting competence rather than one-off skill acquisition.

Although the training programme was developed within the institutional context of TTK UAS, its modular structure and participatory design offer potential for adaptation in other higher education settings. Evidence from the University of Tartu points in a similar direction, where sustained and diverse faculty development activities have led to measurable improvements in AI readiness. This reinforces the value of institutionally grounded, needs-based approaches [31]. The programme's focus on relevant content, ethical foundations, and pedagogical alignment responds to common challenges faced by institutions integrating generative AI. For universities seeking to implement national digitalisation or AI strategies in a meaningful way, the TTK UAS model provides a transferable basis, assuming that local validation, collaborative design, and disciplinary relevance are taken into account.

Some limitations remain. The training model described in this study was developed using an institutionally grounded, design-based approach rather than a controlled experimental framework. While this method ensures contextual relevance and alignment with faculty needs, it limits the generalisability of findings to other institutional types or cultural settings. The results should therefore be viewed as a situated example of translating local faculty input into practice, rather than as a universally validated model. Furthermore, the study does not include a formal evaluation of learning outcomes or behavioural change, as its primary aim was to document the development process. Although informal feedback and iterative adjustments were incorporated, a systematic assessment of long-term impact remains a priority for future research.

Future research should therefore focus on evaluating the sustained effects of the training programme on educators' pedagogical integration of AI. This includes examining how newly acquired competences translate into course design, student guidance, and interdisciplinary collaboration. In particular, future studies could investigate shifts in educators' confidence levels and the sustainability of changes introduced. Comparative research across diverse institutions would further help to clarify how the modular framework can be adapted to different educational settings, including variations in institutional culture, language, and resources. Such studies would strengthen the model's generalisability and contribute to the broader knowledge base on effective faculty development in the age of AI.

6 Conclusion

This paper contributes to the growing body of research focused on supporting higher education institutions in navigating the pedagogical challenges of generative AI. By addressing the gap between faculty awareness and pedagogical readiness, it provides a structured example of how institutions can move from diagnostic insights to concrete instructional improvement.

The proposed training model illustrates a practical pathway from interest to capability, grounded in participatory design, modularity, and attention to ethical concerns. While developed in a specific institutional setting, these principles may be transferable to a range of higher education contexts. Further comparative studies will be essential to evaluate the model's broader applicability.

References

1. Ward, D., et al.: How universities can move forward with generative AI in teaching and learning. Chang. Mag. High. Learn. **56**(1), 47–54 (2024)
2. Aad, S., Hardey, M.: Generative AI: hopes, controversies and the future of faculty roles in education. Qual. Assur. Educ. **33**(2), 267–282 (2025). https://doi.org/10.1108/QAE-02-2024-0043
3. Digital Education Council. What Faculty Want: Key Results from the Global AI Faculty Survey 2025. (2025). https://www.digitaleducationcouncil.com/post/what-faculty-want-key-results-from-the-global-ai-faculty-survey-2025. Accessed 18 June 2025
4. Sutedjo, S.P., Liu, P., Chowdhury, M.: Generative AI in higher education: a cross-institutional study on faculty preparation and resources. Stud. Technol. Enhanc. Learn. **4**(1) (2025). https://doi.org/10.21428/8c225f6e.955a547e. https://stel.pubpub.org/pub/04-01-sutedjo-liu-chowdhury/release/1
5. Petjärv, B., Retsnoi, V., Uukkivi, A., Vilms, M., Safiulina, E., Labanova, O.: Practices, challenges, and training needs of faculty in terms of generative AI. In: 17th International Conference on Computer Supported Education (CSEDU 2025). Springer, Cham (2025). https://doi.org/10.5220/0013287600003932
6. The Design-Based Research Collective: Design-based research: an emerging paradigm for educational inquiry. Educ. Res. **32**(1), 5–8 (2003). https://doi.org/10.3102/0013189X032001005
7. Guskey, T.R.: Professional development and teacher change. Teach. Teach. **8**(3), 381–391 (2002). https://doi.org/10.1080/135406002100000512
8. Webster-Wright, A.: Reframing professional development through understanding authentic professional learning. Rev. Educ. Res. **79**(2), 702–739 (2009). https://doi.org/10.3102/0034654308330970
9. Rahman, M.M., Watanobe, Y.: ChatGPT for education and research: opportunities, threats, and strategies. Appl. Sci. **13**(9), 5783 (2023). https://doi.org/10.3390/app13095783
10. Yan, L., et al.: Practical and ethical challenges of large language models in education: a systematic scoping review. Br. J. Educ. Technol. **55**(1), 90–112 (2023). https://doi.org/10.1111/bjet.13370
11. Yusuf, N., Pervin, M., Román-González, M.: Generative AI and the future of higher education: a threat to academic integrity or reformation? evidence from multicultural perspectives. Int. J. Educ. Technol. High. Educ. **21**(1), 21 (2024). https://doi.org/10.1186/s41239-024-00453-6
12. Slimi, Z., Carballido, B.V.: Navigating the ethical challenges of artificial intelligence in higher education: an analysis of seven global AI ethics policies. TEM J. **12**(2), 590–602 (2023). https://doi.org/10.18421/TEM122-02
13. Holmes, W.: Guidance for generative AI in education and research. (2023). https://doi.org/10.54675/EWZM9535
14. Abu-Orabi, S.T.: Artificial intelligence technologies in higher education: reality and challenges. In: Proceedings of the 17th International Conference on Development of E-System Engineering (DeSE), pp. 479–484 (2024). https://doi.org/10.1109/DeSE63988.2024.10911936
15. Alzakwani, M.H.H., Zabri, S.M., Ali, R.R.: Enhancing university teaching and learning through integration of artificial intelligence in information and communication technology. Edelweiss Appl. Sci. Technol. **9**(1), 1345–1357 (2025). https://doi.org/10.55214/25768484.v9i1.4647
16. Safiulina, E., Labanova, O., Uukkivi, A., Petjärv, B., Vilms, M.: Integrating artificial intelligence in higher education: a literature review of current trends, challenges, and future directions. In: ICERI2024 Proceedings, pp. 1666–1675 (2024). https://doi.org/10.21125/iceri.2024.0492

17. Kohnke, L., Zou, D., Ou, A.W., Gu, M.M.: Preparing future educators for AI-enhanced classrooms: insights into AI literacy and integration. Comput. Educ.: Artif. Intell. **8**, 100398 (2025). https://doi.org/10.1016/j.caeai.2025.100398
18. Akgun, S., Greenhow, C.: Artificial intelligence in education: addressing ethical challenges in K-12 settings. AI Ethics. **2**(3), 431–440 (2022). https://doi.org/10.1007/s43681-021-00096-7
19. Ding, A.-C.E., Shi, L., Yang, H., Choi, I.: Enhancing teacher AI literacy and integration through different types of cases in teacher professional development. Comput. Educ. Open. **6**, 100178 (2024). https://doi.org/10.1016/j.caeo.2024.100178
20. Safiulina, E., Labanova, O., Uukkivi, A., Petjärv, B., Vilms, M.: Deriving a literature-based risk-impact matrix for artificial intelligence in higher education: a focus on challenges and future directions. In: INTED2025 Proceedings, pp. 838–841 (2025). https://doi.org/10.21125/inted.2025.0304
21. Lee, D., et al.: The impact of generative AI on higher education learning and teaching: a study of educators' perspectives. Comput. Educ.: Artif. Intell. **6**, 100221 (2024). https://doi.org/10.1016/j.caeai.2024.100221
22. Durmuş Sarıkahya, S., Özbay, Ö., Torpuş, K., Usta, G., Çınar Özbay, S.: The impact of ChatGPT on nursing education: a qualitative study based on the experiences of faculty members. Nurse Educ. Today. **152**, 106755 (2025). https://doi.org/10.1016/j.nedt.2025.106755
23. Lucas, M., Bem-haja, P., Zhang, Y., Llorente-Cejudo, C., Palacios-Rodríguez, A.: A comparative analysis of pre-service teachers' readiness for AI integration. Comput. Educ.: Artif. Intell. **8**, 100396 (2025). https://doi.org/10.1016/j.caeai.2025.100396
24. Chiu, T.K.F., Xia, Q., Zhou, X., Chai, C.S., Cheng, M.: Systematic literature review on opportunities, challenges, and future research recommendations of artificial intelligence in education. Comput. Educ.: Artif. Intell. **4**, 100118 (2023). https://doi.org/10.1016/j.caeai.2022.100118
25. Pei, B., Lu, J., Jing, X.: Empowering preservice teachers' AI literacy: current understanding, influential factors, and strategies for improvement. Comput. Educ.: Artif. Intell. **8**, 100406 (2025). https://doi.org/10.1016/j.caeai.2025.100406
26. Iskandarova, S., Yusif-zada, K., Mukhtarova, S.: AI into higher education curriculum in developing countries. In: 2024 IEEE Frontiers in Education Conference (FIE), pp. 1–9 (2024). https://doi.org/10.1109/FIE61694.2024.10893097
27. Southworth, J., et al.: Developing a model for AI across the curriculum: transforming the higher education landscape via innovation in AI literacy. Comput. Educ.: Artif. Intell. **4**, 100127 (2023). https://doi.org/10.1016/j.caeai.2023.100127
28. Al-Emran, M., Al-Qaysi, N., Al-Sharafi, M.A., Khoshkam, M., Foroughi, B., Ghobakhloo, M.: Role of perceived threats and knowledge Management in Shaping Generative AI use in education and its impact on social sustainability. Int. J. Manag. Educ. **23**(1), 101105 (2025). https://doi.org/10.1016/j.ijme.2024.101105
29. Sperling, K., Stenberg, C.-J., McGrath, C., Åkerfeldt, A., Heintz, F., Stenliden, L.: In search of artificial intelligence (AI) literacy in teacher education: a scoping review. Comput. Educ. Open. **6**, 100169 (2024). https://doi.org/10.1016/j.caeo.2024.100169
30. Merrill, M.D.: First principles of instruction. Educ. Technol. Res. Dev. **50**(3), 43–59 (2002). https://doi.org/10.1007/BF02505024
31. Hint, H., Leijen, D.A.J.: Understanding and Supporting University Teachers' Use of Generative AI. ISATT 2025, Glasgow (2025) (Unpublished conference presentation; slides shared with permission)
32. Tallinna Tehnikakõrgkool Tallinna Tehnikakõrgkooli arengukava 2021–2025. (2021). https://www.tktk.ee/wp-content/uploads/2022/02/1_15_9_TTK_arengukava_2021_2025.pdf. Accessed 25 June 2025

33. Majandus-ja Kommunikatsiooniministeerium Tehisintellekti ja andmete valge raamat 2024–2030. (2024). https://mkm.ee/et/eesmargid-tegevused/andmed-ja-tehisintellekt. Accessed 25 June 2025
34. Riigikantselei Eesti 2035: Eesti pikaajaline arengustrateegia. (2021). https://www.riigikantselei.ee/eesti2035. Accessed 1 July 2025
35. Haridus-ja Teadusministeerium. Haridusvaldkonna arengukava 2021–2035. (2021). https://www.hm.ee/et/haridusvaldkonna-arengukava-2021-2035. Accessed 1 July 2025
36. Lee, M.M., Jung, Y.H., Park, S.Y.: Understanding faculty's adoption of AI in teaching: the role of self-efficacy, attitudes, and institutional support. Int. J. Educ. Technol. High. Educ. **21**(1), 20 (2024). https://doi.org/10.1186/s41239-024-00490-1
37. Ismail, L., Poth, C., Koot, D.: Teachers' perceptions of using an AI-based educational tool for scientific writing. Front. Educ. **7**, 755914 (2022). https://doi.org/10.3389/feduc.2022.755914
38. Kasneci, E., et al.: ChatGPT for good? on opportunities and challenges of large language models for education. Learn. Individ. Differ. **103**, 102274 (2023). https://doi.org/10.1016/j.lindif.2023.102274
39. Munir, F., Abdulbaki, E., Saiyad, Z., Ipema, H.: Taking the plunge together: a student-led faculty learning seminar series on artificial intelligence. Curr. Pharm. Teach. Learn. **17**(8), 102370 (2025). https://doi.org/10.1016/j.cptl.2025.102370

Personal Learning Environments on a National Scale: Experiences from the Development of a Reference Prototype

Sönke Erdmann, Swathi Krishnaraja, Benja Wiencke, and Ulrike Lucke(✉)

Department of Computational Science, University of Potsdam, An der Bahn 2, 14476 Potsdam, Germany
ulrike.lucke@uni-potsdam.de

Abstract. Personalized learning as an umbrella term is one of the most referenced learning paradigms in educational technologies. Consequently, the variety of Personal Learning Environments (PLE) is also broad. We build on the container character of this term to demonstrate how existing but fragmented learning applications and content can be utilized within a networked digital education ecosystem on a national scale. To identify its values, the Substitution, Augmentation, Modification and Redefinition framework (SAMR) is combined with the Higher Education Reference Model (HERM). A user study was conducted to evaluate the developed reference prototype. The results and future work are outlined.

Keywords: Personal Learning Environments · Digitalisation · Digital Learning Spaces · Educational Infrastructure · Educational Services · Adaptive Learning · Digital Sovereignty

1 Introducing a National Digital Education Ecosystem

The digital infrastructure in the education landscape is fragmented, which complicates cross-institutional cooperation and transitions between institutions along individual learning pathways [23]. Several projects tried to address this problem. Given the complexity of its federated education system and the broad scope of targeted education domains, the German initiative towards a *National Infrastructure for Education* [1] is one of the largest. The aim was to allow learners to seamlessly construct their lifelong learning journeys across all education sectors. This was accompanied by measures to professionalize teaching staff and to strengthen and connect institutional infrastructures. Currently, the Federal Agency for Breakthrough Innovation has been assigned to transfer the results of the funded projects to regular service. The prototype *BIRD* provides a conceptual and technical reference as well as associated research results [7].

C. Meinel et al. (Eds.): CSEDU 2025, CCIS 3148, pp. 121–135, 2027.
https://doi.org/10.1007/978-3-032-39103-2_7

The design of this infrastructure was empirically based on more than 170 fine-grained user stories from a previous project, which were condensed into a prototypical Personal Learning Environment (PLE) [22], and several dozens (107 identified and 27 published) comprehensive scenarios [5,10]. Thus, additional components were added. The Learning Path Finder (LPF) supports users with personalized recommendations for educational offerings [31]. The Buddy Finder (BF) connects users without leaking sensitive personal data [9]. Based on such recommendations for appropriate educational content and learning companions, the shared workspace facilitates collaboration across institutional boundaries [11]. A fundamental premise in the conception of the prototype was not to replace established offerings, but only to interconnect them and thus to supplement existing education infrastructure with new functions, tools or usage options [25]. For this reason, we relied on the SAMR model [28] as a classification schema for educational services, which we align with the HERM model to structure the field. In this article, we compare the idea of expanding existing services both from the empirical perspective of a user survey and from a conceptual point of view, and we condense both into a more nuanced understanding of PLEs.

The remainder of this article is structured as follows. In Sect. 2, we review current strategies for personal, smart or adaptive learning environments. Then we examine selected empirical findings on digital learning spaces in higher education in Sect. 3, focussing on student expectations and experiences. This is further elaborated in Sect. 4 with a description of the BIRD prototype as a realization of a PLE. After a brief recapitulation of the architecture, components and functions of the infrastructure, particular attention is paid to their analysis according to the SAMR model. Based on this differentiated understanding, a concept of a PLE within the national digital education ecosystem is then outlined in Sect. 5. Finally, our findings are summarized and an outlook on future directions for research and development is given.

2 Foundations and Approaches for Personal Learning Environments

As examined in earlier publications [10,21], there are different patterns and terms used for personal or virtual learning environments. Ten years ago the Educause learning initiative proposed a *Next Generation Learning Digital Learning Environment* [4]. As a foundation, EDUCAUSE Technology Research in the Academic Community collaborated with 157 institutions to collect responses from 13,451 faculty respondents in 7 countries about their technology experiences [3]. They identified students wishes and needs regarding learning technologies in higher education institutions (face-to-face, blended and virtual) and proposed blended environments [26].

The Covid pandemic has kickstarted initiatives in Europe in recent years. Besides the German national digital education ecosystem, outlined in Sect. 1, there are also national projects in other regions. For instance, the Finnish project *Digivisio* aims to provide a national digital service platform [18] dedicated to the field of higher education. The Dutch initiative *Npuls* also aims to establish centers of teaching and learning (CTL) [24] in tertiary education. All approaches focus on cross-institutional interoperability within networked learning environments. Thus, personalized and adaptive learning have become fundamental learning paradigms in education technologies [12].

Personalised learning as an "umbrella term" aligns with self-regulated and competence-oriented learning [15]. For example, DigCompEdu provides guidelines from the European Union on the skills that learners should be equipped with in a post-digital society [29]. With the rise of AI in educational fields, digital sovereignty at various levels (individual, institutional and state) is becoming increasingly important. However, most competence models do not yet feature this, although there are initial attempts to incorporate it [14]. On a larger scale, the European Union's EuroStack initiative underscores the importance of a sovereign European infrastructure, particularly in vulnerable areas such as education [2]. Foridi sums it up as follows: "Digital sovereignty is not just a matter of interest for some specialists. It is already affecting everybody. And this is why it is essential to design it as well as possible, together." [13] In summary, while there is no commonly agreed understanding of digital learning environments and the learning theories that underpin them, there is a shared (albeit vague) vision and considerable overlap in the approaches pursued.

3 Empirical Analysis of the Advancement of Networked Learning Spaces

Table 1. Clustering wishes of students for a digital learning space against existing BIRD components.

Component	Ecosystem dimensions	Functionalities
Learning Path Finder	Digital infrastructure	Support in finding suitable digital learning materials; Bundled provision of digital services and offers
Buddy Finder	Communication and Collaboration	Provision of networking opportunities; Provision of digital tools for collaborative work
Data Wallet	Data model	Openness of data; Customization of data handling mechanisms
Personal workspace	Interaction and technical interoperability	Ability to organize learning materials; Ability to structure learning activities
Integration of existing services	Additional tools	Collaborative text/canvas; Personal calendar; Etherpad; Miro/Mind maps; Surveys; Archive management; Integrated zoom; Word-cloud generator; Presentations; Exam administration system

This study builds upon previous research that investigated student expectations and experiences in digital learning environments in higher education (n = 32) [11]. Most participants were indifferent to digital collaboration tools and educational recommendations. However, significant variability was observed in these areas, suggesting that the questions were unclear or insufficient. Agreements were found regarding networking opportunities, adaptability in the self-structuring of learning activities and -materials, and data sovereignty. The initial investigation aimed to identify student needs and inform the redesign of personal learning spaces. Building on the existing structure and functionality of the BIRD prototype components [9,11,23,31], student preferences were systematically categorized. Table 1 shows the main components, dimensions, and the corresponding functionalities derived from the empirical study. The current research aims to evaluate whether the derived BIRD components effectively align with user expectations and needs. In order to assess this, we conducted a usability study focusing on two key components: the Learning Path Finder and the Buddy Finder.

3.1 Usability Study Design Participants

A total of (N =)33 participants took part in the usability study (18 female, 12 male, 2 non-binary/queer, 1 prefer not to answer). Participants represented a diverse range of age groups: 6 were university students in their first degree (18–22 years), 15 were young professionals or recent graduates (23–30 years), and 12 were adults in continuing education (31–45 years). All participants had prior experience with digital learning environments. Participants were recruited using online links distributed to student institutions within Berlin and Brandenburg.

3.2 Study Procedure

The study used a fully functional, interactive prototype of the platform, which provided access to all developed features and components. Although the prototype included the full range of tools, the usability evaluation focused exclusively on two core features: the Learning Path Finder (LPF) and the Buddy Finder (BF). Tasks were derived from realistic user scenarios (see Table 2). The session began with a short pre-questionnaire capturing demographic data, followed by the three usability tasks (one for LPF, and two for BF).

To gain a comprehensive understanding of user experience, we adopted a mixed-methods approach, combining:

- **Behavioral Data:** Usage logs and event metrics collected within the system
- **Quantitative Self-Report:** Custom questions on each feature within LPF and BF and MeCUE questionnaire on usability, aesthetics, and emotions
- **Qualitative Feedback:** Open post-task responses

For each task, participants first received a written scenario description and then completed the interaction within the prototype. After completing each task,

Table 2. Mapping relevant scenarios to the usability tasks.

Scenario(s)	Learner Goal(s)	Usability Task
SZ-HB-I-01 SZ-HB-I-02 SZ-HB-I-03	Researching Language Requirements for a Study Abroad Searching for a Master's Program Searching for a Second Degree Program	Imagine you are a student who is currently registered at a German university. You would like to study the German language as you are new to the language. Find a suitable German course and select it for registration.
SZ-HB-III-02-01 SZ-SB-III-02-01	Search for Other Students for Exam Preparation Search for Other Students	Imagine you are pursuing your master's degree in computer science. You are currently in your final semester and would like to take up a visual computing course. You find the course to be difficult and would like to search for a learning partner who could learn together with you. Find a suitable partner for your situation by going over the icons on the left panel of the BIRD portal. Send a contact request right away if you find a partner.
SZ-SB-III-01-01	Self-Assessment Test and Tutor Search	Imagine you are pursuing a bachelor's degree in computational science. You are an expert in mathematics, and would like to support other students who struggle with mathematics. Go over the icons on the left panel, and find a suitable feature to offer yourselves as a tutor or mentor for helping other students.

the participants answered a structured set of follow-up questions related to the feature they had just used. For the LPF task, this consisted of two custom 5-point Likert-scale questions assessing ease of use and relevance of results, and four open questions exploring perceptions, challenges, and improvement suggestions. For each BF task, participants responded to five custom 5-point Likert-scale questions, five yes/no questions, and eight open questions probing partner search experiences, perceived match quality, and communication options. Upon completion of all three tasks, participants filled out the MeCUE questionnaire, which measured four dimensions: Instrumental Qualities (usefulness, ease of use), Non-Instrumental Qualities (visual aesthetics, innovation), Emotional Response (positive and negative feelings during use), and Global Evaluation (overall satisfaction and recommendation likelihood).

All user interactions during task completion were captured using embedded Google Analytics event logging. This included every navigation action, search query, click, and selections made while using the LPF and the BF. The resulting behavioural data set allowed for the detailed analysis of user paths, the identification of friction points and the mapping of retention or drop-off within each function. All event data was linked to anonymized participant IDs to ensure confidentiality.

3.3 Data Analysis

In the following, we focus specifically on two of the components: the Learning Path Finder (LPF) and the Buddy Finder (BF). They were selected as focal points for this usability study due to their direct alignment with user needs identified in the prior empirical investigation [11]. Furthermore, LPF and BF represent high-interaction user-facing components where users most directly engage with learning content and social functionality.

- **Learning Path Finder (LPF):** The LPF is designed to support students in discovering personalized educational resources and learning pathways. It offers a focussed view of relevant digital services, tailored to the previous achievements and current needs of the user, and aims to reduce fragmentation across tools and platforms [31]. By addressing the need for guided access to learning materials, the LPF contributes to a more seamless and self-regulated learning experience [32]. The behavioural outcomes measured for the LPF in our empirical study include: Search duration, search flow abandonment rate, search participation rate, number of LPF suggestions viewed, session duration, session dropout rate, and overall engagement rate. These metrics help to evaluate how effective the LPF guides users through search tasks and maintains their engagement.
- **Buddy Finder (BF):** The BF introduces a novel way of enabling anonymous peer connections, promoting informal learning interactions within digital environments [9]. The BF is designed to foster a sense of community and support through structured matchmaking and interaction opportunities. The behavioural outcomes measured for BF include: Search/offer completion rate, search/offer completion time, offer key data viewing duration, search criteria duration, search/offer abandonment rates, search/offer participation rates. These indicators assess both the efficiency and quality of user interactions during peer connection processes.

In order to evaluate the effectiveness of the LPF and BF components, we mapped each one to specific user interactions derived from the representative user scenarios. Table 3 summarizes this mapping along with the key insights.

Overall, the results indicate that the LPF achieved consistently high levels of task completion and engagement, despite minor issues with terminology. In contrast, the Buddy Finder revealed a notable discrepancy between the reported ease of use and the actual level of engagement. Behavioural data showed significant drop-offs after the search criteria were selected, low contact request

Table 3. Mapping existing scenarios to the behavioral insights derived from the usability study.

Component	Scenario Actions (Derived)	Usability Study Insight
Learning Path Finder	SZ-HB-I-01: Open Lernpfadfinder → Search "Spracheignungstest Französisch" (analogous to German) → Compare suggestions → Choose online test → Register via form	Unclear naming ("Lernpfadfinder"). Despite this, Google Analytics (GA) shows high engagement and full task completion.
Buddy Finder: Search	SZ-HB-III-02-01: Open BIRD landing page → Select Buddy Finder → Start Search process → Create profile → Fill in Key Data (subject, semester, etc.) → View suggested buddies → Send contact request	GA data shows drop-offs after search criteria selection; very few contact requests sent. Only 47% found matches appropriate; 41% connected with buddies.
Buddy Finder: Offer Creation	No directly relevant scenarios. Example scenario SZ-SB-III-01-01: Available tutor profiles in Buddy Finder panel → Person selects tutor → Chat begins	High completion rates.
Connecting with Buddies	SZ-HB-III-02-01, SZ-SB-III-01-01	59% of users did not connect; low contact events recorded.

rates and that 59% of the participants did not establish connections. Qualitative insights suggest that the search creation process introduced minor technical and cognitive barriers (e.g. users thinking that all fields were mandatory), which contributed to the observed drop-off rates.

Table 4. Participants' MeCUE evaluations and ANOVA results across age groups.

Category	Mean Score	ANOVA (F, p)
Instrumental Qualities	5.30	$F(2,30) = 0.39$, $p = .680$
Non-Instrumental Qualities	3.70	$F(2,30) = 0.12$, $p = .885$
Emotional Response	3.10	$F(2,30) = 0.29$, $p = .751$
Global Evaluation	7.36	–

Subjective assessments through the MeCUE questionnaire echoed these patterns: instrumental qualities received the highest ratings ($M = 5.30$), indicating that users found the platform useful and easy to navigate, while non-instrumental qualities such as aesthetics scored moderately ($M = 3.70$), and emotional engagement was low ($M = 3.10$). Participants' MeCUE evaluations are summarized in Table 4. The ANOVA tests showed no significant differences across age groups for any dimension (all $p > 0.05$), indicating evaluations were consistent regardless of age.

A few more functionalities for the BF were planned, such as an autofill function to simplify the input of search criteria, but these were not yet implemented in the tested version of the prototype. Similarly, data transfer from the wallet to the BF search (as successfully implemented for the LPF search) could not yet be tested.

While this section focused on the functional design and empirical evaluation of two key components (namely LPF and BF), a broader analysis of used applications within such a national digital education ecosystem is conducted in the following Sect. 4 along with a contextualization of the research results.

4 Cross-Institutional Integration of Educational Services

In this section, we provide an overview of the technical aspects of the developed prototype. Subsect. 4.1 explains its architecture. The resulting ecosystem is then analyzed by using the SAMR and HERM models in Subsect. 4.2.

4.1 Reference Architecture

The architecture of the BIRD prototype is vertically and horizontally structured [17], as depicted in Fig. 1 below. Vertically, we distinguish five layers from the entry zone (user-centric, with a focus on broad accessibility and flexibility) downward to the hosting zone (server-centric, with a focus on security and stability). A connection is only allowed between neighboured layers. Horizontally, there are several administrative domains, like existing education institutions or service providers (in gray), and the new infrastructure provided by the BIRD prototype (in blue). Here, we distinguish between central services (like certification infrastructure), personal devices (containing, for instance, a wallet), and the distributed infrastructure that connects to value-adding services. Thus, the autonomy of existing stakeholders is maintained while connecting available content, tools, and services in a heterogeneous ecosystem. At the same time, the zero trust architecture guarantees high robustness of the overall system.

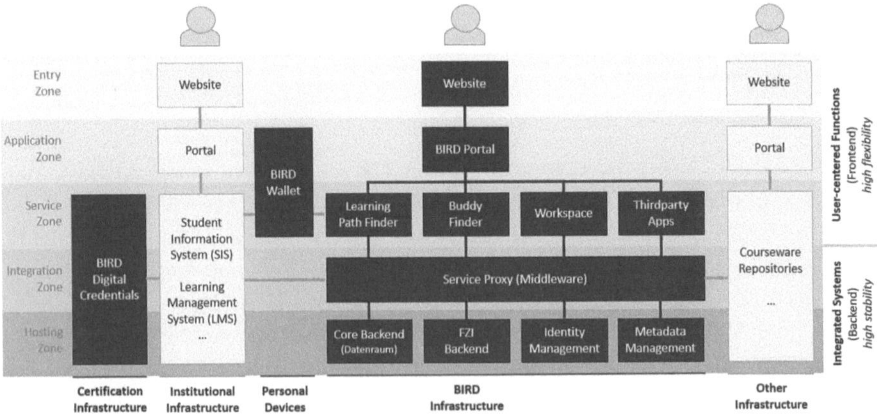

Fig. 1. Reference Architecture for a National Digital Education Ecosystem [17].

At the heart of this reference implementation is a portal that connects a number of educational services to a PLE. This web-based application demonstrates how ecosystem services can be invoked by existing platforms to help users discover relevant educational offerings or engage in exchange with others. The prototype is based on the Liferay framework because of its high degree of flexibility. However, the provided interfaces can be accessed in a similar way by any tools or platforms. Other providers can connect their services with the infrastructure via the defined interfaces to single sign-on, metadata management and wallet. Depending on the depth of integration, these services either retain their existing user interfaces and merely benefit from the data exchange across the infrastructure, or they are integrated more seamlessly as an infrastructural component using the shared front-end of the portal. Thus, the added value relies on the existence of third-party educational repositories and other educational services, that shall not be replaced, but connected and extended.

4.2 Positioning in the Media Ecosystem

As examined in an earlier publication [11], systemic enhancement of educational services or applications can be visualized with the SAMR (substitution, augmentation, modification, and redefinition) model [28] and different integration depths. To go further and determine the values added to the technologies of educational institutions, this analysis is now combined with the Technology Reference Model (TRM) of the Higher Education Reference Model (HERM) [6].

Table 5. Transfer of SAMR categories to infrastructural perspective.

Category	Original explanation	Derived mapping criteria
Substitution	Technology acts as a direct tool substitute, with no functional change.	BIRD replaces existing applications without any change in their functionality or capabilities. There is no further interoperability with other institutions, users or systems.
Augmentation	Technology acts as a direct tool substitute, with functional improvement.	BIRD brings new applications to institutional infrastructure. Thus, teachers and learners gain access to new capabilities within their common environment and processes.
Modification	Technology allows for significant task redesign.	BIRD adds new functionality to existing applications, for instance by plug-ins or interfaces to other systems. Thus, it allows for creation of educational settings that existing applications were not designed for.
Redefinition	Technology allows for the creation of new tasks, previously inconceivable.	BIRD enables new learning and teaching methods and creates new educational spaces, e.g. by reaching target groups or allowing for interactions that were impossible before. This is the most complex category.

Thus, it can be assessed if and how technologies are substituted or transformed in digital learning environments from a systemic perspective.

To map the SAMR framework to the present study, appropriate criteria [16] are needed in order to assign components to these categories. As the common understanding of the levels is to compare analogue methods and tools with digital ones, these criteria will be adapted. The definitions of Puentedura [27] were used as a starting point and modified according to the infrastructural nature of the prototype on a broader scale, i.e. to address existing components in educational institutions and new components brought in by the connecting infrastructure. This is depicted in Table 5.

To obtain an intersubjective mapping, four project team members (two from the technical field and two from the pedagogical field) applied the derived criteria independently. These results were then merged. The results are shown in Fig. 2. Our analysis was limited to the parts of HERM that were identified as the core focus of the BIRD prototype in an previous study [19] by automatically mapping the BIRD scenarios [10] to HERM [6].

There is a wide variety of components that have been augmented or modified by BIRD. Few communication channels are candidates for substitution (or rather, parallel existence). Redefinition only maps, to some extent, to extended reality applications. Many basic components could not be mapped since the prototype simply relies on them without further effect.

It is important to clarify that the taxonomic nature of the SAMR model is not consistent with the 'primacy of pedagogy' [20]. This is not to suggest that greater technical improvement leads to better teaching and learning outcomes. Rather, it provides a framework to help understand what aspects of teaching and learning this approach changes.

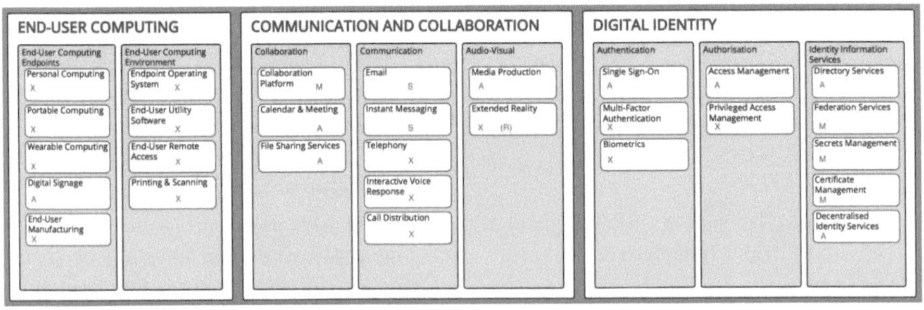

Fig. 2. Section of the HERM Technology Reference Model with added SAMR mapping.

5 Evolved Conception of Personal Learning Environments

Below, the parts of the TRM in HERM that are most affected by changes through a national digital education ecosystem are addressed. From the perspective of the BIRD prototype, it is explained how their understanding can be reframed as components in a cross-institutional PLE.

5.1 End-User Computing

As the proposed infrastructure is a virtual software solution, it only affects one aspect of end-user computing: digital signage. Moreover, an integrated dashboard can facilitate communication between institutions and learners. When used alongside recommender systems, dashboard solutions can adapt to learners' starting points and learning goals.

5.2 Communication and Collaboration

The effects of a networked educational infrastructure are most visible in the communication and collaboration aspects. LMS and cloud storage do not provide learners with genuine communication and collaboration features. This is where a Personal Learning Environment (PLE) comes in, providing a cross-application and cross-institutional network and stimulating broad access to learning offers, tools and people in that network.

In the sense of 'bring your own service', a wide variety of tools can be used for collaboration and communication. Additional applications that are not well established in the field of education are being developed to support this network, such as the aforementioned Buddy Finder. Currently, there are no extended reality (XR) applications connected to the PLE, but these could enhance the possibilities in this category even further by facilitating immersive learning.

The 'bring your own service' approach addresses sovereignty at various levels. To provide one example, if the content of LMS is separated from the operation in institutions, it can assist educators in (re-)gaining autonomy over their content. Therefore, an LMS within a PLE can be viewed as a workplace and a storage for courses that mirrors content to productive LMS. This further enhances the digital sovereignty of educators.

5.3 Digital Identity

One of the project's main objectives was to establish a single digital identity for lifelong learning. It's therefore no surprise that this approach augments authorisation and authentication. The IDM solution developed provides a digital basket ID, into which all connected identity services can be integrated and used seamlessly with single sign-on (SSO). Access management is enhanced by the global SSO, which provides access to infrastructures that were previously restricted, where affiliation metadata is important in determining a user's access rights.

The Self-Sovereign Identity (SSI) digital wallet [30] enhances identity information services. Users regain autonomy over their data and certificates by storing and managing them on their own devices. Certificates are not simply substituted by digital ones. The digital version serves as an enhanced copy of the analogue version. It is machine-readable and carries additional metadata, such as achieved competencies and skills.

6 Conclusion, Limitations and Remaining Work

Adding up all the evaluation measures of this and previous publications provides a holistic view of the affordances of personal learning environments on a national scale. However, there are still some blank spaces that need to be considered.

The SAMR analysis of the parts of the Technology Reference Model in HERM showed that recontextualizing established applications within a networked educational ecosystem increases users' freedom of usage and, therefore, their digital sovereignty. New developed applications can be easily located in the TRM framework, like the Learning Path Finder, the Buddy Finder or the digital wallet. This allows us to pinpoint specific starting points within institutional infrastructures where new educational scenarios can be introduced without the need for significant technical changes.

Generalisations of the study results are difficult due to the specialised case and the small sample size of the study. In addition, the workspace was not a focal point of the usability study due to delays in its implementation. Therefore, relevant insights are still lacking. Feedback gained on the prototype would usually trigger a new iteration in software development. However, since funding for the prototype has ended and rollout has been transferred to a federal agency, these results can be used as a valuable foundation for future endeavours. The concepts and source code of the prototype have been published and are freely available. However, additional motivational and volitional studies must be conducted to better understand and prevent users from drop-off or non-use.

To validate the overlaps between the different approaches, a comparative study on international level is currently being conducted. As none of the European national digital learning environments are operational yet, it is unclear what practical changes they may bring to the education system. Such approaches may help to achieve benchmarks like the Digital Targets 2030 of the European Union. Otherwise, there is still work to be done to address the digital divide. Equal opportunities are needed, as well as educational fairness in the sense of internal differentiation. To achieve this, additional applications tailored for learners with worse starting points are required. These could include learning guidance systems, such as content-independent tutorial systems for self-regulated learning [11]. Current research shows that digital ready conditions are steadily improving in Germany [8], as it does elsewhere. However, it seems that a shift in focus from learners to teachers is still necessary, given that measures to professionalise teachers are lagging behind in European rankings. During the design process, we focused more on pupils and students than on educators. Out of the 15 created personas, 60% were learners, 27% were educators, and 13% were other stakeholders like parents [10]. Consequently, a considerable amount of research and development work is still required to promote the sustainable provision and targeted use of cross-institutional Personal Learning Environments (PLEs) through a national digital education ecosystem.

Acknowledgements. This work was partially funded by the European Union - NextGenerationEU through the German Federal Ministry of Research, Technology and Space (BMFTR) as part of the Digital Education initiative under grant number 16NB001. We are deeply grateful to our partners in the project for the valuable exchange.

References

1. BMBF: Richtlinie zur Förderung von Prototypen für eine Bildungssektorübergreifende, transdisziplinäre Meta-Plattform für kollaborativen, kompetenten und digital gestützten Zugang zu innovativen Lehr-/Lernformaten und unterstützenden Lerntechnologien: "Initiative Nationale Bildungsplattform" (2021). https://www.bmbf.de/bmbf/shareddocs/bekanntmachungen/de/2021/04/3567_bekanntmachung.html
2. Bria, F., Trimmers, P., Gernone, F.: Eurostack – a european alternative for digital sovereignty. Bertelsmann Stiftung (2025). https://doi.org/10.11586/2025006
3. Brooks, C., Pomerantz, J., Galanek, J.: Student and faculty technology research studies. Educ. Center Anal. Res. (2017). https://library.educause.edu/resources/2017/10/ecar-study-of-undergraduate-students-and-information-technology-2017
4. Brown, M., Dehoney, J., Millichap, N.: The next generation digital learning environment. Rep. Res. ELI Paper **5**(1), 1–13 (2015)
5. Bustorff, A., Tille, R., Wisniewski, S., Blum, F., Lucke, U.: Nutzungsanforderungen, pädagogische überlegungen und Grobstruktur einer digitalen Vernetzungsinfrastruktur für die Bildung. eleed (2023)
6. CAUDIT: higher education reference models, V3.1.1. CAUDIT (2025). https://www.caudit.edu.au/EA-Framework
7. Degen, K., Lutzens, R., Beschorner, P., Lucke, U.: Public education data at the crossroads of public and private value creation: orchestration tensions and stakeholder visions in germany's emerging national digital education ecosystem. Electron. Mark. **35**(19) (2025). https://doi.org/10.1007/s12525-024-00752-w
8. Eickelmann, B., et al.: ICILS 2023 #Deutschland. Computer- und informationsbezogene Kompetenzen und Kompetenzen im Bereich Computational Thinking von Schüler*innen im internationalen Vergleich. Waxmann, Münster; New York (2024). https://doi.org/10.25656/01:32046
9. Eilebrecht, S., Beskorovajnov, W.: A formal treatment of homomorphic encryption based outsourced computation in the universal composability framework. Cryptology ePrint Archive, Paper 2025/109 (2025). https://eprint.iacr.org/2025/109
10. Erdmann, S., et al.: Szenarienübersicht aus dem BIRD Projekt. zenodo (2025). https://doi.org/10.5281/zenodo.10075885
11. Erdmann, S., Krishnaraja, S., Wiencke, B., Lucke, U.: Redesigning personal learning environments: Consolidation of empirical findings and conceptual research against the background of a national educational infrastructure. In: Proceedings of

the 17th International Conference on Computer Supported Education - Volume 1: CSEDU, pp. 92–101. INSTICC, SciTePress (2025). https://doi.org/10.5220/0013297200003932
12. Fariani, R., Junus, K., Santoso, H.: A systematic literature review on personalised learning in the higher education context. Technol. Knowl. Learn. **28** (2022). https://doi.org/10.1007/s10758-022-09628-4
13. Floridi, L.: The fight for digital sovereignty: what it is, and why it matters, especially for the EU. Philos. Technol. **33** (2020). https://doi.org/10.1007/s13347-020-00423-6
14. Frederking, V.: Von TPACK und DPACK zu SEPACK.digital. Ein Alternativmodell für fachdidaktisches Wissen in der digitalen Welt nebst einigen Anmerkungen zu blinden Flecken und Widersprüchen in den KMK-Initiativen zur digitalen Bildung in Deutschland. In: Frederking, V., Romeike, R. (eds.) Fachliche Bildung in der digitalen Welt. Digitalisierung, Big Data und KI im Forschungsfokus von 15 Fachdidaktiken. Allgemeine Fachdidaktik Band 3., Fachdidaktische Forschungen., vol. 14, pp. 481–522. Waxmann, Münster/New York (2022)
15. Galle, M.: Personalisiertes Lernen als pädagogisch-psychologisches didaktisches Konzept, pp. 29–37. Springer Fachmedien Wiesbaden, Wiesbaden (2021). https://doi.org/10.1007/978-3-658-35070-3_3
16. Hamilton, E., Rosenberg, J., Akcaoglu, M.: The substitution augmentation modification redefinition (SAMR) model: a critical review and suggestions for its use. TechTrends **60** (2016). https://doi.org/10.1007/s11528-016-0091-y
17. Hartmann, A., von der Heyde, M., Nguyen, D., Zimmermann, H., Lucke, U.: The reference architecture of a national digital education ecosystem. In: Proceedings of the EUNIS, EPiC Series in Computing (2025)
18. Hautakangas, S., Nordlund, H.: Enabling collaboration with enterprise architecture and interoperability: Digivisio 2030 programme in Finland. In: Proceedings of European University Information Systems Congress 2023. pp. 301–310. EPiC Series in Computing (2023). https://doi.org/10.29007/c3r7
19. von der Heyde, M., Matthias: ontology based mapping of herm. In: Proceedings of the EUNIS 2025 – European University Information Systems. EPiC Series in Computing (2025)
20. Irion, T., et al.: Professionalisierung für das Primat des Pädagogischen in der Digitalen Grundbildung. Projekteinführung und -überblick zum BMBF-Projekt "Grundsatzfragen und Gelingensbedingungen in der Professionalisierung von pädagogischen Akteur:innen für Kinder im Grundschulalter" (P3DiG), pp. 77–112 (2023)
21. Kiy, A., Lucke, U.: Technical approaches for personal learning environments: Identifying archetypes from a literature review. In: IEEE 16th International Conference on Advanced Learning Technologies (ICALT), pp. 473–477 (2016). https://doi.org/10.1109/ICALT.2016.122
22. Kiy, A., Lucke, U., Zoerner, D.: An adaptive personal learning environment architecture. In: International Conference on Architecture of Computer Systems (ARCS), pp. 60–71 (2014). https://doi.org/10.1007/978-3-319-04891-8_6
23. Knoth., A., Blum., F., Soldo., E., Lucke., U.: Structural challenges in the educational system meet a federated it-infrastructure for education: Insights into a real lab. In: Proceedings of the 14th International Conference on Computer Supported Education - Volume 1: CSEDU, pp. 369–375 (2022). https://doi.org/10.5220/0011085800003182
24. Kottmann, A., Jappe, A.: Implementing digital transformation through development projects. Transcending Boundaries Sustain. Future High. Educ. **6**, 207 (2025)

25. Lucke, U.: Digital education ecosystems: visions and decision needs. Weizenbaum J. Digit. Soc. **4**(4) (2024)
26. Pomerantz, J., Brown, M., Brooks, D.C.: Foundations for a next generation digital learning environment: faculty, students, and the lms, pp. 1–4. EDUCAUSE Publications (2018)
27. Puentedura, R.: (2014), https://www.hippasus.com/rrpweblog/archives/2014/08/22/BuildingTransformation_AnIntroductionToSAMR.pdf
28. Puentedura, R.: Transformation, technology, and education (2006). http://www.hippasus.com/resources/tte/
29. Redecker, C., Punie, Y.: European framework for the digital competence of educators: Digcompedu. Scientific analysis or review, Policy assessment, Technical guidance KJ-NA-28775-EN-N, Luxembourg (2017). https://doi.org/10.2760/159770
30. Walia, D., Neumann, K., Walia, V., Rathjens, M., Weidner, S., Turowski, K.: Unveiling the potential: assessing the role of ssi wallets in promoting sustainability in federated learning environments. In: Proceedings of the 16th International Conference on Computer Supported Education - Volume 1: CSEDU, pp. 502–509. INSTICC, SciTePress (2024). https://doi.org/10.5220/0012693400003693
31. Ziemann, F., Nguyen, D., Blum, F., Lucke, U.: Personalized recommendations for individual learning pathways: supporting Ukrainian refugee students in continuing their university education. In: Proceedings of European University Information Systems Congress 2023. EPiC Series in Computing, vol. 95, pp. 170–180 (2023). https://doi.org/10.29007/98hp
32. Zimmerman, B.: Dimensions of academic self-regulation: a conceptual framework for education. In: Schunk, D., Zimmerman, B. (eds.) Self-Regulation of learning and performance. Issues and Educational Applications, pp. 3–24. Routledge, New York (1994)

Integrating Network Visualization and GPT-4 in an Adaptive Kanji Learning Tool

Sigrid L. Klinger(✉) and Sven Strickroth

Ludwig-Maximilians-Universität München, Munich, Germany
{sigrid.klinger,sven.strickroth}@ifi.lmu.de
https://www.tel.ifi.lmu.de/

Abstract. Mastering Kanji remains a persistent challenge for learners of Japanese, particularly for those from alphabetic language backgrounds. We present KanjiCompass, an etymology-driven, adaptive learning environment that combines four core innovations: (1) an interactive network visualization of the hierarchical structure and graphemic components of all 2,136 Jōyō Kanji, (2) minimal, context-sensitive learning recommendations based on the learner's current knowledge level, (3) seamless synchronization with the spaced-repetition software Anki to support long-term retention, and (4) GPT-4 Turbo–generated example sentences tailored to beginner proficiency. This paper outlines the system architecture, data model, visualization pipeline, and mechanisms for adaptive content generation. We also present results from a two-week field study ($n = 19$) conducted with German-speaking learners of Japanese. Participants who set explicit learning goals engaged more actively with the tool and used the adaptive features more extensively. Learners preferred the focused subgraph over the global network and found the sentence suggestions relevant and valuable. These findings highlight the potential of adaptive, visualization-based tools to support exploratory learning and motivate learners in mastering the complex Kanji system.

Keywords: Adaptive Learning · Self-Regulated Learning · AI-Generated Content

1 Introduction

Mastering Japanese Kanji remains one of the most difficult challenges for learners of Japanese [31], whether they follow formal instruction or pursue self-study. Unlike phonographic writing systems, where each symbol corresponds to a sound, Kanji is a complex morphographic script [31], each representing the smallest unit of meaning in the Japanese language. The standard set of 2,136 Jōyō Kanji covers the characters encountered in everyday texts. Among those, the 500 most frequent account for about three-quarters of actual usage [5]. The complexity of Kanji arises from the fact that each character simultaneously encodes meaning,

C. Meinel et al. (Eds.): CSEDU 2025, CCIS 3148, pp. 136–161, 2027.
https://doi.org/10.1007/978-3-032-39103-2_8

form, and sound. Take the character 末: it conveys the concepts of "end", "close", and even "powder" in specific contexts (semantics), it bears a strong visual resemblance to the character 未 (morphology), and it may be read for example as *sue*, *matsu*, or *ura* depending on the word in which it appears (phonology). Although Kanji originated in Chinese, their usage in Japanese has evolved in distinctive ways. For example, a single character can have multiple related meanings and several pronunciations, and it is most often encountered not on its own but as part of a compound with other Kanji [33]. These intertwined semantic, morphological, and phonological dimensions must all be considered, which means that learning Kanji differs fundamentally from learning ordinary vocabulary, where learners typically associate one word form with a single meaning and pronunciation.

Traditional approaches to Kanji acquisition, such as rote flashcards or visual mnemonics, focus on individual characters in isolation and overlook the etymological relationships that bind characters into a coherent semantic network [31]. Learners who attempt to infer these connections on their own may develop misconceptions or become overwhelmed by the script's inherent complexity.

To address these challenges, we introduced KanjiCompass [17], an etymology-driven adaptive learning environment that integrates three innovations. First, it represents the hierarchical structure of Kanji and their graphemic components as an interactive network, allowing learners to explore both global layouts and focused subgraphs on demand. Second, it provides minimal, context-sensitive guidance through brief on-screen learning recommendations. Third, it synchronizes seamlessly with spaced-repetition software (Anki) to support long-term retention. Additionally, this paper examines learners' perceptions of beginner-level example sentences generated by GPT-4 Turbo.

Building on our earlier work, this article extends the prototype's system architecture and database design, details the mechanics of LLM-based content generation, and presents more detailed empirical insights into learner behavior. To structure our analysis, we address the following research questions:

- How do the tool's visualizations shape learners' motivation and exploration in Kanji learning?
- To what extent do minimal, on-demand recommendations encourage exploratory learning behaviors in the study of Kanji?
- How do GPT-4 Turbo generated example sentences compare to freely available resources regarding relevance, clarity, and learner acceptance?

By highlighting the etymological connections that underlie individual characters, KanjiCompass offers both independent learners and students in formal education a framework for grasping Kanji as an integrated system rather than an isolated set of symbols. In doing so, it tries to reduce extraneous cognitive effort and curbs the formation of hollow character associations. This prototype is designed to augment rather than supplant established study practices by introducing an explorative environment tailored to the script's inherent complexity.

This paper contributes (1) a graph-based visualization approach for exploring Kanji structure and relationships, (2) a minimal recommendation mechanism to support exploratory learning, (3) an integration with spaced-repetition software (Anki), and (4) an empirical study on learner motivation and the reception of GPT-4 Turbo–generated example sentences.

The study was conducted at a German university with participants who were native German speakers and learners of Japanese. While all example sentences generated by GPT-4 Turbo were in Japanese, translations of Kanji and compound words were provided in German to match participants' learning context. Consequently, this paper focuses on the Japanese–German language pair, and the evaluation reflects learners' perceptions based on this configuration.

The paper is structured as follows: Sect. 2 provides background on Kanji learning, Sect. 3 reviews related work, Sect. 4 presents the prototype, Sect. 5 details evaluation and results, followed by discussion and future research.

2 Background on Kanji Learning

To contextualize current approaches to Kanji learning, this section outlines the structure of the Japanese writing system and summarizes key research on how Kanji are acquired. Japanese script comprises four systems: Hiragana, Katakana, Rōmaji, and Kanji [8]. Hiragana and Katakana each contain 45 basic symbols, while Rōmaji is the romanized representation of Japanese words. Kanji differ substantially in nature: their total number is undefined, with some digital dictionaries listing over 28,600 characters.[1] For everyday literacy, however, the standardized set of 2,136 Jōyō Kanji is most relevant. Mastery of Kanji involves recognizing each character's meaning, pronunciation, and written form.

Most Kanji are not atomic but consist of several smaller graphical units, including a radical. A grapheme-defined as "the smallest unit in a system of writing a language that can express a difference in sound or meaning" [2]–serves as the fundamental element that conveys semantic or phonetic information. For example, in English, the words "there" and "these" differ in meaning and pronunciation due to a single graphemic change. Radicals offer structural classification and semantic hints in a Kanji, while other graphemes contribute directly to a character's meaning or phonetic reading. This layered construction creates a hierarchical relationship (see Fig. 1). Radicals and pictographs typically serve as roots, supporting more complex characters that build upon them.

The distinction between etymologically meaningful graphemes and visually identifiable components has been discussed in detail in our previous work, where we highlighted its importance for understanding Kanji composition [17]. Likewise, the role of the three major etymological categories–pictorial, metaphorical, and phonological–was introduced to illustrate the pedagogical potential of an etymology-driven approach to Kanji learning. Representative examples include: 山 ("mountain"), a pictographic depiction of a mountain range; 炭 ("charcoal"), combining 山 ("mountain") and 灰 ("ash") metaphorically; and 崖 ("cliff", pronounced *gai*), composed of 山 and the phonetic grapheme 厓 (also pronounced

[1] https://kanji.jitenon.jp/ (accessed: 2025-07-14).

[2] https://dictionary.cambridge.org/dictionary/english/, (accessed: 2025-07-14).

gai). Building on that foundation, the present section examines how such structural features influence the design and use of different Kanji learning strategies in practice.

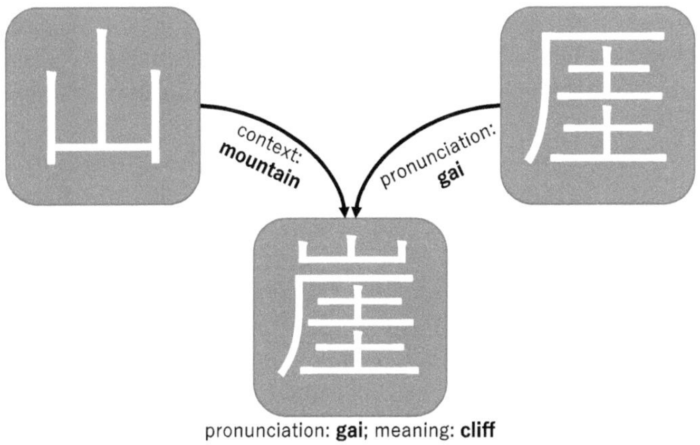

Fig. 1. Visualization of the graphemes 山 and 厓, which combine to form the Kanji 崖, illustrating their parent–child relationship.

For effective learning, it is essential to differentiate the three stages of memory: encoding, storage, and retrieval [25]. Understanding these stages is crucial, as they reflect the progression from initial character recognition to long-term recall in Kanji learning. Kanji learners employ a wide variety of strategies that reflect their individual learning styles, goals, and prior knowledge. Research on Kanji learning methods has produced divergent conclusions, partly because studies often neglect to differentiate between Kanji categories or learner backgrounds when evaluating effectiveness [31]. While some approaches aim to identify the "best" method, this overlooks the complexity of the learning process and the contextual suitability of each technique.

Following Rose's classification [31], three learning strategies can be distinguished: visual association, component analysis, and mnemonic sentences. Each of these supports the encoding stage of memory formation but differs in its assumptions, applicability, and cognitive demands.

Visual association methods involve linking the appearance of a Kanji character with a mental image, a symbol, or another known Kanji. This strategy is prevalent among beginners [31], who often encounter pictorial Kanji early in their learning journey. However, a common misconception, reinforced by oversimplified claims in textbooks, is that all Kanji are pictographs (cf. [11]). Studies have shown that learners sometimes attempt to form such connections even when the Kanji is not pictographic [31]. Identifying truly pictographic Kanji may help learners build more accurate associations and avoid frustration when visual cues are absent or misleading.

Component analysis refers to breaking Kanji into smaller elements such as radicals and graphemes. While this method is beneficial for non-pictographic Kanji, it suffers from inconsistent definitions and applications across research. Some studies limit the analysis to radicals [36], while others consider all components, often ignoring their etymological relevance [31]. Learners may also misidentify graphemes due to misleading interfaces in digital dictionaries, such as Jisho.org[3], which lists all components instead of graphemes. This can result in confusion and false analogies, such as associating unrelated characters based on visual similarity.

Mnemonics are verbal aids that help encode both the meaning and/or the reading of a Kanji. While widely used, they are most effective when applied in a structured and meaningful way [30]. Their use is often combined with component analysis. However, overly abstract or arbitrary mnemonic sentences can become counterproductive [31]. As with visual associations, mnemonics benefit from learner-generated content: forming one's own sentences generally leads to better retention than relying on pre-made examples [21].

Individual Kanji convey only limited semantic information in isolation. Their whole meaning is usually accessed when they appear in compound words rather than as standalone characters [27]. Precise semantic activation emerges only at the compound level, not at the level of the individual characters [27]. This makes example sentences indispensable for effective vocabulary learning [2]. Unfortunately, freely available corpora of sentences such as Tatoeba[4] often contain sentences whose grammatical and lexical complexity exceeds beginner proficiency and still fail to cover every target compound.

3 Related Work

While language learning technologies offer diverse methods, the majority are designed for vocabulary acquisition or grammar instruction [4], making them ill-suited for the specific demands of Kanji. Effective Kanji learning tools must account for the distinctive features of Kanji, including the etymological composition of characters and their structural interrelations.

As outlined in Sect. 2, Kanji are either indivisible characters or composed of graphemes. This creates a structural hierarchy: standalone Kanji form the roots, and more complex characters are built from these and other compounds. Such a hierarchy can be modeled as a directed graph, where nodes represent Kanji and edges encode compositional relationships. This graph structure can support learners in understanding relationships [19]. Several studies [8,20,22,40] have attempted to model character relationships using network analysis, particularly in the context of Chinese (Hànzì) and Japanese Kanji, given their shared roots.

Li and Zhou [22] constructed a large-scale Hànzì network with 6,652 characters and 1,624 components. Their analysis covered several structural properties:

[3] https://jisho.org/ (accessed: 2025-07-14).
[4] https://tatoeba.org (accessed: 2025-07-14).

(1) The graph was extremely sparse. (2) The network showed small-world characteristics (cf. [38]). (3) The clustering coefficient was around a hundred times higher than a comparable random graph. (4) Semantic graphemes had higher degrees than phonetic ones, revealing hubs with major functional roles. And (5) highly connected nodes tended to link to less-connected ones. While their results underscored the writing system's linguistic richness and structural regularity, their visualizations were limited to selected subgraphs (see Fig. 2). A complete rendering was deemed too dense, resulting in a visual "hairball".

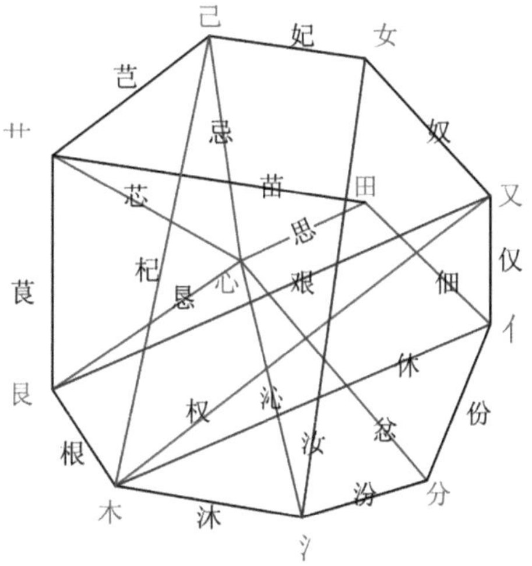

Fig. 2. Subgraph of the Hànzì network by Li and Zhou [22], visualizing graphemes as nodes and characters as edges.

In contrast, Yan et al. [40] developed a Hànzì graph with 3,687 nodes and 7,024 edges to derive a learning sequence. Nodes were connected when one character served as a phonetic or semantic component of another. Edges were weighted according to a theoretical "learning cost", based on stroke count. While visually compelling, the graph was static, and its learning path recommendations were not empirically validated. A supplemtary website allowed users to explore individual character graphs with color-coded semantic or phonetic links and radial layouts. Yet, the network did not visualize hierarchical parent-child relationships or adapt to user knowledge.

Beyond graph-based visualizations, traditional flashcard tools remain widely used in Kanji learning as they're an effective tool for memorization [7]. Among them, Anki[5] is one of the most popular open-source programs. Users can create highly customizable multimedia cards and benefit from a large ecosystem of add-ons and shared decks. When cards transition from the learning to review phase, they are assigned an "ease factor" that dynamically adjusts review intervals,

[5] https://apps.ankiweb.net/ (accessed: 2025-07-14).

starting at 250 % and dropping as low as 130 % depending on recall success. Despite the emergence of gamified tools, studies such as [43] suggest that learners often prefer these simple, self-paced systems and may not benefit from more elaborate learning games.

Prior work has explored the use of Intelligent Tutoring Systems (ITS) and adaptive learning technologies to personalize instruction in language education. As detailed in [17], such systems have been successfully applied to vocabulary and grammar learning, and their underlying models–including student, domain, and pedagogical–offer a foundation for adaptation in Kanji learning. While most research focuses on English and STEM domains [13], a few studies have investigated adaptive tools for Japanese, targeting vocabulary acquisition or character writing [23,26]. These tools, while promising, often lack clear criteria for adapting learning paths or fail to engage users over time fully. As discussed in the earlier work, the potential of adaptive systems to respond to learner diversity in Kanji acquisition remains underexplored, especially concerning structural and etymological features.

Large language models such as OpenAI's GPT-4 have been shown to perform competitively in translation tasks. Jiao et al. [9] compared GPT-3.5 and GPT-4 with commercial systems like DeepL, finding that GPT-4 produces similarly high-quality translations while making fewer errors. Its output is particularly fluent and robust for resource-rich languages such as German and Japanese [9,29], which exceed one million articles on Wikipedia.[6] Robinson et al. [29] compared GPT-3.5 with Google Translate and Meta's NNLB across 204 languages and reported only minor differences in performance between German and Japanese under different prompting conditions. Beyond translation, several studies have explored GPT's potential for generating example sentences. Rüdian and Pinkwart [32] evaluated GPT-3.5's ability to produce A1-level German sentences using up to three specified words and a prompt limiting output to 12 words. In over 200 generated sentences, 80.5 % were grammatically correct and 83.5 % contextually appropriate. However, the model sometimes omitted one of the target words or slipped beyond the A1 level. Because the prompt didn't constrain formatting, it occasionally prefaced its answers with word counts or framing phrases. These inconsistencies were attributed more to the prompt's ambiguity than to any inherent limitation of GPT-3.5.

Building on this foundation, Klinger and Strickroth [16] assessed GPT-4 Turbo's ability to produce three types of learning content: (1) German definitions for individual Kanji, (2) German translations of the most frequent compound words, and (3) Japanese example sentences tailored to the Japanese Language Proficiency Test (JLPT) N5 level, where N5 denotes beginner proficiency and N1 denotes the most advanced level. In a systematic evaluation covering 50 randomly selected Kanji (10 per JLPT level N5–N1), GPT-4 Turbo delivered consistently high accuracy. Most definitions and translations were entirely correct, and most generated sentences were grammatically sound and pedagogically

[6] See Wikipedia statistics: https://w.wiki/7dGH and https://w.wiki/3uxA (accessed: 2025-07-17).

appropriate. These results demonstrate that, with careful prompt engineering, GPT-4 Turbo can effectively support both meaning associations and contextual sentence generation in adaptive Kanji instruction.

However, while the technical feasibility of using GPT for Kanji-related sentence generation has been demonstrated, learner-facing evaluation remains an open question. How learners perceive, interpret, and benefit from such dynamically generated example sentences is poorly understood. This gap motivates the present study's integration of GPT-based sentence generation into a broader adaptive Kanji learning environment, where structural relationships and learner perspectives are considered.

4 An Etymology-Driven Adaptive Kanji Learning Tool

This section presents the design decisions for our prototype, which addresses the research gap identified above. It aims to support mnemonic creation through etymological insights and to foster self-regulated learning of Jōyō Kanji (characters used in everyday Japanese) (cf. [42]). The tool accommodates diverse learning strategies and adapts to users' varying knowledge levels by allowing them to search for Kanji, explore related characters, and export selected items for later review. Learners can track their progress by viewing previously studied Kanji and receive personalized learning recommendations based on their known characters. Simple example sentences generated with GPT-4 Turbo provide essential contextual cues for vocabulary acquisition; these sentences are kept at a JLPT N5 level so beginners can follow them easily. Although large, freely available corpora such as Tatoeba offer many example sentences, they often include grammar and vocabulary that are too advanced for novices and do not cover every target word.

Beyond the basic functionality described in our previous work [17], this section provides additional details on the system architecture, database schema, and GPT integration. The prototype is implemented as a platform independent single-page web application built on the MEAN stack, consisting of MongoDB, Express.js, and Node.js. It offers two Kanji lookup methods: users can enter characters via a Japanese keyboard or draw them with a mouse or touch input. The drawing interface uses Kanjicanvas.js [15], which tolerates imprecise strokes and suggests the intended characters. Export and import operations with Anki enable seamless flashcard synchronization, and adaptive features draw on the internal student model to generate personalized learning-path recommendations.

4.1 Overview

The tool layout is shown in Fig. 3. At the top center (1), users can enter Kanji into the search bar. The central panel (2) displays the Kanji graph–either the complete set or a filtered subset–together with their relationships. As explained in Sect. 4.4, known Kanji nodes are highlighted automatically. A legend in the lower left corner (3) describes the different node and edge styles according to etymological category; it is visible by default but can be hidden. On the right (4), selecting a Kanji opens the information box, or "Kanji card", which presents further details about that character.

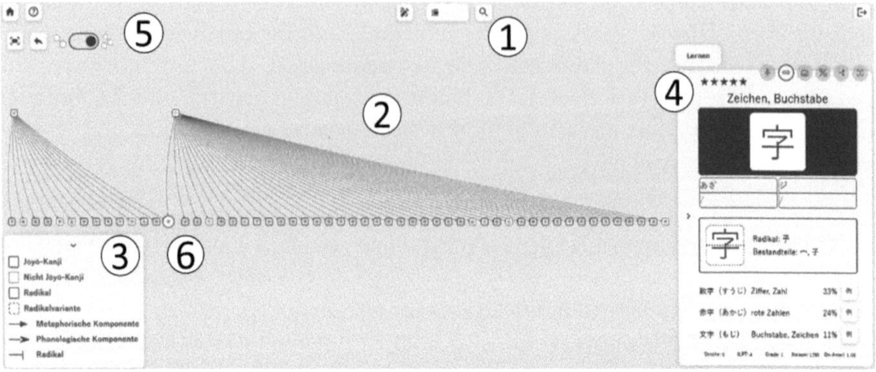

Fig. 3. The prototype's user interface after searching for the Kanji 字 [17].

The Kanji card is like an interactive flashcard (see Fig. 4). Hovering over elements reveals additional information. At the top left (1), the Kanji's usage frequency (sourced from [34]) is shown in quintiles, visualized by one to five stars. An icon next to it (2) represents the Kanji's etymological category. Two German meanings (3) generated by GPT-4 are below the icons. The character is then displayed in large font (4), followed by a table of its Japanese readings (5). In the center (6), an ancient pictorial form or a graphemic decomposition illustrates the Kanji's structure. Further down (7), example words and sentences–also produced by GPT-4–offer contextual practice. Finally, at the bottom (8), general data such as stroke count and JLPT level are listed.

4.2 Database Structure

The prototype uses MongoDB hosted on MongoDB Atlas to store and manage all learning content and user data. As a NoSQL database, MongoDB allows for flexible document-based schemas, making it suitable for storing the semi-structured linguistic data used in the system. Indexes are applied to optimize query performance.

The core collection includes all 2,136 Jōyō Kanji. Fields include radical, graphemes, stroke counts, readings, JLPT levels, grade levels, and etymological classifications. The data are primarily based on Tamaoka et al. [34] and enhanced by the CHISE Project's[7] graphemic decomposition API. Because CHISE focuses on structure rather than etymology, every entry was manually reviewed against the Shin Kango-rin dictionary [10]. During this review, we corrected graphemes,

[7] https://chise.org/ (accessed: 2025-07-14).

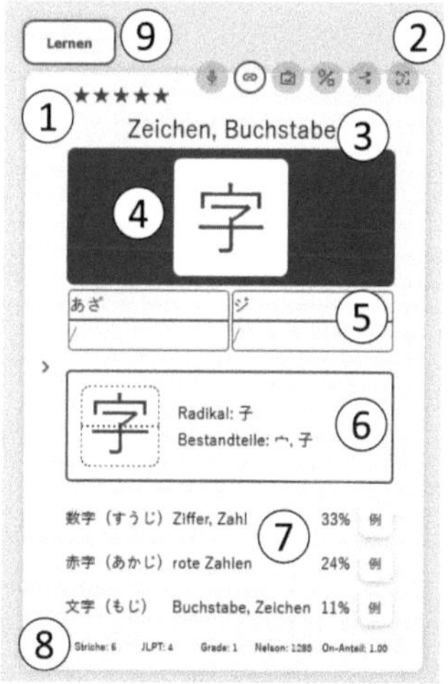

Fig. 4. The information card for the Kanji 字 .

added 520 previously uncatalogued subcomponents, and reassigned categories for conceptual consistency. German meanings of Kanji are generated on first access by GPT-4 Turbo, which provides the two most common German meanings for each character [16], and then stored permanently for reuse. We selected GPT-4 instead of traditional dictionary sources because it can generate concise, reader-friendly definitions by focusing on each Kanji's primary meaning rather than listing every possible interpretation. This approach delivers a uniform format, integrates seamlessly into the application, and reduces the manual effort required for definition curation.

A separate collection stores compound words linked to each Kanji, including their readings, absolute frequency, and computed relative frequency. Translations for the compound words are also generated by GPT-4 Turbo (for details see [16]) and stored in a separate collection to avoid redundancy, since one compound word may appear under multiple Kanji.

Two additional collections manage user data. One stores user credentials. The other records learned Kanji per user, storing the corresponding Anki ease factor. This collection is updated when users export Kanji to Anki or import data from their existing decks.

4.3 The Kanji Graphs

The interactive Kanji graph is a central component and entry point of the tool. This graph visualizes the structure of the Jōyō Kanji as a network based on graphemic decomposition. Each Kanji and grapheme is represented as a node, while the edges depict etymological relationships. These relationships include both semantic and phonological graphemes. The interactive graph is implemented using Cytoscape.js (v3.29.0), a widely used open-source graph library optimized for performance and developer usability [6]. The prototype uses two main types of graphs: the complete graph and the detail graph.

The complete graph appears on the homepage and includes all Jōyō Kanji along with their graphemes. It uses a concentric layout that positions nodes with the most outgoing edges in the center. These nodes are typically high-frequency graphemes that occur in many Kanji. This design emphasizes the structural centrality of frequently reused graphemes, helping learners understand that a small set of components accounts for a large portion of all Jōyō Kanji. Node appearance is differentiated to enhance accessibility. Jōyō Kanji, radicals, non-Jōyō Kanji, and radical variants are represented using different border colors, line styles, and background patterns. Edges vary in color and arrow style depending on whether they indicate metaphorical, phonological, or radical-based relationships. The graph includes 2,658 nodes and 8,950 directed edges, yielding an average node degree of 3.37. Its edge density is approximately 0.13 %, which aligns with comparable studies such as [40], indicating a highly sparse but meaningful structure.

Rendering performance has been optimized using Cytoscape's batch processing mode and hardware-aware settings. For instance, the minimum font size was limited to preserve legibility, and the "haystack" edge style was chosen to minimize rendering cost without affecting visual clarity. A texture cache is generated at the start of viewport transformations to improve responsiveness during pan and zoom interactions. Graph generation is the most computation-intensive task in the tool. It begins with a query to the MongoDB database, retrieving only the relevant data. Nodes are created first, followed by edges to avoid referencing nodes that have not yet been instantiated. Unnecessary edge connections are omitted, such as self-loops for Kanji that are their own radicals or indirect links with only radical variants. This helps reduce visual clutter and improves interpretability.

When a Kanji is selected, the detail graph displays that character and its immediate neighbors; a toggle lets users include indirect neighbors as well (Fig. 3 (5)). The visual style of nodes and edges remains consistent with the complete graph. Still, the selected Kanji is highlighted: it is shown in red, enlarged by a factor of 1.6, and given a circular shape to improve visibility in complex graphs (Fig. 3 (6)). The detail graph is generated using the same Cytoscape object as the complete graph. Unused nodes and edges are deactivated rather than deleted, preserving performance and enabling smooth transitions between views.

The layout of the detail graph is calculated using the Klay Layered Algorithm [14], accessed via the Cytoscape-klay.js extension (v3.1.4). This algorithm organizes nodes into layers based on their dependency depth. Nodes with more parent components appear deeper in the layout, reflecting the internal structure of the Kanji. A unique feature of the detail graph is its use of compound nodes to represent radical-variant relationships. For instance, radicals and their graphical variants (such as 水 and 氵) are grouped into a parent node, visually encapsulated with a dashed gray border. This design avoids unnecessary edge complexity while conveying the connection between a visible component and its canonical radical form. In total, 31 such compound nodes are used for radical families. When the indirect neighbor view is activated, Kanji composed of radical variants from other groups are excluded to preserve local structural clarity.

4.4 Adaptivity

The adaptive functionalities of the prototype can be divided into two main areas: (1) generation of example sentences and (2) personalized adaptation based on the user's knowledge level as inferred from their Anki data, providing tailored learning recommendations and visual adjustments. The prototype follows the adaptive learning framework proposed by Martin et al. [24], which distinguishes between a *Domain Model*, a *Student Model*, and an *Instructional Model*. In this case, the *Domain Model* consists of a database containing the Jōyō Kanji, their meanings, and etymologies. The *Student Model* represents the set of Kanji the learner is familiar with, while the *Instructional Model* encompasses algorithms for learning recommendations and example sentence generation.

Each Kanji flashcard includes up to three example word blocks in the information card's lower section. Each block contains five elements: the compound word, its reading, a translation into German, its frequency, and a corresponding *example sentence*.

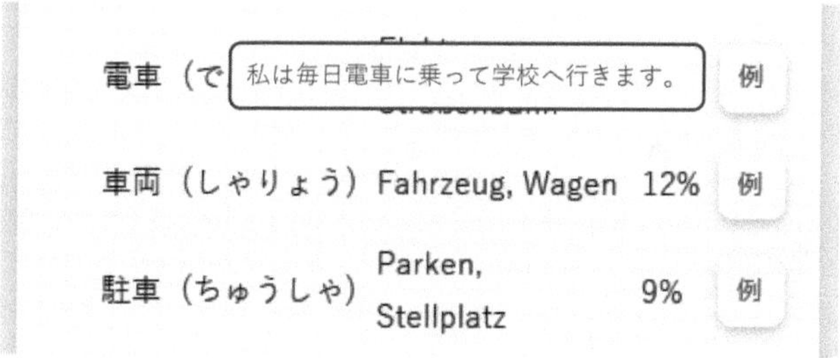

Fig. 5. Lower section of the Kanji card for 車 ("car"), showing a GPT-4 Turbo–generated example sentence overlay for the compound 電車 ("train"): 私は毎日電車で学校へ行きます。 ("I go to school by train every day"). The sentence illustrates the compound word in a JLPT N5–level context.

A small button labeled 例 ("example") is attached to each block and can be used to display the example sentence. When the user clicks the button, a compact overlay shows the sentence in context (see Fig. 5). These example sentences are generated using GPT-4 Turbo with the following prompt: "*Please create a Japanese example sentence at JLPT N5 level regarding grammar and vocabulary that includes the word {compound}. The sentence should clearly convey the meaning of the word through its context, without requiring additional explanations.*".

Here, we present only the basic rationale behind this prompt. Its full development and evaluation are described in detail by Klinger and Strickroth [16]. In brief, specifying JLPT N5 ensures that the sentences use only simple grammar patterns, everyday vocabulary, and approximately 100 Kanji, which is appropriate for beginners. Early tests showed that removing this level constraint yielded more advanced structures.

The prompt's second clause–"without requiring additional explanations"–is equally important, as it prevents GPT-4 from producing minimal or context-free examples. For instance, the sentence 電車がある。 ("There's a train.") is grammatically correct but fails to illustrate the meaning of 電車 ("train") in context, which diminishes its pedagogical value.

A key element of the prototype's adaptivity is its integration with the open-source flashcard software *Anki*. The prototype supports importing Kanji that the learner has already studied in Anki and exporting newly learned Kanji to it. This dual functionality ensures a seamless exchange between the two tools and aligns the learning process with the user's existing study habits. The integration is implemented using the Anki-Connect plugin[8], which provides an HTTP API for local communication with Anki. To use this functionality from within a web-based application in a browser, the domain must be manually added to the plugin's allowlist for cross-origin resource sharing (CORS) headers. Anki uses an algorithm (cf. [39,41]) that schedules card reviews based on a metric known as the *Ease Factor*, which reflects how well a flashcard has been learned (cf. Section 3. The prototype adopts this value to indicate the learner's current knowledge. Kanji with an Ease Factor below 190 % are considered poorly learned and are visually marked in the interface.

Import and export actions are always user-initiated; the prototype does not access Anki in the background without the learner's knowledge. When exporting a flashcard to Anki, a pop-up dialog allows users to select which information (e.g., meaning or etymological details) should be included on the flashcard. The flashcards are automatically generated using a predefined HTML/CSS layout. When importing Kanji from Anki's flashcards, the prototype displays the list of available Anki decks for the user to select. Kanji from the chosen deck and their associated ease factors are used to update the internal student model. These Kanji may originate from flashcards designed for learning individual characters or cards focused on compound words, accommodating different learning strategies.

Learned Kanji are highlighted in the main graph using a yellow background to visualize the user's knowledge. A dedicated grid view also displays all learned Kanji sorted by Ease Factor. Poorly retained Kanji are shown in red and appear toward the top-left, while the best-learned items are placed in the bottom-right. This way, the prototype suggests which Kanji should be reviewed and encourages users to create personalized mnemonics and adjust the flashcards in Anki. By omitting node connections, the grid focuses purely on learner progress rather than on parent-child relationships between Kanji. Selecting any character in this overview immediately opens its detailed graph.

[8] https://foosoft.net/projects/anki-connect/ (accessed: 2025-07-14).

The prototype provides *personalized learning recommendations* based on the learner's current knowledge and the structure of the Kanji, promoting an exploratory approach to learning. These suggestions appear immediately after the user exports a Kanji to Anki by clicking the button shown in Fig. 4 (9). A subtle, pulsating pop-up invites users to study a follow-up Kanji or component that fits their learning trajectory. To prevent cognitive overload, only one recommendation is made per exported Kanji. The logic behind these suggestions is guided by a prioritization framework and updated dynamically based on the user's progress.

The system generates recommendations using a rule-based algorithm that considers four categories, listed below in descending order of importance. Each possible suggestion is checked against the user's existing knowledge to ensure that only unfamiliar Kanji are recommended (see Fig. 6:

(1) *Recommendations based on radicals*: Radicals form the structural and semantic foundation of many Kanji. The prototype's database contains 208 radicals and 36 radical variants. The frequency of each radical and variant was analyzed to determine their relevance. Only radicals and variants appearing in at least 1 % of the Jōyō Kanji are considered for recommendation purposes. This results in a high-priority set of 25 items (19 radicals and six variants) that collectively account for around 61 % of all Jōyō Kanji. Because radicals are directly tied to a Kanji's overall meaning in the majority of cases [31], their broad applicability makes early mastery of these elements essential in the learning process.

(2) *Phonological graphemes*: Despite evidence suggesting the pedagogical value of phonological components, they are rarely emphasized in traditional instruction [35]. To address this, the prototype selectively recommends highly useful phonological graphemes. These are based on a utility score developed from four factors identified by Toyoda et al. [35]: (1) Frequency of appearance in commonly used vocabulary, (2) Number of consistent readings across different Kanji, (3) Reliability of pronunciation transfer, and (4) Total number of Kanji sharing the same phonological cue. Components scoring above average (80 out of 174 candidates) were classified as "highly useful" in the prototype and prioritized for recommendation. This approach aims to counteract learner skepticism by focusing only on those phonological components with high practical value and consistent pronunciation patterns.

(3) *Kanji in example words presented on the Kanji card*: When exporting a Kanji to Anki, learners can choose which example words should appear on the flashcard. If one of the selected compound words contains a Kanji unknown to the learner, the prototype suggests learning that Kanji next. This reinforces learning through contextual association and promotes exploration of vocabulary structures. If multiple unknown Kanji are detected, the system selects the one from the most frequently used word.

(4) *Phonological usage*: If the exported Kanji functions as a phonological grapheme in other Kanji, one such derivative is recommended for further study. This supports cognitive linkage between known and unknown characters that share pronunciation and structure. Only Kanji that exactly match the reading

of the exported character are considered. These recommendations should help reinforce mental associations and strengthen recall by capitalizing on existing phonological familiarity.

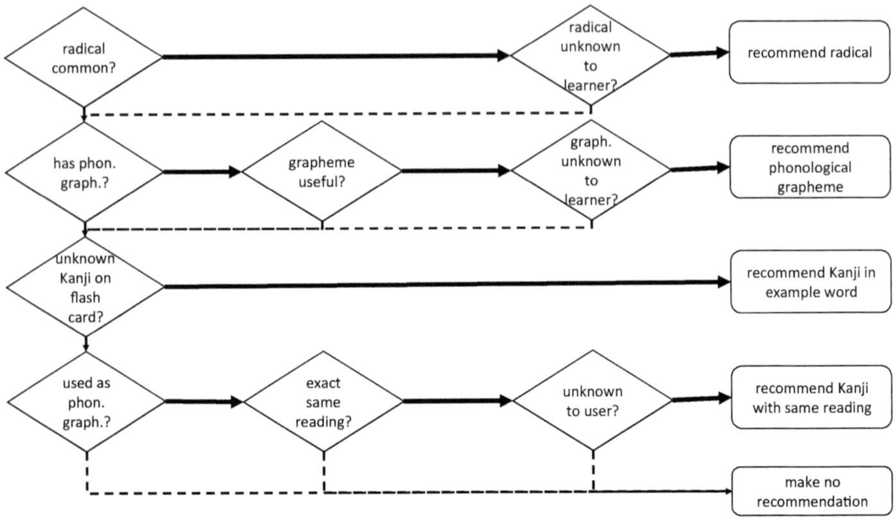

Fig. 6. Flow diagram of the rule-based recommendation algorithm. Thick lines represent the "yes" path, while thin dashed lines indicate the "no" path.

These four recommendation types are designed to support an exploratory and scaffolded learning process. They help users discover patterns, expand their vocabulary network, and deepen their structural understanding of Kanji. The adaptive logic also addresses typical learner needs such as identifying meaningful study paths, building on familiar elements, and uncovering semantically, phonologically, or contextually relevant Kanji. Through this system, the prototype creates a personalized and responsive learning environment that evolves with the learner's progress.

The prototype addresses key use cases, such as repeatedly searching for Kanji, exploring the component-based structure, contextualizing known Kanji with new characters, and using the provided resources for educational and personal interests.

5 Evaluation

We presented an excerpt of findings in our study published in April 2025 [17]. The evaluation aimed to understand how learners perceive and use the tool's visualization and recommendation features in a realistic setting and to determine to what extent these features motivate and engage them to explore and learn Kanji in depth. This paper provides more details and examines how learners perceive the example sentences generated by GPT-4 Turbo. Assessing the direct impact on learning outcomes was beyond the scope of this work owing to the methodological and operational challenges involved in quantifying such effects.

Before conducting the user study, an expert interview was held with a specialist in Kanji pedagogy for non-native speakers. She has been a lecturer at a German university for 18 years, focused on teaching Japanese as a second language. The aim was to gather expert feedback from someone familiar with teaching and learning perspectives. The conversation lasted approximately one hour and was conducted in Japanese. During the session, the entire prototype was presented in the order a learner would typically explore, starting with Kanji lookup, then focused study, and concluding with the review of previously learned Kanji.

The user study was conducted in May 2024 with 19 participants, following a field experiment using a within-subject design. Participants interacted with two versions of the Kanji learning tool: one featuring the adaptive functionalities described in Sect. 4, and one without them. The non-adaptive version was visually identical, but learners could not import and export Kanji via Anki. Additionally, instead of GPT-generated example sentences, the non-adaptive version displayed a randomly selected sentence from the Tatoeba database containing the target compound word.

All 19 participants tested both prototype versions in randomized order over two weeks, with each version used for one week. At the end of each week, participants completed a questionnaire. Participants were instructed to integrate the tool into their existing study routine. No specific Kanji or tasks were assigned, allowing for naturalistic usage. Usability and user experience were assessed using the System Usability Scale (SUS) [3], Likert-scale ratings of specific features (e.g., the Kanji graph, example sentences), and open-ended questions. In addition, participants were asked to define a weekly learning goal and rate their motivation to achieve it on a Likert scale. All closed responses were standardized to a scale from 0 to 4, with 0 representing the most negative and 4 the most positive rating. Participant activity within the prototype was tracked by logging click interactions.

All 19 participants completed both weekly surveys. Thirteen had received formal Japanese instruction, while six were self-taught. Participants were recruited through personal networks and snowball sampling, and all were German-speaking young adults. The median self-reported Kanji knowledge was 350, with five participants reporting knowledge of more than 1,000 Kanji, reflecting a broad range of proficiency levels.

Non-parametric statistical tests were used for analysis. The Wilcoxon-Mann-Whitney and Wilcoxon Signed-Rank tests were applied to compare groups and conditions, while Spearman's rank correlation coefficient (ρ) was used to examine associations between variables. These non-parametric tests are more robust to violations of distributional assumptions than their parametric counterparts [12], and are appropriate for small samples and ordinal data. The significance level was set to $\alpha = .05$, and medians are reported as $\tilde{x}$.

5.1 Results of the Expert Interview

The expert praised GPT's integration, Kanji relationships' visualization, and the Anki connection as valuable features that promote a comprehensive and flexible learning experience. She especially emphasized the value of the tool in promoting self-regulated learning: "The program and the information it contains are well executed throughout. You don't need to look things up in different places. You can get everything at once in KanjiKompass, like a real compass. [...] Ultimately, I think it's good for learning that you have to think for yourself. The tool doesn't just tell you what to do; it requires you to decide for yourself. That's not always comfortable, but that's what learning is."(translated from Japanese). She highlighted that this level of learner autonomy is essential for students of Japanese Studies and encouraged further development in that direction.

5.2 Results of the User Study

This section presents the results of the user study, beginning with overall findings on usability and user experience, followed by an analysis of participant groups based on their use of the tool's adaptive features, including the example sentences generated by GPT.

The participants used the prototype for a median of 57 min and rated it favorably, with a SUS of 72.1, indicating a good user experience [1]. Ten participants rated the usability as good, and four as excellent. SUS scores improved over time, rising from 70.1 in the first week to 74.1 in the second week. Thirteen participants indicated they would use the tool regularly ($\tilde{x} = 3.0$), finding it easy to use and its functions well integrated ($\tilde{x} = 3.0$).

Participants evaluated the overall Kanji graph positively regarding presentation, loading time, and interactivity ($\tilde{x} = 3.0$). However, 48 % of participants, especially those who did not set a specific learning goal, found the graph overwhelming ($\tilde{x} = 1.0$). In the second week, these participants rated the full graph as significantly more overwhelming ($p = .035$, $r = .76$, $\tilde{x}_{\text{goal}} = 3.0$, $\tilde{x}_{\text{no goal}} = 1.0$). The detail graph, by contrast, received consistently higher ratings for presentation, loading time, and interactivity (all $\tilde{x} \geq 3.0$), and was perceived as significantly less overwhelming ($p < .001$, $r = .05$) (see Fig. 7). It was also considered more motivating and helpful for learning, particularly among participants who had defined a learning goal and actively used the adaptive features. Participants highlighted the detail graph's support in understanding Kanji relationships ($\tilde{x} = 4.0$) and in visualizing the connection between radicals and their variants ($\tilde{x} = 3.5$). During the second week, users who engaged with adaptive features rated the detail graph as significantly more motivating ($p = .041$, $r = .51$, $\tilde{x}_{\text{adaptive}} = 3.0$, $\tilde{x}_{\text{non adaptive}} = 2.0$) and more supportive of their learning ($p = .041$, $r = .51$, $\tilde{x}_{\text{adaptive}} = 3.5$, $\tilde{x}_{\text{non adaptive}} = 2.5$). The level of detail provided was also considered appropriate ($\tilde{x} = 3.0$), and participants with high learning goal motivation rated it significantly more positively than those without a defined goal ($p = .038$, $r = .76$, $\tilde{x}_{\text{goal}} = 4.0$, $\tilde{x}_{\text{no goal}} = 3.0$).

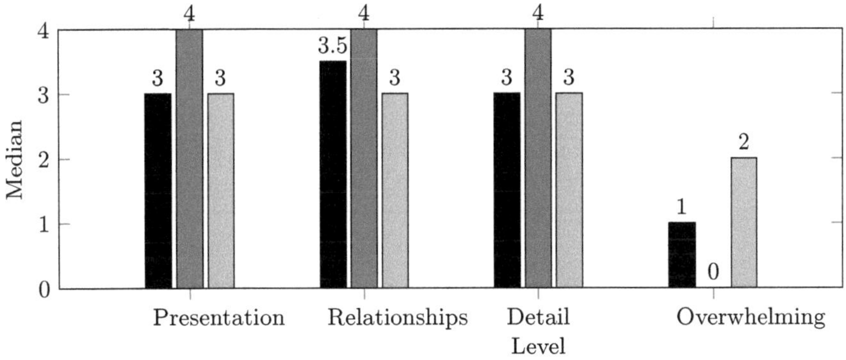

Fig. 7. Median ratings for the detailed graph: overall (black), with (gray) and without (light gray) learning goal motivation [17]. *Presentation*: overall satisfaction; *Relationships*: support in identifying Kanji connections; *Detail Level*: appropriateness of detail; *Overwhelming*: perceived overload. (Color figure online)

Seven participants used the Anki export feature and rated it as highly useful ($\tilde{x} = 4.0$) and efficient ($\tilde{x} = 4.0$). They appreciated the ability to generate flashcards with customizable content ($\tilde{x} = 4.0$), and three of them actively used this customization option before exporting. For two participants, the prototype served as an initial incentive to install Anki, which they subsequently began using regularly. Those who chose not to use the export function cited existing flashcard routines (33.3 %), lack of current Anki use (33.3 %), or other individual reasons. Participants who engaged with the export function received an average of 35.2 adaptive learning suggestions and followed 38.9 % of them. These recommendations were perceived as both helpful ($\tilde{x} = 4.0$) and motivating ($\tilde{x} = 4.0$), as well as easy to understand ($\tilde{x} = 3.5$) and unobtrusive ($\tilde{x} = 3.5$). Although highlighting poorly retained Kanji was rated as moderately motivating ($\tilde{x} = 3.0$), only two participants actively followed the suggestion to revise them. This is reflected in a low agreement score on the item "I followed the request to revise poorly learned Kanji" ($\tilde{x} = 2.0$). Participants rated the import function as motivating ($\tilde{x} = 4.0$), particularly because it visualizes which Kanji they have already learned. This made their progress tangible and helped them understand how known Kanji relate to newly introduced ones. A participant commented: "That was especially great" and another noted: "I really liked the progress visualization in the first [adaptive] version, but the second [non-adaptive] one was great too." Other participants who did not use the import function gave various reasons: One was interested but did not find time to explore the feature in detail. One participant could not use the import due to an incompatibility between AnkiConnect and their current Anki setup, which could not be updated due to other installed add-ons.

Only four participants accessed at least two example sentences in both tool versions. The following analysis is therefore limited to their responses. These participants rated the GPT-generated example sentences as equally good or better than the non-adaptive sentences sourced from the Tatoeba database. Ratings were based on three criteria: comprehensibility, clarity of word meaning, and appropriateness to the learner's proficiency level. The median rating was $\tilde{x} = 3.0$ across versions for both comprehensibility and level-appropriateness. The adaptive examples were slightly preferred in clarifying the target word through context ($\tilde{x} = 3.5$). Regardless of whether they used the adaptive sentence feature, some participants shared suggestions for improvement: One noted the absence of example sentences for rarer words in the non-adaptive version and expressed interest in having such support–something the adaptive variant would have provided. Another recommended offering multiple example sentences at varying language levels to accommodate learners with different proficiency levels. To support comprehension, two participants wanted clickable elements within the sentences, such as links to individual words. Several users did not notice the example sentence feature during the first week. In the second week, participants were more likely to look for and use it actively after being made aware of it through the questionnaire. Feedback suggested that the button labeled with the Kanji 例 was not intuitive for all users. Participants proposed using a more obvious label or a visually distinct icon to make the feature easier to identify and access.

In the following, an in-depth analysis is conducted, where the participants are grouped based on their actual use of the tool's adaptive features. Although all users had access to both versions, only nine participants actively used adaptive features, such as exporting to Anki or exploring at least two example sentences. The remaining ten participants interacted with the tool primarily for Kanji lookup and used few or none of the adaptive elements. For instance, 12 participants did not export any Kanji, and 15 viewed fewer than two example sentences.

An exploratory empirical typology was conducted following the approach by Kluge [18] to understand individual differences further. This method aims to identify participant clusters with internal homogeneity and external heterogeneity based on relevant analytical dimensions. In this case, the dimensions were: (1) prior Kanji knowledge, (2) learning goal motivation (indicates whether participants set a learning goal and, if so, their self-rated motivation on a 1–10 Likert scale), (3) time spent using the tool, (4) SUS, and (5) adaptive feature usage.

These categories were further examined for patterns using Spearman's rank correlation coefficient. The full-sample analysis showed consistent relationships among learning motivation, time spent, and usage of adaptivity. Strong positive correlations were found between learning goal motivation and both usage time ($\rho = .66$, $p = .002$), SUS scores ($\rho = .59$, $p = .008$), and adaptive usage ($\rho = .59$, $p = .007$). SUS scores also correlated moderately with usage time ($\rho = .49$, $p = .034$) and usage of adaptive features ($\rho = .44$, $p = .057$). Participants who set a learning goal rated the system significantly higher in usability (SUS $\tilde{x} = 76.9$) than those without a goal (SUS $\tilde{x} = 62.5$, $p = .025$). They also rated the detailed graph lower across several factors, as shown in Fig. 7. Full correlation results are shown in Fig. 8.

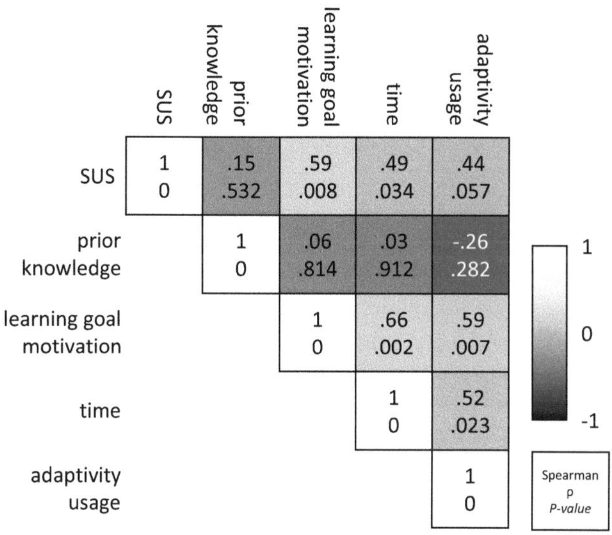

Fig. 8. Spearman correlation matrix (ρ) with corresponding p-values for system usability (SUS), prior knowledge, learning goal motivation, usage time, and adaptivity usage.

Finally, participants suggested improvements in open-ended comments such as integrating stroke order animations, using a font that looks like handwriting, or providing an introductory video. Many appreciated the tool for combining multiple resources. One participant linked the application to Google Maps, describing how it allowed her to recognize Kanji connections and learn radicals from a "bird's-eye view".

6 Discussion

This section discusses the findings concerning the three research questions, focusing on how learners perceived and interacted with the tool's visualizations, recommendations, and generated example sentences.

How do the Tool's Visualizations Shape Learners' Motivation and Exploration in Kanji Learning? The Kanji network visualizations influenced both motivation and navigational behavior. Feedback on the Kanji network visualizations was mixed. While the whole network offered a valuable "big picture"of character interrelations, some users found it overwhelming. A personalized subgraph displaying only known Kanji and their immediate neighbors could reduce cognitive load while offering motivational insights. Instead of showing the full graph by default, the tool could start with a "blank"or minimal graph that grows as learners acquire more Kanji. Alternatively, the initial view could be based on JLPT levels, such as showing only N5 Kanji to beginners. Both approaches would offer a more manageable entry point and could support gradual, self-directed exploration. Indeed, the simplified detailed graph received higher ratings for clarity and engagement due to color-coded progress indicators and focused node sets. This suggests that large-scale overviews can spark curiosity, while personalized and focused subgraphs may provide better support for sustained engagement and exploration.

To What Extent do Minimal, On-Demand Recommendations Encourage Exploratory Learning Behaviors in the Study of Kanji? Minimal recommendations, such as suggestions for related Kanji or important graphemes, were generally well received. Although the visual progress view highlighting poorly retained Kanji based on Anki performance prompted some learners to refocus their study priorities, it was not used consistently. Learners who defined learning goals used these features more actively, explored more Kanji, and reported greater motivation. This indicates that on-demand prompts can support exploratory learning, but their impact depends on learner readiness. Additional onboarding or reflective goal-setting elements could help integrate these recommendations more effectively into learners' study routines.

How do GPT-4 Turbo Generated Example Sentences Compare to Freely Available Resources Regarding Relevance, Clarity, and Learner Acceptance? Only a few participants actively compared GPT-4 Turbo–generated example sentences with those from Tatoeba, which limits generalizability. Within this group, the adaptive sentences were considered equally or more useful in terms of comprehensibility and difficulty level. Learners appreciated that the GPT-based approach offered examples for less common words missing in public repositories. Suggestions for improvement included showing multiple example sentences and adding clickable word explanations. Initially, many users did not notice the sentence feature, and usage only increased after it was explicitly mentioned in the questionnaire. This is surprising, as the chosen label 例 is commonly used in Japanese textbooks to indicate example sentences, for instance, when introducing a new grammar structure. Improving visibility and adding supportive features such as adaptive difficulty could enhance engagement and usefulness.

This study demonstrates that clearly articulated learning goals significantly enhance engagement and feature uptake in an adaptive Kanji learning tool. This finding aligns with prior research showing that specific learning goals foster metacognitive strategy use and improve learning outcomes [28,37]. Participants who entered the study with explicit objectives spent more time interacting with the interface, used adaptive features such as Anki integration and personalized example sentences more, and reported higher overall satisfaction. In contrast, learners without predefined goals exhibited more passive usage patterns, suggesting that embedding goal-setting supports such as onboarding prompts, reflective checklists, or visual goal-tracking indicators could further bolster self-regulated learning in line with Zimmerman's foresight phase [42].

7 Threats to Validity

This study offers important insights into the usability and educational impact of the Kanji learning tool, but several limitations must be considered. Our sample comprised only 19 German-speaking learners of Japanese. Even though we recruited participants with a range of prior Kanji experience, their shared linguistic and cultural background may limit the applicability of these findings to learners from other contexts. Future research should involve larger, more diverse populations to improve generalizability.

Participants used the prototype in their own environments rather than under controlled laboratory conditions. While this ecological approach captures authentic usage patterns, it also introduces variability in how and how often the tool was integrated into participants' study routines. Such uncontrolled factors may have influenced feature exploration and engagement in ways that are difficult to quantify.

Despite randomizing the order of adaptive and non-adaptive tool versions, carryover effects may still have arisen. Initial reactions could have colored participants' perceptions and behaviors in the second week, potentially biasing comparative evaluations.

Differences in Kanji proficiency influenced how users engaged with various features. Advanced learners sometimes deemed certain functions superfluous, whereas beginners struggled with labels like the 例 button.

Moreover, when comparing GPT-generated sentences to those drawn from Tatoeba, participants could not reliably anticipate the difficulty level of the randomly selected Tatoeba examples, since that database contains both straightforward and more complex sentences. Such variability in sentence difficulty may have confounded participants' judgments of relative quality.

It is also important to note that the evaluation of GPT-4 Turbo was limited to generating Japanese sentences with German translations. The model's performance and usefulness may differ for other language pairs or learning contexts, and the findings presented here should not be generalized beyond the Japanese–German use case without further validation.

Finally, the two-week duration provided only a preliminary view of engagement and satisfaction. A longer - term study would be necessary to assess the tool's sustained effects on learning outcomes, retention, and self - regulated study habits.

8 Conclusions and Outlook

In this work, we analyzed KanjiCompass, a learning environment for exploration that integrates network-based visualizations with adaptive support mechanisms to enhance learners' self-regulation in kanji acquisition.

Our user study showed that visualizations influence both motivation and learning behavior. While the graph showing all Jōyō Kanji helped learners understand structural relationships, some found it overwhelming. A progressive visualization strategy, starting with a small, personalized subgraph, may best balance clarity and curiosity.

A key finding of our investigation is that learners value minimal, context-sensitive guidance. Participants reported that short on-screen prompts, triggered only when they decided to export a Kanji for later review, provided the right amount of scaffolding without interrupting their flow. A brief, targeted introduction to the tool's features would have helped to understand the exploratory learning environments better.

GPT-4 Turbo–generated example sentences were perceived as relevant and accessible by the small group of learners who used them actively. The system offered examples for less common compounds that were missing from public repositories. While visibility of this feature was initially low, learner feedback indicates that LLM-generated content can enrich language learning when clearly integrated into the user interface.

Future studies should test KanjiCompass with a larger group of participants and a clearly defined learning task. This would provide deeper insights into learners' interaction with recommendation features when they follow a specific goal or study objective. In particular, the effectiveness of GPT-generated example sentences could be investigated independently of the tool to allow for more targeted evaluation. One promising direction is to increase the adaptivity of these sentences, for example, by including only Kanji that the learner already knows or by selecting topics that match personal interests, such as travel. This personalization may improve the relevance, engagement, and retention of example-based learning materials. The insights gleaned from KanjiCompass offer a roadmap for designing adaptive, network-based learning systems that balance freedom, structure, and intelligent support.

Disclosure of Interests. The authors have no competing interests to declare relevant to this article's content

References

1. Bangor, A., Kortum, P.T., Miller, J.T.: An empirical evaluation of the system usability scale. Int. J. Hum.-Comput. Interact. **24**(6), 574–594 (2008). https://doi.org/10.1080/10447310802205776
2. Benedetti, E., Aizawa, A., Boudin, F.: Automatically suggesting diverse example sentences for L2 Japanese learners using pre-trained language models. In: The 62nd Annual Meeting of the Association for Computational Linguistics: Proceedings of the Student Research Workshop. vol. 4, pp. 114–131. Association for Computational Linguistics, ACL, Bangkok, Thailand (2024)
3. Brooke, J.: Sus - a quick and dirty usability scale. In: Thomas, P.W.J.B., Weerdmeester, B., McClelland, I.L. (eds.) Usability Evaluation In Industry, pp. 189–194. Taylor & Francis Ltd (1996)
4. Cook, V.: Second Language Learning and Language Teaching: Fifth Edition. Routledge, 5 edn. (2016). https://doi.org/10.4324/9781315883113

5. Crowley, D.P.: The occurrence and function of Chinese characters in modern Japanese orthography. J. Newslett. Assoc. Teachers Japanese **5**(3), 1–9 (1968). https://doi.org/10.2307/488736
6. Franz, M., Lopes, C.T., Huck, G., Dong, Y., Sumer, O., Bader, G.D.: Cytoscape.js: a graph theory library for visualisation and analysis. Bioinformatics **32**(2), 309–311 (2015). https://doi.org/10.1093/bioinformatics/btv557
7. Hanson, A.E.S., Brown, C.M.: Enhancing L2 learning through a mobile assisted spaced-repetition tool: an effective but bitter pill? Comput. Assist. Lang. Learn. **33**(1–2), 133–155 (2020). https://doi.org/10.1080/09588221.2018.1552975
8. Jeronimus, M., Westerveld, S., van Leeuwen, C., Bhulai, S., van den Berg, D.: Japanese kanji characters are small-world connected through shared components. In: Bhulai, S., Kardaras, D. (eds.) DATA ANALYTICS 2017: The Sixth International Conference on Data Analytics, pp. 53–58. IARIA (2017)
9. Jiao, W., Wang, W., tse Huang, J., Wang, X., Shi, S., Tu, Z.: Is ChatGPT a good translator? Yes with GPT-4 as the engine (2023). https://doi.org/10.48550/arXiv.2301.08745
10. Kamata, K., Yasuda, N.: [Shinkangorin, 2nd edition, compatible with the "Kaigyōso Stroke Order Dictionary"] [Electronic dictionary]. Taishukan Shoten (2011–2014), from EX-word DATAPLUS9 XD-K7100
11. Kano, C., Takenaka, H., Ishii, E., Fujita, K.: Shinban Basic Kanji Book: Kihon Kanji 500 – Vol.1. Bojinsha, Tōkyō (2018), Basic Kanji Book – Vol. 1 [New edition: Basic Kanji Book – 500 foundational Kanji – Vol.1]
12. Kaur, A., Kumar, R.: Comparative analysis of parametric and non-parametric tests. J. Comput. Math. Sci. **6**(6), 336–342 (2015)
13. Kaur, P., Kumar, H., Kaushal, S.: Technology-assisted language learning adaptive systems: a comprehensive review. Int. J. Cogn. Comput. Eng. **4**, 301–313 (2023). https://doi.org/10.1016/j.ijcce.2023.09.002
14. KIELER Project: Klay Layered. https://rtsys.informatik.uni-kiel.de/confluence/display/KIELER/Klay+Layered (2015). Accessed 20 Apr 2024
15. Klein, D.: The stroke correspondence problem, revisited. arXiv preprint arXiv:1909.11995v3 (2021)
16. Klinger, S.L., Strickroth, S.: Assessing GPT-4's reliability for Japanese kanji instruction: Accuracy, prompt control, and contextual sentences. In: Proceedings of DELFI 2025 – Die 23. Fachtagung Bildungstechnologien. Gesellschaft für Informatik e.V. (2025)
17. Klinger, S.L., Strickroth, S.: KanjiCompass: an etymology-driven adaptive kanji learning tool. In: Proceedings of the 17th International Conference on Computer Supported Education (CSEDU). vol. 1, pp. 472–483. INSTICC, SciTePress (2025). https://doi.org/10.5220/0013341000003932
18. Kluge, S.: Empirisch begründete typenbildung in der qualitativen sozialforschung. Forum Qualitative Sozialforschung/Forum: Qualitative Social Research **1**(1), Artikel 14 (2000). https://doi.org/10.17169/fqs-1.1.1124
19. Komarek, A., Pavlik, J., Sobeslav, V.: Network visualization survey. In: Núñez, M., Nguyen, N.T., Camacho, D., Trawiński, B. (eds.) Computational Collective Intelligence, pp. 275–284. Springer International Publishing, Cham (2015). https://doi.org/10.1007/978-3-319-24306-1_27
20. Kovács, G.: The kanji map. https://thekanjimap.com/ (2024). Accessed 07 July 2025
21. Kuo, A.M.L., Hooper, S.: The effects of visual and verbal coding mnemonics on learning Chinese characters in computer-based instruction. Educ. Tech. Res. Dev. **52**(3), 23–34 (2004). https://doi.org/10.1007/BF02504673

22. Li, J., Zhou, J.: Chinese character structure analysis based on complex networks. Phys. A Stat. Mech. Appl. **380**, 629–638 (2007). https://doi.org/10.1016/j.physa.2007.02.059
23. Li, M., Ogata, H., Hashimoto, S., Yano, Y.: Adaptive kanji learning using mobile-based email. In: Proceedings of the 17th International Conference on Computers in Education, ICCE 2009, pp. 520–526 (2009)
24. Martin, F., Chen, Y., Moore, R.L., Westine, C.D.: Systematic review of adaptive learning research designs, context, strategies, and technologies from 2009 to 2018. Educ. Tech. Res. Dev. **68**, 1903–1929 (2020). https://doi.org/10.1007/s11423-020-09793-2
25. McDermott, K.B., Roediger, H.L.: Memory (Encoding, Storage, Retrieval). In: Butler, A. (ed.) General Psychology (Fall 2018), pp. 117–140. Psychology Curricular Materials, No. 2 (2018)
26. Ng, S.C., Lui, A.K., Wong, Y.K.: An adaptive mobile learning application for beginners to learn fundamental Japanese language. In: Li, K.C., Wong, T.L., Cheung, S.K.S., Lam, J., Ng, K.K. (eds.) Technology in Education. Transforming Educational Practices with Technology, pp. 20–32. Springer Berlin Heidelberg, Berlin, Heidelberg (2015). https://doi.org/10.1007/978-3-662-46158-7_3
27. Ogawa, T., Saito, H.: Semantic activation in visual recognition of Japanese two-kanji compound words: interference and facilitatory effects of neighbors. Psychologia **49**(3), 162–177 (2006). https://doi.org/10.2117/psysoc.2006.162
28. Panadero, E.: A review of self-regulated learning: six models and four directions for research. Front. Psychol. **8**, 422 (2017)
29. Robinson, N.R., Ogayo, P., Mortensen, D.R., Neubig, G.: ChatGPT MT: Competitive for high- (but not low-) resource languages (2023). https://doi.org/10.48550/arXiv.2309.07423
30. Rose, H.: L2 learners' attitudes toward, and use of, mnemonic strategies when learning Japanese kanji. Mod. Lang. J. **97**(4), 981–992 (2013). https://doi.org/10.1111/j.1540-4781.2013.12040.x
31. Rose, H.: The Japanese Writing System: Challenges, Strategies and Self-regulation for Learning Kanji, vol. 116, Multilingual Matters (2017)
32. Rüdian, S., Pinkwart, N.: Auto-generated language learning online courses using generative ai models like ChatGPT. In: 21. Fachtagung Bildungstechnologien (DELFI), pp. 65–76. Gesellschaft für Informatik e.V., Bonn (2023). https://doi.org/10.18420/delfi2023-14
33. Shibatani, M.: The Languages of Japan. Cambridge University Press, Cambridge, Cambridge Language Surveys (1990)
34. Tamaoka, K., Makioka, S., Sanders, S., Verdonschot, R.G.: www.kanjidatabase.com: a new interactive online database for psychological and linguistic research on Japanese kanji and their compound words. Psychol. Res. **81**, 696–708 (2017). https://doi.org/10.1007/s00426-016-0764-3
35. Toyoda, E., Firdaus, A.M., Kano, C.: Identifying useful phonetic components of kanji for learners of Japanese. In: Japanese Language and Literature, pp. 235–272 (2013)
36. Toyoda, E., Kubota, M.: Learning strategies employed for learning words written in kanji versus kana. Aust. Rev. Appl. Linguist. **24**(2), 1–16 (2001). https://doi.org/10.1075/aral.24.2.01kub
37. Urgo, G., Lund, K., Arguello, J.: Goal setting improves learning outcomes by supporting self-regulated learning. In: Proceedings of the 2024 Conference on Human Information Interaction and Retrieval (CHIIR), pp. 213–223. ACM (2024). https://doi.org/10.1145/3624918.3627605

38. Watts, D.J., Strogatz, S.H.: Collective dynamics of 'small-world' networks. Nature **393**(6684), 440–442 (1998). https://doi.org/10.1038/30918
39. Wozniak, P.A.: Optimization of learning. Master's thesis, Poznan University of Technology, Poland (1990)
40. Yan, X., Fan, Y., Di, Z., Havlin, S., Wu, J.: Efficient learning strategy of Chinese characters based on network approach. PLoS ONE **8**(8), e69745 (2013). https://doi.org/10.1371/journal.pone.0069745
41. Ye, J., Su, J., Cao, Y.: A stochastic shortest path algorithm for optimizing spaced repetition scheduling. In: Proceedings of the 28th ACM SIGKDD Conference on Knowledge Discovery and Data Mining (KDD '22), pp. 4381–4390. ACM (2022). https://doi.org/10.1145/3534678.3539081
42. Zimmerman, B.: Attaining self-regulation: A social cognitive perspective. Self-regulation: Theory, research, and applications/Academic (2000). https://doi.org/10.1016/B978-012109890-2/50031-7
43. Zimmerman, E., McMeekin, A.: A review of Japanese call for kanji, vocabulary, and reading: findings, best practices and future directions. JNCOLCTL **29**, 34–68 (2020)

Citizen Science Inquiry: Participation and Democratization

Eileen Scanlon(✉), Christothea Herodotou, Kevin McLeod, and Peter Devine

Open University, Milton Keynes MK7 6AA, United Kingdom
eileen.scanlon@open.ac.uk

Abstract. In this paper, we describe the development over time of our approach to Citizen Science Inquiry and the iterative development of a platform to support and instantiate the necessary features of such an approach. In this endeavour, we have adopted a design-based research (DBR) paradigm to guide our work. We also describe the consequences of our approach for the participation and engagement of participants, volunteers and stakeholders and the potential for increasing the democratic benefits from involvement.

We review contemporary approaches to citizen science and the proposed drawbacks and benefits outlined in these approaches, drawing out the ways in which we have met some of these challenges. As a consequence of our DBR approach, we have a significant number of case studies which illustrate the approach and its outcomes. We present some of these within the paper. We conclude by describing the extent to which our ambitions for this significant work have been fulfilled and outline the next steps in our approach.

Keywords: Citizen Science · Informal Learning · Participation Models

1 Citizen Science and Citizen Inquiry

1.1 Introduction

Citizen science (CS) is a growing trend developed over the past twenty years in involving the public in different types of collaboration with scientists. The growth of this activity has consequences for data collection and data analysis but also for the way in which science itself is carried out.

Citizen inquiry is located at the intersection between 'citizen science' and 'inquiry-based learning' and refers to mass, public scientific investigations. Specifically, '*it fuses the creative knowledge building of inquiry learning with the mass collaborative participation exemplified by citizen science, changing the consumer relationship that most people have with research to one of active engagement*' (Sharples et al., 2013 [1], p.7). The 'citizen inquiry' paradigm shifts the emphasis of scientific inquiry from scientists in control to the general public, by having non-professionals (of any age and level of experience) determine their own research agenda and devise their own science investigations underpinned by a model of scientific inquiry.

C. Meinel et al. (Eds.): CSEDU 2025, CCIS 3148, pp. 162–182, 2027.
https://doi.org/10.1007/978-3-032-39103-2_9

From the perspective of the past 15 years, the new possibilities opened by developing IT led to many actors making extensive use of web 2.0 and mobile technologies to facilitate massive participation of the public of any age, including youngsters, in collective activities. This shift allowed many providers to develop online inquiry-based activities (see e.g., Galaxy Zoo and others reviewed in Curtis (2017) [2].

From our perspective, we could foresee the potential impact on what, and how, citizen scientists learn about science when engaged in such online inquiry activities. In research at the Open University UK, we are interested in the links between formal and informal learning, the growth of such learning opportunities and the approaches that have been taken to assess informal learning associated with citizen science. Citizen inquiry aims to leverage the pedagogical potential of inquiry-based learning – a productive approach which could lead to the development of learners' knowledge of the world and the enhancement of higher-order thinking skills – through opening-up massive participation in inquiry-based activities (Herodotou et al.,2021) [3].

These considerations led us to a number of research questions studied over time. In this paper we report on:

RQ1: *How can citizen science expand its reach and become more democratic and inclusive? and RQ2: How can technology, specifically online platforms, in collaboration with professional scientists, enable the above*?

1.2 The Case for Citizen Science as a Democratic Activity

There is often a blurred line in terms of how citizen science differs or is similar to other research activities and paradigms. Nascimento et al. (2016) [4] detail three ways citizen science provides added value to current research practices: a) citizen science can expand and accelerate science; citizen scientists help collect and analyze data making research faster and broader while collected data are geographically and temporarily extensive (something that cannot be done by professional scientists). Also, new types of research can be pursued as perceived or defined by citizens and their needs; b) citizen science can address societal challenges; the involvement of the public in research means that real-world problems and research questions that matter to people become the focus of research. This type of participation can bring benefits to people such as scientific literacy, behavioral changes and community building; c) citizen science can democratize science and policy; it can make research transparent and inclusive and build trust in evidence-based policy making. This means that policies will more likely be adopted and they will be informed by scientific knowledge co-produced with citizens.

With the growth of citizen science, there has been a corresponding growth in terms of the purposes which citizen science activities might advance. Right from the beginning, there has been an interest in the potential for involving citizens in citizen science with the purpose of enabling more democratic purposes. For example, Irwin produced one of the first books and description of citizen science in 1995: "*a form of science developed and enacted by citizens themselves*" (Irwin1995, p.xi) [5] and in 2001, [6] reviewed the relationship between science and democracy as influenced by issues of public confidence. In his 2001 paper he reminds us of Nelkin [7] writing in the mid-1970s:

> "*The complexity of public decisions seems to require highly specialized and esoteric knowledge, and those who control this knowledge have considerable power. Yet democratic ideology suggests that people must be able to influence policy decisions that affect their lives.*" (p.12) [7]

Raap et al. (2022) [8] discusses the work of Irwin as follows:

> "*Irwin considers gaps between privileged expert knowledge and citizens or lay knowledge as a problem of democracy. How this gap is mediated when citizens become scientific knowledge producers themselves is an important question of citizen science*", (p.2) [8]. also notes the potential of citizen science as "*a democratizing practice allowing for new definitions of public problems, according to some critics, the CS language of democratization hides the logic of platform capitalism, in which citizens, under the banner of CS, perform cheap labor.*"(p.2)

Chilvers and Kearnes (2015) [9] reviews the potential, particularly in the transformation in participation models (reviewed later) which would "*build more socially responsive and responsible science and innovation.*" (p.347)

Mirowski (2018) [10] is more doubtful about the precise nature and benefits of the open science movement and what it means for the so-called power structures in the development of science: "*The layers of confusion surrounding open science rival a millefeuille, and can be just as sticky. The quickest way to cut through the confection is to acknowledge that science has been constituted by a sequence of historical regimes of epistemic and logistical organization, long before the current craze for 'openness'*" and he continues.

> "*Thus we come to the new-found fascination amongst the open science advocates for so-called 'democratization' through so-called 'citizen science'. They assert that 'citizen science advocates are arguing implicitly and explicitly for a radical change to the structures of political power' ([11]Cavalier and Kennedy, 2016: 117). What is especially noteworthy in these instances is the distinctly impoverished notion of democracy inherent in all of their pleas. Many of their assertions boil down to the format that the more outsiders are somehow folded into the scientific process in whatever capacity, the more that the public will come to appreciate and support science, and the better off democracy will flourish.*"(p.172)

This skepticism from Mirowski is important to include in the discussion, and it is important to hold up to scrutiny a notion that more participation, in principle, makes science more democratic. First, he challenges us to consider the nature of this increased participation, and second, he challenges us to consider what 'more democracy' might look like beyond involving more of the public in citizen science activities. What indeed do we make of claims around power and control? The key to answering this question lies in the nature of participation in CS, which is outlined in the next section. In terms of what more involvement in science leads to or might be expected to lead to, we have some evidence from our studies, and those of others, to indicate that involvement in some citizen science activity leads to learning about science (Scanlon et al. 2014, on iSpot [12]), (Herodotou et al. 2022 [13]). Yet, if we truly aim to bring learning and other benefits to participants, citizen science activities need to be designed from the outset with this objective in mind. In our exploration of what democratic citizen science should look like, we concluded in a framework and vision with five key dimensions: to achieve democratization through citizen science, what needs to be in place are functions to support 1) learning and networking, 2) research, 3) facilitation, 4) funding and 5) innovation (Herodotou et al., 2024) [14]. However, in practice, this is far from straightforward, as several key challenges need to be addressed before it can be realised. In our work, we detail challenges related to the time needed to engage with communities and citizen scientists, the identification and selection of citizen scientists to ensure these are not "the usual suspects" or the "loudest voices", the need to find ways to actively engage citizens with varied skills and knowledge in research, the need to train them to ensure data collected are robust and of good quality, and efforts to intentionally enable equitable participation by developing trust between researchers and citizen scientists (ibid). Some of these challenges could be overcome with the use of technologies and the advent of Artificial Intelligence (AI). AI is currently used in citizen science projects to support processes of automatic data collection and analysis, and provision of 24/7 support to the community of volunteers involved in a citizen science project (Fortson et al., 2024) [15]. From our perspective, this is a key driver for our involvement as OU researchers, and we will refer later more to the origins of the project in our desire to explore science learning and how it is impacted by modern technology.

2 Issues

2.1 Data Issues

There are both benefits and challenges associated with the proliferation of data enabled by modern technology. This is similar to the challenges offered by multimodal records of collaborative learning in action which are a challenge for methodologies of data collection but also for data analysis. In the case of data collection, the richness of the data is seductive and it is potentially too easy to assume that what **can** be recorded is what **should be** recorded without further consideration for analysis. The drawback is that the volume of data leads us to a crisis of data overload and that the illusion of completeness, the illusion that what has been captured contains all the elements of what has influenced learning in an individual or a network. (see e.g. Blake et al. [16], Nov et al. (2014) [17]).

Kelling et al. (2015) [18] makes the argument that, for some biology research, the scale and quantity of the data from citizen science projects is required: *"Data from well-designed experiments provide the strongest evidence of causation in biodiversity studies. However, for many species the collection of these data is not scalable to the spatial and temporal extents required to understand patterns at the population level. Only data collected from citizen science projects can gather sufficient quantities of data."*

Recognizing the inherent issues with providing quality assurance he writes:

> *"The lack of well-defined hypotheses to define data collection protocols and individual variability in skill levels and data collection processes are major obstacles in accurately interpreting citizen science data that must be recognized and addressed during analysis."* (ibid p.2)

Their proposal is that using Big Data methods demonstrated a wider potential for using post hoc calibration in analysis of data from citizen science projects, and illustrating their approach using the eBird citizens science project is appealing.

Herodotou, Scanlon and Sharples (2021) [3] reviewing these issues in relation to the nQuire project have the view that: "*The accuracy of collected data should be judged project-by-project, considering several factors. In large-scale CS projects, high quality data can be achieved through a simple process of data collection and post-hoc data quality controls such as computational modelling, while in small-scale CS projects with complex data collection processes, expert-led training, and good quality materials can generate good quality science outcomes (Parrish et al., 2018)* [19]."

2.2 The Different Models of Participation

One further difficulty with encouraging wider participation in the development of science through citizen science speaks directly to consideration of the different participation models in use in the field of citizen science. The notion of a ladder of participation was first introduced by Arnstein (1969) [20] and in recent years has been elaborated on by Haklay et al. (2021) [21]. However, there are other issues to be unpacked about the nature of participation in citizen science. A stated aim of our nQuire development has been to extend the possibilities for democracy in research (Herodotou, Kenny & Scanlon, 2024) [14] and this is predicated on the support, that our platform can give, for citizens to own their investigations and perhaps even set them up. Yet, participation of the public as creators of research is, at least at the moment, rather uncommon and challenging for participants even to consider much less enact (Herodotou et al., 2022) [22]. Yet, some participants would be interested in being supported to do so, should there be support and time availability (ibid). There are interesting examples of how such hurdles can be overcome. For example, Sharma et al. (2022) [23] specifically discuss online citizen science issues of species identification through consensus building and identified ways of improving accuracy and consensus building on identification tasks among volunteers.

The European Commission (EC 2020) [24] points out that citizen science has the potential to improve research and its outcomes and increase science literacy and confidence of the public in research. Many voices in citizen science are echoing this desire and there are some bold attempts to operationalize the support necessary to accomplish this shift. But there are also additional considerations. The democracy movement in citizen science has not won over all scientists involved in citizen science projects, some of whom query whether members of the general public should be encouraged or allowed to participate in different ways from the traditional role of data collector under the supervision of professional scientists. For example, Shaw et al.(2020) [25] reviews case studies applying to Landscape research and although they involved different models of participation they note that "each of them was limited to just one stage of the research process."

Resnik (2019) (p.1) [26] gives an interesting commentary on this expansion of types of participation and highlights the ethical implications of the mixture of roles:

> "*Citizen involvement in research raises novel ethical issues for human studies, because individuals have traditionally occupied the role of researcher or subject,*

but not [both] at the same time. The confluence of these two different roles in the same person poses challenges for investigators and oversight committees because legal rules and ethical guidelines focus on protecting the rights and welfare of human subjects and do not address issues that fall outside this domain, such as study design, data quality and integrity, reporting misconduct, authorship, or publication."

It is also not appropriate to assume that ideas of co-design or co-construction or participation are limited only to the world of citizen science, or any other type of citizen inquiry. Heiss et al. (2017) (p.21) [27] describes how: *"the discussion has moved away from a classical 'public understanding of science' approach, aiming at transferring knowledge about scientific processes to the public, to a 'science in society' approach (Felt* et al. *2013)* [28]*"*. This links to discussions around knowledge production as a mode two activity which means that:

"... *knowledge is no longer produced exclusively in scientific institutions, but in transdisciplinary collaborations, which aim to solve existing practical problems. Such transdisciplinary collaborations may not only involve interactions between scientific disciplines, but also between scientific and non-scientific actors (Hurni and Wiesmann 2014)* [29]. *The concept of 'transformative science' builds on these observations and argues that such transdisciplinary collaborations become more important in modern societies, which are characterized by the increasing penetration of scientific results and processes within society. In order to ensure the external legitimacy of institutionalized scientific research, scientific actors have to open up to societal actors and actively involve them."* (p.21)

Outside of the specific research practices of citizen science, there are paradigm shifts in research design in the social science more generally. In medicine, in social research and in the practices of design-based research there are also ways of working, aligned with moves towards more co-production of research. Palmer and colleagues (2019, p.247), [30] writing about medical research, capture this shift in the zeitgeist as follows:

"Participatory methods increasingly used in healthcare improvement coalesce around the concept of co-production, and related practices of co-creation, co-design and co-innovation. These participatory methods have become the new Zeitgeist—the spirit of our times in quality improvement. The rationale for this new spirit of participation relates to voice and engagement (those with lived experience should be engaged in processes of development, redesign and improvements), empowerment (engagement in co-design and co-production has positive individual and societal benefits) and advancement (quality of life and other health outcomes and experiences of services for everyone involved) should improve as a result."

Roche et al., in a 2020 [31] review of citizen science progress in this area has a clear prescription of what needs to be done in terms of practices and that is:

"to align educational learning outcomes with citizen science project goals at the planning stage of the project using co-creation approaches to ensure issues of accessibility and inclusivity are paramount throughout the design and implementation of every project. Only then can citizen science realise its true potential to empower citizens to take ownership of their own science education and learning." (p.1)

Jenkins (2011) [32] points out the increased possibilities in citizen science for making students see science as relevant to their own lives, and with Archer et al. (2015) [33] sees the possibility of increasing *science capital*, an important potential pathway to change. However, Hall (2024) [35] points out the paradox between scientists aiming for science discovery, often publishing relatively little from citizen science studies.

"Citizen science yields increased scientific capacity in exchange for science literacy and promises of a more responsive science to society's needs. Yet, citizen science projects are criticized for producing few scientific outputs and having exploitative relationships with the citizens who participate" [p.1527]

They propose a model of engagement for citizen science aiming to result in benefits for citizens and scientists alike. Their example relates to a case study of citizen involvement on a hydrology project. Heywood (2016) [35], like others, considers that there is a need for better cooperation between scientists and the public.

In one of the first studies of the motivation of citizens for participation, Curtis (2017) [2], in her thesis work, noted the growing trend in online citizen science projects responding in part to the data deluge offering scientists both an opportunity and a challenge and which coincided with the availability of digital tools both for communication with others and for analysis of data. The move to online citizen science was particularly intriguing. Her particular interest was in the opportunities for participation and engagement of members of the public and their motivations for participation. One key feature was that, for volunteers, participating in online citizen science projects offers them an opportunity to become involved in authentic scientific research for altruistic purposes but also to learn more about science. Curtis [2] writes that the volunteers she surveyed valued this aspect of their participation and comments:

"*projects have enabled scientists to process large amounts of data, utilise the diversity of human pattern recognition and problem-solving skills, and on occasion, have resulted in contributions to knowledge*" (p.314)

3 The Open University Context

So often we engage in trying to understand what people have learned when they engage in an activity as part of a formal learning opportunity. However, it is obvious that these opportunities have changed. No longer do learners need to be physically co-located with instructors, or even with other learners. No longer do we see learners as being required to be part of a formal accredited program of study. In the past, these opportunities for learning were often examined as discrete lessons taking place in classrooms. However, the opportunities for learning have become more widespread and often exist in many different forms. In recent years, new learning opportunities in relation to collaboration, inquiry and location-based learning have emerged as practical possibilities. The concept of learning journey supported by technology, in the sense that learners may be engaged in moving between different settings while learning, is a powerful one. While we might wish to ensure that learners engage enthusiastically with science and that they are satisfied with their participation in science activities and see learning as fun and enjoyable, this is not automatically a benefit of informal settings. It is also difficult to track learning in these settings.

Going forward, we need to address the challenges of evidencing learning in informal settings, or connecting learning across settings, and the concept of learning journey supported by technology, in ensuring that this learning is enjoyable and engaging. The sense that learners may be engaged in moving between different settings is appropriate, and in the sense that multiple learning experiences, rather than learning from isolated incidents, are important. We are particularly interested in the ways in which technology tools can support these new learning journeys, and particularly the prospects for citizen science. Citizen science is an interesting approach which serves multiple purposes and can play an important part in learning journeys. One purpose is that, by becoming involved in citizen science projects, members of the public can become volunteers to a wide range of activities which contribute to the development of science. As such they are a valuable resource.

We are interested in the other potential benefits from this activity, of using the participation in such activities to help participants learn science and learn about science. Aristeidou et al. (2017) [36] provides a review of platforms produced for online citizen science. Masters et al. (2016) [37] reviewing on-line citizen science activities notes that because new technologies allow for much higher levels of participation, collaboration, and interaction in citizen science, the form that these activities take can be important. In their paper, Masters et al. conduct a discussion which: "*explores what online citizen science projects reveal about the 'democratisation' of science and distributed engagement with authentic research. Analysing the wider appeal of these projects as well as their potential for informal science learning and creating communities of practice, [...] asks whether 'citizen' and 'researcher' will ever be on equal footing.*" [p. 1]

A consequence of our approach to informal learning, in our exploration of the topic, we have developed tools to support this activity of participation in science, and we suggest that the tools involved need to be considered also from the perspective of technology enhanced learning. "*.... Technology-enhanced learning consists of much more than a set of research-informed products. It is a complex system, which includes communities, technologies and practices that are informed by pedagogy (the theory and practice of teaching, learning and assessment)*" (Scanlon et al. 2013) [38]. The potential learning environments to be studied are complex, and as described in Scanlon et al. (ibid) [38], we appreciate that the uptake of technology enhanced learning tools is influenced by the 'persistent intent' evident in the description of the development of the tool provided in a later section.

3.1 Methods of Assessing Learning in Citizen Science

Learning from citizen science projects is assessed using a variety of methods, often combining qualitative and quantitative approaches. The field is still maturing, and a key challenge is the lack of a standardised framework for evaluation across diverse projects (Hoedoafia et al., 2024) [39]. The main assessment methods used are: pre/post surveys to capture baseline understanding of knowledge and skills and how this evolves after participation; qualitative feedback such as interviews and focus groups with participants reflecting and documenting their own experiences of learning; observations by researchers while a project runs and participants engage with it and analysis of participants' contributions – the quality and quantity of contributions can be seen as a proxy of their understanding and skills development) (Ivanjko et al., 2025) [40]. When it comes to defining learning from participation in citizen science, this often refers to the following six areas: content knowledge, nature of science knowledge, skills of science inquiry, self-efficacy, interest/motivation, and behaviours/stewardship (Philips et al., 2018) [41].

Capturing learning is not straightforward; a systematic review by Aristeidou & Herodotou (2020) [42] showed that the methods currently used in citizen science projects are mainly self-reports, content analysis of contributed data and of forum posts, accuracy checks of contributed data, quizzes, and instruments for measuring scientific attitudes and beliefs. The authors noted a lack of experimental and long-term studies as well as studies that take place in formal education settings. As an example, the iSpot project (Silvertown et al., 2015) [43] has made efforts to assess learning. Having users observe (spot) organisms, identifying them and finding out their name is an initial step towards learning more about them and engaging with observation as a learning process. iSpot operates a reputation system, which provides an indication of each user's expertise on the site using its recording of observations. This 'reputation' encourages engagement. This alongside other aspects of reputation (relevant biology qualifications or membership of organizations) provide a way to motivate learning the skills of observation and understanding of species.

An estimation of learning which is taking place as a consequence of using iSpot is set out in Scanlon et al. (2014) [44]. This paper approaches an estimation of learning from the users' success in identifications as follows: "*analysis of a sample of 407 users as they progressed through submitting and identifying their first fifty observations within iSpot is strongly suggestive of learning. ..., users showed improvement in their ability to identify other people's observations over the period that they submitted observations.*"(p. 4)

In addition [Silvertown et al. 2015] [43] comments on learning as follows: "*We also have evidence that the effective operation of iSpot is becoming less dependent upon the limited number of experts whom we seeded with high reputations at the start. In January 2010, designated experts were contributing to 60% of determinations, but four years later 60% of observations were being determined without their help.*" (p.142). Silvertown et al. (2015) [43] writing about the difficulty of assessing the influence of his platform iSpot on the learning of contributors states "*While we have anecdotal evidence from comments made by participants that they have learned, we do not have direct, quantitative evidence of learning in iSpot yet.*" (p.142)

3.2 Our Approach: The nQuire Platform

What is nQuire? nQuire is a community and citizen science platform developed in the Institute of Educational Technology at the Open University UK. People can use it to design their own research or take part in research studies designed by other people, including scientists. Using nQuire, people have the possibility to design and manage their own scientific study, with, if necessary, support from experts who can review the studies from members of the public to ensure it is scientifically robust before it goes live, or people can participate and contribute to studies of others. This software was developed using insights from our inquiry learning project *Personal Inquiry* (Sharples et al. 2015) [45] where we postulated that an effective way of motivating younger people to engage in learning science would be using inquiries and making the inquiries personally relevant to them in terms of their community, their environment, and themselves

Access to nQuire and Authoring. nQuire has been through a 15-year development cycle. In its first iteration, we produced a support for inquiry learning in formal school settings. Over the years, we have deployed it in many citizen science settings and in a sequence of design-based research experiments improved its usability and functionality. See e.g. Aristeidou, Scanlon & Sharples (2021) [46], Herodotou et al., (2018) [47]. We designed a tool to help people to engage in citizen science activities and in doing so learn about how research is done. They can do that by taking part in studies set by others, receive feedback, data visualizations, peer learning, as well as set up their own studies through an authoring functionality. It is free to use and provides support from scientists.

Access and Authoring. nQuire is available to anyone who registers to create a mission who is over the age of 16. The 'Create mission' function is supported by an authoring tool which has a number of features. The author starts by choosing a mission name, provides a description and explanation of the purpose of what the mission is designed to achieve and a request for people to help by taking part. The author can then use the 'Build' phase to design the mission with a range of pre-defined response types and potentially enhance further by using more advanced features and customizations suitable for the data which is to be collected.

Two types of mission are possible, one described as confidential, the other social. Social missions use open data meaning each contribution is visible to everyone. Visualisations of the collected data can be displayed to encourage discussion, and users can interact by liking or commenting on specific contributions. Confidential missions, by contrast, keep all submitted data private. Only the mission author can download the responses, and access is limited to the answers themselves – excluding any user-identifying details. No contributions from other participants are shared or displayed: Ethical approval is required before a mission is launched, and each mission is carefully reviewed to ensure compliance. In cases where missions are not affiliated to a research institution, ethics can be obtained via the OU's ethics board. This approach aims to enable individuals and communities who want to use citizen science, yet they are not affiliated to an institution, to do so in an ethical manner and after appropriate approvals are in place. Ethics approvals are accompanied by a general process of approvals by the nQuire team. The latter entails feedback by the nQuire team regarding the mission structure, questions, language that aim to help authors improve the quality of their citizen science studies. These mechanisms aim open-up research to a more diverse demographic through the provision of scaffolding and tangible support. It is our ambition to enable close collaborations between the university and the general public to enable the latter to act as citizen scientists by setting up their own missions on nQuire.

A mission can be linked to social media and if there is an obvious connection to the Open University's social mission, links will be added to an 'Open Societal Challenge', part of the Open University's research strategy. The OU's mission is to be open to people, places, methods, and ideas. The three facets of our Societal Challenges are focusing on addressing three significant challenges that impact people worldwide, tackling inequality, driving sustainability and removing barriers to people living well. Societal challenges are added to each mission for the purpose of aligning with broader research goals in the wider community and potentially attracting more people to the mission. nQuire can be accessed via www.nquire.org.uk. (See Scanlon & Herodotou (2024) [49] for more details.)

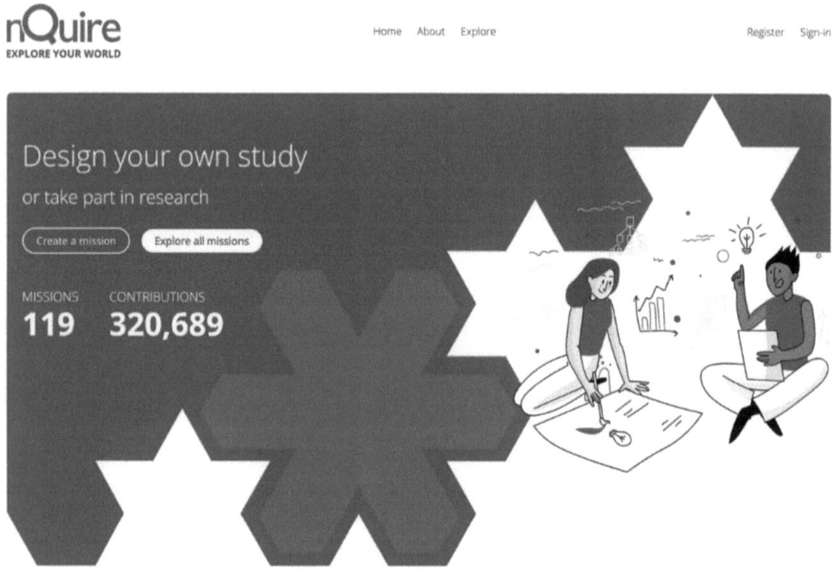

Fig. 1. nQuire home screen.

We want to help people to start thinking critically and scientifically, to understand and assess information around them, change their attitudes to science, and develop scientific literacy. We designed the tool to help people to learn. Within this overall ambition we can see potential for learning science but also learning about how research is done.

3.3 Our Approach to Design

In all our work on this theme we have approached the developments in nQuire using a design-based research (DBR) paradigm (Herodotou et al., 2018) [47], with the following characteristics: iterative design, real-world context for testing, focus on learning for volunteers, scaffolding learning processes, and operationalising the concept of citizen inquiry. Wang and Hannafin (2005) [48] describe DBR this as:

"A systematic but flexible methodology aimed to improve educational practices through iterative analysis, design, development, and implementation, based on collaboration among researchers and practitioners in real world settings, and leading to contextually sensitive design principles and theories"(p. 6). Therefore, our work is distinguished by its attachment to the idea of developing solutions to problems and then testing these solutions (or prototypes) with users and then iterating. To date we have 119 missions. contributions and these iterations to improve the design have been developed. The next Figure gives a timeline for missions conducted since 2018.

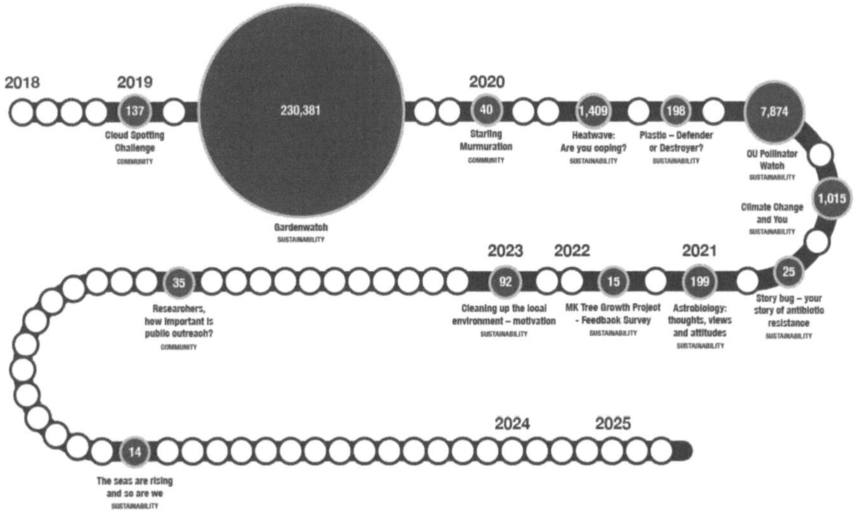

Fig. 2. A representation of the missions run since 2018 highlighting in green which have received most contributions and those dealing with sustainability and community.

To date, since 2018 there have been 119 missions with a total of 320,677 contributions. These are distributed as follows: 30 launched still accepting contributions, and overall the majority are confidential as opposed to social missions. The graph in Fig. 3 provides an interesting angle on nQuire use over the period as it displays how many missions were being published per year regardless of the mission duration. We have an interesting number of the average missions per year (17) and lockdown doubled the average (33).

Figure 3 also notes the points at which the nQuire tool had significant design features added or improved e.g. the authoring tool in 2019 and in 2023 a more extensive redesign.

Table 1 represents the project titles and funding influencing the development of work on nQuire since its inception as part of the Personal Inquiry project. Missions have been launched in six subjects (education, environment, literature, medicine, psychology and technology) and categorized in five themes (community, learning, equality, sustainability

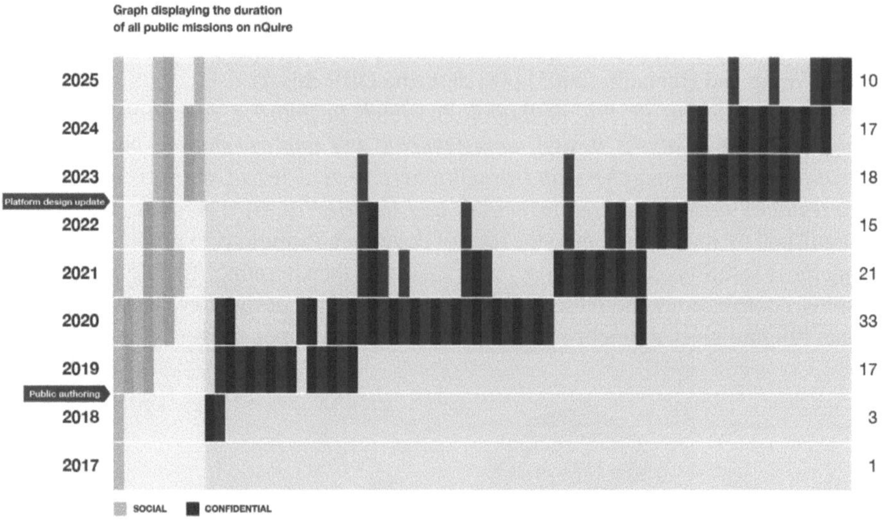

Fig. 3. Graph displaying the duration of missions.

Table 1. Funding for major projects during which we have been developing our approach.

Year	Funder	Project Title
2008–12	ESRC	Personal Inquiry
2012–13	Wolfson	Open Science Lab
2013–15	Nominet	Young People's citizen science
2017–2021	NSF	Learn CitSci
2020–221	Mental Health Scotland	Democratising research: a mental health pilot
2020–21	BBSRC	EDU Cit Sci
2022–2025	EU	Extending Design Thinking Through Digital Technologies
2024–2028	SEPUB	Peace of Mind

and well-being.) In the next sections, we present examples of citizen science projects hosted on nQuire. For this paper, we have chosen some of our case studies related to the societal challenge of sustainability.

4 Case Studies

4.1 Case Study: Forest 404

The Forest 404 study (or, as we called an exploration using nQuire, a 'mission') was a collaboration between the BBC Radio 4, the University of Bristol, the University of Exeter, and the Open University. The aim of the investigation was to understand how people feel when listening to various sounds. These included the sounds of nature such as wind in the trees, birds singing, or waves washing on to the beach, in addition to poems or stories about nature. The nQuire mission was structured around several sections each one asking participants to reflect on a listening experience. The listening experience was enabled by audio files uploaded to the mission. Follow-up questions such as *How pleasant do you find the experience of listening to this sound? Do you find this sound boring or exciting?* were asked. Questions were answered by using sliders and multiple-choice items. People who participated could slide left or right to indicate their agreement with statements. Participants were asked about personal information such as age and gender.

The motivation behind the mission was to enable scientific understanding of the therapeutic potential of nature on wellbeing. 7,596 people took part in the study, mainly from the South-East, South -West of the UK and London. The mission brief included the following.

> "*.... A large body of evidence shows that spending time in natural environments can have positive effects on people's wellbeing. But we know very little about the importance of sound in this relationship. How might listening to birdsong or waves lapping on the beach help people who are stressed or tired? The effects won't be the same for everyone, so we want as many people as possible to take part and help us uncover what works and why.*" Lead researcher from Exeter University

Findings from the study showed that people's responses to the mission were overwhelmingly positive, and in some cases, they reported on behavior changes after taking part in the *Forest 404* experience. One participant explained "*My ears seem more attuned to nature now. On my morning dog walk I could hear nothing but birdsong, I don't think this is any different than before I think I've just noticed it now.*" The study funding were published by Smalley et al. (2020) [49] so participants had the incentive of contributing to the development of scientist's understanding of an important topic. What seemed to be important to engagement with the mission was the involvement of the media in this case the British Broadcasting Company (BBC) for the associated radio broadcasts. The connection between the development of the nQuire tool and its redesign to cope with participation at scale was due to a partnership between the OU and the broadcaster and this has had significance in determining public engagement with some of the larger scale missions or investigations.

4.2 Case Study: OU PollinatorWatch

OU staff launched a mission to explore the topic of pollinators with a view also to help people learn. It was titled Pollinator watch and it was promoted in the popular BBC2 TV series Springwatch. It is an example of our many citizen science projects related to the theme of sustainability. The potential for citizen science projects to make a contribution in this area has been recognized. (See e.g. Austen et al., 2024 [50].)

The interest of OU scientists in biodiversity focused on insect pollinators which are essential, and under threat and a team was brought together to design a mission. The aim of the mission was to help people to learn about different types of pollinators. By

Fig. 4. The Forest 404 experiment. (Figure 4 is taken from Fig. 1 Scanlon and Herodotou. 2025, [53] p 494)

people sharing observations and uploading photographs, data were collected on where pollinators were seen in the UK.

> The mission brief included the following statement: *"We designed this mission to help you learn more about insect pollinators and the benefits they bring; benefits that are largely taken for granted. Whilst observing current Government guidance on restricted movement, social distancing and washing your hands as soon as you get home, we would like you to spend some time in your outdoor spaces looking for insect pollinators. Anyone can take part whether you have a small window-box, balcony, or garden."*
>
> *We are asking you to share your observations or upload photographs of the insect pollinators you see and answer some questions. In doing so, you will help us understand which pollinators are commonly observed and where, as well as how much we know about these important species. This mission will help you learn about different types of pollinating insects, why they are important and why they need our help."*

This mission attracted contributions from 7,824 participants and the summary of findings reported that observations of pollinators were submitted from all across the UK, from 123 of the 124 postcode areas. Bumblebees were the most common. In terms of participants, it was interesting that there was a high level of engagement amongst dedicated wildlife watchers. However, researchers found that 19.2% of participants wouldn't normally observe or identify pollinators and 10.9% were not previously aware of the threats they faced.

(https://nquire.org.uk/mission/oupollinatorwatch/findings)

Fig. 5. OU Pollinator Watch. (Figure 5 is taken from Fig. 1 Scanlon and Herodotou, 2025, [53] p 494)

We have hosted a number of other missions on the platform related to the environment and sustainability. These include, *GardenWatch*, *Climate Change and You*, *MK trees*, *Heatwaves: are you coping?* and *The Sea is rising and so are we*, and most recently *Eco Anxiety*. As we can see from Fig. 2 these have attracted considerable public attention and range from examples where the design of the mission involved co-creation at a workshop (e.g. *Climate Change and you* and *Heatwaves: are you coping?*), design changes such as the introduction of the authoring tool (e.g. *Climate Change and you*) or more intensive co-design by the stakeholder community (c.g. *Youth Mental Health* and *The Sea is rising and so are we*).

Media campaign involvement – such as in *Forest 404* and *GardenWatch* has proven to be a powerful driver for public participation.

4.3 Discussion

There has been much activity and writing around citizen science as a movement since the early nineties. From the early commentaries about the potential of the citizen science movement to a more recent discussion of the prospects for technology enhancement of the processes associated with various steps in the activities, these trends have resulted in the contemporary landscape of so many, and so varied citizen science related projects.

In response to our first RQ, much is written about extending the model of participation for citizen science projects to include all the stages of the inquiry process beyond merely data collection and in some cases analysis. The two examples we have chosen to illustrate above provide the opportunity to consider what is meant by participation and what the benefits of these activities are. In each case, there is a benefit to the scientists of specific data on interesting topics, in the case of *Forest 404* an investigation into the impact of sound leading to a publication on the topic. In the case of *OU Pollinator Watch*, good quality information on insect pollinators in the UK with representation of the whole country, but even more is the intent of the scientists to develop an activity that engaged the volunteers, providing opportunities to develop skills in observation but also to learn about what makes a difference to the societal problem of decrease in insect pollinators and what behaviours might have significant impact. This is in the nature of a call to action around environmental issues. Both these examples therefore give a purpose to the activity beyond data collection opportunities for scientists presented by public engagement events in the media combined with citizens science activity.

We have conducted a survey of 150 of our volunteers to establish what, in their opinions, participation in nQuire had meant for them. Herodotou et al. (2022) [22] reports on this work detailing self-perceived learning benefits for half of participants in relation to increased awareness about the topic of the citizen science project, a desire to learn more about the topic, a change in everyday habits and taking action to support biodiversity. Yet, it is worth noting that perceived it as highly unlikely for them to design their own studies as they do not have the time and skills or because this was seen as an activity not for them.

We need to further establish what is learned in participation in specific missions across a theme, whether about the science involved in the missions or learning about the process of science inquiry, to understand more about the nature of science knowledge and the processes of scientific discovery. In our 2022 study we asked about their confidence in their ability to conduct inquiries and their intention to conduct them in the future. This needs more investigation with the increase in the number of investigations now available and with an increase in participation in missions.

In response to RQ2, we showcased how technological and human support can work complementarily to enable participation of the public in setting up, managing or taking part in citizen science investigations. We believe that tools such as the nQuire platform can tackle some of the key challenges citizen science is facing, in particular, the lack of skills and knowledge of volunteers and the need to actively engage them in the research cycle (Herodotou et al., 2024) [14] as well as the collection of robust and good quality data, in our case enabled through the tool and the provision of feedback by professional scientists. The cultivation of close collaborations between research institutions and volunteers/communities should be a next step towards enabling more democratic and inclusive forms of citizen science. In practice, this would mean that professional scientists encourage volunteers to engage with citizen science and provide them with scaffolding as to how to do so, including the right tools and mechanisms to support them throughout the research journey. This requires an acknowledgement that the expertise of volunteers lies in their own experiences, needs and requirements of the topic they wish to examine, whereas professional scientists have the research expertise and they are asked to communicate it and negotiate it with volunteers in meaningful and easy to grasp ways.

5 Conclusions

The endeavour we are engaged in is to explore ways in which our tools can contribute to improving the public's understanding of science and how scientific knowledge develops. Our ultimate aim is to identify sustainable ways in which citizen science can become more democratic and inclusive. Part of this endeavour is how best to engage individuals and communities with limited or no research expertise and interest in scientific investigations with the process of designing and implementing a scientific investigation. With our research work's origins in personal inquiry learning in schools, bringing together approaches to developing understanding of science concepts and processes, this continuing research work on citizen science was started with a recognition of the possibilities of combining inquiry learning with citizen science and collaboration. Harnessing these components could provide more opportunities for participants' learning from engaging with citizen science.

With many nQuire 'missions' completed (69 to date), we have developed a usable and effective tool and we have developed the possibility of making progress on the democratization of the research process by enabling enhanced levels of participation and by turning volunteers into co-researchers. This work presents two key challenges. The first is whether participation in a mission leads to learning. The second is whether technologies like nQuire can support more substantive citizen engagement in scientific inquiry.

With regards to the first challenge, we have established as described above evidence which suggests learning can result from participation. For the second challenge we can point to several encouraging case studies which exemplify how this approach can enhance citizen involvement in science. Like many others we have begun experimenting with AI tools, to accelerate and enhance data analysis in missions with many participants as reflected in the recent systematic reviews of the potential of Generative AI in learning settings e.g., Bond et al. (2024) [52]. We are also working on versions of the tool that would support more projects exploring design thinking, youth mental health, eco-anxiety, and policy prioritization in funded research (https://learn.nquire.org.uk/signin.)

Future Work. We are currently concluding a project which has explored the use of nQuire and other emerging technologies in design thinking in eight schools across Europe, returning to our roots in schools with a specially designed *nQuire for schools* platform. Our latest project initiative, *Peace of Mind,* builds on our past work co-creating a mission with interested young participants and engages youth on the island of Ireland in an investigation of programs to promote resilience. Across all of our work, we remain deeply committed to our goal of widening participation in scientific endeavors and democratizing research through citizen science inquiry.

Acknowledgements. Our thanks are due to the participants and collaborators in all our citizen science investigations, and especially to our major Funders summarized in Table 1. This paper is an extension of a short paper presented at CSEDU 2025 and reprinted in the conference proceedings as Scanlon and Herodotou (2025) [53]. Figure 4 is taken from Fig. 1 Scanlon and Herodotou. P 494 and Fig. 5 is taken from Fig. 1 Scanlon and Herodotou, p 494. The Conference link is at **https://csedu.scitevents.org** and the Proceedings are available at **www.scitepress.org**

Disclosure of Interests No competing interests.

References

1. Sharples, M., McAndrew, P., Weller, M., Ferguson, R., FitzGerald, E., Hirst, T., et al.: Innovating Pedagogy 2013. Open University, Milton Keynes (2013)
2. Curtis, V.: Online citizen science and the widening of academia: distributed engagement with research and knowledge production. In: Palgrave Studies in Alternative Education. Palgrave Macmillan, Cham, Switzerland (2018). https://doi.org/10.1007/978-3-319-77664-4
3. Herodotou, C., Scanlon, E., Sharples, M.: Methods of promoting learning and data quality in citizen and community science. Front. Clim. Sci. **3**.–2021 (2021). https://doi.org/10.3389/fclim.2021.614567
4. Nascimento, S., Cuccillato, E., Schade, S., Guimarães Pereira, A.: Citizen Engagement in Science and Policy-Making. Publications Office of the European Union, Luxembourg (2016)
5. Irwin, A.: Citizen Science. Routledge, London (1995)
6. Irwin, A.: Constructing the scientific citizen: science and democracy in the biosciences. Public Underst. Sci. **10**(2001), 1–18 (2001)
7. Nelkin, D.: The political impact of technical expertise. Soc. Stud. Sci. **5**, 37 (1975)
8. Raap, S, Knibbe, M and Horstman, K. Representing neighborhood health: exploring citizen science as a democratic force. Citiz. Sci.: Theory Pract., **9**(1): 12, 1–12. doi:10.5334/ (2024)
9. Chilvers, J., Kearns, M.: Remaking Participation: Science, Environment and Emergent Publics (2015)
10. Mirowski, P.: Social studies of science the future of open science. **48**(2) (2018)
11. Cavalier, D., Kennedy, E.: The Rightful Place of Science: Citizen Science. Arizona Consortium for Science, Policy and Outcomes, Tempe, AZ (2016)
12. Scanlon, E., Woods, W., Clow, D.: Informal participation in science in the UK: identification, location and mobility with iSpot. Educ. Technol. Soc. **17**(2), 58–71 (2014)
13. Herodotou, C., et al.: Online community and citizen science supports environmental science learning by young people. Comput. Educ. **184**, 104515 (2022). https://doi.org/10.1016/j.compedu.2022.104515
14. Herodotou, C., Kenny, I., Scanlon, E.: Democratising research practices through community citizen science. In: Proceedings of the 2024 International Conference on Information Technology for Social Good, pp. 68–75. Association for Computing Machinery, New York, NY, USA
15. Fortson, L., Crowston, K., Kloetzer, L., Ponti, M.: Artificial intelligence and the future of citizen science. Citiz. Sci.: Theory Pract. **9**(1) (2024)
16. Blake, C.T., Scanlon, E.: Enriching accounts of computer supported collaboration by using video data. ALT-J: Res. Learn. Technol. **11**(2), 5–13 (2003)
17. Nov, O., Arazy, O., Anderson, D.: Scientists@Home: what drives the quantity and quality of online citizen science participation? PLoS One. **9**(4), e90375 (2014). https://doi.org/10.1371/journal.pone.0090375
18. Kelling, S., Fink, D., La Sorte, F.A., Johnston, A., Bruns, N.E., Hochachka, W.M.: Taking a "big data" approach to data quality in a citizen science project. Ambio. **44**, 601–611 (2015). https://doi.org/10.1007/s13280-015-0710-4
19. Parrish, J.K., Burgess, H., Weltzin, J.F., Fortson, L., Wiggins, A., Simmons, B.: Exposing the science in citizen science: fitness to purpose and intentional design. Integr. Comp. Biol. **58**, 150–160 (2018). https://doi.org/10.1093/icb/icy03220
20. Arnstein, S.: A ladder of citizen participation. J. Am. Inst. Plan. Assoc. **35**(4), 216–224 (1969)

21. Haklay, M., Fraisl, D., Greshake, T.B., Hecker, S., et al.: Contours of citizen science: a vignette study. R. Soc. Open Sci. **8**, 202108 (2021). https://doi.org/10.1098/rsos.202108
22. Herodotou, C., Twiner, A., Scanlon, E., McLeod, K., Seale, J.: From participants to creators: considerations for community-led citizen science. In: Chinn, C., Tan, E., Chan, C., Kali, Y. (eds.) Proceedings of the 16th International Conference of the Learning Sciences-ICLS 2022, pp. 11–18. International Society of the Learning Sciences, Hiroshima, Japan (2022)
23. Sharma, N., Colucci-Gray, L., van der Wal, R., Siddharthan, A.: Consensus building in online citizen science. Proc. ACM. Hum. Comput. Interact. **6**(CSCW2), 434 (2022)
24. EC (European Commission): Citizen Science: Elevating Research and Innovation Through Societal Engagement. Publications Office of the European Union (2020)
25. Shaw, B.J., Draux, H., García Martín, M., Martin, J., Bieling, C.: Contributions of citizen science to landscape democracy: potentials and challenges of current approaches. Landsc. Res. **42**(8), 831–844 (2017)
26. Resnik, D.B.: Citizen scientists as human subjects: ethical issues. Citiz. Sci.: Theory Pract. **4**(1), 11–1–7 (2019). https://doi.org/10.5334/cstp.150
27. Heiss, R., Mathess, W.: Citizen science in the social sciences: a call for more evidence. GAIA-Ecol. Perspect. Sci. Soc. **26**(1), 22–26 (2017). https://doi.org/10.14512/gaia.26.1.7
28. Felt, U., et al.: Science in Society: Caring for Futures in Turbulent Times. ESF Policy Briefing 50. European Science Foundation, Strasbourg (2013)
29. Hurni, H., Wiesmann, U.: Transdisciplinarity in practice. experience from a concept-based research programme addressing global change and sustainable development. GAIA. **23**(3), 275–277 (2014)
30. Palmer, V.J., et al.: The participatory zeitgeist. Med. Humanit. **45**, 247–257 (2019). https://doi.org/10.1136/medhum-2017-011398
31. Roche, J., et al.: Citizen science and learning: challenges and opportunities. Front. Sociol. Sec. Sociol. Theory. **5** (2020). https://doi.org/10.3389/fsoc.2020.613814
32. Jenkins, L.L.: Using citizen science beyond teaching science content: a strategy for making science relevant to students' lives. Cult. Stud. Sci. Educ. **6**, 501–508 (2011). https://doi.org/10.1007/s11422-010-9304-4
33. Archer, L., Dawson, E., DeWitt, J., Seakins, A., Wong, B.: "Science capital": a conceptual, methodological, and empirical argument for extending bourdieusian notions of capital beyond the arts. J. Res. Sci.Teach. **52**, 922–948 (2015). https://doi.org/10.1002/tea.21227
34. Hall, D.M., Avellaneda-Lopez, P.M., Ficklin, D.L., Knouft, J.M., Lowry, C.: How to close the loop with citizen scientists to advance meaningful science. Sustain. Sci. **19**, 1527–1542 (2024)
35. Heywood, B.K.: Beyond data points and research contributions: the personal meaning and value associated with public participation in scientific research. Int. J. Sci. Educ., Part B. **6**(3), 239–262 (2016). https://doi.org/10.1080/21548455.2015.1659
36. Aristeidou, M., Scanlon, E., Sharples, M.: Profiles of engagement in online communities of citizen science participation. Comput. Hum. Behav. **74**, 246–256 (2017). https://doi.org/10.1016/j.chb.2017.04.044
37. Masters, K., Eun Young, O., Cox, J., Simmons, B., et al.: Science learning via participation in online citizen science. J. Sci. Commun. **15**(3) ISSN 1824-2049 (2016)
38. Scanlon, E., et al.: Beyond Prototypes: Enabling Innovation in Technology-Enhanced Learning (2013). https://doi.org/10.13140/2.1.1026.8163
39. Hoedoafia, M.A., Martell, M., Perko, T.: Evaluating citizen science projects: insights from radon research. Front. Environ. Sci. **12**, 1436283 (2024)
40. Ivanjko, F., et al.: Research on Citizen Science: Integration, Evaluation, and Challenges. https://eu-citizen.science/blog/2025/02/18/research-on-citizen-science-integration-evaluation-and-challenges/ (2025)

41. Phillips, T., Porticella, N., Constas, M., Bonney, R.: A framework for articulating and measuring individual learning outcomes from participation in citizen science. Citiz. Sci.: Theory Pract. **3**(2) (2018)
42. Aristeidou, M., Herodotou, C.: Online citizen science: a systematic review of effects on learning and scientific literacy. Citiz. Sci.: Theory Pract. **5**(1), 11–1–12 (2021). https://doi.org/10.5334/cstp.224
43. Silvertown J., et al.: Crowdsourcing the identification of organisms: a case-study of iSpot. ZooKeys **480**: 125–146. doi:10.3897/Strasse, Politische Analyse 1/2018 3 Citizen Science: Expertise, Demokratie und öffentliche Partizipation (2015)
44. Scanlon, E., Woods, W., Clow, D.: Informal participation in science in the UK: identification, location and mobility with iSpot. J. Educ. Technol. Soc. **17**(2), 58–71 (2014)
45. Sharples, M., et al.: Personal inquiry: orchestrating science investigations within and beyond the classroom. J. Learn. Sci. **24**(2), 308–341 (2015)
46. Aristeidou, M., Scanlon, E., Sharples, M.: Technologies for citizen inquiry: participatory research in online communities. In: Burns, D., Howard, J., Ospina, S.M. (eds.) The SAGE Handbook of Participatory Research and Inquiry, pp. 496–512. SAGE Publications, London (2021)
47. Herodotou, C., Aristeidou, M., Sharples, M., Scanlon, E.: Designing citizen science tools for learning: lessons learnt from the iterative development of nQuire. Res. Pract. Technol. Enhanc. Learn. **13**(4) (2018)
48. Scanlon, E., Herodotou, C.: Enhancing participation through inquiry learning and citizen science: science for everyone. In: Proceedings of the 16th International Conference on Computer Supported Education, vol. 1, pp. 557–563. SciTePress (2024)
49. Wang, F., Hannafin, M.J.: Design-based research and technology-enhanced learning environments. Educ. Technol. Res. Dev. **53**(4), 5–23 (2005)
50. Smalley, A., et al.: Forest 404: using a BBC drama series to explore the impact of nature's changing soundscapes on human wellbeing and behaviour. Glob. Environ. Chang. **74**, 102497 (2020)
51. Austen, K., Janssen, A., Wittmayer, J.M., Hölke, F.: The potential of citizen science to transform science: lessons for a sustainable future. People Nat. **6**, 435–445 (2024)
52. Bond, M., Khosravi, H., De Laat, M., et al.: A meta systematic review of artificial intelligence in higher education: a call for increased ethics, collaboration, and rigour. Int. J. Educ. Technol. High. Educ. **21**, 4 (2024). https://doi.org/10.1186/s41239-023-00436-z[57]
53. Scanlon, E., Herodotou, C.: Citizen science and democracy: participation with a purpose. In: Proceedings of the 17th International Conference on Computer Supported Education, vol. 1.: CSEDU; ISBN 978-989-758-746-7; ISSN 2184-5026, pp. 492–499. SciTePress (2025). https://doi.org/10.5220/0013350800003932

Reimagining Writing Pedagogy with ChatGPT: Expanding Pedagogical Possibilities and Learning Outcomes

Alexandra Jeikner(✉)

Deree-The American College of Greece, 6 Gravias Street, Aghia Paraskevi, Athens GR-153 42, Greece

ajeikner@acg.edu

Abstract. Following the initial upheaval caused in academia by the appearance of GenAI tools such as ChatGPT, literature demonstrates increasing support for the inclusion of GenAI tools into the teaching pedagogy. The arguments range from thereby preventing surreptitious usage to improving the learning environment to preparing students for their professional future. The literature – and personal experience – also demonstrates, however, lingering skepticism among educators of these tools, which often stems from lack of understanding of these tools and their application. This article presents three class activities where use of ChatGPT is integrated into the teaching pedagogy and Learning Outcomes include the acquisition of writing skills as well as ChatGPT usage skills; it also presents two assessments rubrics that evaluate both critical writing and engagement with AI. Since students' writing skills and subject knowledge as well as digital and AI literacy skills at the undergraduate level, in the specific academic context, is relatively low, activities were created, based on an active learning paradigm, which involve low to moderate ChatGPT-use, where the students retain a leading role. This is a position paper which bases its evidence on existing literature, not experimental results, since the activities have not been yet tested owing to departmental restrictions regarding use of GenAI tools.

Keyword: AI-Based Writing Activities

1 Introduction

ChatGPT, one of the most well-known generative AI (GenAI), made its appearance in late 2022 and initially this new technology seemed to be the mightiest foe of the academic world yet. A review of the literature at the time reveals mostly panic and disapproval, reflecting deep anxieties about the implications of this new tool. Educators worried that while academic shortcuts such as plagiarism or outsourcing to ghostwriting services had existed before, ChatGPT – cheap to use and seemingly undetectable would normalize a mindset that devalues the intellectual effort and ethical responsibility integral to education. Numerous academic institutions, reacting to the perceived new threat, implemented strict policies that banned all use; educators reported students for violations

C. Meinel et al. (Eds.): CSEDU 2025, CCIS 3148, pp. 183–212, 2027.
https://doi.org/10.1007/978-3-032-39103-2_10

of academic integrity if Gen-AI detectors reported that one or more paragraphs had been generated by AI; and while some students admitted using ChatGPT, others insisted that the writing was their own.

The following two years saw a gradual change of attitudes, with an increasing number of academics becoming less defensive and more curious. A significant body of research emerged which argues that GenAI tools should be used within the academic environment as they can help enhance learning. For instance, in a review of the literature published March 2024, Karataş et al. claim that we are now faced with "a landscape of cautious optimism tempered by skepticism" where "the need for AI in education" is clear (p. 19344). By 2025, bewilderment remains but it is tempered with curiosity and even praise. GenAI tools are increasingly presented as a valuable educational tool and authorized usage is permitted in many university courses. The literature shows that educators are increasingly including tools such as ChatGPT in their classrooms (for a review, see for instance Deng et al., 2025). At the same time, both traditional and AI-Powered plagiarism detection tools, such as Turnitin and Copyleaks respectively, are condemned as unreliable and counter-pedagogical owing to (false) accusations of cheating made on predictions instead of evidence (Reinhardt & Guartuche, 2024; Leong and Zhang, 2025); furthermore, the detection algorithms cause further concern since linguistic patterns of EFL-students may be misclassified as AI-generated (Deans et al., 2024; Raqif et al., 2025). False accusations can in fact lead to legal challenges (Hanafi et al., 2025; Raqif et al., 2025).

Yet, individual instructors and sometimes whole departments continue to prohibit all use. The main reasons, besides lack of familiarity and lack of "innovation consciousness: a conscious awareness of new technologies" (Nissim & Simon, 2025, p. 383, referring to Olugbara et al. 2020), usually involve concerns about plagiarism and security as well as the impact on content accuracy, critical thinking and academic integrity (for a review, see for instance Deng et al., 2025).

This article is based on personal experience in the Writing Program (WP) of a private undergraduate educational institution in S. Europe, where the language of instruction is English. While the educational institution overall permits and even encourages authorized use, in the WP, such use is discouraged. The rationale is that students should first develop their own writing skills, such as the drafting of thesis statements or the structuring of paragraphs, before being asked to request, evaluate and use GenAI output as well as that if students are taught to rely on GenAI tools for their writing, very soon writing classes will no longer be needed. While the author of this paper understands this reasoning and even agrees to some extent, they support that such attitudes toward GenAI are unrealistic and pedagogically counterproductive. Experience confirms what the literature demonstrates. For one, students in higher education (HE) institutions struggle to draft well-organized texts, supported by well-researched and effectively integrated sources, in precise and academically appropriate language. Second, students for whom English is a foreign language (EFL-students) may be even more challenged when asked to produce academic writing. Limited language proficiency means that they often have their first language (L1) in mind when writing essays in a second language (L2). This not only results in low linguistic precision and wordy sentences that obscure meaning, but also means that significant effort is invested in language instead of content (Chung &

Ahn, 2021; Lee & Briggs, 2020; Kaur & Newell, 2024). This in turn increases anxiety and reduces self-confidence (Baek et al., 2024). Personal experience has also shown that even when academic policy prohibits it, both native and non-native speakers often turn to GenAI tools. The literature confirms this is a global phenomenon, since access, time and cost-efficiency of GenAI tools outweigh concerns about output quality or academic integrity.

This paper argues that since it is our responsibility as educators not only to teach students critical thinking but also prepare them for their professional life, it is also our responsibility to help students use AI-tools. Just as once educational institutions "helped students acquire basic technological proficiency", they now need to promote "more advanced digital competence" (Kohnke et al., 2023, p. 546). A few decades ago, members of Generation X (born approximately 1965–1980), who grew up without computers and the internet, were labelled digital immigrants who needed to be taught to use these technologies. In contrast, members of Generation Y, otherwise known as Millennials (born approximately between 1981–1996), which grew up with computers and access to the internet, were called digital natives and seen to possess a kind of innate digital literacy. Today, members of Generation Z (born approximately 1997 to 2010) are considered to be even more digitally literate, and it is tempting to assume that this knowledge extends to GenAI. However, just as it was not true that Generation Y members possessed innate digital literacy, so it is not true that Generation Z members possess innate GenAI literacy. They are, just as members of the Generation X were digital immigrants, GenAI immigrants. As such, they need to be taught effective, safe and ethical GenAI use before they enter the workforce.

2 Literature Review

2.1 GenAI Tools in Higher Education

Nloy et al. (2024), reviewing several studies, identify ChatGPT as the choice of GenAI tools owing to its "high accessibility, being a free tool" and "easily accessible globally" as well as its user-friendly interface (p. 4). ChatGPT is described as a valuable tool as it "entails an evolution of current educational practices where information is increasingly available to users, not only in a query but also in a synthesised form, ready for use" (García-López et al., 2025, p. 3). Access-disparity concerns mostly students from the lowest income group (Baek et al., 2024).

It should be noted that while "[m]ost reviews provide comprehensive analyses of the technology's implications for education" and "contribute to a broader understanding of ChatGPT in education" (Deng et al., 2025, p. 5, referring to Chen et al., 2024; Grassini, 2023; Lo, 2024), they not necessarily establish causality and might not offer sufficient insight into "the *actual* impact of ChatGPT on student learning" (Deng et al., 2025, p. 5, italics in the original). This is said to concern particularly cross-sectional studies that are said to present inaccurate correlations in contrast to experimental studies (Deng et al., 2025). Jin et al. (2025) also note that "the small body of existing research on GenAI in academic writing has various limitations" as studies focus mostly on the benefits of the use of GenAI tools as well as that studies do not take into account that groups from different disciplines, using the tools for different purposes, may have different perceptions as well as that most studies focus on participants from "a single cultural context" (p.2). Overall, an examination of a wide range of recent literature reviews indicates that Gen AI tools are considered, despite being associated with several challenges, as offering significant benefits for the educational environment (Bittle & El-Gayar, 2025).

Concerning challenges, these range from data security, accuracy and bias, copyright and ownership, academic integrity and ownership, as well as individuality and critical thinking. For one, especially the use of free tools, such as ChatGPT, involve issues of data privacy and security. In a review of the literature, García-López et al. (2025) explain that an ethical challenge of using ChatGPT in education is that sensitive information of students can be compromised (García-López et al., 2025). Other important challenges involve content bias, weak reliability and accuracy as well as (un)traceability (Cong-Lem et al., 2025; García-López et al., 2025). ChatGPT, with its ability to provide answers quickly, is said to pose risks to the development of critical thinking, problem-solving skills as well as research skills since students might be tempted to prefer convenience to exploration and reflection (Li, 2025). This compounds the challenge posed owing to the superficial, unreliable and biased content ChatGPT may produce (Cong-Lem et al., 2025). ChatGPT has been shown to provide not only superficial answers (Kovari, 2025; Cong-Lem et al., 2025) but also to generate for instance fake references, also referred to as hallucinations, as well as to provide inaccurate answers (in Cong-Lem et al., 2025). While sources show that newer versions have improved, the output provided is still not always accurate (Malfatti, 2025). It should be noted that Deng et al. (2025), having reviewed existing literature, warn that insufficient data exists whether ChatGPT indeed enhances higher-order thinking skills or leads to higher quality, suggesting for instance that self-appraisal might not be a reliable indicator. Another problem identified is that tools such as ChatGPT can perpetuate biases given that it is not necessarily trained on data that includes perspectives of "racial, gender, and socioeconomically diverse communities" (in García-López et al., 2025). When one considers that ChatGPT may encourage lack of critical engagement, the argument that students may come across and perpetuate misinformation (Deng et al., 2025; Li, 2025) seems highly reasonable. One more, significant, challenge concerns "authenticity and academic integrity" (Li, 2025). While higher education institutions emphasize the need for academic originality and respect of intellectual ownership, they cannot prevent students from turning to ChatGPT for assistance (see for instance Barus et al., 2025; Holland and Ciachir, 2024). ChatGPT content can be so refined and personalized that it cannot be distinguished from student-produced content (see Cong-Lem et al., 2025; Evangelista, 2025; Weber-Wulff et al., in Kartelj et al., 2025).

Nonetheless, the literature shows that the inclusion of GenAI tools in the learning environment offers educators and learners significant opportunities. A significant body of research proposes that ChatGPT can enhance the learning environment (Garcia-Lopez, 2025). For educators, for instance, ChatGPT can help develop "lesson plans and instructional materials tailored to different learning styles, thereby promoting differentiated instruction as well as "customise lessons and objectives while fostering interactive learning through simulations" (in Nissim & Simon, 2025, p. 382–83) and offer suggestions for improving teaching practices (see for instance Kayalı et al., 2023).

For students, ChatGPT is also identified as offering several pedagogical benefits. Some of its advantages range from "facilitating learning" and "creating rich learning environments" (for a review of the literature, see for instance Kayalı et al., 2023, p.21 & p. 27). Chatbots such as ChatGPT can be used in the classroom as an educational and learning tool to increase students' efficiency in task-completion of the writing process, by helping improve language and coherence, by providing textual and subject explanations as well as reference material, even by creating outlines (Albadarin et al., 2023; Huang and Tan, 2023; Kohnke et al., 2023; Prananta et al., 2023; You, 2024). Its ever-present availability also means that students can "learn at their own pace, ask questions at their convenience, and navigate topics without undue pressure" (Li, 2025, p. 4). According to review of the literature conducted by Holland and Ciachir (2024), the albeit few – studies suggest an overall positive attitude among students regarding the usefulness of ChatGPT. Students appreciate that ChatGPT provides them with answers and material quickly, removing the need for what is considered time-consuming internet-search (Holland & Ciachir, 2025). They view it as helping them save time by completing tasks they consider as less important, such as summarizing academic articles and thereby giving them time to focus thoroughly on academic tasks they consider more important (Holland & Ciachir, 2025). Additionally, ChatGPT appears to be considered a "co-creator" since students view it as a tool that can aid them in generating ideas for their writing (Holland & Ciachir, 2025, p. 487). Although the possibility exists that the novelty of ChatGPT plays a role, studies suggest that ChatGPT can also foster motivation (Deng et al., 2025). This can be explained through the perception of students that ChatGPT can serve as a "personal academic tutor" since it can help students evaluate the quality of an idea or of their work and overcome a "brain freeze" (Holland & Ciachir, 2025, p. 487, italics in the original), without the need for a human educator. However, it has been noted that the inclusion of ChatGPT may also enhance demotivation, with some students feeling that if ChatGPT is used, then grades no longer reflect hard academic work (Holland & Ciachir, 2025).

ChatGPT is also identified as contributing to critical engagement. Studies show that educators can employ GenAI tools to engage students in reflective writing and encourage critical thinking (Albadarin et al., 2023; Graefen & Fazel, 2024; Zhao et al., 2023). For instance, students can "review the changes made by ChatGPT and decide whether to accept or reject them based on their own judgment" (Barrot, 2023, p. 4). Of interest for writing classes such as ours, which are based on the flipped-classroom method, are findings that ChatGPT can help students improve student performance and attitudes toward learning and self-confidence (Li, 2023). In a review of empirical studies, Lo et al. (2024) note that ChatGPT was identified as mostly contributing to improved writing performance and permitting "to scaffold the writing process" (p.12). Since ChatGPT involves interactive conversations, it "foster[s] deeper understanding and empower[s] students to take ownership of their learning journey" (in Li, 2025, p. 5); since these conversations may also take place outside the classroom setting, ChatGPT is said to encourage further exploration and enhance participation (in Li, 2025,; Rahman & Watanobe, 2023 and Sullivan et al., 2023; Dergaa et al., 2023; Perera & Lankathilaka, 2023; Ray, 2023). ChatGPT is even said to be a knowledge acquisition partner, encouraging students to question assumptions, challenge conventions, and explore new ideas. This cultivates the essence of critical thinking the ability to analyze, synthesize, and evaluate information from multifaceted perspectives (in Li, 2025). For sure, ChatGPT is changing the educational landscape by offering personalized learning experiences as well as interactive engagement and dialogue instead of the traditional information delivery flow instructor-to-student (Bittle & El-Gayar, 2025; Li, 2025).

The literature shows that GenAI tools can be of particular assistance to EFL students. Deng et al. (2025) conclude that a review of studies indicates that the use of ChatGPT is particularly pronounced in language education and claim that this "suggests that this field might be particularly well-suited for ChatGPT integration" (p. 17). There is consensus that GenAI tools should become part of the teaching process in L2 learning (for a systematic review of studies, see Karataş et al., 2024; Yang & Li, 2024). GenAI tools such as ChatGPT are said to "revolutionize language pedagogy" through the learner-centered nature (Karataş et al., 2024, p. 19355). Even before the advent of GenAI tools, the use of technology in the classroom was described as helping students (Song & Song, 2023). For instance, even simple online machine translations (MT), such as Google Translate (GT), can help improve linguistic accuracy and increase student satisfaction within the higher education (HE) environment (Chung & Ahn, 2021; Lee & Briggs, 2020). Now, ChatGPT is said to help "break […] down geographical […] barriers" by allowing students to translate content into their native language (Li, 2025, p. 7). EFL-learners can use ChatGPT to identify and correct language errors (Li, 2025). ChatGPT can also help "students organize their thoughts more clearly and communicate them more effectively, of particular benefit for EFL-students, and that this "support reduces cognitive strain, enabling students to concentrate more on the substance of their writing rather than on the linguistic complexities" (in García-López et al., 2025, p. 8). They offer new and more effective ways to "address the challenges associated with developing writing proficiency through traditional training methods" by assisting in the development and internalization of academic writing skills (Song & Song, 2023, p.2). For instance, chatbots such as ChatGPT can be used to acquaint students with differences between academic and casual writing (Yan, 2023, in You, 2024), translate explanations into the L1-language and create vocabulary notes (Kohnke et al., 2023). Even prompt writing can enhance "the ability to effectively express ideas and communicate intentions" (Michalon & Camacho-Zuñiga, 2023, in You, 2024, p. 2). Interestingly, ChatGPT instruction is overall claimed to benefit EFL students more than traditional instruction (Song & Song, 2023; Vera, 2023) and to be considered by students as improving "motivation and learning engagement" (Karataş et al., 2024, p. 19353). Lo et al. (2024) point out that some studies have shown that students are dissatisfied with ChatGPT for being inaccurate and challenging owing to prompt writing issues but also that "a teacher-mediated writing class" offers more opportunities for interaction" (p. 13). Yet, other studies have shown that students appreciate the personalized responses as well as the instant and individualized feedback which in turn makes the learning experience more "meaningful and effective" (Karataş et al., 2024, p. 19358). Teng's study (2024) shows that students viewed feedback provided by ChatGPT as more substantial than their educators'. Its ever-present accessibility furthermore provides "unlimited opportunities" for practice (Yang & Li, 2024, p. 8). Some studies claim it helps "learners to acquire […] speaking, listening, reading, and writing [skills]" and improve "grammar accuracy, vocabulary size, and formulaic sequence"

(Hong, 2023, in Zhao et al., 2023). Other studies limit its value to "writing and grammar skills", but not speaking or listening (Karataş et al., 2024).

We argue that the literature shows that for classes that involve writing, ChatGPT can clearly be helpful for both L1 and L2 writers, when used as a practice platform and writing assistant tool (Barrot, 2023; Karataş et al., 2024; You, 2024). Instead of checking their writing for linguistic errors, students have time to invest in content creation (You, 2024). It is important though to ensure that these technologies are adapted to the needs of a particular classroom and a particular student body; educators also need to be equipped with the necessary skills to evaluate the safety issues as well as legal and ethical implications of incorporating GenAI tools into the teaching pedagogy.

2.2 Best Practices for Integrating GenAI Tools in EFL Writing Classes

The need for thorough understanding of GenAI tools and careful implementation into the classroom becomes evident when reviewing the literature. It is vital for educators to "adopt innovative pedagogical practices" and use "a technology-integrated teaching approach" (Song & Song, 2023, p. 12). Higher education institutions need to replace the emphasis on AI detection and punishment with the inclusion of ethical AI usage in the teaching pedagogy (Raqif et al., 2025). As Bittle and El-Gayar stress, "ethical guidelines and best practices for GenAI use in education must be developed and rigorously evaluated in real-world settings" (p. 10). Both educators and students need to be "provided with the necessary resources to critically assess and question these technologies, maximizing their benefits while mitigating risks" (Garcia-Lopez, 2025, p. 8). Educators furthermore need to be able to evaluate the usefulness and the ethical implications in practice (in Garcia-Lopez, 2025). If ChatGPT is to be used as a writing assistant, educators need to be trained in effective and responsible use (Baek et al., 2024). Since studies have shown that when educators lack AI-skills, the students' learning experience is negatively impacted, educators need "to attain a high level of proficiency in incorporating chatbots, such as ChatGPT, into their classrooms to create inventive, well-structured, and captivating learning strategies" (Albadarin et al., 2023). ChatGPT may have evolved considerably the last two years, but it is still prone to inaccuracies and biases. It is therefore vital for educators to ensure that students do not rely on it for content creation and instead engage critically with the content produced (Li, 2025). This means that educators must carefully consider the strategies employed and activities designed. Reviewing the literature on the collaboration between educators and ChatGPT in language education, Jeon and Lee (2023) stress that benefits to learning depend on the educators' decisions on how to integrate GenAI tools into the classroom, rather than the specific tool alone. Graefen & Fazal (2024) identify the need for "case-based advice" on the usage of GenAI (p. 49). Overall, educators need to understand both the role of GenAI tools and their own in the classroom (Jeon & Lee, 2023).

To begin with, educators need to understand the differences in and levels of usage of GenAI tools within the specific teaching context so that these complement their pedagogical expertise. Different suggestions exist regarding the extent of using a Gen AI tool (Paulsen, 2024; Forbes and Brandauer, 2023). Overall, the choice requires educators to use their pedagogical expertise to a) effectively integrate ChatGPT into their teaching, b) teach the students to be active and effective "investigators" and not "passive recipients" and c) teach students ethical use (Jeon & Lee, 2023, p. 15885–6). One example of usage-extent is choosing between 'Closed' when instructors deem these tools as not compatible with learning outcomes; 'Restricted' which means it can be used for specific tasks; 'Conditional', implying that it should not be used for specific tasks; 'Open', with usage permitted as the student chooses (Forbes and Brandauer, 2023). A similar observation is made by Paulson (2024), who differentiates different usage-levels: "1) Limited or Guided, 2) Measured, and 3) Integrated". Closely related to the usage-extent is the role that ChatGPT is given. One suggestion is that ChatGPT can have four roles within the classroom: "interlocutor, content provider, teaching assistant, and evaluator"; within each role, ChatGPT can have a variety of functions (Jeon and Lee, 2023, p. 15881). Another suggestion is that GenAI tools are employed as "1) idea or design aid, 2) critical thinking or discussion partner, 3) editing or feedback partner, 4) research aid, 5) personal learning support, or 6) group work support" ((Paulsen, 2024).

The level and usage extent selected depend on the learning outcomes of the respective task, the students' familiarity with the topic, and their AI literacy skills (Paulsen, 2024). For instance, limited use is more appropriate when "learning outcomes primarily emphasize human capabilities", while low AI literacy skills and limited subject knowledge mean guidance and scaffolding are required; a measured use is appropriate for students with intermediate AI literacy skills and some familiarity with the subject so that they can interact with ChatGPT as a "conversation partner" (Paulsen, 2024). Furthermore, limited or guided use is recommended when assessment is "AI-vulnerable" and student output can easily be replaced with AI output, while the measured use is recommended when assessment is "AI-tenable" and students cannot "shortcut" their learning (Paulsen, 2024).

Clear communication of expectations and policies is vital. As Huang and Tan (2023) point out, GenAI tools do not "inherently increase the risk of plagiarism" (p. 1151). However, the integration of ChatGPT into the teaching environment can encourage and facilitate academic dishonesty (Kovari, 2025). Students need to know how and how not to use GenAI tools. Educators need to provide guidelines and set rules regarding the permitted usage (Albadarin et al., 2023; Bittle and El-Gayar, 2025). Breaches of academic integrity can also be mitigated if students are taught to appropriately use and attribute AI-produced output (Barrot, 2023). Educators need to communicate the extent and manner to which students should and should not employ ChatGPT (Yang & Li, 2024; You, 2024; Zhao et al., 2023) so that students can overcome fear of having breached academic integrity principles (in Graefen & Fazal, 2024). They need to create an atmosphere that encourages students to indicate ChatGPT-output instead of hiding it (Jeon & Lee, 2023). Educators also need to explain the consequences of breaching academic integrity (in Graefen & Fazal, 2024).

The implementation of assignments that involve different tasks can help mitigate attempts at cheating as well as discourage overreliance on GenAI tools and encourage critical engagement. When an assignment is "AI-vulnerable", meaning that usage cannot be prevented or detected, limited usage is considered more appropriate (Paulsen, 2024). The existing research indicates that educators need to create activities that ensure that students remain the authors of the work produced and ChatGPT the assistant or tutor (Yang & Li, 2024). Educators can create tasks where ChatGPT is a "supportive tool" so that cognitive engagement is not undermined (Albadarin et al., 2023). Assignments should promote higher-order thinking, creativity and problem-solving skills to maintain academic integrity and also protect the students' learning experience (Bittle and El-Gayar, 2025). Assessments can include oral presentations and the submission of a portfolio that includes material produced over a specific time period (Bittle and El-Gayar, 2025; Kovari, 2025). Cheating can be discouraged and critical engagement encouraged by designing tasks with specific instructions for prompt phrasing that lead to desired output (Barrot, 2023; Bozkurt & Sharma, 2023; Jeon and Lee, 2023; Kayalı et al., 2023; Rowland, 2023; Yang & Li, Y2024).

Educators must also clearly convey the rationale for permitting, restricting, or requiring GenAI use (Sharpe, 2024). While we came across assignments where ChatGPT is given a leading role, we argue that in undergraduate courses where students lack subject knowledge and have limited AI literacy skills, ChatGPT should have only a supplemental role. This can prevent overreliance (Albadarin et al., 2023; Barrot, 2023; Jeon and Lee, 2023; Karataş et al., 2024; Song & Song, 2023). A task for instance could require students to write their own material and then use ChatGPT as an editing tool (Barrot, 2023).

Instructors also need to emphasize that even if ChatGPT presents its output as definitive, this output should be critically evaluated and not necessarily accepted (Albadarin et al., 2023; Graefen & Fazal, 2024; Kayalı et al., 2023; Kohnke et al., 2023; Yang & Li, 2024). Given that (undergraduate) students' subject knowledge might be limited, this is a challenging task. Tasks therefore should also require educators to maintain oversight over content generated (Li, 2025; Huang & Tan, 2023).

Furthermore, even if GenAI usage is involved, tasks must encourage relationships between students and educators. Studies confirm the importance of "human interaction and collaboration" (Albadarin et al., 2023). Students in fact do not appreciate the lack of "human touch" of "ChatGPT's responses" (Teng, 2024, p. 9). The literature indicates that educators need to find a way "that incorporates both technology and human interaction" (Karataş et al., 2024, p. 19357). This can be done by using ChatGPT "in group projects and peer review sessions, where students refine their drafts with AI-generated feedback before engaging in peer discussion" (Teng, 2024, p. 9).

Educators furthermore need to create assessment methods that evaluate student and machine input and communicate these beforehand to students. The objective should be to develop and assess both disciplinary knowledge and AI-usage competence (Rowland, 2023). Different proposals exist, such as the writing continuum model which assesses human involvement and use of AI on a one-dimensional continuum, ranging from no AI-assistance over to different levels of usage such as proofreading and writing-assistant, up to entirely AI-generated (Rowland, 2023). The "stages of writing + continuum model" is more nuanced, assessing the extent to which GenAI tools were used within each writing stage (Rowland, 2023). Students should be informed of the assessment methods (Sharpe, 2024).

Lastly, educators need to explain that copyright and privacy laws do not apply when GenAI tools are used, which means that device data, usage data, log data as well as content may be stored (Kayalı et al., 2023; You, 2024).

3 Activities Explained

3.1 Learning Outcomes and Learning Objectives (LOs)

This manuscript responds to recent studies that emphasize the need for educators to redefine their role by including GenAI technology in their pedagogical approach as well as to contribute to the creation of a community where experiences and case-based activities are shared (Kasneci, in Graefen & Fazal, 2024). We acknowledge that (writing) courses should teach and promote critical writing, but also that it is vital to integrate GenAI tools into the teaching process. We fear that on the one hand, a refusal to do so only perpetuates surreptitious usage and that on the other, adamant support of the traditional college essay and traditional assessment practices will result in writing courses writing themselves out of existence and failing to prepare students for a future with GenAI integrated into the academic, work and personal environment.

Before deciding on the design of activities, it is important to be aware of desired learning outcomes, which refer to the overall knowledge, skills and abilities students are expected to acquire in a class. Learning outcomes in our case are predetermined by our course syllabus. However, specific learning objectives (LOs) can be set for specific classes and activities, which specify the knowledge and skills a specific lesson should help develop. Effective technology-integration into teaching has been shown to involve the creation of assignments which include the use of this technology in the LOs. We first consulted a revised version of Bloom's taxonomy (1999) which expresses educational outcomes, moving from factual acknowledge to procedural and then meta-cognitive knowledge (Fig. 1). Then, we consulted the many lists of action verbs available to use to define the intended LOs in each activity (Fig. 2).

We also consulted a more recent revision of Bloom's taxonomy that considers AI capabilities to align course activities to revised LOs that account for GenAI capabilities (Fig. 3). The aim was to identify the AI capabilities at each stage and combine them with the human skills at the respective stage. So, for instance, in two of the suggested activities, at the stages of understanding and application, students are asked to apply their understanding of ethical considerations of academic integrity to the application of prompt writing, while ChatGPT at this stage can offer a translation.

3.2 Rationale for the Proposed Activities

We are aware that several such activities already exist, but we feel that given the skepticism that persists among faculty regarding the usefulness of incorporating GenAI tools into the classroom pedagogy, need exists for the provision of a variety of very specific assignments. Research suggests for instance that educators fear that students will misuse GenAI tools, by cheating or becoming dependent on it; they also fear that they themselves might misuse ChatGPT and create inappropriate educational material since the content generated could be inaccurate, biased or plagiarized; consequently, they are more hesitant to employ GenAI tools (Verano-Tacoronte et al., 2025). By presenting three exercises that contain very specific guidelines, this manuscript helps demonstrate ways of maintaining academic integrity and limiting the possibility that ChatGPT produces

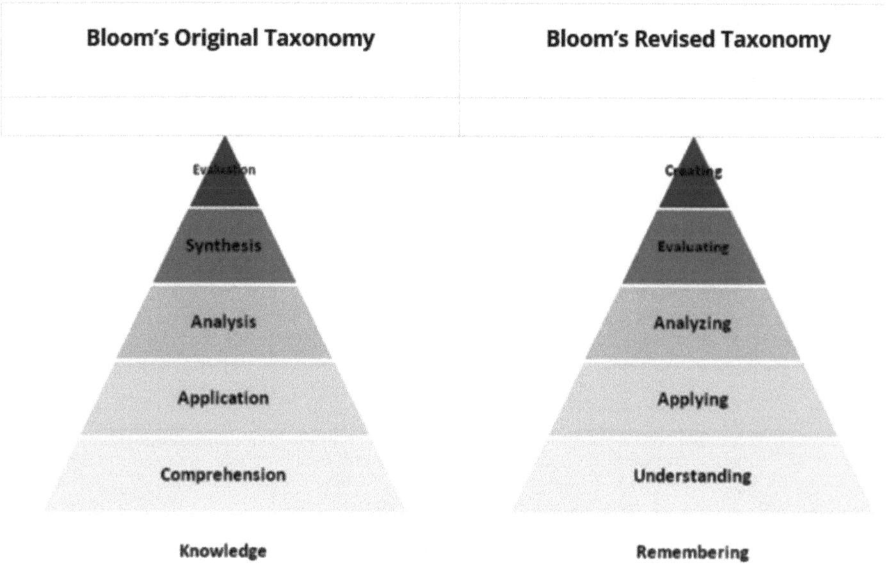

Fig. 1. Shank, n.d.

inaccurate or biased content as well as encouraging human interaction and critical reflection. Furthermore, we hope to demonstrate how Learning Outcomes, reflecting Bloom's Taxonomy, can be achieved despite, or rather through, the inclusion of ChatGPT in the learning process.

This manuscript presents three AI-based activities for a first year HE writing course, where the language of instruction is for most students L2, two designed solely by the author and one by a colleague and the author. Two activities are phrased for students, one for instructors. The first and the last are designed for both L1 and L2 students, while the second is designed for L2 students specifically. While the first and the second activity instruct students on how to write their own prompt, the third activity presents them with a pre-written prompt. This is meant to demonstrate different ways of acquainting students with the importance of prompt writing for ensuring privacy of data and ethical usage.

The activities demonstrate how a GenAI tool such as ChatGPT can be used to acquaint students with effective but also ethical use. The activities also ensure human collaboration and critical thinking. This manuscript further provides an assessment-example that evaluates the writing process, the use of AI, and the students' critical engagement. The structure of the activity, starting with in-class work and then/or peer work, followed by individual work, and concluding with a brief class discussion where students share experiences should encourage engagement and concentration. The first part, consisting of theory, is short; the second requires students to collaboratively immerse themselves in the learning, thereby reducing anxiety; the third part should allow students to share experiences and thereby see their own learning experiences in context.

Remembering	Understanding	Applying	Analysing	Evaluating	Creating
acquire	arrange	apply	analyse	appraise	calculate
choose	categorize	calculate	appraise	argue	change
collect	change	change	break down	assess	combine
complete	chart compile	choose	classify	compare	compose
copy	conclude	classify	combine	conclude	constitute
define	convert	compute	compare	contrast	create
describe	defend	conduct	contrast	critique	derive
detect	determine	construct	criticize	decide	devise
distinguish	diagram	demonstrate	deduce	discriminate	discover
duplicate	differentiate	develop	defend	interpret	document
find	document edit	discover	detect	judge	generalize
identify	estimate	employ	differentiate	justify	modify
indicate	explain	generalize	distinguish	recommend	originate
isolate	extrapolate	manipulate	evaluate	relate	plan
label	formulate	modify	formulate	standardize	produce
list	generalize	operate	generate	validate	rearrange
mark	give example	organize	illustrate		relate
match	illustrate	predict	infer		revise
name order	interpret	prepare	outline		signify
outline place	organize	produce	paraphrase		specify
recall recognize	paraphrase	relate	plan		synthesize
reproduce select	predict	restructure	relate		tell
state underline	prepare	show	save		write
	relate	solve transfer	separate		
	summarize	use	shorten		
	update		structure		
			subdivide		

Fig. 2. Imperial, n.d.

3.3 Theoretical Context of the Proposed Activities

These activities have not been implemented in the classroom since for the time being, our department discourages all use of GenAI tools. They are based on the review of existing literature presented before which provides evidence for the need to design and implement Gen-AI based educational technologies in HE. They were inspired by resources and guidelines offered for instance by Alby (n.d.), Atlas (2023), Gibson (n.d.), Hernandez (2024), Rowland (2023); Schaper (2024), Wang et al. (2024). Similarly, material provided by universities such as NC State University (n.d.) and Brandeis University as well as the Teaching and Learning site of Conestoga, for instance by Sharpe (2024) and Paulson (2024), was of immense value.

We designed the activities using the active learning paradigm and the concept of learning and writing as a process as our theoretical framework. Our writing courses are already based on the active learning paradigm, where flipped classroom practices, which engage students actively through scaffolding activities completed both in class and at home, have been part of the course design for years. Learning and writing are approached in these courses as a process which means that instead of focusing only on the end product, we require students to produce prewriting and a first draft before the final version.

Cao & Dede's proposal (2023), based on Wegerif's dialogic theory, offered further theoretical context that we considered as echoing the concept that within the flipped

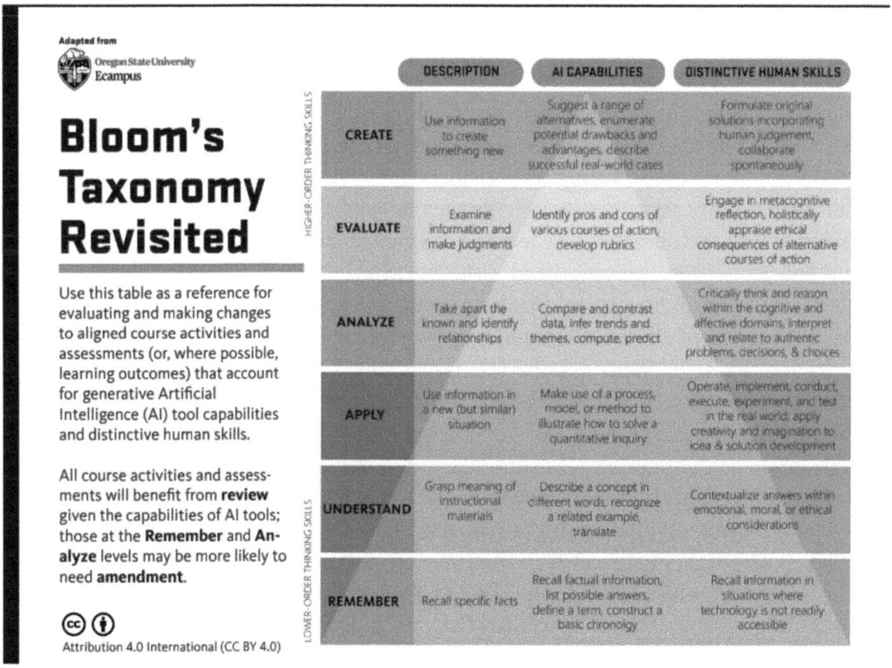

Fig. 3. Artificial Intelligence Tools (CC BY 4.0), Oregon State University

classroom, educators can shift their role to facilitators instead of the traditional instructor imparting information in a one-directional manner. Wegerif (2019) posits that in the age of the internet, which disrupts the traditional approach to education as dependent on the concept of one true reality, education should introduce students to an environment of multiple perspectives and uncertainties and encourage them to engage in dialogue. Cao and Dede (2023) propose to approach teaching and learning as a dialogic practice and employing GenAI-tools as "dialogue partner" rather than output-provider (p.7). To note, however, is that given our particular student body – with its limited content knowledge and limited digital and AI literacy skills as well as limited exposure to critical engagement – we decided to assign ChatGPT only limited and very specific dialoguing opportunities. While ChatGPT can indeed engage in very engaging dialogue, the student body we have in mind cannot be expected to evaluate whether the content provided is accurate and unbiased.

Ethan Mollick's concept of Co-Intelligence (2024) helped contextualize GenAI within the – possibly very near – future classroom. Mollick (2024) posits that we should engage with AI as a creative partner, a co-worker, co-teacher and coach since the development of Large Language Models (LLMs) like ChatGPT means that we have created an artificial intelligence that can augment human abilities. For that to happen, according to Mollick (2024), we need to use AI in our activities, give it a specific role, maintain oversight, and be prepared for AI to improve rapidly. We consider that Mollick is very correct in claiming that ChatGPT can be used to augment human capabilities. While for the time being we do not consider ChatGPT to be reliable enough to be considered a creative partner – or at least not by our student body with its specific characteristics outlined above – we agree that we, as educators, need to be prepared for rapid leaps of improvement in AI capabilities. As such, we propose conservative use of ChatGPT in the classroom, giving it a specific role mostly as coach. This will acquaint students with the technology and also help them see how this tool can be used to augment their writing abilities without, however, losing ownership of their work.

The first activity addresses the challenges L1 and L2 students face when it comes to understanding and summarizing a text. Experience shows that this task is considered challenging for reasons ranging from difficulty concentrating on a long or demanding text to difficulty in understanding; lack of awareness regarding proper quoting and citing techniques; difficulty in distinguishing important from unimportant information; difficulty in organizing ideas in coherent paragraphs. The task requires students to ask ChatGPT for a translation of a short article into L2, if English is not their native language, or a simplified but exact paraphrased version in English. Here, ChatGPT is initially used as a translation or paraphrase tool. After that, the students will use ChatGPT as an editing and lastly as a feedback tool. The students will not be required to rate the translation or the feedback initially; they will evaluate the ChatGPT-output (feedback provided and suggestions offered) only after receiving specific guidelines.

The second activity addresses the challenges that L2 students, face in terms of transitions and wordiness. The task requires students to ask ChatGPT to translate an introduction for an essay written in L1 to L2 and then use it as a language assistant to improve transitions and reduce wordiness. In other words, they will use ChatGPT as a translation tool, not unlike GT, as well as an editing and feedback partner. The students will not be required to rate the translation provided; rather, the translation step was selected for the mere reason that L2 students may find it difficult to get the ideas they have in their native language on paper in the English language. They will evaluate the ChatGPT-output (its translation from L1 to L2) only after receiving specific guidelines.

The third activity addresses the difficulties L1 and L2 students have with effectively integrating sources into their writing. This is a crucial skill as it enhances the quality and credibility of students' work. However, integrating sources into academic writing requires both technical skills, such as for citations and paraphrasing, as well as critical thinking, such as for evaluating sources and connecting ideas. This activity is designed to address these concerns using ChatGPT but also to guide students to use ChatGPT as a supplementary tool, focusing on ethical usage and critical evaluation of AI-generated content.

These activities are considered appropriate for several reasons. First, they require development according to specific guidelines, including ChatGPT-use. Having students engage with prompt-writing, also obliges them to review the assignment and the evaluation criteria. Second, the tasks do not require students to develop their own arguments, which means they are not encouraged to turn to ChatGPT for content that requires critical thinking. Educators thereby do not oblige students to upload their individualized intellectual property to a platform which does not guarantee copyright and privacy laws. Third, the three tasks ask are appropriate for collaborative work and peer review which, as the literature has shown, is important for maintaining a healthy relationship between students and machine learning. Since students are asked to document each step of the writing process, these activities also emphasize the importance of ethical usage. Students are given clear guidelines on how to identify material written by ChatGPT by submitting screenshots of the chats and their use of this output. Critical reflection is encouraged through tasks that involve collaboration in evaluating ChatGPT output and reflecting on the experience. Educators need to review material submitted to Blackboard (Bb) Portfolio – the Learning Management System used in our HE institution after every class. Thereby, they maintain oversight and guide students when need be.

3.4 Rationale for Choice of ChatGPT and Access Considerations

In these activities, the use of a computer/laptop and access to the internet are required. Students are also required to upload personal output to an external AI-platform such as ChatGPT where privacy is not ensured.

Concerning issues of access: The rationale is that almost all students have access to a smartphone. Should this not be the case, the activities can be done in a computer lab. Since the activities will be completed on campus, students will have internet access through the free college wi-fi. None of the activities require students to use ChatGPT at home; in fact, students will be instructed to limit their use of ChatGPT to within the classroom and only for the tasks specified.

Concerning the choice of GenAI tool: ChatGPT was selected as the most useful tool. We draw attention to the fact that not every institution has a private and free AI-platform where privacy is ensured. The rationale for our choice is that ChatGPT has been identified in the literature as a popular tool among students and a substantial number of studies have used ChatGPT. We decided against using more than one GenAI tool to help students become more familiar with the one tool; furthermore, we took into consideration potential lack of familiarity with GenAI tools among educators and arising reluctance to use it.

Concerning required engagement with ChatGPT: Students do not have the option of opting out of these activities without incurring a grade penalty. The rationale is that since the literature indicates that educators need to redefine their role and include use of GenAI tools in the assignment, GenAI tools must be integrated into the learning experience and the learning objectives must involve the use of GenAI tools.

3.5 Rationale for Extent of AI-use

These are AI-supported activities, where students retain the leading role and are responsible for the final product. ChatGPT has a supportive role as an assistant and feedback provider.

It was decided to combine a mixture of guided and limited usage as well as measured ChatGPT usage. The rationale for the guided usage was first that the writing courses are directed at first-year, mostly L2, students with limited knowledge of academic writing conventions; therefore, students require clear guidelines and continuous scaffolding. Second, their digital and particularly AI literacy skills are usually limited owing to limited or no practice in high school. Furthermore, the rationale is that the proposed activities are meant to be used by instructors who might also feel insecure and uncertain about introducing such activities into their classroom.

Guided and limited usage includes tasks where ChatGPT, as an idea aid, helps identify ideas and structure; as an editing and a feedback partner, identifying errors and limitations. We included some measured or conditional usage, since the specific assignments would still not allow students to "shortcut" their learning and since students would be required to disclose usage by uploading their interactions with ChatGPT (Paulsen, 2024). Measured usage was considered necessary to assist students in developing higher order thinking skills that included "content development, refinement, or enhancement". (Paulsen, 2024). ChatGPT as idea aid can revise student work; and as an editing and a feedback partner improve the clarity and coherence of student writing.

3.6 Rationale for Duration of Activities

By being designed for three classes, these activities engage students in process writing. The scaffolding approach, which also breaks down the assessment into smaller tasks, prevents students from feeling overwhelmed. Independent writing is promoted by asking students to employ feedback they have received from both human and machine.

3.7 Assessment

The designed grading rubrics reflect the integration of ChatGPT into the learning environment. It is a two-tiered evaluation process that evaluates the students' documentation of collaboration with ChatGPT as well as engagement with and evaluation of ChatGPT output during the writing process, while it also requires critically reflection of the learning experience. This can be achieved by approaching the first part as formative writing and the second part as summative writing; or, the whole proposed activity can be considered as formative writing, leading up to a summative essay-assignment. In either case, the assessment, communicated to students beforehand, ensures that students understand the repercussions of inappropriate use of such tools.

Points:

0: None
1: Basic
2: Satisfactory to competent
3: Good to very good
4: Excellent (Tables 1 and 2)

Table 1. Documentation of the writing process plus engagement with and evaluation of ChatGPT output (Jeikner, 2025).

	0	1	2	3	4
Submission of all required documents, on the day and time requested					
Assigned prompt reproduction, following guidelines.					
Collaborative engagement with ChatGPT output and peer illustrated through incorporation of ChatGPT output and feedback as well as peer feedback.					
Individual writing.					

Table 2. Critical reflection of the writing process (Jeikner, 2025)

	0	1	2	3	4
Description					
Reflection					
Structure					
Language					

4 Sample Instructions Page

Note: This document may be downloaded and reused as long as it is cited as a model

Guidelines for Instructors

The activities were created for a Writing course but can be adjusted to any class that involves writing. The activities should be completed over the course of three 50-min classes and the steps outlined below be followed. Students should be provided with activity guidelines in print and/or electronic format from the start of the activity. Students should be made aware of the necessity of submitting required material at the time assigned. Students should be reminded not to use ChatGPT or any other GenAI tool for this or another assignment.

After each class, student submissions to Bb Portfolio should be reviewed and a brief comment should be provided. If students fail to submit, this should be addressed in the following class.

4.1 Guidelines for Students

Assignment Rationale
As students in a higher educational institution, you are expected to produce several written assignments. However, many of you may not have been exposed to academic writing in high school. Furthermore, for many of you, English is a second language which makes writing even more challenging. You may have considered using generative AI (GenAI) tools such as ChatGPT, hoping to achieve a higher grade, even if you know this is considered cheating. This assignment is intended to show you how to employ AI-tools in an effective as well as ethical manner, thereby helping you acquire AI-literacy skills that you will need in your future career.

Choice of GenAI Tool
ChatGPT was chosen to acquaint you with GenAI-tools. The reason is its high accessibility due to free access and user-friendly interface. You should not use other AI-tools for this activity.

Activity Structure
This assignment will be completed over three classes. Your task will be to [...]. At the end of the assignment, you will submit a reflective essay, analyzing and evaluating your learning experience.

Security Considerations
Be aware that privacy and intellectual property are not protected on free GenAI platforms. Do not upload full assignments, yours or someone else's, to such platforms. Furthermore, since device, usage and log data are stored, do not share personal information, yours or someone else's.

Authorized and Unauthorized use of ChatGPT
The extent of permitted use of ChatGPT and the required documentation apply to this course and activity. Other courses may have other policies. See College policies on academic integrity: [link]

All use of ChatGPT needs to be documented.

Authorized use:

Use of ChatGPT for the activities assigned.
Use of ChatGPT in the classroom during the activities.

Unauthorized use:

Use of ChatGPT for any other activity other than the ones assigned.
Use of ChatGPT outside the classroom environment.
Use of other GenAI tools.

As defined in the Student Handbook, the unauthorized use of GenAI tools is considered to grant unfair advantage and to constitute an academic offence. As such, and just as other breaches of academic integrity, any unauthorized use is reported to the Committee on Standing and Conduct.

If you have any questions regarding un/authorized use, please contact me.

Learning Objectives

[...]

Submissions and Evaluation

At the end of each class, you will upload material produced by you and a copy of your ChatGPT chat sessions to Blackboard (BB), E-Portfolio. Once the three-class activity has been completed, you will submit to Bb Portfolio a reflection paragraph.

Assessment Rubrics

[...]

Limitations

The activities were created for undergraduate writing classes in a private higher educational institution where the language of instructions, English, is the L2 for most students. While the writing skills practiced are for sure important in other courses, it should be noted that in writing classes, subject knowledge is writing skills, which means that these activities are designed to develop writing skills and not any other subject knowledge. The socio-cultural environment of the student population we had in mind is furthermore very country-specific, as we assume that most students have limited digital and AI literacy skills and have also not been encouraged in high school to engage in critical reading and writing. They were also designed for a very specific class schedule of 50 min classes.Therefore, we acknowledge that if the proposed activities are adapted to other courses, in other institutions, in other geographical and socio-cultural environments, they will need to be altered and adapted (Tables 3, 4 and 5).

5 Sample Activities

Table 3. Writing a thematic summary, phrased for (L1 and L2) students (Jeikner, 2025)

Class 1

- We revisit, using a handout, basic principles of summarizing chronologically and thematically; versus paraphrasing and quoting. 5 min.
- Read the article (about 500 words) for basic understanding. 5 min.
- Reread and annotate the article, using handout (summary-sentences for each point, use own words, no quotes; author-attribution in every sentence). 10 min.
- Share your annotations with a peer. 5 min.
- Copy your and your peer's annotations (=summary sentences) into a document, in chronological order and upload to your Bb Portfolio. 5 min.
- Ask ChatGPT to translate the article into your native language; if English is your native language to paraphrase the article into a simpler style. In either, the same sentence pattern and the same information should be included. 10 min.
- To make sure that you use ChatGPT ethically and safely, you must:
  - o Be clear in articulating what you want it to do and not do.
  - o Set the context.
  - o Include key details of the assignment.
  - o Do not include personal information (e.g. name, address).
- Tell ChatGPT (in your native language) that:
  - o You are a student at a university where English is the language of instructions, in a writing course, in the first semester.
  - o You have to write a thematic summary.
  - o You are uploading the article for the summary.
  - o You need a translation into your native language or a paraphrase using simpler English. In either, the exact same sentence pattern and the exact same information should be included.
  - o It should not provide any summary.
- Upload conversation with ChatGPT and ChatGPT output to Bb Portfolio.
- Class discussion. 5-10 min.

Learning outcomes of this class are to:

- Read for understanding.
- Understand the chronological and the thematic summary.
- Demonstrate textual understanding by annotating an article.
- Identify levels of permitted and not-permitted ChatGPT usage.
- Apply information on effective and ethical prompts for ChatGPT by writing a prompt for ChatGPT.
- Use ChatGPT as a writing assistant, but not an author.

Class 2

- We revisit, using a handout, the difference between chronological and thematic summary. 5 min.
- Read the ChatGPT output. 5 min.
- With your peer, and using the ChatGPT version of the article, you will begin with the thematic summary. 15 min.
  - o Identify the author's overall argument.
  - o Restructure summary sentences according to sub-arguments.
  - o Upload your document to your Bb Portfolio.
- Upload the same document to ChatGPT and ask it to identify strengths and any weaknesses in your work. 5 min.
  - o It should consider content and structure (which should be centered around arguments).

(*continued*)

Table 3. (*continued*)

- o It should identify if time words are used.
  - o It should identify if there is reference to the author in every single sentence.
  - o It should not offer any suggestions.
  - o Upload to ChatGPT also the grading criteria.
- Write a paragraph on your experience of working with ChatGPT. 15 min.
  - o Describe initial understanding of the article.
  - o Describe the experience of telling ChatGPT what to do (prompt writing).
  - o Compare/contrast your understanding of the text with the ChatGPT version.
  - o Explain the usefulness of ChatGPT version and the feedback.
- Upload your paragraph as well as your conversation with ChatGPT and the ChatGPT output to your Bb Portfolio.
- Class discussion. 5 min.

Learning outcomes of this class are to:

- Identify levels of permitted and not-permitted usage within a specific class.
- Apply information on effective and ethical prompts for ChatGPT by writing a prompt for ChatGPT.
- Apply understanding of summary techniques by rearranging annotation sentences into thematic order, while respecting attribution.
- Utilize ChatGPT output.
- Analyze ChatGPT output.
- Use ChatGPT as a writing assistant, but not an author.

Class 3

- We discuss transitions in the thematic summary using a handout. 5 min.
- With your peer, and using your writing and the ChatGPT output, turn the thematic sentences into a coherent thematic summary paragraph. 15 min.
- Upload the same document to ChatGPT and ask it for advice on how to improve the paragraph. 5 min.
- Rewrite the passage on your own, using the handouts received, the work done in class, and the suggestions provided by ChatGPT. 15 min.
- Write an evaluation (2-3 sentences) of the ChatGPT advice. 5 min.
- Upload your evaluation and the summary paragraph as well as your conversation with ChatGPT and the ChatGPT output to your Bb Portfolio.
- Class discussion. 5 min.

Learning outcomes of this class are to:

- Create a thematic summary, step 2.
- Identify levels of permitted and not-permitted ChatGPT usage.
- Apply information on effective and ethical prompts for ChatGPT by writing a prompt for ChatGPT.
- Analyze and evaluate ChatGPT suggestions.
- Engage in process writing.
- Use ChatGPT as a feedback partner, but not an author.

Reflective assignment

- Write a reflective paragraph discussing the value of working with ChatGPT and its output. You should now consider in three body paragraphs:
- Regarding your writing in general:
  - o Any challenges you experienced initially when asked to write the summary.
  - o The experience of the revision process in general.
- Regarding ChatGPT use:
  - o The useful of the ChatGPT output.
  - o The experience of using ChatGPT as writing assistant and feedback partner.

(*continued*)

Table 3. (*continued*)

• Submit this writing to Bb Portfolio.
Learning outcomes of this class are to:
• Analyze the writing process and the engagement with ChatGPT.
• Connect thinking to writing to arrive at a holistic learning experience.

Table 4. Writing an introduction, phrased for EFL students (Jeikner, 2025)

Class 1

- Using a handout, we discuss the basic elements of an introduction. 5 min.
- Write the introduction for [… essay] in your native language. 20 min.
- Ask ChatGPT to translate the article into your native language.
- To make sure that you use ChatGPT ethically and safely, you must:
  - o Be clear in articulating what you want it to do and not do.
  - o Set the context.
  - o Include key details.
  - o Do not include personal information (e.g. name, address).
- Tell ChatGPT in your native language that:
  - o You are a student at a university where English is the language of instructions, in a writing course, in the first semester.
  - o You have to write an introduction to a [type of] essay that [essay task].
  - o You are uploading the introduction to this essay in your native language.
  - o You need a translation into English.
  - o It should not change or improve anything.
  - o Upload to ChatGPT also the prompt, the introduction in your native language and the grading criteria.
- Read ChatGPT output (translation). 5 min.
- Upload conversation with ChatGPT and ChatGPT output to Bb Portfolio.
- Class discussion. 15-20 min.

Learning outcomes of this class are to:

- Apply information on introductions by writing your own introduction.
- Apply information on effective and ethical prompts for ChatGPT by writing a prompt for ChatGPT.
- Use ChatGPT as a writing assistant, but not an author.

Class 2

- You receive a handout on wordiness and transitions. Discussion. 10 min.
- With a peer, and using the handout received, locate instances of wordiness and weak transitions in each other's translated introductions. 15 min.
- Ask ChatGPT to identify weaknesses regarding wordiness and transitions in its own output, but not provide suggestions. 5 min.
- With your peer, in bullet form, compare what you identified and what ChatGPT identified – note down similarities and differences: 15 min.
- End of class: Upload to Bb Portfolio:
  - o Original translation with weak instances underlined and highlighted.
  - o Your comparison and notes.
  - o Your conversation with ChatGPT and the ChatGPT output.
- Class discussion. 5 mins.

(*continued*)

Table 4. (*continued*)

Learning outcomes of this class are to: • Identify and improve weak transitions and instances of wordiness. • Compare writing. • Use ChatGPT as a writing assistant and tutor, but not an author. **Class 3** • You receive a handout on the revision process. Discussion. 5 min. • Ask ChatGPT for improvement suggestions on the translated version. 5 min. • Rewrite the passage on your own, using the handouts received, the work done in class, and the suggestions provided by ChatGPT. 15 min. • Upload the passage to Bb Portfolio. • Ask ChatGPT for a revised version of the original passage it wrote, addressing the weaknesses identified and suggestions offered. • With your peer, compare each other's rewritten passage with that of ChatGPT and identify differences and similarities in bullet form. 15 min. • Upload the document with the similarities and differences to Bb Portfolio. **Learning outcomes of this class are to:** • Engage in process writing. • Use feedback to revise. • Engage with ChatGPT critically. **Reflective assignment** • Write a reflective paragraph discussing the value of working with ChatGPT and its output. You should now consider in three body paragraphs: • Regarding your writing in general: o Any challenges experienced initially when asked to write the introduction. o The experience of the revision process in general. • Regarding ChatGPT use: o The useful of the ChatGPT output. o Experience of using ChatGPT as a writing assistant and feedback partner. • Submit this writing to Bb Portfolio. **Learning outcomes of this class are to:** • Analyze the writing process and the engagement with ChatGPT. • Connect thinking to writing to arrive at a holistic learning experience.

Table 5. Working with sources, phrased for instructors (Jeikner, 2025)

Class 1: Writing and Analysis

- Introduction to the task. 10 min.
  - Explain the goal of integrating sources into an academic essay. Provide a handout with guidelines on effective source integration.
- Writing Exercise. 20 min.
  - Students write a short paragraph integrating at least two sources provided by the instructor (e.g., excerpts from articles or books).
- AI-Assisted Review. 15 min.
  - Students upload their paragraph to ChatGPT, asking for suggestions on improving integration, transitions, and clarity.
  - It is important to stress that students should not provide any personal information such as their name or location to maintain data privacy.
  - Students should also be informed that they should also tell ChatGPT what to do and what not do to maintain academic integrity.
- Example Prompt for ChatGPT
  - Here is a paragraph where I've integrated two sources. Please identify areas where the integration of sources, transitions, or clarity could be improved and suggest how I might revise it to strengthen my argument. Please do not provide me with complete sentences or a paragraph.
- Students review suggestions, noting what aligns with guidelines provided.
- Class Discussion. 5 min.
- Students upload their original writing, their conversation and ChatGPT output to the Bb Portfolio for instructor feedback.

Learning outcomes of this class are to:

- Practice paragraph writing with source integration.
- Identify levels of permitted and not-permitted ChatGPT usage.
- Apply information on effective and ethical prompts for ChatGPT by writing a prompt for ChatGPT.
- Use ChatGPT as a writing assistant and coach, but not an author.

Class 2: Peer Review and Revision

- Review of Key Concepts. 10 min.
  - Provide students with examples of strong and weak source integration. Discuss strategies for improving.
- Peer Review. 20 min.
  - Students exchange paragraphs with peers.
  - Each pair identifies areas where source integration could be clearer, better cited, or more effectively connected to the argument.

(*continued*)

Table 5. *(continued)*

- Revision. 20 min.
  - Using feedback from their peers and suggestions from ChatGPT, students revise paragraphs.
- Submission:
  Students upload their revised paragraphs to the Bb Portfolio for instructor feedback.

Learning outcomes of this class are to:

- Analyze strengths and weaknesses in writing.
- Apply revision suggestions to writing.
- Compose revised writing.

Class 3: Reflection and Comparison

- Final AI Check. 10 min.
  - Students ask ChatGPT to rewrite their revised paragraphs for clarity and conciseness.
  - They compare ChatGPT's version with their own, noting differences and improvements or weaknesses.
- Group Activity. 20 min.
  - In small groups, students discuss the strengths and weaknesses of their paragraphs versus ChatGPT's version.
- Reflection Writing. 20 min.:
  - Each student writes a reflective paragraph discussing their experience with source integration and ChatGPT influenc on their learning process.
- Questions to guide reflection:
  - What did you learn about integrating sources?
  - How did ChatGPT's suggestions help or hinder your understanding?
  - How did the ChatGPT version differ from your own?
  - Why or why not would you use the ChatGPT version instead of your own?
  - What would you do differently in future assignments?
- Submission:
  - All materials (original, revised, ChatGPT version, and reflection) are compiled and submitted as part of the activity to Bb portfolio.

Learning outcomes of this class are for students to:

- Identify levels of permitted and not-permitted ChatGPT usage.
- Distinguish between using ChatGPT as a writing assistant/ coach v. author.
- Compare quality of human to machine writing.
- Analyze the writing process and the engagement with ChatGPT.
- Connect thinking to writing to arrive at a holistic learning experience.

6 Conclusions

Technological developments are proceeding at a rapid pace. When this author was preparing an early version of this manuscript for a conference, it was still 2024. Already in 2023, the ChatGPT Plus paid model had offered enhanced capabilities for complex tasks and was said to provide more factually correct information and demonstrate less hallucinations that the 2022-model– developments clearly pointing toward the importance of acknowledging its impact on the educational field. By the end of 2024, both the free ChatGPT and the Plus paid models, while still not free of problems, demonstrated further improvements. Now, mid-2025, the release of GPT-5, with further capabilities, is eagerly anticipated. This new model is said for instance to come with enhanced text-creation abilities and a more human-centric approach, which will result in more genuine interactions as well as more accurate and personalized content. Here it should be noted that having to pay for a better version should not be considered a significant deterrent. Pricing for ChatGPT Plus (the cheaper paid version, compared to ChatGPT Pro) for example ranges between 20 to 7.5 US dollars monthly, depending on whether it is a monthly or annual subscription. Given that students might well be using ChatGPT for personal and professional purposes besides educational ones, they might very well consider using the paid version. Regardless of which version students may use, it is important to acknowledge that even if students are aware that the ChatGPT output of might be flawed, they are still likely to turn to it for assistance, especially when they feel challenged by assignment requirements and time constraints. Furthermore, course policies that prohibit its use will not prove a deterrent.

The literature clearly shows that instead of trying in vain to prevent students from using GenAI tools, effective GenAI literacy skills need to be taught. Still, our experience demonstrates that many instructors are hesitant to do so. Reasons range from fear of rendering human educators and writing classes obsolete to fear of the impact on student learning and integrity up to a simple lack of knowledge of how to use GenAI tools. This manuscript will hopefully contribute to a community that shares experiences on the integration of GenAI into the classroom by providing very specific examples that might help such hesitant educators. The choice of ChatGPT is only indicative, meant to acquaint hesitant instructors with different ways of using one tool.

While ChatGPT remains flawed, given that since it is trained on data it receives, which can for instance be biased, it is nonetheless important to acknowledge that ChatGPT and GenAI tools overall have altered the educational experience forever. We also agree with the literature that suggests that using GenAI tools as a creative partner and a dialogue partner will usher in exciting new educational opportunities, with the caveat that familiarity with usage must first be established.

Looking into the future, we argue that the only solution to remain relevant as writing educators and ensure that students do not sacrifice their critical thinking and their writing skills to the ease of GenAI tools such as ChatGPT, is in fact to integrate ChatGPT into the educational pedagogy. This will also ensure that students learn ethical, safe, and effective usage of GenAI tools. We should not repeat the mistake made about 25 years ago that members of Generation Y were all digital natives and believe that members of Generation Z are all GenAI-natives. It is our responsibility to help students learn appropriate use of GenAI tools and to prepare them for a future where AI is integrated into their professional life.

Acknowledgments. A first draft of this paper was presented at CSEDU 2025 17th International Conference on Computer Supported Education 2025, as Saving writing classes from extinction: ChatGPT as part of the teaching pedagogy. The author thanks her colleague Dr. Sakellari for the third activity as well as her suggestions. GenAI tools were not used to write this manuscript. ChatGPT was used only in the context of the testing the proposed activities.

Disclosure of Interests The author has received no funding and has no competing interests to declare that are relevant to the content of this article.

References

Albadarin, Y., Saqr, M., Pope, N., Tukianen, M.: A systematic literature review of empirical research on ChatGPT in education. Discov. Educ. **3**(1) (2023). https://doi.org/10.1007/s44217-024-00138-2

Alby, C.: AI prompts for teaching: a spell book. https://docs.google.com/document/d/1Lo4aeiWT4f5xhcsAbWAfQRITghBhcmFN2m-JEX5OkJA/edit?tab=t.0. (n.d.) Last accessed 15 Apr 2025

Artificial Intelligence Tools (CC BY 4.0), Oregon State University.: https://ecampus.oregonstate.edu/faculty/artificial-intelligence-tools/meaningful-learning/. Last accessed 1 June 2025

Atlas, S.: ChatGPT for higher education and professional development: A guide to conversational AI. College of Business Faculty Publications. https://digitalcommons.uri.edu/cba_facpubs/548?utm_source=digitalcommons.uri.edu%2Fcba_facpubs%2F548&utm_medium=PDF&utm_campaign=PDFCoverPages. (2023) Last accessed 15 Apr 2025

Baek, C., Tate, T., Warschauer, M.: "ChatGPT seems too good to be true": college students' use and perceptions of generative AI. Comput. Educ.: Artif. Intell. **7**, 1–9 (2024). https://doi.org/10.1016/j.caeai.2024.100294

Barrot, J.S.: Using ChatGPT for second language writing: pitfalls and potentials. Assess. Writ. **57** (2023). https://doi.org/10.1016/j.asw.2023.100745

Barus, O.P., Hidayanto, A.N., Handri, E.Y., Sensuse, D.I., Yaiprasert, C.: Shaping generative AI governance in higher education: insights from student perception. Int. J. Educ. Res. Open. **8** (2025). https://doi.org/10.1016/j.ijedro.2025.100452

Bittle, K., El-Gayar, O.: Generative AI and academic integrity in higher education: a systematic review and research agenda. Information. **16**(4), 296 (2025). https://doi.org/10.3390/info16040296

Bozkurt, A., Sharma, R.C.: Generative AI and prompt engineering: the art of whispering to let the genie out of the algorithmic world. Asian J. Dist. Educ. **18**(2), i–vii (2023)

Brandeis University: Center for teaching and learning, https://www.brandeis.edu/teaching/resources/syllabus/ai-statements.html. (n.d.) Last accessed 25 May 2025

Cao, L., Dede, C.: Navigating a world of generative AI: Suggestions for educators. Next Level Lab. Harvard University. https://nextlevellab.gse.harvard.edu/2023/07/28/navigating-a-world-of-generative-ai-suggestions-for-educators/. (2023) Last accessed 25 May 2025

Chung, E.S., Ahn, S.: The effect of using machine translation on linguistic features in L2 writing across proficiency levels and text genres. Comput. Assist. Lang. Learn. **34**(3), 2239–2264 (2021). https://doi.org/10.1080/09588221.2020.1871029

Cong-Lem, N., Soyoof, A., Tsering, D.: A systematic review of the limitations and associated opportunities of ChatGPT. Int. J. Hum.-Comput. Interact. **41**(7), 3851–3866 (2025). https://doi.org/10.1080/10447318.2024.2344142

Deans, K.R., Jones, J., Harvey, J.B.: Artificial intelligence in higher education: a comparative study on the performance and detectability of AI-generated graduate-level coursework utilizing ChatGPT. J. Health Adm. Educ. **40**(4), 613–630 (2024)

Deng, R., Jiang, M., Yu, X., Lu, Y., Liu, S.: Does ChatGPT enhance student learning? a systematic review and meta-analysis of experimental studies. Comput. Educ. **227** (2025)

Evangelista, E.D.L.: Ensuring academic integrity in the age of ChatGPT: rethinking exam design, assessment strategies, and ethical AI policies in higher education. Contemp. Educ. Technol. **17**(1), ep559 (2025). https://doi.org/10.30935/cedtech/15775

Forbes, M., Brandauer J.: What's my stance on genAI in this class? Gettysburg College Johnson Center for Teaching and Learning. https://genai.sites.gettysburg.edu/positions-and-policies/. Last accessed 15 May 2025. (2023) Last accessed 17 May 2025

García-López, I.M., González González, C.S., Ramírez-Montoya, M., Molina-Espinosa, J.-M.: Challenges of implementing ChatGPT on education: systematic literature review. Int. J. Educ. Res. Open. **8** (2025). https://doi.org/10.1016/j.ijedro.2024.100401

Gibson, R.: AI prompt book. https://rise.articulate.com/share/rd3oV4df9xf5hr_7gVtBL_O4_ZcDzU-K#/. (n.d.) Last accessed 14 May 2025

Graefen, B., Fazal, N.: From chat bots to virtual tutors: an overview of chat GPT's role in the future of education. Arch. Pharm. Pract. **15**(2), 43–52 (2024). https://doi.org/10.51847/TOuppjEDSX

Hanafi, A.M., Al-Mansi, M.M., Al-Sharif, O.A.: Generative AI in academia: a comprehensive review of applications and implications for the research process. Int. J. Eng. Appl. Sci.-October 6 Univ. **2**(1), 91–110 (2025). https://doi.org/10.21608/ijeasou.2025.349520.1041

Hernandez, M.: Generative AI prompt book. https://docs.google.com/document/d/1xRAmnya_exvqCcIwTV78JAZqCpX5jz2ko574R3SWuwE/edit?tab=t.0#heading=h.f234k44nnc1c. (2024) Last accessed 13 May 2025

Holland, A., Ciachir, C.: A qualitative study of students' lived experience and perceptions of using ChatGPT: immediacy, equity and integrity. Interact. Learn. Environ. **33**(1), 483–494 (2024). https://doi.org/10.1080/10494820.2024.2350655

Huang, J., Tan, M.: The role of ChatGPT in scientific communication: writing better scientific review articles. Am. J. Cancer Res. **13**(4), 1148–1154 (2023)

Imperial: Choosing action verbs. Educational Development Unit. https://www.imperial.ac.uk/staff/educational-development/teaching-toolkit/intended-learning-outcomes/choosing-action-verbs/ (n.d.). Last accessed 15 May 2025

Jeikner, A.: Saving writing classes from extinction: ChatGPT as part of the teaching pedagogy. In: du Boulay, B., et al. (eds.) CSEDU 2025 17th International Conference on Computer Supported Education 2025, vol. 1, pp. 500–511. Scitepress, Portugal (2025)

Jeon, J., Lee, S.: Large language models in education: a focus on the complementary relationship between human teachers and ChatGPT. Educ. Inf. Technol.: Off. J. IFIP Tech. Committee Educ. **28**(12), 15873–15892 (2023). https://doi.org/10.1007/s10639-023-11834-1

Jin, F., Sun, L., Pan, Y., Lin, C.-H.: High heels, compass, spider-man, or drug? metaphor analysis of generative artificial intelligence in academic writing. Comput. Educ. **228** (2025). https://doi.org/10.1016/j.compedu.2025.105248

Karataş, F., Yaşar Abedi, F., Ozek Gunyel, F., Karadeniz, D., Kuzgun, Y.: Incorporating AI in foreign language education: an investigation into ChatGPT's effect on foreign language learners. Educ. Inf. Technol. **29**, 19343–19366 (2024)

Kartelj, A., Mladenović, M., Vujičić Stanković, S.: Comparison of algorithms for the recognition of ChatGPT paraphrased texts. J. Big Data. **12**(1), 1–17 (2025). https://doi.org/10.1186/s40537-025-01082-0

Kayalı, B., Yavuz, M., Balat, S., Çalışan, M.: Investigation of student experiences with ChatGPT-supported online learning applications in higher education. Australas. J. Educ. Technol. **39**(5), 20–39 (2023). https://doi.org/10.14742/ajet.8915

Kohnke, L., Moorhouse, B.L., Zou, D.: ChatGPT for language teaching and learning. RELC J. (2023). https://doi.org/10.1177/00336882231162868

Kovari, A.: Ethical use of ChatGPT in education-best practices to combat AI-induced plagiarism. Front. Educ. **9**, 1–7 (2025). https://doi.org/10.3389/feduc.2024.1465703

Lee, S.M., Briggs, N.: Effects of using machine translation to mediate the revision process of Korean university students' academic writing. ReCALL First View. **33**(1), 18–33 (2020). https://doi.org/10.1017/S0958344020000191

Leong, W.Y., Zhang, J.B.: AI on academic integrity and plagiarism detection. ASM Sci. J. **20**(1), 1–10 (2025)

Li, H.: Effects of a ChatGPT-based flipped learning guiding approach on learners' courseware project performances and perceptions. Australas. J. Educ. Technol. **39**(5), 40–58 (2023). https://doi.org/10.14742/ajet.8923

Li, M.: The impact of ChatGPT on teaching and learning in higher education: challenges, opportunities, and future scope. In Encyclopedia of Information Science and Technology, 6th edn (2025). DOI:https://doi.org/10.4018/978-1-6684-7366-5.ch079

Lo, C.K., Yu, P.L.H., Xu, S., Ng, D.T.K., Jong, M.S.: Exploring the application of ChatGPT in ESL/EFL education and related research issues: a systematic review of empirical studies. Smart Learn. Environ. **11**(50), 1–24 (2024). https://doi.org/10.1186/s40561-024-00342-5

Malfatti, F.I.: ChatGPT, education, and understanding. Soc. Epistemol., 1–15 (2025). https://doi.org/10.1080/02691728.2025.2449599

Mollick, E.: Co-intelligence: Living and Working with AI. WH Allen, London (2024)

NC State University: Teaching resources. https://teaching-resources.delta.ncsu.edu/designing-assignments-with-ai-in-mind/. (n.d.) Last accessed 15 Apr 2025

Nissim, Y., Simon, E.: The diffusion of artificial intelligence innovation: perspectives of preservice teachers on the integration of ChatGPT in education. J. Educ. Teach. **51**(2), 381–401 (2025). https://doi.org/10.1080/02607476.2025.2469128

Paulsen, E.: The optional use of generative artificial intelligence (GenAI) in assessments. faculty learning hub. Teach. Learn. Conestoga.. https://tlconestoga.ca/spectrum-ai-learning-tasks/. (2024) Last accessed 17 Apr 2025

Prananta, A.W., Megahati, S.R.R.P., Susanto, N., Raule, J.H.: Transforming education and learning through chat GPT: a systematic literature review. Jurnal Penelitian Pendidikan IPA. **9**(11), 1031–1037 (2023). https://doi.org/10.29303/jppipa.v9i11.5468

Reinhardt, K.S., Guartuche Jr., O.: Curriculum Integration of AI Technology for Student Autonomy and Self-efficacy. Texas Association of Teacher Education. https://txate.org/resources/Documents/The%20Forum%20Volume%2016%20Winter%2024.pdf#page=40Shepherd. (2024) Last accessed 14 May 2025

Rowland, D.R.: Two frameworks to guide discussions around levels of acceptable use of generative AI in student academic research and writing. J. Acad. Lang. Learn. **17**(1), T31–T69 (2023)

Shank, P.: eLearning Guild Research: Reconsidering Bloom's Taxonomy (old AND new). Learning Guild. https://www.learningguild.com/articles/1105/elearning-guild-research-reconsidering-blooms-taxonomy-old-and-new/. (n.d.) Last accessed 15 May 2025

Schaper, N.: Using ChatGPT to create constructively aligned assessment tasks and criteria in the context of higher education teaching. In: Artificial Intelligence and Education-Shaping the Future of Learning (2024)

Sharpe, A.: The optional use of generative artificial intelligence (GenAI) in assessment. faculty learning hub. Teach. Learn. Conestoga. https://tlconestoga.ca/the-optional-use-of-generative-artificial-intelligence-genai-in-assessments/. (2024). Last accessed 15 May 2025

Song, C., Song, Y.: Enhancing academic writing skills and motivation: assessing the efficacy of ChatGPT in AI-assisted language learning for EFL students. Front. Psychol. **14** (2023). https://doi.org/10.3389/fpsyg.2023.1260843

Teng, M.F.: "ChatGPT is the companion, not enemies": EFL learners' perceptions and experiences in using ChatGPT for feedback in writing. Comput. Educ.: Artif. Intell. **7** (2024). https://doi.org/10.1016/j.caeai.2024.100270

Vera, F.: Enhancing english language learning in undergraduate students using ChatGPT: a quasi-experimental study. In: Red Internacional de Investigadores en Educación, I Congreso Internacional de Aprendizaje Activo CIAA 2023, pp. 18–21 (2023)

Verano-Tacoronte, D., Bolívar-Cruz, A., Sosa-Cabrera, S.: Are university teachers ready for generative artificial intelligence? unpacking faculty anxiety in the ChatGPT era. Educ. Inf. Technol. (2025). https://doi.org/10.1007/s10639-025-13585-7

Wang, S.J., Bankard, J.S., Bui, E., Nye, B.: Writing with AI: what college students learned from utilizing ChatGPT for a writing assignment. Educ. Sci. **14**(9), 976 (2024). https://doi.org/10.3390/educsci14090976

Wegerif, R.: Toward a dialogic theory of education for the internet age. In: Mercer, N., Wegerif, R., Major, L., Mercer, N., Wegerif, R., Major, L. (eds.) The Routledge International Handbook of Research on Dialogic Education, 1st edn, pp. 1–13. Routledge, London (2019)

Yang, L., Li, R.: ChatGPT for L2 learning: current status and implications. System. **124** (2024). https://doi.org/10.1016/j.system.2024.103351

You, S.: A systematic review of the impact of ChatGPT on higher education. Int. J. Technol. **3**(1), 1–14 (2024). https://doi.org/10.4018/IJTEE.343528

Zhao, R., Yunus, M.M., Rafiq, K.R.M.: The impact of the use of ChatGPT in enhancing students' engagement and learning outcomes in higher education: a review. Int. J. Acad. Res. Bus. Soc. Sci. **13**(12), 3734–3744 (2023). https://doi.org/10.6007/IJARBSS/v13-i12/20258

Between Scientific Complexity and Misinformation: The Role of ChatGPT in Climate Communication

Dionisia Laranjeiro[1](✉), Ana I. Lillebø[2], and Helena Vieira[3]

[1] CIDTFF – Research Centre on Didactics and Technology in the Education of Trainers, Department of Education and Psychology, University of Aveiro, Aveiro, Portugal
dionisia.mendonca@ua.pt

[2] ECOMARE, CESAM - Centre for Environmental and Marine Studies, Department of Biology, University of Aveiro, Aveiro, Portugal

[3] CESAM - Centre for Environmental and Marine Studies, Department of Environment and Planning, University of Aveiro, Aveiro, Portugal

Abstract. Climate communication faces several challenges that make it difficult for people to understand and act on climate change in an informed way. These include scientific complexity, misinformation and lack of personal connection. Such difficulties are not overcome by traditional media or social networks, which are the main chosen ways of accessing information and news on the subject. This study was conducted to ascertain whether Generative AI may facilitate public understanding and reduce barriers to climate communication. We used ChatGPT to ask a series of questions aimed at the general public, the educational community and climate scientists that need to communicate to policy makers and politicians. The results suggest that ChatGPT can be a useful tool for communicating climate change, providing clear, accurate and informative answers and excluding conspiracy theories. However, some answers were too brief or general and needed to be complemented with more information for better understanding. Generative AI seems to serve as a good first approach to the topic of climate change, synthesizing key concepts and clarifying doubts. As Generative AI depends upon open access information, academia has a key role ensuring the availability of accurate science-based knowledge.

Keywords: Generative AI · ChatGPT · Climate Change · Climate Communication · Climate Education · Climate Policy

1 Introduction

This article is an extended and revised version of the paper Generative AI in Climate Communication and Education, presented at the CSEDU 2025 - International Conference on Computer Supported Education [1]. A key difference in this version is the inclusion of science communication strategies aimed at politicians and policymakers, in addition to the original focus on the general public and the educational community.

C. Meinel et al. (Eds.): CSEDU 2025, CCIS 3148, pp. 213–242, 2027.
https://doi.org/10.1007/978-3-032-39103-2_11

This broadens the scope of the study and reflects the need to engage decision makers in climate issues. New prompts were added to capture this dimension. The overall structure - from the introduction to the methodology, results, discussion, and conclusion - has been strengthened to address the specifics of communicating climate science in policy contexts.

1.1 Climate Change Communication Challenge

Climate change is one of the greatest challenges for humanity, with severe consequences, widespread impacts and risks predicted. The global temperature of the earth is rising, mainly due to human activities related with the emission of greenhouse gases. This global warming causes changes in the atmosphere, land and oceans and affects weather and climate extremes, with considerable damage to nature and people [2]. According to the Organization for Economic Cooperation and Development working paper on people's understanding of and support for climate policies [3], the implementation of climate-related policies has been challenging, and communication, specifically information and explanations addressing citizens major concerns, can increase the support for climate policies.

It is acknowledged that there are barriers to climate change communication, resulting in the topic being perceived as ambiguous, uncertain and complex, making public understanding incomplete, distant in space and time, and disconnected from their personal experiences [4]. Some barriers and challenges to climate communication with implications on people's understanding and willingness to adopt climate-friendly practices have already been identified. In traditional media, such as television and newspapers, the frequency of communication on climate change is uneven and unsystematic, marked by cyclical moments such as extreme weather events, conferences and political meetings, and the publication of scientific reports [5]. The media's tendency towards alarmist and sensationalist reporting, combined with the journalistic pursuit of balance, often portrays climate sceptics and climate change scientists as equal in number and influence [4], which doesn't accurately reflect the actual scientific consensus, given that over 95% of climate scientists attribute global warming to human activity [6]. Interest in the topic varies from country to country: it is higher in Portugal, Greece, and Chile, and lower in the United States, the United Kingdom, and Germany. The difference in interest is attributed to the effects of climate change felt in the first countries, such as major fires, but also to political polarization. In the United States and Australia, where the left-right divide is more pronounced, people are generally less interested in climate change news [7].

News consumption habits are changing, with television losing ground to the internet. Young people are using social networks as their main source of news, with X (former Twitter) being the most widely used for this purpose. News about climate change is on the rise. Climate scientists are intensifying efforts in public engagement and communication, but they compete with a multitude of subjective opinions on social media, making it difficult to establish themselves as an expert authority [8]. Newman [9] carried out a study that is consistent with these findings. When analyzing the posts and most active actors on X during the release of the IPCC Fifth Assessment Report[1], he concluded that the majority came from bloggers, activists and concerned citizens, suggesting that large audiences were more exposed to non-traditional voices than scientists. Also, Meyer et al. [10] analyzed the public discourse on X choosing five climate events from 2017 to 2021. Results showed that discussions were heavily politicized, frequently called for action while criticizing administrations, and highlighted potential negative future scenarios. The microblogging platform was centered around controversial debates and polarizing personalities such as Greta Thunberg and Donald Trump.

A review on the role of online and social media in climate communication contrasts optimistic scholars who see these tools, with audiovisuals and interactivity, as a means to improve science communication and empower unprivileged groups to be heard, against the pessimists, who focus on fragmentation and manipulation of those who may have difficulty distinguishing scientific information from misinformation. From more than 100 publications examined, the study concludes that the amount of online climate content is significant and increasing, but the quality of communication is poor. Climate scientists and scientific institutions play a limited role in the online debate, while climate NGOs communicate extensively online to inform, build support, change behavior and mobilize action [11]. The study also suggests that online communication contributes to raising awareness and improving knowledge but claims that there is little empirical evidence that it has an effect in changing climate-related behavior and action. Bushell et al. [12] also found that although climate communication is improving, there is still a gap between awareness of scientific knowledge and action by governments, industry and people. Causes cited relate to the nature of the problem (e.g. long-term challenge requiring action now and lack of immediate evidence) and the narratives used to communicate, which are not effective in changing behavior (e.g. doomsday and alarmism). A more recent paper [13] reported on the adoption of mitigation and adaptation actions by individuals, such as travelling by public transport and cycling, installing solar panels, switching to high efficiency vehicles or changing to a plant-based diet. Even so, the primary motivation was economic rather than environmental.

In addition to media communication, interpersonal communication may also play an important role in beliefs and feelings about climate change. A survey study with a US nationally representative sample reports that discussing global warming with friends and family influences knowledge about the topic, about the scientific consensus on anthropogenic causes, and encourages further discussion and deeper engagement [14]. Regarding the family, it is worth highlighting the role that children can play in transferring knowledge and changing their parents' attitudes. Lawson et al. conducted a study with 238 families over two years, in which middle school children received a climate change curriculum designed to promote intergenerational learning. The discussion between parents and children during the educational intervention increased parents' concerns about climate change, especially among more conservative fathers [15]. In fact, engaging in deliberative discussion is considered one of the most effective climate change education strategies [16].

[1] IPCC Fifth Assessment Report https://www.ipcc.ch/assessment-report/ar5/

1.2 What Does Generative AI Bring to Climate Change Communication?

Generative AI refers to a class of artificial intelligence (AI) systems that can generate new data based on existing data, often using deep learning models. This means that the new content is not copied from the training data but is based on patterns and structures learned during the training process. Generative AI can be applied to text generation. A prominent example is ChatGPT[2], a large language model (LLM) that has been trained to produce text optimized for dialogue, using terabytes of data written by humans, and obtained from different sources such as websites, books and research articles. ChatGPT was chosen for this study by its prevalent use[3]. In January 2025, ChatGPT had around 3.66 billion visits per month. It is important to highlight that these LLM are trained solely on predictive tasks that do not require an understanding of meaning. This would involve linking linguistic forms to communicative intents, that these models currently are not equipped to do [17]. ChatGPT answers user-generated questions, using natural language processing techniques that makes the interaction sound like human conversation, even though it is artificial communication [18]. This versatile tool is being used for many applications, including the creation of stories and poetry, programming code, as a translator or a calculator, as a creative generator in marketing campaigns, in scientific writing and in business predictions. It is also used as an advanced search tool that presents the results in a narrative way [19].

Regarding climate, as an AI, ChatGPT has the advantage of accessing large amounts of information, from various scientific disciplines such as atmospheric science, oceanography and ecology, to quickly relate seemingly independent information, in order to reach conclusions [20] and present the most likely sequence of words based on its training data. In this way, it can present relevant and contextualized answers, synthesizing and explaining complex concepts [21]. One good advantage is the capability of summarizing information from long texts, identifying key points and main themes to facilitate comprehension [22]. Because ChatGPT can store input/output responses, it enables continuous conversation [19], making the experience more dynamic and interesting for the user. Immediate feedback makes it possible to clarify and deepen the topic of climate change in real time, as new questions arise. Due to this interactive nature, ChatGPT has great potential for active learning, as the user actively investigates the problem.

A growing body of studies has highlighted the relevance of using Generative AI in the educational context. Professor Oscar A. Acar, in his Harvard Business Review article [23], proposed the PAIR framework for using Generative AI in education, emphasizing the need to use AI in education, rather than prohibiting it. PAIR (Problem, AI, Interaction, Reflection) is designed to proactively integrate AI into students' curriculum, developing skills such as the ability to formulate problems, explore different AI tools, think critically and reflect on AI results. For students, chatbots have been suggested to improve learning and motivation, as they can provide personalized learning experiences with content tailored to their needs and learning style [24]. For teachers, Generative AI can help to

[2] ChatGPT https://chat.openai.com/

[3] https://explodingtopics.com/blog/chatgpt-users - Exploding Topics identifies and tracks emerging trends and issues. Its trustworthiness is based on transparency (explanations of data collection and analysis), reputation and credibility. It is often cited by professionals and companies looking for market trends.

address science education topics such as climate change and also be used as a tool for creating educational resources. A good example is given by Cooper [25], who asked ChatGPT to create a teaching unit on renewable and non-renewable energy sources for 7th graders based on the 5E instruction model [26]. He obtained the design of a unit, divided into rubrics, with a sequence of activities for each phase (engage, explore, explain, elaborate, evaluate) and quizzes for a final (self-)evaluation. This type of content and functionality can be extremely useful for teachers with mixed ideas or insufficient understanding of the subject. In the USA, a country where only about half the population believes that climate change is mainly due to human activity, a nationally representative survey of science teachers on climate change was conducted. It found that most teachers lacked training in the subject, had little knowledge of the evidence, and were unaware of the scientific consensus on anthropogenic global warming. This was reflected in the differing approaches taken by teachers in the classroom, with some teaching that climate change is mainly caused by human activity (54%), others using mixed messages and attributing equal importance to natural and anthropogenic causes (31%) or denying the issue (10%) and avoiding it (5%) [27].

Generative AI can also play a role in climate policy. The Paris Agreement [28], signed by 195 countries, set a global target of limiting temperature rise to between 1.5 °C and 2.0 °C, which is not being met. Each country has the autonomy to define its climate action according to national circumstances, and the political response has fallen short of expectations [29]. Although politicians take the scientific evidence into account, they have limited time to implement a certain number of actions and will choose to focus on issues that their electorate considers a priority. ChatGPT may be used by scientists to write policy briefs, presenting arguments about the urgency and challenges of climate change. A policy brief is a short policy document used as a tool to persuade informed non-researcher audiences, such as decision makers, politicians or journalists [30]. ChatGPT can extract information from research long papers and present it in an engaging, succinct form, with a clear and simple language understandable by a broad knowledgeable audience. As this tool can generate text that is grammatically correct, coherent and contextually appropriate, it can be used for abstracts, arguments and social media posts promoting research findings [31]. In this way, Generative AI may also be used by policymakers to communicate with citizens about climate policies, which have historically been difficult to implement. A study based on 40.000 interviews with citizens of 20 countries (representing 72% of CO2 emissions) sought to understand this difficulty. Citizens showed little willingness to reduce CO2 emissions, namely driving less, reducing the heating and cooling of their homes, or limiting beef consumption. The lack of support for climate policies was related to a perception of economic regression, and unpopular measures such as energy taxation and carbon pricing. An important finding was that informing the public about the mechanisms and benefits of climate policies significantly increases their overall support. Hence, it becomes essential to launch informative campaigns that elucidate how these policies effectively reduce emissions and outline the individual costs and gains associated with climate measures [3]. Governmental communication campaigns seek to raise awareness, promote engagement and motivate behavior change. It may involve partnerships with companies, NGOs, communication agencies and public figures and combine a variety of strategies, channels and media. A challenge for policy makers is to reach different audiences with incomplete knowledge, inform of key facts and concepts and engage the public according to their characteristics and differences [32]. ChatGPT can be part of a scalable, tailored and automated climate communication, combined with other communication tools in a concerted intervention. It can be used to create articles and posts with reasons for climate action, providing informative content on impacts and proposed policies. Nisbet and Spaiser also claim that it can answer people's doubts about policies and may generate convincing moral arguments, appealing to compassion and fairness, to encourage behavior change [33]. Nevertheless, it is proposed that the content generated by ChatGPT may be utilized as a first draft, with subsequent editing by specialists to ensure relevance and accuracy in accordance with the stated objectives [34].

It is important to recognize some limitations and ethical concerns associated with ChatGPT. Sometimes it generates inaccurate or even false information, such as references, links and DOI, therefore the veracity of the facts should always be checked by comparing them with other sources [22]. The quality of the content depends on the data with which it was trained. Direct use of ChatGPT generated content without scientific verification may risk perpetuating or amplifying existing biases and inaccuracies [34]. A major concern is the risk of political bias. In several political orientation tests, ChatGPT was classified as having left-leaning political views. Political bias in a widely used tool can be dangerous for society, as it can impact human perception and increase the spread of misinformation. Ethical AI should present balanced, neutral arguments based on available scientific evidence and not favor particular political viewpoints [35]. There is also the issue of plagiarism. When using ChatGPT we may not recognize and give due credit to the authors of the content used [25]. Another concern related to the origin of the training data is whether ChatGPT's filtering ability will exclude manipulative information [22]. To mitigate this limitation and to ensure accuracy, relevance and coherence, ChatGPT is trained in a multi-stage process, using advanced machine learning techniques. It is pre-trained with a large corpus of Internet text. It undergoes supervised fine-tuning with human trainers, to enhance the conversation. It also uses a Reward Model Construction, where the generated responses are reviewed and ranked by humans. Finally, the model uses a reinforcement learning technique called Proximal Policy Optimization, which uses the reward model to maximize predicted quality and generate knowledgeable and contextually appropriate conversations [22].

Sometimes the tool is used to aid decision making, but it can be inconsistent and contradictory, yet people tend to trust and let their judgement be influenced by ChatGPT advice [36]. The issue of trust in ChatGPT is important to consider. The study by Choudhury and Shamszare [37] aimed to understand the impact of user's trust in ChatGPT, through a survey answered by 607 adults in the USA. The results suggest that trust is critical to the adoption of this tool. The authors highlight the importance of the issue, emphasizing that blind trust can have severe consequences, for example, in decision-making contexts, just as a lack of trust can lead to under-use and loss of opportunities. In education, the trend towards acceptance by students is noteworthy. A survey of university students in the USA found that 89% used ChatGPT for schoolwork, which may raise new ethical issues. On the one hand, it can be used as a pedagogical complement that increases students' motivation and self-efficacy. On the other hand, it can be used to produce homework, projects and reports, which can lead to more superficial learning and weaken critical thinking, representing a new challenge for teachers in terms of assessment [38]. A final ethical issue relates to the carbon impact of ChatGPT due to its high energy consumption. GPT-3 training consumed approximately 190,000 kWh of energy and produced 85,000 kg of CO2 [40]. A study of the carbon impact of various GPT models, based on GPT3 and GPT2, aimed to determine the energy efficiency of each. The power (watts) used for each query varied between 48.9 and 61.7 [41]. As a technology that is growing rapidly on the market, the environmental cost cannot be ignored.

1.3 Why This Study?

In this article, and considering all potential limitations, we seek to check whether ChatGPT, as a text-generating AI, can generate information and explanations to support climate communication, to help people understand and act on climate change in an informed way, by targeting three different audiences: the general public, the educational community and climate scientist that need to communicate to politicians and policy makers. The research team is part of BESIDE, an ERA Chair project for research and development in environmental economics with the aim to foster multidisciplinary and transdisciplinary research in themes related to climate change, sustainability and socioeconomic sciences. One of the research areas is focused on science communication of related topics, particularly for strategy and policy making. With the rise of Generative AI, the team aimed to explore its impact on the science communication of climate change. As Schäfer recently reflected, Generative AI is influencing academia, science, teaching and science communication, but articles on the role of Generative AI in science communication are relatively scarce [11]. Science communication researchers should explore it from the users' perspective and how it is used to obtain information on science-related topics.

We have created three sets of prompts to address specific objectives for each audience. Prompts with generic and useful information about climate change were created for the general public. For teachers, we have chosen a prompt to assist with teaching climate change in a formal educational setting. Additionally, prompts were created to assist climate scientists in communicating with policy makers and politicians about climate change. We then analyzed the answers generated and the results were compared with the content of scientific publications and recent grey literature. Finally, this study allowed us to conclude that, overall, the generated information and explanations are sufficient for the objectives and the chosen targeted audience.

2 Method

This is an exploratory study that reports on our experience of interacting with ChatGPT about climate change and reflects on its possible implications as a reliable source of information and explanations for climate communication. Through the chatbot we asked pre-selected questions related to climate change, that could be useful for communication, namely, to inform the general public, for educational goals and to support science policy targets, i.e., to overcome academic jargon and raise awareness for policy makers and politicians. Table 1 summarizes the target audiences and specific goals associated with the prompts created.

Table 1. Target audiences and specific goals associated with the prompts created.

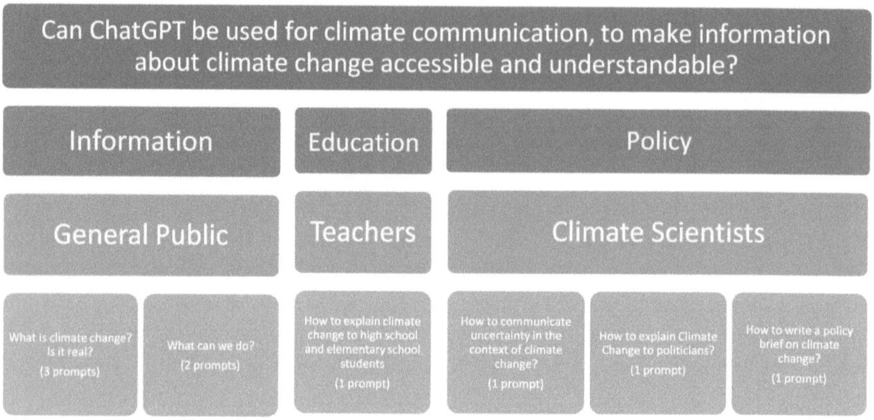

The first set of questions was designed to understand how ChatGPT generates answers about climate change, assuming that the general public would use it to obtain information. The following prompts were used:

- What is climate change?
- What are the real problems associated with climate change?
- What can we do to reduce climate change? What can I do to reduce climate change?
- Is climate change a hoax?

For the educational community, we used ChatGPT as a potential tool to support teachers by asking for suggestions on how to approach the topic with students. We selected the elementary and high school as these grades are identified as having the majority of climate change education interventions [16], and Climate Change education should inform and prepare these generations to understand, make lifestyle changes and adaptations to reduce GhG emissions and other ongoing and upcoming impacts [42]. The chosen prompt was:

- How can I explain the concepts of climate change, climate adaptation and climate change mitigation with concrete examples to high school students versus elementary school students?

For academics to transfer science-based knowledge for policy makers and politicians' awareness on climate change, a combination of two questions and one task was used:

- How to communicate uncertainty in the context of climate change?
- As a climate scientist, how can I explain climate change to politicians so that they understand the urgency and prioritize the issue?

- Write a policy brief on climate change for non-environmental politicians, with the aim of getting them to fund more sustainable projects. I need three A4 pages readable by them in a clear and concise manner.

We conducted an initial session with ChatGPT-3.5 in August 2023, as it was the most accessible version but limited to pre-2021 data. In June 2024, we repeated the questions with the free version of ChatGPT-4.0, a more advanced version with improved data coverage, though still constrained by session length and response complexity. For each of the three goals (information, education, policy), we reset ChatGPT and started a new conversation. We then analyzed differences between versions and compared the content generated with scientific publications and recent grey literature, including reports from IPCC, OECD and UNESCO. Table 2 lists the consulted literature, with the main themes addressed. The complete references are available in the bibliography.

In the presentation of the results, ChatGPT responses are boxed in tables, in italic and edited/cut to reduce the text length. We present ChatGPT-4 responses (July 2024), as they are more recent, but for interpretation, answers from ChatGPT-3.5 (August 2023) were also consulted to verify consistency and evolution (completed answers available by emailing the authors).

Responses were evaluated based on relevance (whether the answers addressed the questions, matched the required knowledge level, and were clear for different audiences), completeness (whether they covered key scientific facts), and scientific accuracy (whether they aligned with peer-reviewed literature and official reports). Overall, our findings indicate that ChatGPT provides sufficiently relevant information for the intended audiences. Due to the characteristics of a LLM, repeating the questions to ChatGPT will not result in the same answers.

3 Results

3.1 Generative AI for Public Communication of Climate Change (Table 3)

[Prompt 1] What Is Climate Change?

The first question was asked to understand how ChatGPT provides a general introduction to the topic of climate change. The answer gives us a definition, presents the causes and a set of consequences, introduces some possible adaptation and mitigation measures. The information is accurate and relevant, but not complete. As this was a general question, with no indication to go deeper, it resulted in an equally general answer, good for a first approach to the topic. It also introduces some terms that may not be familiar for the general public, like Greenhouse Gases, and then give examples and explains the greenhouse effect, which may be important for better understanding of the theme and opens possibilities to be explored with new prompts. There are some differences between answers from ChatGPT-3.5 (2023) and ChatGPT-4 (2024). The language in version 3.5 was simpler and attributed the causes of climate change mainly to human activity, whereas the new version begins by mentioning that Climate Change can result from natural and human activities. This may lead to believe that these have equal importance, which is not accurate. However, throughout the explanation, the focus is indeed

Table 2. List of consulted literature used to verify the answers of ChatGPT.

	Climate Comm.	Climate educ.	Climate Policy
Biswas, Som S. 2023. "Potential Use of Chat GPT in Global Warming"	x	x	
Change, N. C. (2019). Scientific uncertainty.			x
Cooper, Grant. 2023. "Examining Science Education in ChatGPT: An Exploratory Study of Generative Artificial Intelligence."		x	
Dechezleprêtre, Antoine, Adrien Fabre, Tobias Kruse, Blueberry Planterose, Ana Sanchez Chico, and Stefanie Stantcheva. 2022. "Fighting Climate Change: International Attitudes Toward Climate Policies."	x	x	x
DeMarco, Rosanna, and Kimberly Adams Tufts. 2014. "The Mechanics of Writing a Policy Brief."			x
IPCC. 2023. "Summary for Policymakers." Climate Change 2023: Synthesis Report. A Report of the Intergovernmental Plane on Climate Change	x	x	x
IPCC, 2023: Sections. In: Climate Change 2023: Synthesis Report. Contribution of Working Groups I, II and III to the Sixth Assessment Report of the Intergovernmental Panel on Climate Change	x	x	x
Kooli, Chokri. 2023. "Chatbots in Education and Research: A Critical Examination of Ethical Implications and Solutions."		x	
Longnecker, Nancy. 2016. "An Integrated Model of Science Communication-More than Providing Evidence."	x		
Nerlich, Brigitte, Nelya Koteyko, and Brian Brown. 2010. "Theory and Language of Climate Change Communication."	x		

(continued)

Table 2. (*continued*)

	Climate Comm.	Climate educ.	Climate Policy
Paris Agreement. 2015. "Paris Agreement."	x		
Robertson, C. T. 2022. "How People Access and Think about Climate Change."	x		
Stoknes, Per Espen. 2014. "Rethinking Climate Communications and the 'Psychological Climate Paradox.'"	x		
Thompson, Jessica, and Sarah Schweizer. 2008. "The Conventions of Climate Change Communication."	x		
Tosun, Jale, and B Guy Peters. 2021. "The Politics of Climate Change: Domestic and International Responses to a Global Challenge."			x
UNESCO Climate Change Initiative. (2010). Climate change education for sustainable development.		x	
Wong, Shale L., Larry A. Green, Andrew W. Bazemore, and Benjamin F. Miller. 2017. "How to Write a Health Policy Brief."			x
Young, E., & Quinn, L. (2017). An essential guide to writing policy briefs.			x
Yu, H. (2024). The application and challenges of ChatGPT in educational transformation: New demands for teachers' roles.		x	
Zhu, Jun Jie, Jinyue Jiang, Meiqi Yang, and Zhiyong Jason Ren. 2023. "ChatGPT and Environmental Research."	x	x	x

on anthropogenic causes. In 2023, the response included a call to action, adaptation and mitigation measures and a reference to the Paris Agreement, offering a broader perspective. The 2024 version presents a more direct answer to the question.

[Prompt 2] What Are the Real Problems Associated with Climate Change? The second question intended to increase understanding of the problem of climate change and verify if ChatGPT added and deepened information to the first question, which happened.

Table 3. Answer to prompt "What is Climate change?" (Source: [1]).

Climate change refers to significant and lasting changes in the Earth's climate, particularly in temperature, precipitation patterns [...] ranging from decades to millions of years. It can result from natural processes, such as volcanic eruptions [...] as well as from human activities, particularly the burning of fossil fuels and deforestation. Here are some key points: *1. Greenhouse Effect: Human activities, especially the burning of fossil fuels [...] and deforestation, have increased concentrations of greenhouse gases (GHGs) like carbon dioxide (CO2) [...]. These gases trap heat in the atmosphere, leading to a warming effect known as the greenhouse effect.* *2. Temperature Rise: [...] increase in global average temperatures [...] with the last few decades being the warmest on record.* *3. Sea Level Rise: As temperatures rise, polar ice caps and glaciers melt, contributing to higher sea levels [...]* *4. Extreme Weather Events: [...] increase in the frequency and intensity of [...] hurricanes, droughts, heatwaves, [...] devastating impacts on ecosystems and human societies.* *5. Ocean Acidification: Increased CO2 levels [...] dissolve in oceans, leading to ocean acidification [...] harm marine life [...] such as corals and some plankton species.* *6. Impact on Ecosystems: [...] Species may be forced to migrate to new areas, adapt, or face extinction.* *7. Human Health and Socioeconomic Impact: [...] increased heat stress, the spread of diseases, and food and water insecurity. [...] economic losses and social instability [...] on agriculture, infrastructure, and livelihoods.* *Understanding and addressing climate change involves reducing GHG emissions (mitigation), adapting to its effects (adaptation), and enhancing resilience to its impacts through policy measures, technological innovations, and international cooperation.*

While the first answer focused on environmental and health problems, the second repeated information from the first answer, but went into more detail on the economic, social and cultural aspects, all connected with anthropogenic actions. The answer from ChatGPT-3.5 had minimal differences (e.g., the cultural impact was not mentioned, but all the other points were presented in both answers, although organized differently) (Table 4).

[Prompt 3a] What Can We Do to Reduce Climate Change? (Table 5)

There were several differences between the 2023 and 2024 responses. In 2023, ChatGPT-3.5 provided a shorter response with mostly global actions and only one individual measure. It listed 13 actions without distinguishing mitigation from adaptation, and some points lacked detailed explanations. In 2024, the ChatGPT-4 generated a longer list of measures but focused on giving instructions without explaining why they should be implemented. Additionally, some points such as 'Choose products with lower carbon footprints' were treated in a superficial manner, which may make them difficult for the public to understand due to a lack of context or suitable explanation and may compromise behavior change and action.

Table 4. Answer to prompt "What are the real problems associated with climate change?" (Source: [1]).

1. *Rising Temperatures: [...] heat-related illnesses and deaths, particularly among vulnerable populations like the elderly and children.*
2. *Sea Level Rise: [...] threatens coastal communities with increased flooding, erosion, and the loss of habitat [...]. It can also lead to the displacement of populations and the loss of arable land.*
3. *Extreme Weather Events: [...] can cause significant damage to infrastructure, disrupt livelihoods, and lead to loss of life.*
4. *Impact on Water Resources: [...] more severe droughts [...] and increased flooding [...] affect freshwater availability for drinking, agriculture, and sanitation [...]*
5. *Agricultural Disruption: [...] alter growing seasons, reduce crop yields, and affect food security [...] reduce the predictability of food production, leading to higher food prices and increased hunger and malnutrition.*
6. *Biodiversity Loss: Many species are unable to adapt quickly [...] leading to shifts in distribution, population declines, or even extinction [...]*
7. *Ocean Acidification: [...] affects marine life [...] corals, mollusks, and some plankton species that rely on calcium carbonate to form their shells and skeletons.*
8. *Health Impacts: [...] spread of infectious diseases [...], worsening air quality (leading to respiratory issues) [...] can strain public health systems.*
9. *Economic Costs: [...] Damage to property and infrastructure [...], loss of agricultural productivity, and increased health care costs [...] reduced tourism revenues and increased costs for disaster relief and adaptation measures.*
10. *Social and Political Instability: [...] Resource scarcity [...] can lead to migration, social unrest, and even violent conflict over resources.*
11. *Loss of Livelihoods: [...] Climate change can disrupt fishing, farming, and forestry activities, leading to loss of income and increased poverty.*
12. *Cultural Impacts: [...] rising sea levels and extreme weather can damage historical monuments and archaeological sites, while changing environmental conditions can disrupt traditional ways of life.*

[Prompt 3b] What Can I Do to Reduce Climate Change? (Table 6)

This question was intended to prompt the AI to present individual measures and encourage behavioral change. The answer presents a set of twelve actions to combat climate change. Again, some points briefly explain the reasons for the proposed measure (e.g., points 1, 4, 6 and 8), others would benefit from a more detailed explanation (e.g., point 7). Some measures are either too vague (points 5 and 10), difficult to understand (point 11) or difficult to operationalize without additional information (point 9 and 12), which may compromise behavior change and action from the reader recipient.

[Prompt 4] Is Climate Change a Hoax?

This question was asked with the intention of understanding ChatGPT's answers related to *fake news* and conspiracy theories about climate change. The answer indicates that ChatGPT training excludes fake news or conspiracy theories about climate change. When we raised the question about the veracity of climate change, it responded based

Table 5. Answer to prompt "What can we do to reduce climate change? (Source: [1]).

Mitigation Strategies

1. *Reduce Greenhouse Gas Emissions: [...] Transition to Renewable Energy like solar, wind, hydroelectric, and geothermal power to reduce dependence on fossil fuels. [...] Improve energy efficiency in buildings, transportation, and industries. [...] Electrify transportation and other sectors currently dependent on fossil fuels. [...] Implement carbon pricing mechanisms, such as carbon taxes or cap-and-trade systems, to incentivize the reduction of greenhouse gas emissions.*
2. *Sustainable Agriculture and Forestry: [...] Reduce deforestation and promote reforestation and afforestation. [...] Adopt sustainable agricultural practices that reduce emissions, such as no-till farming, crop rotation, and organic farming. [...] Agroforestry: Integrate trees and shrubs into agricultural landscapes to enhance carbon sequestration.*
3. *Carbon Capture and Storage (CCS): [...] Develop and deploy technologies that capture CO2 directly from the atmosphere and store it underground. [...] Bioenergy with CCS (BECCS): Combine bioenergy production with carbon capture and storage to create negative emissions.*
4. *Reduce Waste [...] Increase recycling rates and compost [...] to reduce methane emissions from landfills. [...] Promote a circular economy where products are designed for reuse, repair, and recycling, minimizing waste.*
5. *[...] Support and strengthen international climate agreements, such as the Paris Agreement [...] Implement national policies and regulations that promote renewable energy, energy efficiency, and emissions reductions.*

Adaptation Strategies

1. *Climate-Resilient Infrastructure: Building Standards [...] ensure infrastructure can withstand extreme weather events. Invest in flood defenses, such as levees, sea walls, and stormwater management systems.*
2. *Implement water conservation practices [...] drought management plans to ensure water availability during dry periods.*
3. *Agricultural [...] plant drought-resistant crop varieties. [...] Improve irrigation systems to use water more efficiently.*
4. *Community Preparedness [...] Develop and implement emergency response plans [...] Increase public awareness and education [...]*

Individual Actions

1. *Reduce Energy Consumption: [...] Improve home insulation, use energy-efficient appliances, and switch to LED lighting. [...] Use public transportation, carpool, bike, or walk instead of driving alone. Consider electric or hybrid vehicles.*
2. *Sustainable Consumption: [...] Reduce meat and dairy consumption [...] Choose products with lower carbon footprints, avoid single-use plastics, and support companies with sustainable practices.*
3. *Advocacy and Education: Raise Awareness, Educate others [...] advocate for strong climate policies. Political Engagement: Support and vote for leaders and policies that prioritize climate action.*

Technological Innovation

1. *Invest in research and development of new technologies that can reduce emissions or help adapt to climate change.*
2. *Accelerate the deployment of existing green technologies, such as renewable energy systems and electric vehicles.*

International Cooperation

1. *Global Collaboration [...] share knowledge, technology, and resources.*
2. *Provide financial support to developing countries for climate mitigation and adaptation efforts.*

Table 6. Answer to prompt "What can I do to reduce climate change?"

1. ***Reduce energy consumption***: *Use energy-efficient appliances, turn off lights and electronics when not in use, and consider using smart power strips to eliminate standby power. Lowering your energy consumption reduces greenhouse gas emissions from fossil fuel-based electricity generation.*
2. ***Use renewable energy***: *If possible, install solar panels on your home or support renewable energy sources offered by your utility company. This can significantly reduce your reliance on fossil fuels.*
3. ***Opt for energy-efficient transportation***: *Use public transportation, carpool, bike, or walk whenever possible. If you need a car, consider an electric or hybrid vehicle, as they produce fewer emissions compared to traditional gasoline-powered cars.*
4. ***Reduce, reuse, recycle***: *Minimize waste generation by buying products with minimal packaging, reusing items, and recycling materials whenever possible. Reducing waste reduces the need for resource extraction and waste disposal, both of which contribute to emissions.*
5. ***Support sustainable practices***: *Choose products and services from companies that prioritize sustainability and environmentally friendly practices.*
6. ***Eat a more plant-based diet:*** *Reduce meat consumption, especially beef and lamb, as livestock agriculture is a significant source of methane, a potent greenhouse gas.*
7. ***Conserve water:*** *Be mindful of water usage, repair leaks promptly, and consider installing water-saving fixtures in your home.*
8. ***Plant trees and support reforestation***: *Trees absorb carbon dioxide from the atmosphere, making reforestation efforts vital for carbon sequestration.*
9. ***Advocate for climate-friendly policies:*** *Get involved in local and national climate advocacy efforts, urging policymakers to implement climate-friendly policies and support renewable energy initiatives.*
10. ***Educate yourself and others***: *Stay informed about climate change, its impacts, and solutions. Share your knowledge with friends, family, and community to raise awareness.*
11. *Offset your carbon footprint: Consider offsetting the emissions you cannot eliminate by investing in projects that reduce or capture greenhouse gases, such as renewable energy or reforestation projects.*
12. *Support renewable energy initiatives: Invest in renewable energy projects or participate in community solar initiatives.*

on scientific consensus, pointing out the evidence to justify the veracity of the facts. It mentioned the IPCC as the authority on climate change and briefly explained why there are groups that deny climate change. Comparing responses from ChatGPT-3.5 and 4, the latest version offers more developed and accurate content, mentioning different scientific organizations and relevant scientific support and provides ways to refute skeptical claims (Table 7).

3.2 Generative AI for Educational Goals of Climate Change

[Prompt 6] - How Can I Explain the Concepts of Climate Change, Climate Adaptation and Climate Change Mitigation with Concrete Examples to High School Students Versus Elementary School Students? (Table 8)

Table 7. Answer to prompt "Is Climate change a hoax?" (Source: [1]).

Climate change is not a hoax. The overwhelming consensus among scientists is that climate change is real, primarily caused by human activities, and has significant and measurable impacts on the planet. [...]

Scientific Consensus

1. *Intergovernmental Panel on Climate Change [...] reports, which are compiled by hundreds of experts from around the world, conclude that climate change is happening, largely driven by human activities such as burning fossil fuels and deforestation.*
2. *[...] Major scientific organizations worldwide, including NASA, the National Oceanic and Atmospheric Administration (NOAA), the American Association for the Advancement of Science (AAAS), and the Royal Society, agree on the reality of climate change and its human causes.*
3. *[...] Thousands of peer-reviewed studies [...] provide robust evidence of climate change [...] data from various sources, including temperature records, ice cores, satellite observations, and climate models.*

Evidence of Climate Change

1. *[...] past few decades being the warmest on record [...] aligns with increased concentrations of greenhouse gases in the atmosphere.*
2. *Glaciers and polar ice caps are melting at an accelerating rate [...]*
3. *Sea levels have risen due to melting ice and the thermal expansion of seawater [...]*
4. *[...] extreme weather events [...] have increased. Climate change influences the severity and occurrence [...]*
5. *Oceans absorb about a quarter of the CO2 emitted by human [...] leads to ocean acidification, which affects marine life [...].*
6. *Many species are shifting their geographical ranges, migration patterns, and seasonal behaviors in response to changing temperatures and habitats.*

Addressing Skepticism

[...] arguments often stem from misunderstandings, misinformation, or vested interests in maintaining the status quo. Here are common rebuttals to skeptical claims:

1. *Natural Variability: While natural factors do influence the climate, the rapid warming [...] cannot be explained by natural variability alone. Human activities are the primary driver of recent changes.*
2. *Historical Climate Changes: The Earth's climate has changed throughout its history, but the current rate of change is unprecedented [...]. Past changes were often driven by natural factors over much longer timescales.*
3. *Scientific Integrity: Climate science is subject to rigorous peer review and transparency. The scientific method involves constant testing, validation, and refinement of theories and data.*

Climate change is supported by a vast body of scientific evidence [...]. Dismissing it as a hoax undermines efforts to tackle the significant challenges it poses.

The answer is relevant to educational purposes as it presents essential content for an initial learning of the topics proposed by the teacher. The content was adapted to the students' schooling levels and age groups, using distinct language and appropriate examples, aligned with contemporary theories of cognitive development and learning. The

Table 8. Answer to prompt 6 (Source: [1]).

Climate Change

High School Students:

- *Explanation: Climate change refers to significant changes in global temperatures and weather patterns over time [...] rapid increase in global temperatures largely due to human activities like burning fossil fuels, deforestation, and industrial processes.*
- *Example: [...] impact of the greenhouse effect. Explain how gases like carbon dioxide (CO2) and methane (CH4) trap heat in the Earth's atmosphere, leading to a rise in global temperatures. Use data and graphs showing rising global temperatures over the past century.*
- *Discussion Point: Talk about the melting of polar ice caps and glaciers, rising sea levels, and the increased frequency and intensity of extreme weather events, such as hurricanes, heatwaves, and floods.*

Elementary School Students:

- *Explanation: Climate change means the Earth's weather is getting warmer or changing in other ways, and it's happening faster because of things people do.*
- *Example: Describe how burning things like coal, oil, and gas to run cars and factories puts more "bad" gases into the air. These gases act like a blanket, making the Earth warmer.*
- *Discussion Point: Talk about simple effects, like how polar bears' homes (ice) are melting and how this makes it hard for them to live. [...] how more wildfires can start because it gets too hot and dry.*

Climate Change Adaptation

High School Students:

- *Explanation: Climate change adaptation involves making adjustments in our social, economic, and environmental practices to minimize the damage [...].*
- *Example: [...] building seawalls and levees to protect coastal cities from rising sea levels [...] developing drought-resistant crops to ensure food security in areas prone to drought.*
- *Discussion Point: [...] different countries [...] adaptation strategies based on their specific vulnerabilities and needs [...] Netherlands' extensive use of dikes and water management systems to prevent flooding.*

Elementary School Students:

- *Explanation: Adaptation means changing how we live so we can handle the changes in the weather.*
- *Example: [...] in places where it's getting really dry, farmers are planting special plants that don't need as much water. In cities near the ocean, people are building big walls to keep the water out [...]*
- *Discussion Point: Use simple visuals, like pictures of drought-resistant plants or seawalls [...]*

Climate Change Mitigation

High School Students:

- *Explanation: [...] efforts to reduce or prevent the emission of greenhouse gases to slow down global warming.*
- *Example: [...] renewable energy sources [...] produce electricity without emitting greenhouse gases. [...] importance of energy efficiency, such as using LED lights and electric cars.*

(*continued*)

Table 8. (*continued*)

• *Discussion Point: [...] international agreements, like the Paris Agreement, in setting targets for reducing emissions. [...] impact of individual actions, such as reducing meat consumption, using public transportation, and recycling.*
Elementary School Students:
• *Explanation: Mitigation means doing things to stop climate change from getting worse.*
• *Example: [...] solar panels on houses can make electricity from the sun, which doesn't make "bad" gases. [...] planting trees helps because trees take in the "bad" gases and give us oxygen.*
• *Discussion Point: Show pictures or videos of wind turbines and solar panels. Encourage simple actions, like turning off lights when not needed and riding bikes instead of using cars.*
Summary
• *High School: Provide detailed explanations with scientific terms, data, and real-world examples. Encourage critical thinking and discussion about global and local impacts and solutions.*
• *Elementary School: Use simple language, relatable examples, and visual aids. Focus on basic concepts and easy-to-understand impacts and actions.*

2024 version is again more developed, introducing explanations, examples and discussion points on climate change, adaptation and mitigation. It concludes with pedagogical tips to tailor the complexity and examples to the appropriate school level. Limitations are addressed in the discussion.

3.3 Generative AI for Policies of Climate Change

[Prompt 7] How to Communicate Uncertainty in the Context of Climate Change? (Table 9)

The answer emphasizes the importance of effectively communicating uncertainty in the context of climate change and presents eight key guidelines. These include acknowledging the existence of uncertainty, using probabilities, incorporating quantification and visual aids, explaining the different types and sources of uncertainty, highlighting robust findings, and tailoring messages to specific audiences.

The main difference between the two versions of ChatGPT lies in their focus. The earlier version presented 12 points, placing greater emphasis on using clear language and engaging in dialogue with the public to build trust and understanding. The more recent version distinguishes between different audiences and stresses the importance of taking action, for example, by noting that uncertainty should not lead to stagnation or be used as an excuse for inaction.

Table 9. Answer to prompt 7.

Communicating uncertainty in the context of climate change is essential to maintaining credibility, fostering trust, and enabling informed decision-making [...]: 1. *Be Honest, Not Paralyzing: Acknowledge uncertainty [...] Emphasize what is known with high confidence (e.g., human activities are warming the planet) alongside areas where uncertainty remains (e.g., the exact pace of future sea-level rise).* 2. *Use Probabilistic Language Thoughtfully: [...] "There is a 90% chance that..." can be more relatable than "very likely." Combine probabilities with ranges to convey variability (e.g., "Global temperatures are projected to rise by 2.1°C to 3.5°C by 2100 under current policies").* 3. *Distinguish Between Types of Uncertainty: Known unknowns (e.g., future emissions scenarios, policy choices); Model uncertainty (e.g., different models give slightly different outcomes); Natural variability (e.g., short-term climate fluctuations). [...] helps audiences understand that uncertainty doesn't mean ignorance—it often means complexity.* 4. *Highlight Robust Findings: Emphasize conclusions that remain consistent across scenarios and models (e.g., "Regardless of emission pathway, Arctic Sea ice will continue to decline").* 5. *Visual Tools Help: [...]Include simple, annotated visuals (e.g., the "burning embers" diagram used by the IPCC to show risk levels under different warming scenarios).* 6. *Frame Risk, Not Just Uncertainty: [...] Use risk language (e.g., low probability but high impact) similar to how financial or insurance sectors discuss risk.* 7. *Tailor to Your Audience: Policymakers may want decision-relevant ranges. The general public may prefer clarity and relevance over statistical detail. Scientists may appreciate a deeper dive into methodologies and data sources.* 8. *Avoid Common Pitfalls: Don't downplay the seriousness of climate change by overemphasizing uncertainty. Don't imply that uncertainty is a reason for inaction—highlight how precautionary principles apply.*

[Prompt 8] As a Climate Scientist, How Can I Explain Climate Change to Politicians So that They Understand the Urgency and Prioritize the Issue? (Table 10)

There were some differences between the answers from ChatGPT3.5 and ChatGPT 4. The latest one considers challenges that politicians face, such as limited time, economic pressures and preference for actionable measures with local relevance. It frames climate change in terms of risk, cost-benefit analysis and immediate consequence, using a pragmatic approach for persuasion, aligned with existing political agendas. The 2023 version had a more educational tone, focusing on building relationships and empathy, using evidence and storytelling to build understanding and long-term engagement, but also offering instructions and actionable policies.

[Prompt 9] As a Climate Scientist, How Can I Explain Climate Change to Politicians So that They Understand the Urgency and Prioritize the Issue? (Table 11)

Table 10. Answer to prompt 8.

[...] balancing scientific accuracy with strategic communication. Politicians are time-constrained, decision-oriented, and often influenced by policy implications, public opinion, and economic concerns. *1. Frame It in Terms of Risk, Not Just Science: [...] Emphasize climate change as a high impact, escalating risk, not a far-off environmental issue. Use analogies they understand: "Just like national security, climate risk requires acting before every detail is certain."* *2. Focus on Local and Immediate Relevance: Translate global models into local impacts: rising insurance costs, infrastructure vulnerability, crop losses, or heat-related health crises in their region. Use real, recent extreme events (droughts, floods, fires) linked to climate trends—not as proof, but as illustrations of increasing risks.* *3. Quantify Economic Consequences (and Opportunities): Politicians respond to cost-benefit framing - Cost of inaction (damage to economy, health, agriculture) and Benefits of action (job creation, clean tech leadership, avoided future costs). Reference trusted bodies like the IPCC, World Bank, or insurance industry reports.* *4. Lead with Solutions, Not Just Problems: [...] we have tools to act now (clean energy, urban planning, adaptation strategies). Present policy levers they control (e.g., zoning laws, energy incentives, transport policies). Show examples of [...] leaders succeeding with climate-forward policies [...].* *5. Emphasize Urgency Without Despair: [...]early action reduces costs and damage. Avoid doom-laden language.* *6. Use Clear, Confident Language: [...] Say "We know" rather than "The models suggest." Be concise. You often have less than 5 minutes to make your point. Prepare one-pager summaries with visuals, short bullet points, and a "bottom line" recommendation.* *7. Build Relationships, Not Just Briefings: Be available for follow-up. Politicians often return to people they trust when shaping policy. Understand their priorities and constraints—reframe climate to align with what they already care about (e.g., jobs, national security, public health).*

ChatGPT 4 fulfilled the task of creating a backbone of a policy brief on sustainable projects for non-environmental politicians. The content was well structured, divided in three pages, starting with general information, and then presenting pragmatic concerns with examples, ending with concrete recommendations. The style is adapted to the political target, with a clear language, quick to read, appealing to responsibility and impact. In comparison, the ChatGPT3.5 version had a few limitations. It did not meet the three-page requirement, being too short and general, nor did it co-substantiate its affirmations with concrete data. Further limitations are explored in the discussion.

Table 11. Answer to prompt 9.

Policy Brief: Climate Action as a Strategic Investment
Securing Our Economy, Infrastructure, and Public Safety through Sustainable Projects

- *Executive Summary: Climate change is no longer a future problem—it is a current economic, security, and infrastructure risk. The good news: investing [...] now will reduce costs later, create jobs, and protect public assets.*
- *This brief outlines: Why climate change matters for all sectors[...]. What's at stake for our economy [...] and communities. How smart investments [...]deliver long-term value. Actionable recommendations for funding [...]*
- *The Context: Climate Risk Is Now a Core Governance Issue: Disasters are escalating [...]. Local impacts are growing [...] The financial sector is shifting [...]*

[PAGE 2: ECONOMIC AND POLICY CASE FOR ACTION]

1. *Climate Change Affects All Portfolios: Economic Development - Rising heat lowers labor productivity [...], Investing [...]creates more jobs [...]. Health and Safety - Heat-related illnesses and air pollution are straining healthcare systems [...]. Infrastructure - $1 spent on climate-resilient infrastructure avoids $4–$7 in disaster recovery costs.*
2. *Sustainable Projects - smart, scalable investments that align with economic growth and fiscal responsibility. Example: Renewable Energy (solar, wind) - Lower long-term energy costs, energy Independence [...]*
3. *Political Momentum Is Building - scaling green infrastructure spending. [...] job-creating, clean-tech projects. Not acting increases our exposure to liability, public discontent, and future costs.*

[PAGE 3: RECOMMENDATIONS & NEXT STEPS]

1. *Expand Funding for Proven Sustainable Infrastructure: Prioritize projects with a clear cost-benefit profile: energy upgrades, resilient roads, cooling interventions, water management.*
2. *Establish a Climate-Resilience Fund in Every Ministry - Even non-environmental departments [...]Transport can fund heat-resistant materials; Housing can invest in passive cooling.*
3. *Remove Regulatory Barriers to Green Investment [...]Offer tax or permitting incentives for local governments adopting climate-smart plans.*
4. *Monitor, Evaluate, and Report Outcomes - Require performance metrics for publicly funded sustainability projects*

Climate action is no longer just about carbon—it's about cash, continuity, and competitiveness. By funding sustainable projects, we reduce risk exposure, boost local economies, and build trust with the public. This is not an expense—it's an investment with immediate and long-term returns.

Contact for Technical Guidance. If your office needs help identifying shovel-ready projects or assessing climate risk exposure in your domain, a team of scientists and policy advisors is available for consultation.

4 Discussion

In this study, we used ChatGPT to understand its potential contribution to climate communication, literacy and critical thinking, targeting three different audiences with different objectives: information about climate change (used by the general public); teaching about climate change in a formal educational context (used by teachers); communication for policy makers and politicians about climate change (used by climate scientists).

For the first objective, some prompts were created to emulate what the general public could ask ChatGPT to get information about climate change. Simple questions with little context were deliberately asked. The results allowed a qualitative evaluation of the relevance, accuracy and scientific acumen of ChatGPT replies to climate related questions and showed some aspects worth highlighting.

The user gets clear and general information about what climate change is and its main causes, and more specific information about the consequences, adaptation and mitigation measures, as well as potential individual actions. Accessible language, selection of essential information and clarity of content presentation are benefits commonly associated with Generative AI [20, 22] and mentioned as good practices in various existing models of science communication [43].

The information presented is correct and relevant, with facts widely recognized in the scientific community (e.g., IPCC[4], NOAA[5]). One aspect that caught our attention in Prompt 1 of ChatGPT-4 was the way it included natural and human causes for this phenomenon, but without developing the theme equally for both, providing only additional content for the anthropogenic related causes. While the answer is not wrong, this may lead the public to consider natural and human causes with equal importance, which is not accurate, as the acceleration of climate change is mainly due to human activity [44]. Nevertheless, in Prompts 4 and 5, the emphasis is again, and appropriately, only focused on human action.

Analyzing the set of information resulting from Prompts 1 to 4 in terms of completeness, the information is sufficient for the objectives and the chosen target, as a very detailed approach could overwhelm and demotivate this public. Regarding climate communication, Stoknes [45] advises not to overwhelm people with the catastrophic scenarios but instead focus on a positive message of a greener future, in a smart society, using less resources and having a better quality of life. To understand perceptions of climate change and the factors influencing behavior change, Dechezleprêtre et al. [3] conducted a large-scale survey involving 40.000 respondents from 20 countries. They concluded that support for climate policies depends on people's beliefs about the effectiveness of the policy (in reducing emissions), concerns about inequality (impact on low-income households) and personal interests (impact on household). Explaining climate policies and their benefits to the average citizen increases the willingness to support them, while simply informing about the impacts of climate change seems to be ineffective. But, as concluded by Robertson [46, p. 57] 'Climate change is a difficult news topic to cover, and it is not clear that there is a one-size-fits-all approach to it'. When analyzing the types of measures, 10 of the 12 proposals for individual actions focus on changing individual

[4] Intergovernmental Panel on Climate Change https://www.ipcc.ch/

[5] National Oceanic and Atmispferic Administration https://www.noaa.gov/

consumer behavior at household level. Advocacy is mentioned, but in a general way, not elaborated with subtypes such as protesting or calling representatives, among others. This reinforces the privileging of individual consumer behavior change over potentially more effective advocacy.

When addressing measures towards climate mitigation (i.e., enhance decarbonization by reducing the GhG emissions) and/or adaptation (i.e., take actions to minimize present and future impacts)[6] both collective (Prompt 3a) and individual (prompt 3b) most points were presented in an instructional way, indicating what needs to be done without justifying why the measure is needed or how it impacts the overall goal, which may not be motivating enough to change behavior. Individual measures are presented without distinguishing degrees of importance, but they clearly have different impacts, which would be interesting for the public to understand. Measures such as asking people to unplug appliances have been questioned, as the impact of this action is minimal compared to others of higher impact such as using renewable energy or public transportation to reduce the carbon footprint. This may lead to distrust or confusion among individuals [32].

Another issue to underline relates to the content of the reply to Prompt 4. We questioned the veracity of climate change, and the answer reinforces the fact that ChatGPT has been trained to not promote *fake news* or respond/apply to conspiracy theories, related to the theme. Additional prompts were made to test the robustness of ChatGPT regarding climate change conspiracies (1 - Regarding climate change, it is too late to do something. 2 - Why is the Antarctic Sea ice increasing? 3 - Plants requires CO_2, thus fossil fuel emissions will be beneficial for plants? – complete answers available by email), and it seems to be robustly trained in this theme. This may be related with the algorithm's automatic filters, the training of humans to improve the quality of the answers and the pre-training text corpus [39], as the field of climate science has a substantial number of state-of-the-art summaries and assessment reports publicly available [11]. As a tool that evolves with the corpus of text available on the internet, it is necessary to ensure that the programming and training techniques exclude misinformation and offer scientifically correct information [47–49].

This represents an advantage in the current digital and social media era, where citizens use them as quick access to information and most trust the content provided, as contradicting *fake news* circulating on social networks is of uttermost importance to education and awareness on climate change. In contrast, it's important to recognize that ChatGPT can be exploited by malicious actors to spread false climate change information and manipulate public opinion. Like other GenAI tools, its ability to rapidly generate large volumes of text makes it easier to flood online platforms with misleading, persuasive, and deceptive content [50].

Regarding the use of ChatGPT for educational purposes, a more elaborate prompt [Prompt 5] was created to address the topic of climate change, as well as adaptation and mitigation measures, at different levels of education.

[6] European Environmental Agency - https://www.eea.europa.eu/en/about/contact-us/faqs/what-is-the-difference-between-adaptation-and-mitigation

The content of the answer is relevant and respects the students' ages, presenting appropriate language and examples depending on whether it was elementary or high school education.

In terms of development and learning, elementary school children (7–11 years) are beginning to think logically, but they are still very attached to the concrete and have difficulty understanding abstract concepts. Therefore, the content of teaching should be simple, using examples from everyday life and practical activities [51]. In secondary school, students are developing the capacity for abstract, hypothetical-deductive and systematic thinking. An appropriate lesson can include critical analysis of concepts, problem solving, debates and abstract and ethical questions [52]. At both levels of education, students learn best through interaction with peers and teachers [53], so discussion is essential. The ChatGPT response considers the developmental levels of the age groups concerned. For elementary education, it includes simple and concrete explanations *(e.g., 'Adaptation means changing how we live so we can handle the changes in the weather')*, with real examples (e.g., *'In cities near the ocean, people are building big walls to keep the water out')* and discussion. For high school, it introduces more complex terms and examples (e.g., '*gases like carbon dioxide (CO2) and methane (CH4) trap heat in the Earth's atmosphere*'), also encouraging discussion (e.g., '*Discussion Point: different countries adaptation strategies on their specific vulnerabilities and needs')*. One point that could be improved in the high school response would be to encourage collaborative learning by suggesting group projects that promote the exchange of ideas, as well as the use of research tools, such as books and technology, that help to develop critical thinking and autonomy [54].

ChatGPT's response also considers the evolution of learning over time. For Bruner, all concepts can be taught to younger children as long as the content is appropriate to their level of development, and it can be deepened in the future [55]. The role of the adult is to provide scaffolding for the child's construction of knowledge, interacting with them and helping them to progress to higher levels. Ausubel [56] reiterates the importance of prior knowing in the construction of knowledge. For meaningful learning to occur, new information must relate to the knowledge the child has already acquired. Content gains meaning when it is learned in interaction with relevant concepts that already exist in the learner's cognitive structure. There is then a process of knowledge modification. Meaningful learning facilitates the retention and use of information in other learning. Even if it is forgotten, it is easier to relearn. In ChatGPT's response, there is an evolution of content, with increasing complexity from elementary to secondary education, respecting these highly accepted theories of learning.

However, as the answer is too concise, it only serves as a starting point for the teacher to organize ideas and structure an educational plan or activity, reinforcing the need to complement it with other resources. As Haluza and Jungwirth [21] suggest, it is important to formulate the questions accurately, to provide sufficient context, and to indicate the specifics intended in the answer, such as length, preferred structure, and key content. Writing effective prompts to get the desired results requires some thought [57]. It is important to use an elaborate, specific prompt to achieve the defined goal. It is also possible to regenerate answers and give feedback on the answer (thumbs up and down) to improve results. A way to get a more structured response could be to ask ChatGPT to generate a hierarchical table of contents and then elaborate on each point in subsequent iterations. In our case, one way to overcome the limited answer obtained would be to continue the dialogue in subsequent prompts, asking ChatGPT to elaborate on each point and to supplement it with teaching and learning activities. However, this could still result in a limited pedagogical activity, as ChatGPT being a LLM lacks human skills such as creativity, empathy and critical thinking. Therefore, it is advisable to use it mostly as a complementary tool. Once used, it is essential that teachers critically evaluate and adjust the content generated to their objectives [58]. Cooper reached a similar conclusion. After generating a teaching unit with ChatGPT, available in [25], he found it to be a valuable tool for educators in designing science units, rubrics and quizzes, as long as they review AI-generated content to ensure alignment with their educational context. When entering the level of detail, it is important to verify ChatGPT responses, either with expert support or by consulting other sources, to ensure accuracy and consistency [34]. Furthermore, for educational purposes ChatGPT can be complemented with creative GenAI apps to create images, like DALL-E, LENSA or similar, in addition to standard teaching support material.

For our third goal, using Generative AI for climate change communication to politics and policy makers, we've created two questions and a task for climate researchers interested in communicating with this audience.

Climate science is a complex field that involves uncertainties due to the complexities of the Earth's climate system and the uncertainty associated to predictions, namely when forecasting climate half-a-century or a century ahead. Politicians are often faced with the challenge of balancing competing interests, economic considerations, and scientific information. In most situations, decisions are taken using scenario modelling with the best available knowledge but where uncertainty is clearly a large portion of the context [59]. It is important for climate scientists to understand the politicians' perspective, build a trusting relationship, and work collaboratively towards solutions. Communicating uncertainty effectively to politicians in the context of climate change is crucial for informed decision-making [60].

Prompt 7 provides guidelines for communicating uncertainty. Some of these recommendations overlap with good practices of science communication, such as tailoring the message to the audience, using visual aids, numbers and graphics. Other tips are more related to uncertainty, such as acknowledging the issue, differentiating types of uncertainty, and explaining the causes. It is also suggested that the message uses probabilities, quantifications and highlight robust findings.

In Prompt 8, ChatGPT was asked to explain climate change to politicians so that they understand the urgency and prioritize the issue. The answer suggests that explaining climate change to this target requires ("*balancing scientific accuracy with strategic communication... use clear, confident language... be concise... with visuals... use analogies... show examples*"). Thompson and Schweizer make similar claims for effective public communication specific to climate change [61]. ChatGPT also presents scientific arguments relatable and urgent for politicians ("*Focus on local and immediate relevance... quantify economic consequences... cost-benefit framing... job creation*"). This response rather than overwhelming politicians with data or abstract models, contextualizes climate science as a matter of risk management, which is a language familiar to political decision-making. These arguments are also used in the task proposed in Prompt 9, to create a policy brief (*"investing now will reduce costs later, create jobs, and protect public assets... every $1 spent on climate-resilient infrastructure avoids $4-$7 in disaster recover costs... not acting increases our exposure to liability, public discontent, and future costs."*).

The policy brief backbone generated by ChatGPT follows some good practices for writing this type of document [30, 62, 63]: it includes an executive summary, states its objectives, contextualizes the problem, outlines possible actions, and provides general recommendations, all this using language and arguments adapted to the target audience. However, we identified some limitations in the generated policy brief, namely the lack of a more detailed content and usage of very brief text, lack of illustrative graphics to support the argument and increase its appeal and impact, as well as the lack of references to other studies. A data-driven policy brief should include evidence-based content [63]. These shortcomings of the policy brief may be related to the initial prompt provided to ChatGPT. One way to address this would be to improve the prompt, for instance, requesting ChatGPT to provide visual elements, graphics and bibliographic references. Prompt engineering is key to solve challenges in generative AI. A prompt should be comprehensive and clearly formulated to ensure that the generated answer meets the intended requirements. Still, it is advisable to evaluate the generated content and specifically to confirm all stated references, as ChatGPT may fabricate citations as confirmed by other authors [64, 65]. Nevertheless, we consider the result to be a good starting point for defining a conceptual plan and structure and then to further develop a policy brief on climate change for policy makers, when combined with data from other sources.

5 Conclusion

This study has shown that Generative AI, and ChatGPT in particular, can contribute to overcoming barriers in climate change communication to different audiences. By answering a set of prompts defined by the researchers, with different levels of depth and demand, ChatGPT was able to provide reliable information on climate change to support people's understanding and willingness to adopt more climate-friendly practices.

For the general public, it offered explanations of the causes, impacts and potential responses to climate change. In the context of formal education, it provided teachers a valuable starting point for structuring learning activities adapted to different school levels. In both cases, ChatGPT proved useful in providing an initial overview of the topic and for summarising concepts and clarifying initial doubts. It makes complex content more accessible and stimulates further engagement through continuous dialogue, while allowing educators and learners to add depth by combining it with other trusted resources.

The study also highlights the opportunities and challenges that generative AI brings to climate communication in policy contexts. By incorporating science communication strategies tailored to climate policy, ChatGPT can facilitate dialogue with decision-makers by providing arguments aligned with political reasoning. For scientists, these generated texts help translate complex science based knowledge into narratives that are both relatable and urgent, thereby increasing the likelihood that policymakers and politicians will prioritize climate issues. The policy brief proposed by ChatGPT followed good practice guidelines in science communication for policy and could be used as a starting point in terms of conceptual plan and structure to further develop a more comprehensive policy brief, to be complemented with data from additional sources. However, some aspects must be considered when using Generative AI in policy-oriented communication, including accuracy, accessibility, the appropriateness of language, framing and trust.

Our comparison between ChatGPT-3.5 and ChatGPT-4 also revealed some differences. While version 3.5 tended to offer broader contextualisation, version 4 produced more literal and provided stronger scientific supported information, though requiring more carefully elaborated prompts or continuous dialogue to achieve depth and relevance. A major advantage of both versions over social media is that their learning database and programming algorithm seem to exclude most common fake news on climate change.

At the same time, some limitations identified, such as brevity, a lack of depth in some responses and an absence of critical thinking, mean that generative AI-drafted texts must remain complementary to human expertise. Academic institutions therefore play a decisive role in ensuring that accessible, peer-reviewed knowledge continues to inform these AI tools.

Future research should examine how different audiences perceive and act upon AI-generated content, whether it can foster meaningful behavioural change, and how it might support innovative policy solutions, such as mitigation and adaptation strategies. At the same time, concerns regarding accuracy, bias, copyrights and the environmental impact of AI must be addressed if such tools are to be integrated responsibly into climate communication, where scientific rigour, ethical considerations and societal trust remain essential.

Acknowledgments. The authors acknowledge financial support from FCT/MCTES, through national funds of CIDTFF (UIDB/00194/2020) and CESAM (UID Centro de Estudos do Ambiente e Mar (CESAM) + LA/P/0094/2020).

Disclosure of Interests The authors have no competing interests to declare that are relevant to the content of this article.

Funding. This work was funded by the ERA Chair BESIDE project financed by the European Union's Horizon 2020 under Grant Agreement ID: 951389, DOI: 10.3030/951389.

References

1. Laranjeiro, D., Lillebø, A., Vieira, H.: Generative AI in climate change communication and education. In: Proceedings of the 17th International Conference on Computer Supported Education, pp. 123–134. SciTePress - Science and Technology Publications (2025). https://doi.org/10.5220/0013478400003932
2. IPCC: Summary for Policymakers. IPCC, Geneva, Switzerland (2023)
3. Dechezleprêtre, A., Fabre, A., Kruse, T., Planterose, B., Sanchez Chico, A., Stantcheva, S.: Fighting Climate Change: International Attitudes Toward Climate Policies, p. 1714. OECD Publishing, Paris (2022). https://doi.org/10.2139/ssrn.4165337

4. Wibeck, V.: Enhancing learning, communication and public engagement about climate change - some lessons from recent literature. Environ. Educ. Res. **20**(3), 387–411 (2014). https://doi.org/10.1080/13504622.2013.812720
5. Horta, A., Carvalho, A.: Climate change communication in Portugal. Oxf. Res. Encycl. Clim. Sci., 1–32 (2017). https://doi.org/10.1093/acrefore/9780190228620.013.316
6. Cook, J., et al.: Quantifying the consensus on anthropogenic global warming in the scientific literature. Environ. Res. Lett. **8**(2) (2013). https://doi.org/10.1088/1748-9326/8/2/024024
7. Newman, N., Fletcher, R., Robertson, C.T., Eddy, K., Nielsen, R.K.: Digital News Report 2022. Reuters Institute for the Study of Journalism, Oxford (2022) [Online]. Available: https://reutersinstitute.politics.ox.ac.uk/digital-news-report/2022
8. Alinejad, D., Van Dijck, J.: Climate communication: how researchers navigate between scientific truth and media publics. Commun. Public. **8**(1), 29–44 (2023). https://doi.org/10.1177/20570473221138612
9. Newman, T.P.: Tracking the release of IPCC AR5 on Twitter: users, comments, and sources following the release of the working group I summary for policymakers. Public Underst. Sci. **26**(7), 815–825 (2017). https://doi.org/10.1177/0963662516628477
10. Meyer, H., Peach, A.K., Guenther, L., Kedar, H.E., Brüggemann, M.: Between calls for action and narratives of denial: climate change attention structures on Twitter. Media Commun. **11**(1), 278–292 (2023). https://doi.org/10.17645/mac.v11i1.6111
11. Schäfer, M.S.: Online communication on climate change and climate politics: a literature review. Wiley Interdiscip. Rev. Clim. Chang. **3**(6), 527–543 (2012). https://doi.org/10.1002/wcc.191
12. Bushell, S., Buisson, G.S., Workman, M., Colley, T.: Strategic narratives in climate change: towards a unifying narrative to address the action gap on climate change. Energy Res. Soc. Sci. **28**, 39–49 (2017)
13. Brown, H., Austhof, E., Luz, P., Ferguson, D.: Economics, health, or environment: what motivates individual climate action. PLOS Clim. **2**(8) (2023). https://doi.org/10.1371/journal.pclm.0000177
14. Goldberg, M., van der Linden, S., Maibach, E., Leiserowitz, A.: Discussing global warming leads to greater acceptance of climate science. Proc. Natl. Acad. Sci. **116**(30), 14804–14805 (2019)
15. Lawson, D., Stevenson, K., Peterson, M., Carrier, S., Strnad, R., Seekamp, E.: Children can foster climate change concern among their parents. Nat. Clim. Chang. **9**(6), 458–462 (2019)
16. Monroe, M., Plate, R., Oxarart, A., Bowers, A., Chaves, W.: Identifying effective climate change education strategies: a systematic review of the research. Environ. Educ. Res. **25**(6), 791–812 (2019)
17. Bender, E.M., Koller, A.: Climbing towards NLU: on meaning, form, and understanding in the age of data. In: Proceedings of the 58th Annual Meeting of the Association for Computational Linguistics, pp. 5185–5198 (2020)
18. Esposito, E.: Artificial Communication. MIT Press, Cambridge (2022)
19. Dwivedi, Y.K., et al.: 'So what if ChatGPT wrote it?' Multidisciplinary perspectives on opportunities, challenges and implications of generative conversational AI for research, practice and policy. Int. J. Inf. Manage. **71** (2023). https://doi.org/10.1016/j.ijinfomgt.2023.102642
20. Biswas, S.S.: Potential use of Chat GPT in global warming. In: Annals of Biomedical Engineering, pp. 1126–1127. Springer International Publishing (2023). https://doi.org/10.1007/s10439-023-03171-8
21. Haluza, D., Jungwirth, D.: Artificial intelligence and ten societal megatrends: an exploratory study using GPT-3. Systems. **11**(3) (2023). https://doi.org/10.3390/systems11030120
22. Zhu, J.J., Jiang, J., Yang, M., Ren, Z.J.: ChatGPT and environmental research. Environ. Sci. Technol., 1–4 (2023). https://doi.org/10.1021/acs.est.3c01818

23. Acar, O.: Are Your Students Ready for AI?: A Four-Step Framework to Prepare Learners for a ChatGPT World? Harvard Business Publishing Education (2023) [Online]. Available: https://hbsp.harvard.edu/inspiring-minds/are-your-students-ready-for-ai?
24. Kuhail, M.A., Alturki, N., Alramlawi, S., Alhejori, K.: Interacting with Educational Chatbots: A Systematic Review, vol. 28, p. 1. Springer US (2023). https://doi.org/10.1007/s10639-022-11177-3
25. Cooper, G.: Examining science education in ChatGPT: an exploratory study of generative artificial intelligence. J. Sci. Educ. Technol. **32**(3), 444–452 (2023). https://doi.org/10.1007/s10956-023-10039-y
26. Bybee, R.W., et al.: The BSCS 5E Instructional Model: Origins and Effectiveness. Biological Sciences Curriculum Study, Colorado Springs (2006)
27. Plutzer, E., McCaffrey, M., Hannah, A.L., Rosenau, J., Berbeco, M., Reid, A.H.: Climate confusion among U.S. teachers. Science. **351**(6274), 664–665 (2016). https://doi.org/10.1126/science.aab3907
28. UNFCCC: Paris Agreement, in Report of the Conference of the Parties to the United Nations Framework Convention on Climate Change (21st Session). UNFCCC, Paris (2015)
29. Willis, R.: The role of national politicians in global climate governance. Environ. Plann. E: Nat. Space. **3**(3), 885–903 (2020). https://doi.org/10.1177/2514848619887464
30. Young, E., Quinn, L.: An Essential Guide to Writing Effective Policy Briefs. Open Society Foundations (2017)
31. Zenni, R.D., Andrew, N.R.: Artificial intelligence text generators for overcoming language barriers in ecological research communication. Austral Ecol. **48**(7), 1225–1229 (2023). https://doi.org/10.1111/aec.13417
32. Nerlich, B., Koteyko, N., Brown, B.: Theory and language of climate change communication. Wiley Interdiscip. Rev. Clim. Chang. **1**(1), 97–110 (2010). https://doi.org/10.1002/wcc.2
33. Nisbett, N., Spaiser, V.: How convincing are AI-generated moral arguments for climate action? Front. Clim. **5** (2023). https://doi.org/10.3389/fclim.2023.1193350
34. Salvagno, M., Taccone, F.S., Gerli, A.G.: Can artificial intelligence help for scientific writing? Crit. Care. **27**(1), 1–5 (2023). https://doi.org/10.1186/s13054-023-04380-2
35. Rozado, D.: The political biases of ChatGPT. Soc. Sci. **12**(3), 148 (2023)
36. Krügel, S., Ostermaier, A., Uhl, M.: ChatGPT's inconsistent moral advice influences users' judgment. Sci. Rep. **13**(1), 1–5 (2023). https://doi.org/10.1038/s41598-023-31341-0
37. Choudhury, A., Shamszare, H.: Investigating the impact of user trust on the adoption and use of ChatGPT: survey analysis. J. Med. Internet Res. **25** (2023). https://doi.org/10.2196/47184
38. Yu, H.: The application and challenges of ChatGPT in educational transformation: new demands for teachers' roles. Heliyon. **10** (2024). https://doi.org/10.1016/j.heliyon.2024.e24289
39. OpenAI: ChatGPT-4 System Card. OpenAI. [Online]. Available: https://cdn.openai.com/papers/gpt-4-system-card.pdf (2023)
40. Quach, K.: AI me to the moon… Carbon footprint for 'training GPT-3' sames as driving to our natural satellite and back. Register. (2020) [Online]. Available: https://www.theregister.com/2020/11/04/gpt3_carbon_footprint_estimate/
41. Everman, B., Villwock, T., Chen, D., Soto, N., Zhang, O., Zong, Z.: Evaluating the carbon impact of large language models at the inference stage. In: IEEE International Performance, Computing, and Communications Conference (IPCCC), pp. 150–157 (2023)
42. UNESCO: Climate change education for sustainable development. In: The UNESCO Climate Change Initiative. With Assistance of Julia Heiss. UNESCO (2010) [Online]. Available: https://unesdoc.unesco.org/ark:/48223/pf0000190101
43. Longnecker, N.: An integrated model of science communication-more than providing evidence. J. Sci. Commun. **15**(5), 1–13 (2016). https://doi.org/10.22323/2.15050401

44. IPCC: AR6 Synthesis Report: Climate Change 2023. IPCC (2023) [Online]. Available: https://www.ipcc.ch/report/ar6/syr/
45. Stoknes, P.E.: Rethinking climate communications and the 'psychological climate paradox'. Energy Res. Soc. Sci. **1**, 161–170 (2014). https://doi.org/10.1016/j.erss.2014.03.007
46. Robertson, C.T.: How people access and think about climate change. In: Digital News Report 2022, pp. 54–57 (2022) [Online]. Available: https://reutersinstitute.politics.ox.ac.uk/digital-news-report/2022
47. OpenAI: ChatGPT-4. OpenAI. [Online]. Available: https://openai.com/index/gpt-4-research/ (2023)
48. Raman, R., et al.: Fake news research trends, linkages to generative artificial intelligence and sustainable development goals. Heliyon. **10**(3) (2024). https://doi.org/10.1016/j.heliyon.2024.e24727
49. Montoro-Montarroso, A., et al.: Fighting disinformation with artificial intelligence: fundamentals, advances and challenges. Profesional de la informaci6n. **32**(3) (2023). https://doi.org/10.3145/epi.2023.may.22
50. Goldstein, J.A., Sastry, G., Musser, M., DiResta, R., Gentzel, M., Sedova, K.: Generative language models and automated influence operations: emerging threats and potential mitigations. arXiv:2301.04246. (2023) [Online]. Available: http://arxiv.org/abs/2301.04246
51. Piaget, J.: The Origins of Intelligence in Children. International Universities Press (1952)
52. Piaget, J., Inhelder, B.: The Psychology of the Child. Basic Books (1969)
53. Vygotsky, L.S.: Mind in Society: The Development of Higher Psychological Processes. Harvard University Press (1978)
54. Johnson, D.W., Johnson, R.T.: Learning Together and Alone: Cooperative, Competitive, and Individualistic Learning. Prentice-Hall, Inc. (1987)
55. Wood, D., Bruner, J.S., Ross, G.: The role of tutoring in problem solving. J. Child Psychol. Psychiatry. **17**(2), 89–100 (1976)
56. Ausubel, D.P.: Aquisição e Retenção de Conhecimentos: Uma Perspectiva Cognitiva. Plátano Editora, Lisbon (2003)
57. Lin, Z.: Why and how to embrace AI such as ChatGPT in your academic life. R. Soc. Open Sci. **10**(23658) (2023). https://doi.org/10.1098/rsos.230658
58. Kooli, C.: Chatbots in education and research: a critical examination of ethical implications and solutions. Sustainability (Switzerland). **15**(7) (2023). https://doi.org/10.3390/su15075614
59. Tosun, J., Peters, B.G.: The politics of climate change: domestic and international responses to a global challenge. Int. Polit. Sci. Rev. **42**(1), 3–15 (2021). https://doi.org/10.1177/0192512120975659
60. Scientific uncertainty. Nat. Clim. Chang. **9**, 797 (2019)
61. Thompson, J., Schweizer, S.: The conventions of climate change communication. In: National Communication Association National Convention, San Diego, California, pp. 1–32 (2008)
62. Wong, S.L., Green, L.A., Bazemore, A.W., Miller, B.F.: How to write a health policy brief. Fam. Syst. Health. **35**(1), 21–24 (2017). https://doi.org/10.1037/fsh0000238
63. DeMarco, R., Tufts, K.A.: The mechanics of writing a policy brief. Nurs. Outlook. **62**(3), 219–224 (2014). https://doi.org/10.1016/j.outlook.2014.04.002
64. Bhattacharyya, M., Miller, V.M., Bhattacharyya, D., Miller, L.E.: High rates of fabricated and inaccurate references in ChatGPT-generated medical content. Cureus. **15**(5) (2023). https://doi.org/10.7759/cureus.39238
65. Gravel, J., D'Amours-Gravel, M., Osmanlliu, E.: Learning to fake it: limited responses and fabricated references provided by ChatGPT for medical questions. In: Mayo Clinic Proceedings: Digital Health, pp. 226–234 (2023). https://doi.org/10.1016/j.mcpdig.2023.05.004

European Digital Credentials in Non-formal Education: More than Badges, Towards Better Acceptance

Tina John(✉)

Institute for Interactive Systems, Technische Hochschule Lübeck, Mönkhofer Weg 239, Lübeck 23562, Germany
tina.john@th-luebeck.de

Abstract. The Digital Learning Campus (DLC) implements micro-credentials based on open badges, which are enriched with additional metadata, transferred to the European Learning Model (ELM) and finally issued as European Digital Credentials (EDCs). It is a procedure that documents learning outcomes from non-formal educational offers in a Europe-wide standardised, interoperable and forgery-proof format. The credentials issued in this way have a clear value, as they meet the requirements of the EU Council Recommendation on Micro-Credentials of 2022 and are based on internationally recognized standards.

At the same time, this value is often not recognized in practice. The cause is not so much the technical or conceptual design, but rather the perception of badges and micro-credentials in general. Their use as gamification or marketing tools in other contexts resulted in a loss of image, which leads to skepticism and a lack of acceptance. The article shows that the EDCs issued in the DLC are not just any badges, but quality-assured certificates that are comparable to formal education certificates. Increased communication and education is therefore crucial to avoid misunderstandings and to make the added value of EDCs visible to learners, employers and educational institutions.

Keywords: European Digital Credentials · Micro Credentials · Open Badges · Non-formal Learning · Europass · Digital Learning Campus · Moodle Badges · European Learning Model · Educational Technology

1 Introduction

In the educational context, a distinction between formal, non-formal and informal learning raised in the late 1960s [1]. Although non-formal learning is becoming increasingly important in the 21st century, the educational landscape still shies away from recognising non-formal learning outcomes. This thesis will address this problem using the example of the Digital Learning Campus, with the hope of creating more acceptance.

Formal learning takes place in the main education and trainings system and lead to the acquisition of a formal qualification, whereas non-formal learning takes place outside the main education and training systems and does not necessarily lead to the

C. Meinel et al. (Eds.): CSEDU 2025, CCIS 3148, pp. 243–258, 2027.
https://doi.org/10.1007/978-3-032-39103-2_12

acquisition of a formal qualification [2–6]. Given this paradigm informal learning takes place everywhere and does not lead to the acquisition of any formal qualification. It is the acquisition and accumulation of knowledge, skills and attitudes from daily experiences and exposure to the environment [7].

Formal and non-formal learning is therefore essentially distinguished by the place of learning and the associated mediation system [3]. However, regardless of the form of learning, similar or even identical learning outcomes can be achieved. However, this does not apply to the certificates associated with them [6]. Formal learning leads to certificates from the public education system [8]. More and more professional skills are not acquired before entering the labour market through formal learning in traditional educational institutions, but continuously, during work and self-organised. However, certification is still firmly linked to educational institutions that show little willingness to recognise learning outside their educational programmes [9].

The different methods of performance assessment and document assessment are used for the recognition of competencies and the assessment of experience [6]. While performance assessment involves demonstrating competencies in an examination or test situation and then drawing conclusions about competencies based on the behavior (performance) displayed, document assessment involves submitting written evidence and checking it for compliance with requirements and authenticity. Procedures for documenting and certifying certificates acquired in a non-formal way often take a back seat to formal qualifications. This poses challenges for the acceptance and recognition of competences, especially those acquired through non-formal learning and recognised by document assessment.

For internationally active companies, however, even conventional education certificates for formal qualifications are often of little significance, as they rarely precisely reflect individual competence profiles [10]. In the context of higher education, the Diploma Supplement was developed by an initiative of the European Commission, Council of Europe, and UNESCO to ensure the recognition of qualifications by universities, authorities and employers at home and abroad [11]. It provides comprehensive, standardized information about a student's qualification, learning outcomes, institutional context, and the national education system, promoting transparency and facilitating degree recognition internationally.

The fast-paced society and a labour market that is constantly changing requires the individual to acquire additional skills outside formal and general vocational training. Companies on the labour market are increasingly looking for partial qualifications or certain combinations of partial qualifications, the qualification profiles rather than full occupational profiles [12]. Individual competencies must therefore be demonstrable and also be recognized.

Suitable solutions for the certification of partial qualifications and individual competencies already exist in the form of micro-credentials and diploma supplements as well as procedures that can simplify the discovery and recognition of these. Digital certificates of competence and digital procedures can meet the need for flexible recognition solutions to complement the traditional system [13]. For example, there are digital solutions for micro-credentials in the form of badges, for the Diploma Supplement in the form of

European Digital Credentials and for the storage and sharing of educational certificates in the form of data wallets.

An example of an implementation of digital credentials for non-formal learning that makes use of these digital tools is the implementation of a prototype for European Digital Credentials in Non-Formal Education for the Digital Learning Campus (DLC) [14]. This is intended to create the possibility of issuing digital certificates for micro-credentials for non-formal learning as well. As digital certificates, they are intended to bring benefits to learners for lifelong learning and professional development by being recognised throughout Europe.

A discussion about the European Digital Credentials for the DLC with actors from the educational context raised the following questions, among others, which can already be found in the literature in the discussion of micro-credentials in Australia [15]:

- Who needs these badges?
- What should an employer or educational institution do with an accumulation of micro-credentials?
- What are they worth?
- Is non-formal learning not just for oneself?

While the technical implementation of the prototype was not questioned in the educational landscape, the added value of micro-credentials was doubted all the more.

The emergence of these questions is to be counteracted with this thesis using the example of the prototype of the European Digital Credentials for the DLC. The challenges will be shown, why these questions could arise and use cases will be shown in which the benefits of digital evidence for micro-credentials will be presented. In order to make the most of the added value of the digital tools available, it is crucial to intensify educational work and to clearly communicate the benefits of digital credentials [13] and also to strengthen the acceptance and recognition of competences acquired through non-formal learning.

1.1 Educational Certificates

When one talks about the issuance of educational certificates, one first thinks of school leaving certificates, university degrees or professional qualifications. Thus, the first thought in the context of educational credentials is the idea of formal learning. This is associated with educational certificates such as a transcript of records, which are usually issued by schools, vocational schools or universities. They certify a person's achievements in a certain area or a specialist area. They provide a summary of people's performance in different subjects or courses, including grades and other assessments.

But what about skills or competencies that you have acquired outside of formal learning? In this area of non-formal learning, when we issue educational certificates, we usually speak of credentials issued by professional associations, organizations or companies. They document the acquisition of certain skills or abilities.

However, educational certificates are also certificates, which are usually also issued by companies or organizations, and document the completion of a training program or training, for example. The difference between all these educational certificates is, on the one hand, the formality provided by the issuing institution, but also the way in which these educational certificates can be obtained. For example, in the case of certificates, it may be sufficient to have participated, whereby in the case of credential, a successful participation is awarded and in the case of transcript of records, even a qualified successful participation is awarded.

1.2 Challenge

The problem of acceptance is built up across several pillars, namely the pillar of acceptance of digital certificates per se, the pillar of certification of non-formally acquired skills, and the pillar of acceptance of skills acquired outside formal learning.

Acceptance of Skills Acquired Outside Formal Learning. An example from the analogue reality in Germany, which can still be observed. A master craftsman is a master craftsman if he or she has a master craftsman's certificate. A journeyman is a journeyman if he has a journeyman's certificate. A craftsman is a craftsman if he has learned a craft. All three levels assume that the qualification was acquired in the context of formal learning at a corresponding training institution.

The master craftsman's certificate, the journeyman's certificate, the craft certificate are the documents that qualify the holder and are relevant for the recognition process of competencies with employers and educational institutions through document verification.

However, with the new media, the Open Educational Resources, learning opportunities in the field of non-formal learning and informal learning "Working by Doing", as they say in German, for example, you can acquire the same skills as a journeyman and also a master craftsman, although there is a lack of documents that identify them. Or not?

In the employer and employee relationship, it is not yet the case that skills play the decisive role, but the submitted proof of qualification, although skills acquired without a formal qualification at work and in leisure time may be more important for professional competence than formally certified knowledge [9]. Even with the same skills, the salary with proof of qualification is higher. A study by the Bertelsmann Stiftung shows that people without a formal degree often do the same jobs as colleagues with a degree, but still earn an average of 7–11% less. The salary is mainly based on the proof of qualification submitted, not on actual skills [16].

Certification of Non-formally Acquired Skills

Learning outcomes of formal learning, which go hand in hand with the acquisition of qualifications and enrichments, are recorded in a standardised manner, "regardless of the person" [3]. The form in which these types of educational certificates are issued is usually highly formalised. Traditionally, this type of educational evidence is issued in the form of certificates, certificates or certificates in writing. They are usually provided with a signature, a seal or an official certification and are often available in several languages in an international context.

Non-formal learning certificates are mainly issued in the form of certificates of participation, certificates or general certificates. The different manifestations range from analogue standard slips of paper, to electronic certificates in the form of pdf documents, to signed pdf documents and digital certificates with machine-readable data that are subject to a standardized data model.

Less commonly, there is evidence that explicitly documents acquired skills. Digital certificates can also have this shortcoming. A particular challenge lies in the lack of standardization. So far, there is no uniform, cross-sectoral certificate system, so the form and quality of the certificates depend heavily on the respective issuer, the region or the industry.

The significance, transparency and comparability of the qualifications acquired in the non-formal sector therefore depend to a large extent on the scope and level of detail of the information contained in the certificate. Overall, these certificates document the acquired skills and learning outcomes in a comprehensible way, but their design and binding nature vary greatly. Standardised and transparent forms that create better comparability are still developing, but have not yet been established across the board.

Acceptance of Digital Certificates. There is still limited acceptance of digital certificates compared to traditional paper certificates, especially in certain education sectors, employers and traditional institutions. Despite an overall increase in digitization, a study from 2017 shows that the degree of digitization in the area of learning materials and certificates in schools and vocational training is still comparatively low. Many players therefore continue to rely on printed media and analogue evidence.

The low acceptance of digital certificates compared to classic paper certificates is based on an interplay of technical, legal and cultural factors. Often, questions of trust are in the foreground. Digital certificates are considered less secure by many players because visible features such as signatures or seals are missing. Although technical solutions such as digital signatures exist that guarantee tamper protection, they have not yet been introduced nationwide or are generally known.

In addition, the legal framework for the use of digital evidence is not yet fully established. Uncertainties regarding recognition and binding nature mean that digital certificates are often handled more carefully than classic documents. This is exacerbated by technical hurdles and a lack of standardization. The large number of institutions involved makes uniform processes difficult, and not all educational institutions have the necessary infrastructure to create and manage digital certificates.

In addition, a cultural inertia is at work. Many employers, educational institutions or even authorities continue to prefer paper formats, which have been established and manageable for decades. This attitude is often also an expression of a more general reluctance towards digitization in the education sector. Finally, existing digitization gaps exacerbate the problem: In rural regions, in less digitized organizations or among older target groups, the prerequisites for reliable use of digital certificates are often lacking.

Overall, it can be seen that the low prevalence of digital evidence is not due to a single factor, but is due to an interplay of legal uncertainties, technical barriers, cultural reservations and unequal infrastructural conditions.

2 Suitable Solutions for the Certification of Partial Qualifications and Individual Competencies

2.1 Micro-credentials

The term micro-credential has been appearing increasingly since the early 2010s, but it was only through political and higher education developments from 2018 onwards that it systematically found its way into the European education debate [17–19]. Originally from the English-speaking world, it has been used since 2013 in the context of growing online educational offerings, such as Massive Open Online Courses (MOOCs), to describe small-scale digital evidence of competencies and learning success.

In the European context, the topic was officially addressed for the first time with the *Paris Communiqué* 2018 and has been actively developed by the European Commission since 2020. The decisive policy framework finally emerged with the EU Council Recommendation of June 2022: Since then, micro-credentials have been clearly outlined by a consolidated definition, standardised elements and ten universal principles.

Among other things, information on the identification of the learners, title, issuer, date of issue, learning outcomes, workload (ideally in ECTS), level or cycle (e.g. EQF, QF-EHEA), forms of examination and assessment, form of participation and quality assurance are mandatory. In addition, other elements such as participation requirements, exam proctoring, grades or stackability can be added.

The ten principles set by the EU emphasise quality, transparency, relevance, valid and traceable examinations, stackability and recognition, transferability, learner centricity, authenticity, and comprehensible information and guidance. Quality assurance is to be based on established procedures such as ECTS and the European Standards and Guidelines (ESG). At the same time, it is recommended that, if possible, micro-credentials should be issued as digital certificates in the European *Digital Credentials for Learning standard* in order to ensure comparability and recognition throughout Europe.

With the EU definition of 2022, a micro-credential is considered quality-assured proof of learning outcomes from a clearly defined, manageable learning offer. However, the concept goes back further in its idea, as earlier educational certificates – such as language certificates or driving licences – already fulfilled similar functions. However, it was only through digitization and the need for modularized, flexible learning paths that it was anchored in education policy.

Today, the term is firmly established both politically and strategically. At the European level as well as in national higher education strategies (e.g. HRK 2020), it forms the basis for a coherent framework that positions micro-credentials as high-quality, comparable and recognizable building blocks in the European Higher Education Area.

Micro-credentials are already being used and recognized internationally in industry organizations, educational institutions and commercial exhibitors, with employers playing a decisive role in the recognition of micro-credentials issuers. Industry organisations and educational institutions are trusted more than commercial exhibitors [20].

2.2 Open Badges Infrastructure

Open Badges were introduced by the Mozilla Foundation in 2011 as an open standard to make digital credentials of competency interoperable and verifiable. They contain more than one image, namely machine-readable metadata on issuer, recipient, award criteria and links to competence frameworks such as ESCO. This makes it possible to classify competencies more precisely and compare them with the requirements of the labor market. The underlying Open Badges Infrastructure makes it possible to create badges online and share them in various contexts, such as via career networks such as LinkedIn. The open standard stands for transparency, cooperation and worldwide usability [21].

The distribution is increasing rapidly, with the majority of badge offers being in the USA. Today, they are widely used – from professional development to corporate training and modernized certification programs. At the same time, they serve as a visible marketing tool for educational offers and help to make digital certificates better known and accepted [13, 22].

2.3 European Digital Credentials Infrastructure

While certificates and certificates are traditionally established in the formal education system, the question arises as to how learning outcomes from non-formal learning can be documented in such a way that they are comparable, recognised and transferable. In recent years, a comprehensive infrastructure has emerged in Europe that enables digital educational certificates in a standardised framework.

An essential basis for this evidence is the concept of micro-credentials. They make it possible to map learning outcomes in a granular way and thus make visible which competencies have been acquired in a particular course or offer. The European Commission does not see micro-credentials as a substitute for traditional qualifications, but as a complement that is particularly suitable for lifelong learning and professional development. It is crucial that micro-credentials are not just simple certificates of participation, but that they are linked to transparent learning objectives and verifiable performance.

The technical basis for such evidence is the European Digital Credentials Infrastructure (EDCI). It is part of the Europass framework and allows educational institutions to issue digital, tamper-proof certificates. These certificates are based on the European Learning Model (ELM), a comprehensive semantic data model that uses over 480 attributes to map all relevant information on learning processes and qualifications in a structured manner [23]. Diploma supplements are also digitized with this data model. The ELM ensures that both formal and non-formal and informal learning can be described in a uniform data structure. This ensures interoperability: educational certificates issued according to this model can be read, shared and checked throughout Europe.

Another central component of this infrastructure is the Europass Wallet. It acts as a digital wallet where learners can securely store, manage, and share their certificates when needed [24]. This gives them access to their certificates at any time and allows them to present them to potential employers or educational institutions, for example. The wallet also ensures the authenticity of the documents, as issued credentials are provided with electronic seals that correspond to the physical stamp or signature.

The strength of this infrastructure lies in the combination of different levels: learning offers are described in a structured manner using metadata and the EDCI ensures that digital, verifiable certificates are created from them. Europass Wallet and Viewer make these credentials accessible and verifiable for learners and institutions. In addition, there is the link to European frameworks such as the European Qualifications Framework (EQF) or the ESCO taxonomy, which systematically classify skills, qualifications and occupations [25].

This shows that digital educational certificates have long since outgrown an experimental phase. With Europass, EDCI and ELM, there is a functioning infrastructure that makes it possible to issue certificates in the field of non-formal learning that are trustworthy, interoperable and understandable throughout Europe. For the Digital Learning Campus, this opens up the opportunity not only to document the diverse learning activities, but also to make them visible in a format that is valid beyond the local context and can be recognized by employers as well as educational institutions.

3 European Digital Credentials for the Digital Learning Campus

3.1 Digital Learning Campus

The Digital Learning Campus (DLC) in Schleswig-Holstein combines digital and physical learning spaces and represents a platform for open, non-formal educational offerings. The programme is made up of learning opportunities offered by universities, universities of applied sciences and regional learning venue networks. In addition, media institutions are involved in the teaching of digital skills. Foundations and non-governmental organizations as well as technical institutions also expand the range of topics offered. Freelance trainers are also trained and can generate offers [14, 26].

The DLC is a network and thus not a formal education or training institution. However. some courses are organized in such a way that they can be very close to the formal system, although the scope of education of a course of study will not be covered in one offer. The DLC itself distinguishes between different educational certificates for participation in offers, for successful participation and qualified successful participation.

3.2 Implementation of European Digital Credential

The aim is to document learning outcomes from the DLC's offerings through European Digital Credentials (EDC) in a comprehensible, secure and Europe-wide way [14]. It uses the technical infrastructure of the European Commission, in particular the Europass ecosystem, the European Digital Credentials Infrastructure (EDCI) and the European Learning Model (ELM).

The central basis for the implementation are the Moodle badges, which are already used in the DLC to document learning successes. Moodle [27] provides native functions with which learners can receive awards according to defined criteria, such as after completing courses or certain activities. These badges are technically based on the Open Badge standard [22] and already contain metadata, but are not sufficient to fully meet the requirements of the ELM.

In order to achieve compatibility with the EDCI, a Moodle plugin was developed that integrates additional metadata from the course information. This includes information on learning objectives, acquired competences, scope of the offer, references to competence frameworks such as Future Skills 2021 [28] as well as structural information on courses and providers. This information is translated into the JSON format of the ELM. This creates a standardized data set that forms the basis for issuing a valid EDC.

The next step is to use the EDCI Issuer, an open-source application provided by the European Commission. This issuer will be integrated into the DLC infrastructure. It validates the created JSON data according to the specifications of the ELM and generates the actual digital certificate from it. To ensure authenticity and integrity, the certificate is provided with a qualified electronic seal (eSeal), which takes on the role of the institutional stamp. This seal is applied through the integration of the Connecting Europe Facility Digital Signature Service (CEF DSS). This gives the credential the same status as a signed and stamped paper certificate.

The credentials issued can be sent directly to learners via email or stored in their Europass Wallet. There they have the opportunity to securely store the certificates, access them at any time and share them with employers, educational institutions or other institutions. The standardised structure ensures that the evidence is readable and verifiable throughout Europe. In addition, the electronic seal protects against manipulation.

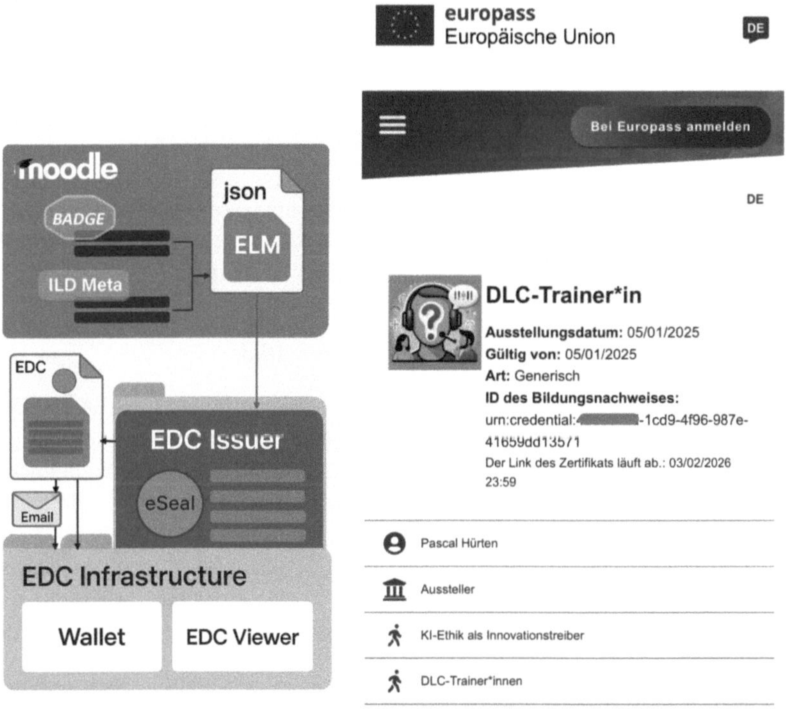

Fig. 1. The technical components and workflow for the creation of an EDC in Moodle adapted [14:616] (left) and an example of a European Digital Credential in the Europass Viewer obtained by completing several online courses in the DLC (right).

An example of this implementation is the issuance of an EDC for the successful completion of several online courses in the DLC in Fig. 1. The certificate appears in the Europass Viewer and transparently shows the learning path completed. Learners will thus be able to demonstrate competences acquired in the context of non-formal education in the DLC in a format recognised throughout Europe.

The implementation process (see Fig. 1) thus comprises four technical and organizational levels:

1. Moodle badges as a starting point for learning success.
2. Enrichment with further ELM necessary metadata from ILD Meta.
3. Transformation of the data into the ELM format via a special Moodle plugin.
4. Issuance and signature of the EDC by the EDCI issuer with subsequent entry in the Europass Wallet.

This structure combines the already established functions of Moodle with the European standards for digital educational certificates. The result is an interoperable and forgery-proof credentialing process that makes non-formal education visible and usable.

4 Discussion

The Digital Learning Campus issues micro-credentials for non-formal learning outcomes that meet the requirements for micro-credentials. The basis is Open Badges, which are equipped with the necessary additional metadata that follows the European Learning Model, the standardized data model that is also used for the digital mapping of the Diploma Supplement, as it was also developed for this purpose. The issuer is the network of universities, universities of applied sciences, regional learning venue networks, media institutions, non-governmental organizations and technical institutions. Nevertheless, there is a lack of general acceptance for these micro-credentials.

4.1 Perception of Open Badges and Micro-credentials

Open badges and micro-credentials are not differentiated by everyone at all times, but are perceived as synonyms [29]. Although open badges can be understood as a digital implementation of micro-credentials, they are more flexible and broadly defined.

Both formats make competences, skills and learning successes visible and certifiable–especially in non-formal contexts. They are based on digital structures with metadata such as issuer, date, learning content or certificates, which increases their verifiability and trustworthiness. At the same time, they give learners the opportunity to create personal competence profiles and use them flexibly, for example in the professional environment.

However, Open badges are often used as gamification elements in non-formal learning. This means that in some contexts there is a veritable flood of badges, which can reduce the value and credibility of individual badges [15, 20]. If badges are awarded for very small or superficial learning progress, they threaten to be devalued into pure "virtual trophies". In addition, clear standards and quality criteria are often missing, so that the significance of the information cannot be uniformly understood. Employers and educational institutions are then faced with the challenge of reliably assessing the actual value of individual badges.

Another reason for the loss of credibility lies in the focus on marketing: If badges are used primarily for the visibility of educational offers without representing a relevant proof of competence, trust in the seriousness of the format decreases [20]. In addition, the large number of badges increases the problem of information overload – badges are thus more likely to be hidden than actively considered in the selection process.

The flood of badges, the use of badges as a marketing tool and as a gamification element in e-learning, and the association of badges with the concept of micro-credentials lead to a bad reputation for badges and micro-credentials and can lead to statements:

- Who needs these badges?

To counteract this development, a stronger focus on quality instead of quantity is necessary. Educational institutions should set clear, transparent award criteria and only issue badges if they are associated with an actual gain in competence. Equally important is the transparent communication of the badge content and its criteria, so that learners and employers alike can better assess the value. Finally, badges should not be isolated but embedded in broader competency profiles or portfolios, reinforcing their relevance in the overall context.

Despite the risk of a "badge flood", Open Badges can thus fulfil their role as credible digital proof of competence and at the same time as motivating elements in the learning process and further expand their relevance for educational institutions as well as for the world of work.

Open badges, which are used as gamification elements or marketing tools in non-formal learning, should not be equated with the concept of micro-credentials. However, the Open Badge Standard infrastructure forms the technological backbone for the design, verification and dissemination of micro-credentials.

4.2 Perception of Micro-credentials Versus Qualifications

Micro-credential are often only seen in the context of non-formal learning. Furthermore, they are often only mentioned in connection with digital evidence. The lack of acceptance of learning outcomes from non-formal learning as well as for digital evidence then also leads to a lack of acceptance of micro-credentials.

Even though they were only anchored in education policy through digitization and the need for modularized, flexible learning paths, they are comparable to the traditional analogue seminar certificates handed out on paper at universities. The collection of examination certificates or "certificates" for academic achievements is traditionally a strongly German phenomenon, which is particularly widespread in the German higher education system. These certificates serve as formal proof of participation and achievement and are usually a prerequisite for successfully completing the studies. They contain the identification of the learner, the title of the seminar, the name of the exhibitor, the date of issue, the amount of work, the form of examination and evaluation as well as the form of participation. It usually did not include learning outcomes, level or cycle, which are more likely to emerge from the curriculum of the degree program.

In the Anglo-American world, a system with credit points, course degrees and official transcripts dominates, and there are also comparable certificates of achievement in other European countries, but they are almost identical to the concept of micro-credentials in their own business. All these certificates of achievement are inherently stackable, as they indicate partial qualifications prescribed by the curriculum. They serve as a prerequisite for admission to courses in higher semesters and must be recognized accordingly. The same applies to the year report cards at school. Each annual report card is an admission requirement for the new school year if the minimum criteria are met. Only when all partial qualifications have been achieved is a qualification or degree shown, for example in the form of a certificate.

The second part of the definition of micro-credentials of the International Standard Classification of Education (ISCED) covers this use case: A micro-credential is a certification of assessed learning that is additional, alternate, complementary to or a component part of a formal qualification. Such micro-credentials are also distinguished in the literature as "university-sponsored transcripted micro-credentials" [20] oder "credit-bearing micro-credentials" [15].

The concept of micro-credentials should therefore not be rejected. However, it is used in a very inflationary way and is often applied to all kinds of learning experiences in a shorter form [15, 29].

4.3 Benefits and Added Value of European Digital Credentials for the DLC

Digital educational certificates, especially in the form of European Digital Credentials (EDCs), are a central building block for the recognition, visibility and comparability of learning outcomes. They record acquired skills, qualifications or achievements in a structured, machine-readable and forgery-proof form. The consistent use of international standards such as the European Learning Model (ELM) ensures that these certificates are interoperable, portable and verifiable in the long term. In contrast to purely digitized versions of traditional certificates, EDCs extend the functionality of educational credentials by providing a semantically unique description of learning performance via metadata and enabling its contextual embedding.

A significant added value results from the simplified international verification. Because EDCs include digital signatures and verification mechanisms, their authenticity can be verified globally without the need to contact the issuing institution directly. This is particularly important for transnational mobility, recognition procedures and international cooperation.

The benefits for the actors involved are manifold. Apprentices receive transparent and accessible documentation of their learning outcomes, which they can use in a targeted manner in application and qualification processes. Employers benefit from more efficient validation of relevant competencies and can integrate this information into recruiting or personnel development processes. Education providers gain new options for modular recognition and crediting, which makes the offer more flexible. For political decision-makers, data-based foundations are created for the further development of education and labour market strategies.

The possible applications of EDCs are wide-ranging. They range from complete formal degrees to professional certificates to small-scale, targeted micro-credentials that document specific competencies. In the context of non-formal education offerings such as the DLC, micro-credentials that follow a standard that can also reflect formal qualifications deserves to be considered for the recognition of learning achievements.

- What are they worth?

Since the DLC only issues micro-credentials for qualified learning outcomes, the value is comparable to the value of a partial qualification such as that of university-sponsored transcripted micro-credentials. The decision-makers are the providers of the learning opportunities themselves, which are based on the EU's ten principles for the allocation of micro-credentials.

If there were trust in these micro-credentials new perspectives open up: they enable modular certification that supports flexible learning paths, facilitates mobility between education systems and promotes the recognition of individual competences. A granularity that the labor market needs when looking for suitable employees.

- What should an employer or educational institution do with an accumulation of micro-credentials?

Use a digital infrastructure that enables semiautomatic validation of relevant competencies and integrate this into recruiting or personnel development processes. For educational institutions the infrastructure might automatic recognize skills for course of study recommendations.

4.4 The Cycle of Learning and Motivation

Education can be described as a recurring cycle (see Fig. 2) that begins with the extrinsic motivation to learn, continues with the acquisition and documentation of competencies and finally includes their verification and recognition. The recognition of acquired competences opens up further learning paths, as well as further educational and professional paths, which can lead to an intrinsic motivation to continue one's education in order to meet new professional requirements or to facilitate working life through expanded skills [13].

Digital educational credentials in the DLC directly support this cycle, as they can be generated automatically after completing a learning activity and made available in EDC-compliant form, so that they can be made visible to employers and educational institutions in the data wallet. By changing one's own portfolio of skills, new job or training offers can be automatically matched in the EDC infrastructure. From a civil society perspective, it is becoming increasingly important to be able to react flexibly to developments in the labour markets [10]. The world needs more granular certified learning [15] so that everyone can upgrade themselves quickly and adapt to the labour market situation without further vocational training or studies. The motivation for non-formal learning will increase if learners can trust that the micro-credentials they receive are recognised.

- Is non-formal learning not just for oneself?

The answer is both yes and no. Although you study for your own benefit, the job market values well-trained employees with specific skills in addition to formal qualifications, which are becoming increasingly important. Good employees find it easier to progress in their jobs and climb the career ladder.

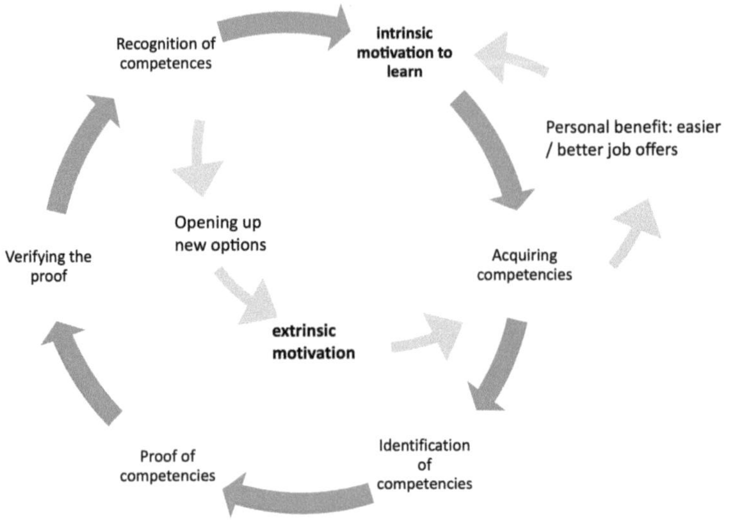

Fig. 2. A cycle of motivation, learning, recognition and new opportunities.

5 Conclusion

The example of the Digital Learning Campus shows that micro-credentials based on open badges have a high potential to make non-formal learning outcomes visible, verifiable and comparable. The transfer of the data to the European Learning Model and the use of European Digital Credentials will support interoperability, quality assurance and international recognition. This provides learners, employers and educational institutions with tools that strengthen individual competence profiles and at the same time promote permeability between formal and non-formal learning contexts.

At the same time, the lack of acceptance remains a key challenge. The inflationary use of badges, their use as a gamification or marketing element, and unclear standards have weakened trust in digital credentials. In order to establish micro-credentials as a credible and sustainable educational currency, it is therefore necessary to comply with clear award criteria, transparent communication and consistent quality assurance. Only when the focus is more on relevance and value can micro-credentials establish themselves in the long term as a recognised link between non-formal learning and formal qualifications.

Disclosure of Interests. The authors have no competing interests to declare that are relevant to the content of this article.

References

1. Norqvist, L., Leffler, E.: Learning in non-formal education: is it "youthful" for youth in action? Int. Rev. Educ. **63**(2), 235–256 (2017)
2. Kommission der Europäischen Gemeinschaften.: Memorandum über lebenslanges Lernen. Brüssel. (2000)

3. Leu, H.R.: Non-formales und informelles Lernen–unverzichtbare Elemente frühpädagogischer Professionalisierung. Eine Analyse vor dem Hintergrund des Deutschen Qualifikationsrahmens. Weiterbildungsinitiative Frühpädagogische Fachkräfte (WiFF) Expertisen 40. München. (2014)
4. Johnson, M., Majewska, D.: Formal, Non-formal, and Informal Learning: What Are they, and how Can we Research them? Cambridge University Press and Assessment, Cambridge (2022)
5. Tillmann, A., Eichhorn, M., Weiß, D.: Zertifizierung von informellen und non-formalen Lernprozessen. In: Schulz, S. (ed.) Proceedings of DELFI Workshops 2019, p. 91. Workshopbeitrag, Bonn: Gesellschaft für Informatik e.V. (2019). https://doi.org/10.18420/delfi2019-ws-111
6. Annen, S.: Anerkennung von Kompetenzen: Kriterienorientierte Analyse ausgewählter Verfahren in Europa. W. Bertelsmann Verlag, Bielefeld (2012)
7. Coombs, P.H., Ahmed, M.: Attacking Rural Poverty: how Nonformal Education Can Help. Johns Hopkins University Press, Baltimore (1974)
8. Dohmen, G.: Das informelle Lernen: Die internationale Erschließung einer bisher vernachlässigten Grundform menschlichen Lernens für das lebenslange Lernen aller. BMBF Publik, Bonn (2001)
9. Gaylor, C., Schöpf, N., Severing, E.: Wenn aus Kompetenzen berufliche Chancen werden. Wie europäische Nachbarn informelles und non-formales Lernen anerkennen und nutzen, Bertelsmann Stiftung, Gütersloh (2015)
10. Buchem, I., Orr, D., Brunn, C.: Kompetenzen sichtbar machen mit Open Badges. Abschlussbericht der HFD Community Working Group Kompetenz-Badges. Hochschulforum Digitalisierung, Berlin. https://hochschul-forumdigitalisierung.de/sites/default/files/dateien/HFD_AP_Nr48_Open_Badges_Bericht_2019_DE_web.pdf. (2019) Last accessed 02 Sept 2025
11. European Higher Education Area (EHEA): Diploma Supplement. I. Principles and General Guidelines for Those Producing Supplements. Paris Communiqué Appendix IV. https://ehea.info/Upload/document/ministerial_declarations/EHEAParis2018_Communique_AppendixIV_952782.pdf. (2018) Last accessed 03 Sept 2025
12. Ziegler, M., Horstmann, K., Wehner, C.: Machbarkeitsstudie: Teilqualifikationen in Online-Jobanzeigen (OJA). Humboldt-Universität zu Berlin, Berlin (2022)
13. Buchem, I.: Zukunft der Anerkennung? micro-credentials, open badges und data-wallets. weiter bilden. DIE Zeitschrift für Erwachsenenbildung. **31**(1), 32–36 (2024)
14. John, T., Hürten, P.: Implementing European digital credentials in non-formal education: a prototype for the digital learning campus. In: Proceedings of the 17th International Conference on Computer Supported Education-Volume 1., ISBN 978-989-758-746-7, ISSN 2184-5026, pp. 612–619 (2025)
15. Oliver, B.: Making Micro-credentials Work for Learners, Employers and Providers. Deakin University, Melbourne. https://dteach.deakin.edu.au/wp-content/uploads/sites/103/2019/08/Making-micro-credentials-work-Oliver-Deakin-2019-full-report.pdf. (2019) Last accessed 05 Sept 2025
16. Bürmann, M., Wiek, J.: Ungelernte Fachkräfte–Formale Unterqualifikation in Deutschland. Bertelsmann Stiftung, Gütersloh (2018)
17. Rentzsch, R.: Microcredentials auf Hochschulniveau–Ansätze zum Umgang mit einem bildungspolitischen Trend. Studie im Auftrag der Hochschulrektorenkonferenz (HRK) im Rahmen des Projekts MODUS. HRK, Bonn. https://www.hrk-modus.de/media/redaktion/Downloads/Publikationen/MODUS/Microcredentials_Studie_WEB.pdf. (2023) Last accessed 05 Sept 2025

18. Hochschulrektorenkonferenz (HRK): Microcredentials an Hochschulen – strategische Entwicklung und Qualitätssicherung. Ergebnisse der Zukunftswerkstatt Microcredentials. HRK, Bonn. https://www.hrk-modus.de/media/redaktion/Downloads/Publikationen/MODUS/Ergebnisse_der_ZW_Microcredentials_WEB_01.pdf. (2023) Last accessed 05 Sept 2025
19. Council of the European Union: Recommendation of 16 June 2022 on a European approach to micro-credentials for lifelong learning and employability. https://eur-lex.europa.eu/legal-content/DE/TXT/PDF/?uri=CELEX:32022H0627(02). (2022) Last accessed 05 Sept 2025
20. Narayanaswamy, R., Albers, C.S., Knotts, T.L., Albers, N.D.: Sustaining and reinforcing the perceived value of higher education: E-learning with micro-credentials. Sustainability. **16**(20), 8860 (2024). https://doi.org/10.3390/su16208860
21. Rentzsch, R.: Digitale Bildungsnachweise–Der Stand 2020 in Deutschland und Europa. Institut für Innovation und Technik, Berlin (2021)
22. Jovanovic, J., Devedzic, V.: Open badges: challenges and opportunities. In: Advances in Web-Based Learning–ICWL 2014: 13th International Conference, Tallinn, Estonia, 2014, Proceedings, vol. 13, pp. 56–65. Springer International Publishing, Cham (2014)
23. Gottlieb, M., Bacharach, G.: Cleaning up: interplay between European standards and verifiable credentials for higher education institutions. In: Auer, M.E., Pachatz, W., Rüütmann, T. (eds.) Learning in the Age of Digital and Green Transition, pp. 777–788. Springer International Publishing, Cham (2023). https://doi.org/10.1007/978-3-031-26190-9_81
24. Bildungsbüro Erasmus+: Kleiner Leitfaden Europass. https://www.erasmusplus.bayern.de/fileadmin/user_upload/erasmus/180506_kleiner_Leitfaden_Europass.pdf. (2018) Last accessed 05 Sept 2025
25. European Commission: ESCO Handbook: European Skills, Competences, Qualifications and Occupations. Publications Office of the EU, Luxembourg (2019)
26. Filk, C.: Digital learning campus Schleswig-Holstein (DLC-SH): Ein Zukunftsmodell für Bildung und Innovation? Medienimpulse. **63**(4) (2024)
27. Moodle: Moodle–Open-source learning platform. https://moodle.org. (n.d.) Last accessed 05 Sept 2025
28. Stifterverband für die Deutsche Wissenschaft e.V.: Future Skills 2021|Stifterverband. (2021), https://www.stifterverband.org/medien/future-skills-2021. Last accessed 05 Sept 2025
29. Varadarajan, S., Koh, J.H.L., Daniel, B.K.: Correction: a systematic review of the opportunities and challenges of micro-credentials for multiple stakeholders: learners, employers, higher education institutions and government. Int. J. Educ. Technol. High. Educ. **20**, 24 (2023). https://doi.org/10.1186/s41239-023-00393-7

Haphazard Notes. An Overview on Note-Taking Practises, Teaching and Training in Academia

Yannic Jäckel(✉), Daniel Schiffner, and Jan Schneider

DIPF, Leibniz-Institut für Bildungsforschung und Bildungsinformation, Rostocker Straße 6, 60323 Frankfurt am Main, Germany
y.jaeckel@dipf.de

Abstract. This paper explores how participants in a small-scale survey (N = 76) take notes during reading. All participants either had an academic education or were currently in the process of receiving it. The sample consists of persons currently actively engaged in research, people formerly engaged in research and students. This paper provides an overview of common note-taking techniques and practices in literature and their use in our participants. It also provides a discussion on how writing and typing proficiency influences effective note-taking. The Main findings of this paper are a lack of use of structured note-taking techniques and a lack of formal note-taking education in schools and universities alike, which presented itself in the results of our survey. The authors argue that through dedicated educational tools and note-taking software, this lack of education and training may be mitigated, but such tools do not exist yet.

Keywords: Note-Taking · Academic Writing · Knowledge Management · Information Gathering · Critical Reading · Learning · Spaced Repetition · Retrieval Practise

1 Introduction

Research and scientific advancement further the collective understanding of phenomena in any given society [11], researchers and scholars within a society make statements on phenomena in the world [35]. These statements are based on prior knowledge, axioms, and ongoing discourse a researcher has learnt in their education: the Paradigm [23]. The Paradigm is acquired through study and textbooks [23] and, as Walter Pauk puts it, a student's notes may become their own 'handwritten textbook' [33]. Notes are ephemeral knowledge made persistent through the information technology of writing [12].

In following Bloom's taxonomy of learning, we argue that to create scientific advancement, a researcher must first remember, understand, apply, analyse, and evaluate knowledge they have acquired previously through reading, discussion, or other means [22].

C. Meinel et al. (Eds.): CSEDU 2025, CCIS 3148, pp. 259–287, 2027.
https://doi.org/10.1007/978-3-032-39103-2_13

For centuries, scholars and students have achieved this through notes and note-taking. Greek and Roman sophists, rhetors, philosophers, and their students took notes and even shared them with each other to learn and teach [7]. As we explored in a recent study [14], contemporary scholars still take notes while reading and writing, and still consider them an essential part of scholarly work [36]. However, we also found that structured note-taking was not widely used among our participants [14], making it difficult to share and reuse notes.

Ancient students and scholars relied on their intuition to take notes, as many students still do today [42], who use very basic note-taking techniques [16]. There are, however techniques that have been developed in more recent history to make learning and studying faster, more efficient, and more reliable. Research shows that despite having many tools at our disposal, in today's world, where critical thinking and reading may be regarded as more important than ever [2], we see that researchers, teachers, and students alike are ill-taught to perform these vital tasks [2,3,10,14,25,37].

That said, reading is not as simple an act as it may appear. In 2019 Ahmad, referencing previous research, differentiated between two types of reading: **literal or mechanical reading**, done simply to obtain factual knowledge from texts, and **critical reading**, which is done to develop an analytical and neutral comprehension of the text [2].

Critical reading is a scholarly technique that involves the ability to distinguish facts from fiction, opinion and belief. It also involves questioning the intentions of the authors, disseminating their arguments and word choices, and finding conclusions based on what the authors have written and what is implied. Thus, critical reading does not only provide an understanding of the text, but also requires an understanding of the context in which the text was produced [2].

Structured Note-taking, as both Ahmad and Tiruneh show, is an excellent tool to teach students both reading comprehension and critical reading at the same time [2,40]. Yet, all too often, note-taking is only considered as the process of simply encoding knowledge, i.e. writing down information, often by hand [16,17,28,29,34,42]).

1.1 Contribution

Previous research indicates that the use of structured note-taking techniques that enforce review has a positive effect on reading comprehension and critical reading proficiency in students [2,37,40]. Previous research also indicates benefits of handwritten notes over typed notes [24,25].

Thus, we want to recontextualize and expand our findings and take the opportunity to discuss them in the context presented above. In doing so, we want to explore how structured note-taking techniques are differentiated from the simple encoding of knowledge and how they facilitate meaningful engagement with a topic through systematic revision. We will also explore how the use of these techniques may overcome alleged shortcomings of our modern way of writing, which is typing [3,24,25,29].

To achieve a meaningful and grounded discussion, we want to present the results of a survey we performed in 2024 and already partially published in 2025 [14] and analyse them in the context of the discourses mentioned above, which were largely left unexplored in the original publication [14].

2 Survey

This publication is an extension to a paper we presented at the 17th CSEDU conference in Porto (Portugal) in April 2025, in which we performed a small-scale survey on the note-taking habits and tool usage of active researchers with an academic education mostly from Germany [14]. There, we presented findings from purely academic backgrounds, which we want to extend in this paper by re-examining key findings concerning note-taking practices and training in academic education. To this end, we extended the analysis of our survey to include cohorts we previously excluded.

We based a questionnaire on a paper by Mosleh and Baba, published in 2013 [14,28], which provided an overview of 'common' note-taking techniques. While the authors do not provide any indication as to why they considered the methods to be popular, our survey found none of the more structured methods widely used. The whole questionnaire can be found in the appendix of our previous publication [14].

The techniques we explored ranged from unstructured methods like the Sentence and Outline Methods, to highly structured, column-based approaches, like the Cornell Method or REAP.

Since the inner workings of these techniques are important in the discussion, we will provide short explanations in the following sections.

2.1 Common Note-Taking Methods

Sentence and Outline Methods. The Sentence Method represents the most basic form of note-taking. Each note is written on a single line, constructing a list of bullet points [16,28] without any particular order or schema.

The Outline Method acts on the same principle, while ordering the sentences under headlines using indentations to indicate the pertinence of a sentence to a topic or concept [16,17,28].

Referred to as 'conventional notes' [16,17], these methods are regarded by Kauffmann et al. as methods employed by students, who have not yet learned a more effective technique [16].

Results, regarding the effectiveness of Outlines [17] compared to the Sentence Method, seem to be mixed and inconclusive [4].

Two-Column Reading and Cornell Method. The Cornell Method was developed by Cornell University Professor of Education, Walter Pauk to enhance students' learning while reading or during lectures. The first edition of his book, 'How to study in college' appeared in 1962 [33,38].

Similar to Two-Column Reading [14,28,37] or 'split-page' notes [37], where a notebook page is split into a note-taking column and a 'recall column' [32], the Cornell Method involves dividing the page into three areas, one on the left, one on the right and a bottom section for summaries. The area on the right, as in Two-Column-Reading, is designated for the reader's notes and constitutes the primary note-taking area. The left column, called the 'cue column' was designated by Pauk to be a section where note-takers write questions during a later review process that are answerable by the notes that have taken in the right-hand section of the paper. These questions act as study cues and are formulated in a second step after the lecture, during study-time [33]. The third section at the bottom of the page is used to summarize the contents of the notes and cues on this particular page. It is filled in during study time, after reviewing the notes and cues [32].

Ahmad's interpretation of the Cornell Method gives more credit to the use of the 'cue column' in critical reading. Here, the 'cue column' also contains thoughts, keywords, observations, and questions [2]. Also, based on previous research, Ahmad extends the Cornell Method yet again to include a second review step, wherein the page is turned around, and the whole page is contextualized by writing down reflections on how the page pertains to a note-takers own knowledge [2].

While we did not expect these modifications to be present in the minds of our survey participants, they illustrate the flexibility and adaptability of note-taking methods to deepen understanding on a topic and enforce reflection and engagement with a subject.

The Cornell method has recently received scientific attention regarding its effectiveness as a note-taking and teaching strategy in teaching for critical reading to school children [2,27]. However, a systematic survey done by Reed et al. in 2016 does not mention studies involving the Cornell Method in college-level students [37]. It would seem that further research is needed to further our understanding of this method in an academic working context.

Four Column Reading. Four Column reading is a note-taking strategy that can be traced back to a pamphlet on scientific writing circulated by the German Leibniz-University of Hannover [1]. Király et al. gave a very recent introduction for students at the Technische Universität Dresden [18], referencing the booklet as a base for their Four-Column approach to critical reading. However, on closer examination the source that this booklet provides, and the technique explained by Király et al. differ considerably, which causes us to believe that this method originated with Király et al. in Dresden under this name.

Four Column Reading splits a page into four columns, as the name suggests. The general layout is tabular and presented below (Table 1).

This technique is presented as ideal for the reuse of notes because the annotated part itself, as well as the reasoning of the note-taker, are present for re-examination and reuse in another context [18]. However, the information given by Király et al. seems a bit contradictory, since the notes are taken to be used for

Table 1. Four Column Reading according to Király et al.

Original Text	Page No.	My comments	In my work
Paraphrase or Quotation of a passage to be annotated	The page where the passage is to be found	Questions, comments, annotations, reasoning	Where does this fit in the paper to be written

a specific publication, with designates slots for their use in said publication [18]. Being a somewhat new method and not mentioned elsewhere, we did not expect it to be too commonly used, but we included it in the survey on the chance that it might have gained a following among students.

REAP Read Encode Annotate Ponder. REAP was developed by Eanet and Manzo in 1976 to increase students' comprehension and higher-order thinking and writing skills [8,40]. Thus, it is specifically designed to teach students critical reading and thinking.

The main steps, according to Tiruneh [40], who paraphrases Eanet and Manzo [8] are as follows:

1. **Read** through the text quickly and get an overview of the writer's main idea(s).
2. **Encode**, by putting the main ideas into your own words. Use the text margin to write and highlight cues and keywords.
3. **Annotate** by writing short summaries of important points, share with others and discuss.
4. **Ponder**, by reflecting on what you read and by thinking and discussing with others.

According to Eanet and Manzo, at the heart of the REAP strategy lies teaching students how to annotate and summarize a text. Writing and sharing annotations forces students to consider multiple aspects and viewpoints of a text, which might otherwise be overlooked. In sharing thoughts and notes with others, students are encouraged to write their notes in a way that others can understand. They also gain insights in different perspectives, as they read and discuss notes by other students. The ponder stage allows students to cement their knowledge and synthesise what they have read with existing knowledge or new knowledge from other sources [8,40].

While this method seems the most time-consuming and requires collaboration from other students, we argue that it can be of great value to academic work in the context of research-groups. In contrast to all other note-taking techniques we present, it enforces a review-process that is not self-centred and only includes knowledge that the note-taker themselves have, but allows for other interpretations, understandings, and viewpoints to be included in a discussion.

As Tiruneh has shown, this technique provides advantages as a teaching method, when it comes to reading comprehension [40] because it enforces a more in-depth engagement with the text than simply reading through and reading aloud, followed by direct questioning [40].

Mapping and Charting Methods. According to Mosleh and Baba, Mapping Methods are note-taking methods that organize notes and information in graphical representations [28]. In the context of this paper, we use the term Mapping Method as a collective noun for all forms of directed and connected graphical notes, such as concept maps [30,33] or mind maps [5,33].

Reed et al. found in their 2016 review that research on guided note-taking showed students with partially filled out graphic organizers (maps) to outperform those with outlines or completed maps [37].

Similarly, we used the term Charting method, as described by Mosleh and Baba [28], to mean any method that organizes knowledge and information in tabular form, where each column is assigned a specific category. Information classified into one of these categories is stored in the respective column. Thus, it acts as a catch-all for column-based methods that are not specifically mentioned.

While we were unable to find a scientific background for this particular method, we found evidence for their use in teaching on university and college websites like: https://subjectguides.york.ac.uk/note-taking/charting or https://learningessentials.auckland.ac.nz/key-study-skills/note-taking/charting/

2.2 Findings

In this publication, we wanted to provide a broader picture on the general state of note-taking training and tool usage in academic education. In contrast to our previous publication, where we were more interested in how notes are used in the writing process of active researchers and in how they reused their notes [14], we want to focus more on how note-taking methods are employed and learned by those who have received a university education. Thus, we added cohorts we previously omitted to our analysis, namely those having received a university education, but are no longer active in the field (**Former Academics**) and those, currently receiving an academic education (**students**).

Academic Career Stage. Our sample consists of 76 participants with academic background, of which 33 are active researchers and 12 are students, as shown in Table 2.

The two biggest cohorts were Computer Science (N = 13), Psychology (N = 10) and History (N = 5), with the wider spread ranging from Humanities like History of Art, Archival studies, Linguistics, Sociology and Education to sciences like Chemistry among others. While being a decently broad spread, it did not provide any reasonable insights or correlations.

Table 2. Career stages of participants.

Career stage	Number of participants in cohort
Active Researchers	33
Former Academics	31
Students	12
Total	76

Reading and Note-Taking Strategies. One of our crucial questions was whether the described note-taking techniques were in use by our participants.

Since some of the techniques we mention are made for note-taking in lectures and some for reading, we allowed multiple strategies to be selected. However, the answer 'None of the above' excluded all others. The results can be seen in Tables 3 and 4

Table 3 gives an overview over participants that do not employ any of the reading strategies we were looking for. To put the numbers in Table 4 into perspective, we subtracted those participants who did not employ reading strategies from our sample.

Table 3. Q. 11: Participants employing note-taking strategies.

	Active Researchers	Former Academics	Students
Cohort size	33	31	12
None of the above	11	10	5
Participants with reading strategies	22	21	7

Table 3 indicates that many of our participants either did not use or know of the techniques we proposed as answers.

Only the Outline- and Sentence- and Mapping Methods can be considered widely used across all cohorts.

However, we find in our former academics and students cohorts, that more structured note-taking strategies seem slightly more popular than among our active researchers. However, the use of Cornell and REAP is almost absent or fully absent in all cohorts.

Four Column Reading was used by some participants (N = 5) in our Former Academics cohort. We analysed, whether there would be a specific field in which this technique could have been taught, but there was no clear correlation. Furthermore, among these participants, only one (N = 1) stated to have received any note-taking training in university, while 2 (N = 2) stated to have no formal training at all.

Table 4. Usage of note-taking techniques.

	Active Researchers	Former Academics	Students
Participants with reading strategies	22	21	7
Four Column Reading	1	5	2
Two Column Reading	3	2	2
Cornell Method	1	1	0
REAP Method	1	1	0
Outline Method	11	11	5
Mapping Method	8	4	1
Sentence Method	9	10	5

Handwritten Notes and Writing Media. Most note-taking techniques we described above were designed to be used with handwritten notes, and research indicates potential benefits to handwritten notes, though evidence remains inconclusive overall [25,37].

With Q.5 and Q.6, we wanted to see if handwriting was still prevalent in our participants. We found that only students read primarily on print-outs (N = 5) or on both (N = 6), while in all other cohorts, most participants stated to either read on both media equally or primarily on screen. However, the differences are small in all cohorts if 'both' is counted both ways (Table 5).

Table 5. Q. 5: Primary reading media.

	Active Researchers	Former Academics	Students
Cohort size	33	31	12
Both/Can't really say	12	16	6
Primarily Print	8	8	5
Primarily Screen	13	7	1

While annotations were not as prevalent as word-processors or handwriting, it still seems to be employed widely in our participants.

Concerning handwriting, we observe that both typing and handwriting were employed quite equally, with only our former academics cohort showing a stronger tendency towards handwritten notes as shown in Table 7 the same trend manifests itself in those participants, who stated not to use any note-taking techniques (see Tables 7 and 8).

Roughly a third of our participants (N = 23 out of 76) did state to not use handwritten notes at all. We wanted to see if, similar to tool usage in the next section, a trend could be observed in the scientific fields of these participants. For

Table 6. Q. 6: Distribution of note-taking habits (Multiple Answers allowed).

	Active Researchers	Former Academics	Students
Cohort size	33	31	12
Handwritten notes	22	23	8
Word processor	20	16	3
Annotations	10	11	5
Dedicated Software	4	6	3

Table 7. Q. 6: Distribution of note-taking habits (Multiple Answers allowed) among participants without note-taking techniques.

	Active Researchers	Former Academics	Students
Participants w/o note-taking technique	11	10	5
Handwritten notes	9	9	3
Word processor	6	8	1
Annotations	5	2	2
Dedicated Software	2	2	1

the sake of readability, we aggregated smaller fields in larger fields of study like 'humanities' or 'Computers & Technology'. While a large group of participants not using handwritten notes stems from a technology background, they do not represent a majority.

As hinted at in our introduction, the benefits of handwriting over typing are an ongoing discussion. This prompted us to ask those participants who claimed to take handwritten notes, to specify on what writing surface they took their notes (Q. 7). Table 10 shows that throughout all cohorts, our participants stated to either take their notes on predominantly paper, or both on screen and paper.

Table 8. Q. 6: Distribution of note-taking habits (Multiple Answers allowed) among participants without note-taking training.

	Active Researchers	Former Academics	Students
Participants w/o note-taking training	24	21	6
Handwritten notes	16	15	5
Word processor	13	12	2
Annotations	7	6	3
Dedicated Software	5	5	1

Table 9. Q. 6, 3: Scientific Field of participants who used no handwritten notes.

Field	Number of participants
Participants not using handwritten notes	23
Humanities	5
Chemistry	1
Computers & Technology	9
Social Sciences Education	4
Psychology	4

Table 10. Q. 7: Distribution of handwritten notes on paper vs. on screen (Multiple Answers allowed).

	Active Researchers	Former Academics	Students
Cohort size	22	23	8
Handwritten notes on paper	19	20	6
Handwritten notes on screen	11	14	3
Both	9	11	1

Similarly, we asked those participants if they did so on paper or on screen. While all cohorts claim to still annotate print-outs, we cannot observe a clear trend towards one or the other, as can be seen in Table 11.

Table 11. Q. 9: Distribution of annotations on paper vs. on screen.

	Active Researchers	Former Academics	Students
Cohort size	10	11	5
Annotations on paper	6	8	3
Annotations on screen	8	9	5
Both	3	6	3

Tool Usage. We assumed that data on the use of dedicated tools would allow us to draw conclusions to employed note-taking strategies, even if they were not specifically mentioned in previous questions, since they might simply be implemented in the tool, without the user's knowledge.

As shown in Table 13, the spread of tools is dominated by word-processors like MS Word and LibreOffice Writer (N = 35), with MS Word being dominant by far (N = 27).

The spread of dedicated note-taking tools is very broad, but shows a very slight tendency towards RoamResearch based tools like Logseq (N = 2), Notion (N = 3), Obsidian (N = 4), and Org-Roam (N = 1), which implement the Outline- and Sentence Methods. With no particular review step. While they allow tags and links to be included in notes, as well as a full-text search, these tools still implement only the most basic form of intuitive note-taking. The tools were closely followed by reference management Systems like Citavi or Zotero (N = 6).

We found that, with few exceptions (N = 4), all participants who used dedicated note-taking software came from technology-adjacent fields, as shown in Table 12. We aggregated technology-adjacent fields into 'Computers & Technology', to provide better readability.

Table 12. Q. 6, 3: Scientific Field of participants who used note-taking software.

Field	Number of participants
Participants using dedicated tools	14
Computers & Technology	8
Educational Science	1
German Studies/Philosophy	1
Psychology & Psychometrics	1

Note-taking functionalities embedded in operating systems were also popular (N = 7) among our participants, and considered 'dedicated note-taking tools' for research purposes.

Training. Since one of the main foci of this paper is how note-taking is taught and what techniques result from this training, we decided to have a closer look at the results of our survey.

Our results are compiled in Tables 14, 15 and 16 and show that the vast majority of participants (N = 51) either consider themselves self-taught only (N = 20) or received no training at all (N = 31), through all cohorts, leaving only a minority of participants (N = 25) with any formal training, either in school or university.

Participants who claimed to have received formal training did not necessarily receive note-taking training in university, where it could be expected to be taught with special focus on scientific practise and critical reading (see Table 16).

Former academics with formal training (N = 10) claimed to have learned note-taking mainly in school (N = 6), whereas active students with formal training (N = 6) claimed to have learned note-taking in school and/or university equally.

Table 13. Q. 6, 8, 10: Tool used among Participants (Multiple Answers allowed).

Tool	Occurrences
Participants using only word-processors or editors	29
MS Word	27
LibreOffice	8
VS Code	3
Google Docs	2
Participants using dedicated tools	14
Apple Notes (incl. iOS)	4
Citavi	4
MS OneNote	4
Obsidian	4
LaTeX	3
Notion	3
Evernote	2
Google Keep	2
Logseq	2
Miro	2
MS Notes	2
Zotero	2
Atlassian Jira	1
Atlassian Confluence	1
Epikur	1
Foxit PDF-Reader	1
GoodNotes	1
Google Workspace	1
Jupyter Notebooks	1
MS Excel	1
MS Teams	1
Org Roam	1
Retext	1
Trello	1
Windows Sticky notes	1
Vivaldi Browser	1

Of special interest are participants who stated to use none of the note-taking techniques we explored (N = 26). They, as shown in Table 14, did in the majority (N = 20) not receive any formal training. Those, who claimed to have received training, did so in school. Only one of these participants claimed to have learned note-taking in university, while still not employing any of the note-taking techniques we explored.

Table 14. Qs. 15 + 11: Number of participants not using note-taking techniques and their formal training.

	Active Researchers	Former Academics	Students
No note-taking technique	11	10	5
School	2	2	2
University	1	0	0
No formal training (self-taught only + no training)	9	8	3

Table 15. Q. 15: Number of participants having received any training.

	Active Researchers	Former Academics	Students
Cohort size	33	31	12
I did not receive any training	17	10	4
Self-taught only	7	11	2
Participants with formal training	9	10	6

Table 16. Q. 15: Formal Note-taking training received.

	Active Researchers	Former Academics	Students
Participants with formal training	9	10	6
School	2	6	3
University	3	3	2
Both	4	1	1

Quality of Notes. To assess the quality of notes that our participants took, the question was posed whether participants did publish their notes (Q.16). As there is no clear definition for the quality of notes, we chose the publication of notes as a proxy measure. We argue that if our participants published their notes, they would hold them to the same high standard they hold the rest of their publications.

It turns out that the vast majority (N = 71) did not publish their notes, with only a small number (N = 5) publishing them (see Table 17).

Table 17. Q. 16: Do you publish your notes?

	Active Researchers	Former Academics	Students
Cohort size	33	31	12
Yes	4	0	1
No	29	31	11

To further assess, what issues may be a reason to not publish notes, we asked participants that did not publish their notes, why they choose to do so (Q. 18). Multiple reasons were offered, with one specifically referring to errors in notes, which we considered another proxy measure for note quality. An "other" option was given to allow participants to give individual reasons.

Table 18. Q. 18: Reasons why notes would not be published.

	Active Researchers	Former Academics	Students
Participants not publishing notes	29	31	11
My notes are private	21	23	6
My notes may contain errors	13	17	10
They may contain cues for further research	5	6	0
They would not make sense to others	4	5	1

As seen in Table 18, most participants overall (N = 50) considered their notes to be private. Curiously, less active researchers thought errors in their notes to be a reason for not publishing them (N = 13 of 29) than former academics (N = 17 of 31) or students (N = 10 of 11). This may indicate a growing confidence in notes, the longer the academic career.

Only a small minority over all cohorts stated that their notes were useless due to being idiosyncratic (N = 10).

However, participants only voiced this concerned in using the "other" option, since "They would not make sense to others" was purposefully not given as a multiple choice question. The reason was that we considered it to be a 'catch all' answer that may mask all other options.

Interestingly, only a minority across all groups seemed to be concerned about the reuse of their notes for further research (N = 11).

In our former academics cohort, two participants voiced general scepticism towards publishing notes, asking "what for?" (N = 1) or "why would I publish my notes?" (N = 1).

Reasoning. In designing the survey, we assumed that the names for individual note-taking techniques may not be familiar, but that participants still employed principles from the described techniques regardless. Thus, we asked if participants took notes that included their mental disposition at the time of reading or their own reasoning (Qs. 12–14).

The inclusion of their own reasoning was of particular interest to us, since pondering notes is a feature common to all structured techniques we described. To see if participants did not include their own reasoning in notes, would allow us to argue that these notes were simply copied from the original source material, but not necessarily engaged with.

Through all cohorts, the majority of our participants (N = 54), claimed to include their own reasoning in their notes. However, roughly a quarter of our participants (N = 19), stated not to include their own reasoning in their notes.

Due to this large percentage, we wanted to see if any participant falling into this group employed note-taking strategies that would normally enforce the inclusion of their own reasoning. We found that they did not employ any of the structured techniques, or none of the given strategies at all. One former academic gave Four Column Reading as a method they used, thus indicating that they may have made one of their answers accidentally (Table 19).

Table 19. Note-taking methods employed by participants not including their own reasoning.

	Active Researchers	Former Academics	Students
Participants not including reasoning	8	6	5
Four Column Reading	0	1	0
Outline Method	2	1	0
Mapping Method	1	0	0
Sentence Method	4	2	1
Charting Method	0	1	1
None of the above	3	2	3

Note Usage. Another area of interest for us was how notes are used in the writing processes of our participants (Q. 19). We assume that if notes are taken as text snippets, note-takers may paraphrase more and may thus engage deeper with the source, creating more in-depth understanding.

Since both usages as text snippets or memory aid may coexist, multiple answers were allowed. Only one valid answer was given in the open-ended option. It was given as 'I use my notes as outlines', which we encoded as 'text snippet' (See Table 20).

Table 20. Note usage.

	Predoc	Postdoc	Professor	Former Academics	Students
Cohort size	20	9	4	31	12
Use as snippets (only)	4	0	1	3	0
Use as memory aid (only)	6	6	1	16	5
Both	10	2	1	11	7
Other (invalid)	1	1	0	1	0

In Table 20, we split our active researcher cohort by their current position in academia because it could be observed that participants currently doing their PhD were the only cohort to show a wide-spread usage of notes as text snippets or both snippet and memory aid ($N = 14$). Postdocs and Professors, used their notes mainly as memory aids ($N = 6$ and $N = 2$ respectively).

3 Discussion

Expanding on our previous work [14], we found that the employment of structured and guided note-taking techniques and a lack of formal training to be present in all of our participants. Only a minority received formal training, and even those participant did not mainly employ note-taking techniques that are geared towards better learning and critical reading.

While the sample is not very big, due to its broad spread of fields and the random way in which the survey-link was distributed, we still consider our results to be meaningful.

In this analysis, we focus on specific shortcomings in training and note-taking behaviour, which have previously not been discussed in this much detail.

3.1 How Revision and Reflection in Note-Taking Helps Us Learn and Research

The column-based techniques and REAP, which we presented earlier, all share one common feature: They require note-takers to take at least one additional step to reflect on the notes they have taken. While their implementations and complexity differ, they all are designed to offer guidance during note-taking and learning. This guidance is often literal, through splitting the page in distinct regions for distinct purposes (Column-based approaches), or figurative through spelled out steps to be taken (REAP).

What this guidance achieves is a deeper and more critical engagement with the source material by linking notes to existing knowledge, or by discussing the contents of notes through annotation and reflection (with others). The latter is explicitly enforced in the **Ponder-phase** of the REAP method, as well as the last step in the modified approach to the Cornell method, presented by Ahmad [2]. Both encourage the embedding of new information in the network of a note-takers own knowledge through retrieval practise and Active Learning [31], creating the same evaluation, discussion and understanding, described in Bloom's taxonomy [22], that we identified as key parts of scientific advancement earlier.

That said, we acknowledge the possibility that those participants, who claimed to use none of the techniques we asked about (N = 26) may employ techniques similar to index cards or Zettelkasten, which would still provide the enforced review step, which is absent in the Sentence- and Outline Methods, which are most commonly in use among our participants. We posit, that this review step can be considered a 'Desirable Difficulty' in note-taking, which is shown to facilitate and benefit learning [24].

However, we concur with previous research [2,3] in the assumption that complex and structured methods are not very intuitive and need specialized training to be implemented and used effectively. We see this assumption confirmed in our findings. Most of our participants did not receive formal training and rely on intuitive and basic methods without any particular structure. We will explore this phenomenon in greater detail in the following section.

3.2 The Use of Note-Taking Techniques and Formal Training

Our findings show almost an absence of formal training in note-taking, which aligns well with previous research [2,3,10,36,40,42]. This absence explains the relative prevalence of intuitive methods, such as Outline- and Sentence-Methods, and relative absence of structured techniques that require formal training [2,3, 40].

Considering that Fix and Dittmann observed a lack of training as early as 2008 [10], the deficit we perceive has persisted for quite some time in Germany. However, this lack of training in note-taking is not a localized phenomenon, as other researchers have found in their more recent studies [2,3,40,42].

That this phenomenon may be due to teachers having received little to no formal training in note-taking themselves is indicated by our findings. Nobody in our professor cohort and only four participants from our PostDocs cohort (N = 4), who could be lecturers, received any formal training. The vast majority of our participants overall (N = 51) did not receive any formal training, which is not entirely surprising considering the teachers themselves have no formal teaching.

We see a large percentage of participants not using any method (N = 26 of 76), including academics (N = 11), not even the most basic form of notes: Sentences. We cannot say for certain that these participants do not use personalized methods like the filing cabinets described by Umberto Eco [9], the Zettelkasten, popularized by Niclas Luhmann [15,34] or the combinatorial technique on index cards described my McCarty [26]. We did, however, not find these or similar methods represented as answers to open-ended questions.

This would leave highlights or keywords as possible notes to be taken. While Umberto Eco specifically encourages note-takers to underline in books and photocopies, he also cautions note-takers to annotate these highlights and make notes on index cards to sort them into filing cabinets [9]. Thus, he circumvents the 'photocopier effect' [9], adding a dedicated ponder step, which allows for critical engagement with the text, akin to REAP. While we cannot say, for certain, that highlights and underlines are the only notes taken by participants who stated to use 'none of the above' (N = 26), it seems a logical conclusion. Especially if it is taken into account that the vast majority of these participants (N = 20 out of 26) of these participants, have not received formal training in note-taking.

Interestingly, participants who stated to use none of the presented note-taking techniques still took mainly handwritten notes or used word-processors and did not make annotations, as shown in Table 7. Since we did not ask how note-takers took their notes specifically, but whether they used any of the structured techniques we were interested in, we can only speculate about the actual process, but would assume it to be suboptimal. More research is direly needed to understand this phenomenon further.

That said, we argue that participants may use structured note-taking methods inadvertently by employing tools that implement these methods. The following section will provide a discussion on the benefits of the tools in use and the relative lack of tool use shown in our findings.

3.3 Tool Usage

As we discussed in the previous sections, the review of notes is a crucial step that creates engagement with the material to be learned. More importantly, methods like Cornell and REAP actively encourage multiple review steps, to facilitate learning. These steps, much like in the personalised methods we presented, happen after some time has elapsed and can thus both be considered Retrieval Practise and Spaced Repetition [31]. In taking away the original text that was read and relying only on the notes to review, a 'Desirable Difficulty' [24] is created to foster a better understanding and linking of knowledge [31]. However, we must not forget that the systems we described are designed to create notes for learning, which implies an active and, most crucially, ongoing review process. It is this ongoing process, we argue, that creates knowledge and understanding, not the one-off process of taking notes. We consider it important to have a reproducible system in place, so note-takers can actively review notes and understand the system, even years after the notes were taken. Dedicated note-taking software offers such a system, even though most software only offers an implementation of Sentence and Outline Methods with no encouragement for review and synthesis. Thus, we consider these tools to be suboptimal, but still an improvement over a simple word processor because they offer the ability to link and search notes. Even so, we cannot observe a lack of tools on the market with dozens of dedicated tools available via a simple search on the internet[1]. However, it would seem that researchers wish for tools that implement their own idiosyncratic way of taking notes [15,26,34], sometimes going through great lengths to adapt tools at their disposal to the purpose [15,36]. We see this reflected in our data as well, where (sticky-)note systems that are included in a computer's operating system are in use (see: Table 13), a behaviour that Qian et al. also describe for one of their participants [36].

That said, we found that even the dedicated tools available were not used much by our participants (see Table 13). This can indicate two things: either the tools are not known to most of our participants, or not perceived as useful. The first indication is supported by our data. With few exceptions, participants who used dedicated note-taking software came from technology adjacent fields of study (see: Table 12. This does not discount that tools were tried by participants from other fields and not found to be useful. However, together with the observed lack of training we discussed above, it appears more likely that even suboptimal tools are not known to our participants because systematic note-taking is not part of the curriculum. This is further corroborated by the predominant use of word-processors as note-taking tools (see: Table 13). We already argued that people will use the tools they know and learned to use in the course of their education, e.g., a word-processor or handwriting [3].

The reason why we consider tools like word-processors to not be effective note-taking tools is that they were in no way designed to be. Moreover, as we already discussed, even specific tools like the RoamResearch based tools, or reference management systems, that are in use among our participants, do not facilitate active and constant review. While they allow for links and search in notes, which is an improvement over a word processor, their interface is still the same as MS-Word or similar tools. If these systems are used with one of the structured note-taking methods, it needs heavy adaptation. This degree of tech-savvyness is not usually present in users, we argue. In addition to that, if note-takers need to spend significant time in adapting a tool to their use, they learn about the tool and not about the material they study.

[1] A simple search on DuckDuckGo using the term 'note-taking tools' resulted in two listicles that could be archived, among others, within the first 10 results, providing 15 and 17 'best note-taking apps in 2025', respectively. A simple search on GitHub, using the same term, returned 38.8k repositories. The pages have been archived on archive.org and are accessible through these links: https://web.archive.org/web/20250720025053/https://niftypm.com/blog/best-note-taking-apps/, https://web.archive.org/web/20250806120031/https://hive.com/blog/best-note-taking-apps/, and https://web.archive.org/web/20250806121035/https://github.com/search?q=Note-taking&type=repositories (All saved on Aug 6, 2025).

We identify two conflicting goals here. On the one hand, software developers create tools that are easy to use and offer a minimal amount of friction to perform the task. This task is 'encoding information' and is performed through note-taking. However, as Mueller and Oppenheimer showed in 2014, learning is more than encoding [29]. When learning is considered, the convenience of the tool conflicts with repeated interaction and critical engagement required. As we argued above, learning and understanding requires a repeated and constant review of one's own knowledge, relinking it whenever new information is acquired [31], in a constant struggle against forgetting [32]. However, if note-takers constantly need to fiddle with a software to facilitate something it was not designed to do, it takes away focus from the topic that should be understood and learnt and creates friction [36] which is less than ideal in a research and learning environment.

We conclude that this might be a reason why researchers mainly engage in simple, intuitive and basic methods of note-taking. They avoid Undesirable Difficulty, provided by suboptimal tools, and use convenient technologies they are all familiar with. The following section will provide a discussion about the most familiar tool for note-taking there is: Pen and paper.

3.4 Pen or Keyboard Which Is Mightier?

The practise of handwritten notes is well represented in our data. This corresponds well with the prevalent use of basic note-taking techniques, since handwritten notes in themselves can be considered a very basic and intuitive technique, as we will discuss in the following sections.

As discussed in the previous section, our findings suggest that note-takers use the tools they are familiar with, even if they are a less than ideal fit for the purpose. Further exemplified by a strong use of handwritten notes and analogue writing media (Table 6) among our participants: Around 70% of our participants overall (N = 53 out of 76) took notes by hand (Tables 11 and 10, with around 17% of our total sample (N = 13 out of 76) stating to use handwritten notes only.

Interestingly, among participants, who employed none of the structured techniques we presented (N = 26) the percentage of handwritten notes is much higher at around 81% (N = 21 out of 26, see Table 7), with around 15% (N = 4 out of 26) employing handwriting only.

This is contrasted by around 36% (N = 27 out of 76) of participants who stated to use both digital and handwritten notes and around 30% (N = 23 out of 76), who used no handwritten notes at all. The latter group stems from various academic fields (see: Table 9, which is not dominated by fields from science and technology.

This relative prevalence of handwriting fits in with the use of basic and intuitive note-taking methods and tools, generally employed by our participants, which we discussed in the previous sections. Yet, it also warrants a deeper look into the discourse concerning the effectiveness of handwritten notes over typed notes. While research within this discourse is extensive, as indicated by the encompassing reviews of Marano et al. and Reed et al. [25,37], it is mainly concerned with younger age groups and provides a somewhat blind spot in the age groups we targeted, according to Marano et al. [25].

Concerning the benefits of handwritten notes, an often cited study, performed by Mueller and Oppenheimer in 2014 indicates a benefit of handwritten notes over typed notes, when they analysed if students performed better at learning assessments using laptops or long form writing [29]. What they found was that students using a laptop were prone to transcribing parts of the lecture verbatim, which lead to ineffective notes and poor recollection in comprehension tasks [29], an effect found by other studies as well [3, 25]. Verbal interventions to stop students from transcribing proved ineffective [29].

We find this urge to transcribe similar to something Walter Pauk mentions as early as 1984, when he strongly advises students to not forego note-taking by using tape recorders to record lectures 'for later' [32, 33]. Umberto Eco observes similarly in 1977 with the use of photocopiers, where students and researchers alike consider a text read, once they made a photocopy of it [9]. In a later revision of his work from 2001, Walter Pauk advises students not to 'keyboard' (i.e. to transcribe) handwritten notes, since he considered it a waste of hours because the act of 'keyboarding' would be "mentally, physically and emotionally exhausting" to students [33]. Interestingly, earlier revisions of 'How to study in college' (1984, 1993, 1997) containing no such provision against 'keyboarding', while even encouraging students to type first drafts, because of quickness. We would link this to laptops becoming more frequent in the early 2000s, thus becoming more of the 'problem' in classrooms that Mueller and Oppenheimer will observe in 2014 [29].

But while laptops have since become omnipresent, it appears that systematic typing skills have not. A recent study conducted by Bouriga and Olive in 2021 indicates that the act of systematic typing is still unfamiliar to students, leaving them with suboptimal, idiosyncratic typing systems [3]. This is a stark contrast to a general proficiency in handwriting, which is taught as early as kindergarten [3]. This is an important observation because both handwriting and typing reside in procedural memory [19] if properly taught, meaning that both do not require active focus, when performed by a proficient practitioner [19, 31]. Consequently, a non-proficient typist would need to focus on the act of typing, rather than on what is currently being typed [3]. Bouriga and Olive confirmed this hypothesis by observing a higher mental load in typists, which they link to a lack of proficiency and overwhelming user interfaces of word-processing software [3].

Disregarding the level of proficiency, the argument often presented as beneficial in handwriting is its 'inherent slowness', which forces writers to synthesise and reflect while writing [3, 24, 25, 29, 38], which is put somewhat into question by a recent study performed by Tindle and Longstaff, who found that in handwriting, the brain uses the same resources for writing, as it does for keeping information in working memory [39], causing a split in attention. Nevertheless, following the argument of beneficial 'inherent slowness', it would be the comparative speed of typing, which encourages mindless verbatim transcription [3, 25, 29, 38]. This also aligns with the research shown in the usage of AI tools [20].

In following this argument, the benefit of handwriting would neither lie in psychomotor skills, or graphical representations of words and information attached to the process of handwriting [21,25,42], nor the writers inherent proficiency outlined above, but simply in bodily limitations of the writer, namely muscle fatigue and sore wrists. This would mean that, similar to a German proverb "Was sehrt, das lehrt" (What hurts me, teaches me), which originated in swordplay [13], writers would avoid a sore wrist in writing as little as possible, but still encoding as much information as possible, but not so much they end up in pain. We think the latter would sound familiar to most readers from school experience, the dull ache of a wrist after writing a long term paper. So, to avoid pain and suffering, writers would, in this line of argument, synthesise information on the spot, creating an impromptu, immediate, review step.

While the above argument maybe sounds plausible in theory, it is somewhat defeated by the very study cited to prove it. In 'Study 3' [29] Mueller and Oppenheimer specifically state that there is little 'relative lack of verbatim overlap in longhand notes' [29], implying that note-takers still tried to transcribe as much as possible, when handwriting. We find the reason for this in the study's methodology. Mueller and Oppenheimer created a time-constrained environment for their participants in tasking them to take notes on TED-Talks [29]. We argue that any environment like this would create the urge in note-takers to take as many notes as possible. We would expect this, especially for untrained note-takers. Thus, the bodily limitations described above would only hamper an untrained note-takers, desire to write down as much as possible, while a keyboard would allow the same untrained note-takers to follow this desire without limitation. The writing media make no difference in the desire, apparently.

Let us consider an internal perspective of both note-takers: 'scribe'[2] and 'typist'. Both would like to write down as much information as possible because they both know they will be asked questions later. Both are under the same pressure to transcribe verbatim, but the ability of the 'scribe' to do so would be severely hampered by their pain tolerance and muscle training. Notwithstanding the comparative mechanical slowness of handwriting, [38] in the first place. This 'mechanical disadvantage' would, in theory, force them to listen more carefully for cues as to why information may or may not be relevant, enforcing synthesis on the spot [36], but also allowing for the linking of the heard information to what is already in long-term memory [31]. Now we compare the 'typist' in the other corner. They would, in theory, be able to transcribe the full lecture verbatim, had they the required systematic typing skills, without any fear of a sore wrist and quicker typing movements than the 'scribe' could ever move their pen. In practise, however, they would be looking for the correct keys on their keyboards and have suboptimal movement routines for their fingers, slowing them down. Also, they would be distracted by red and blue lines under the words they just typed in their word-processor, requiring immediate attention. Considering this

[2] We use this outdated term deliberately because the English language defaults to 'writer'.

inner perspective, it is no wonder they perform worse on assessment. While they can recollect factual knowledge [3,29], which they may have collected simply by listening, they perform worse when time elapses and after note review [29].

To sum up, we argue that after considering the evidence, all that can be seen is that any uneducated user of a tool, will use said tool to its full potential within their abilities to use it. If users are not educated on the use of their tools, they will use them in the way it provides the best convenience for them. The argument Pauk and Eco present is that students should forego this convenience because it was detrimental to learning by taking away the active engagement with the material to be read or learned, while not arguing for a ban of the technologies they caution against [9,32,33].

Thus, we find that it is not the act of typewriting that creates ineffective notes, rather than a general lack of note-taking, typing and review skills [2,3,10,40]. We maintain that 'Mindless transcription' [29], tape recordings [32,33], and photocopies [9] all represent the same argumentative category of 'tool misuse because the user has not learned differently', which stems from an unawareness about pitfalls of simply 'storing information for later' and the resulting inability to recognize the ineffectiveness of their tool use, which leads to sticking to suboptimal methods. We can buttress this argument by observing our findings. The propensity for the use of intuitive and basic tools or methods and the general lack of education on more effective note-taking go hand in hand in our participants.

3.5 Trust in Notes and (re)Use

To review notes, note-takers need to trust the system they use to an extent that gives them confidence in their notes. Research notes are a researcher's thoughts, understanding and reasoning made persistent through the act of writing. They can be an indicator to a researcher's attention [42] and reading focus.

Following this, it is all the more important that researchers can reuse their notes in reviewing information and critically questioning their own understanding of the world, their 'epistème' [11], their interpretation of the world [41], their paradigm [23].

To assess if researchers and those with academic backgrounds trusted their notes to the same extent they trusted their publications, we asked if participants published their notes. Publication acts, as explained in the findings section above, as a proxy measure for the confidence our participants had in their notes. We found that almost no participant published their notes (N = 5 out of 76) and many stating concerns about errors in their notes as a reason not to publish (N = 39 out of 76). This contrasts somewhat with notions in previous research, that identified unintelligibility as a more pressing concern [10,28], which was only mentioned by some of our participants (N = 10 out of 76) (see: Table 18).

While privacy concerns may also include a notion on unintelligibility, 'being wrong' seemed to be a bigger concern to our participants. Bigger than specifically voicing an opinion about others not being able to understand one's notes.

We find this circumstance particularly interesting from an epistemological point of view. If notes are a glimpse in a reader's 'Weltbild' [41], i.e. their interpretation of the world, then they cannot really contain 'errors' to begin with. They may contain interpretations and notions that are falsified by observation [35], but these are, given a review of notes, identifiable and correctable, which in turn would constitute a learning process. This would necessitate an ongoing review of a researcher's note-base. What could also be an 'error', would be a misquotation from a text, which would probably go unnoticed in a regular review, but could be spotted if compared with the source material. The latter may even be automated because, in accordance to the arguments we presented earlier, the act of transcribing does not seem to benefit learning anyway.

We can combine this line of argument with the observation that among our participants, the majority (N = 54 out of 76) includes their own reasoning in their notes, even without employing techniques that would compel them to do so. This reasoning would constitute the interpretations and notions, we mentioned, which cannot be 'wrong' strictly speaking, but may simply change with an influx of more knowledge.

However, a fear of 'errors' in notes may be a hint to the perception of insufficiency in correcting and reviewing notes by the participants who stated this fear. We find implied in this fear an apprehension towards a possible observed assessment, represented by the publication of notes and fear of reprimand. While this cannot be proven by our data, we consider this likely, given the propensity of an academic education to lead to the so-called impostor phenomenon [6]. We find this all the more likely, when observing the answers of participants from our Student cohort, who almost unanimously voiced a concern of 'error's in their notes. We argue that students show a trend in this perception of constantly being assessed that continues on into an active career in research.

In this context, it is even more interesting to see that in our findings our participants have a tendency to use their notes as text-snippets, especially present in the Active Researcher cohort (see: Table 20). This is somewhat puzzling because on closer inspection of the data, 17 participants who voice their fear of 'errors', still used their notes as text snippets in writing. We have no indication to know whether these participants fixed their 'errors' in their publications, but would presume they do so.

Qian et al. observed a similar lack of trust, when they studied the note-taking techniques of their participants who often went back to the original publication because they found their notes lacking [36].

In this discussion, we have explored how structured note-taking methods like REAP, Cornell and the other column-based methods provide a scaffold for ongoing, critical and meaningful review and discussion of notes in students and researchers alike. While our findings suggest that researches may already include parts of these scaffolds in their work, the tools and methods they use are basic and idiosyncratic and do not support the shareability and reusability necessary to provide meaningful discourse based on notes and a specialised tool that would aid in the process of creating the required structure has not yet been defined or finds use in our participants.

4 Conclusion

Expanding the research in our original publication [14], we argue that a Virtual Research Environment (VRE) would allow researchers to make better use of their notes and maybe address the issues we presented then. On re-examining the full dataset, and the surrounding discussion concerning proficiency in note-taking, typing and learning we presented here, we maintain this argument, but emphasize the need to include dedicated reviews within such a tool. Based on our discussion, we conclude that the act of simply encoding knowledge does result in good learning and research outcomes, as Mueller and Oppenheimer have already shown [29] in contrast to works by Kiewra and others that proposed encoding theory [16,17]. We argue that simply encoding knowledge with the Sentence- and Outline Methods, which are implemented in a great number of note-taking tools, does not provide an optimal basis for research and scholarly work, if used without ongoing review and integration of new knowledge. Without this step, any knowledge encoded in a tool will inevitably become another recorded tape [32] or photocopy [9] or photo of a lecture slide.

Both Ahmad [2] and Tiruneh [40] show the importance of note-taking in critical reading, even in a non-academical context, and both employ methods we discussed in this paper [2,40]. While both do not explicitly state whether they employed digital means to take notes, we would surmise from the context of their publications, that they employed handwritten notes. However, with look at our discussion of the matter, we conclude that the main driving factor behind the perception of digital note-taking as less effective [3,24,25,29] is not the act of digital writing, but a lack of proficiency in typing and tools badly suited for the process. Yet, being Computer Scientists in Education, we argue that educational technology may offer guard rails to note-takers that would encourage more structured and beneficial techniques to be used and make them more pleasant to use at the same time. While we agree that learning requires a 'Desirable Difficulty' [24], the difficulty offered by cluttered and bad user interfaces cannot be considered desirable.

From what we see presented in our findings and discussion, we conclude that at least our participants do not use their notes to their full potential [14], but moreover do not **create** them to their full potential, too. In employing a known algorithm for taking structured, reviewed and synthesised notes, embedded in a network of a researches own knowledge, notes become the most powerful tool at a researchers' disposal when creating new scientific literature. They also become more shareable and allow more profound discussion among peers. Would researchers employ methods like REAP in a digital form, which our findings suggest they do not, discussion would be a bigger part of their daily work and notes would become a tool for collaboration, rather than a private affair as it currently seems to be.

And while the perception of 'errors' in a researcher's notes currently hampers this open discussion, we think it paramount to share and discuss our understanding of scientific works, especially in the raw form provided by notes. The chance that notes may offer a glimpse into the 'epistème' [11] or 'Weltbild' [41] of other researchers, may today remain unharnessed because we, as researchers, do not adhere to the things we should be teaching our students. Generations of college educators like Walter Pauk, Eanet and Manzo, Umberto Eco dedicated time and effort to design note-taking systems that generate effective, collaborative and reusable notes. But today we still see, at least in the small bubble we can observe, a lack of training in note-taking and critical reading around the globe [2, 10, 40] and the resulting knock-on effects of teachers being unable to teach something they do not know themselves [10, 14]. The proliferation of suboptimally designed tools further exacerbates this circumstance by claiming to solve the problem, while instead entrenching suboptimal note-taking techniques through their implementation that encourages basic, intuitive and badly reusable notes like Sentence and Outline Methods with no easy and convenient option for review and synthesis. Incompatibility issues between tools make it even more difficult to change track, once note-takers decided on a tool to use.

Thus, we think that a VRE may be a solution for a better use of our research-notes, if it is built implementing the scaffolds that are provided by REAP, Cornell, or the other structured methods we described, including multiple spaced review steps taken by the researcher to engage with their own knowledge. Something that compels students and researchers alike to **not** only use the keyboard to its full potential in transcribing, to **not** only summarise texts with LLMs and **not** only take screenshots or photos of slides, but to engage with the material in a critical manner, creating real understanding, synthesis and learning.

The need for tools to navigate an ever-growing fond of knowledge is clear, and we should not rely on old and possibly outdated ways of teaching and learning, by banning technology from classrooms [29]. Yet, we agree with previous research [2, 3, 10, 40] in arguing that we need special and specific training in note-taking, typing and critical thinking and reading in a digital age, as well as tools that would encourage and compel us to really take the small inconvenience that is learning of the easy solution offered by simple tools.

More research in this field is needed to see if digital note-taking can become the best possible tool available if meaningful interaction and deliberate revision were employed, and the resulting notes could become the personal textbook Pauk mentions [33], that helps researches to recognise the limits of their own Paradigm [23] to work around it and expand their knowledge.

References

1. Starthilfe Schreiben.: Leibniz Universität Hannover, Zentrale Einrichtung für Qualitätsentwicklung in Studium und Lehre (ZQS) (2021). https://www.zqs.uni-hannover.de/fileadmin/zqs/PDF/Schluesselkompetenzen/Starthilfe_Schreiben.pdf

2. Ahmad, S.Z.: Impact of cornell notes vs. REAP on EFL secondary school students' critical reading skills. Int. Educ. Stud. **12**(10), 60 (2019). https://doi.org/10.5539/ies.v12n10p60. http://www.ccsenet.org/journal/index.php/ies/article/view/0/40869
3. Bouriga, S., Olive, T.: Is typewriting more resources-demanding than handwriting in undergraduate students? Read. Writ. **34**(9), 2227–2255 (2021). https://doi.org/10.1007/s11145-021-10137-6. https://link-springer-com.dipf.idm.oclc.org/article/10.1007/s11145-021-10137-6
4. Bui, D.C., McDaniel, M.A.: Enhancing learning during lecture note-taking using outlines and illustrative diagrams. J. Appl. Res. Mem. Cogn. **4**(2), 129–135 (2015). https://doi.org/10.1016/j.jarmac.2015.03.002. https://www.sciencedirect.com/science/article/pii/S2211368115000200
5. Buzan, T., Buzan, B.: The Mind Map Book: Unlock Your Creativity, Boost Your Memory, Change Your Life. Pearson/BBC Active, Harlow Munich, nachdr edn (2012)
6. Cisco, J.: Exploring the connection between impostor phenomenon and postgraduate students feeling academically-unprepared. High. Educ. Res. Dev. **39**(2), 200–214 (2020). https://doi.org/10.1080/07294360.2019.1676198
7. Cribiore, R.: Listening to the Philosophers: Notes on Notes. Cornell University Press (2024). http://www.jstor.org/stable/10.7591/jj.5233150
8. Eanet, M.G., Manzo, A.V.: REAP - a strategy for improving reading/writing/study skills. J. Read. **19**(8), 647–652 (1976). https://www.jstor.org/stable/40032892
9. Eco, U.: How to Write a Thesis. The MIT Press, Cambridge (Mass.) London, translation edition edn. (2015)
10. Fix, G., Dittmann, J.D.: Exzerpieren. Eine empirische Studie an Exzerpten von GymnasialschülerInnen der Oberstufe. Linguistik Online **33**(1) (2008). https://doi.org/10.13092/lo.33.529, https://bop.unibe.ch/linguistik-online/article/view/529
11. Foucault, M.: Die Ordnung der Dinge: eine Archäologie der Humanwissenschaften. No. 96 in suhrkamp taschenbuch wissenschaft, Suhrkamp, Frankfurt am Main, 26. auflage edn (2020)
12. Harari, Y.N.: Nexus: A Brief History of Information Networks from the Stone Age to AI. Fern Press, London (2024)
13. Amberger, J.C.: The Secret History Of The Sword (1998). http://archive.org/details/the-secret-history-of-the-sword
14. Jäckel, Y., Schiffner, D., Schneider, J.: Our notes leave too much to say: investigating note-taking practices and technological tools in academia. In: Proceedings of the 17th International Conference on Computer Supported Education, pp. 493–503. SCITEPRESS - Science and Technology Publications, Porto, Portugal (2025). https://doi.org/10.5220/0013218600003932, https://www.scitepress.org/DigitalLibrary/Link.aspx?doi=10.5220/0013218600003932
15. Kadavy, D.: Digital Zettelkasten: principles, methods, & examples. Kadavy Inc. (2021)
16. Kauffman, D., Zhao, R., Kauffman, Y.: Effects of online note taking formats and self-monitoring prompts on learning from online text: using technology to enhance self-regulated learning. Contemp. Educ. Psychol. **36**, 313–322 (2011). https://doi.org/10.1016/j.cedpsych.2011.04.001
17. Kiewra, K.A., Benton, S.L., Kim, S.I., Risch, N., Christensen, M.: Effects of note-taking format and study technique on recall and relational performance. Contemp. Educ. Psychol. **20**(2), 172–187 (1995). https://doi.org/10.1006/ceps.1995.1011. https://www.sciencedirect.com/science/article/pii/S0361476X85710119

18. Király, R.S., Hösl, P., Beerbaum, T., Samuelsson, U.: Jump-Start Your Writing: Tips and Methods for Planning and Writing Academic Texts. Dresden University of Technology, 2 edn. (2023). https://doi.org/10.25368/2023.150, https://tud.qucosa.de/id/qucosa:87238
19. Knowlton, B.J., Schorn, J.M.: Procedural and motor learning. In: The Oxford Handbook of Human Memory. Oxford University Press, Oxford (2024)
20. Kosmyna, N., et al.: Your brain on chatgpt: accumulation of cognitive debt when using an AI assistant for essay writing task (2025). https://arxiv.org/abs/2506.08872
21. Koziol, L.F., Budding, D.E., Chidekel, D.: From movement to thought: executive function, embodied cognition, and the cerebellum. The Cerebellum **11**(2), 505–525 (2012). https://doi.org/10.1007/s12311-011-0321-y
22. Krathwohl, D.R.: A revision of bloom's taxonomy: an overview. Theory Into Pract. **41**(4), 212–218 (2002). https://doi.org/10.1207/s15430421tip4104_2. https://www.tandfonline.com/doi/full/10.1207/s15430421tip4104_2
23. Kuhn, T.S., Hacking, I.: The Structure of Scientific Revolutions, 4th edn. The University of Chicago Press, Chicago; London (2012)
24. Limbu, B., Chounta, I.A.: Can the mighty pen be mightier? Investigating the role of haptic senses in multimodal immersive learning environments. In: Proceedings of the 17th International Conference on Computer Supported Education, pp. 72–82. SCITEPRESS - Science and Technology Publications, Porto, Portugal (2025). https://doi.org/10.5220/0013285600003932. https://www.scitepress.org/DigitalLibrary/Link.aspx?doi=10.5220/0013285600003932
25. Marano, G., et al.: The neuroscience behind writing: handwriting vs. typing—who wins the battle? Life **15**(3), 345 (2025). https://doi.org/10.3390/life15030345. https://www.mdpi.com/2075-1729/15/3/345
26. McCarty, W.: Pursuing a combinatorial habit of mind and machine. In: Nyhan, J., Rockwell, G., Sinclair, S., Ortolja-Baird, A. (eds.) On Making in the Digital Humanities, pp. 251–266. The scholarship of digital humanities development in honour of John Bradley, UCL Press (2023). https://doi.org/10.2307/j.ctv2wk727j.16. https://www.jstor.org/stable/j.ctv2wk727j.16
27. Miller, E., Kelly, A.M.: Flipped science classrooms and the cornell note-taking method. Sci. Scope **47**(6), 43–49 (2024). https://doi.org/10.1080/08872376.2024.2407297
28. Mosleh, M., Baba, M.S.: Overview of traditional note taking. Educ. Psychol. Rev. (2013)
29. Mueller, P.A., Oppenheimer, D.M.: The pen is mightier than the keyboard: advantages of longhand over laptop note taking. Psychol. Sci. **25**(6), 1159–1168 (2014). https://doi.org/10.1177/0956797614524581
30. Novak, J.D., Gowin, D.B.: Learning How to Learn. Cambridge University Press, Cambridge (1984). https://doi.org/10.1017/CBO9781139173469. https://www.cambridge.org/core/books/learning-how-to-learn/D4E082D454735D8CC7FEDADFA25A3B99
31. Oakley, B.A., Rogowsky, B., Sejnowski, T.J.: Uncommon sense teaching. Tarcher-Perigee, an imprint of Penguin Random House LLC, New York (2021)
32. Pauk, W.: How to study in college. Houghton Mifflin, Boston (1984). http://archive.org/details/howtostudyincoll0000pauk
33. Pauk, W.: How To Study In College. Houghton Mifflin Co (2001). http://archive.org/details/howtostudyincoll00pauk_1
34. Pitura, J.: Digital Note-Taking for Writing. Springer (2023)

35. Popper, K.: The Logic of Scientific Discovery. Routledge, London, special indian edition edn (2010)
36. Qian, X., Fenlon, K., Lutters, W., Chan, J.: Opening up the black box of scholarly synthesis: intermediate products, processes, and tools. Proc. Assoc. Inf. Sci. Technol. **57**(1), e270 (2020). https://doi.org/10.1002/pra2.270. https://onlinelibrary.wiley.com/doi/abs/10.1002/pra2.270
37. Reed, D.K., Rimel, H., Hallett, A.: Note-taking interventions for college students: a synthesis and meta-analysis of the literature. J. Res. Educ. Effect. **9**(3), 307–333 (2016). https://doi.org/10.1080/19345747.2015.1105894
38. Saran, M., Krentz Gober, M., McCarty, E.B.: An introduction to the cornell note system. Ear Nose Throat J. **101**(9_suppl), 37S–41S (2022). https://doi.org/10.1177/01455613221146457. http://journals.sagepub.com/doi/10.1177/01455613221146457
39. Tindle, R., Longstaff, M.G.: Working memory and handwriting and share a common resource: an investigation of shared attention. Curr. Psychol. **42**(5), 3945–3956 (2023). https://doi.org/10.1007/s12144-021-01733-4
40. Tiruneh, D.T.: The effect of explicit reading strategy instruction on reading comprehension of upper primary grade students. Int. J. Educ. **6**(3), 81–100 (2014). https://doi.org/10.5296/ije.v6i3.5989. https://www.macrothink.org/journal/index.php/ije/article/view/5989
41. Wittgenstein, L.: Über Gewißheit. No. 250 in Bibliothek Suhrkamp, Suhrkamp Verlag, Frankfurt am Main, 15. auflage edn (2020)
42. Ślęzak Świat, A.M.: Development of digital literacy - translanguaging and transmedia note taking formats for academic reading. Theory Pract. Second Lang. Acquisition **8**(1) (2022). https://opus.us.edu.pl/info/article/USL71db3a3cbc64436581e515d296676a6d/

The Hack4CBL Framework: A Challenge-Based Learning Approach for Multidisciplinary Hackathons in Higher Education

Efraín Ortíz-Pabón[1], Lady Fernández-Mora[2], Nestor Armando Nova-Arévalo[3], and Juan E. Gómez-Morantes[1(✉)]

[1] Facultad de Ingeniería, Pontificia Universidad Javeriana, Bogotá, Colombia
{efrain.ortiz,je.gomezm}@javeriana.edu.co
[2] Instituto Tecnológico de Costa Rica, CTEC Campus San Carlos, Alajuela, Costa Rica
lfernandez@itcr.ac.cr
[3] Facultad de Comunicación y Lenguaje, Pontificia Universidad Javeriana, Bogotá, Colombia
novanestor@javeriana.edu.co

Abstract. This paper introduces the Hack4CBL framework, integrating Challenge-Based Learning (CBL) principles into hackathon design for multidisciplinary higher education. By aligning hackathon stages with CBL domains (engage, investigate, act, transfer), it fosters collaboration and diverse learning outcomes. We illustrate Hack4CBL's effectiveness through the "Second International Hackathon of Intelligent Solutions for the Promotion of Agribusiness 4.0," involving 142 undergraduate students from Colombia and Costa Rica across Systems Engineering, Business Administration, and Agronomic Engineering. Its application in a formal undergraduate course is also discussed. Over 16 weeks, interdisciplinary teams tackled real-world agribusiness challenges, developing minimum viable products. Results show that CBL integration enhances collaboration, deepens domain knowledge, and accelerates professional skill development. The framework offers a replicable model for educational hackathons aligned with professional realities. Emotional challenges were identified, suggesting a need for explicit guidance.

Keywords: Hackathon · Challenge-Based Learning · Prototyping · Minimum Viable Product · Digital Innovation · Agribusiness 4.0

1 Introduction

Hackathons are time-bounded, collaborative events where diverse participants come together to create solutions and develop software or functional prototypes, usually within one to three days [12]. Over time, their formats and durations

C. Meinel et al. (Eds.): CSEDU 2025, CCIS 3148, pp. 288–308, 2027.
https://doi.org/10.1007/978-3-032-39103-2_14

have diversified, evolving from strictly in-person gatherings to virtual and hybrid experiences with flexible time frames adjusted to project complexity.

While popular in industry settings, hackthons have become a highly relevant tool in higher education for experiential learning and bridging the gap between theory and practice. The complexity of challenges, team dynamics, and logistics involved in hackathons contributes to the development of essential skills such as problem-solving, teamwork, leadership, communication, adaptability, and technical proficiency. As a result, they are increasingly adopted as educational strategies in undergraduate and graduate programs [20]. However, integrating their intense, competitive format into academic curricula poses significant pedagogical and logistical challenges. Realizing these outcomes requires intentional design, robust coordination, and appropriate communication tools to manage organizational demands effectively.

A key challenge in large-scale hackathons involving students from diverse disciplines and backgrounds is the alignment of varied expectations, competencies, and—specially—learning objectives. In such settings, overly narrow or linear challenges may lead to disengagement and limited skill development. Addressing this issue requires complex, multifaceted problems—such as designing an application to improve healthcare access by integrating patient records, telemedicine, social services, and data analytics—thus encouraging collaboration, leveraging diverse viewpoints, and promoting interdisciplinary innovation.

While traditional hackathons can foster intense collaboration and rapid prototyping, their short duration often limits opportunities for deep, sustained learning [7]. Challenge-Based Learning (CBL) [18] offers a pedagogical framework designed precisely to bridge this gap by guiding learners through an iterative process of engaging with a "big idea," formulating essential questions, investigating real-world contexts, and taking action to create viable solutions. The collaborative, multidisciplinary, and problem-driven nature of hackathons aligns naturally with these stages, suggesting that a CBL-inspired structure could enhance their educational value. Furthermore, unlike traditional hackathon formats that may impose uniform challenges or narrow technical focuses, CBL naturally accommodates the varied expectations and competencies of participants from different disciplines by centering the learning process around complex, multifaceted real-world problems that require diverse expertise to solve.

Building on this alignment, we present the Hack4CBL framework, which systematically integrates CBL principles into hackathon design. This framework ensures that multidisciplinary teams engage with complex challenges that span technology, ethics, business, and domain expertise, while allowing each participant to pursue discipline-specific learning objectives within the same collaborative project.

The proposed framework was validate through two large-scale, binational hackathons involving students from Colombia and Costa Rica—one centered on Tourism 4.0[1] and another on Agribusiness 4.0 (presented in this paper). These complementary case studies provide a comprehensive basis for analyzing the

[1] This case was presented in depth at the CSEDU 2025 Conference [19].

framework's design, application, and impact. Through this multi-faceted approach, we highlight how CBL-guided hackathons function as agile spaces for prototyping and as structured platforms for interdisciplinary learning and institutional innovation, and how the Hack4CBL es an appropriate methodological tool to guide the development of these hackathons.

After this introduction, Sect. 2 discusses CBL as a general pedagogical framework and its relevance for hackathon design. Section 3 then explores hackathons as a general pedagogical strategy, outlining their potential and limitations. Later, Sect. 4 discusses the challenges of integrating CBL principles into hackathon design. Section 5 presents the Hack4CBL framework based on CBL principles, while Sect. 6 details the framework's application in two large-scale binational hackathon. Finally, Sect. 7 discusses the main lessons and findings from this experience, followed by Sect. 8 on conclusions and future perspectives.

2 Challenge-Based Learning

Fostering soft skills in engineering students remains a critical yet complex educational goal. In response to evolving demands, engineering curricula have incorporated diverse pedagogical models aimed at promoting practical, entrepreneurial, and real-world learning experiences [16]. Approaches such as experiential learning [8, 11], along with project-based and service learning [3], have become prominent strategies. Among these approaches, hackathons have emerged as a particularly promising format for experiential learning, yet they require careful pedagogical structuring to maximize their educational potential.

To transform a hackathon from a competitive event into a structured learning experience, a robust pedagogical framework is required. Challenge-Based Learning (CBL), as articulated by Nichols and Cator [18], provides this essential framework by immersing students in authentic, context-specific problems that demand the design and implementation of viable solutions. It is uniquely suited for the dynamic, fast-paced, and multidisciplinary nature of educational hackathons.

Challenge Based Learning is defined as "an engaging multidisciplinary approach to teaching and learning that encourages students to leverage the technology they use in their daily lives to solve real-world problems" [18][2]. It is a pedagogical model that immerses students in authentic, context-specific problems, challenging them to design and implement viable solutions [18]. Its focus on real-world relevance, interdisciplinary teamwork, creativity, and reflective practice has contributed to its adoption across STEM education [4]. CBL emphasizes collaboration among students, instructors, and stakeholders, fostering divergent thinking. Crucially, it values not only the final outcome but the entire learning journey, encouraging continuous reflection on progress and understanding [3].

The CBL process follows a structured progression that starts with a big idea and moves through stages such as the formulation of an essential question,

[2] See [6] for a more complex discussion about the various definitions of CBL and their implications.

definition of the challenge(s), development of guiding questions, activities, and resources; and culminates in the creation, implementation, and evaluation of a solution [18]. Table 1 summarizes each of these elements. This process is commonly organized around three fundamental domains that guide learning activities [5]:

- **Engage:** Students connect with big ideas and essential questions that resonate with their interests and societal needs. This domain focuses on understanding the context and significance of challenges, fostering emotional and intellectual investment in the learning process.
- **Investigate:** Students develop guiding questions and conduct research to build the knowledge foundation necessary for addressing their chosen challenge. This involves exploring multiple perspectives, gathering relevant resources, and understanding the complexity of real-world problems.
- **Act:** Students design, develop, and implement solutions while documenting their process and reflecting on their learning. This domain emphasizes the creation of tangible outcomes and the practical application of acquired knowledge.

One of CBL's most significant strengths lies in its capacity to accommodate diverse learning objectives within the same project [15]. The collaborative nature of this approach allows students to take on different roles and responsibilities based on their expertise and learning needs. For example, while one student might focus on technical implementation, another might concentrate on market analysis or user experience design. This flexibility supports multidisciplinary teamwork, enabling students from various backgrounds to contribute their specialized knowledge while developing cross-disciplinary competencies. This is particularly valuable in engineering education, where essential skills like teamwork and leadership are learned through collaboration but are incredibly difficult to quantify, despite being critical for professional success.

The CBL model is commonly applied through either dedicated CBL courses or standalone CBL projects [6]. In the former, the challenge supports the learning of core course content; in the latter, solving the challenge is the main objective, often in the form of graduation work or extracurricular initiatives. While hackathons are a frequent type of extracurricular CBL project [6], implementing CBL in large-scale, multidisciplinary settings presents several challenges that require careful consideration and strategic solutions. These will be explored in Sect. 4.

Having outlined the principles of CBL, we now examine the specific characteristics of hackathons to demonstrate their natural alignment and potential for integration.

3 Hackathons

Hackathons are traditionally understood as "events where computer programmers and others collaborate intensively over a short period to develop software

Table 1. Components and Descriptions of Challenge-Based Learning. Source: [18].

Component	Description
Big Idea	Broad concept that can be explored in multiple ways, has the quality of being appealing, and is important to the students and society at large. Examples of big ideas include identity, sustainability, creativity, violence, peace, power, among others.
Essential Question	Questions generated from the big idea. They should reflect the interests of the students and the needs of the community. The essential questions identify what is important to know about the big idea.
The Challenge	A challenge is articulated from each essential question, asking students to create a specific response or solution that can result in concrete and meaningful action.
Guiding Questions	Generated by the students, these questions represent the knowledge students need to discover in order to successfully address the challenge.
Guiding Activities	Lessons, simulations, games, and other types of activities that help students answer the guiding questions and lay the foundation for them to develop innovative, insightful, and realistic solutions.
Guiding Resources	This focused set of resources may include sources, databases, experts, etc., that support the activities and help students develop a solution.
Solutions	Each challenge is broad enough to allow for a variety of solutions. Each solution should be thoughtful, concrete, viable, clearly articulated, and presented in a publishable multimedia format, such as an enhanced podcast or a short video.
Assessment	The solution can be assessed based on its connection to the challenge, the accuracy of the content, the clarity of communication, the applicability for implementation, and the effectiveness of the idea, among other factors. In addition to the solution, the process that individuals and teams went through to reach a solution can also be evaluated, capturing the development of key skills or competencies.
Publication	The challenge process provides multiple opportunities to document the experience and publish it for a wider audience. Students are encouraged to publish their results online and seek feedback. The idea is to expand the learning community and foster discussion about solutions to challenges that are important to students.

projects" [12]. Originally emerging from the software development community as competitive coding events, hackathons have evolved significantly in both format and purpose. This evolution has been particularly notable in their transition from purely technical, competition-focused events to educational tools that emphasize learning, collaboration, and problem-solving [17]. Modern educational hackathons increasingly involve non-programmers (e.g., designers, business students, and domain experts) fostering interdisciplinary collaboration and enriching collective problem-solving capabilities. This shift reflects a growing recognition that complex real-world challenges require diverse perspectives and expertise beyond technical programming skills.

Hackathons do not follow a universal format. Variations in structure and purpose are common across academic and corporate contexts, depending on expected outcomes [21]. These events may also appear under different names—such as hackfests, code camps, datathons [1], or jams. Jams, while sometimes including programming, are often discipline-specific and may focus on areas like video game development or service design [12].

The typical hackathon process follows a structured sequence: team formation and ideation during the pre-hackathon phase, core development activities during the hackathon itself, and a post-hackathon phase where teams evaluate outcomes and consider future development [12]. This three-phase structure, illustrated in Fig. 1, provides a foundation for organizing activities but often lacks the pedagogical rigor necessary for sustained educational impact.

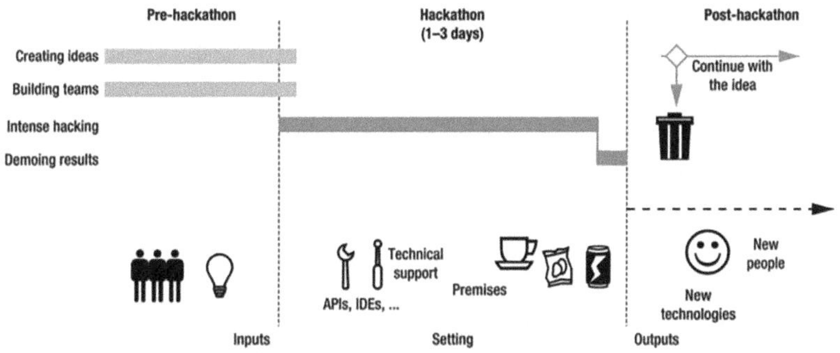

Fig. 1. The typical hackathon process, in terms of the essential activities, phases, and supporting elements. Surce: [12].

Hackathons have gained significant adoption in higher education due to their capacity to foster experiential learning through authentic problem-solving scenarios that mirror professional environments [2]. Their intensive, collaborative nature naturally develops essential 21st-century skills including teamwork, communication, leadership, adaptability, and creative problem-solving, while effectively bridging the theory-practice gap by requiring students to rapidly apply theoretical knowledge to practical challenges. The collaborative environment encourages peer learning and knowledge sharing, often proving more effective than traditional instructor-led approaches for technical skills and creative problem-solving strategies [17].

The time-restricted format effectively simulates professional work environments, exposing students to real-world pressures, deadlines, and collaborative dynamics while teaching them to manage scope, make trade-offs, and deliver functional solutions under time constraints. This, while desirable, comes with significant drawbacks.

Despite their educational potential, traditional hackathons present significant pedagogical challenges. Their typically short duration prioritizes rapid solution development over deep learning and reflection, often leading to superficial problem analysis and quick-fix solutions [7]. Furthermore, short-duration hackathons tend to reward pre-existing skills rather than developing new competencies. Assessment represents another challenge, as traditional grading mechanisms are poorly suited to the collaborative, iterative nature of hackathon outputs, while the competitive format can create tension between winning and learning. In multidisciplinary settings, these challenges are amplified by communication barriers between disciplines and differences in success metrics that can lead to conflict rather than synergy.

Traditional hackathons also lack structured reflection and knowledge transfer activities, representing missed educational opportunities where students may complete events without fully understanding their learning process [22]. The format struggles with diverse learning objectives, potentially favoring certain disciplines while marginalizing others, and requires complex, multi-faceted problems that genuinely need diverse expertise—yet traditional evaluation criteria often focus on technical innovation or presentation quality, failing to capture the full range of valuable contributions from multidisciplinary team members [14]. Finally, the emphasis on rapid prototyping can promote a "move fast and break things" mentality that conflicts with educational values of careful analysis, ethical consideration, and sustainable solution development.

4 The Challenges of Hackathon Design Using the CBL Framework

At first look, most of the challenges discussed at the end of Sect. 3 can be solved by extending the hackathon duration, thus providing more breathing room for the learning process to occur. Longer timeframes allow for more thorough problem analysis, iterative development, user testing, and reflection. Students can pursue more ambitious projects, learn new technologies, and engage with real stakeholders. However, while offering opportunities for deeper learning, extending hackathons introduces new challenges that require careful pedagogical consideration.

Extended hackathon formats create cascading organizational complexities that fundamentally differ from traditional short-term events. Unlike conventional hackathons that rely on intense bursts of energy sustained over 1–3 days, longer formats require sustained institutional support across weeks or months, including securing physical and virtual spaces, coordinating faculty involvement, and managing student schedules across multiple academic commitments. This creates inherent tension between the spontaneous, high-energy nature that makes hackathons effective and the structured, systematic approach necessary for sustained educational experiences. The logistics become more complex as the timeline extends, requiring robust project management systems and institutional coordination mechanisms that traditional hackathons can bypass through their compressed format.

Beyond logistics and organization, the main challenge of long-format hackathons is maintaining student motivation and engagement throughout the duration of the hackathon. Traditional hackathons capitalize on adrenaline, competition, and time pressure to sustain participant energy, but longer formats must navigate inevitable "motivation valleys"—periods of technical frustration, team conflicts, or creative blocks that would be temporary inconveniences in short events but can become project-threatening obstacles over extended timelines. This requires implementing structured motivation mechanisms such as milestone celebrations, regular mentoring touchpoints, and iterative feedback loops that maintain momentum while allowing for the deeper reflection and learning that CBL demands.

Assessment and evaluation approaches become significantly more complex in CBL-inspired hackathons compared to traditional formats. While conventional hackathons can rely primarily on final product evaluation and competition-based ranking, extended hackathons must assess learning processes, individual contributions within collaborative teams, discipline-specific learning objectives, and the iterative development of both technical solutions and soft skills. This creates multidimensional evaluation challenges that require balancing formative and summative assessment, individual versus team contributions, and technical achievements against learning growth. The framework must accommodate diverse learning objectives across multidisciplinary teams while maintaining fairness and pedagogical rigor throughout the extended timeline.

Finally, CBL's emphasis on authentic, real-world problem solving necessitates sustained stakeholder engagement that adds another layer of complexity to extended hackathons. Traditional hackathons can limit external involvement to initial problem presentation and final judging, but CBL-integrated formats require ongoing coordination with industry partners, community organizations, and domain experts throughout the development process. This includes managing regular feedback cycles, facilitating stakeholder-student interactions, accommodating potential project pivots based on real-world input, and ensuring that external partners remain engaged over extended timelines. The pedagogical benefits of authentic problem-solving must be balanced against the logistical challenges of maintaining these relationships and the potential disruptions they can introduce to student learning processes.

5 The Hack4CBL Framework

As exposed in Sect. 4, navigating the organizational, motivational, and assessment challenges inherent in extended-format events requires a more intentional design. We therefore developed Hack4CBL, a framework that integrates the structure of hackathons with the pedagogical principles of CBL to create a cohesive learning experience. Hack4CBL is a unifying framework that integrates the three hackathon stages (pre-, hackathon, post-) shown in Fig. 1, the CBL framework (summarized in Table 1), and the three domains of engage, investigate, and act. A fourth domain, 'transfer,' was added to ensure that learning and outcomes extend beyond the event, fostering long-term impact and knowledge sharing.

The Hack4CBL framework, shown in Fig. 2[3], structures hackathons for challenge-based learning in three stages: pre-hackathon, hackathon, and post-hackathon. Each stage includes activities in four domains, which may be executed in any order, preferably in parallel. Once outputs of a stage are secured, the team can move on, and multiple iterations may be conducted at each stage as needed.

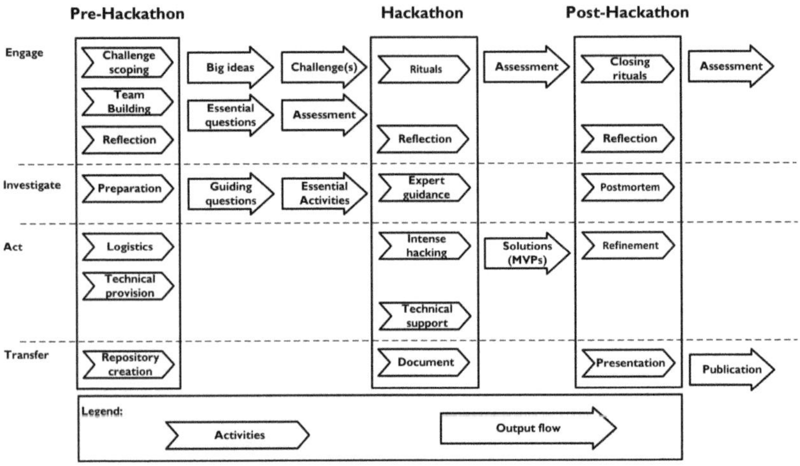

Fig. 2. The Hack4CBL framework. Adapted from [19].

5.1 Four Learning Domains

The framework operates through four interconnected learning domains that guide activities throughout all phases: engage, investigate, act, and transfer.

The "engage" domain focuses on establishing meaningful connections between participants and the challenge at hand. Activities include identifying the "big idea" that resonates with societal needs and participants' interests, formulating essential questions that drive inquiry, and fostering emotional and intellectual investment in the learning process. This domain ensures that participants understand the broader context and significance of their work, moving beyond mere technical problem-solving to address real-world impact.

Building upon initial engagement, the "investigate" domain emphasizes research and knowledge acquisition necessary for informed solution development. Participants develop guiding questions, identify andexplore multiple perspectives, gather relevant resources, and conduct systematic research to understand

[3] It is important to note that this new version of the Hack4CBL framework includes lessons learned and incremental improvements based on the experience presented in [19].

the complexity of their chosen challenge. This domain supports evidence-based decision-making and ensures solutions are grounded in thorough understanding of the problem space.

The "act" domain centers on the practical application of acquired knowledge through solution design, development, prototyping, and implementation. Participants create tangible outcomes, document their development process, and engage in iterative refinement based on feedback. This domain emphasizes hands-on learning through the creation of functional prototypes and viable solutions.

Finally, the "transfer" domain, added to the traditional CBL framework, focuses on extending learning and outcomes beyond the immediate event. Activities include knowledge dissemination, solution presentation to broader audiences, reflection on learning processes, and consideration of long-term implementation possibilities. This domain ensures that hackathon outcomes have lasting impact and contribute to ongoing innovation ecosystems.

5.2 Three-Phase Implementation Structure

The four learning domains presented above are implemented across three distinct phases: pre-hackathon, hackathon, and post-hackathon. Each phase serves specific pedagogical purposes while maintaining continuity across all four domains, ensuring that engagement, investigation, action, and transfer activities are distributed throughout the extended learning experience.

The pre-hackathon phase establishes the foundation for meaningful challenge-based learning. In the engage domain, organizers identify overarching "big ideas" that align with societal needs and participant interests, while teams begin connecting with specific challenges that resonate with their interdisciplinary composition. The investigate domain involves preliminary research into challenge contexts, exploration of relevant technologies and methodologies, and identification of key stakeholders and resources. Act domain activities include team formation strategies, initial ideation sessions, and establishment of collaborative tools and communication channels. The transfer domain begins with the creation of knowledge repositories and documentation systems that will support ongoing learning throughout the hackathon.

The hackathon phase emphasizes intensive collaborative work guided by CBL principles. Engage activities involve continuous refinement of challenge understanding and maintenance of team motivation through structured milestone celebrations and peer interaction. The investigate domain features deep exploration of technical solutions, stakeholder consultation, user research, and iterative validation of assumptions. Act domain work centers on MVP development through progressive versioning, implementation of functional prototypes, and integration of multidisciplinary contributions. Transfer activities include documentation of development processes, preparation of communication materials, and ongoing reflection on learning outcomes.

The concluding post hackathon phase focuses on evaluation, reflection, and knowledge transfer. Engage domain activities involve celebration of achievements, reflection on collaborative experiences, and consideration of long-term commitment to developed solutions. The investigate domain includes evaluation of outcomes, analysis of lessons learned, and identification of areas for future exploration. Act domain work involves final solution refinement, presentation preparation, and demonstration to evaluation panels. Transfer activities encompass formal presentation of results, publication of outcomes for broader audiences, creation of lasting documentation, and establishment of pathways for continued development.

5.3 Framework Flexibility and Iteration

A key strength of the Hack4CBL framework lies in its flexible, non-linear structure. While the three phases provide temporal organization, the four domains operate as parallel, interconnected streams of activity that can be pursued simultaneously within each phase. This design recognizes that learning is not linear and that different teams may progress through domains at varying rates based on their specific challenges and team dynamics.

The framework explicitly supports iterative development, allowing teams to cycle back through domains as their understanding deepens or as new challenges emerge. For example, initial investigation may reveal the need for refined engagement with stakeholders, or early prototyping activities may generate new questions that require additional research. This iterative approach aligns with both agile development methodologies and contemporary understanding of how learning occurs in complex contexts.

5.4 Multidisciplinary Integration Mechanisms

The Hack4CBL framework specifically addresses the challenges of multidisciplinary collaboration through several integrated mechanisms. The engage domain ensures that "big ideas" are sufficiently broad and complex to require diverse expertise, while essential questions are formulated to draw upon different disciplinary perspectives. When provided enough time to work (months instead of weeks), this structure provides enough space for each discipline to identify the guiding questions that can be answered from their respective knowledge base. This promotes collaborative inquiry where participants contribute specialized knowledge while learning from other disciplines.

The act domain structures collaborative work to leverage diverse skills through defined roles and responsibilities that align with disciplinary strengths while promoting cross-disciplinary learning. Team composition strategies balance disciplinary representation while ensuring that all participants can contribute meaningfully to solution development. The transfer domain provides multiple pathways for different types of contributions to be recognized and valued, moving beyond traditional technical evaluation criteria to encompass business viability, social impact, and collaborative effectiveness.

5.5 Assessment and Evaluation Integration

Unlike traditional hackathons that rely primarily on final product evaluation, the Hack4CBL framework integrates assessment throughout all phases and domains. The engage domain assessment focuses on the quality of challenge articulation, and depth of contextual understanding. Investigate domain evaluation examines research thoroughness, stakeholder engagement, and evidence-based decision-making processes.

Act domain assessment encompasses both technical implementation quality and collaborative development processes, recognizing individual contributions within team contexts. The transfer domain evaluation considers communication effectiveness, knowledge documentation quality, and potential for long-term impact. This comprehensive assessment approach supports both formative learning during the hackathon and summative evaluation of outcomes, while accommodating diverse learning objectives across multidisciplinary teams.

5.6 Institutional Implementation Considerations

The framework provides guidance for institutional implementation while remaining adaptable to different educational contexts. Pre-hackathon phase planning requires sustained institutional support for extended timelines, coordination of faculty involvement across disciplines, and establishment of external stakeholder relationships. The framework addresses logistical challenges through structured project management approaches while maintaining the creative, collaborative spirit that makes hackathons effective learning experiences.

Implementation considerations include faculty development for mentoring roles that support CBL principles, establishment of assessment criteria that value process as well as product, and creation of institutional policies that support innovative pedagogical approaches. The framework also addresses resource requirements including physical and virtual collaboration spaces, technology infrastructure, and ongoing support systems that extend beyond traditional event-based models.

Through this comprehensive structure, the Hack4CBL framework transforms hackathons from competitive events into structured learning experiences that maintain their collaborative, innovative character while providing the pedagogical rigor necessary for meaningful educational impact in higher education contexts.

6 Case Study and Results

To illustrate the framework's validity and contributions in a higher education setting, the Hack4CBL framework was use to design and execute two large-scale bi-national hackathons.

The first hackathon was bi-national educational event centered on Tourism 4.0 that engaged 210 undergraduate students from Colombia's Pontificia Universidad Javeriana and Costa Rica's Instituto Tecnológico de Costa Rica, Campus San Carlos. Students from diverse disciplines including systems engineering, computer engineering, business administration, tourism management, and data science were organized into 27 interdisciplinary teams of 6–7 members each. The event spanned approximately four months and was structured using the Hack4CBL framework as an initial validation case. The hackathon was notably student-managed, with five teams of students handling project management and logistics, creating an additional learning opportunity that emulated a corporate environment. The results of this experience is presented in [19].

As a second validation case, the "Second International Hackathon of Intelligent Solutions for the Promotion of Agribusiness 4.0" is presented in the remaining of this section. This hackathon aimed to foster interdisciplinary and international collaboration among students from Colombia and Costa (see Table 2 for details about disciplines included in the project teams). Over a 16-week period, each team selected an agribusiness problem and developed a comprehensive solution. The process involved analyzing the social, economic, and technological context; conducting market research to define target audiences, entry barriers, and internationalization options; and formulating a solution proposal combining information technologies with agro-industrial product development while ensuring technical, commercial, and social viability.

Table 2. Number of students involved in the hackathon (per academic course).

Course	Institution	# of students
Strategic IT managment	Pontificia Universidad Javeriana, Colombia	75
International Commerce	Pontificia Universidad Javeriana, Colombia	30
Project Formulation and Evaluation	TEC de Costa Rica, Campus Cartago	25
Agricultural Product Processing	TEC de Costa Rica, Campus Cartago	12

6.1 Pre-hackathon Phase

Team conformation was done by the professors of the courses shown in Table 2 ensuring a uniform distribution of disciplines across teams. This formed twelve teams of 10–11 members, strengthening knowledge exchange. Twenty additional students acted as the event management team to coordinate logistical elements and provide support to participants and external stakeholders of the hackathon. This management team was divided into five management areas in a hierarchical way (see Fig. 3): General (strategic direction), Control (monitoring deadlines and quality), Logistics (managing spaces, supplies, and webinars), Marketing (event website and promotional materials), and Information Technologies (digital infrastructure).

During this phase, the management team coordinated interactive spaces with external experts, including five webinars on market trends, cross-border logistics, and technology adoption. Guiding questions on scalability, environmental

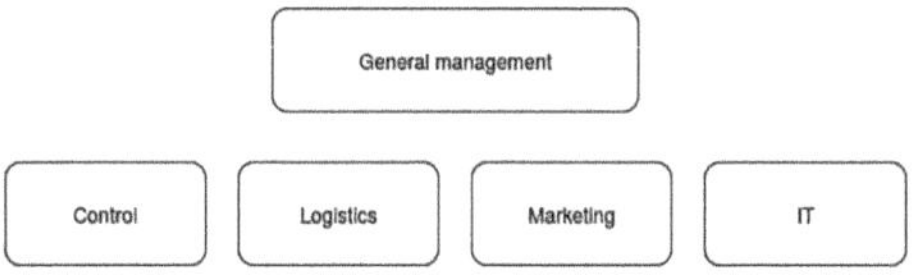

Fig. 3. Managment team structure.

impact, and financial viability were designed for each session. Investigative activities applied Design Thinking tools like actor mapping, and value chain analysis to ensure solution relevance. Basic content and reference materials was published in a collaborative repository.

Big Idea and Challenges. The hackathon's "big idea" was using technologies from the fourth industrial revolution [10] to solve real issue in agricultural setting, hence the "agribusiness 4.0" moniker. This big idea was latter decomposed in five challenges:

Challenge 1. addresses the need for Latin American tropical fruit producers and exporters, particularly small-scale farmers in Colombia and Costa Rica, to transform their business models beyond basic fruit export. While global demand for tropical fruits is growing across Europe, Asia, and other regions, producers currently export mostly fresh or dried fruits with low added value. The challenge calls for participants to develop digital solutions and strategic approaches that help producers sophisticate their entire business model—from production and processing to branding and market knowledge—to increase value-added operations, improve profit margins, and create more sustainable and equitable supply chains that benefit producers, exporters, and end consumers alike.

Challenge 2. addresses the global aging population by challenging multidisciplinary teams to create comprehensive solutions for elderly nutrition using agricultural products from Colombia and Costa Rica. Teams must develop an innovative food product specifically designed for seniors that ensures high nutritional value, safety, and ease of consumption, incorporating functional ingredients from tropical fruits and agricultural products (such as passion fruit, physalis, dragon fruit, star fruit, ginger, turmeric, papaya) that provide specific health benefits like bone strengthening, healthy digestion, or glucose control. The solution must include market research for a selected international market, covering demand analysis, competition, export requirements, sustainable packaging, and efficient logistics, alongside a comprehensive digital strategy utilizing e-commerce, AI-based digital marketing, mobile apps, and/or blockchain for traceability to position and sell the product globally.

Challenge 3. targets the rapidly growing global nutricosmetics market (expected to exceed \$10 billion by 2027) that combines nutrition and beauty through products improving skin, hair, and nail health from within. Teams must design an innovative nutricosmetics product using natural ingredients from Costa

Rica and/or Colombia (preferably fruits) in drinkable, capsule, or powder form that meets European quality standards. The solution requires targeting a specific European market with a comprehensive strategy covering positioning, branding, export compliance, and regulatory adherence, plus developing a functional digital prototype (app, AI personalization, or interactive e-commerce) and data-driven digital marketing strategy.

Challenge 4. addresses the booming global pet food market where North America and Europe lead demand for premium, natural, and sustainable options. Teams must develop an innovative dog and cat nutrition product combining tropical fruits (papaya, mango, guava) with sustainable animal proteins (insects, responsibly farmed fish, or meat industry by-products) in innovative formats like kibble, snacks, or functional supplements. The solution requires targeting North American and/or European markets with comprehensive export and marketing strategies that comply with international regulations (FDA, AAFCO, EFSA) and capitalize on trends like functional diets, sustainability, and animal welfare. Teams must integrate ICT solutions such as digital traceability systems for sustainable ingredient sourcing, mobile/web apps for personalized diets based on breed, weight, and age, and AI/big data-driven digital marketing for optimized market segmentation.

Challenge 5. addresses the growing global market for high-quality cacao and coffee derivatives in North America, Europe, and Asia, where consumers value sustainability and fair trade. Teams must design an innovative high-value-added product (functional chocolates, specialty beverages, healthy snacks, natural cosmetics) that can be easily manufactured by rural or vulnerable communities while promoting fair trade and sustainable practices. The solution requires targeting a specific regional market with a comprehensive strategy emphasizing social impact, sustainability, and quality certifications (organic, Fair Trade, denomination of origin). Teams must develop a digital platform prototype featuring blockchain traceability, a fair trade marketplace connecting producers with global buyers, and AI-driven marketing analytics, delivering product specifications, export/marketing strategy, and the functional platform prototype.

6.2 Hackathon Phase

During the Hackathon, teams critically reviewed their chosen challenge's initial contextualization. Challenges were assigned based on team preferences, but guaranteeing at least two teams per challenge. Teams deeply explored assigned agro-industrial problems, identifying social, logistical, economic, and technological factors to redefine objectives and adjust solution scopes. User-centered methodologies were applied to identify key needs, leading to initial use scenarios and functional mockups that aligned team expectations and generated valuable input for subsequent investigation and prototyping stages.

Once the preliminary solution vision was structured, teams deepened their investigation phase by exploring relevant technological tools and methodological approaches for their challenges. This included evaluating applicable emerging technologies (blockchain, mobile platforms, traceability systems, e-commerce, among others) and agile validation and prototyping frameworks. Active participation in webinars and technical advisory sessions with invited experts was fundamental. These sessions offered updated information on agro-industrial sector trends, sustainability, international trade, and digital transformation, serving as a basis for design and implementation decisions. They also fostered critical thinking and the ability to adapt theoretical knowledge to each challenge's specific context. This phase also facilitated the recognition of technical and operational limitations, allowing development efforts to focus on higher-impact or viable components.

This phase focused on the iterative construction of the Minimum Viable Product (MVP), following a progressive version scheme: v0.0 (basic functional structure), v1.0 (semi-complete validated prototype), and v2.0 (consolidated version of the prototype for final pitch). This approach allowed teams to refine their solutions as they received internal and external feedback, balancing creative ambition with technical realism. Validations were executed through user simulations or consultations with key sector stakeholders, allowing for adjustments to functionalities, improved user experience, and incorporation of scalability, sustainability, and impact criteria. Collaborative meetings and workshops provided direct feedback, contrasting proposals with expert and potential user perspectives. Concurrently, preliminary business models were structured, identifying revenue sources, value propositions, and commercial viability. This integrated approach ensured MVPs addressed challenges and had future evolution potential. Furthermore, this highlighted the non-technical contributions of all the disciplines involved in the hackathon.

The stage concluded with final pitch preparation, including documentation and functional demos.

6.3 Post-hackathon Phase

During this final phase, formal presentations were conducted before a jury of technology, agribusiness, and entrepreneurship experts, simulating investor panels. Teams defended solutions via audiovisual pitches and MVP demos, fostering communication, technical argumentation, and strategic thinking. Evaluators assessed innovation, social impact, technical scalability, and commercial viability, providing realistic experience. Post-presentation feedback sessions highlighted the importance of intercultural communication, agile methodologies, and clear sprint objectives. Recommendations included strengthening project management training, active webinar participation, improved inter-institutional coordination, and clearer evaluation criteria for future editions.

This phase involved each team creating a video pitch (3–5 minutes) to contextualize their MVP, solution, value proposition, and societal impact for jurors and students. This condensed weeks of work into an understandable format. An official event website published all projects, including descriptions, mockups, repository links, and final pitches, documenting the hackathon and encouraging external feedback.

The remote closing event featured finalist presentations to experts. Twelve teams were initially presented in four simultaneous rooms, with the highest-scoring team from each advancing. The four finalists then repeated their defense before all jurors. This activity concluded the project and significantly strengthened students' collaborative, argumentative, and communicative competencies.

7 Discussion of Results and Key Findings

The Hack4CBL framework successfully addressed the primary challenges of long-format hackathons through its structured four-domain approach. The progressive MVP versioning (v0.0 → v1.0 → v2.0) and student-managed organizational structure maintained engagement throughout the 16-week duration, avoiding the "motivation valleys" typical of extended projects. The framework enabled genuine interdisciplinary collaboration, with systems engineering students developing market understanding while business students gained technical appreciation, evidencing T-shaped professional development. This is consistent with the observations of previous hackathon in which the Hack4CBL framework was used [19].

Most significantly, the framework demonstrated concrete real-world impact: three teams progressed to the Pontificia Universidad Javeriana's innovation hub for continued product development, validating the transition from academic exercise to potential commercial innovation as suggested by the "transfer" domain (see Fig. 2).

7.1 Assessment and Pedagogical Implications

The multi-dimensional assessment approach proved both effective and challenging. Each professor evaluated individual inputs within their disciplinary courses, creating distributed assessment that captured discipline-specific contributions. However, this was significantly more time-demanding and difficult to navigate than traditional hackathon assessment, as each team presented unique dynamics requiring individualized evaluation strategies. The complexity of coordinating assessment across multiple faculty while ensuring consistency represents a significant implementation challenge.

Faculty roles evolved from content deliverers to CBL facilitators and mentors, requiring new competencies in cross-disciplinary mentoring and agile project management support—a substantial professional development requirement for institutional implementation. The contribution of the student-lead management teams was vital in this aspect.

7.2 Cross-Cultural Collaboration Challenges

The binational implementation revealed significant cross-cultural challenges alongside educational benefits. Communication barriers extended beyond language to encompass distinct communication patterns and expectation-setting approaches. Different work cultures created problems with varying attitudes toward deadlines, meeting structures, and collaborative decision-making. This was worsen by the mismatch of academic calendars and schedules between the participating institutions. While the extended timeline allowed cultural adaptation impossible in short-format hackathons, these challenges required constant mediation.

Observations also revealed interpersonal conflicts within teams. The nature of these conflicts varied; some were internal, stemming from personal deficiencies or perceived incompetence in teamwork, while others were external, related to specific task requirements or the inherent dynamics of the team itself. This aligns with prior research [13], which highlights the mediation of different team conflicts regarding collaboration performance. The study also noted that cultural dimensions, particularly differences in ways of thinking and approaches to solutions, could significantly influence students' communication patterns, collaborative effectiveness, and overall innovation capacity, especially in a binational context [9].

The framework's structure provided some mitigation—shared "big ideas" created common ground and diverse perspectives enriched solutions—but highlighted the need for explicit intercultural competency development and structured cross-cultural team management guidance in future implementations.

The process of navigating these challenges, even imperfectly, contributes significantly to the development of critical soft skills such as resilience, emotional intelligence, and nascent conflict resolution abilities. These competencies are highly valued and indispensable in contemporary professional environments. This transforms a potentially negative observation into an actionable pedagogical improvement, indicating that the Hack4CBL framework, while robust in its design, can be further refined to provide enhanced support to students in these non-technical, yet critically important, areas of personal and interpersonal development.

7.3 Implementation Requirements and Scalability

The framework's success depended on complete institutional support from both universities, enabling coordination across disciplines, technological infrastructure provision, and sustained resource allocation. This comprehensive backing proved essential but represents a significant requirement for potential adopters, as the framework demands resources exceeding traditional hackathon requirements. Once again, the creation of a student-lead management team was a vital success factor for this hackathon.

External stakeholder coordination through webinars and expert consultations enhanced authenticity but required dedicated coordination resources. The progression of three teams to continued development demonstrates the value of these connections while highlighting institutional capacity needs for ongoing industry relationships.

The framework offers strong scalability potential, contingent on institutional readiness to provide comprehensive support and commitment to extended-format educational innovations. Success requires careful evaluation of institutional capacity and commitment levels, but the comprehensive structure provides a replicable model adaptable to diverse educational environments and disciplinary combinations.

8 Conclusions

The Hack4CBL framework is conclusively demonstrated as an effective pedagogical strategy for multidisciplinary teams, capable of accommodating diverse learning outcomes. Its successful implementation, as shown in the case studies presented in [19] and this paper, highlights its capacity to foster an ideal context for multidisciplinary learning, bridging academia and real-world impact. This framework cultivates T-shaped professionals by ensuring digital students understand technology's real-world entanglement and other disciplines appreciate its transformative impact. Hack4CBL offers a robust, replicable model for higher education, promoting real-world problem-solving, genuine multidisciplinary collaboration, and iterative development. It consistently enhances diverse learning outcomes, cultivates essential soft skills, and prepares students for professional life. This structured approach addresses the limited guidance on adapting CBL to hackathons, providing a concrete blueprint for scalable and effective implementation in complex, multi-institutional settings.

While this work highlights the immediate educational benefits of Hack4CBL, comprehensive research is needed to fully understand its long-term effects. Future longitudinal studies are essential to assess the sustained influence of these experiences on participants' professional trajectories and overall career development. Such studies would provide stronger empirical evidence of the framework's efficacy, solidifying its position as a transformative pedagogical innovation and guiding future educational reforms and investments in experiential learning models.

Acknowledgments. We sincerely thank all stakeholders–students, professors, and industry experts–for their role in this project's success. Special thanks to Pontificia Universidad Javeriana (Colombia) and Instituto Tecnológico de Costa Rica for their support, and to the student organizers for their project management efforts. Finally, we acknowledge the contributions of the Gemini 2.5 Pro LLM by Google in the editing of the paper, which assisted with translation, grammar, spelling, and readability improvements, without any influence on the ideas, structure, or arguments presented here.

Disclosure of Interests. The authors have no competing interests to declare that are relevant to the content of this article.

References

1. Anslow, C., Brosz, J., Maurer, F., Boyes, M.: Datathons: an experience report of data hackathons for data science education. In: Proceedings of the 47th ACM Technical Symposium on Computing Science Education, pp. 615–620 (2016). https://doi.org/10.1145/2839509.2844568

2. Araújo, A.A., Kalinowski, M., Baldassarre, M.T.: Embracing experiential learning: hackathons as an educational strategy for shaping soft skills in software engineering. In: 2025 IEEE/ACM 37th International Conference on Software Engineering Education and Training (CSEE&T), pp. 319–324 (2025). https://doi.org/10.1109/CSEET66350.2025.00040
3. Chanin, R., Sales, A., Santos, A., Pompermaier, L., Prikladnicki, R.: A collaborative approach to teaching software startups: findings from a study using challenge based learning. In: CHASE 2018: Proceedings of the 11th International Workshop on Cooperative and Human Aspects of Software Engineering, pp. 9–12 (2018). https://doi.org/10.1145/3195836.3195844
4. Conde, M., Rodríguez-Sedano, F.J., Fernández-Llamas, C., Gonçalves, J., Lima, J., García-Penalvo, F.J.: Fostering STEAM through challenge-based learning, robotics, and physical devices: a systematic mapping literature review. Comput. Appl. Eng. Educ. **29**(1), 46–65 (2021). https://doi.org/10.1002/cae.22354
5. Dikilitaş, K., Marshall, T., Shahverdi, M.: CBL framework today and CBL learning outcomes. In: A Practical Guide to Understanding and Implementing Challenge-Based Learning, pp. 27–53 (2025). https://doi.org/10.1007/978-3-031-67011-4_2
6. Doulougeri, K., Vermunt, J.D., Bombaerts, G., Bots, M.: Challenge-based learning implementation in engineering education: a systematic literature review. J. Eng. Educ. **113**(4), 1076–1106 (2024). https://doi.org/10.1002/jee.20588
7. Gama, K., Zimmerle, C., Rossi, P.: Online hackathons as an engaging tool to promote group work in emergency remote learning. In: Proceedings of the 26th ACM Conference on Innovation and Technology in Computer Science Education V. 1, pp. 345–351 (2021). https://doi.org/10.1145/3430665.3456312
8. Jamison, C.S.E., Fuher, J., Wang, A., Huang-Saad, A.: Experiential learning implementation in undergraduate engineering education: a systematic search and review. Eur. J. Eng. Educ. **47**(6), 1356–1379 (2022). https://doi.org/10.1080/03043797.2022.2031895
9. Jones, G., Chirino Chace, B., Wright, J.: Cultural diversity drives innovation: empowering teams for success. Int. J. Innov. Sci. **12**(3), 323–343 (2020). https://doi.org/10.1108/IJIS-04-2020-0042
10. Kagermann, H., Wahlster, W., Helbig, J.: Recommendations for implementing the strategic initiative INDUSTRIE 4.0. Technical report (2013)
11. Kolb, D.A.: Experiential Learning: Experience as the Source of Learning and Development, 1st edn. Prentice Hall (1983)
12. Komssi, M., Pichlis, D., Raatikainen, M., Kindström, K., Järvinen, J.: What are hackathons for? IEEE Softw. **32**(5), 60–67 (2015). https://doi.org/10.1109/MS.2014.78
13. Lee, D., Huh, Y., Reigeluth, C.M.: Collaboration, intragroup conflict, and social skills in project-based learning. Instr. Sci. **43**(5), 561–590 (2015). https://doi.org/10.1007/s11251-015-9348-7
14. Lyndon, M.P., et al.: Hacking hackathons: preparing the next generation for the multidisciplinary world of healthcare technology. Int. J. Med. Inform. **112**, 1–5 (2018). https://doi.org/10.1016/j.ijmedinf.2017.12.020
15. Martin, D.A., Bombaerts, G.: What is the structure of a challenge based learning project? A shortitudinal trajectory analysis of student process behaviours in an interdisciplinary engineering course. Eur. J. Eng. Educ. **50**(1), 51–81 (2025). https://doi.org/10.1080/03043797.2024.2376222
16. Martínez, M., Crusat, X.: Work in progress: the innovation journey: a challenge-based learning methodology that introduces innovation and entrepreneurship in

engineering through competition and real-life challenges. In: 2017 IEEE Global Engineering Education Conference (EDUCON), pp. 39–43 (2017). https://doi.org/10.1109/EDUCON.2017.7942821
17. Nandi, A., Mandernach, M.: Hackathons as an informal learning platform. In: Proceedings of the 47th ACM Technical Symposium on Computing Science Education, pp. 346–351 (2016). https://doi.org/10.1145/2839509.2844590
18. Nichols, M.H., Cator, K.: Challenge based learning: take action and make a difference. Technical report, Apple (2008). https://www.challengebasedlearning.org/wp-content/uploads/2019/03/CBL_Paper_2008.pdf
19. Ortíz-Pabón, E., Fernández-Mora, L., Nova-Arévalo, N., Gómez-Morantes, J.: From big idea to prototype: a challenge-based learning framework for hackathons in higher education. In: Proceedings of the 17th International Conference on Computer Supported Education - Volume 2: CSEDU, pp. 670–677 (2025). https://doi.org/10.5220/0013233400003932
20. Paganini, L., Gama, K.: Female participation in hackathons: a case study about gender issues in application development marathons. IEEE Revista Iberoamericana de Tecnologias del Aprendizaje **15**(4), 326–335 (2020). https://doi.org/10.1109/RITA.2020.3033209
21. Porras, J., et al.: Hackathons in software engineering education: lessons learned from a decade of events. In: Proceedings of the 2nd International Workshop on Software Engineering Education for Millennials, pp. 40–47 (2018). https://doi.org/10.1145/3194779.3194783
22. Sotaquirá-Gutiérrez, R., Beltran, L.M., Garzon Ruiz, J.P.: Hackathons as experiential learning platforms for engineering design skills. Cogent Educ. **12**(1), 2442187 (2025). https://doi.org/10.1080/2331186X.2024.2442187

Supporting Educators in Building Algorithm Design Tests for Novice Programmers

Caio Oliveira, Leandra Silva, Bianca Pachêco, and João Brunet(✉)

Department of Systems and Computing, Federal University of Campina Grande, Campina Grande, Brazil
{caio.oliveira,leandra.silva,bianca.pacheco}@ccc.ufcg.edu.br, joao.arthur@computacao.ufcg.edu.br

Abstract. High enrollment in introductory programming courses presents significant challenges for providing personalized feedback to students. While automated assessment systems are extensively adopted, they predominantly emphasize functional verification over algorithmic design quality—including proper function utilization and appropriate data structure selection. This focus can result in students developing functionally correct yet structurally problematic solutions that impede their educational progress. To bridge this educational gap, we implemented design tests as a mechanism for automatically identifying nonconformities with pre-established rules in student algorithms. Our framework, PyDesignWizard, offers an API that utilizes Python's Abstract Syntax Tree (AST) to facilitate the development of design tests. Our empirical validation involved analyzing 1,714 student solutions from an introductory programming course at the Federal University of Campina Grande, yielding 98.6% accuracy, a 0.99 true negative rate, 77% precision, and 84% recall. We further conducted qualitative assessment via interviews with 16 programming faculty members employing the Think Aloud Protocol. The outcomes demonstrated substantial comprehension and encouraging responses: 15 instructors rapidly assimilated the approach, and 8 underscored the academic advantages of recognizing structural problems. To foster the adoption of Design Tests, we built a catalog of design tests derived from content analysis of multiple programming courses and structured interviews with educators. This catalog provides instructors with ready-to-use tests for common scenarios in introductory programming education. The catalog tests were validated against real student programs to ensure their practical applicability.

Keywords: Design Test · Introductory Programming Courses · Tests · Feedback · Assessment

C. Meinel et al. (Eds.): CSEDU 2025, CCIS 3148, pp. 309–335, 2027.
https://doi.org/10.1007/978-3-032-39103-2_15

1 Introduction

The significance of programming education has grown substantially in recent years, driven by rapid technological progress and expanding interest in computer science. This expansion has led to considerably larger enrollment in introductory programming courses, creating a substantial increase in the volume of assignments and assessments that educators must evaluate, review, and score [19]. To illustrate, within the academic environment where this research was conducted—the Introduction to Programming course at the Federal University of Campina Grande (UFCG)—each semester typically accommodates approximately 90 students. The curriculum emphasizes hands-on learning through regular programming assignments that students must complete and submit for evaluation. This pedagogical approach generates an average of 270 assignment submissions per class session, all requiring instructor review, detailed feedback, and assessment. Such substantial evaluation demands underscore the scalability challenges that educators encounter when attempting to maintain comprehensive assessment standards while delivering prompt and meaningful feedback to students.

Research conducted by Leite [11] and Papastergiou [14] indicates that enhancing the regularity of coding assignments can contribute to advancing students' programming competencies, yet this approach simultaneously amplifies the assessment burden for educators. Automatic evaluation systems, as discussed by Janzen [7] and Singh [16], are commonly employed to mitigate this challenge. Educators routinely utilize Online Judge platforms [8], where student code submissions undergo automated assessment through test cases that predominantly emphasize functional accuracy, potentially overlooking crucial elements concerning code organization and algorithmic methodology. In essence, these approaches tend to evaluate exclusively 'what' students' programs accomplish, rather than examining 'how' they achieve these results. Although investigations exist regarding the application of static code analysis in computer science education [17], such methodologies concentrate mainly on code quality metrics instead of examining algorithmic design principles [2].

Beyond functional correctness, assessing algorithmic design plays an important role in programming education. Design encompasses the components within the algorithm and the manner in which the algorithm is constructed and arranged in code. Given the restricted attention in academic literature regarding automated verification of algorithmic design, and since Online Judge systems concentrate predominantly on functional validation, numerous students consequently develop solutions that deviate from anticipated design patterns, impeding the cultivation of problem-solving capabilities. For instance, imagine an educator requesting students to develop the Merge Sort algorithm using Python [6], yet a student opts to create the Bubble Sort algorithm alternatively. While the implementation remains functionally accurate—successfully ordering a sequence—the student fails to satisfy the instructor's design requirements. In certain situations, the issue becomes worse when students resort to utilizing built-in libraries or methods (such as sort() in this scenario) that perform the entire task they were intended to accomplish independently.

Our previous work address this gap by proposing an automated approach for inspecting algorithm design, based on static code analysis, with a focus on the educational context [12]. Our tool, *PyDesignWizard*, offers an interface that enables the development of structural assessments to examine algorithmic organization, extending beyond mere functional validation. In contrast to conventional testing methods, our methodology encompasses elements ranging from parameter definitions and variable declarations to identifying iterative constructs and recursive patterns, facilitating comprehensive evaluation of syntactic and semantic adherence. This capability empowers educators to automatically verify design characteristics of student implementations, including control structure utilization, recursive call depth, computational complexity, code modularization, and additional architectural considerations.

The *PyDesignWizard* API was built based on Python's abstract syntax tree (AST) [3,15], facilitating code reading and manipulation. Using our tool, educators can develop customized tests to examine both the operational behavior and structural design of student algorithms, guaranteeing the authenticity of their implementations while speeding up the evaluation process.

To evaluate the ability of our approach to detect design issues, we elaborated the following research questions:

- **RQ1:** Can the structure of students' solutions be effectively assessed through design tests?
- **RQ2:** Do educators perceive the concept of design tests as intuitive and easy to grasp?
- **RQ3:** Does a tool based on design tests offer tangible benefits in educational contexts?

To validate our approach and address these research questions, we conducted two complementary empirical studies. The first study assessed the precision of algorithm detection across 1,714 programs developed by 90 students enrolled in the Introduction to Programming course at the Federal University of Campina Grande, which operates one of Brazil's five largest Computer Science programs. To examine instructor perceptions of our methodology, we performed a qualitative investigation involving semi-structured interviews with 16 educators from various academic institutions. We employed the Think Aloud Protocol [5] to systematically collect and analyze interview data.

The findings demonstrate that our tool achieved substantial effectiveness in identifying algorithmic characteristics, with design-based assessments significantly reducing false negative occurrences. Quantitatively, the system attained 98.6% accuracy, with 77% precision and 84% recall in sorting algorithm detection tasks. Through qualitative evaluation, instructors characterized the design assessments as intuitive and acknowledged the tool's pedagogical value within programming education contexts. Eight participants emphasized the system's utility for verifying student code structure, while four indicated intention to integrate the tool into their curricula. An additional four participants proposed incorporating the system into software testing and architecture courses, suggesting complementary integration with established practices such as unit testing methodologies. Only two participants failed to identify clear applications within their educational environments. Collectively, the feedback indicates that our tool can serve as a valuable pedagogical resource for enhancing programming education quality by promoting algorithmic design best practices and improved code organization.

This extended version of our previous conference publication [12] presents a comprehensive catalog[1] of 21 design tests that can be applied to Python programs. These tests reflect common concerns identified in introductory programming courses, which we systematically gathered through curriculum analysis of 21 academic programs and in-depth interviews with experienced professors from UFCG. Our objective is to provide ready-to-use tests that address frequently encountered pedagogical issues, including the detection of prohibited function usage, identification of auxiliary data structures, recognition of excessive conditional statement patterns, and other structural concerns commonly observed in novice programming solutions. This catalog serves as a foundational resource for instructors seeking to implement automated design evaluation without requiring extensive technical expertise in test development.

This paper is organized as follows. Section 2 introduces the concept of Design Tests. Section 3 describes their application in education and the tool we developed for Python. Section 4 presents our quantitative and qualitative evaluations. Section 5 introduces a catalog of design tests based on curriculum analysis. We discuss related work in Sect. 6, and conclude in Sect. 7 with key findings, threats to validity, and future directions.

2 Background: Design Tests

Our prior research [4] presented design tests as a novel testing methodology specifically developed to validate the conformance of software implementations with established architectural principles and design specifications. Unlike traditional functional testing approaches that primarily concentrate on input-output correctness verification, design tests extend the validation scope to encompass the structural and architectural integrity of the system implementation. This testing paradigm serves to maintain consistency in architectural decision enforcement, particularly valuable in development environments characterized by high team member turnover, thereby minimizing the risk of overlooked or misinterpreted design constraints. The integration of design tests within routine testing procedures enables early identification of discrepancies between intended design specifications and actual implementation, consequently enhancing the overall quality assurance process.

To enable the implementation of design tests for architectural conformance, we developed DesignWizard, an API that integrates seamlessly with the JUnit testing framework [9] for Java-based software systems. This framework enables developers to articulate design principles and architectural decisions using familiar programming constructs, thereby ensuring that design constraints remain

[1] Available at https://github.com/biancacpacheco/design-wizard-catalog.

both executable and maintainable as executable documentation. Figure 1 illustrates an overview of the design tests approach. It enables developers to construct automated design tests that systematically validate adherence to architectural specifications. The tooling relies on two fundamental architectural components: a code structure analysis API that performs metadata extraction from the codebase and provides programmatic access to structural information, and a comprehensive testing infrastructure that delivers assertion mechanisms, orchestrates automated test execution, and generates detailed validation reports.

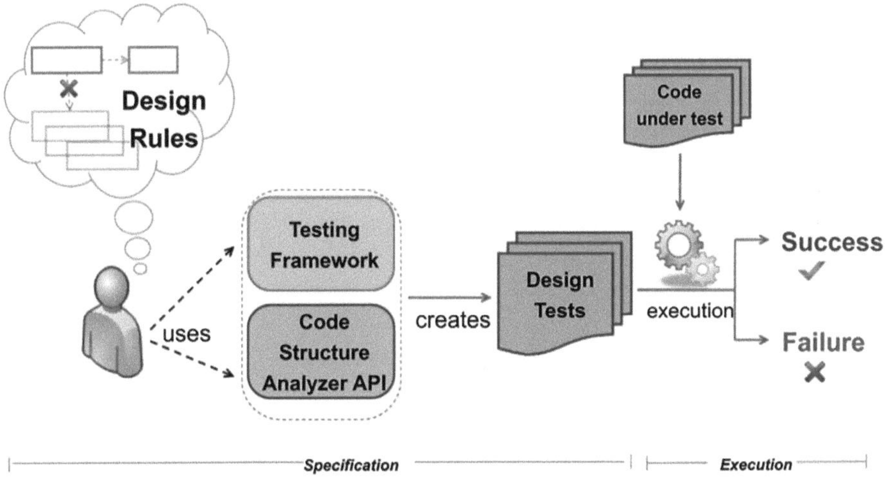

Fig. 1. Design Test Overview (reproduced from the conference version of this paper [12]).

For the sake of clarity, let us analyze a concrete example. The design test below (Listing 1.1) illustrates this: a design rule establishes that classes in the `dao` package should only be accessed by classes within the `controller` or `dao` packages. This rule is verified through a design test that checks all method calls to ensure compliance.

To provide a concrete illustration, we present a practical example demonstrating the application of design tests in architectural validation. The design test presented in Listing 1.1 exemplifies this approach: an architectural constraint specifies that classes residing within the `dao` package must exclusively receive access requests from classes located in either the `controller` or `dao` packages. This architectural restriction is systematically validated through a design test implementation that performs comprehensive analysis of method invocations to verify adherence to the established access control policy.

Listing 1.1. Design Test pseudo-code for communication rule between dao and controller package.

```
daoPackage = myapp.dao
controllerPackage = myapp.controller
FOR each class in daoPackage DO
  callers = class.getCallers()
  FOR each caller in callers DO
    assert caller in controllerPackage ||
        caller in daoPackage
```

The development of this design test follows an approach that begins with the identification of target package structures, followed by the analysis of calling relationships for each class within the `dao` package. Validation assertions are subsequently implemented to ensure that invoking classes originate exclusively from the permitted `controller` or `dao` package domains. The testing mechanism leverages static code analysis capabilities provided by the DesignWizard framework to extract structural metadata, while utilizing the JUnit testing infrastructure for process automation and execution control.

The next section presents our methodology for adapting and extending the design testing concept to the domain of programming education. We have refined the conceptual framework of design tests to operate at the algorithmic level, thereby enabling educators to formulate and evaluate granular pedagogical constraints related to the utilization of iterative constructs, variable declarations, conditional statements, and other fundamental programming elements.

3 Design Tests for Education

Context. Considering the educational context, instructors face a scenario analogous to that of software developers: there exists a number of tools and mechanisms to verify whether students' programs are functionally correct, but, there are only a few to systematically examine the internal aspects (the algorithmic design) of the solutions they develop using the same programming language and testing infrastructure employed by the target program. In this work, we propose, implement, and evaluate the necessary tooling to extend the concept of design tests to the educational domain. We also provide a catalog of 21 design tests for Python programs. These tests address common pedagogical concerns, including prohibited function usage, auxiliary data structures, and other structural issues in novice solutions. We developed this catalog to bridge the gap between theoretical design testing concepts and practical educational implementation, providing instructors with immediately applicable tools rather than requiring them to develop tests from scratch.

Design at Algorithm Level. The concept of design encompasses multiple abstraction levels and contexts. While design tests, as presented in Sect. 2, target high-level architectural constructs such as modules, packages, and subsystems, introductory programming education operates at a fundamentally different granularity level. In educational settings, instructors focus on structural aspects that, while more fine-grained, remain inherently design-oriented. These pedagogical concerns encompass (not limited to):

- the elements students use to implement the program, such as conditionals, loops, variables, data types, and operators;
- the choice and manipulation of data structures; and
- the usage of specific functions, classes, and modules.

The Problem. Let us take as a concrete example the Introduction to Programming course from the Federal University of Campina Grande. A specific course unit focuses on linear iterations over lists for tasks such as filtering and element retrieval. Consider a fundamental exercise requiring students to locate and return the index of the minimum element within a list. The canonical algorithmic approach involves initializing the first element as minimum, then systematically traversing the list to compare each subsequent element against the current minimum candidate. When a smaller element is encountered, its corresponding index is recorded as the new minimum position. Upon completing the traversal, the algorithm returns the stored index representing the location of the minimum value.

Since instructors typically use Online Judges to assess students' code output, they are limited to checking if the output is the value expected, once they use input/output tests. Through classroom observation, instructors identified that students often deviated from the expected linear search by adopting sorting-based strategies: some developed custom implementations of classical sorting algorithms, while others—more problematically from a pedagogical perspective—utilized Python's built-in `sort()` function. Consequently, although both approaches demonstrated in Listing 1.2 and Listing 1.3 achieve functional correctness and pass automated tests, they fundamentally violate the specific algorithmic design constraints established by the instructors.

Listing 1.2. Finding Smallest with Bubble Sort.

```
def get_smallest(sequence):
  n = len(sequence)

  for i in range(n-1):
    for j in range(0, n-i-1):
      if sequence[j] > sequence[j+1]:
        swap(sequence, j, j+1)

  return sequence[0]
```

Listing 1.3. Finding Smallest with Python's built-in *sort()* function.

```
def get_smallest(sequence):
  sequence.sort()
  return sequence[0]
```

The course instructors[2] consider design adherence essential to the pedagogical process, as it reinforces fundamental computational concepts such as linear

[2] The last author was actively involved in the introductory programming course discussed in the paper.

time complexity and the avoidance of unintended side effects. Given the substantial volume of student submissions, manual code inspection becomes prohibitively time-consuming and impractical for systematic evaluation. This scenario necessitates automated validation mechanisms, such as design tests, to systematically verify the correspondence between pedagogical expectations and student implementations.

Design Tests for Education. We developed **PyDesignWizard**, a Code Structure Analyzer API that performs syntactic parsing of Python programs and provides comprehensive methods for querying structural information about the analyzed codebase. This framework enables the development of design tests for scenarios such as the previously described case. **PyDesignWizard** employs Python's Abstract Syntax Tree (AST) for static code analysis and seamlessly integrates with *Unittest*, Python's native testing framework, to incorporate unit testing methodologies into the design validation process.

The **Python Design Wizard** API offers a comprehensive suite of methods that enable systematic inspection of algorithmic structures, thereby allowing instructors to assess adherence to prescribed design rules in student implementations. Some of the key methods include:

- `get_calls_function(function_name)`: This method checks if a specific function, such as `sort()`, has been called within the student's code. It is useful for ensuring that students do not use built-in functions when the goal is to manually implement the algorithm.
- `entity_has_child(parent_entity, child_type)`: This method checks whether a given entity (such as a loop or function) contains specific child elements, such as an assignment variable. It can be used to verify the complexity or modularity of the code.
- `get_relations(relation_type)`: With this method, it is possible to inspect relationships between different code entities, such as nested loops or function calls. It allows the detection of complex patterns, like sorting algorithms that use multiple loops.
- `get_entity(entity_name)`: This method identifies and returns a specific entity in the code, such as a function or class, enabling detailed analysis of that entity in terms of parameters, variables, and control structures.

Let us revisit the previous example and present a design test that determines whether an implementation employs a quadratic sorting strategy or Python's built-in `sort()` function. While instructors could develop tests targeting specific structural patterns—such as the presence of `for` loops, `if` statements, or variables storing minimum elements—the pedagogical objective in this scenario was to maintain flexibility in student approaches rather than imposing overly restrictive constraints. The primary goal was to prevent the adoption of sorting-based strategies when a single linear traversal would suffice algorithmically. Consequently, the design test targets two critical characteristics: the occurrence of nested loop structures, which may indicate sorting algorithm implementation, and the invocation of Python's `sort()` function. The design test implementation using PyDesignWizard is presented in Listing 1.4.

Listing 1.4. Design Test to check sorting strategies.

```
1  def test_sort_algorithm(self):
2    dw = PyDesignWizard("student-submission.py")

3    outer_loop = dw.get_entity('for1')
4    if outer_loop = None:
5      outer_loop = dw.get_entity('while1')
6    self.assertTrue(outer_loop != None)

7    inner_loop = outer_loop.get_relations('HASLOOP')
8    self.assertTrue(inner_loop != None)

9    change_list = dw.entity_has_child(inner_loop,\
       'assign_field')
10   self.assertTrue(change_list)

11   sort_calls = dw.get_calls_function('sort')
12   self.assertTrue(sort_calls == 0)
```

Line 2 instantiates a PyDesignWizard object, initializing it with the target file "student-submission.py". Upon instantiation, the PyDesignWizard framework performs static analysis on the code's Abstract Syntax Tree (AST) to extract structural metadata, representing the codebase as a collection of entities and their interconnections. The framework subsequently provides query methods for examining these entities and relationships, thereby facilitating systematic inspection of the code's structural properties and behavioral characteristics.

Lines 3 to 6 implement a search mechanism to identify an outer iterative construct within the student's implementation, initially attempting to locate a for loop ('for1') and, upon failure, searching for a while loop ('while1'). The subsequent assertion validates that an outer loop construct was successfully identified. Should neither iterative structure be present, the test execution will terminate with a failure condition.

Lines 7 and 8 attempt to find an inner loop within the outer loop by checking for a 'HASLOOP' relationship. If an inner loop is detected, the test continues; otherwise, the assertion in line 8 causes the test to fail.

Lines 9 and 10 validate the presence of assignment operations within the inner iterative construct. Line 9 searches for a child entity labeled `assign_field` within the inner loop structure, which indicates the occurrence of an assignment operation. Line 10 enforces this requirement through an assertion; failure to locate such an assignment results in test termination.

Lines 11 and 12 examine the utilization of the `sort` function within the student's implementation. Line 11 quantifies the number of `sort` function invocations using the method `dw.get_calls_function('sort')`. Line 12 asserts that the invocation count equals zero, thereby enforcing the constraint that implementations must not depend on built-in sorting functionality. An assertion failure indicates that the student's solution inappropriately employs the `sort` function, violating the intended algorithmic approach.

Identifying the use of specific functions, such as the `sort()` function, is relatively straightforward and leaves little room for errors in the tests. However, note that the absence of nested loops does not necessarily mean that the student did not sort the sequence. They could have used different sorting strategies, such as Merge or Quick sort. Therefore, a design test may fail to detect some cases (false negatives), as well as flag instances where nested loops are used but are not actually sorting the sequence (false positives). For this reason, we evaluated our approach using these types of tests to assess precision and recall within the context of more complex scenarios

The detection of specific function invocations, such as the `sort()`, presents a relatively straightforward validation scenario with minimal potential for test implementation errors. However, the absence of nested loop constructs does not definitively indicate that students avoided sorting-based approaches, as alternative sorting algorithms such as Merge Sort or Quick Sort may not exhibit the characteristic nested loop patterns. Consequently, design tests may experience both false negatives—failing to identify sorting implementations that do not conform to expected structural patterns—and false positives—incorrectly flagging nested loop constructs that serve purposes other than sorting operations. To address these inherent limitations, we conducted a comprehensive evaluation of our methodology using such test cases to quantify precision and recall metrics within increasingly complex algorithmic scenarios.

4 Evaluation

To evaluate our approach, we focus on three key aspects to assess its effectiveness and practicality.

First, we employed unit testing to evaluate our tool's capacity for detecting fundamental code constructs. This assessment examines the accuracy with which the framework identifies specific programming elements within student submissions, including iterative structures, conditional statements, variable declarations, and command sequences.

Second, we analyze the performance of a particular design test within a complex evaluation scenario characterized by inherent uncertainty. This examination enables us to assess our approach's robustness when processing ambiguous or incomplete code structures, thereby simulating realistic pedagogical challenges where algorithmic patterns may not conform to expected structural conventions.

Finally, we investigate instructors feedback regarding their experience with test development using the proposed methodology. This evaluation encompasses their assessment of the tool's usability and pedagogical value, as well as their perspectives on how this approach may enhance instructional practices and student assessment procedures.

4.1 Methodology

We conducted our evalution guided by the following research questions:

- **RQ1**: Can the structure of students' solutions be effectively assessed through design tests?
- **RQ2**: Do educators perceive the concept of design tests as intuitive and easy to grasp?
- **RQ3**: Does a tool based on design tests offer tangible benefits in educational contexts?

This section presents the two empirical studies conducted to investigate the research questions. The first study addresses the initial research question, while the second study examines the remaining two questions. The studies comprise: (1) a quantitative evaluation of the API that measures the reliability and accuracy of test results generated by PyDesignWizard, and (2) a qualitative investigation in which educational professionals assess the tool's pedagogical applicability and effectiveness within instructional contexts.

Quantitative Study: Answering RQ1. Our API enables the identification of specific functions, data types, data structures, and other code elements, leveraging static analysis to significantly reduce the likelihood of errors. We conducted a comprehensive testing process to ensure high accuracy in these fundamental yet critical scenarios, reinforcing confidence in the tool's reliability. To systematically evaluate the API, we generated synthetic Python programs encompassing a variety of language constructs, including loops, variable usage, data structures, and function definitions. We applied the API to extract information from these programs and manually verified the correctness of the retrieved data. In addition, the unit tests we developed play a key role in mitigating risks associated with the tool's development. The results of our coverage tests are summarized as follows:

- 33 unit tests;
- 100% function coverage; and
- Approximately 86% branch/code coverage.

Nonetheless, we consider it equally important to assess the performance of design tests in more complex scenarios—particularly those in which determining whether a solution meets a given specification requires deeper analysis, and multiple valid implementation strategies may exist. To this end, we evaluated the precision of a design test specifically crafted to detect whether a given code implements a sorting strategy. The sorting context was chosen for several reasons. First, sorting a sequence typically involves loops, conditional logic, and manipulation of data structures, providing a rich and varied landscape for analysis. Second, there are numerous ways to perform sorting, ranging from classic algorithmic implementations to the use of built-in language functions. Finally, instructors of the introductory programming course at UFCG have frequently observed that students tend to apply sorting algorithms to problems that do not warrant such complexity—a practice they actively seek to discourage. For these reasons, we focused our evaluation on the design test presented in Listing 1.4, as introduced in Sect. 2.

Dataset. We automatically collected a sample of 1,714 Python solutions from our Online Judge system. We focused our analysis on 21 specific problems, selected based on their tendency to prompt students to use sorting as a shortcut, rather than employing the most appropriate problem-solving strategy. These are tasks where sorting is not required, yet often appears in student submissions as a way to simplify the solution. Representative examples include: (i) identifying the smallest or largest element in a list, (ii) determining whether a list is already sorted, (iii) counting the number of distinct elements, and (iv) verifying whether all elements in a list are unique, among others.

Procedures and Metrics. After executing the selected design test, we manually reviewed all 1,714 student solutions to verify whether the test correctly identified the presence of a sorting strategy. Based on this analysis, we recorded the number of true positives, false positives, true negatives, and false negatives in order to compute the test's precision, recall, and accuracy. In this context, a true positive corresponds to a case in which the test correctly detected a sorting strategy in a solution that indeed employed one. A false positive occurs when the test erroneously flagged a solution as using sorting when no such strategy was present. True negatives represent cases where the absence of a sorting strategy was correctly identified, while false negatives indicate instances in which the test failed to recognize a sorting strategy that was actually implemented in the student's code.

Results and Discussion. Table 1 presents the confusion matrix used to classify test results in terms of true positives (TP), false positives (FP), true negatives (TN), and false negatives (FN).

Table 1. Confusion Matrix for Test Results (reproduced from the conference version of this paper [12]).

	Detected Positive	Detected Negative
True Positive (TP)	49	9 (FN)
True Negative (TN)	15 (FP)	1695

Precision, defined as the ratio of true positives (TP) to the sum of true positives and false positives (FP), was 77% (49/(49 + 15)). Recall, which measures the ratio of true positives to the sum of true positives and false negatives (FN), was 84% (49/(49 + 9)). Finally, accuracy, the ratio of all correctly classified instances (true positives and true negatives) to the total number of instances, reached 98,6% ((49 + 1641)/(49 + 15 + 1641 + 9)). The results indicate that the design test is effective at correctly detecting sorting strategies in student solutions, achieving high accuracy with minimal classification errors.

Our manual inspection revealed two main categories of programs that the test incorrectly identified cases as involving sorting:

- Modifications to the array during iteration: These programs performed changes to the array elements while looping through them; however, these changes were not intended to reorder the elements and did not reflect a sorting procedure.
- Use of supplementary data structures: In these instances, the algorithm relied on additional structures—such as hash maps or secondary arrays—initialized before the main loop. Although these structures supported unrelated computations, their presence led the test to incorrectly infer a sorting strategy.

Listing 1.5 shows an example of false positive. Note that the code does have two loops, but it does not manipulate the list `numbers` to sort its elements.

Listing 1.5. False positive example.

```
def split_sequence(numbers, divs):
  for i in range(len(numbers)):
    num = numbers[i]
    for div in divs:
      if div != 0:
        num /= div
    numbers[i] = num
```

These observations underscore the difficulty of accurately distinguishing genuine sorting strategies from other forms of iterative modifications or auxiliary computations, reinforcing the need to further refine the static analysis tests. Nonetheless, it is worth noting that although these student solutions did not implement sorting per se, they still deviated from the instructors' intended design, often introducing unnecessary quadratic complexity for problems that could be solved more efficiently.

Regarding the false negatives, in 8 of them the students used either native functions or custom implementations that performed operations on the list, which the test failed to detect. Examples include the use of functions like `insert`, `pop`, or custom implementations of such operations. In one particular case, a student utilized a lambda function, and our API did not capture this instance due to the lack of implementation for handling the structure of lambda expressions.

Concerning the false negatives, in eight cases students employed either built-in functions or custom implementations that manipulated the list, which the test was unable to detect. Examples include the use of functions such as `insert` and `pop`. Notably, in one instance a student used a lambda function, which our API failed to identify due to the absence of support for analyzing the structure of lambda expressions.

Listing 1.6 shows an example of false negative. Note that the student implemented the insertion sort, but used the insert function instead of moving the elements applying swaps (`assign_field`).

Listing 1.6. False negative example.

```
def my_insertion_sort(arr):
  for i in range(1, len(arr)):
    value = arr.pop(i)
    j = i -1
    while j >= 0 and arr[j] > value:
        j -= 1
    arr.insert(j+1, value)
  return arr
```

The limitation observed in false negatives is not related to the API itself, but rather from the specificity of the design test. The test could have been more comprehensive by explicitly including functions such as insert and pop, which were inadvertently omitted. This situation highlights an important consideration regarding the trade-off between developing highly detailed tests that aim to cover numerous cases and designing more general tests that, while simpler, are susceptible to both false positives and false negatives.

In contrast, the instance involving the lambda function reveals a clear need to enhance the API. This case demonstrates that the current implementation does not adequately handle certain language constructs, and extending the API to support lambda expressions would likely improve its precision and breadth of coverage.

Qualitative Study: Answering RQ2 and RQ3. Depending exclusively on practitioners' perceptions of the tool's documentation would not address our research questions concerning the usefulness and usability of the solution. For this reason, we conducted a qualitative study in which we interviewed 16 professionals in order to evaluate and collect deeper insights on the design test approach for education. Next, we give details on the participants, the procedures applied to collect and analyze data, and the results of this study.

Participants. Our study involved 16 educators from three distinct Brazilian universities. Participants (P1, P2, ...P16) were recruited via email invitations distributed through mailing lists across these three Brazilian institutions, guaranteeing diverse institutional representation. All participants are education professionals possessing direct expertise in delivering programming-related instruction. This group includes both university professors and graduate students who serve as instructors for programming disciplines.

Interviews and Data Collection. We assessed whether educators possess the ability to comprehend the design testing concept, develop their own design tests, and their viewpoints regarding our approach. For this purpose, we requested that instructors complete two activities: (i) reviewing 3 previously constructed design tests and providing explanations for these tests, and (ii) creating 4 design tests based on particular scenarios that we offered.

The 3 previously developed tests were selected based on their progressive complexity, beginning with an examination for basic function invocations and advancing to more sophisticated structures including loops and sorting algorithms, given that sorting algorithms are fundamental to confirming structural comprehension of code. This selection was deliberate, as the third test, which necessitated identifying sorting algorithms, enabled us to determine whether educators could comprehend and articulate a more sophisticated concept. In the activity of developing 4 new tests, the provided scenarios encompassed verification of variable assignments through validation of appropriate function and loop implementation. These activities were chosen to mirror typical educational circumstances, ensuring that educators could implement the design testing concept within practical environments.

We applied the think-aloud protocol [5] to gather data regarding their experiences during task completion. The think-aloud protocol represents a qualitative research methodology wherein participants articulate their cognitive processes while performing a task. This technique enables the capture of reasoning, challenges, and strategies employed by participants, offering insights into their interaction with the material. Each session averaged approximately 20 min in duration. We documented the sessions, encompassing both task execution and subsequent interviews, and subsequently transcribed the audio recordings. These transcriptions underwent accuracy verification before being subjected to coding procedures. We employed predetermined tags concerning API usability and design test comprehension to maintain consistency in response categorization. Coding constitutes a systematic procedure utilized in qualitative research to classify textual data into themes or patterns. Through coding implementation, we organized participants' responses into meaningful categories that supported our analysis of educators' understanding of the design testing process, their approach to test development, and their overall perceptions of the methodology.

Results. We mapped participants' verbalization to 7 pre-defined tags: Positive feedback (tool or approach), Negative feedback (tool or approach), Difficulty (use or understanding), Ease (use or understanding), Correct response, Incorrect response, and Response close to correct. The observations from the data are the following.

Observation 1: Instructors can easily understand the concept of design tests.

Among 16 participants, 15 indicated understanding the concept effortlessly, and 10 educators were capable of considering implementations prior to examining the documentation. This demonstrates the intuitive character of the concept for educational professionals.

The data we collected shows a significant amount of positive feedback. There were 103 comments categorized under "Ease of Understanding". 8 educators posed questions or provided comments that demonstrated deeper engagement with the design testing concept, indicating a high degree of comprehension. In contrast, one participant (P12) experienced difficulty understanding the approach and characterized it as confusing.

P1: *"From what I understand, 'for' is also an entity, so in this line here, I am grabbing all occurrences of 'for' and returning a list with those occurrences, and I check if they are different from an empty list."* This demonstrates the participant's ability to interpret the role of programming structures as entities in the design tests and understand their functional use within the tool.

P2: *"[...] I really liked it, I found the way of doing these tests interesting, I think it's cool. My feedback is entirely positive."* This feedback emphasizes the enthusiasm for the design test approach and its perceived usefulness.

Observation 2: Design tests are seen as a valuable tool for educational use.
Multiple educators indicated that they could identify immediate applications for design tests within their instruction. Among the 16 participants, 8 explicitly identified potential educational implementations, including automating the structural assessment of student assignments. Additionally, 4 educators expressed willingness to consider incorporating the tool into their instructional practices, especially in courses involving programming methodologies.

P3: *"Thinking quickly, for correction, the first thing that comes to mind is grading exams."* Snippet showing that the instructor quickly identified practical applications for design tests, specifically for automating and enhancing the feedback process on student submissions.

P4 reflected on the broader use of the tool in programming courses: *"I think in the Programming II course, it could be interesting to use these design tests along with unit tests, because they abstract the idea of what needs to be tested."* This suggests that design tests could represent a beneficial enhancement to conventional unit tests, offering a supplementary level of feedback that emphasizes the architecture of learners' code.

Observation 3: Some instructors experienced minor difficulties with the API, but the overall concept remained clear.
A minority of participants encountered slight difficulties when utilizing particular API functions, despite the fact that most of them perceived the design testing concept as straightforward to comprehend. To illustrate, 6 educators reported experiencing some uncertainty regarding the manipulation of specific relationships between entities, which hindered their capacity to develop the tests.

P5: *"I had some doubts about how to manipulate some of the relationships between the entities, but I think it's something that can be understood with more practice."* Despite these difficulties, the participants generally found that the concept was clear and the tool was accessible.

P6: *"I didn't understand the last one, do you want me to check if there's at least one 'for' inside 'func1'?"* This indicates that while there were occasional misunderstandings, they were more about the technical details of implementation rather than the core concept of design tests.

Observation 4: Instructors see potential in combining design tests with other educational tools.
Educators would be enabled to evaluate both solution accuracy and code architecture through this approach, rather than merely verifying correctness. As an illustration, participants proposed integrating design tests with unit tests to

deliver more thorough feedback to learners. Several participants contemplated how design tests might supplement current educational tools and approaches.

P7: *"I think design tests could be used to detect when students are using functions they shouldn't, like built-in libraries."* Students can be motivated to concentrate on acquiring fundamental programming principles while simultaneously reinforcing particular coding standards through design tests, as this implies.

Participants demonstrated enthusiasm for integrating design tests into their instructional practices, resulting in an overall favorable response despite slight API difficulties. Educators were capable of engaging in critical analysis regarding its implementation in programming education, and the methodology was broadly comprehended. To summarize, educator responses provide strong evidence supporting the notion that design tests constitute an intuitive and beneficial instrument for academic environments.

5 Design Tests Catalog

In this section, we present our design tests catalog, which complements the framework described in the previous sections. We begin by presenting the motivation that drove us to create this catalog and its intended purposes. We then describe the methodology we employed to develop and validate the catalog entries. Finally, we detail the key characteristics of the catalog and provide concrete examples of design tests that address common pedagogical concerns in introductory programming courses.

Motivation. While our approach provides instructors with the flexibility to create custom design tests tailored to their specific pedagogical goals, we recognized that many introductory programming courses share common concerns about algorithmic design and coding practices. To facilitate adoption and reduce the initial effort required from instructors, we developed a catalog of reusable design tests that address frequently encountered issues in novice programming solutions. This catalog serves as both a practical toolkit that instructors can immediately deploy and a collection of exemplars that demonstrate the range and versatility of design testing patterns, thereby enabling broader adoption of design-focused assessment in introductory programming education.

Method. To ensure our catalog addresses common needs of introductory programming education, we drew from two complementary sources of information. First, we conducted a systematic analysis of syllabi and course materials from 21 introductory programming courses across five different institutions. Second, we conducted detailed interviews with two professors who have been teaching Introduction to Programming at the Federal University of Campina Grande for over 10 years, a course that serves 90 students per semester and includes, as of this writing, 1,041 practical programming problems.

The first step involved an analysis of course materials to understand the scope and depth of topics covered in introductory programming courses. We collected and examined syllabi and course plans from each of the 21 courses in our sample. Through this analysis, we identified and tagged the core topics taught across courses, including fundamental data structures (arrays, lists), control structures (loops, conditionals), algorithmic techniques (searching, sorting), along with concepts such as functions, modularization, and basic input/output operations, among others. Table 2 summarizes the frequency distribution of the main topics found in our analysis.

Table 2. Distribution of core topics across 21 introductory programming courses from different institutions.

Topic	Frequency
Data Structures	16
Theory and Concepts	10
Sorting Algorithms	9
Search Algorithms	8
Control Structures	8
Functions and Modularization	7
Input/output Operations	5
Algorithm Complexity	4
Object Oriented Programming	3

As shown in the table above, the most common topic among the courses we analyzed is related to data structures. These range from simple implementations, such as linear lists (e.g., *"basic operations on linear lists and algorithm analysis"* as extracted from one of the collected curricula), to more complex structures, including binary search trees, heaps, and graphs (e.g., *"this stage will cover the concept of binary search trees and heaps"* extracted from the instructional materials of another course to which we had further access). Our catalog focused on the verification of simple data structures, as we aimed to design tests suitable for more universal assessments and, in contrast, more complex structures often require more granular verification, depending on the specific problems presented to students.

Theoretical concepts were also fairly common across the courses, which is entirely expected, as a foundational understanding of how computers work is essential for students beginning to learn programming. However, as the name suggests, these topics do not involve practical code implementations. Rather, they provide context to the other topics listed in the table.

The third most common topic observed in our analysis is related to classic sorting algorithms: in nine of the courses we observed, it is possible to see that learning algorithms such as bubble sort, insertion sort, merge sort, counting sort, etc. were a key part of these courses' programs.

Next, topics on classical search algorithms - specifically linear and binary search were also very frequent among the courses, followed by standard flow control structures - usage of conditional commands ('if'/'else' implementations) and finite and infinite loops ('for' and 'while'). There was also a frequent number of courses, focused on either an imperative paradigm or an object-oriented paradigm, that somehow discussed function creation and code modularization.

The last three more observed topics were on input/output operations - to which traditional online judges work perfectly well to assert, algorithm complexity - prioritizing teaching how to calculate the operational cost of algorithms, and object-oriented programming.

From this analysis, we were able to identify key topics on programming problems proposed to students and that could benefit from complementary design tests instead of using solely the classic online judge implementations that focus on input/output information. For example, when studying sorting algorithms, design tests can guarantee that the student is not using python's built-in sort() function, and more than that, they help verifying if certain structures - such as auxiliary arrays and nestled loops are being used when expected.

Another example of usage derived from this analysis is related to teaching finite and infinite loops to students. In one of the introductory programming courses offered by the Federal University of Campina Grande, this two structures are separated into two different units - in one of them, the student is expected to implement solutions utilizing solely 'for' loops, in the following one, the problems need to use 'while' loops to be solved. However, certain problems can be solved with either solutions, and a typical input/output verification could fail to detect a problem. We developed design tests in our catalog that guarantee usage of predefined structures and functions - that includes conditionals, loops, operations in lists as well as usage of pre-established functions if verbally required for a solution.

From this step, we defined the main categories of tests that would be in our catalog: sorting algorithms, search algorithms, prohibited structures and functions, code smells (such as an exaggerated amount of 'return' statements) and usage of specific elements in code (e.g., 'for' loops, lists).

The second step involved conducting semi-structured interviews with the two experienced professors from the Federal University of Campina Grande focused on eliciting their pedagogical expertise regarding common student mistakes while designing their algorithm. During the interviews, we asked the professors to reflect on recurring issues they observe in student solutions, the design principles they try to instill, and the specific criteria they use when evaluating code conformance beyond functional correctness.

From these interviews, we were able to extract well-defined design rules that capture expert knowledge about good programming practices in introductory contexts. These rules encompass various aspects of code design, including appropriate algorithm selection, efficient use of data structures (e.g., recognizing when auxiliary structures add unnecessary complexity), and adherence to problem constraints (e.g., respecting prohibited function usage).

From this two-step process, we identified 24 potential tests that are candidates for inclusion in our test catalog and successfully developed 21 of them.

Next, we provide a detailed description of the catalog and present concrete examples of these implemented tests.

The Catalog. Table 3 summarizes the test catalog data, including the frequency of each test type and their respective implementation characteristics.

Table 3. Test catalog summary with frequencies and characteristics.

Topic	Frequency	Description
Usage of specific elements	9	Declaration of functions, manipulation of lists, usage of finite and infinite loops, auxiliary structures, pre-established functions
Sorting Algorithms	6	Classic sorting algorithm implementations
Search Algorithms	2	Linear and binary search approaches
Prohibited Structures and Functions	2	Verifies if a student implements structures our functions to solve a problem without the expected approach
Code Smells	2	Verifies characteristics such as the size of the list of arguments and list of returns

The catalog is divided into five topics: Usage of Specific Elements, where tests focus on verifying if a student's implementations follow specific guidelines - such as the definition of one or more functions, manipulation of lists, and declaration of auxiliary structures in the solution. Sorting Algorithms, which verify if implementations of bubble sort, insertion sort, selection sort, merge sort, quick sort and counting sort follow expected structures such as the usage of auxiliary lists, nestled loops, etc. Search Algorithms verify if a student is implementing a solution based on linear or binary search approaches. Prohibited Structures and Functions asserts that a student is not using prohibited elements - like the built-in sort function or casting a list to a set to manipulate its values. Lastly, Code Smells verify if a student is overusing return statements or exaggerating the number of arguments of their defined functions.

In this paper, we will focus on further explaining two of the catalog's tests: one in verification of a sorting algorithm and another in guaranteeing the usage of a predetermined structure. Motivated by the previously mentioned challenge mentors commonly face when a student implements a solution that functionally works, but does not follow more specified details (e.g., implementing a bubble sort instead of a selection sort; using 'for' loops when it was expected to use 'while' loops). However, all of the implementations are available in the catalog on Github, followed by their description and example codes that can be analyzed.

The catalog is organized with the same topics shown in Table 3, every test of the catalog is displayed with the definition of the test, it's implementation, an example of code that passes the design test and an example of code that does not.

For simplification purposes, Listing 1.7 demonstrates the pseudo-code for the verification of a selection sort implementation, the real code is available on Github:

Listing 1.7. Selection Sort Code Verification.

```
def selectionsort_verification(filepath):
  dw = PyDesignWizard("student-submission.py")

  function_names = dw.get_all_functions()
  args = function_names[0].args.args
  args_names = [i.arg for i in args]

  for_entities = dw.get_entities_by_type("for")

  nestled_fors = False
  aux_variable = False

  if len(for_entities) == 2:
    relations = dw.design_get_callees_from_entity_\
      relation('for1', 'HASLOOP')
    if len(relations) > 0:
      if relations[0].get_name() == for_entities[1]\
       .get_name():
        nestled_fors = True
    if (nestled_fors):
      body = for_entities[0].get_ast_node().body
        for node in body:
          if dw.verify_instance(node, "assign"):
            for t in node.targets:
              if dw.verify_instance(t, "name"):
                if t.id not in args_names:
                  aux_variable = True

  selection_sort = nestled_fors and aux_variable

  return selection_sort
```

In this code, after the tool parses the file, we first verify if there are two 'for' loops in the implementation, and, if so, it is checked if they are nestled loops. Should the verification of nestled loops be true, the code then searches for the presence of auxiliary variables - which is how it differentiates a selection sort from a bubble sort implementation. After verifying both values, it returns the result based on the existence of two nestled 'for' loops and an auxiliary variable.

Listing 1.8 is an example of code that passes this test and is successfully identified as a selection sort:

Listing 1.8. Selection Sort Example.

```
def selection_sort(array, size):
    for ind in range(size):
        min_index = ind
        for j in range(ind + 1, size):
          if array[j] < array[min_index]:
            min_index = j
            (array[ind], array[min_index]) =\
                (array[min_index], array[ind])
    return array
```

Listing 1.9, on the other hand, is a script that does not pass this test, as it is a bubble sort implementation:

Listing 1.9. Bubble Sort Example.

```
def bubble_sort(arr):
    for i in range(len(arr)):
        for j in range(len(arr) - 1 - i):
            if arr[j] > arr[j + 1]:
                arr[j], arr[j + 1] = arr[j + 1], arr[j]
    return arr
```

Another test present in our catalog is the one to verify the exclusive use of a 'for' loop in a student's implementation, as shown in listing 10:

Listing 1.10. Exclusive Use of 'For' Loop Verification.

```
def exclusively_for_verification(filepath)

  dw = PyDesignWizard("student-submission.py")

  for_use = len(dw.get_entities_by_\
   type("for")) > 0
  while_use = len(dw.get_entities_by_\
    type("while")) > 0

  exclusively_for = for_use and not while_use

  return exclusevily_for
```

This script is smaller—first, it identifies the presence of entities of type 'for', then entities of type 'while', and determines whether a code exclusively uses 'for' loops based on this information. Although it may seem simple, this test can be helpful in introductory programming courses, as students often face challenges that could, technically, be solved using either 'for' or 'while' loops. By designing tests that ensure the use of one or the other, the instructor can be confident that students are indeed practicing the specified control structure while programming. Listings 11 and 12 exemplify two cases that would be accepted in a traditional input/output based online judge, but not on verification of exclusive use of one of the two loop structures:

Listing 1.11. Listing Multiples of a Number Using 'For' Loop.

```
def filter_multiples(list, number):
    results = []
    for i in list:
        if i % number == 0:
            results.append(i)
    return results
```

Listing 1.12. Listing Multiples of a Number Using 'While' Loop.

```
def filter_multiples(list, number):
    results = []
    i = 0
    while i < len(list):
        if list[i] % number == 0:
            results.append(i)
        i += 1
    return results
```

As seen above, both functions take a list of numbers and a single number as arguments. They iterate through the list, checking whether each value is a multiple of the given number. If the condition is met, the value is added to a secondary list. While both implementations would pass a functionality test, only one of them adheres to the constraint of using 'for' loops exclusively. We next detail the evaluation process of the catalog as well as the results obtained.

Evaluation. To evaluate the effectiveness of our design tests catalog, we implemented a two-phase validation methodology. The first phase focused on establishing the internal validity of our test implementations by creating unit tests for each catalog entry. These unit tests were designed to verify that our design tests correctly identify both positive cases (code that should be flagged) and negative cases (code that should not be flagged) under controlled conditions. We developed 63 tests to mitigate threats to internal validity that could arise from implementation errors.

The second phase involved executing all catalog tests against our dataset of student solutions and conducting manual analysis on a sample of 100 of these solutions to classify each result, the decision to utilize a smaller sample was taken as our previous study already provided us with reliability on the tool. The sample provided results of 2100 executions (21 tests on 100 files) in total. For every test execution, we manually identified true positives (correctly flagged design assertions), false positives (incorrectly flagged solutions), true negatives (correctly not observed a design constraint), and false negatives (missed design verifications). This comprehensive classification enabled us to calculate accuracy, true negative rate, precision, and recall, providing quantitative evidence of the catalog's diagnostic effectiveness and reliability in real-world educational contexts. Table 4 presents the confusion matrix resulting from this validation process.

Table 4. Confusion Matrix for Catalog Test Results.

	Detected Positive	Detected Negative
True Positive (TP)	497	45 (FN)
True Negative (TN)	33 (FP)	1525

For the catalog evaluation, the calculated precision was 93.77% (497/(497+33)), the recall was 91.70% (497/(497+45)), and the overall accuracy was 96.29% ((497+1525)/(497+1525+33+45)). The findings suggest that the efficacy of the tests in identifying structures and components implemented and utilized by students is noteworthy. However, we underscore the significance of instructors assessing and employing suitable tests for particular scenarios. To illustrate, when encountering two nested 'for' loops within a problem concerning matrix searches, a false positive may arise, leading the tests to identify the implementation as either bubble sort or selection sort. However, no cases were observed in which two sorting algorithms were identified simultaneously. This finding indicates that the tests would be highly effective for assessing whether a student is implementing an appropriate sorting technique, for example.

Nonetheless, it was observed that the tests are capable of reliably identifying the use of forbidden functions and structures, verifying whether the student actually used expected ones, whether the program was modularized into one or more functions, and whether the implementations follow the patterns of classical sorting and searching algorithms when such are expected.

6 Related Work

The evaluation of student programs in introductory programming courses has long been a subject of academic interest [1,10,13,18]. A widely adopted strategy involves Online Judges, which automatically determine whether a program behaves as expected by comparing its outputs to predefined results. For instance, Janzen et al. [7] and Singh et al. [16] advocate for this output-driven validation, where correctness is defined solely in terms of input-output matching. While effective for checking functionality, this approach does not account for how solutions are implemented, leaving out important structural aspects such as recursion, control flow, and modular decomposition.

An alternative line of research investigates static code analysis as a means of assessment. Truong et al. [17] examine the benefits of evaluating software metrics like cyclomatic complexity and code coverage in learning environments. This methodology emphasizes general code quality and adherence to good programming practices but does not explicitly assess the underlying algorithmic strategies used by students.

Building on these efforts, Araújo et al. [2] argue for the inclusion of algorithmic reasoning in evaluation criteria. Their findings suggest that many students opt for technically correct but pedagogically inadequate solutions, especially when design expectations are not clearly articulated. Such practices can impede the development of essential problem-solving and abstraction skills.

To overcome these challenges, our research introduces a novel tool designed to verify structural aspects of student code through static analysis. Rather than replacing functional tests, the tool supplements them by identifying when a solution deviates from the algorithmic patterns expected by instructors. This integrated assessment strategy enables richer, more targeted feedback, supporting both correctness and conceptual understanding.

7 Conclusion and Future Work

In this study, we introduced the Python Design Wizard, a tool designed to assess the structural features of student code in introductory programming courses. Unlike traditional approaches focused solely on functional correctness, our tool leverages design tests to verify whether students xffg' implementations align with specific algorithmic strategies expected by instructors. Through static analysis, the tool detects structural deviations, offering a complementary perspective to output-based evaluation and enabling more comprehensive feedback.

To support and encourage the use of design tests in educational settings, we also developed a catalog of design tests. This catalog was constructed through content analysis of multiple introductory programming courses and informed by structured interviews with experienced educators. It provides a collection of ready-to-use tests that reflect common instructional goals and algorithmic patterns. We validated the catalog using real student submissions to ensure both its relevance and effectiveness in practice.

Together, the tool and the catalog provide a foundation for integrating structural assessment into programming education, supporting instructors in promoting better coding practices and deeper algorithmic understanding among students.

7.1 Threats to Validity

Our study presents encouraging evidence for the use of design tests in structural assessment, but some limitations must be considered when interpreting the results.

One limitation lies in the scope of our dataset: the analysis was based on 1,714 student submissions related to sorting algorithms, all collected from a single academic institution. Although this dataset offered sufficient variety for initial evaluation, it does not capture the full spectrum of problems, strategies, and coding habits that might appear in different educational contexts or algorithmic topics. As such, the generalizability of the tool to other types of exercises or institutions remains an open question.

The qualitative component of our study also involved a limited number of instructors, which may restrict the diversity of pedagogical viewpoints captured. Broader engagement with educators from varied backgrounds and teaching environments could provide a richer understanding of how design tests align with different instructional goals.

Another important consideration concerns the catalog of design tests we developed. Although it provides a valuable foundation for structural assessment, it is not intended to be universally applicable across all introductory programming courses. Different institutions may emphasize distinct programming paradigms, learning outcomes, or assessment philosophies. To address this, we constructed the catalog based on content analysis of introductory programming courses from five well-established Brazilian universities.

7.2 Future Work

Future work should expand both the dataset and the range of instructor perspectives, as well as explore the application of the tool and catalog across diverse curricula and programming languages. These steps are crucial to validating the broader applicability of the approach and refining it for wider adoption.

Furthermore, it would be interesting to investigate the integration of this tool into other programming paradigms and languages, as well as expanding its capabilities to more complex scenarios that go beyond sorting algorithms. We also aim to explore the possibility of developing more specific tests that could handle different levels of complexity, providing a more granular evaluation of algorithm design.

References

1. Ala-Mutka, K.M.: A survey of automated assessment approaches for programming assignments. Comput. Sci. Educ. **15**(2), 83–102 (2005)
2. Araujo, E., Serey, D., Figueiredo, J.: Qualitative aspects of students' programs: can we make them measurable? In: 2016 IEEE Frontiers in Education Conference (FIE), pp. 1–8. IEEE (2016)
3. Beazley, D.: Python Essential Reference. Addison-Wesley (2012)
4. Brunet, J., Guerrero, D., Figueiredo, J.: Design tests: an approach to programmatically check your code against design rules. In: 31st International Conference on Software Engineering - Companion Volume, pp. 255–258 (2009). https://doi.org/10.1109/ICSE-COMPANION.2009.5070995
5. Ericsson, K.A., Simon, H.A.: Protocol Analysis: Verbal Reports as Data, revised edn. MIT Press, Cambridge (1993)
6. Python Software Foundation: Python 3 Documentation (2023). https://docs.python.org/3/
7. Janzen, S., et al.: Automated grading systems in competitive programming contests. In: Proceedings of the 8th International Symposium on Educational Software Development (2013)
8. Juiz, A., et al.: Online judge and its application to introductory programming courses. ACM SIGCSE Bull. (2014)
9. JUnit Team: JUnit 5: The Next Generation of JUnit (2023). https://junit.org/junit5/. Accessed 11 Nov 2024
10. Keuning, H., Jeuring, J., Heeren, B.: A systematic literature review of automated feedback generation for programming exercises. ACM Trans. Comput. Educ. (TOCE) **19**(1), 1–43 (2018)
11. Leite, L.: A proposal for improving programming education with frequent problem solving exercises. In: Brazilian Symposium on Computer Education (2015)
12. Oliveira, C., Silva, L., Brunet, J.: Beyond functionality: automating algorithm design evaluation in introductory programming courses. In: Proceedings of the 17th International Conference on Computer Supported Education (CSEDU 2025). SCITEPRESS (2025)
13. Paiva, J.C., Leal, J.P., Figueira, Á.: Automated assessment in computer science education: a state-of-the-art review. ACM Trans. Comput. Educ. (TOCE) **22**(3), 1–40 (2022)
14. Papastergiou, M.: Digital game-based learning in computer programming: impact on educational effectiveness and student motivation. Comput. Educ. (2009)
15. van Rossum, G.: The Python Language Reference Manual. Network Theory Ltd. (2009)
16. Singh, J., Gupta, P., Sharma, M.: Online judge system for learning and practicing programming. Int. J. Comput. Appl. (2013)

17. Truong, N., Roe, P., Bancroft, P.: Static analysis of students' java programs. In: Proceedings of the Sixth Australasian Conference on Computing Education-Volume 30, pp. 317–325. Citeseer (2004)
18. Wasik, S., Antczak, M., Badura, J., Laskowski, A., Sternal, T.: A survey on online judge systems and their applications. ACM Comput. Surv. (CSUR) **51**(1), 1–34 (2018)
19. Watson, C., Li, F.W.: Failure rates in introductory programming revisited. In: Proceedings of the 2014 Conference on Innovation & Technology in Computer Science Education, pp. 39–44 (2014)

Preparing Citizens to Access Digital Public Services: A Virtual Reality Serious Game

Ilenia Fronza(✉), Shiva Saket Parida, and Aziya Mehboob

Free University of Bozen, Bolzano, Italy
{ilenia.fronza,shivasaket.parida,aziya.mehboob}@unibz.it

Abstract. Many citizens lack the digital skills needed to access public services, which limits the successful implementation of smart cities and smart villages. To address this issue, we have developed a Virtual Reality (VR) serious game aimed at helping citizens develop the essential skills needed for accessing digital public services. As its web-based version, *DigiVillage VR* is set in a fictional smart village where the player participates in digital activities related to public services and learns how to navigate the platforms that offer these services in real life. In this paper, we present an overview of the serious game, evaluate its quality, and compare it with its web-based version. The transition to VR successfully delivers a more immersive and realistic experience.

Keywords: Serious Game · Virtual Reality (VR) · Digital Skills · E-government · Smart Village · Computing Education

1 Introduction

Digital services that enable access to various commercial and public services through online platforms have reached rural communities, where *smart villages* integrate smart technologies, infrastructure, and services to promote sustainable development and strengthen local economies [2,5]. In particular, smart villages use innovative and smart solutions to deliver public services [28]. However, e-government initiatives may fail to engage citizens if they do not possess the necessary skills [30,31]. Serious games can enhance skills, deliver significant objectives, and allow learners to practice scenarios by providing an environment where they can address real problems, explore solutions, and learn from mistakes by gaining new perspectives without fear of real-life consequences [11,18]. Although serious games have been proposed to enhance citizens' understanding of public processes (for example, [9,24]) and encourage participation (for example, [3]), there is a notable lack of games that focus on accessing digital public services and improving citizens' digital skills. For this reason, our previous paper [13] proposed *DigiVillage Chronicles*, a web-based serious game to enhance the acquisition of digital skills needed to access public services by stimulating real-life scenarios through in-game activities and tasks.

C. Meinel et al. (Eds.): CSEDU 2025, CCIS 3148, pp. 336–352, 2027.
https://doi.org/10.1007/978-3-032-39103-2_16

In this paper, we build on [13] by developing a Virtual Reality (VR) version of the serious game to enhance immersion and user engagement. *DigiVillage VR* transforms 2D gameplay into a more immersive experience by allowing players to explore environments with real-time visual clues, interact with voice-responsive characters, and obtain immediate feedback through a points-based reward system and challenge-oriented mechanics. Additionally, to improve the educational goals of the original game [13], *DigiVillage VR* features a focused activity mode, realistic digital interaction, and more complex multi-step activities that reflect the usage of digital public services in the real world.

We describe the enhanced gameplay mechanics, visual design, and VR controls introduced in *DigiVillage VR*. Moreover, we discuss the results of a comparison between the VR and web-based versions of the game, focusing on usability and engagement. Finally, we present the evaluation of the serious game based on the criteria for high-quality serious games [6]. *DigiVillage VR* offers an improved balance between learning goals and engaging gameplay, enhancing the original version with a more immersive environment and improved game mechanics. The addition of new activities along with points-lives system reinforces better learning through feedback.

The rest of this paper is organized as follows: Sect. 2 provides background information and related work. Section 3 describes the *DigiVillage VR*, focusing on story telling, game mechanics, player interaction, and a comparison with the web-based version of the game. Section 4 describes the evaluation of *DigiVillage VR*, and Sect. 5 concludes the paper and outlines ideas for future work.

2 Background and Related Work

The term "serious games" was introduced in 1987 by Clark C. Abt [1], who defined them as games where the main objective is education in its diverse forms rather than entertainment. Unlike traditional games, serious games focus on problem-solving and learning, utilizing similar media and interactive elements to make the experience engaging and enjoyable [4]. Serious games utilize game design to achieve educational goals through gameplay; they are applied across diverse fields, including healthcare [21], education [10,25,29], the military [17], and language teaching [15,33].

The digital era has further enhanced the use of serious games, particularly through immersive simulations such as Virtual Reality (VR), to improve learning and training experiences [8]. VR provides a three-dimensional(3D) simulated environment in which users experience the illusion of being part of that setting by interacting with it as if they were present there [22]. The key attributes of VR technologies are *immersion, presence, and interactivity*, and they are known to influence learning outcomes [27]. For example, the use of an immersive head-mounted display (HMD) facilitates engagement and skill development [14,16].

Studies have investigated the impact of VR and traditional formats, often reporting improvements in engagement and motivation when using VR. For example, Cheng et al. [7] analyzed a video game designed for learning the

Japanese language and culture in two formats: computer and VR. They found enhanced engagement with cultural learning when using the VR format. Raya et al. [26] reported that a VR experience designed to immerse users in artwork showed increased motivation compared to traditional methods. Some studies have shown that VR improves learning compared to other formats. For instance, Yu et al. [32] used videos to educate their students about the natural world. These videos were presented on two different platforms: a computer and a VR HMD. The findings suggest that using VR devices enhances learning and increases the environmental awareness of participants. Liou and Chang [19] reported that VR experiences in science education produce improved results in motivation and learning achievement compared to traditional lectures.

Nevertheless, studies found no significant differences in learning outcomes between VR and traditional formats. For instance, Hernandez et al. [23] examined the effectiveness of various virtual laboratory formats for engineering education. They evaluated the use of both computer application-oriented labs and VR-based labs for industrial engineering learning, concluding that both methods are equally effective. Similarly, López-Fernández et al. [20] conducted a comparative study involving 289 students to teach the Scrum methodology using two versions of a game: one VR-based and the other web-based. Their findings showed that both versions were effective in gaining knowledge. Damianova and Berrezueta-Guzman [8] highlighted the efficacy of VR-based serious games in improving experiential learning, engagement, and knowledge retention across various domains, including education, healthcare, and professional training. This is evident in examples like biology-themed escape rooms and molecular manipulation simulations, which support the visualization of abstract concepts and skill development, as well as VR-based fire extinguisher training that enables safe, hands-on practice with real-time feedback.

Based on these insights, we created a VR version of our previously designed web-based serious game [13], which aimed to improve digital skills to access public services in smart villages and was developed in a point-and-click 2D format. The goal of transitioning our serious game to VR is to offer a more immersive and realistic experience that is consistent with the best practices identified in the current literature.

3 DigiVillage VR

Building on top of the web-based game presented in [13], *DigiVillage VR* is a VR serious game aimed at helping citizens of smart villages in developing essential skills for accessing digital public services. Figure 1 shows the splash screen. *DigiVillage VR* targets adults looking to improve their understanding of public services, particularly those in rural areas having limited familiarity with digital public services. As in [13], the game is set in a fictional smart village, named DigiVillage, where the local government's operations have undergone digital transformation. This transformation involves the implementation of innovative and smart solutions to enhance the delivery of public services.

Fig. 1. *DigiVillage VR* splash screen.

3.1 The Story Telling

Once known for its vineyards and rolling hills, DigiVillage has evolved into a smart village that offers digital access to all public services, along with a *Digital Competence Platform* that assists residents in learning about digital services. Figure 2 displays the map of DigiVillage, highlighting the public services available in *DigiVillage VR*, in line with the guidelines from the European Union [12]. Specifically, the youth services allow users to browse and apply for jobs, the bank services enable users to transfer money, and the health services facilitate the online booking of doctor's appointments.

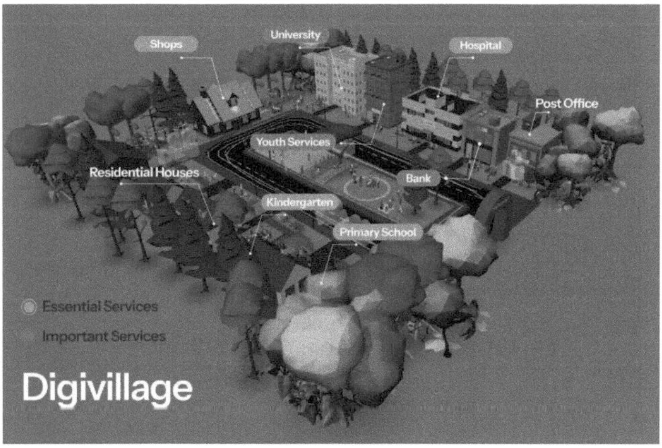

Fig. 2. Map of DigiVillage and its public services [12].

As in the original version of the game [13], the main character, Giulio, lives in DigiVillage and appreciates the convenience of living in a digital world, but he is still acquiring the necessary skills. The player controls Giulio as he navigates around Digivillage and faces various digital challenges in his daily life. The story has three scenarios, each starting with Giulio receiving a text from a supporting character in the story, which sets the objective to meet and interact with them. The meeting sets the stage for Giulio to learn about a new digital service [13]. The game includes the following three scenarios, each centered on a digital activity.

Scenario 1. Learning How to Search for Jobs Online

Narrative: The story begins with Giulio receiving a text from Anna to meet her near the cafe (Fig. 3). Anna had invited him to celebrate the occasion of starting her first job. During the chat, Giulio mentions to Anna that he has visited several companies in Digivillage to hand in his CV but has not found a suitable position yet. Anna recommends the Youth services, where she found valuable guidance and support to explore and apply for jobs. After their meeting, Giulio visits the youth services building, where a staff member introduces him to the Digital Competence platform, which offers step-by-step guidance for developing digital skills for many public services, including online job search. Giulio explores the job search process and, after completing a job application, earns a digital badge. Thankful for the help, he downloads the mobile application to seek any future assistance with public services.

Fig. 3. Scenario 1: Giulio interacts with Anna, who tells him about the Digital Competence Center in town.

Activity: Giulio completes the following steps to learn how to apply for a job online (Fig. 4):

- Creating an account on the Municipal job portal;
- Searching for job positions with location and keywords;
- Using filters to narrow down the search results;
- Viewing the job description;
- Creating an effective resume relevant to the position;
- Uploading the resume and sending a job application.

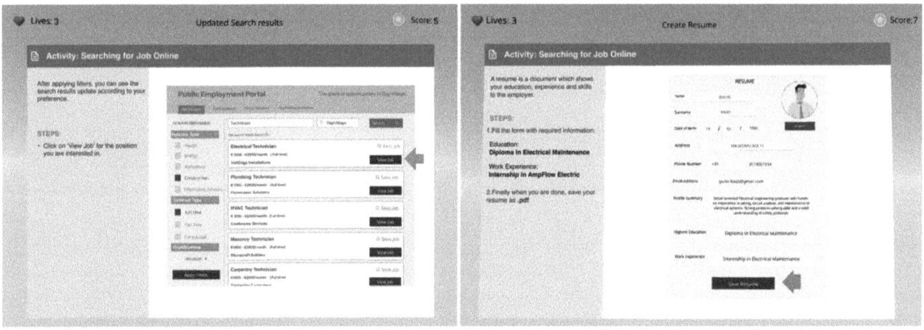

Fig. 4. Scenario 1: Giulio searches for a job online and applies for it.

Scenario 2. Learning How to Make an Online Money Transfer.

Narrative: Giulio receives a text from his friend Mark asking to meet at the park. When they meet, Mark explains that he urgently needs money. Since it is a public holiday, he suggests that Giulio send it through an online transfer. Not being familiar with online banking, Giulio decides to learn how to set up an online banking account from the Digital Competence platform and make the transfer (Fig. 5).

Activity: Giulio completes the following steps to learn how to set up an online bank account and transfer money (Fig. 6):

- Providing the necessary personal information;
- Verifying the phone number with a one-time password;
- Providing bank account information;
- Uploading an identity document for verification;
- Creating a strong password for the account;
- Signing in with user ID and password;
- Providing the recipient's details for transfer;
- Confirming the bank transfer with a one-time password.

Fig. 5. Scenario 2: Giulio meets Mark, who asks him to make an online money transfer.

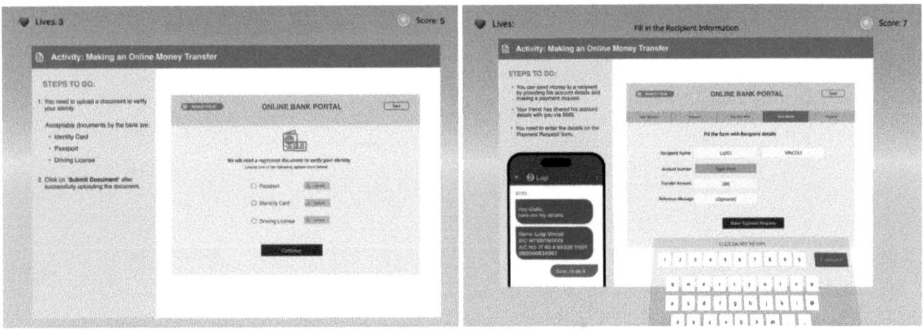

Fig. 6. Scenario 2: Giulio sets up his online banking and transfers money online.

Scenario 3. Booking a Doctor Appointment Online.

Narrative: Giulio receives a text from his mother inviting him over for lunch. While they eat, she asks him to visit the clinic and book a doctor's appointment for her (Fig. 7). Giulio mentions that he can do that online. Curious to learn how this is possible, his mother watches as he shows her the Digital Competence platform. After completing the activity, Giulio earns a digital badge.

Activity: Giulio completes the following steps to learn how to book an appointment with the doctor online (Figs. 6 and 8):

- Choosing a login method for the Public Health portal;
- Providing health card number and tax ID code to login;
- Navigating to the *book appointment* page;
- Choosing date and time of the appointment;
- Confirming and viewing appointment details.

3.2 Game Mechanics

Each scenario presents a challenge focused on accessing and navigating a specific digital public service. For each challenge, guided step-by-step activities introduce

Fig. 7. Scenario 3: Giulio's mother needs to book a doctor's appointment.

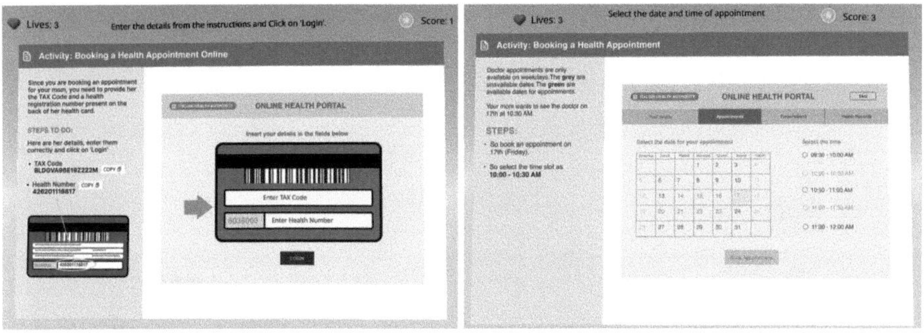

Fig. 8. Scenario 3: Giulio schedules a doctor's appointment for his mom online.

essential processes such as uploading required documents, entering the necessary information, and navigating the website of the digital services (Fig. 9).

Progress in the game depends on making the correct choices: players earn points for correct actions and lose lives for incorrect ones. If all lives are lost, the activity restarts. This encourages players to complete each step carefully, reinforcing learning through gameplay. The game also provides the player with immediate feedback when an incorrect choice is made (Fig. 10).

Some steps in the activity may have more than one correct option, with better choices earning higher scores. For instance, when registering for an online bank account, the player is required to create a password and is awarded points based on its strength: the stronger the password, the more points they receive (Fig. 11). Upon successful completion of all steps in an activity, the player is rewarded with a digital badge.

3.3 Player Interaction

The game uses two types of interaction. With *in-game UI interactions*, the player points to the ray cast and presses the trigger button of the VR controller to interact with diegetic UI elements inside the game, like a virtual keyboard (Fig. 12).

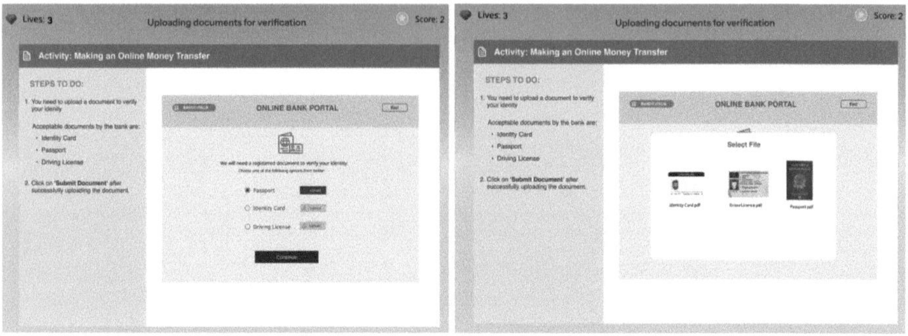

Fig. 9. The player uploads a document to register for online banking.

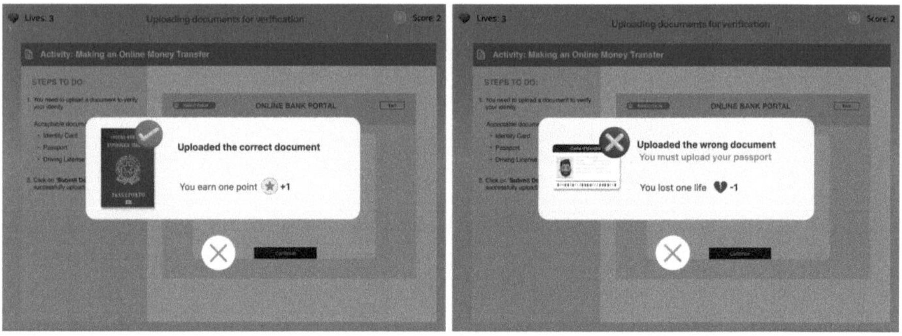

Fig. 10. Players earn points for correct actions (on the left) and lose lives for incorrect ones (on the right).

With *movement inside the game world*, the player moves freely in the virtual environment by looking in the desired direction of movement and using the thumstick of the VR controller (Fig. 13). The player's movement in the VR version feels more immersive due to the 3D environment and first-person view. However, using raycasting or a virtual keyboard instead of clicking or typing on a physical keyboard (as in the original version) deviates from how digital public services are accessed in real life.

3.4 Comparison with the Web-Based Version of the Game

As detailed in Table 1, the comparison between the web-based game [13] and the redesigned VR version highlights key improvements across various design aspects.

Overall, the player's sense of immersion has been enhanced through VR, a 3D environment, voice-acted dialogues, and animations (Fig. 14). In addition, the gamification elements and learning outcomes have been strengthened through gameplay mechanics and new challenges, respectively. Usability has also

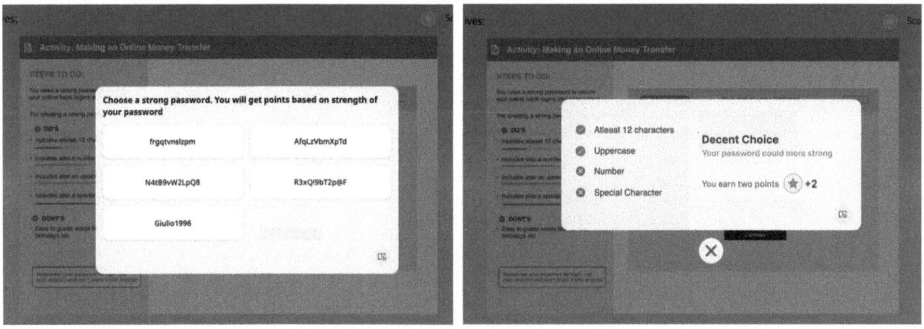

Fig. 11. The player gets more points based on the strength of the password.

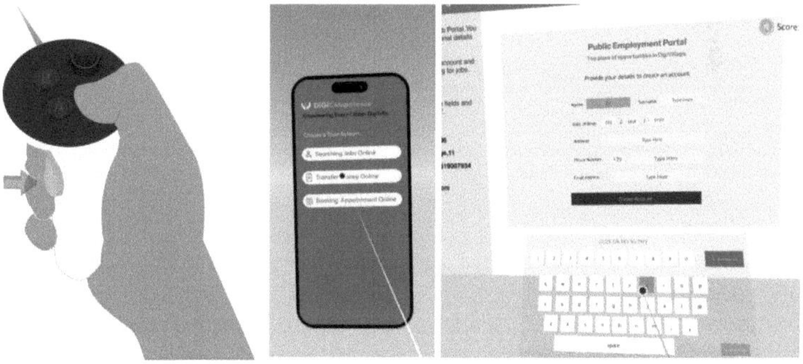

Fig. 12. The player can interact with UI elements using ray casting in VR.

improved due to multiple game modes, an updated UI, and a more intuitive navigation system. However, in *DigiVillage VR*, the user input transitioned from mouse and keyboard to VR controllers. This change represents a deviation from real-life user interactions when navigating digital services.

4 Evaluation

For evaluating the game, we focus on its new features and, as in our previous paper [13], we used the criteria for high-quality serious games [6] to evaluate the *serious* aspect, the *game* aspect, and the *balance* between these two aspects. Table 2 shows the results of the evaluation of the *serious part.*

The learning outcomes have been enhanced with additional steps in the activities that more accurately simulate real-life interactions with digital public services. For example, while registering for online banking, the VR version has an additional step of uploading an identity card for verification. Similarly, the online job application process includes a further step in creating an effective resume. The method of delivery has also been improved with a new game mechanic of granting points for correct choices and deducting lives for incorrect ones. This encourages the player to pay attention and learn from mistakes during the steps

Fig. 13. The player can move in the virtual environment with the thumstick.

Fig. 14. Comparison between the original 2D third-person point-and-click interface (left) and the enhanced 3D first-person VR experience (right), showcasing the shift in visual design and interaction format.

of the activity. In summary, as indicated in Table 2, all core elements of the *serious part* of the game have seen improvements in the VR version.

The core elements of the *game part* include enjoyable gameplay and appropriate media presentation (Table 3). *DigiVillage VR* enhances overall enjoyment with a vibrant 3D environment, animated characters, and voice-acted dialogues, creating a more immersive and lifelike virtual world with dynamic elements. The media presentation is improved with step-by-step voice guidance that supports the learning process by offering immediate feedback on player actions, while a clear navigation system helps maintain focus without confusion. Additionally, the ability to copy-paste long-form data while filling in details brings it closer to real-world digital service use, making the experience both engaging and authentic. In summary, as indicated in Table 3, both the core elements of the *game part* have seen improvements in the VR version.

Table 1. Comparison between *DigiVillage VR* and the web-based game [13].

Design Aspect	Web-based game	Feature implemented in *DigiVillage VR*	Images from *Digivillage VR*
Navigation	Players explore freely but often get lost.	**Real-time navigation arrow:** The game always points the player to the next goal, reducing confusion and improving flow during the game.	
Dialogue system	Text-based dialogues only	**Voice dialogue system:** Fully voiced characters with animations enhance immersion and storytelling.	
Gameplay flexibility	Only linear narrative	**Multiple game modes:** Players can go through the story or jump directly to activities for faster gameplay	
Gamification	Rewarded only after completing the activity	**Point system:** Players are rewarded for correct actions during the activity, increasing motivation.	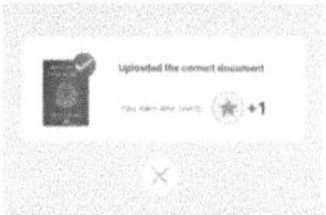
Challenge mechanism	No penalty for incorrect actions	**Lives system:** Players lose lives for incorrect actions, encouraging attentiveness and precision in tasks.	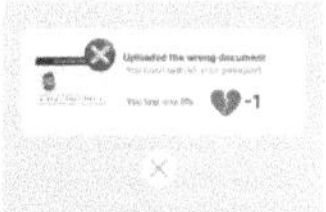
Flow of experience	Activities interrupted by quizzes	**No quizzes:** The absence of quizzes helps maintain immersion and reduces the risk of cognitive overload. .	
Digital Literacy Stimulation	Simple task-based activities	**Extended activities:** Players go through multi-step processes, similar to real-life digital services.	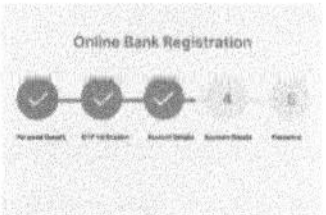
Data Entry Process	Manual text entry	**Copy-paste system:** Mimicking real-world digital interactions for authentic learning practice	

The criteria for *balance between serious and game parts* evaluate how well the two components of a serious game are integrated and interconnected (Table 4). The learning activities in the game are presented as narrative-driven scenarios, ensuring seamless integration into the game play. In terms of integration, *Digivillage VR* enhances the original version by removing quizzes that previously disrupted the flow of the game. However, the interaction technology has shifted to VR controllers, which deviates from real life interaction of using keyboard and mouse to navigate digital services. In summary, as shown in Table 4, one element has improved in the VR version, while the other presents some

Table 2. Evaluation of *DigiVillage VR*: serious part [6].

Element	Game feature	How *Digivillage VR* fulfills the criterion	Improved (↑)/reduced (↓)
Goal	New challenges	New challenges have been incorporated to improve learning outcomes and provide a more accurate stimulation that reflects the real-life interactions encountered when using digital services.	↑
Method	Lives system	A lives mechanism deducts lives for incorrect choices during the activity. If all lives are lost, the player must restart the activity. This encourages the player to learn from mistakes and pay close attention while filling in details and making choices during the steps of the activity	↑
Quality	Point system	Granting/deducting points for correct/incorrect choices encourages players to learn the proper procedures to advance in the activity. Players earn a badge upon finishing the activity to recognize of their learning achievements.	↑

Table 3. Evaluation of *DigiVillage VR*: game part [6].

Core elements	Game feature	How *Digivillage VR* fulfills the criterion	Improved (↑)/reduced (↓)
Enjoyment	Lively atmosphere, voice acted dialogues	The enjoyment quality of the game is further deepened with a vibrant 3D environment, animated characters and voice-acted dialogues. While exploring the environment, the player can encounter town residents engaged in everyday activities such as: children playing in the park, vehicles moving and other dynamic elements, which improves the immersion in the virtual world.	↑
Media presentation	Voice guidance, navigation system, improved data input	Step-by-step voice guidance during activities, provides players with immediate feedback for correct and wrong choices. An easy navigation system points the player towards the current objective, helping them to stay on track without feeling overwhelmed. This version also allows the player to copy-paste long form data in the form like (IBAN, address) during the activity providing a more closer stimulation of our everyday digital interaction.	↑

critical issues. Overall, *DigiVillage VR* qualifies as a high quality serious game. It offers an improved balance between learning goals and engaging gameplay, enhancing the original version with a more immersive environment and improved game mechanics. The addition of new activities along with a points-lives system reinforces better learning through feedback. Although the transition to VR controllers slightly reduces realism compared to keyboard use, the overall experience is more enjoyable and educationally effective.

Table 4. Evaluation of *DigiVillage VR*: balance between game and serious parts [6].

Core elements	Game feature	How *Digivillage VR* fulfills the criterion	Improved (↑)/reduced (↓)
Integrated serious part with game play	Story scenario based activities	The in game activities where learning takes place are presented as scenarios in the story through which the player is introduced to a digital public service. This helps the player to learn in context, making it more relatable and applicable in the real world. By presenting learning activities as part of the narrative, educational tasks are seamlessly integrated into the gameplay, which maintains emotional engagement.	↑
Interaction technology	VR controls	The player's movement in the VR version feels more immersive due to the 3D environment and first person view, closely resembling the experience of walking through a village. However, the UI interaction such as using raycasting or a virtual keyboard instead of clicking or typing on a physical keyboard (as in the original version), deviates from how digital public services are typically accessed in real life.	↓

5 Conclusion and Future Work

This paper presented *DigiVillage VR*, a serious game designed to train users to access digital public services in smart villages. The goal of transitioning from web-based to VR is to enhance immersion and user engagement.

The application of the quality criteria for serious games [6] shows improvement in both the serious and the game parts, particularly in balancing learning objectives with gameplay. The serious part was improved through in-depth activities that more accurately reflect real-world digital services, while the point-lives game mechanic encourages learning through feedback. The game component presents enhanced visual aesthetics through a dynamic 3D environment and improved usability via voice-guided activities and an intuitive navigation system. The evaluation of the balance between gameplay and learning shows an improvement due to the exclusion of quizzes and the seamless integration of activities into the game narrative. The use of VR controllers feels more immersive due to the 3D environment and first-person view. However, this interaction method differs from conventional mouse and keyboard inputs typically used to access digital services, as featured in the original game.

One of the possible limitations of this study is expert bias since the evaluators were also the authors of this work. To ensure objectivity, future evaluations should include independent experts who have had no prior involvement in the development process. In addition, user-based evaluation should be conducted to complement the assessment of engagement and usability. Furthermore, this study did not measure the effectiveness of the game in facilitating learning, which we should investigate in future research. To better align the solution with actual requirements and regulatory standards of real public services, it is also crucial to involve public administrations and collect their feedback.

In the future, the scope of the game can be expanded with a wider variety of interactive scenarios that reflect the diversity of digital public services in the real world. This could include activities designed for mobile interaction, missions where players assist others, and scenarios that promote awareness of online safety. These additions would enrich the learning experience, facilitate the deeper transfer of digital skills to real-life contexts, and foster digital inclusion for a diverse group of residents in smart villages. Furthermore, to improve the game, a future iteration could implement an "adaptive difficulty" feature, which would dynamically modify the difficulty level according to the player's performance and better accommodate players with varying degrees of digital literacy. Social interaction mechanics, such as multiplayer support, could further improve the educational value of the game by introducing cooperative problem solving. An additional area of investigation could also focus on cybersickness, commonly experienced in VR environments.

Acknowledgments. This research has been carried out within the PNRR research activities of the consortium *iNEST (Interconnected North-East Innovation Ecosystem)* funded by the European Union *Next-GenerationEU* (Piano Nazionale di Ripresa e Resilienza (PNRR) Missione 4 Componente 2, Investimento 1.5 D.D. 1058 23/06/2022, ECS_00000043 Spoke1, RT1A, CUP I43C22000250006). This manuscript reflects only the Authors views and opinions, neither the European Union nor the European Commission can be considered responsible for them.

References

1. Abt, C.: Serious Games. University Press of America (1987)
2. Adamowicz, M., Zwolińska-Ligaj, M.: The "smart village" as a way to achieve sustainable development in rural areas of Poland. Sustainability **12**(16), 6503 (2020)
3. Aguilar, J., Díaz, F., Altamiranda, J., Cordero, J., Chavez, D., Gutierrez, J.: Metropolis: an emerging serious game for the smart city. Dyna **86**(211), 215–224 (2019)
4. Bergeron, B.: Developing serious games (game development series). Charles River Media, Inc. (2005)
5. Bokun, K., Nazarko, J.: Smart villages concept—a bibliometric analysis and state-of-the-art literature review. Prog. Plan. **175**, 100765 (2023)
6. Caserman, P., et al.: Quality criteria for serious games: serious part, game part, and balance. JMIR Serious Games **8**(3), e19037 (2020)
7. Cheng, A., Yang, L., Andersen, E.: Teaching language and culture with a virtual reality game. In: Proceedings of the 2017 CHI Conference on Human Factors in Computing Systems, pp. 541–549 (2017)
8. Damianova, N., Berrezueta-Guzman, S.: Serious games supported by virtual reality-literature review. IEEE Access (2025)
9. De Classe, T.M., De Araujo, R.M., Xexéo, G.B., Siqueira, S.W.M.: Public processes are open for play. Digit. Gov. Res. Pract. **2**(4), 1–18 (2021)

10. Deshpande, A.A., Huang, S.H.: Simulation games in engineering education: a state-of-the-art review. Comput. Appl. Eng. Educ. **19**(3), 399–410 (2011)
11. Deterding, S., Dixon, D., Khaled, R., Nacke, L.: From game design elements to gamefulness: defining "gamification". In: Proceedings of the 15th International Academic MindTrek Conference: Envisioning Future Media Environments, pp. 9–15 (2011)
12. European Union: European union access factsheet (2022). https://ec.europa.eu/enrd/sites/default/files/enrd-factsheet_access-to-services.pdf
13. Fronza, I., Parida, S., Mehboob, A.: Digivillage chronicles: a serious game designed to improve digital skills for accessing public services. In: Proceedings of the 17th International Conference on Computer Supported Education - Volume 2: CSEDU, pp. 745–751. INSTICC, SciTePress (2025). https://doi.org/10.5220/0013290600003932
14. Hamstra, S.J., Brydges, R., Hatala, R., Zendejas, B., Cook, D.A.: Reconsidering fidelity in simulation-based training. Acad. Med. **89**(3), 387–392 (2014)
15. Hung, H.T., Yang, J.C., Hwang, G.J., Chu, H.C., Wang, C.C.: A scoping review of research on digital game-based language learning. Comput. Educ. **126**, 89–104 (2018)
16. Jensen, L., Konradsen, F.: A review of the use of virtual reality head-mounted displays in education and training. Educ. Inf. Technol. **23**, 1515–1529 (2018)
17. Johnson, W.L., Rickel, J.W., Lester, J.C., et al.: Animated pedagogical agents: face-to-face interaction in interactive learning environments. Int. J. Artif. Intell. Educ. **11**(1), 47–78 (2000)
18. Knight, J.F., et al.: Serious gaming technology in major incident triage training: a pragmatic controlled trial. Resuscitation **81**(9), 1175–1179 (2010)
19. Liou, W.K., Chang, C.Y.: Virtual reality classroom applied to science education. In: 2018 23rd International Scientific-Professional Conference on Information Technology (IT), pp. 1–4. IEEE (2018)
20. López-Fernández, D., Mayor, J., García-Pérez, M., Gordillo, A.: Are virtual reality serious video games more effective than web video games? IEEE Comput. Graphics Appl. **43**(2), 32–42 (2023)
21. Maheu-Cadotte, M.A., et al.: Effectiveness of serious games and impact of design elements on engagement and educational outcomes in healthcare professionals and students: a systematic review and meta-analysis protocol. BMJ Open **8**(3), e019871 (2018)
22. Mazuryk, T., Gervautz, M.: Virtual reality-history, applications, technology and future (1996)
23. Hernández-de Menéndez, M., Vallejo Guevara, A., Morales-Menendez, R.: Virtual reality laboratories: a review of experiences. Int. J. Interact. Des. Manufact. (IJIDeM) **13**, 947–966 (2019)
24. Pflanzl, N., Classe, T., Araujo, R., Vossen, G.: Designing serious games for citizen engagement in public service processes. In: Business Process Management Workshops: BPM 2016 International Workshops, Rio de Janeiro, Brazil, 19 September 2016, Revised Papers 14, pp. 180–191. Springer (2017)
25. Rajaravivarma, R.: A games-based approach for teaching the introductory programming course. ACM SIGCSE Bull. **37**(4), 98–102 (2005)
26. Raya, L., García-Rueda, J.J., López-Fernández, D., Mayor, J.: Virtual reality application for fostering interest in art. IEEE Comput. Graphics Appl. **41**(2), 106–113 (2021)
27. Ryan, M.L.: Narrative as virtual reality 2: revisiting immersion and interactivity in literature and electronic media. JHU Press (2015)

28. Satoła, Ł, Milewska, A.: The concept of a smart village as an innovative way of implementing public tasks in the era of instability on the energy market—examples from Poland. Energies **15**(14), 5175 (2022)
29. Schäfer, A., Holz, J., Leonhardt, T., Schroeder, U., Brauner, P., Ziefle, M.: From boring to scoring-a collaborative serious game for learning and practicing mathematical logic for computer science education. Comput. Sci. Educ. **23**(2), 87–111 (2013)
30. Sundberg, L.: Electronic government: towards e-democracy or democracy at risk? Saf. Sci. **118**, 22–32 (2019)
31. Yu, T.K., Lin, M.L., Liao, Y.K.: Understanding factors influencing information communication technology adoption behavior: the moderators of information literacy and digital skills. Comput. Hum. Behav. **71**, 196–208 (2017)
32. Yu, Z., Lin, X.: Impact of environmental education with VR equipment on learning performance and environmental identity. In: Cyber Security Intelligence and Analytics: Proceedings of the 2020 International Conference on Cyber Security Intelligence and Analytics (CSIA 2020), Volume 2, pp. 3–9. Springer (2020)
33. Zou, D., Huang, Y., Xie, H.: Digital game-based vocabulary learning: where are we and where are we going? Comput. Assist. Lang. Learn. **34**(5–6), 751–777 (2021)

Perceptions and Experiences on Teaching and Learning of a Experimental HCI Course Focusing on Collaborative Practices

Gabriela C. dos Santos[1](✉), Deivid Eive dos S. Silva[2], and Natasha M. C. Valentim[1]

[1] Department of Informatics, UFPR, Federal University of Paraná, Curitiba, PR, Brazil
dessilva@inf.ufpr.br
[2] Federal University of Western Pará, UFOP, Oriximiná, PA, Brazil
{gcsantos,dessilva,natasha}@inf.ufpr.br

Abstract. This article presents an experience report obtained in the course Experimental Human-Computer Interaction, offered to Computer Science and Biomedical Informatics undergraduate students and to graduate students in Informatics at the Federal University of Paraná located in southern Brazil. The course was organized with four Practical Works (PWs), focusing on the planning, execution, and analysis of primary studies and secondary studies. The PWs addressed the planning, execution and presentation of a Systematic Mapping Study (PW1), the planning, execution and presentation of a pilot study (PW2), the quantitative analysis of a primary study (PW3), and the qualitative analysis of a primary study (PW4). Perceptions of students, assistants, and the teacher were gathered through direct observations. In this sense, it was possible to observe that students faced difficulties in understanding open and axial coding processes in qualitative analysis. Additionally, collaborative work in pairs was a key factor, making the experience more productive and beneficial.

Keywords: Experimental Human-Computer Interaction · Research Education · Practical Works

1 Introduction

Understanding experimental research is crucial for training future researchers and professionals, enabling them to plan, execute, and analyze studies—key components of the scientific discovery process [21]. Experimental studies can be classified as primary, when they empirically investigate specific research questions, or as secondary, when they synthesize and analyze evidence from multiple primary studies addressing the same question [17,21].

C. Meinel et al. (Eds.): CSEDU 2025, CCIS 3148, pp. 353–375, 2027.
https://doi.org/10.1007/978-3-032-39103-2_17

To engage with these types of research, students must not only understand methodological principles but also develop collaborative and reflective practices. In this context, peer collaboration is fundamental for knowledge construction, as it allows students to share experiences, discuss challenges, and develop joint solutions [15]. This exchange enriches the learning process, offering diverse perspectives and fostering an active, engaging educational environment. Such practices are indispensable for preparing professionals to tackle the dynamic and complex challenges of the Human-Computer Interaction (HCI) field.

To empower students to meet these challenges, the Experimental HCI course was offered in the first semester of 2024, for undergraduate and graduate students. Thus, the objective of the Experimental HCI course was to enable students to plan, execute, and analyze primary and secondary studies on Experimental HCI through four Practical Works (PWs). The course methodology involved four PWs, each focusing on a specific stage of the research process: (1) planning, executing, and presenting a Systematic Mapping Study (SMS); (2) planning, executing, and presenting a pilot study; (3) conducting a quantitative analysis of a primary study; and (4) conducting a qualitative analysis of a primary study. Each PW followed a structured sequence of steps with clear instructions and appropriate tools, requiring students to submit detailed reports upon completion. The assignments were completed both individually and in pairs. In this sense, the course was designed to develop students' critical thinking and analytical skills, both of which are fundamental to scientific research.

This article presents the perceptions of students, the assistants, and teacher of the Experimental HCI course regarding the observed and lived experiences. Analysis of the PWs was conducted to identify the difficulties students faced. Difficulties such as understanding the open and axial coding processes were observed in the qualitative analysis. Furthermore, one student who worked in pairs considered the experience more productive, highlighting collaboration as a key factor in making the course more enjoyable. Thus, through this experience report, we hope to contribute by presenting lessons learned and good practices so that other teachers and researchers can make classes more dynamic and promote greater student engagement, contributing to a more meaningful learning of Experimental HCI.

In summary, this work contributes to the field of HCI by enabling students to develop HCI research skills through a practical and collaborative approach, essential for tackling real-world challenges in academia and industry. It also reinforces the importance of educational practices that promote collaboration and active learning through educational tools and resources. This article is an extended and revised version of the paper published at CSEDU 2025 [31].

This paper is structured as follows: Sect. 2 presents related work, Sect. 3 describes the teaching methodology for the course Experimental HCI, Sect. 4 details the results, Sect. 5 discusses the lessons learned, Sect. 6 concludes with final considerations and future directions.

2 Related Works

This section showcases examples of educational initiatives focused on disseminating content and fostering learning through diverse pedagogical approaches, such as constructionism and the flipped classroom. These studies leveraged interactive resources in both in-person and online settings to enrich teaching and learning processes.

Perin et al. (2021) [25] documented their experience using tools to support practical work in an Experimental HCI course. Delivered remotely, this course for undergraduate and postgraduate computing students employed a flipped classroom model, where students accessed content prior to class sessions. A questionnaire gathered student perceptions of the tools, revealing that challenges could be overcome by engaging with support materials, further studying the tools, and interacting with tutors, teachers, and assistants.

Girvan and Savage (2019) [9] presented a constructionist approach to learning experiences within virtual worlds. This study involved 24 postgraduate students in a Technology and Learning course. Over four weeks, students, most of whom lacked prior programming or Second Life platform experience, worked in pairs. This activity was part of a course module designed to integrate theory and practice, including orientation phases, workshops, and an open assessment where students collaborated to create interactive installations in the virtual world. These installations were built on specific platforms with visible spaces to promote collaboration and socialization. Students presented their projects and reflections at the conclusion, highlighting both programming skills acquired and practical application of concepts.

Martinelli and Zaina (2021) [23] introduced an approach based on a virtual flipped classroom for teaching HCI. This approach incorporated elements for both in-class and out-of-class engagement. Thirty-three undergraduate and ten postgraduate HCI students participated. Before class, students independently interacted with HCI course material, focusing on a new unit each week. During class, students attended a synchronous online meeting. After the lesson, they organized into different online rooms to complete practical exercises in small groups. Data was collected twice: first, after the fifth week, using a questionnaire about their experience with various material and activity formats in the classroom, employing the Self-Assessment Manikin (SAM) [19]; and second, through interviews with each group at the end of the course.

Similar to the works by Martinelli and Zaina (2021) [23] and Perin et al. (2021) [25], the methodology used in this study also employs flipped classroom dynamics and support tools to foster active learning. However, it distinguishes itself by focusing on student observations and perceptions across various PWs, ranging from SMSs to primary studies and quantitative analyses. Unlike Girvan and Savage's (2019) [9] approach, which emphasized virtual worlds, this work integrated both virtual and traditional tools, combining in-person experiences with activities conducted outside the classroom. While Martinelli and Zaina (2021) [23] explored the teaching of HCI, our methodology offered students greater flexibility in choosing tools and methods for the experimentation process. This combination of techniques and the careful assessment of each PW reinforce students' technical skills, preparing them to tackle real-world challenges in HCI research with a cohesive and systematic integration of theory and practice.

3 Teaching Methodology for the Course Experimental HCI

The Experimental HCI course has a 60-hour workload, distributed across 30 weekly sessions of four hours each. The course ran from February 28 to August 9, 2024. It is an elective course offered to undergraduate students in the Computer Science and Biomedical Informatics (CS & BI) programs and to graduate students in Informatics and Computer Science at the Federal University of Paraná (UFPR) in Brazil.

The main objective of the Experimental HCI course is to equip students with the skills to plan, execute, and analyze both primary and secondary studies. To assist in achieving the overall objective, four specific objectives were presented: (1) The student should be able to plan and execute a controlled experiment from an HCI perspective; (2) The student should be able to analyze the results of an experiment both quantitatively and qualitatively, using appropriate techniques and tools for this purpose; (3) The student should be able to plan, execute, and analyze a Systematic Literature Review (SLR) or SMS; (4) The student should demonstrate the ability to critically analyze and make decisions informed by theoretical or empirical knowledge

According to the scope of the Experimental HCI course, the main topics covered are: Introduction to Experimental HCI; Controlled Experiments in HCI; Statistical Methods Applied to Experimental HCI; Qualitative Analysis; Quantitative and Qualitative Analysis Tools; SLR and SMS; and Topics in Experimental HCI.

3.1 Readings and Bibliographies

The basic bibliographies are: Lazar et al. (2009) [20], Cairns and Cox [2], Purchase (2012) [27] and Soegaard and Rikke (2017) [32][1]. The supplementary bibliographies for students who were interested in increasing their knowledge on the topics presented in the discipline were: Gergle and Tan (2014) [8], Hornbaek (2011) [12], Da Rocha and Baranauskas (2003) [36], Rogers et al. (2013) [28], Barbosa and Silva (2010) [1], Wazlawick (2009) [37], Wöhlin et al. (2000) [39], Juristo and Moreno [14], and Petersen et al. (2015) [26].

Regarding quantitative analysis, the teacher suggested reading Chaps. 9 and 15 of Field's (2009) book [7], which covers topics such as mean comparisons and nonparametric tests. For additional material on qualitative analysis, the teacher suggested the work of Valentim et al. (2015) [34]. Regarding data analysis and representation, the teacher suggested Chap. 8 of Creswell's (2014) book [6].

[1] https://www.interaction-design.org/.

3.2 Teaching Procedures

The classes followed a lecture-dialogue strategy. This strategy is characterized by the presentation of content with the active participation of students, considering their prior knowledge. The teacher serves as a mediator, allowing students to question, interpret, and discuss the topic of study [11]. Furthermore, the course had four group-based PWs on the topics covered in class. The course was organized with PWs to allow for group discussion and practice of solutions.

Classes were held in person in UFPR classrooms and computer labs. The professor used whiteboards/chalkboards, laptops, and multimedia projectors as support materials. Finally, students were required to register and follow the course through Moodle C3CL[2]. Moodle served as a virtual classroom where the professor provided materials and supplementary reading material. Students could also interact, share assignments, and hold discussions through forums.

3.3 Pratical Works

The course was planned with four PWs (Fig. 1). For each PW completed, the students submitted a report and a presentation. The report detailed all the documentation for the PW development. And the PW presentation consisted of a detailed explanation of all the documentation used for the PW development to the other classmates. Each PW had specific requirements and deliverables, forming the basis for evaluating student outcomes. Undergraduate students were given the flexibility to complete these assignments individually or in pairs, as they preferred.

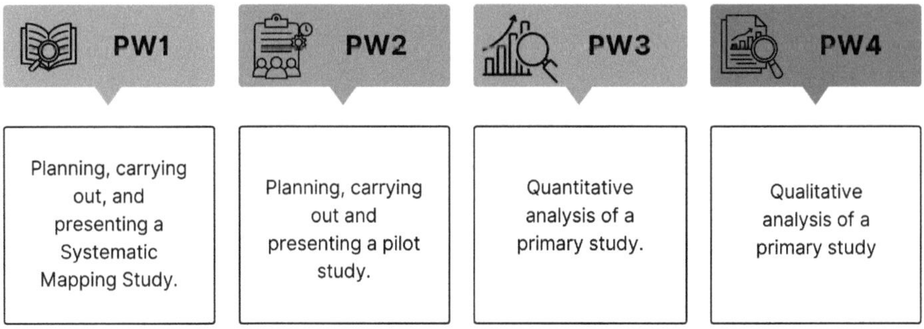

Fig. 1. Context [31].

Pratical Work 1 (PW1). PW1 focused on planning, executing, and presenting a SMS. Students were required to use the Porifera tool[3] [3] (detailed in Subsect.

[2] https://moodle.c3sl.ufpr.br/.
[3] https://porifera.app.br/.

3.4). In which, the teacher presented the tool and also gave the necessary instructions for its use. For the planning phase, the instructor mandated that the SMS protocol meet several key requirements: (1) defining the context and need for the SMS, setting its objective using the Goal-Question-Metric (GQM) approach [16] (Fig. 2), formulating main and secondary research questions, defining the search string, selecting data sources, describing criteria and restrictions for data source selection, justifying publication languages, outlining inclusion criteria (IC) and exclusion criteria (EC) for articles, and detailing the article selection procedures (1st and 2nd filters). For collaboration, students added the instructor as a collaborator in Porifera. They also conducted pilot searches to refine the search string, constantly observing results in digital libraries.

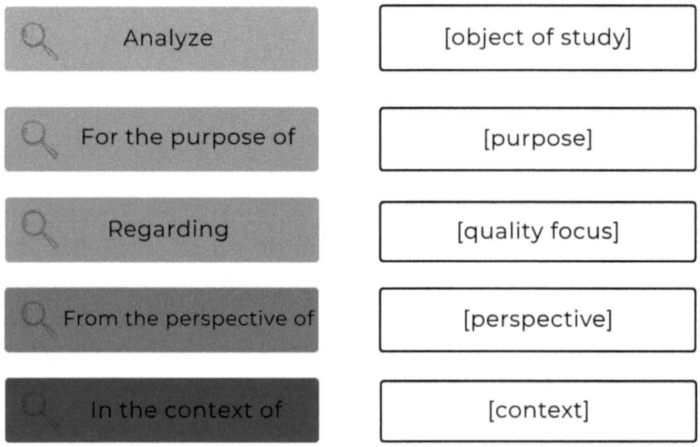

Fig. 2. GQM.

For the execution of the SMS, students had to fulfill several items: altering or adding selection criteria (inclusion and exclusion), defining a data extraction form, choosing one of the digital libraries specified in the protocol, and conducting the search with their defined string. They considered the first 30 articles returned by the digital library, exporting them in Bibtex format for import into Porifera. Students then performed the 1st filter (reading titles and abstracts) of these 30 articles in Porifera, informing the instructor for consensus. Subsequently, they carried out the 2nd filter (full reading) on articles that passed the 1st filter, again informing the instructor for consensus. The report had to describe the information from both the 1st and 2nd filters (Fig. 3), indicating which articles passed or failed and based on which inclusion/exclusion criteria. They also interpreted agreement and reliability indices (Kappa) in Porifera. Finally, they extracted data from at least one article that passed the 2nd filter and described it in their report. For the SMS presentation, students developed and shared slides with their classmates.

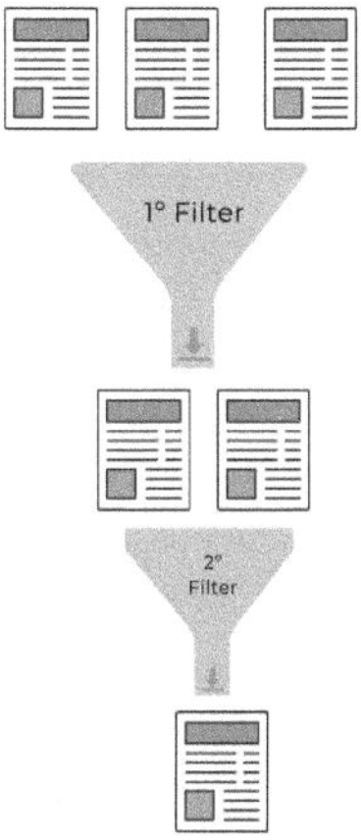

Fig. 3. 1st and 2nd Filters the SMS.

Pratical Work 2 (PW2). PW2 involved planning, executing, and presenting a pilot study. The planning of the pilot study required students to define the study's objective using GQM [16], formulate null and alternative hypotheses, select dependent and/or independent variables (and how they were collected/calculated), specify the study design as either between-group or within-group [21], select participants and the study environment/location, define and prepare instruments, develop instructions, and outline measurement procedures. They also assessed threats to validity. For the execution of the pilot study, each student invited at least two people to participate and carried it out. In their report, they described the personal characteristics and experiences of the pilot participants, detailing the preparation for the pilot, including training and instructions, and explaining how the experimental procedures were conducted. For the pilot study presentation, students developed and shared slides with their classmates.

Pratical Work 3 (PW3). PW3 consisted of a quantitative analysis of a primary study. In this PW, students had to identify a scientific article relevant to their research topic that described a statistical analysis and contained quantitative data suitable for reproduction. They were then required to study the statistical tests from the identified article and reproduce them using statistical software like SPSS[4] or R[5] (detailed in Subsect. 3.4). Finally, they developed a report documenting the reproduction of these tests, describing each step performed in the statistical software and presenting the achieved results.

Pratical Work 4 (PW4). PW4 involved developing and presenting a qualitative analysis of a study. Students could choose qualitative data from a study

[4] https://www.ibm.com/br-pt/spss.
[5] https://www.r-project.org/.

related to their research. This could be qualitative data from their own pilot study (PW2) if sufficient data was available, or from a reported study in the literature with accessible raw data. If neither option was available, they could collect qualitative data through an interview, questionnaire, or observation related to their research topic. Next, students had to analyze and code the qualitative data, identifying, naming, and recording recurring content in the complete dataset (open coding). Afterward, they examined their results to find more abstract categories into which the codes (classes of evidence) from the previous stage were grouped (axial coding), and they also identified significant relationships between categories. Students were generally instructed to proceed in the way they found most productive, always maintaining systematicity and rigor in their analysis. Finally, students wrote a report describing (a) the analysis process, (b) the results, and (c) the conclusions drawn from their work. Atlas.ti[6] was suggested software for coding and categorizing the data (detailed in Subsect. 3.4). For the qualitative analysis presentation, students developed and shared slides with their classmates.

In addition to these assignments, students were responsible for further readings and presentations. To ensure everyone was engaged and ready to participate actively in discussions, a drawing was held in each class to determine the presenter, excluding students who had already presented from subsequent draws. This format encouraged students to read beforehand and be prepared to discuss the content, fostering mutual understanding and collaborative learning—fundamental aspects of the flipped classroom's success. Each student had between 20 and 30 min for their presentation.

3.4 Suggested Tools for PWs

To facilitate PW1, students were instructed to utilize the Porifera[7] tool [3]. This tool is designed for researchers conducting SMS or Systematic Literature Reviews (SLR). Campos et al. (2022) [3] highlight several advantages of Porifera, including its capability to calculate the Kappa coefficient [5]. Kappa is a Concordance Test that evaluates interobserver or intraobserver reliability (reproducibility) for nominal categorical variables [5]. Porifera supports both the planning and execution phases of an SMS. In the planning definition, researchers can specify objectives, search strategies, search sources, and criteria for selecting primary studies. For objectives, the tool suggests using the GQM approach, along with defining the main research question. Regarding search strategies, it recommends employing PICOC (Population, Intervention, Comparison, Outcome, and Context) to aid in forming the search string. The tool also allows users to add the digital libraries intended for use as research sources. Finally, it supports adding and consulting inclusion and exclusion criteria, which are crucial during the article selection process. Campos et al. (2022) [3] recommend using the Bibtex format for importing digital library files into Porifera. A notable advantage

[6] https://atlasti.com/.

[7] https://porifera.app.br/.

during import is that the tool flags records with incomplete data, prompting users to check and adjust them if necessary. The SMS execution is based on the imported files, essentially the list of publications. Article selection is organized into two phases, labeled "First" and "Second" filter within the tool. Researchers select a criterion and can optionally add a comment on their evaluation. When there's agreement between evaluations, the tool prompts for confirmation. If disagreement arises, the tool highlights it, making it clear that researchers need to discuss and reach a consensus. The authors also ensured that researchers cannot view other researchers' reviews before conducting their own, a distinguishing feature that allows for stability and independent evaluations from each researcher. Throughout the selection process, Porifera displays a dashboard to track information about each phase, including the concordance index and reliability index, as shown in Fig. 4.

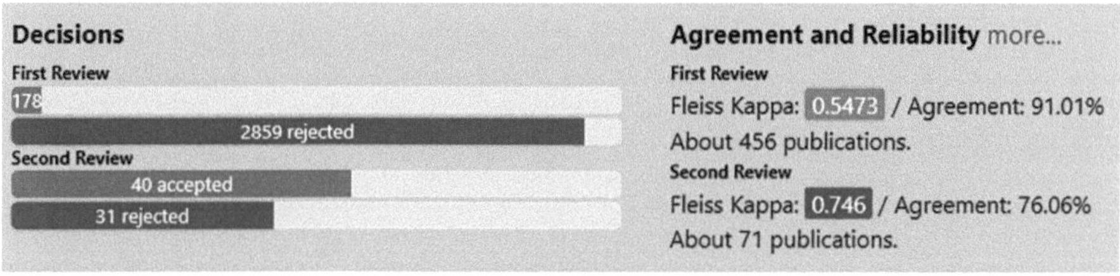

Fig. 4. Porifera software [31].

For PW3, two statistical software tools were suggested for conducting statistical tests: SPSS[8] and/or R[9]. The Statistical Package for the Social Sciences (SPSS) is a statistical software program that enables data analysis, graph and report creation, and various statistical tests. One of its advantages is the ability to import and export data from other programs and merge files with different subjects and variables. Developed in the 1960s and currently maintained by IBM as IBM SPSS Statistics [35], its disadvantage is that it can be challenging for beginners, requiring computer skills for full management [35]. An example of its interface is shown in Fig. 5.

The R software is a free software environment for statistical computing and graphics (Fig. 6) [4]. A key distinguishing feature is its ability to compile and run on various platforms, including UNIX, Windows, and MacOS. R supports a wide array of statistical techniques such as linear and non-linear modeling, classical statistical tests, time series analysis, classification, clustering, and graphics, and is highly extensible [4]. An advantage of using R is the ease with which it produces high-quality, publication-ready graphics, including mathematical symbols and formulas when needed [4].

[8] https://www.ibm.com/br-pt/products/spss.
[9] https://www.r-project.org/.

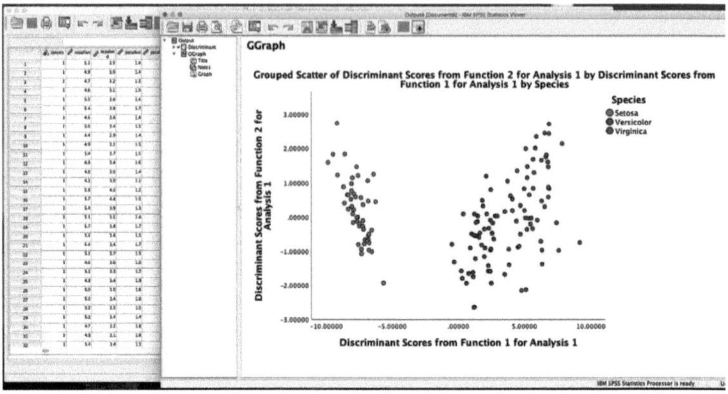

Fig. 5. SPSS software [13].

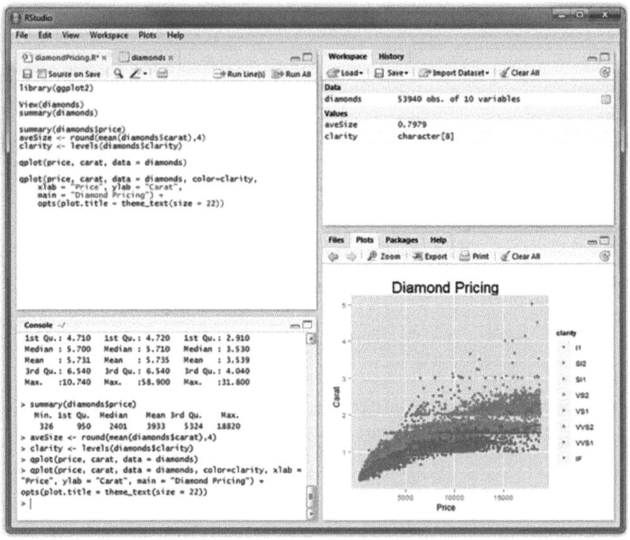

Fig. 6. R software [31].

Finally, for PW4, the Atlas.ti tool[10] was suggested (Fig. 7). Atlas.ti is a qualitative data analysis software capable of searching and analyzing rich textual, graphic, audio, and video data. It helps organize and manage data systematically and creatively, optimizing the analytical process. Among Atlas.ti's distinct features are its advanced coding, multimedia analysis, visualization, and real-time collaboration capabilities.

[10] https://atlasti.com/.

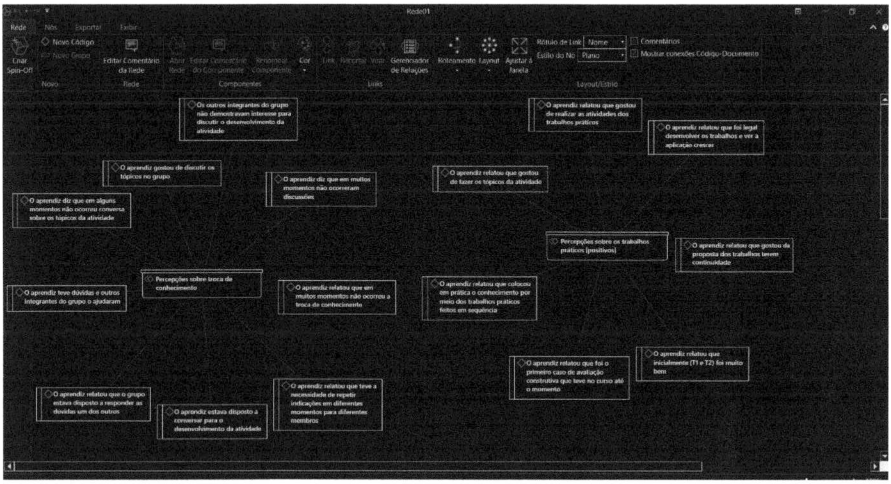

Fig. 7. Atlas.ti software Version 9 (in Portuguese).

4 Results: Perceptions and Measures Taken

This section introduce the participants in the Experimental HCI course. It also discuss the students' comprehension difficulties during the PWs, the completeness and progress of each student and work pair, and finally, a quantitative analysis of the topics covered in each PW.

4.1 Population

Our study analyzed the perceptions of students, teaching assistants, and the instructor involved in the TExperimental HCI course. This course, offered at the Federal University of Paraná (UFPR), included five undergraduate students from UFPR and one external student. Additionally, two PhD students in Computer Science from UFPR's Postgraduate Program in Informatics served as teaching assistants (Fig. 8).

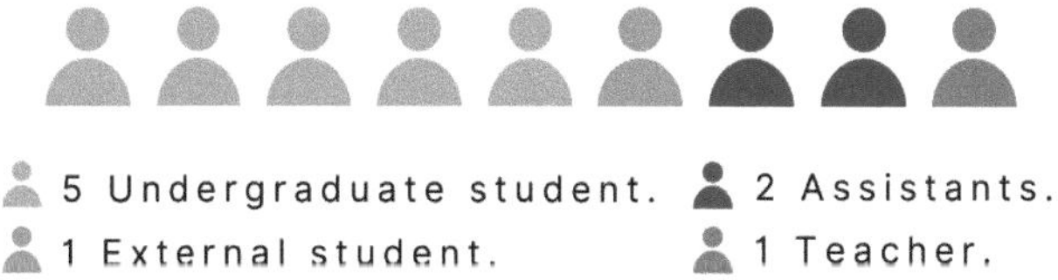

Fig. 8. Population and sample.

4.2 Main Difficulties of Understanding

As for the main difficulties observed during the development of the PWs (Fig. 9), it's important to highlight that in PW1, students faced challenges in using the GQM method, particularly with the phrase "for the purpose of". To address this, the teacher provided in-class examples to help clarify their understanding and reinforce the correct application of GQM. Another difficulty arose when students were required to use the PICOC framework to develop the search string. To assist, the teacher used the students' own topics to demonstrate how to formulate a proper search string, familiarizing them with the PICOC approach and its relevance.

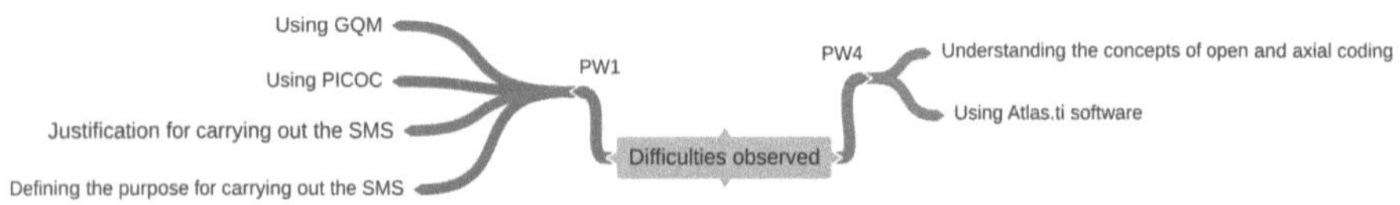

Fig. 9. Main difficulties of understanding.

Additionally, some students struggled with understanding the purpose of conducting a SMS and the justification for its importance. To help address this, the teacher introduced relevant article examples, guiding students to reflect on the significance of the SMS in the context of their research topics. In PW4, the main difficulties were associated with the qualitative analysis process. During the presentation on qualitative coding, some students had trouble grasping the concepts of open and axial coding. To aid comprehension, the teacher conducted a hands-on coding exercise on the whiteboard, encouraging all students to participate. This interactive approach helped improve their understanding of the coding process.

Another difficulty reported by students was in using the suggested tool for qualitative analysis, Atlas.ti. One student had trouble finding the option for axial coding within the software, resorting to alternative methods. For example, another student found it easier to use spreadsheets for both open and axial coding instead of Atlas.ti, as they felt more comfortable with this approach. These challenges underscore the importance of offering additional practice, demonstrations, and flexibility in tool usage to ensure students can effectively engage with the methodologies and tools being taught.

4.3 Completeness and Evolution of the Students in Each PW

We analyzed the completeness and evolution of students across each PW, examining both the pair (PA) and the four individual students (P1, P2, P3, and P4).

In PW1, several items were either missing or incompletely described in the reports. These included: the need for the SMS topic (PA, P2), the study's aim according to the GQM framework (PA, P1, P4), the search string developed with the PICOC framework (PA, P1, P3, P4), the selection of data sources (P1), the justification for choosing these sources (P3, P4), the description of study restrictions (PA, P2, P3, P4), the selection of languages (P2), the selection procedures and criteria (P1, P2, P3, P4), the execution of the pilot study (P1, P2), modifications or additions to selection criteria (P1), defining the data extraction form (PA, P1, P3, P4), running the search with the string (P1), selecting and exporting 30 articles in Bibtex format and importing them into Porifera (P1), running the first filter (P1, P2, P4), running the second filter (P1, P2, P4), interpreting concordance and reliability indices (P1, P3, P4), and extracting an article that passed the second filter (PA, P1, P3, P4).

Moving to PW2, the following items were either incomplete or absent: the study's objective according to the GQM framework (P3, P4), the formulation of null and alternative hypotheses (P3, P4), the selection of dependent and independent variables (P3), how these variables would be collected or calculated (PA, P1), the specification of the study design (P1, P4), the definition of instruments (P1, P3), the assessment of threats to validity (P4), and the description of pilot study participants' personal characteristics (P1). For PW3, all students who undertook this PW completed it fully, though P2 and P4 did not carry out this specific assignment. In PW4, only P1 fully completed the task but did not present their study, while the other students completed it as expected.

These results indicate that in the first two PWs, the student pair failed to complete a few items—six in PW1 and one in PW2. However, for the subsequent PWs, they completed all required tasks. This leads to some conjectures: it's possible the pair faced initial challenges in communication and collaboration, which were addressed during the course, ensuring better performance in later PWs. Another possibility is that the initial PWs (1 and 2) were inherently more complex and demanded more time, contributing to students' struggles. As the number of items increased in each subsequent PW, students may have dedicated more time and effort to ensure completion.

Conversely, analyzing the students who completed the PWs individually reveals they faced more significant challenges in task completion. It was only in PW3 and PW4 that these individual students managed to complete nearly all required items. This suggests that, as undergraduates, individual students might have struggled more due to the heavy workload of the PWs. In contrast, the student pair found it easier to manage the workload and complete most tasks. Therefore, for future iterations of the course, it's recommended that students be encouraged to complete the PWs in pairs, which would likely enhance their ability to manage the workload effectively and complete tasks more efficiently.

Finally, one student from the pair shared their experience, stating: "I found it more productive because when I had doubts, I would ask my partner, and he would either have the answer or help me figure it out. This collaboration made the subject more useful". The student also emphasized the importance of the practices carried out in the course, remarking: "This subject is something that I believe should be mandatory in the program because reading and understanding articles, conducting tests, and understanding statistical and qualitative analysis are essential skills in academia".

4.4 Quantitative Analysis of Practical Works

To plan and execute the SMS (PW1), students followed instructions provided by the course instructor. After developing the SMS research question, students develop subquestions to help answer the main question. Subquestions are important in an SMS because they allow them to identify in detail the current state of the literature on the research topic in question and also guide the researcher in adapting the proposed research based on the body of knowledge [16]. In this sense, Table 1 presents the number of subquestions developed by students. There were variations between five (P1, P2, P3, P4) and six (PA) subquestions per SMS. It is believed that there was no discrepant number of subquestions because it was an SMS developed during a course.

Table 1. List of number of subquestions, EC, IC and total articles returned in the SMS for PW1.

Students	Subquestions of number	Criteria		Total articles returned
		I	E	
PA	6	1	8	35
P1	5	2	3	-
P2	5	1	5	297
P3	5	4	4	31
P4	5	1	3	78

Table 1 also presents the CI and CE by SMS. The number of CI varies between one (PA, P2, P4) and four (P3), and the number of CE varies between three (P1, P4) and eight (PA). CI and CE should be based on the research question. They should be piloted to ensure they can be reliably interpreted and that they classify studies correctly [16]. It is believed that the number of CE was higher than the CI because the students developed specific CIs with a restricted scope, directly influencing the development of the CE.

Furthermore, Table 1 presents the total number of articles returned when applying the search string in the digital libraries. In this sense, there is a variation of 297 articles (P2) and 31 articles (P3). The results demonstrate that the search string for each SMS underwent a process of refinement and testing until this result was reached. This demonstrates the students' and the teacher's concern with encouraging them to search for articles related to the research scope, as well as the concern with removing articles that are not related to the research scope.

Based on these results, the students performed the 1° filter, which consisted of reading the titles and abstracts of the articles and performing the analysis based on the CE and CI. The teacher's guidance for the 1° filter was to read the first 30 articles. However, some students read more than requested (Table 2), such as P3 and P4 with 31 articles and 78 articles, respectively. This additional number of articles applied in the 1° filter, carried out by two students, can demonstrate the importance they gave to this PW.

Table 2. Quantitative listing of the 1st and 2nd SMS Filters for PW1.

Students	1° Filter			Kappa 1°	2° Filter			Kappa 2°
	Analyzed	Accepted	Rejected		Analyzed	Accepted	Rejected	
PA	30	15	15	0.9111	15	3	12	1
P1	-	-	-	-	-	-	-	-
P2	30	13	17	1	13	3	10	1
P3	31	23	8	1	23	19	3	1
P4	78	15	63	-	15	11	4	-

Still regarding the first filter, it was observed that the PA accepted (15) and rejected (15) the same number of articles (Table 2). There is a student, P3, who accepted (23) more articles than he rejected (8). And also, there are students, such as P2 and P4, who rejected (17, 63) more articles than they accepted (13, 15). Some students performed the Kappa index indicating that there was almost perfect agreement with the range of 0.81 to 1.00 [18].

The second filter consisted of reading the entire article, and based on the EC and IC, the students carried out the evaluations (Table 2). In this sense, the majority of students (PA, P2, and P4) rejected (12, 10, and 4) more articles than they accepted (3, 3, and 11). Only P3 accepted (19) more articles than it rejected (3). Furthermore, the Kappa reliability index remained stable, as occurred in the first filter. The results of the second filter showed that the students maintained the same behaviors and responsibilities when continuing with the SMS.

Regarding PW2, the teacher asked the students to define the study goal using GQM (Fig. 2). Table 3 presents the analysis performed on this topic, where the "x" represents the behavior performed by the students. In this case, only PA, P2, and P4 followed the recommendations. The other students (P1 and P3) defined the objective independently. In this scenario, it is believed that the teacher could have reinforced the importance of using GQM to define the objective.

Also for PW2, the students defined the null and alternative hypotheses, variables dependente and independente and the study design. Table 4 presents these results. Lazar et al. (2017) [21] states that an experiment is normally possible if it has at least one null hypothesis and one alternative hypothesis. With a hypothesis defined, it influences the development of the study's dependent and independent variables [21]. The independent variables ranged from one (PA, P1, P3, P4) to two (P2) (Table 4). The dependent variables ranged from one (P4)

Table 3. Goal and GQM Results for PW2.

Students	Goal	GQM
PA	-	x
P1	x	-
P2	-	x
P3	x	-
P4	-	x

to four (P2). The independent variables are generally the treatments or conditions that researchers can control, while dependent variables are generally the outcomes that researchers need to measure [21,24].

Table 4. Hypotheses, Variables and Group Design for PW2.

Students	Hypotheses		Variables		Between group	Within group
	Null	Alternative	Independent	Dependent		
PA	1	1	1	2	-	x
P1	1	1	1	3	x	-
P2	1	1	2	4	-	x
P3	1	1	1	3	x	-
P4	1	1	1	1	-	x

Another request from the professor was to define the study design. Table 4 presents the analysis carried out on this topic, where "x" represents the definition made by the students. P1 and P3 defined the between-group design, where each study participant is exposed to only one condition [21]. PA, P2, and P4 defined the within-group design, where each study participant is exposed to multiple conditions [21]. It is common for experimenters to argue among themselves when deciding which of the two design approaches to adopt in a study. The decision is often difficult because the advantages and disadvantages of the between-group design and the within-group design are exactly opposite [21]. In this sense, each experiment is unique, and the decision must be made on a case-by-case basis, with full consideration of the specific context of the experiment.

For PW2, the students developed the instructions and training to be carried out with the participants in their studies. Table 5 shows that only P2 did not concern herself with the preparation of the participants. Therefore, it is believed that the participants may have been influenced by external factors to carry out the study, since there was no training and preparation for the study. Furthermore, the number of participants in the pilot study varied between two (PA, P3, P4) and eight (P1), as detailed in Table 5. One of the teacher's guidelines was that at least two people participate in the pilot study. It is clear that some students put in more effort and dedication than requested, enriching the pilot study with the participation of more people, such as P1 (8) and P2 (5).

Table 5. Procedures adopted for the execution and number of participants in the pilot study for PW2.

Procedures adopted for the execution of study pilot	PA	P1	P2	P3	P4
Trainings	-	x	-	x	-
Instructions	x	x	-	x	x
Number of participants of study pilot	2	8	5	2	2

For PW2, the students also defined and prepared the instruments to be used in the pilot study. All students used the Informed Consent Form (ICF) and the characterization questionnaire (Table 6). The use of the ICF by all students reaffirms the importance of informing participants that they are voluntarily participating in a pilot study and giving their consent. Furthermore, collecting data on the characterization of pilot study participants emphasizes that participant profiles can influence study results.

Table 6. Instruments defined for the pilot study for PW2.

Instruments	PA	P1	P2	P3	P4
ICF	x	x	x	x	x
Characterization questionnaire	x	x	x	x	x
During-use Questionnaire			x		
Post-Use Questionnaire	x	x	-	x	
Interview	-	-	-	-	x

According to Table 6, the instrument used by P2 was an in-use questionnaire, in which participants had to identify whether the image presented in the questionnaire was developed by human beings or generated by Artificial Intelligence (AI). It is believed that the use of the in-use questionnaire impacted the results of P2's pilot study with important findings, such as 73% of participants having a higher accuracy rate for human-generated images than for AI-generated images.

PA, P1, and P3 used the post-use questionnaire in their pilot studies (Table 6). It is believed to have been the most widely used due to its practicality, ease of data collection, and ability to maintain participant anonymity [30]. Only P4 conducted interviews with the participants. It is believed that P4 chose to use this instrument to obtain specific information about the participants, such as their history with technology and their social context.

For PW3, students selected a study and reproduced the quantitative analysis. Therefore, students received software suggestions to aid in this reproducibility of analysis. However, the students chose to use JASP[11] (PA) and R[12] (P1, P3) (Table 7). JASP is free software for statistical analysis and is familiar to SPSS software [10]. It is believed that due to the students' profiles, they chose to use the software with which they were already familiar.

Table 7. Softwares used for data analysis for PW3.

Students	JASP	R
PA	x	-
P1	-	x
P2	-	-
P3	-	x
P4	-	-

Still on PW3, the students reproduced the statistical tests. Table 8 presents the tests performed, with Analysis of Variance (ANOVA) performed by P1 and P3; Mann-Whitney U and Shapiro-Wilk (SW) tests performed by PA; and Discriminant Function Analysis (DFA) performed by P3. ANOVA is a statistical technique used to compare means of three or more groups. It assesses whether the observed variability between group means is greater than the variability within the groups themselves, indicating whether the differences are statistically significant [33]. The Mann-Whitney U test is a nonparametric test used to compare two independent samples, assessing whether they may have been drawn from the same population [22].

Table 8. Tests reproduced by students in PW3.

Students	ANOVA	Teste U de Mann-Whitney	SW	DFA
PA	-	x	x	-
P1	x	-	-	-
P2	-	-	-	-
P3	x	-	-	x
P4	-	-	-	-

Furthermore, still for PW3, the students reproduced the SW test. The SW test is used to verify whether a data set follows a normal distribution. It is widely

[11] https://jasp-stats.org/.
[12] https://www.r-project.org/.

used in statistical analysis to validate the assumption of data normality, and is a requirement for many parametric tests [29]. DFA is a statistical method used to classify data into predefined groups based on independent variables. It is a powerful technique for predicting group composition and understanding which variables are most effective in distinguishing between groups [38].

For the final PW4, the students conducted a qualitative analysis. Table 9 presents the source of the analyzed data. In this sense, PA, P2, and P3 analyzed data from an open-ended questionnaire. P1 and P4 analyzed data from interviews. The choice between a questionnaire and an interview is crucial for qualitative data collection, depending on the depth and type of information sought. In this sense, it is believed that the students explored the diversity of qualitative research designs.

Table 9. Source of qualitatively analyzed data for PW4.

Students	Interview	Questionnaire
PA	-	x
P1	x	-
P2	-	x
P3	-	x
P4	x	-

In summary, the analysis presented in this section provided a detailed overview of the methodological approaches, instrument choices, and statistical tools adopted by students in each PW. The variations observed in the data and the way students approached the different stages of the PWs offer valuable insights into the learning process and the challenges inherent in empirical HCI research. The next section, "Lessons Learned" (Sect. 5), will delve deeper into these insights, discussing the main conclusions and pedagogical implications derived from these observations and results.

5 Lessons Learned

The analysis of the results obtained throughout the course revealed a set of important lessons about the teaching and learning process in contexts focused on experimental research in HCI.

First, it was observed that completing the PWs in pairs can be improved student performance, especially for undergraduate students. Students who opted for collaborative work showed greater completeness in their submissions, greater consistency throughout the course, and reported a more productive experience. The exchange of knowledge and mutual support contributed to overcoming doubts and completing the proposed activities, indicating that collaboration is a key element for developing investigative skills in this context.

In contrast, students who completed the PWs individually faced more difficulties, especially in the initial PWs. This difference in performance highlights the need to consider paired work as a recommended teaching strategy for courses involving more complex practical and analytical activities. Furthermore, the data indicated that the first PWs —especially PW1 and PW2— had a higher incidence of incomplete or missing items, such as the definition of objectives using the GQM approach, the construction of the search string based on the PICOC model, and the description of methodological elements such as hypotheses, variables, and experimental design. These findings suggest that the initial stages of the course require greater pedagogical support from the instructor, with more detailed instructions, applied examples, and opportunities for formative feedback.

Another relevant aspect concerns the use of the tools recommended for conducting the PWs. Although the course suggested the use of specific software such as Porifera, Atlas.ti, SPSS, and R, not all students were able to use them easily. Some opted for alternative solutions, such as spreadsheets for qualitative analysis, highlighting the need for flexibility in the tools used, as long as the methodological procedures were properly followed. This flexibility proved beneficial in ensuring the continuity of analyses, respecting students' varying levels of technological familiarity and prioritizing conceptual understanding of the methods.

The implementation of PW4, focused on qualitative analysis, highlighted the importance of demonstrative approaches in teaching analytical techniques. During this work, many students reported difficulty understanding the open and axial coding processes. In this sense, the adoption of a practical strategy—with demonstrations on the board and exercises conducted in class—proved effective in promoting understanding of concepts and guiding the appropriate application of the analytical steps. Such strategies reinforce the importance of active and interactive methodologies in teaching abstract or less familiar content.

Finally, it was observed that, throughout the course, students showed progressive improvement in terms of autonomy and content appropriation. While the first PWs revealed methodological gaps and difficulties in performing tasks, the final PWs revealed greater initiative, a diversification of instruments, and the use of different statistical and qualitative techniques. This training path suggests that the gradual organization of activities—beginning with more structured tasks and progressing to more open-ended proposals—favors student development and the consolidation of skills essential to HCI research. Thus, the lessons learned from this experience can inform future offerings of the course, contributing to the improvement of research methods teaching in the field of HCI.

6 Final Considerations and Future Work

The main objective of the Experimental HCI course was to prepare students to conduct primary and secondary studies through practical activities involving the planning, execution, and analysis of empirical research. Based on the analysis of the four PWs developed throughout the course, it was possible to identify recurring challenges faced by students, as well as significant advances in their training.

The results indicated that students experienced initial difficulties in tasks such as defining research objectives using the GQM approach, formulating search strings based on the PICOC model, and conducting qualitative analyses with open and axial coding. These difficulties were overcome, in part, through specific pedagogical interventions, such as practical classroom demonstrations, interactive activities, and guided discussions. These strategies proved effective in promoting conceptual understanding and encouraging the appropriate application of research methods.

The lessons learned throughout the process highlight the relevance of collaborative work, especially for undergraduate students, as a way to enhance learning, distribute analytical effort, and foster knowledge exchange. The importance of offering flexibility in the choice of technological tools used was also highlighted, allowing students to opt for more accessible approaches, as long as they maintain the methodological quality of the analyses. A gradual increase in student autonomy was also observed throughout the course, reflected in the greater completeness of the final PWs, the diversification of instruments, and the use of different analytical techniques. This development points to the effectiveness of a pedagogical organization that begins with more structured activities and evolves into more open-ended and personalized challenges, respecting the learning pace and encouraging the development of scientific skills.

However, this study has some limitations that should be considered. The sample analyzed was small, consisting of a small number of students in a single offering of the course, which limits the generalizability of the results. Furthermore, student perceptions were obtained indirectly, through observations and analysis of assignments, without the use of specific opinion-gathering instruments such as interviews or structured questionnaires. Finally, the time available for completing the PWs, given the semester-long format of the course, may have impacted the depth of some steps.

As future work, we intend to systematize these lessons into pedagogical guidelines to guide the offering of courses with a practical and investigative focus in the field of HCI. These guidelines may include recommendations on teaching strategies, tool integration, encouraging collaboration, and gradual structuring of activities, contributing to the improvement of research methods teaching in undergraduate and graduate Computer Science programs. Furthermore, it is recommended that new studies be carried out with larger groups and specific assessment instruments, in order to deepen the understanding of the impacts of the methodologies adopted in the training of students in experimental research in HCI.

Acknowledgements. We would like to thank the Coordination for the Improvement of Higher Education Personnel (CAPES) - Academic Excellence Program (PROEX) and the Center for Scientific Computing and Free Software (C3SL). The Gemini Artificial Intelligence tool was used for the spelling review of the article.

References

1. Barbosa, S., Silva, B.: Interação humano-computador, Elsevier (2010)
2. Cairns, P., Cox, A.L.: Research Methods for Human-Computer Interaction, vol. 10. Cambridge University Press, Cambridge (2008)
3. Campos, T., Damasceno, E., Valentim, N.M.: Proposta e avaliação de um si colaborativo para apoio a revisões sistemáticas e estudos de mapeamento, Anais do XVIII Simpósio Brasileiro de Sistemas de Informação (SBSI) (2022)
4. Chambers, J.M.: Software for Data Analysis: Programming with R, Springer (2008)
5. Cohen, J.: A coefficient of agreement for nominal scales. Educ. Psychol. Measur. **20**(1), 37–46 (1960)
6. Creswell, J.W.: Investigação Qualitativa e Projeto de Pesquisa-: Escolhendo entre Cinco Abordagens. Penso Editora, (2014)
7. Field, A.: Discovering statistics using SPSS: Book plus code for E version of text, vol. 896. SAGE Publications Limited London, UK (2009)
8. Gergle, D., Tan, D.S.: Experimental research in HCI. In: Ways of Knowing in HCI, pp. 191–227. Springer (2014)
9. Girvan, C., Savage, T.: Virtual worlds: a new environment for constructionist learning. Comput. Hum. Behav. **99**, 396–414 (2019)
10. Han, H., Dawson, K.J.: Jasp (software). PsyArXiv, (2020)
11. Hartmann, A.C., Maronn, T.G., Santos, E.G.: A importância da aula expositiva dialogada no ensino de ciências e biologia. II Encontro de Debates sobre Trabalho, Educação e Currículo Integrado **1**(1) (2019)
12. Hornbæk, K.: Some whys and hows of experiments in human-computer interaction. Found. Trends® Hum.-Comput. Interact **5**(4), 299–373 (2011)
13. IBM: Software de análise estática - spss statistics. https://www.directindustry.com/pt/prod/ibm/product-15019-921417.html
14. Juristo, N., Moreno, A.M.: Basics of Software Engineering Experimentation. Kluwer, Dordrecht (2001)
15. Kaptelinin, V., Nardi, B.A.: Acting with Technology: Activity Theory and Interaction Design, MIT Press (2009)
16. Kitchenham, B., Charters, S.: Guidelines for performing systematic literature reviews in software engineering. Citeseer, (2007)
17. Kitchenham, B., Madeyski, L., Budgen, D.: Segress: software engineering guidelines for reporting secondary studies. IEEE Trans. Software Eng. **49**(3), 1273–1298 (2022)
18. Landis, J.R., Koch, G.G.: An application of hierarchical kappa-type statistics in the assessment of majority agreement among multiple observers. Biometrics **363**, 374 (1977)
19. Lang, P.: Behavioral treatment and bio-behavioral assessment: computer applications. In: Technology in Mental Health Care Delivery Systems, pp. 119–137. (1980)
20. Lazar, J., Feng, J.H., Hochheiser, H.: Research Methods in Human-Computer Interaction, Wiley (2009)
21. Lazar, J., Feng, J.H., Hochheiser, H.: Research Methods in Human-Computer Interaction, Morgan Kaufmann (2017)
22. MacFarland, T.W., Yates, J.M.: Mann–whitney u test. In: Introduction to Nonparametric Statistics for the Biological Sciences Using R, pp. 103–132. Springer (2016)
23. Martinelli, S.R., Zaina, L.A.: Learning HCI from a virtual flipped classroom: improving the students' experience in times of covid-19. In: Proceedings of the xx Brazilian Symposium on Human Factors in Computing Systems, pp. 1–11. (2021)

24. Oehlert, G.W.: A first course in design and analysis of experiments. Retrieved from the University Digital Conservancy, (2010)
25. Perin, A., Paim, P., Valentim, N.: Experiência sobre o uso de ferramentas de apoio à pesquisa experimental em uma disciplina de ihc. In: Anais do XXXII Simpósio Brasileiro de Informática na Educação, pp. 1297–1307. SBC, Porto Alegre, RS, Brasil (2021). https://doi.org/10.5753/sbie.2021.218615. https://sol.sbc.org.br/index.php/sbie/article/view/18151
26. Petersen, K., Vakkalanka, S., Kuzniarz, L.: Guidelines for conducting systematic mapping studies in software engineering: an update. Inf. Softw. Technol. **64**, 1–18 (2015)
27. Purchase, H.C.: Experimental Human-Computer Interaction: A Practical Guide with Visual Examples, Cambridge University Press (2012)
28. Rogers, Y., Sharp, H., Preece, J.: Design de interação, 3th edn. Bookman Editora, (2013)
29. Royston, P.: Approximating the shapiro-wilk w-test for non-normality. Stat. Comput. **2**(3), 117–119 (1992)
30. Santos, G., Silva, D., Valentim, N.: Um mapeamento sistemático da literatura sobre iniciativas que avaliam a experiência do aprendiz. In: Anais do XXXIII Simpósio Brasileiro de Informática na Educação, pp. 621–633. SBC, Porto Alegre, RS, Brasil (2022). https://doi.org/10.5753/sbie.2022.224673, https://sol.sbc.org.br/index.php/sbie/article/view/22445
31. dos Santos, G.C., Silva, D., Valentim, N.: Teaching topics in human-computer interaction: a practical experience with a focus on experimental research. In: Proceedings of the 17th International Conference on Computer Supported Education - Volume 2: CSEDU, pp. 776–783. INSTICC, SciTePress (2025). https://doi.org/10.5220/0013340300003932
32. Soegaard, M., Dam, R.F.: The encyclopedia of human-computer interaction. The Encyclopedia of Human-Computer Interaction (2017). https://www.interaction-design.org/
33. St, L., Wold, S., et al.: Analysis of variance (anova). Chemom. Intell. Lab. Syst. **6**(4), 259–272 (1989)
34. Valentim, N.M.C., Conte, T., da Silva Estácio, B.J., Prikladnicki, R.: How do software engineers apply an early usability inspection technique? A qualitative study. In: SEKE, pp. 686–691 (2015)
35. Verma, J.P.: Data Analysis in Management with SPSS Software, Springer (2012)
36. Vieira, H., Baranauskas, M.C.C.: Design e avaliação de interfaces humanocomputador. Unicamp, Campinas (2003)
37. Wazlawick, R.S.: Metodologia de pesquisa para ciência da computação, vol. 2. Elsevier, Rio de Janeiro (2009)
38. White, J.W., Ruttenberg, B.I.: Discriminant function analysis in marine ecology: some oversights and their solutions. Mar. Ecol. Prog. Ser. **329**, 301–305 (2007)
39. Wohlin, C., Runeson, P., Höst, M., Ohlsson, M.C., Regnell, B., Wesslén, A.: Experimentation in Software Engineering, vol. 236, Springer (2012)

A Shift in Mindset? Assessing the Impact of a Computer Science Program on Primary School Teachers

Marina Unterweger(✉), Corinna Hörmann, Lisa Kuka, and Barbara Sabitzer

Department of STEM Education, Johannes Kepler University, Altenberger Straße 68, 4040 Linz, Austria
{marina.unterweger,corinna.hoermann,lisa.kuka,barbara.sabitzer}@jku.at

Abstract. This study explores the impact of the "COOL CS Circus", an innovative Computer Science outreach initiative developed in Austria, on primary school teachers' perceptions of computer science (CS) and their readiness to incorporate CS content into classroom instruction. In response to widespread concerns about a lack of teacher preparedness, persistent gender stereotypes, and limited early exposure to CS, the program employed creative, unplugged activities to introduce foundational CS concepts in an engaging format. A total of 202 teachers who participated in the program completed a survey assessing their experiences, perceived effectiveness of the program, changes in mindset, and confidence in implementing CS. Quantitative results revealed overwhelmingly positive responses to the program's clarity, relevance, and student engagement. While prior CS experience correlated with implementation readiness, professional development emerged as a key enabler across all groups. Notably, many teachers reported at least a partial shift in their perception of CS and embraced creative pedagogical approaches, particularly for increasing inclusion and engagement among girls. Qualitative feedback supported these findings and highlighted logistical suggestions for program improvement. The study concludes that informal, immersive learning environments can successfully foster teacher motivation and self-efficacy, thereby contributing to more equitable and effective CS education in primary schools.

Keywords: Computer Science Education · Professional Development · Primary School · Early CS Education · CS Unplugged

1 Introduction

Globally, there is growing recognition that digital education and computer science (CS) must begin at an early age to prepare learners for an increasingly technology-driven world. Introducing computing concepts in primary school not only supports cognitive development, such as logical thinking, creativity, and

C. Meinel et al. (Eds.): CSEDU 2025, CCIS 3148, pp. 376–394, 2027.
https://doi.org/10.1007/978-3-032-39103-2_18

problem-solving, but also plays an important role in preparing the future workforce and reducing educational inequalities [13,24].

This idea fits into a broader discussion about the importance of STEM education (science, technology, engineering, and mathematics). Many researchers point out that early experiences in STEM can spark children's interest and influence their later career choices [25,33,38]. Early contact with STEM subjects is seen as essential for building future motivation and knowledge in these areas, helping to support continued learning and interest later in life [2,6].

However, many students do not have a clear understanding of what a computer scientist does [26,29]. There are still many myths and stereotypes about the CS field [4], which can create wrong ideas and discourage students from becoming interested in it. For this reason, it is important to show CS in a positive and realistic way, especially at a young age [4].

Another strong reason for including CS in early education is the growing lack of skilled workers in STEM and ICT. In 2021, around 9 million people were working as ICT experts in the European Union. The EU has set a goal to increase this number to 20 million by 2030, which would mean about 10% of the total workforce. At the same time, the gender gap remains a problem: only one in five ICT professionals and graduates are women. This lack of diversity can also affect how digital tools are created and used [14].

To solve these problems, schools must make changes. A good starting point is to offer CS education that is open to everyone and that motivates all students, including girls. Some researchers highlight that interesting and well-designed teaching materials can help attract girls to CS [5,22,32]. However, success also depends on the teachers. Many primary school teachers say they do not feel ready to teach CS. Studies show that they often lack subject knowledge, have low confidence, or do not have enough time or access to training [36,40]. Even teachers who are interested in the topic may have difficulty bringing CS into their classrooms without the right support.

To support teachers and help students discover CS in a fun and easy way, the "COOL CS Circus" workshop was developed. It is a creative, unplugged activity for Austrian primary schools that teaches key computing ideas through movement, storytelling, and body-based learning. This playful and inclusive method is designed to make CS less intimidating, easier to understand, and more enjoyable for both students and teachers.

This study looks at how primary teachers experienced the "COOL CS Circus". A total of 202 educators who took part in the workshop answered a survey. The goal was to find out how useful and clear the program was for them, how their students reacted, and how the workshop influenced their views on CS. The study also explored what experience teachers had with CS before the workshop, and whether this affected how ready they felt to teach the content. Finally, the role of professional development (PD) in supporting teachers' readiness was also examined.

The structure of the paper is as follows: Sect. 2 provides an overview of the theoretical background relevant to the study. Section 3 describes the research design and methodology. Section 4 presents the main findings, followed by a discussion of the results and study limitations in Sect. 5. Finally, Sect. 6 concludes the paper with key takeaways and suggestions for the future.

2 Theoretical Framework

2.1 Mindset and Belief Change in Teacher Education

In teacher education, it is important not only to teach content and methods, but also to help teachers change the way they think about teaching and learning. This is especially important in Computer Science (CS), a subject where many stereotypes and misconceptions are still common. For example, many teachers believe that girls are naturally less interested in CS than boys [28,35]. These beliefs can influence how teachers present the subject and who they think will succeed. As a result, such assumptions may limit girls' participation, reduce their confidence, and widen the gender gap in computing [12,27,28] Research shows that gender differences in CS attitudes and participation start early, even in primary school [12,18,35]. These differences are often not based on actual ability, but rather on social expectations and classroom experiences. Teachers, often unintentionally, play a key role in shaping these early experiences and beliefs. One strategy to reduce these gaps is to provide early exposure to CS or STEM through creative, hands-on, and engaging activities. Studies suggest that such interventions can spark interest in computing and help all students, especially girls, see themselves as capable and welcome in technical fields [17, 25,33]. However, for early CS experiences to be truly inclusive and impactful, teachers themselves must first shift their own beliefs about the subject and about who can succeed in it. Therefore, teacher education must go beyond teaching programming or CS content. It must also focus on changing teachers' mindsets and expectations.

The Conceptual Change Theory offers a useful explanation for how this shift can occur. According to Posner et al. [30], people change their beliefs when new experiences create cognitive conflict with existing conceptions. For change to happen, the new ideas must be seen as intelligible (understandable), plausible (believable), and fruitful (useful in practice). In CS teacher training, this conflict can occur when teachers are introduced to learning activities that do not match their original views of computing. For instance, when teachers see that young children can successfully code using storytelling or creative games, or when they see girls engaging enthusiastically with programming tasks, their previous beliefs may be challenged. If the new methods are easy to understand and clearly support learning goals, teachers are more likely to replace their old views with new, more inclusive ones.

In addition to the cognitive and social aspects of belief change, it is also important to consider culture and identity. Teachers may hold unconscious biases about who belongs in computing, and these beliefs often reflect broader societal stereotypes, for example, the persistent idea that boys are more naturally inclined toward CS than girls [28,35]. Such gendered assumptions, even when unintentional, can shape teachers' expectations and influence how they interact with students. Culturally Responsive Pedagogy [15] and Culturally Responsive Computing [34] offer valuable frameworks to help teachers reflect critically on these biases. By becoming more aware of the cultural and gender-based influences on student participation, teachers can begin to question the narrow image of who CS is for. This reflection supports a broader, more inclusive view of computing; one that values diverse interests, talents, and backgrounds. When belief change includes attention to equity and identity, teachers are more likely to adopt inclusive practices that make CS education accessible and engaging for all learners.

2.2 Situated Learning and Informal Professional Growth

Recent research confirms that teacher learning occurs across a spectrum of settings, including formal, non-formal, and informal environments [1]. While formal professional development (PD), such as university coursework or in-service training, continues to play a critical role, informal learning experiences rooted in authentic practice are increasingly recognized as essential for sustained professional growth. These diverse pathways enable teachers to develop pedagogical content knowledge, adapt to new curricular demands, and build confidence in integrating emerging subjects such as computer science [1].

Situated learning theory provides a useful lens for understanding these processes. As Lave and Wenger (1991) argue, learning is not merely the acquisition of abstract knowledge but a social process that occurs through participation in meaningful activities within a community of practice. Teachers engaging in authentic, contextually embedded experiences, such as co-teaching, observing student engagement, or experimenting with new methods, are not passive recipients of knowledge. Instead, they are active participants in a dynamic, identity-shaping learning process. This is especially relevant for subjects like CS, where many educators may lack formal training and benefit from immersive exposure to the discipline in low-stakes, supportive settings [23].

This framework has particular resonance in the context of computer science (CS) education, where teacher familiarity with disciplinary content and pedagogical strategies may be limited. Grover and Pea (2018) argue for the importance of practice-based learning opportunities that demystify CS concepts by situating them in accessible and meaningful contexts [16]. Similarly, Hwang et al. (2023) emphasize the need for professional learning environments that integrate computational thinking into interdisciplinary and culturally relevant pedagogies [20].

Moreover, research shows that socio-demographic characteristics influence how teachers engage with various forms of professional learning, which in turn affects their self-efficacy and job satisfaction [44]. These findings emphasize the need for differentiated, accessible PD models that go beyond traditional formats. Conventional workshops and seminars are often characterized by one-size-fits-all delivery, limited interaction, and a disconnect from day-to-day teaching realities [44]. In contrast, innovative models promote active engagement, collaboration, and relevance by integrating mentoring, coaching, professional learning communities, and teacher-led research [41]. Such approaches support teachers in contextualizing new knowledge and transferring it effectively into their classroom practice.

Altogether, the integration of situated learning theory with recent empirical findings points toward a multidimensional understanding of teacher development. Informal, immersive, and socially grounded learning opportunities, particularly those embedded in authentic practice, can complement and, in some cases, surpass formal PD in fostering deep, lasting professional change.

The COOL CS Circus exemplifies such an innovative approach to teacher learning, offering educators an immersive, low-stakes environment in which to encounter CS not as abstract content but as a socially embedded, performative, and embodied teaching practice. Unlike conventional PD models that often emphasize transmissive learning through lectures and isolated workshops, the CS Circus creates space for teachers to engage informally, yet meaningfully, with new content and pedagogical methods.

Crucially, the CS Circus unfolded outside the habitual constraints of school routines and curricular pressures, fostering what can be termed an "informal professional learning space". Here, teachers could explore new subject matter, observe student engagement in real time, and critically reflect on pedagogical strategies without the performative burden of being formally evaluated. This mirrors the call by Grover et al. (2018) and Hwang et al. (2023) for professional development in computer science education that is embedded in authentic teaching experiences, rather than abstracted from practice.

Furthermore, the embodied and creative nature of the workshop, featuring dance, storytelling, and tactile exploration, supports a broader understanding of what it means to "teach computer science". CS was presented not as a rigid discipline but as a living, interactive domain accessible to all learners. This reframing enabled teachers to witness firsthand how interdisciplinary and affective dimensions of learning (e.g., movement, surprise, play) can enhance both understanding and inclusivity, especially for students traditionally underrepresented in STEM.

Ultimately, the CS Circus functioned as an innovative site of informal professional growth. It allowed teachers to experiment with novel instructional ideas, reflect on their own assumptions about CS, and develop new pedagogical dispositions, without requiring formal certification, top-down mandates, or extended release from teaching duties. As such, it offers a compelling model for future PD initiatives that aim to combine subject-specific knowledge, creativity, and equity-oriented practice through immersive and contextualized learning environments.

2.3 Motivation and Implementation Readiness

Teachers' motivation and readiness to adopt computer science (CS) in primary education is shaped by several internal and external factors [21,37]. To better understand these dynamics, two complementary theoretical frameworks are particularly useful: Expectancy-Value Theory [43] and the Technology Acceptance

Model (TAM) [11]. Expectancy-Value Theory explains motivation as the result of individuals' beliefs about their ability to succeed (expectancy) and the importance they place on the task (value). TAM extends this by highlighting two key factors that influence user acceptance of technology: perceived usefulness and perceived ease of use. When teachers believe they can successfully teach CS and see it as a valuable part of the curriculum, their willingness to engage increases significantly [37].

In addition to theoretical models, individual teacher characteristics play a substantial role in determining motivation and readiness for innovation. Intrinsic motivation, such as a teacher's curiosity, autonomy, and desire for professional growth, often drives the willingness to explore new content areas like CS [7,10]. When educators perceive opportunities for meaningful learning and professional development, they are more likely to actively engage with new instructional practices. Self-efficacy [3], or the belief in one's ability to master and apply unfamiliar content or pedagogical approaches, is another critical factor. Teachers with higher self-efficacy are more likely to experiment with new methods and persist through challenges [10,45]. Furthermore, job engagement, teachers' emotional and cognitive involvement in their profession, also influences their openness to innovation [10,19]. Teachers who are engaged tend to be more resilient, proactive, and receptive to pedagogical shifts, making them prime candidates for adopting new content like computer science.

These motivational and personal factors are particularly relevant when examining the impact of the "COOL CS Circus". By observing and participating in innovative, age-appropriate learning experiences, teachers increase their expectancy of success and they begin to believe that teaching CS is achievable and rewarding. At the same time, the program highlights the value of CS education by linking core CS concepts to creative problem-solving, logical thinking, and student engagement, aligning with teachers' broader educational goals.

The CS Circus also addresses key components of the Technology Acceptance Model by enhancing both perceived usefulness and ease of use. Through interactive workshops and performances, teachers experience firsthand how CS content can be delivered in a way that is accessible and engaging for young learners. This exposure helps demystify CS topics and provides practical models that teachers can adapt, thereby lowering perceived complexity and boosting confidence in their ability to implement CS in their own classrooms.

Besides internal factors, external factors, such as professional development is another critical aspect influencing readiness. Especially ongoing, high-quality professional development has shown to be crucial for teachers' readiness to integrate new approaches in their classroom [37]. Consistent with these findings, primary school teachers participating in the "COOL CS Circus" program reported a pronounced need for ongoing professional development opportunities to support the successful incorporation of computer science education [40]. The CS Circus offers a novel form of situational professional learning by immersing teachers in an innovative instructional setting without the immediate pressure of leading activities themselves. Beyond professional development, additional external factors have been identified as significant contributors to teacher motivation and implementation readiness. A supportive work environment characterized by professional autonomy, constructive feedback, recognition, clear instructional goals, and manageable demands can enhance teacher motivation while minimizing resistance to change [8]. Moreover, positive social dynamics, such as collegial support, peer modeling, and a culture of collaboration and knowledge sharing, further encourage the adoption of new practices [42]. Leadership also plays a central role; school leaders who actively promote innovation and cultivate a collaborative school culture can significantly bolster teachers' willingness and capacity to embrace curricular change [39].

In summary, the CS Circus effectively leverages core motivational drivers; self-efficacy, intrinsic motivation, job engagement, perceived value, and ease of use, grounded in both the Expectancy-Value Theory [43] and the Technology Acceptance Model [11]. By providing teachers with engaging, hands-on experiences and professional exposure in a supportive environment, the program fosters the confidence and commitment necessary to integrate CS meaningfully in primary education.

3 Methods

3.1 Setting

The present study was conducted within the framework of the COOL CS Circus "Clear the Ring for Computer Science" (German: "Manege frei für die Informatik"), an outreach initiative developed by the COOL Lab at Johannes Kepler University Linz (JKU) in Austria within the project "Let IT Dance!" funded by the Austrian Federal Chancellery (German: Bundeskanzleramt) [40]. The COOL Lab is a dedicated teaching and learning environment focused on computer science, computational thinking, and digital education, addressing learners of all ages, including primary and secondary students, as well as (prospective) teachers. The CS Circus was specifically designed for primary school children and teachers, with the goal of introducing fundamental CS concepts through creative, playful, and engaging activities.

Fig. 1. Circus Show.

The CS Circus premiered in March 2022 and has since become a regular part of the "Linz Aktion", a city-wide campaign that allows fourth-grade pupils to explore Linz's cultural and educational institutions over the course of one or two days. As part of this campaign, the CS Circus takes place three times a week from February to June, though the start was delayed to March in 2022 due to pandemic restrictions. Events are hosted at the Circus of Knowledge, Johannes Kepler University's dedicated event venue, or in lecture rooms on campus. The program is offered in two formats: a circus show with performative and interactive elements (see Fig. 1), and a station-based workshop (see Fig. 2), which enables more direct student participation through hands-on activities [31].

Fig. 2. Station-based Workshop.

Both formats of the CS Circus are structured to deliver core CS topics such as algorithms, programming logic, coding, and encryption [31]. The content is tailored to be age-appropriate and accessible to young learners, often incorporating movement, storytelling, and visual performance to ensure engagement and comprehension. The program also serves a dual purpose of teacher education, allowing educators to experience innovative approaches to teaching CS within a live learning environment.

3.2 Research Design

This study was conducted during the 2022 and 2023 iterations of the "Linz Aktion", with the objective of exploring how participation in an CS outreach program influences primary school teachers' perceptions of CS and their willingness to implement related content in their classrooms. In addition to investigating teachers' knowledge and confidence, the study also examines how professional training and prior experience relate to teaching readiness. Five research questions guided the study:

1. How do primary teachers evaluate the informativeness, comprehensibility, and reception of the program by themselves and their students?
2. To what extent did the program influence teachers' perceptions of CS?

3. What prior knowledge and teaching experience did teachers have with CS concepts, and how does this correlate with their readiness to implement these topics?
4. What role do professional training opportunities play in teachers' willingness to include CS in the classroom and how can the circus program be improved?

To answer these questions, a paper-based questionnaire was administered, employing a mixed-methods design that combined quantitative and qualitative data. The quantitative section consisted of dichotomous (yes/no) items and 5-point Likert-scale items, allowing teachers to express varying degrees of agreement with specific statements. The Likert items were coded numerically from 1 ("does not apply") to 5 ("completely applies"). The survey also included optional open-ended questions to gather qualitative feedback on barriers to implementation and suggestions for improving the program.

The instrument was developed in German and later translated into English for the purposes of this paper. Participants completed the questionnaire anonymously, using a unique alphanumeric code for identification. This paper analyzes only the subset of survey items that directly address the research questions related to the circus workshop and its impact. The remaining sections of the questionnaire focused on broader topics such as the current state of digital education and computer science in primary schools, teachers' implementation practices, perceived barriers or relevant content areas. These findings have already been published in a separate article [40]. Additionally, preliminary results based on approximately 30 responses collected during the first month of data collection in 2022 have been published previously and served as a foundation for the more comprehensive analysis presented here [31].

Quantitative data were analyzed using IBM SPSS Statistics, version 23. Descriptive statistics (means, standard deviations, and frequencies) were calculated for all Likert-scale items. Spearman's rank correlation coefficient was used to examine relationships between variables, particularly where data were ordinal or not normally distributed.

Qualitative responses to the open-ended question were analyzed thematically using the method of Braun and Clarke [9]. Initial open coding was followed by the grouping of similar codes into broader categories to identify common themes and patterns related to teachers' suggestions and experiences.

3.3 Sample Description

The sample consisted of 272 primary school teachers who participated in the circus-themed CS workshop "Clear the Ring for Computer Science" at the Lab of the Johannes Kepler University Linz, Austria in the years 2022 and 2023. The workshop was attended collectively by 3,226 children, with each teacher accompanying a group of students. At the end of the program, all teachers were invited to complete the survey. A total of 202 teachers responded, resulting in a response rate of 74.3%.

Among the 202 respondents, 186 identified as female (92.1%), 14 as male (6.9%), and two did not disclose their gender. The teachers reported a wide range of teaching experience, with a mean of 16.03 years and a standard deviation of 11.72 years, indicating a highly diverse sample in terms of career stage.

4 Results

This section presents the findings from the quantitative and qualitative analysis of the teacher survey administered following the "Manege frei für die Informatik" program. The results are structured according to the core areas of interest outlined in the study's research questions, including teachers' evaluations of the program, shifts in perception regarding CS, prior knowledge and experience with CS content, the role of professional development in influencing implementation intentions, as well as considerations for improvement of the workshop.

4.1 Teacher and Student Reception of the Program

To assess how primary school teachers perceived the informativeness, comprehensibility, and overall reception of the program, participants were asked to rate three key statements using a 5-point Likert scale (1 = "does not apply" to 5 = "completely applies"). The items focused on the teachers' personal enjoyment of the workshop, their perception of student response, and the clarity of the content presented (Fig. 3).

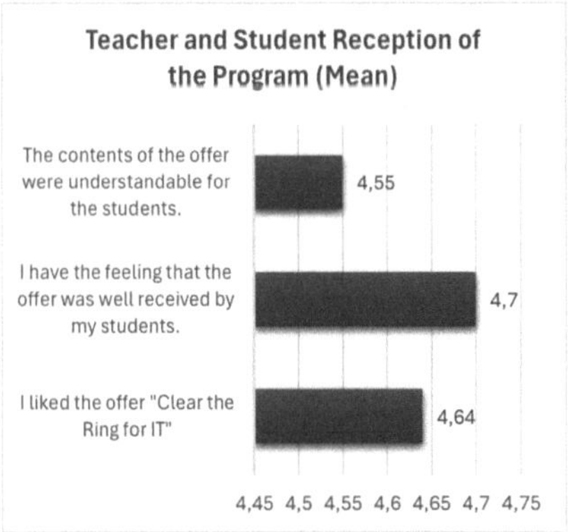

Fig. 3. Mean Score of Teacher and Student Reception of the Program.

The responses revealed a highly positive reception. Of the 202 valid responses, 200 participants provided ratings for the item "Mir hat das Angebot gefallen" ("I liked the offer"), yielding a mean score of M = 4.64 (SD = 0.64) and a median of 5.00, indicating that the overwhelming majority either agreed or strongly agreed with this statement. Similarly, 199 participants responded to the item "Ich habe das Gefühl, dass das Angebot bei meinen Schüler*innen gut angekommen ist" ("I feel that the offer was well received by my students"), with a slightly higher mean of M = 4.70 (SD = 0.58) and the same median of 5.00. These findings suggest that teachers not only found the program personally enjoyable but also perceived it as positively received by their students.

The comprehensibility of the content was also rated very highly. For the statement "Die Inhalte des Angebotes waren für die Schüler*innen verständlich" ("The content was understandable for the students"), the mean was M = 4.55 (SD = 0.66), with a median again of 5.00, based on 200 responses. This consistency across all three items indicates that teachers viewed the workshop as not only engaging and relevant but also appropriately designed in terms of clarity for the primary school audience. The small standard deviations further reflect the homogeneity of positive responses, suggesting a broad consensus among participants regarding the program's quality and accessibility.

4.2 Shifts in Teachers' Perceptions of Computer Science and Attitudes Toward Creative Pedagogy

To evaluate whether participation in the workshop led to a shift in teachers' conceptual understanding of CS, and to assess their openness to interdisciplinary teaching strategies, teachers were asked to rate their agreement with two related statements. The item "Das Bild der Informatik hat sich nach der Vorstellung/nach dem Stationenbetrieb für mich geändert" ("The image of computer science has changed for me after the show/workshop") received a more varied set of responses, with a mean of M = 3.24 (SD = 1.08) and a median of 3.00 (N = 192). This suggests that for a significant portion of participants, the program led to at least a partial shift in how they perceive CS, though the change was not uniform across the sample (Fig. 4).

In contrast, the item addressing interdisciplinary creative methods, "Ich finde es sinnvoll, informatische Inhalte kreativ mit z.B. Bewegung und Tanz zu vermitteln" ("I think it makes sense to teach CS creatively, e.g., with movement and dance"), was rated much more favorably. The mean response was M = 4.18 (SD = 0.83), with a median of 4.00 (N = 201), indicating strong agreement with the pedagogical approach employed in the program.

To further explore the relationship between perception change and attitudes toward creative teaching, a series of Spearman rank correlations were conducted. The results demonstrated significant positive associations between the belief that creative approaches could engage girls in particular and both the valuing of creative teaching ($\rho = .344$, $p < .001$, N = 188) and a reported change in perception of CS ($\rho = .169$, $p = .023$, N = 179). Additionally, there was a moderate positive correlation between perception change and support for creative teaching more broadly ($\rho = .205$, $p = .004$, N = 192).

These findings suggest that participation in the program contributed to a subtle yet meaningful shift in mindset for many teachers. Those who experienced a change in how they view CS were more likely to embrace non-traditional,

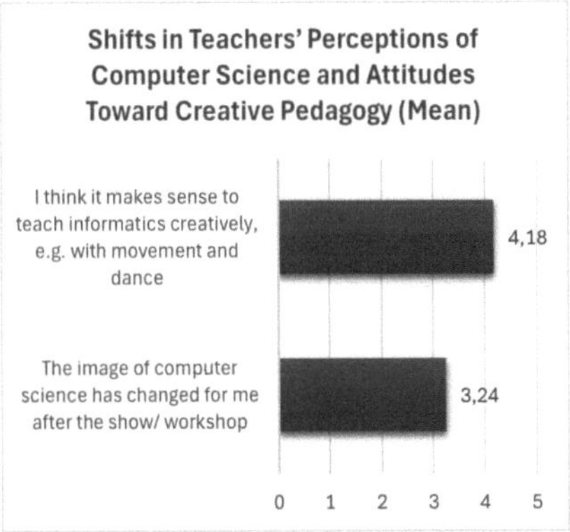

Fig. 4. Mean Score of Teachers' Perceptions of Computer Science and Attitudes Toward Creative Pedagogy.

creative teaching methods, and to see such approaches as particularly valuable for addressing gender imbalances in student engagement.

4.3 The Role of Prior Experience and Knowledge in Implementation Readiness

A key objective of the study was to assess how teachers' prior exposure to CS concepts influenced their perceived ability to implement the content covered in the program in their own classrooms. This was measured through four items assessing familiarity with core concepts, prior integration of such topics into teaching, and perceived readiness to implement the content with and without additional training (Fig. 5).

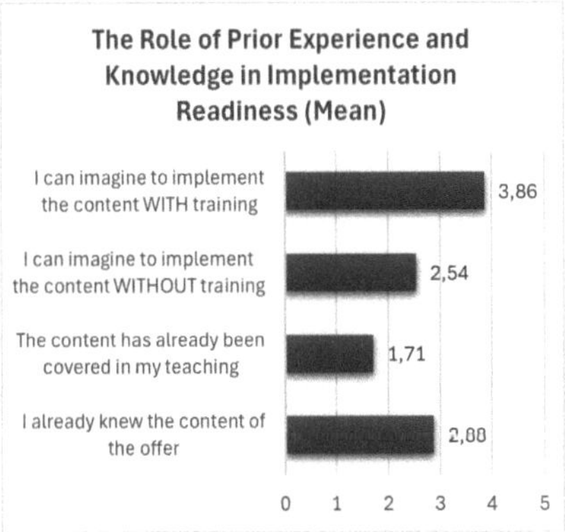

Fig. 5. Mean Score of the Role of Prior Experience and Knowledge in Implementation Readiness.

The statement “Ich kannte die informatischen Konzepte und Inhalte des Angebotes schon vorher” (“I already knew the CS concepts and content of the offer”) received a moderate mean of M = 2.88 (SD = 1.28; N = 199), indicating a relatively even distribution across the scale. However, the extent to which these contents had already been addressed in class was markedly lower. The item “Die Inhalte wurden bereits im Unterricht behandelt” (“The content has already been covered in my teaching”) received a mean of just M = 1.71 (SD = 0.99; N = 195), revealing that for most teachers, the program introduced new or unfamiliar CS concepts.

When asked about their ability to implement the content of the offer without training, teachers reported limited confidence, with a mean of M = 2.54 (SD = 1.13; N = 199). In contrast, the same item with training yielded a much higher mean of M = 3.86 (SD = 1.01; N = 194), indicating that professional development is a crucial factor in teacher readiness.

To explore these relationships more precisely, Spearman’s rho correlations were calculated. Prior experience with the CS content covered in the program (i.e., having taught it before) was moderately correlated with willingness to implement the content without training (ρ = .276, $p < .001$, N = 194), as was prior conceptual knowledge (ρ = .360, $p < .001$, N = 197). Even willingness to implement with training showed small but significant correlations with both prior knowledge (ρ = .180, p = .012, N = 192) and prior use (ρ = .161, p = .026, N = 190).

These results clearly indicate that teachers with more prior experience or knowledge of CS felt significantly more confident in their ability to apply the material, especially without additional support. However, even among experienced teachers, willingness increased further when the option of professional development was included.

4.4 The Influence of Training Opportunities and Suggestions for Program Improvement

Given the differences in willingness to implement CS content with and without support, additional analyses were conducted to evaluate how teachers’ self-efficacy, need for professional development, and intentions to integrate CS were interrelated.

Correlational analysis revealed a strong positive association between self-perceived confidence in CS topics (“I feel confident in CS topics such as coding, algorithms, programming, etc.”, “Ich fühle mich in den informatischen Themen wie Codierung, Algorithmen, Programmieren, etc. sicher”) and willingness to implement the content without training (ρ = .416, $p < .001$, N = 191). A similarly strong correlation was found between confidence and general intention to integrate CS into teaching (“I can imagine incorporating CS content in my own lessons”, “Ich kann mir vorstellen, informatische Inhalte im eigenen Unterricht einfließen zu lassen.”) (ρ = .434, $p < .001$, N = 190). Conversely, the perceived need for additional support or training was negatively correlated with readiness to implement without training ($\rho = .216$, $p = .003$, $N = 188$), and also negatively related to confidence ($\rho = .189$, $p = .009$, $N = 191$).

Interestingly, the correlation between need for support and willingness to implement with training was not significant ($\rho = .034$, $p = .647$, $N = 184$), suggesting that the provision of training may override differences in perceived support needs. Teachers generally felt capable of implementing the content if appropriate training were offered, regardless of their current confidence levels.

These findings underscore the critical role of professional development in facilitating the integration of CS into primary school classrooms. While prior experience and confidence certainly influence readiness, structured training significantly increases the willingness to engage with new and potentially complex subject matter.

In addition to the quantitative items, participants were invited to provide suggestions for improving the "Manege frei für die Informatik" program. A total of 51 teachers responded to the open-ended question. Thematic analysis revealed several key areas for improvement. The most frequently mentioned issue was the noise level and spatial layout of the station-based workshop. Teachers reported that the use of a single, large room for multiple stations led to poor acoustics, which hindered children's ability to concentrate and follow instructions. Many recommended conducting the program in separate or larger rooms to reduce distractions.

Another common theme was the desire for clearer explanations of CS concepts, both for students and teachers. Some participants suggested that the term "computer science" and related concepts such as programming should be explicitly introduced at the beginning, possibly with preparatory materials. Several teachers also emphasized the need for more hands-on activities and opportunities for active participation, expressing a preference for the workshop format over the stage-based presentation. Others recommended delivering the program directly in schools, noting that logistical barriers sometimes hinder external excursions.

Despite these suggestions, many responses were explicitly positive, with numerous teachers praising the clarity, organization, and engagement level of the program. Several stated that they had no improvement suggestions, underscoring the program's overall strong reception.

5 Discussion and Limitations

The findings of this study suggest that creative, unplugged programs such as the "COOL CS Circus" can be effective in shifting primary school teachers' perceptions of computer science and increasing their readiness to engage with computing content in the classroom. This is a critical outcome given that many primary educators are reluctant to teach CS due to several challenges such as lack of training, low self-efficacy, and persistent misconceptions about the discipline [36,40].

A key insight from the study is that even brief, informal exposures to computer science, when embedded in enjoyable, low-stakes environments, can generate meaningful pedagogical shifts. The majority of teachers reported that the program was highly engaging for both themselves and their students, and that it delivered age-appropriate content in a clear and accessible way. These responses align with situated learning theory, which posits that learning is most impactful when it occurs in authentic, social, and contextually relevant settings [23]. The CS Circus enabled teachers to engage with computing not through abstract instruction, but through experiential participation. This embodied and performative mode of learning helped demystify computer science and present it as a creative, interdisciplinary domain.

Importantly, the study showed that for a notable portion of participants, the program influenced how they view computer science. While the overall shift in perception was moderate (M = 3.24), teachers who responded positively to creative pedagogical strategies were significantly more likely to report a change in their image of CS. These findings align with conceptual change theory, which states that belief revision is more likely when learners encounter new ideas that are both intelligible and meaningful in context [30]. Participation in the CS Circus may have served this role by introducing a novel, accessible model of teaching computing that contrasted with some teachers' previous understandings, even if those prior views were not explicitly stereotypical or negative.

Another important finding relates to implementation readiness. Teachers with more prior experience in CS felt significantly more confident about integrating it into their classrooms. However, even those without such experience expressed a willingness to engage, especially when professional development (PD) was offered. The sharp increase in reported readiness with PD underscores its indispensable role. These findings are consistent with the Technology Acceptance Model (TAM), which identifies perceived ease of use and perceived usefulness as critical precursors to adoption [11]. The CS Circus successfully boosted both: it made CS feel accessible and relevant while reducing perceived complexity.

The qualitative feedback echoed the overall enthusiasm for the program but also pointed to areas for improvement, including suggestions for better acoustics, more hands-on activities, and clearer explanations of CS concepts. Notably, although teaching materials were provided to participants ahead of the 2023 sessions, almost none reported using them in their classrooms prior to attending the workshop. This points to a gap between intention and practice that may reflect time constraints, confidence issues, or a need for more integrated support.

Several limitations of the study must be acknowledged. First, the reliance on self-reported data introduces the potential for response bias. Second, the study's participants were regionally concentrated in Austria, which may limit generalizability to other educational contexts. Finally, the study did not examine longer-term implementation, which would be important for future research.

While the central objective of the CS Circus was to introduce primary school pupils to computer science in a fun and approachable way, the program also had a valuable impact on teachers. By engaging with the same content and observing how students responded to creative, unplugged activities, many teachers gained new perspectives on how CS can be taught effectively at the primary level. Although not designed as a formal professional development initiative, the experience allowed teachers to build confidence, reflect on their own teaching practices, and consider new possibilities for integrating computer science into their classrooms. This dual impact of sparking student interest while inspiring teacher reflection highlights the broader educational value of well-designed outreach programs that bring innovative content directly into the learning environment.

6 Conclusion

This study examined the influence of the "COOL CS Circus", a creative, unplugged outreach initiative, on primary school teachers' perceptions of computer science and their readiness to teach computing content. While the central aim of the program was to engage young learners and spark their interest in CS, it also served as an informal learning experience for teachers. By observing and participating in the hands-on, embodied activities alongside their students, teachers were able to experience alternative, accessible approaches to introducing computer science at the primary level.

The findings suggest that even short, informal exposure to well-designed CS content can help shift teacher perceptions and increase willingness to engage, particularly when professional development opportunities are available. The program's creative pedagogy and emphasis on playful learning were especially well received, highlighting the value of non-traditional approaches in demystifying CS and supporting inclusivity.

Overall, the dual benefit of student engagement and teacher reflection points to the broader educational potential of outreach programs like the CS Circus. While not a replacement for comprehensive teacher training, such initiatives can complement professional development efforts by fostering interest, lowering entry barriers, and promoting pedagogical experimentation. Future efforts should explore ways to build on these initial impacts through follow-up support, resource integration, and longitudinal research on classroom implementation and student outcomes.

7 Use of AI Services

During the development of this manuscript, AI-assisted tools such as ChatGPT and DeepL were used solely for language polishing, including grammar correction and clarity enhancement, without contributing to original content, data analysis, or core arguments. The authors take full responsibility for the authenticity and scholarly integrity of the work.

References

1. Abakah, E.: Teachers' informal learning: self-initiated and practice-embedded pathways for professional growth. Teach. Teach. Educ. Leadership Professional Dev. **2**, 100017 (2023). https://doi.org/10.1016/j.tatelp.2023.100017
2. Bagiati, A., Yoon, S.Y., Evangelou, D., Ngambeki, I.: Engineering curricula in early education: describing the landscape of open resources. Early Childhood Res. Pract. **12**(2), n2 (2010)
3. Bandura, A.: Self-efficacy in Changing Societies. Cambridge University Press (1997)
4. Beaubouef, T., McDowell, P.: Computer science: student myths and misconceptions. J. Comput. Sci. Coll. **23**(6), 43–48 (2008)
5. Bollin, A., Kesselbacher, M., Mößlacher, C.: Ready for computing science? A closer look at personality, interests and self-concept of girls and boys at secondary level. In: Kori, K., Laanpere, M. (eds.) International Conference on Informatics in Schools: Situation, Evolution, and Perspectives, pp. 107–118. Springer (2020). https://doi.org/10.1007/978-3-030-63212-0_9
6. Bybee, R.W., Fuchs, B.: Preparing the 21st Century Workforce: A New Reform in Science and Technology Education. Wiley (2006)
7. Chen, S., Abd Rani, N.S.: Exploring the impact of teachers' intrinsic motivation on innovative teaching practices: the mediating role of teacher engagement in Beijing colleges and universities. Uniglobal J. Soc. Sci. Humanit. **4**(1), 1–10 (2025)
8. Chen, X., Wu, L., Jia, L., AlGerafi, M.A.: Flow experience and innovative behavior of university teachers: model development and empirical testing. Behav. Sci. **15**(3), 363 (2025)
9. Clarke, V., Braun, V.: Thematic analysis. J. Posit. Psychol. **12**(3), 297–298 (2017)
10. Daud, S.R., et al.: A conceptual framework for the individual factors fostering the innovative work behaviour of stem teachers. Inf. Manage. Bus. Rev. **16**(1), 252–261 (2024)
11. Davis, F.D., et al.: Technology acceptance model. In: Tam. Al-Suqri, M.N, Al-Aufi, A.S (eds.) Information Seeking Behavior and Technology Adoption, vol. 205, no. 219, p. 5 (1989)
12. De Wit, S., Hermans, F., Aivaloglou, E.: Children's implicit and explicit stereotypes on the gender, social skills, and interests of a computer scientist. In: Proceedings of the 17th ACM Conference on International Computing Education Research, pp. 239–251 (2021)
13. El-Hamamsy, L., et al.: How are primary school computer science curricular reforms contributing to equity? Impact on student learning, perception of the discipline, and gender gaps. Int. J. STEM Educ. **10**(1), 60 (2023)
14. European commission: The digital economy and society index (desi) (2022). https://digital-strategy.ec.europa.eu/en/policies/desi
15. Gay, G.: Preparing for culturally responsive teaching. J. Teach. Educ. **53**(2), 106–116 (2002)
16. Grover, S., Pea, R.: Computational thinking: a competency whose time has come. Comput. Sci. Educ. Perspect. Teach. Learn. School **19**(1), 19–38 (2018)
17. Hinterplattner, S.: Students' perceptions of computer science and the role of gender. In: Uhomoibhi, J. (eds.) International Conference on Computer Supported Education, pp. 125–148. Springer (2022). https://doi.org/10.1007/978-3-031-40501-3_6
18. Hinterplattner, S., Rottenhofer, M., Groher, I., Sabitzer, B.: Exploring students' experiences and perceptions of computer science: a survey of Austrian secondary schools. In: CSEDU (2), pp. 238–247 (2022)

19. Hosseini, S., Haghighi Shirazi, Z.R.: Towards teacher innovative work behavior: a conceptual model. Cogent Educ. **8**(1), 1869364 (2021)
20. Hwang, Y., Das, A., Waite, J., Sentance, S.: Using a sociological lens to investigate computing teachers' culturally responsive classroom practices. In: Proceedings of the 2023 ACM Conference on International Computing Education Research-Volume 1, pp. 206–221 (2023). https://doi.org/10.1145/3568813.3600112
21. Inan, F.A., Lowther, D.L.: Laptops in the k-12 classrooms: exploring factors impacting instructional use. Comput. Educ. **55**, 937–944 (2010). https://api.semanticscholar.org/CorpusID:6128487
22. Kröhn, C., Groher, I., Sabitzer, B., Kuka, L.: Female computer scientists needed: approaches for closing the gender gap. In: 2020 IEEE Frontiers in Education Conference (FIE), pp. 1–4 (2020). https://doi.org/10.1109/FIE44824.2020.9273933
23. Lave, J., Wenger, E.: Situated Learning: Legitimate Peripheral Participation. Cambridge University Press, Cambridge, New York (1991)
24. Lee, S.J., Francom, G.M., Nuatomue, J.: Computer science education and k-12 students' computational thinking: a systematic review. Int. J. Educ. Res. **114**, 102008 (2022)
25. Maltese, A.V., Tai, R.H.: Eyeballs in the fridge: sources of early interest in science. Int. J. Sci. Educ. **32**(5), 669–685 (2010)
26. Martin, C.D.: Draw a computer scientist. ACM SIGCSE Bull. **36**(4), 11–12 (2004)
27. Master, A., Cheryan, S., Meltzoff, A.N.: Computing whether she belongs: stereotypes undermine girls' interest and sense of belonging in computer science. J. Educ. Psychol. **108**(3), 424 (2016)
28. Master, A., Meltzoff, A.N., Cheryan, S.: Gender stereotypes about interests start early and cause gender disparities in computer science and engineering. Proc. Natl. Acad. Sci. **118**(48), e2100030118 (2021)
29. Mitchell, A., Purchase, H.C., Hamer, J.: Computing science: what do pupils think? In: Proceedings of the 14th Annual ACM SIGCSE Conference on Innovation and Technology in Computer Science Education, p. 353 (2009)
30. Posner, G.J., Strike, K.A., Hewson, P.W., Gertzog, W.A., et al.: Accommodation of a scientific conception: toward a theory of conceptual change. Sci. Educ. **66**(2), 211–227 (1982)
31. Rottenhofer, M., Kuka, L., Sabitzer, B.: Clear the ring for computer science: a creative introduction for primary schools. In: Bollin, A., Futschek, G. (eds.) International Conference on Informatics in Schools: Situation, Evolution, and Perspectives, pp. 103–112. Springer (2022). https://doi.org/10.1007/978-3-031-15851-3_9
32. Rottenhofer, M., Sabitzer, B., Rankin, T.: Developing computational thinking skills through modeling in language lessons. Open Educ. Stud. **3**(1), 17–25 (2021)
33. Russell, S.H., Hancock, M.P., McCullough, J.: Benefits of undergraduate research experiences. Science **316**(5824), 548–549 (2007)
34. Scott, K.A., Sheridan, K.M., Clark, K.: Culturally responsive computing: a theory revisited. Learn. Media Technol. **40**(4), 412–436 (2015)
35. Spieler, B., Oates-Indruchovà, L., Slany, W.: Female students in computer science education: understanding stereotypes, negative impacts, and positive motivation. J. Women Minorities Sci. Eng. **26**(5) (2020)
36. Stringer, L.R., Lee, K.M., Sturm, S., Giacaman, N.: A systematic review of primary school teachers' experiences with digital technologies curricula. Educ. Inf. Technol. **27**(9), 12585–12607 (2022)
37. Stumbrienė, D., Jevsikova, T., Kontvainė, V.: Key factors influencing teachers' motivation to transfer technology-enabled educational innovation. Educ. Inf. Technol. **29**(2), 1697–1731 (2024)

38. Swift, T.M., Watkins, S.E.: An engineering primer for outreach to K-4 education (2004)
39. Thoonen, E.E., Sleegers, P.J., Oort, F.J., Peetsma, T.T., Geijsel, F.P.: How to improve teaching practices: the role of teacher motivation, organizational factors, and leadership practices. Educ. Adm. Q. **47**(3), 496–536 (2011)
40. Unterweger, M., Hörmann, C., Kuka, L., Sabitzer, B.: The importance of digital and computer science education in primary schools: Perspectives from educators. In: Proceedings of the 17th International Conference on Computer Supported Education - Volume 2: CSEDU, pp. 545–556. INSTICC, SciTePress (2025). https://doi.org/10.5220/0013353100003932
41. Van Veen, K., Zwart, R., Meirink, J.: What makes teacher professional development effective?: A literature review. Teach. Learn. Matters, 3–21 (2012)
42. Vescio, V., Ross, D., Adams, A.: A review of research on the impact of professional learning communities on teaching practice and student learning. Teach. Teach. Educ. **24**(1), 80–91 (2008)
43. Wigfield, A., Eccles, J.S.: Expectancy-value theory of achievement motivation. Contemp. Educ. Psychol. **25**(1), 68–81 (2000)
44. Yoon, S.W., Kim, D.: Socio-demographic patterns in teacher professional development participation: implications for self-efficacy and job satisfaction. Teach. Teach. Educ., **113**, 103664 (2022). https://doi.org/10.1016/j.tate.2021.103664
45. Yu, H., Zhang, J., Zou, R.: A motivational mechanism framework for teachers' online informal learning and innovation during the Covid-19 pandemic. Front. Psychol. **12**, 601200 (2021)

Motivation Without Overload: Adaptive Gamification with gAmIcode for Non-technical Web Development Learners

Patrizia Sailer[1,2](✉), Thomas Kremsner[3], Franz Knipp[1,2], and Fares Kayali[4]

[1] Department Informationtechnology, University of Applied Sciences Burgenland, Campus 1, Eisenstadt, Austria
patrizia.sailer@hochschule-burgenland.at
[2] Doctoral School Computer Sciences, University of Vienna, Waehringerstrasse 29, Vienna, Austria
[3] Energy Transistion, Forschung Burgenland, Campus 1, Eisenstadt, Austria
[4] Centre for Teacher Education, University of Vienna, Porzellangasse 4, Vienna, Austria

Abstract. Gamification is becoming increasingly relevant in higher education as a way of enhancing learner engagement and motivation, particularly in technical subjects, such as web development. However, many existing implementations rely on generic approaches that do not adequately address the diverse needs of learners, which results in limited effectiveness and reduced engagement. This study presents the conception and evaluation of gAmIcode, a gamified learning platform designed to support students from non-technical study programmes. gAmIcode offers adaptive learning paths, motivational elements and a user-friendly interface. Based on the Octalysis Framework and Cognitive Load Theory, gAmIcode ensures the balanced integration of motivational and instructional design principles. A mixed-methods evaluation using eye-tracking, emotion analysis, and standardised user questionnaires was conducted to assess the platform's usability, user experience, and educational impact. The findings emphasise the importance of personalised gamification and highlight the value of combining motivational design with cognitive accessibility in digital learning environments.

Keywords: Web Development Education · Eye-Tracking · Human-Centered-Design · Gamified Learning Platform · Higher Education

C. Meinel et al. (Eds.): CSEDU 2025, CCIS 3148, pp. 395–425, 2027.
https://doi.org/10.1007/978-3-032-39103-2_19

1 Introduction

In higher education, there has been increasing integration of technical subjects into curricula in various disciplines, including business, environmental sciences, healthcare and technology, despite these curricula not being primarily focused on technical training. An example is the integration of web development courses within non-technical degree programmes. Although the interdisciplinary approach has been shown to facilitate the acquisition of significant digital competencies among its students, it has also given rise to a number of notable instructional challenges. It is important to note that students often enter these courses with a wide range of prior knowledge and technical literacy levels, which makes it challenging to deliver instruction that meets the needs of all learners.

Traditional classroom teaching, with its focus on lectures followed by practical exercises, has proven inadequate for addressing the needs of students from diverse backgrounds. In a qualitative study [54], structured interviews were conducted with ten affected part-time students enrolled in a university course on web development in a non-technical study programme. The objective of the study was to explore students' difficulties and learning needs. The results revealed two major implications. Firstly, the adoption of alternative teaching models like the flipped classroom. Secondly, the development of a gamified learning platform offering customised support and motivational features.

In response to the first recommendation, a follow-up study was conducted to compare the traditional classroom approach with the flipped classroom model [55]. The findings of this study demonstrated improvements in students' academic performance and in-class participation. However, motivation levels remained largely unchanged, indicating that restructuring the teaching format alone may not be sufficient to enhance student engagement on a broader level. In order to address the second recommendation, existing digital learning platforms that offer web development content were reviewed systematically based on the requirements identified during the earlier interviews. The analysis indicated that existing platforms were largely unable to satisfy the identified needs [56]. It was found that common issues included a lack of alignment with curriculum content, the absence of essential elements and barriers related to cost or usability. Consequently, the decision was taken to design a new platform that would reflect the needs identified in the initial interviews. The resulting platform, gAmIcode, incorporates interactive exercises, real-time feedback and motivational mechanisms such as challenges, levels and symbolic rewards. The platform design is informed by the Octalysis Framework and the Cognitive Load Theory.

The purpose of this paper is to present the conception and evaluation of the first functional prototype of the gAmIcode platform. The objective of the present study is to investigate the influence of a gamified digital learning platform, developed on the basis of a student-centred needs analysis and motivational design theory, on perceived usability, user experience (UX) and engagement in a web development course for students without a technical background. In order to address this question, a multi-method evaluation approach is employed. This includes both qualitative student feedback and eye-tracking data. The purpose of this is to assess interaction patterns and attention distribution. The findings will contribute to the ongoing discussion on how gamified learning environments can support heterogeneous learners in technical subjects and will provide insight into future iterations of personalised digital tools in support of inclusive and high-quality education in line with Sustainable Development Goal 4 [1].

2 Related Work

2.1 Use of Gamification in Higher Education

Gamification has become an increasingly valuable strategy in higher education, particularly for enhancing student engagement, motivation and the acquisition of complex skills across technical disciplines. The integration of components such as points, badges, leaderboards and adaptive challenges is a hallmark of gamified environments. These environments are designed to personalise the learning process, foster collaboration and enhance academic performance [6,29,45].

In terms of learning impact and pedagogical benefits, research has repeatedly demonstrated that the incorporation of gamification into educational settings results in enhanced outcomes. In the context of computing and IT-related courses, including programming, cloud computing and modelling, the integration of gamified features has been demonstrated to contribute to enhanced pass rates, augmented problem-solving abilities and elevated learner participation. This assertion is supported by research findings [6,29,49]. The implementation of these effects on digital learning platforms such as Moodle has been shown to be conducive to enhancing their impact. The presence of features such as adaptive feedback and progression tracking has been demonstrated to engender learner satisfaction and sustained engagement [9].

When applied to gamified learning platforms, the integration of gamification elements has been demonstrated to enhance motivation and knowledge retention, provided that these elements are designed to facilitate the learning process rather than hinder it. A fundamental challenge confronting lecturers is the necessity to evaluate student progress and to personalise content in a dynamic manner. Adaptive gamification, a pedagogical approach that customises its methodology according to the learner profile, has been shown to be more efficacious than generalised approaches, particularly during periods of remote learning, such as during the global COVID-19 pandemic [17,30,34]. Avatars, progress indicators and leaderboards represent a small sample of the tools available to designers when creating personalised experiences. However, it is important to exercise caution when employing these tools, as excessive complexity can lead to either learner overload or disengagement [31,32,46].

In the specific context of programming courses, the integration of gamification has been demonstrated to have a positive impact on both the reduction of attrition rates and the enhancement of student engagement. This enhancement is achieved through the implementation of meticulously designed games and gaming-based activities. The integration of game elements, such as points and competition, within blended learning environments has been demonstrated to positively influence learner motivation, irrespective of the player type [13,15]. The utilisation of conceptual models for the purpose of gamifying online programming courses has been demonstrated to hold considerable potential in terms of reducing teacher workload and supporting student autonomy [21,51].

The success of gamification is closely tied to the usability and overall UX of the platform. Research has demonstrated the importance of intuitive navigation, adaptive interfaces and emotional design in enhancing user satisfaction and learning outcomes [5,42]. A well-designed platform supports both pragmatic and hedonic qualities, allowing learners to focus on content while experiencing motivation and enjoyment. A range of evaluative techniques, including questionnaires, heuristic inspections and eye-tracking, are increasingly employed to assess cognitive load and engagement [11]. Furthermore, gamification can enhance UX by increasing activity, reducing user error and creating emotionally engaging learning environments [52]. However, it is important to note that these benefits can only be realised if the gamified elements are appropriately aligned with the needs of the learners and seamlessly integrated into a usable interface [38,48]. It has been established that storytelling, user journey mapping and narrative branching are additional strategies that help personalise learning, in addition to supporting learner autonomy and reflection [63].

Nevertheless, gamification in education is not without its challenges. Technical limitations, motivational disparities and issues of thematic relevance can hinder its effectiveness [3,19]. Moreover, ethical considerations must be addressed to avoid performance pressure, social comparison risks, or manipulation through reward systems [7,39].

2.2 Eye Movements and Emotions in Education

The effectiveness of learning platforms can be assessed not only through gamification, but also by analysing eye movements and emotional responses. Eye-tracking studies show that design elements such as colour coding can enhance learning by helping users to quickly identify key elements [43]. To illustrate, the implementation of colour coding can facilitate the learning process, enabling learners to swiftly identify desired elements in comparison to monotonous designs, as evidenced in an eye-tracking study [47]. Furthermore, positive features such as anthropomorphic illustrations and appealing colours attract attention and focus it on relevant content [50]. However, purely decorative elements can distract from the learning material and reduce motivation, although some studies suggest they can have a positive impact [58]. Graphics with instructional value are generally more effective than decorative ones [61]. Reviews of multimedia content show that learners tend to focus on text rather than images and that dynamic visuals are more attention-grabbing than static ones. Individual differences, such as prior knowledge and processing speed, also influence how learners engage with multimedia content [2].

The incorporation of emotional elements in the design of learning platforms is a crucial aspect that merits consideration, as emotions have been demonstrated to exert a significant influence on human decision-making processes that extend beyond the boundaries of rational interpretation. The enhancement of positive emotions during the learning process has been demonstrated to facilitate the maintenance of motivation and to enhance outcomes. This concept is known as emotional design [2,41]. The visual aspects of a learning platform, including layout, colour and overall design, can influence learners' emotions and motivation [23]. Emotional intensity has been demonstrated to correlate with enhanced recall of content [20]. The available evidence indicates that features such as colours, sound effects and human avatars with facial expressions have the potential to induce more positive emotions, with colours having the most significant impact [66]. Specific design choices, such as the use of warm colours and round shapes, have been found to elicit positive emotions, which are associated with improved learning outcomes. In contrast, neutral designs have been shown to result in neutral attitudes [65].

2.3 Research Gap

Despite the findings of earlier studies that have demonstrated the potential of gamification to enhance learning outcomes and student motivation in technical education, its targeted application within the domain of web development in non-technical study programmes in higher education remains underexplored. Web development presents specific pedagogical challenges, including the need to grasp complex, practice-oriented topics such as responsive design, syntax accuracy and real-time debugging. These requirements indicate a necessity for highly interactive and supportive learning environments that extend beyond generic gamified approaches.

Furthermore, an evaluation of existing digital learning platforms in this field has revealed notable limitations [56]. It is observed that numerous platforms are inadequate in providing fundamental features such as personalised feedback mechanisms, adaptive learning pathways and contextualised guidance that is aligned with the specific requirements of each task. These observations highlight a notable absence in the availability of digital tools designed specifically to address the instructional needs of learners in web development. Therefore, it is evident that there is a necessity for the development and empirical evaluation of a gamified digital learning platform that is specifically tailored to the demands of web development education and informed by both pedagogical theory and student-centred design.

3 Theoretical Framework

3.1 Octalysis Framework for Gamified Learning

The application of gamification has evolved beyond the simplistic utilisation of points, badges and leaderboards to encompass a more profound understanding of human motivation. Therefore, the Octalysis Framework for Gamification and Behavioral Design offers a comprehensive model grounded in eight distinct core drives (CD) that aim to explain why individuals are motivated to engage with certain tasks or systems [10]. These CDs are essential for designing meaningful and engaging user experiences and are particularly relevant in the context of digital learning platforms, like shown in Fig. 1.

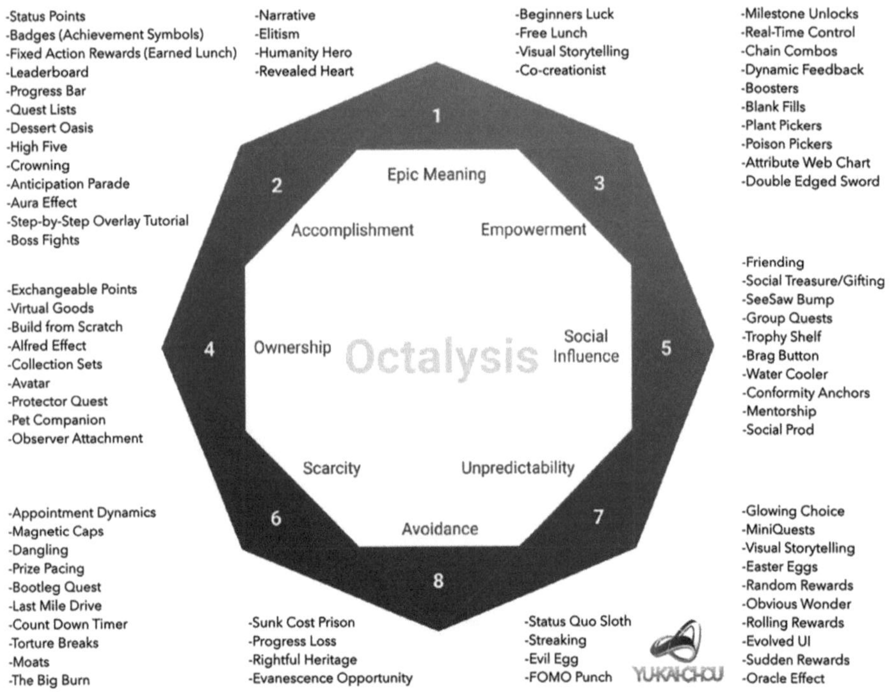

Fig. 1. The Octalysis Framework for Gamified Learning [10].

The Octalysis Framework identifies eight motivational CDs: epic meaning, accomplishment, empowerment, ownership, social influence, scarcity, unpredictability and avoidance. It is important that the purpose of these drives is not to function in isolation, but rather collectively to shape a dynamic and engaging UX. The concept of epic meaning can be addressed through the use of storytelling and learning missions, while accomplishment is supported by progress indicators, badges and levels. The empowerment is encouraged through the implementation of interactive tasks and the provision of timely feedback. Ownership of the learning process is fostered through the creation of customisable profiles and the saving of progress. The concept of social influence includes features like leaderboards and peer interaction, while elements of scarcity and unpredictability are introduced through timed content and surprise elements. Avoidance is theorised to be activated by mechanisms that prevent loss of progress or missed opportunities. In the design of the gAmIcode platform, the Octalysis Framework was systematically applied to map gamification features to these drives. This approach was adopted to ensure that motivational elements were deliberately aligned with learner needs, thereby supporting engagement, participation and sustained involvement with the learning content.

3.2 Cognitive Load Theory and Instructional Design

While gamification frameworks such as Octalysis provide a robust foundation for enhancing learner motivation, effective instructional design must also consider cognitive limitations in the learning process. The Cognitive Load Theory offers a well-established theoretical model that addresses how information is processed in working memory during learning tasks [62]. It is particularly relevant in digital learning environments, where interface design, instructional structure and task complexity can either support or hinder the acquisition of knowledge.

The Cognitive Load Theory differentiates between intrinsic, extraneous and germane cognitive load, with the latter being defined as "the load that is relevant to the task at hand". Intrinsic load arises from the inherent complexity of the learning content and the learner's prior knowledge. This is particularly relevant in tasks that require simultaneous processing, such as coding in web development. Extraneous load arises from suboptimal instructional design and presentation, such as confusing navigation or messy interfaces and should be minimised. Germane load represents the cognitive effort devoted to constructing and automating knowledge structures and it can be enhanced through strategies such as reflection, problem solving and guided practice.

3.3 Implications for Platform Design

The integration of the Octalysis Framework and Cognitive Load Theory provides a comprehensive foundation for designing effective gamified learning environments. The concept of motivational design entails the activation of fundamental drives, such as the pursuit of epic meaning through the medium of storytelling or mission-based tasks, the fulfilment of accomplishment through the presence of visible progress elements like badges and levels and the enhancement of empowerment through the implementation of interactive challenges with real-time feedback. The capacity for ownership is cultivated through the implementation of customisable profiles and the preservation of progress, while the concept of social influence is facilitated by features such as leaderboards, collaboration and peer recognition. The integration of scarcity and unpredictability can be achieved through the implementation of time-limited rewards or surprise challenges. Avoidance mechanisms can be employed to maintain engagement by discouraging loss of progress or missed opportunities.

While gamification boosts motivation, Cognitive Load Theory highlights the need to manage the learner's mental effort. Therefore, an effective learning platforms must manage three main types of load. Firstly, they must introduce concepts in a progressive manner. Secondly, they must reduce extraneous load by ensuring a clear interface, intuitive navigation and minimal distractions. Thirdly, they must support germane load by incorporating reflective tasks and problem-solving exercises that promote schema construction.

4 Methodology

4.1 Human-Centred Design

Human-centred design is a well-established problem-solving methodology that seeks to balance human desirability, technological feasibility and economic viability in the development of products and services. Initially rooted in disciplines such as computer science, visual design and architecture, the concept has since evolved to encompass a broad spectrum of applications, including service design and educational innovation [12,27]. This process is categorised into three fundamental phases: inspiration, ideation and implementation. The inspiration phase is centred on the generation of empathy through qualitative research, with the objective of identifying and understanding the needs, goals and challenges of the target group. This includes the formulation of problems and the communication of specific user requirements, ensuring clarity and focus in the design process. In the ideation phase, creative strategies are employed to generate a range of potential solutions. A key component is the development of prototypes, which serve as concrete representations of proposed concepts and facilitate iterative refinement. The implementation phase involves the testing of prototypes with users. Feedback obtained is systematically incorporated to ensure that the final solution remains closely aligned with user expectations and functional requirements.

In the present study, the principles of human-centred design are applied within the context of a university-level web development course. Lecturers assume the role of designers by creating course content and instructional methods, while students act as users who actively engage with the material and provide formative feedback. This feedback is instrumental in effecting iterative revisions of the course design, including the development of a digital learning platform. As shown in Fig. 2, this approach ensures ongoing alignment with the needs of students and facilitates the continuous enhancement of the learning experience.

4.2 Method Triangulation

This study employs method triangulation by combining eye-tracking, emotion measurement, interviews and questionnaires to evaluate usability and UX.

Eye-Tracking and Emotion Measurement. Eye-tracking is a valuable method for capturing user attention by measuring where and how long participants look at specific areas of a digital interface [43]. It offers precise insights into engagement and potential confusion [26]. Depending on the study, the method can have limitations such as time-consuming data collection and analysis [35,64].

To assess usability and emotional engagement, this study employed the Smart Eye AI-X eye-tracker (60 Hz) in combination with iMotions 10.0 software, which enabled eye-tracking, facial expression analysis and galvanic skin response (GSR) measurement, shown in Fig. 3. Heat maps visualised attention distribution on the interface using colour gradients from green (low) to red (high) [2,53]. Facial

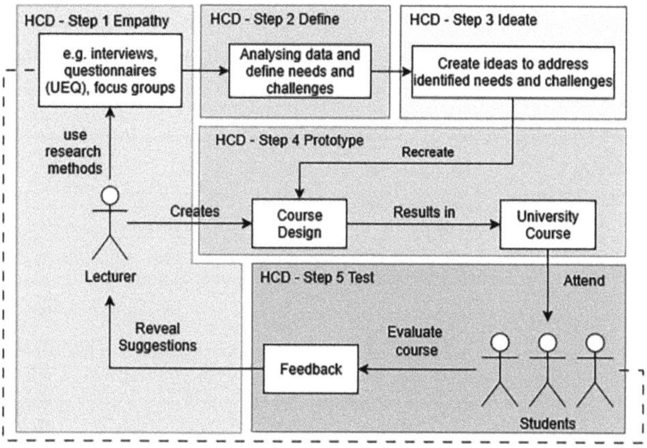

Fig. 2. Visualisation of the use of Human-Centred Design [55,57].

expressions were analysed using the "Affdex" algorithm based on the Facial Action Coding System, allowing detection of emotional states such as positive or negative reactions [8,28]. GSR data, captured via the Shimmer3 GSR+ unit, provided physiological indicators of user arousal through skin conductance changes [18,22]. These multimodal methods offer objective insights into cognitive and emotional user experiences, enhancing traditional usability testing [41].

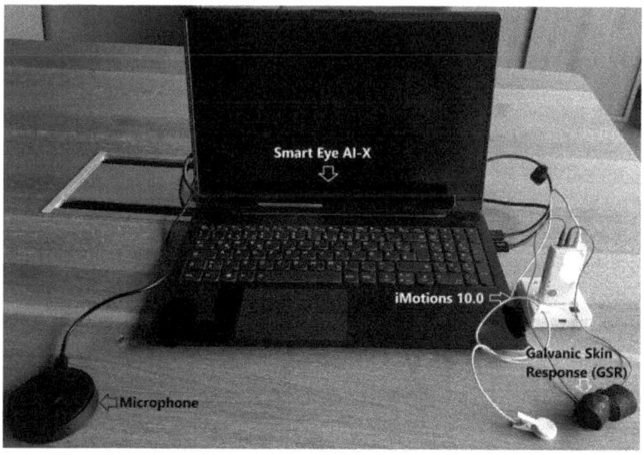

Fig. 3. Setup Eye-Tracking [57].

Methods in Technology Acceptance and User Experience. This study applies the Technology Acceptance Model (TAM) and the User Experience Questionnaire (UEQ) to assess user engagement with the gamified learning platform. TAM, shown in Fig. 4, explains technology acceptance through two main constructs: perceived usefulness and perceived ease of use, which influence attitudes and usage behaviour [4,14,40]. The UEQ evaluates six dimensions of UX: attractiveness, perspicuity, efficiency, dependability, stimulation and novelty, offering insights into both pragmatic and emotional aspects of interaction [59].

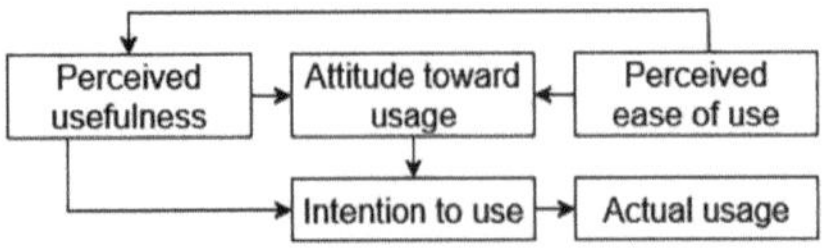

Fig. 4. Visualisation of the Technology Acceptence Model [4,57].

Semi-structured Interviews. They allow for deeper exploration of individual perspectives while maintaining comparability through a predefined guide [37]. Qualitative data were analysed using content analysis supported by MAXQDA to ensure systematic interpretation [33]. This mixed-methods design provides a comprehensive understanding of user perception, motivation and satisfaction.

5 Gamified Learning Platform gAmIcode

This section introduces the gamified learning platform gAmIcode, its design, usability tests and eye-tracking, to assess user interactions and identify improvements. This name was chosen to reflect integrated gamified elements with coding, emphasizing an engaging and interactive learning experience. In the future, AI-driven feedback will be added to personalise and optimise user interactions.

5.1 Requirements

In a previous study [54], interviews with students from non-technical study programs were conducted to explore their challenges in learning web development. A key outcome was the demand for a gamified learning platform tailored to their needs. The students formulated detailed requirements that formed the basis for the platform's design. These included personalised learning paths, a responsive and user-friendly design, integrated coding exercises with real-time feedback, motivational gamification elements such as points, badges, levels, optional leaderboards, social interaction tools, tutorial support and LMS integration. The current study builds on these foundations by implementing and evaluating a first prototype of the platform. Table 1 summarises these findings.

5.2 Usage of Octalysis Framework and Cognitive Load

Table 2 presents a comprehensive mapping of identified platform requirements to their corresponding Octalysis CDs and cognitive load principles. This alignment

Table 1. Overview of Requirements based on previous study [54].

Learning Paths	Visual code Feedback	Responsive Design
Immediate Feedback	Task-related Feedback	Multi-device usage
Realistic challenges	Badges as reward	Levels/Stages
Social Interaction	Leaderboard	Attractive design
Integrated Code Editor	Progress indicators	Colour Scheme
Learning Types	Tutorials, videos	Intuitive UI
LMS Integration	Nicknames	
Scalability, Flexibility	Avoid external tools	

Table 2. Mapping requirements to Octalysis core drives and cognitive load principles

Platform Feature	Octalysis Core Drive								Cognitive Load Principle
	1	2	3	4	5	6	7	8	
Badges		X							Germane load
Progress Indicators		X		X					Reduces extraneous load
Leaderboard (optional)					X				Managed extraneous load
Realistic Challenges			X				X		Germane load
Immediate Feedback			X						Reduces extraneous load
Task-Related Feedback			X						Supports schema construction
Integrated Code Editor			X	X					Minimises extraneous load
Responsive Design									Reduces extraneous load
Attractive, Intuitive UI	X						X		Reduces extraneous load
Colour Scheme	X		X						Reduces extraneous load
Tutorials, Videos	X		X						Manages intrinsic load
Learning Paths		X		X					Manages intrinsic load
Social Interaction					X				—
Nicknames				X	X				—
Scalability, Flexibility	X								—
Integration with LMS				X					Reduces extraneous load
Avoid External Tools			X	X					Reduces extraneous load
Adaption of Prior Knowledge			X	X					Manages intrinsic load
Learning Types				X					—
Visual Code Feedback			X						Reduce extraneous load
Multi-Device Usage								X	Reduce extraneous load
Level/Stages		X		X					Germane load

ensures that motivational and instructional design elements are integrated to create an engaging, cognitively accessible learning environment that is tailored to diverse learner needs.

The platform design systematically translates motivational and cognitive principles into practical features. In order to promote motivation through accomplishment, the platform incorporates a points, badges and levels system to incentivise progress and achievement. The implementation of progress indicators should support the promotion of a sense of ownership, thereby facilitating self-regulation. The provision of immediate, task-related feedback facilitates learners' reflection and adaptation should support schema construction and deep engagement. The integration of programming challenges with interactive feedback should promote empowerment and cognitive load by promoting active problem solving. The integration of social features, including leaderboards and anonymity based on nicknames, should foster collaboration and social influence, thereby reducing stress.

From a cognitive perspective, intuitive navigation, a consistent layout and a responsive interface should reduce extraneous load by preventing distraction. The integration of tools, such as a built-in code editor, obviates the need to switch platforms and ensures cognitive continuity. The utilisation of adaptive content, tutorials and videos should facilitate the management of intrinsic load by aligning task difficulty with learners' prior knowledge. Finally, features such as unlockable content or streak mechanisms enhance engagement through scarcity and loss-avoidance mechanics, all the while keeping cognitive demands balanced.

5.3 Structure of gAmIcode

The development of gAmIcode was initiated on the basis of the defined requirements and with reference to the Octalysis Framework and Cognitive Load Theory. These theoretical models provided a foundation for the alignment of motivational design with cognitive accessibility. The platform has been integrated into the university's LMS using the Learning Tools Interoperability (LTI) standard, ensuring a seamless login experience that aligns with the expectations of users. Furthermore, it enables the automatic transfer of course context and supports the return of grading results to the LMS without the need for separate credentials. In order to support clarity and usability, the interface is structured into seven distinct subpages, as illustrated in Fig. 5. This promotes intuitive navigation and reduced cognitive effort.

Upon logging in, students are directed to an overview page that displays their recent activity, earned badges and current rankings, offering a concise overview of their progress, see Fig. 6. The course page lists all available courses, showing progress for each, while the course detail page provides further information, including course structure, exercises and badges. The ranking page offers a view of student standings at different levels, promoting competition and motivation. It looks similar like the leaderboard on the overview page, but additionally it offers the option to opt out of the leaderboard. The code editor page provides an integrated development environment where students can edit, preview and validate their solutions. Following the completion of a task, the system provides

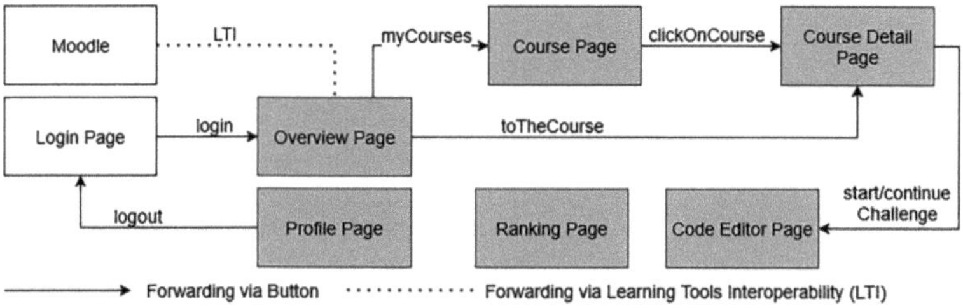

Fig. 5. Subpages of gAmIcode and their interaction via buttons. The grey-shaded subpages indicate sections where navigation is possible from any other grey-shaded page through the menu (adapted from Sailer et al. (Color figure online) [57]).

immediate feedback, confirming success or initiate revisions based on any identified issues. Furthermore, the profile page provides students with the option to personalise their settings, allowing them to adapt the platform to their individual preferences. It is possible to alter the name to a pseudonym, which may then be displayed on the leaderboard under the chosen nickname. This enables users to participate in the leaderboard without revealing their identity.

5.4 Evaluation of gAmIcode Participants and Setup

This chapter builds on an earlier study involving 57 students enrolled on web development courses as part of non-technical degree programmes [54]. To identify concrete platform requirements, ten of these students participated in semi-structured interviews. Their contributions directly informed the design of the platform, which was systematically aligned with the CDs of the Octalysis Framework and the principles of Cognitive Load Theory. This theoretical grounding ensured that motivational and cognitive aspects were embedded in the platform from the outset. The same students were later invited to participate in usability testing, with continuity maintained through the use of their original study IDs. Although only eight participants were available during the summer testing phase, this sample size was sufficient, as five participants are generally enough to detect the majority of usability issues [44]. Each 45-minute session included setup and consent (10 min), a usability test (1020 min) and a concluding interview (15 min). A pilot run was conducted beforehand to refine the procedure and ensure that the study design effectively captured aspects relevant to both Octalysis and Cognitive Load Theory.

During the usability testing, the participants provided detailed feedback on their experience with gAmIcode, highlighting appealing and engaging aspects, as well as missing or improvable features. Their insights revealed user preferences, highlighted both positive and negative aspects of gAmIcode and identified potential usability issues. This feedback forms a critical foundation for refining the design and functionality of gAmIcode in line with learner expectations, while maintaining its theoretical grounding.

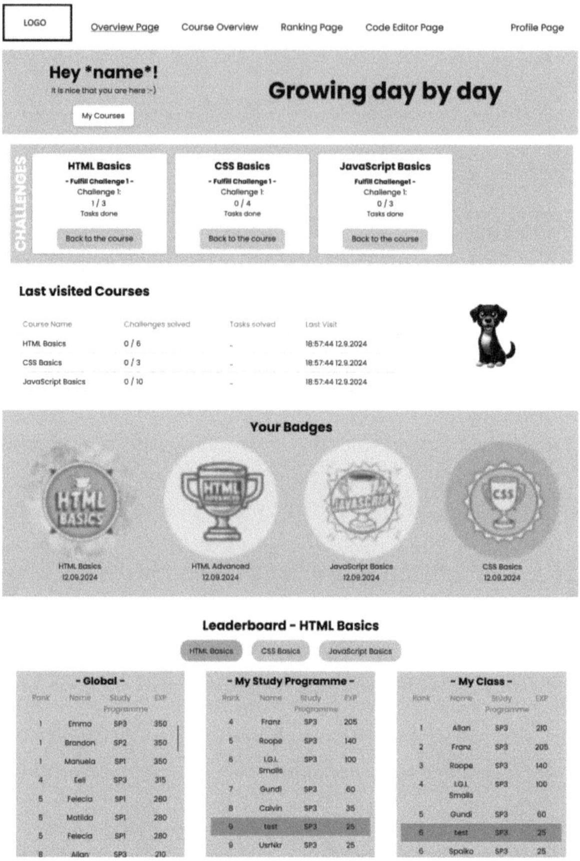

Fig. 6. gAmIcode - Overview Page [57].

5.5 Conducted Usability Tests

The usability study is based on a comprehensive guide that outlined a series of tasks, which are listed in Table 3.

The provided guide was designed to ensure consistency across participants, thereby facilitating a systematic evaluation of the platform's usability and UX. The tasks were read aloud in sequence and participants were asked to solve them. Figure 7 and Fig. 8 display mockups of the platform with the task sequence, showing questions on the left and the platform interface on the right, with colour-coded connections and numbered steps indicating the task order.

Fig. 7 shows simple tasks that required a single action to complete. Task 1 involved changing personal information, which required the user to click on the Profile Page button in the top right-hand corner. Some tasks allowed for multiple approaches. For example, Task 9 required the user to *Start Course 1*. This could be done either by clicking on the *Start Course* button in the Course section or

Table 3. Listing of the tasks carried out during usability testing to explore the platform including expected results [57].

Task	Expected Solution	Figure, color
T1 - Update your data	Go to the profile page	Fig. 7, red
T2 - Change the nickname	Change the name	Fig. 7, blue
T3 - Check the Leaderboard	a) Go to the ranking page b) Scroll to the end of the overview page	Fig. 7, green
T4 - Opt-out of Leader-board	Click the "opt-out" button	Fig. 7, orange
T5 - Look for Course 1	a) Go to the course overview page b) Scroll to the courses on the overview page	Fig. 7, purple
T6 - Start Course 1	Click on the "start course" button	Fig. 7, yellow
T7 - Go to the Editor	Go to the editor page	Fig. 7, darkblue Fig. 8, red
T8 - Reset course progress	Click on the "reset course progress" button	Fig. 8, blue
T9 - Change colour theme	Select another theme in the drop down menu	Fig. 8, green
T10 - Complete challenge	Follow the instruction	Fig. 8, orange

by navigating from the overview page to the course details page. In such cases, an "a" and "b" were added to the item number to indicate the possible paths.

Figure 8 illustrates a similar process, but in this case, Task 7, "Complete the challenge", required multiple steps. The user is first required to locate the instructions (Step 8), select the correct file (Step 9) and enter the necessary code snippet (Step 10), which is displayed in a live preview (Step 11). Upon completion of the task, the user clicks *Check*, which triggers a feedback message in the top right corner. This message, which appears for eight seconds unless hovered over, indicates success with *Well done* or provides a hint if incorrect, allowing the user to attempt the task again. Initially, only Task 1/3 is visible and subsequent tasks are revealed sequentially upon successful completion of the previous ones. This iterative process must be repeated until all tasks are completed correctly.

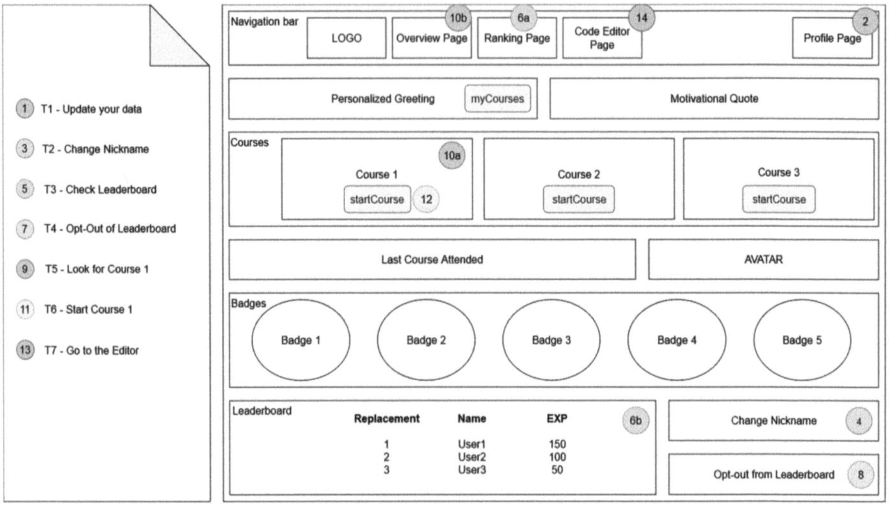

Fig. 7. Mockup of the Overview Page [57].

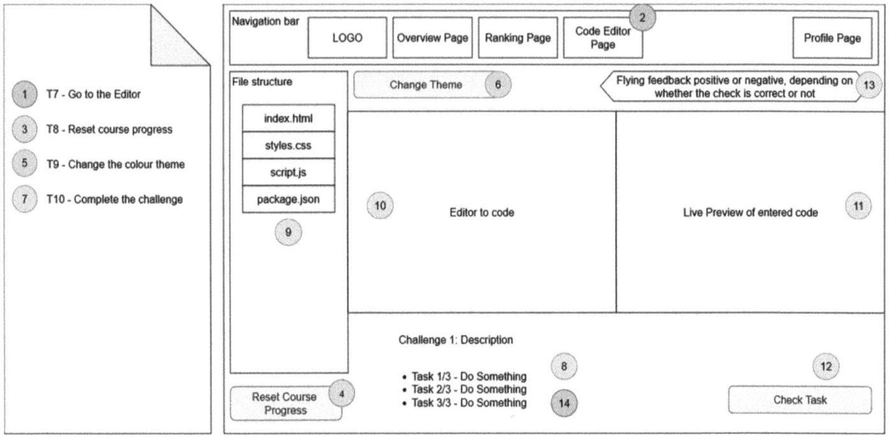

Fig. 8. Mockup of the Code Editor Page [57].

6 Results

The following sections present the results of the usability test for each page of gAmIcode, outlining the specific usability issues identified. Moreover, insights are obtained from the analysis of facial expressions, eye movements, interviews and the TAM and UEQ evaluations. The results are then interpreted through the lens of the Octalysis Framework and Cognitive Load Theory to assess how well the platform supports user motivation and cognitive processing.

6.1 Usability Test with Eye-Tracking

The results of the usability test indicated that most participants completed their tasks successfully. Emotional data, shown in Table 4, revealed varied reactions. The overview page triggered the most negative emotions, likely due to initial disorientation, with an average of 8.2 emotional peaks per minute. The ranking page caused frustration, including 5.7% anger and 9.3% confusion. In contrast, the profile page received the most positive feedback, with 22.3% joy and under 1.5% negative emotions such as fear, disgust, or sadness.

Table 4. Overview of Facial Expressions that were triggered per sub page in % [57].

Subpage	Fear	Confusion	Digust	Sadness	Joy	Contempt	Anger	Surprise
Overview	1.4	15.2	4.7	5.1	19.5	0.9	3.5	1.9
Profile	0.5	4.0	1.1	1.3	22.3	1.1	1.5	0.7
Ranking	1.0	9.3	0.6	3.3	16.0	2.9	5.7	0.6
Course	1.3	6.8	1.5	3.1	15.7	2.6	2.5	1.4
Editor	2.5	6.2	2.3	3.0	18.5	1.6	3.0	2.3

Eye-Tracking Results Overview Page. The preliminary assignment involved a one-minute examination of the website, subsequently followed by participant feedback on the overview page. The heatmap, shown in Fig. 9, confirmed that all elements were viewed, indicating strong visual engagement. The participants described the layout as clear, compact and tidy. While a few suggested using more colours, the muted palette was an intentional design choice. The hover effects on badges and the avatar dog were particularly well received. Only one participant expressed confusion, caused by the visibility of multiple courses.

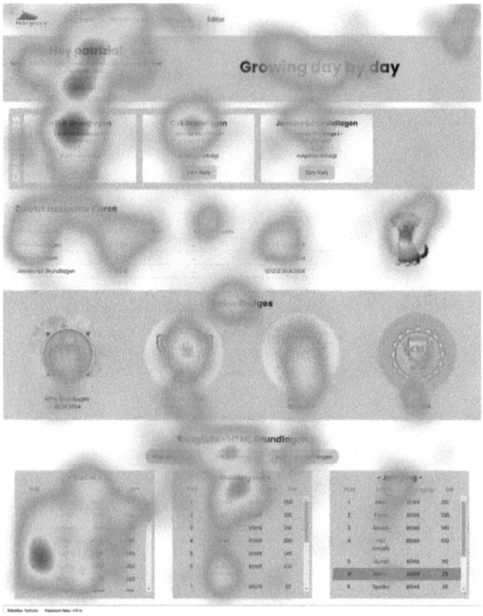

Fig. 9. Heat Map of the overview page (n = 8). Red areas are viewed the most, followed by yellow and green areas [57] (Color figure online).

Eye-Tracking Results Profile Page. Participants were requested to make any necessary updates to their profile information and to indicate their preferred learning type. As demonstrated in the heatmap, shown in Fig. 10 all interface elements were viewed, indicating a high level of user engagement. The majority of participants successfully completed the task and expressed satisfaction with the page's clear and intuitive design. Nevertheless, several improvement suggestions were made: the introduction of an automatic assessment to prefill the user's knowledge level, the addition of a field to specify how often programming languages are used and the expansion of the categorisation of prior knowledge beyond the existing three levels. Participants furthermore recommended a help button to clarify the meaning of the knowledge levels and a drag-and-drop feature for uploading a profile picture to enhance usability.

Eye-Tracking Results Ranking Page. Participants were asked to identify themselves on the leaderboard and explore the option to opt-out of the ranking display. The majority of users found the task straightforward, like shown in Fig. 11. However, opinions on the ranking feature were polarised: while some expressed appreciation for the competitive element, others preferred to avoid comparison with peers. The utilisation of nicknames was identified as a beneficial measure to address privacy concerns. Some terminology, such as "Global Ranking", required further clarification for the participants. The colour-coded ranking system was positively received for its clarity and visual appeal. The

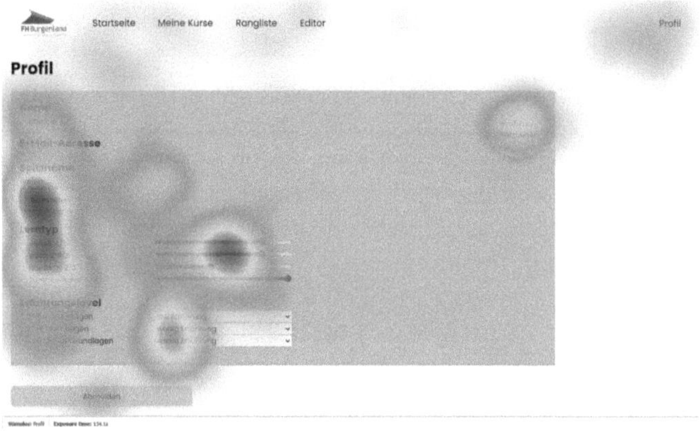

Fig. 10. Heat map of Profile settings (n = 8). Red areas are viewed the most, followed by yellow and green areas [57] (Color figure online).

opt-out process was received positively, however, participants proposed a confirmation step and the enhancement of the visibility of the opt-out button.

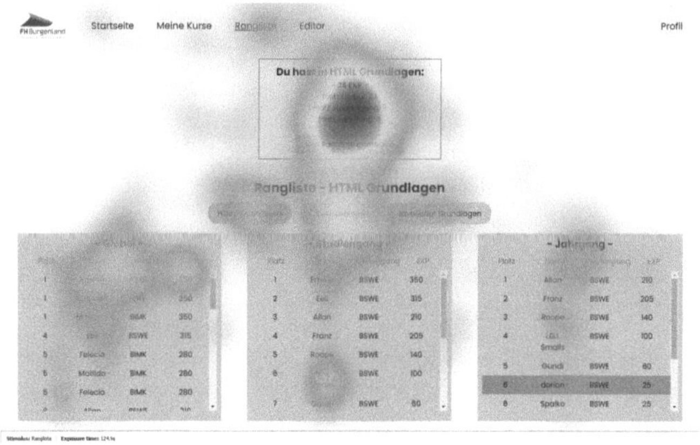

Fig. 11. Heat Map of the Ranking Page (n = 8). Red areas are viewed the most, followed by yellow and green areas [57] (Color figure online).

Eye-Tracking Results Course Page. After the participants had solved the first tasks in the HTML course, they had to go back to the course page and view their progress. The heatmap in Fig. 12 shows that the dashboard and badges were the center of attention during this task, while the text was not read in detail. Respondents were asked to give feedback on how they liked the course overview and whether the progress in the course was displayed clearly. Although the design was rated as visually aesthetic, participants wanted to see the description of the course first and then the progress. This would feel more coherent in terms of order. Furthermore, the size of the headings and the text should be more differentiated, as they were relatively the same size. Some participants found it unclear that stars were used to indicate progress. Stars usually indicate an evaluation of the course and not a progress bar. A pie chart or a filling bar could be used instead, which fills up as the course is completed. Another suggestion for improvement was that the site should be kept more compact and to avoid scrolling. The badges are well accepted, as well as the green colours when a task has been completed. Nevertheless, the term 'Exp.' (Experience Points) is not understood by all participants. It should also be stated which challenge is graded for how much experience in the course. The average time to complete a course would also be helpful to know whether to start the next challenge or not.

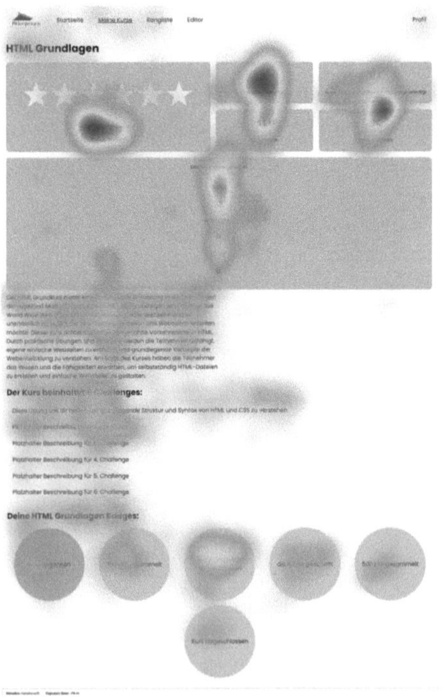

Fig. 12. Heat Map of the Course Page (n = 8). Red areas are viewed the most, followed by yellow and green areas [57] (Color figure online).

Eye-Tracking Results Code Editor Page. The code editor offers immediate feedback on web development tasks and has proven to be very appealing, as demonstrated in Fig. 13. The findings indicated that the participants had a favourable response to the functionality and responsiveness. Nevertheless, participants recommended displaying the number of remaining attempts for incorrect submissions and enlarging error messages to include more detailed explanations. It was proposed that additional measures be taken to enhance the clarity and visibility of the system, like marking error lines with a red exclamation mark, the renaming of the Reset Editor button to Repeat Task and the enhancement of the visibility and accessibility of the colour scheme toggle.

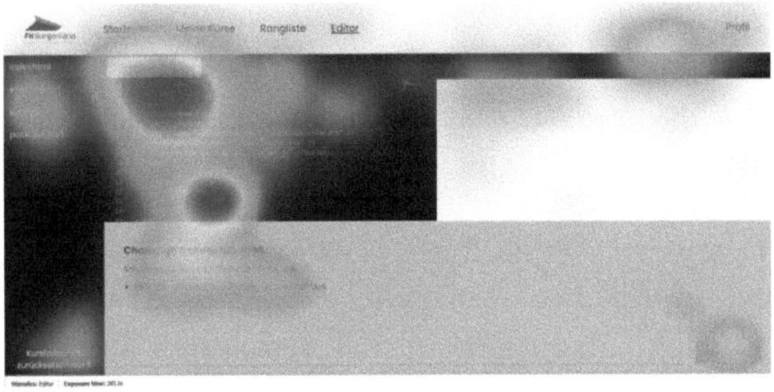

Fig. 13. Heat Map of the Code Editor (n = 8). Red areas are viewed the most, followed by yellow and green areas [57] (Color figure online).

6.2 Semi-structured Interviews

The semi-structured interview contained questions that are grouped into four categories. Regarding design and aestetics, it was noted that, while the layout of the platform was appreciated by some, the colour scheme was found to be too muted by others, lacking in vibrancy. It was recommended to use more dynamic colours, especially with the institution's branding, as well as highlight colours for key elements such as progress indicators, buttons and error messages. The design has also been described as visually monotonous, with insufficient differentiation between components such as courses, leaderboards and badges. The recommendations included enhancing the visibility of the profile section, improving the visual appeal, offering customisable avatars and introducing a dynamic colour scheme that evolves with user progress to boost engagement.

In the category usability and coherence, students evaluated the platform's clarity, organisation, navigation and overall ease of use. The feedback was predominantly positive, with users commending the platform's uncomplicated and intuitive design, minimalist menu structure and well-organised layout that facilitated the identification of features and monitoring of progress. However, suggestions for improvement included more accessible settings for theme customisation and better spacing when receiving multiple badges to enhance the UX.

In the category functionality, the students provided a largely favourable response to the platform's features. The efficacy of badges in promoting a sense of achievement was emphasised and the progress tracking system was positively received. However, some participants found the use of stars confusing, as they were mistaken for course grades. Progress bars or circles were recommended as clearer alternatives. Users recommended a 'jump back' button to facilitate navigation, commended the built-in editor for its convenience and proposed enhancements such as a personal testing environment. Furthermore, participants expressed interest in social features to support peer interaction and group progress tracking. Additionally, they recommended including Frequently Asked Questions, support options for struggling students and the ability to contact course lecturers, especially to assist beginners and those experiencing difficulties.

The overall impression of the platform was largely positive. Users highlighted its essential features, ease of use and professional design. The integrated editor was praised for its functionality, while the muted colour scheme was considered appropriate for the style of the platform. However, some users suggested improvements to make the appearance even more appealing. The leaderboard received a mixed feedback, with the opt-out option and utilisation of nicknames being met with approval. It was recommended that clearer notifications be provided regarding the display of nicknames. A number of recommendations for potential enhancements were proposed, including the refinement of avatars, the incorporation of level-based exercises and the extension of the platform's scope. The use of descriptive keywords, including 'structured', 'clear', 'intuitive' and 'practical', served to emphasise the platform's organised and user-friendly character.

6.3 Technology Acceptance Model

The responses given by TAM are summarised in Table 5, using a scale from 1 (best) to 5 (worst).

Table 5. Results Technology Acceptance Model Mean and Variance [57].

	Q1	Q2	Q3	Q4	Q5	Q6	Q7	Q8	Q9	Q10	Q11	Q12
Mean	2.375	2.500	2.625	2.750	1.000	1.000	1.125	1.000	1.750	1.000	1.250	1.125
Variance	0.839	0.857	1.411	1.929	0	0	0.125	1.071	0	0.214	0.125	0.214
	Q13	**Q14**	**Q15**	**Q16**	**Q17**	**Q18**	**Q19**	**Q20**	**Q21**	**Q22**	**Q23**	
Mean	1.250	1.250	1.625	1.500	1.625	2.000	3.000	3.250	1.875	2.375	3.000	
Variance	0.214	0.214	0.554	0.571	0.554	1.143	1.714	1.357	0.982	1.125	0.857	

The visual aspects included Q1 for visual appeal and Q2 to Q4 for the use of colour. The mean rating for these was moderate, ranging from 2.375 to 2.75. The variability was particularly pronounced in responses pertaining to colour usability, with a variance of 1.929. Conversely, questions pertaining to navigation and readability (Q5 to Q8) were appraised favourably, with mean values ranging from 1.0 to 1.125 and an absence of variance, suggesting unanimous acceptance.

The evaluation of platform usability was conducted through the utilisation of Q10 to Q14. The questions in this category received consistently high ratings, with mean values ranging from 1.125 to 1.25. The participants found the platform easy to use, self-explanatory and enjoyable, and indicated a strong willingness to continue using it and to recommend it to others (Q13).

The questions concerning engagement with technical systems (Q15 to Q18) demonstrated moderate ratings, with mean values ranging from 1.625 to 2.0 and higher variance, indicating divergent levels of comfort among users. The practical usage of the system, measured by Q19 and Q20, received higher mean scores of 3.0 and 3.25, respectively. However, significant disagreement was observed, particularly for Q19, which showed a variance of 1.714.

The final group, Q21 to Q23, addressed the willingness to engage with new systems. The outcomes of this study were heterogenous. Q21 attained a mean score of 1.875, while Q22 and Q23 received higher scores of 2.375 and 3.0, respectively. This finding suggests that the level of long-term commitment exhibited by individuals is contingent upon their perception of the system's functionality.

6.4 User Experience Questionnaire

The UEQ evaluated six dimensions of UX using a scale from 3 (negative) to +3 (positive). All dimensions received positive ratings. The highest-rated aspects were perspicuity (mean: 2.25, variance: 0.79) and efficiency (mean: 2.22, variance: 0.40), indicating that users found the platform easy to understand and effective in task completion. Dependability (mean: 1.88, variance: 1.05) received a positive rating but showed higher variability, suggesting differing perceptions of system reliability. Attractiveness (mean: 1.563, variance: 0.33) and stimulation (mean: 1.563, variance: 0.71) were moderately positive, while novelty (mean: 1.250, variance: 1.41) received the lowest score, pointing to limited innovation.

6.5 Octalysis Framework and Cognitive Load

The platform requirements were implemented based on the Octalysis Framework and Cognitive Load Theory to support motivation and cognitive processing. Features linked to CD2 "Accomplishment", such as progress indicators or badges, were consistently viewed and used by participants. CD3 "Empowerment" was addressed through the integrated code editor and visual feedback mechanisms, both received positive feedback and showed high engagement in eye-tracking data. CD5 "Social Influence", implemented via the leaderboard and nickname functionality, received mixed reactions. Opt-out and anonymisation were appreciated, but clarity issues were noted. In terms of Cognitive Load Theory, features such as immediate feedback or intuitive navigation contributed to a reduction in extraneous load, while structured challenges and task-related feedback supported germane processing and schema construction. Some features, including learning type selection and badge personalisation, were used but also prompted suggestions for improvement, indicating varied effectiveness in meeting motivational and cognitive goals.

7 Discussion

7.1 gAmIcode

The evaluation of gAmIcode not only confirms alignment with key usability expectations but also provides a more nuanced understanding of how platform features fulfil motivational and cognitive principles as outlined in the Octalysis Framework and Cognitive Load Theory. As illustrated in Table 6, the consolidation of data from interviews and eye-tracking with theoretical mappings enables a more targeted analysis of instructional effectiveness.

Table 6. Requirements Evaluation Based on Interview Feedback, Eye-Tracking Data, Octalysis Framework and Cognitive Load Theory.

Requirement	Method	Implementation Status	**Octalysis**		**Cognitive Load**	
			Core Drive	Fulfilled	Category	Fulfilled
Learning Paths	I	Missing	CD2, CD4	–	IL	–
Immediate Feedback	ET/I	Inadequate	CD3	Yes	EL	Yes
Realistic Challenges	I	Missing	CD3, CD7	–	GL	–
Social Interaction	I	Missing	CD5	–	–	–
Integrated Code-Editor	ET/I	Implemented	CD3, CD4	Yes	EL	Yes
Learning Types	I	Partial	CD4	Partial	–	–
LMS Integration	I	Partial	CD4	Yes	EL	Yes
Scalability, Flexibility	I	Implemented	CD1	Yes	–	–
Visual Code Feedback	ET/I	Implemented	CD3	Yes	EL	Yes
Task-Related Feedback	ET/I	Implemented	CD3	Partial	SC	Partial
Badges as Reward	ET/I	Implemented	CD2	Partial	GL	Yes
Leaderboard	ET/I	Implemented	CD5	Partial	EL	Partial
Progress Indicators	ET/I	Inadequate	CD2, CD4	Yes	EL	Partial
Tutorials, Videos	I	Missing	CD1, CD3	–	IL	–
Nicknames	ET/I	Implemented	CD4, CD5	Yes	–	–
Avoid External Tools	ET/I	Implemented	CD3, CD4	Yes	EL	Yes
Responsive Design	ET/I	Missing	–	–	EL	–
Multi-Device Usage	I	Missing	CD8	–	EL	–
Levels/Stages	I	Missing	CD2, CD4	–	GL	–
Attractive Design	I	Inadequate	CD1, CD7	Partial	EL	Partial
Colour Scheme	I	Inadequate	CD1, CD3	Partial	EL	Partial
Intuitive UI	ET/I	Implemented	CD1, CD7	Yes	EL	Yes

I...Interview, ET...Eye-Tracking, CD...Core Drive, IL...Intrinsic Load, EL...Extraneous Load, GL...Germane Load, SC...Schema Construction

Several features displayed a high degree of coherence with both theoretical frameworks and user expectations. The integrated code editor exhibited elevated levels of visual engagement and functional clarity. The platform effectively supported

CD3 "Empowerment" by allowing users to experiment and receive immediate feedback. Furthermore, it reduced extraneous cognitive load by minimising distractions and streamlining the task flow, a finding that aligns with the importance of real-time feedback in digital learning environments [32]. Similarly, characteristics such as the intuitive UI, visual code feedback and the absence of external tools also satisfied both the motivational and cognitive criteria.

However, it is important to note that not all implemented features fully achieved their intended effect. While the badges were generally well received and contributed to CD2 "Accomplishment" and germane cognitive load through milestone recognition, user feedback revealed a desire for more visually distinct and rewarding elements, such as "special" or rare badges. This finding indicates that, while the fundamental mechanism proved effective, the motivational impact could be enhanced by augmenting the sense of progression and reward. This observation is consistent with existing research [3] on the importance of personalisation and variety in gamified rewards.

A similar pattern emerged with the leaderboard, which partially supported CD5 "Social Influence" and helped reduce extraneous load through features such as nicknames and opt-out options. However, the emotional and interview data revealed a mixture of reactions, with some users finding it motivating, while others perceived it as pressuring or unclear, especially with regard to terms such as Global Ranking. This finding aligns with previous research, which suggests that competitive elements necessitate careful personalisation to circumvent adverse motivational outcomes [3,36].

The implementation of progress indicators was technically accomplished, aligning them with CD2 and CD4, in addition to extraneous load reduction. However, their utilisation of stars resulted in erroneous interpretations, for example leading to confusion with grading. The participants recommended the use of clearer visual aids, such as pie charts or bars, to facilitate comprehension. This demonstrates that the simple implementation of a motivational mechanic is inadequate if the visual communication undermines cognitive clarity, as emphasised by visual design studies [43,47].

Regarding task-related feedback, while implemented and linked to CD3 and schema construction, it was rated as partially fulfilled. While the participants expressed appreciation for the explanatory feedback, they made a request for more detailed, beginner-friendly messages. This finding aligns with literature of adaptive feedback in deep learning and schema building [46].

The learning type selector, though partially implemented, highlighted further gaps. This prototype addressed CD4 "Ownership" but did not include any adaptivity or automated assessment. This reduced its cognitive and motivational impact, especially when compared to platforms offering dynamic personalisation. The efficacy of adaptive learning in enhancing engagement and learning outcomes has been demonstrated in numerous studies [31,46].

With regard to visual and emotional engagement, while design aesthetics such as layout and navigation were positively noted, the colour scheme and overall visual appeal were considered to be inadequate. The muted, grey-dominant palette was perceived as professional but lacking vibrancy, thus resulting in a limited emotional impact. The dimensions of attractiveness and stimulation in the UEQ, while positive, did not receive the highest ratings, indicating potential for enhancement of the visual experience in alignment with CD1 "Meaning" and CD7 "Unpredictability". As shown in relevant literature, colour and visual hierarchy have an impact on emotional engagement and cognitive ease [43,65,66].

Finally, Table 6 highlights that the absence of several features, such as learning paths, adaptive levels, social interaction tools or responsive design, hinders the complete realisation of both frameworks. The absence of these had a impact on CD2, CD4 and CD5, resulting in deficiencies in both intrinsic and germane load management. The present findings are in accordance with literature for adaptive and socially integrated learning environments that provide support for learner autonomy and peer support [3,36].

7.2 Future Work

Based on the current evaluation, targeted improvements are planned to further align gAmIcode with motivational and cognitive design principles. While many features were implemented, several failed fully meeting user expectations or fulfilling their intended Octalysis or Cognitive Load Theory roles. Planned enhancements include replacing progress stars with clearer visual indicators, redesigning badges for greater engagement and clarifying terminology such as "Exp.".

Feedback will become more adaptive through targeted hints after repeated errors. The leaderboard will be refined with clearer terms and enhanced opt-out visibility and the learning type selector extended with self-assessment tools to support personalisation and intrinsic load management.

New features will include learning paths, level-based progression, multi-device support, chat tools and peer feedback, addressing gaps in adaptive learning and social interaction. The gamification strategy for usage in classroom will follow the Goal-Access-Feedback-Challenge-Collaboration model [25]. Open-ended tasks, peer assessment and innovative grading will further enhance personalisation and engagement [60]. Large Language Models will be explored for real-time feedback on complex tasks [24] and peer assessment will support collaboration and motivation [16]. These improvements aim to deliver a more adaptive and motivating experience for non-technical learners.

8 Conclusion

Students enrolled in non-technical programmes often encounter considerable difficulties when attempting to engage with technical subjects such as web development. These challenges frequently result in frustration, reduced motivation and poor course evaluations, underscoring the necessity for learning environments that are more closely tailored to the needs of these learners. An analysis of interview data indicated dissatisfaction with conventional teaching methodologies and a pronounced need for more engaging, accessible and supportive learning tools. These insights were instrumental in the development of the gamified learning platform gAmIcode, which was designed to integrate features and motivational elements aligned with learner preferences.

The platform was developed using a HCD approach, ensuring that user feedback guided both functionality and design decisions throughout the process. In addition to the integration of student participation, the theoretical foundations of the Octalysis Framework and Cognitive Load Theory were utilised to inform the design of platform features, with the objective of enhancing motivation, engagement and cognitive efficiency.

The prototype was subjected to a comprehensive evaluation involving eye-tracking, TAM and UEQ assessments and follow-up interviews. The findings confirmed a generally positive UX, particularly with regard to ease of use and interface clarity. Following a thorough evaluation, it has been determined that there are several areas that require refinement. These include, but are not limited to, adjustments to the visual design, the addition of feedback mechanisms and the incorporation of support tools such as an Frequently Asked Questions section. These improvements are scheduled for implementation in the next iteration of the platform, which will undergo testing in classroom settings comprising at least 25 students per group across four classes. The ensuing phase will provide a more robust validation of the effectiveness of gAmIcode and address the limitations of the initial usability test, which was based on a small sample size.

Acknowledgments. The authors would like to thank the University of Applied Sciences Burgenland, the University of Vienna and the UniVie Doctoral School Computer Science (DoCS) for their support in developing and evaluating the gAmIcode platform. Special thanks go to DeepL and DeepL Write for their support with the partial translation and proofreading in terms of spelling and grammar as well as ChatGPT as a reliable sparring partner during the creation process.

References

1. Alcántara-Rubio, L., Valderrama-Hernández, R., Solís-Espallargas, C., Ruiz-Morales, J.: The implementation of the SDGs in universities: a systematic review. Environ. Educ. Res. **28**(11), 1585–1615 (2022). https://doi.org/10.1080/13504622.2022.2063798
2. Alemdag, E., Cagiltay, K.: A systematic review of eye tracking research on multimedia learning. Comput. Educ. **125**, 413–428 (2018). https://doi.org/10.1016/j.compedu.2018.06.023
3. Almeida, C., Kalinowski, M., Uchôa, A., Feijó, B.: Negative effects of gamification in education software: systematic mapping and practitioner perceptions. Inf. Softw. Technol. **156**, 107142 (2023). https://doi.org/10.1016/j.infsof.2022.107142
4. Alomary, A., Woollard, J.: How is technology accepted by users? A review of technology acceptance models and theories, (2015)
5. Alqurni, J.S.: Evaluating the user interface and usability approaches for e-learning systems. Int. J. Inf. Technol. Web Eng. (IJITWE) **18**(1), 1–25 (2023). https://doi.org/10.4018/IJITWE.333638

6. Barna, B., Fodor, S.: An Empirical Study on the Use of Gamification on IT Courses at Higher Education. In: Auer, M.E., Guralnick, D., Simonics, I. (eds.) ICL 2017. AISC, vol. 715, pp. 684–692. Springer, Cham (2018). https://doi.org/10.1007/978-3-319-73210-7_80
7. Blštáková, J., Piwowar-Sulej, K.: Gamification as an innovative idea within human resources management. In: International Scientific Conference Hradec Economic Days 2019 (2019).https://doi.org/10.36689/uhk/hed/2019-01-007
8. Bonnardel, N., Piolat, A., Le Bigot, L.: The impact of colour on Website appeal and users' cognitive processes. Displays **32**(2), 69–80 (2011). https://doi.org/10.1016/j.displa.2010.12.002
9. Bucchiarone, A., Cicchetti, A., Bassanelli, S., Marconi, A.: How to merge gamification efforts for programming and modelling: a tool7mplementation perspective. In: 2021 ACM/IEEE International Conference on Model Driven Engineering Languages and Systems Companion (MODELS-C), pp. 721–726. IEEE, Fukuoka, Japan (2021). https://doi.org/10.1109/MODELS-C53483.2021.00116
10. Chou, Y.K.: Actionable Gamification: Beyond Points, Badges, and Leaderboards, Packt Publishing Ltd (2019)
11. Corrêa, G., Pereira, R., Silveira, M., Gasparini, I.: Exploring usability and user experience evaluation methods: a tertiary study. In: Proceedings of the 26th International Conference on Enterprise Information Systems-Volume 2: ICEIS, pp. 357–368. INSTICC, SciTePress (2024). https://doi.org/10.5220/0012606100003690
12. Dam, R.F.: The 5 stages in the design thinking process (2024). https://www.interaction-design.org/literature/article/5-stages-in-the-design-thinking-process. Accessed 06 Aug 08 2024
13. Dambic, G., Kesscec, T., Kucak, D.: A blended learning with gamification approach for teaching programming courses in higher education. In: 2021 44th International Convention on Information, Communication and Electronic Technology (MIPRO), pp. 843–847. IEEE, Opatija, Croatia (2021). https://doi.org/10.23919/MIPRO52101.2021.9597167
14. Davis, F.D., Bagozzi, R., Warshaw, P.: Technology acceptance model. J. Manag. Sci. **35**(8), 982–1003 (1989)
15. Delroy Chifamba, T., Moosa Motara, Y.: Gamification of functional programming. In: 2020 2nd International Multidisciplinary Information Technology and Engineering Conference (IMITEC), pp. 1–8. IEEE, Kimberley, South Africa (2020). https://doi.org/10.1109/IMITEC50163.2020.9334096
16. Mascio, D., Peretti, T., Temperini, S., M.: The role of intrinsic motivation in peer assessment activity: an empirical evaluation. In: 2021 19th International Conference on Information Technology Based Higher Education and Training (ITHET), pp. 1–7. IEEE (2021). https://doi.org/10.1109/ITHET50392.2021.9759621
17. Dicheva, D., Irwin, K., Dichev, C.: Exploring learners experience of gamified practicing: for learning or for fun? Int. J. Serious Games **6**(3), 5–21 (2019). https://doi.org/10.17083/ijsg.v6i3.299
18. Farnsworth, B.: Galvanic Skin Response (GSR): The complete pocket guide. https://imotions.com/blog/learning/research-fundamentals/galvanic-skin-response/ (2023). https://imotions.com/blog/learning/research-fundamentals/galvanic-skin-response/. Accessed 22 Aug 2024
19. Figueiredo, J., Garcia-Penalvo, F.J.: Increasing student motivation in computer programming with gamification. In: 2020 IEEE Global Engineering Education Conference (EDUCON), pp. 997–1000. IEEE, Porto, Portugal (2020). https://doi.org/10.1109/EDUCON45650.2020.9125283

20. Genç Aksaray, S., Ozcelik, E.: Attention mediates the effect of emotional arousal on learning outcomes in multimedia learning: an eye-tracking study. Educ. Psychol. **43**(1), 38–56 (2023). https://doi.org/10.1080/01443410.2022.2154317
21. Gunnars, F., Palmquist, A., Sundgren, M.: Adult education teacher's perception of gamification implemented in distance education. In: ICERI2021 Proceedings, pp. 3049–3056. IATED (2021). https://doi.org/10.21125/iceri.2021.0759
22. Hamelin, N., Agrawal, S., Patwa, N., Casper Ferm, L.E., Thaichon, P.: Package appearance matter: facial expression and Galvanic Skin Response analysis approach. J. Glob. Scholars Market. Sci. **31**(4), 624–644 (2021). https://doi.org/10.1080/21639159.2021.1939094
23. Heidig, S., Müller, J., Reichelt, M.: Emotional design in multimedia learning: differentiation on relevant design features and their effects on emotions and learning. Comput. Hum. Behav. **44**, 81–95 (2015). https://doi.org/10.1016/j.chb.2014.11.009
24. Hou, X., et al.: Large language models for software engineering: a systematic literature review (2024). https://doi.org/10.48550/arXiv.2308.10620
25. Huang, B., Hew, K.F.: Implementing a theory-driven gamification model in higher education flipped courses: effects on out-of-class activity completion and quality of artifacts. Comput. Educ. **125**, 254–272 (2018). https://doi.org/10.1016/j.compedu.2018.06.018
26. Hyönä, J.: The use of eye movements in the study of multimedia learning. Learn. Instr. **20**(2), 172–176 (2010). https://doi.org/10.1016/j.learninstruc.2009.02.013
27. Ideo, E.: The field guide to human-centered design: design kit. IDEO, (2015)
28. iMotions: Facial expression analysis (2024). https://imotions.com/products/imotions-lab/modules/fea-facial-expression-analysis/. Accessed 6 Aug 2025
29. Iosup, A., Epema, D.: An experience report on using gamification in technical higher education. In: Proceedings of the 45th ACM Technical Symposium on Computer Science Education, pp. 27–32. (2014). https://doi.org/10.1145/2538862.2538899
30. Kamunya, S., Oboko, R., Maina, E.: A systematic mapping of adaptive gamification in e-learning. Open J. Inf. Technol **2**, 53–68 (2019). https://doi.org/10.32591/coas.ojit.0202.04053k
31. Khaldi, A., Bouzidi, R., Nader, F.: Gamification of e-learning in higher education: a systematic literature review. Smart Learn. Environ. **10**(1), 10 (2023). https://doi.org/10.1186/s40561-023-00227-z
32. Kiryakova, G., Angelova, N., Yordanova, L.: Gamification in education. In: Proceedings of 9th International Balkan Education and Science Conference, vol. 1, pp. 679–684. (2014)
33. Fokussierte Interviewanalyse mit MAXQDA. Advances in Intelligent Systems and Computing, Springer, Wiesbaden (2020). https://doi.org/10.1007/978-3-658-31468-2
34. Kumaran, S.S., Nithiya, S.M., Harini, A.: A review on gamification in e-learning: effects and challenges. Jurnal Pendidikan **24**(1), 29–42 (2023). https://doi.org/10.33830/jp.v24i1.3673.2023
35. Li, X.: Eye-tracking research in interactive language learning environments: a systematic review. In" Education and Information Technologies, pp. 20383–20408 (2024). https://doi.org/10.1007/s10639-024-12648-5
36. López-Fernández, D., Gordillo, A., Tovar, E., Alarcón, P.P.: Gamification in computer science education: an empirical study of a meme contest. In: 2023 IEEE Frontiers in Education Conference (FIE), pp. 1–6. (2023). https://doi.org/10.1109/FIE58773.2023.10343279

37. Magaldi, D., Berler, M.: Semi-structured interviews. In: Zeigler-Hill, V., Shackelford, T.K. (eds.) Encyclopedia of Personality and Individual Differences, pp. 4825–4830. (2020). https://doi.org/10.1007/978-3-319-24612-3_857
38. Magylaitė, K., Kapočius, K., Butleris, R., Čeponienė, L.: Towards high usability in gamified systems: a systematic review of key concepts and approaches. Appl. Sci. **12**(16), 8188 (2022). https://doi.org/10.3390/app12168188
39. Mahat, J., Alias, N., Yusop, F.D.: Systematic literature review on gamified professional training among employees. Interact. Learn. Environ. **31**(10), 6747–6767 (2023). https://doi.org/10.1080/10494820.2022.2043910
40. Marangunić, N., Granić, A.: Technology acceptance model: a literature review from 1986 to 2013. Universal Access in the Information Society **14**(1), 81–95 (2014). https://doi.org/10.1007/s10209-014-0348-1
41. Mayer, R.E., Estrella, G.: Benefits of emotional design in multimedia instruction. Learn. Instr **33**, 12–18 (2014). 10/gf4zw9
42. Miya, T.K., Govender, I.: UX/UI design of online learning platforms and their impact on learning: a review. Int. J. Res. Bus. Soc. Sci. **11** (2022). https://doi.org/10.20525/ijrbs.v11iW.2236
43. Molina, A.I., Arroyo, Y., Lacave, C., Redondo, M.A., Bravo, C., Ortega, M.: Eye tracking-based evaluation of accessible and usable interactive systems: tool set of guidelines and methodological issues. Univ. Access Inf. Soc, 1–24 (2024). https://doi.org/10.1007/s10209-023-01083-x
44. Nielsen, J., Landauer, T.K.: A mathematical model of the finding of usability problems. In: Proceedings of the INTERACT 1993 and CHI 1993 Conference on Human Factors in Computing Systems, pp. 206–213. (1993)
45. O'Donovan, S., Gain, J., Marais, P.: A case study in the gamification of a university-level games development course. In: Proceedings of the South African Institute for Computer Scientists and Information Technologists Conference, pp. 242–251. ACM, East London South Africa (2013). https://doi.org/10.1145/2513456.2513469
46. Oliveira, W., et al.: Tailored gamification in education: a literature review and future agenda. Educ. Inf. Technol. **28**(1), 373–406 (2023). https://doi.org/10.1007/s10639-022-11122-4
47. Ozcelik, E., Karakus, T., Kursun, E., Cagiltay, K.: An eye-tracking study of how color coding affects multimedia learning. Comput. Educ. **53**(2), 445–453 (2009). https://doi.org/10.1016/j.compedu.2009.03.002
48. Paiva, L.O.: To the next level! an exploratory study on the influence of user experience on the acceptance of a gamified learning platform. In: CSEDU (1), pp. 281–288. (2022). https://doi.org/10.5220/0011067900003182
49. Paľová, D., Vejačka, M.: Implementation of gamification principles into higher education. Eur. J. Educ. Res. **11**(2), 763–779 (2022). https://doi.org/10.12973/eu-jer.11.2.763
50. Peng, X., Xu, Q., Chen, Y., Zhou, C., Ge, Y., Li, N.: An eye tracking study: positive emotional interface design facilitates learning outcomes in multimedia learning? International Journal of Educational Technology in Higher Education **18**(1), 1–18 (2021). https://doi.org/10.1186/s41239-021-00274-x
51. Piteira, M., Costa, C., Aparicio, M.: A conceptual framework to implement gamification on online courses of computer programming learning: implementation. In: ICERI2017 Proceedings, pp. 7022–7031. IATED (2017). https://doi.org/10.21125/iceri.2017.1865
52. Putri, M.F., Muhammad Razi, A.: The benefits of gamification on user experience: a systematic literature. Jurnal Jurnal Sains Dan Teknologi (JSIT) **2**(3) (2022). https://doi.org/10.47233/jsit.v2i3.353

53. Raschke, M., Blascheck, T., Burch, M.: Visual Analysis of Eye Tracking Data. In: Huang, W. (ed.) Handbook of Human Centric Visualization. AISC, pp. 391–409. Springer, New York (2014). https://doi.org/10.1007/978-1-4614-7485-2_15
54. Sailer, P.: Learning web technologies: overcoming educational challenges. In: EdMedia+ Innovate Learning, pp. 466–475. Association for the Advancement of Computing in Education (AACE), Brussels, Belgium (2024)
55. Sailer, P.: Enhancing web development education in higher education: a comparison of traditional and flipped classroom models. In: Proceedings of the 17th International Conference on Computer Supported Education - Volume 2: CSEDU, pp. 606–617. INSTICC, SciTePress (2025).https://doi.org/10.5220/0013433300003932
56. Sailer, P.: From theory to practice: evaluating gamified platforms through student-centred requirements. In: EdMedia+ Innovate Learning, pp. 874–882. Association for the Advancement of Computing in Education (AACE) (2025)
57. Sailer, P., Kremsner, T., Knipp, F., Kayali, F.: Enhancing learning with gamification: empowering students in web development education. In: Proceedings of the 17th International Conference on Computer Supported Education - Volume 2: CSEDU, pp. 557–568. INSTICC, SciTePress (2025). https://doi.org/10.5220/0013354800003932
58. Schneider, S., Nebel, S., Rey, G.D.: Decorative pictures and emotional design in multimedia learning. Learn. Instr. **44**, 65–73 (2016). https://doi.org/10.1016/j.learninstruc.2016.03.002
59. Schrepp, M.: User experience questionnaire handbook. All you need to know to apply the UEQ successfully in your project (2015). https://doi.org/10.13140/RG.2.1.2815.0245
60. Sharmin, S.: Creativity in CS1: a literature review. ACM Trans. Comput. Educ. **22**(2), 1–26 (2022). https://doi.org/10.1145/3459995
61. Sung, E., Mayer, R.E.: When graphics improve liking but not learning from online lessons. Comput. Hum. Behav. **28**(5), 1618–1625 (2012). https://doi.org/10.1016/j.chb.2012.03.026
62. Sweller, J.: Cognitive load theory. Psychology of Learning and Motivation **55**, 37–76 (2011). https://doi.org/10.1016/B978-0-12-387691-1.00002-8 Elsevier
63. Toledo Palomino, P., Nacke, L., Isotani, S.: Gamification of virtual learning environments: a narrative and user experience approach. In: Proceedings of the XXII Brazilian Symposium on Human Factors in Computing Systems, pp. 1–10. (2023). https://doi.org/10.1145/3638067.3638103
64. Turčáni, M., Balogh, Z., Kohútek, M.: Evaluating computer science students reading comprehension of educational multimedia-enhanced text using scalable eye-tracking methodology. Smart Learn. Environ. **11**(1), 29 (2024). https://doi.org/10.1186/s40561-024-00318-5
65. Um, E., Plass, J.L., Hayward, E.O., Homer, B.D., et al.: Emotional design in multimedia learning. J. Educ. Psychol. **104**(2), 485 (2012). https://doi.org/10.1037/a0026609
66. Uzun, A.M., Yıldırım, Z.: Exploring the effect of using different levels of emotional design features in multimedia science learning. Comput. Educ. **119**, 112–128 (2018). https://doi.org/10.1016/j.compedu.2018.01.002

Adaptive Feedback and Progress Monitoring in MatematiX: Facilitating Customized Mathematics Education Through Serious Games

Daniela Popita(✉) and Adriana Mihaela Coroiu(✉)

Department of Computer Science, Babeş-Bolyai University, Cluj-Napoca, Romania
daniela.popita9@gmail.com , adriana.coroiu@ubbcluj.ro

Abstract. The paper presents an improved version of MathematiX [22], an application developed to help children practice and learn mathematics in primary and secondary school. The application MatematiX incorporates active learning concepts such as serious games, visualizations, storytelling and game-like elements with the purpose of keeping the engagement of the children at a high level while ensuring the rise of their academic level. Learning today focuses only on face-to-face interactions and online platforms are mostly used for document storage. Although the majority of children spend most of their free time on online platforms, there are just a few that offer educative and fun content. The improved version of the application was validated with primary and secondary school students. It provides a feedback system for users and a monitoring system on the progress of each child facilitating the improvements of the application even further. The games and explanations offered by MatematiX involve different mathematical notions from number comparison to basic algebra operations and entry level geometry elements.

Keywords: Serious Games · Feedback · Education · Children · Storytelling · Angle · Arithmetic Operations

1 Introduction

Technology advancements appear every day in various domains, new methods are discovered and more efficient solutions provided to various problems. However, the educational system seems to be forgotten when talking about adapting content and teaching methods [30]. The newly discovered technology resources could improve the learning system regardless of the subject taught.

Children spent a lot of their time online [31] making the importance of developing educational, safe and useful resources [13] even more important. The online environment could be a quality setting for children to learn and enjoy themselves at the same time, as long as the appropriate resources are created [27].

Mathematics, in particular, is a subject that requires a lot of effort in order to be taught properly [26]. Children often find this subject hard unless they

C. Meinel et al. (Eds.): CSEDU 2025, CCIS 3148, pp. 426–442, 2027.
https://doi.org/10.1007/978-3-032-39103-2_20

understand it properly, and even then it's difficult to foster children's interest in it. Especially geometry, which develops critical skills such as logical reasoning, problem-solving, and spatial awareness, often fall short in engaging today's middle school students. As a result, there is a growing need to integrate interactive educational tools that support geometry learning through visual, hands-on, and stimulating experiences [1].

In this paper, we present relevant studies regarding the efficiency of online learning through serious games, storytelling and gamification, through the analysis of the solutions proposed and the general feedback received. We present the enhancements made to the solution proposed by us, the application MatematiX, to incorporate feedback, progress monitoring and the integrated geometry resources.

2 Storytelling, Gamification and Serious Games

Storytelling, the art of communicating information through stories, has become a revolutionary educational method, especially in middle school [14], where it enhances participation, critical thinking, and conceptual comprehension across several subjects. In mathematics [12], particularly geometry, storytelling provides an innovative method to link abstract concepts with familiar, real-world scenarios, enhancing both emotional and cognitive engagement in the learning experience [36].

Research highlights the significance of narratives in enhancing the engagement and retention of learning experiences. Integrating storytelling into geometry classes enables students to relate mathematical issues within familiar contexts, so enhancing curiosity and motivation [33].

Storytelling corresponds to the educational objectives of the 21st century, fostering digital literacy, teamwork, and flexibility. These talents are vital for contemporary learners and are adeptly fostered through collaborative storytelling activities, wherein students enhance their communication skills and teamwork abilities while engaging with academic material [6].

Moreover, digital storytelling—utilizing tools such as iMovie and Audacity—has demonstrated efficacy in promoting creativity and critical thinking. These tools empower students to create, develop, and showcase their tales, enhancing their educational experiences by fostering both technical skills and conceptual comprehension [28].

Defined as the integration of game components, such as rewards, challenges, and progression, into non-game situations, gamification enhances the involvement and increases the motivation of students [19].

The integration of storytelling and gamification offers instant feedback and acknowledgement as the narrative progresses activated upon receiving accurate responses. This mix of narrative and gamification is particularly helpful for children in classes 0–4, who are at a crucial stage of cognitive development.

Serious games are intentionally designed to promote understanding and skill development in multiple areas of education. The players have a game experience where, in order to advance, they must use their knowledge regarding a certain subject [29]. The key element of a serious game is the "playing" aspect, the users do not have the feeling of learning, they are not actually asked direct questions, the questions are embedded in the game and progressing in the game requires the users to use knowledge by solving different tasks [2].

The benefits and advantages of serious games in learning have been proved by various studies, offering resources on various subjects not only mathematics, conducted in the field of education regarding primary [7,16] and middle school education [3,17].

Additionally, serious games have been proven effective for higher education students, for instance, in a study that describes a serious game designed for learning JavaScript by Maskeliūnas et al. [18] the comparison between the test taken by the participants before and after showed increased knowledge of the programming language. Another example with prommising results is League of Emotions Learners (LoEL) [25] is a game designing for improving the skills of communicating emotions in young adults.

During the research process, we identified and focused on two main categories of serious game applications. The first category describes serious games [34] that can be customized, allowing educators or researchers to adapt the game content, structure, or difficulty level based on the specific learning objectives, the targeted content and audience, or context of use. These games focus on providing the educators the resources to practice with their students not only the concepts that the developers deemed important, but also concepts of their choice.

The second category consists of non-customizable serious games, which are developed with a fixed structure and focus on predefined content. These games are typically designed to address a specific subject or learning goal and refer to a certain topic chosen by the developers/researchers based on the context that the game is going to be used. The following section highlights several of the most significant examples for our research.

3 Different Serious Games Platforms

3.1 Apothiquiz

Apothiquiz [5] is a medical quiz serious game designed to ease the drug classification learning process. It was developed by a group of three teachers and five students from University of Franche-Comté as a collaboration between the Faculty of Sciences and Techniques and the Faculty of Health Sciences. The students in pharmacy constructed the database that contains the drug information necessary for the questions of the game and the computer science students designed and implemented the applications.

All users have access to the main quiz questions, and there are some extra features accessible only for users that have an account; we mention one of them, the battleship mode created for students to play with each other. Creating an account is free.

For the application testing, the authors selected on a voluntary basis students from third and fourth years of pharmacy. Each student was assessed before and after using the application through a 20 multiple choice questions test, asking to find the class, indication, side effect, interaction or chemical formula of a drug and in the opposite way, to find a drug from the class, indication, side effect, interaction, or chemical formula.

The results showed the usefulness of an application of this kind. Between the pre-testing and the post-testing, the score increased with 3 points out of a maximum of 20 points (95 # confidence interval of [3.8; 2.7] in the third year and of [4.3; 2.8] in the fourth year). The students responded on average after 22 days [from 14 to 35 days]. 78 of the students that took part in the study completed the test before using the application and 41 completed test after using the application. There were also 18 third year students and 23 fourth year students took the test after using the app.

3.2 PizzaAlLancio

PizzaAlLancio [8] is a serious game developed by a team of students from the University of Padua, Italy. The game is designed to help children understand complementary and equivalent fractions. It tells the story of a delivery boy that eats a part of the pizza while making the delivery and needs the help of the user to complete the part of the pizza that was eaten.

All the information stored is anonymous; the users are identified solely by their device ID. A disadvantage of this approach is that the user progress cannot be tracked on multiple devices and in order to maintain the progress, the user has to use the same device.

The app was tested at the end of May 2018 with 34 children, 17 fourth graders and 17 fifth graders. All children took a written test before using the game to assess their level of knowledge. After using the application, they took another computer based test on fractions. The statistics gathered in the game sessions, suggest that the game is suitable for forth graders.

Later, the application [9] was extended with a complementary web platform that allows the customization of the previously developed game. This platform allows teachers to provide specific input data for the fractions game (the values for the denominators and numerators) through a web form. In order to join the teacher's game, the students need to enter a game room code corresponding to the teacher's session.

The new game data, submitted by the teacher, is stored in the database. Each student device that joins the game room sends a specific request for the game data containing the room ID, such that the server returns the data introduced by the teacher for that specific session.

The web platform provides a new feature that allows the teacher to create an entirely new game using a visual interface. This is achieved through the use of a drag-and-drop canvas that teachers can manipulate to design the layout of the game, define its interactive behavior, and input custom exercises.

3.3 ThimelEdu

ThimelEdu [32] is an interactive single-player educational game, designed for primary and secondary school students, that presents a virtual ancient theater world, where the users can study and learn information about the Ancient Theater. It uses interactive quizzes and questionnaires that do not need the motorization of teachers.

The players can walk around the virtual ancient theater and learn information about arts, ancient objects and architecture.

There are different features accessible for the users depending on whether they have created an account in the application. For the users with an account retrieves all the resources relevant to the user based on the association of the user information (language, grade etc.) and the information addressed by the resource are retrieved and suggested to the user. Users who do not have an account do not benefit of the profile customization, and the users that have not completed their profile, receive a partial customization.

3.4 Pie Framework

Pie framework [20] is an open source toolkit that provides custom UI components compatible with educational purposes. It offers teachers the ability to create quiz-like materials for students and monitor their progress. This framework is used by different e-learning applications to create and present resources on different subjects not only Mathematics.

4 Feedback Collecting Systems

Before presenting the feedback collecting system of different educational applications, there needs to be a distinction between the different types of feedback that our research focused on:

- Structured feedback - precise answers given by the user to clearly defined questions (multiple-choice questions, yes/no questions etc.)
- Unstructured feedback - open-ended comments, suggestions, or free-text input completed by the user
- Implicit Feedback (Behavioral Data) - the user's actions (time spent in the app, results obtained after solving different tasks, etc.)

During the research process, we studied different platforms that collect one or more of the feedback types presented. There are apps that retain the grades of the students and other details to monitor the university/school's performance level or the students' performance level. There are apps that collect different types of feedback directly from the user. We present the implementation of a few of them.

4.1 Siberian Federal University's Feedback System

In the article [15] the authors try to create the best database management system for a Higher Educational Institution, the Siberian Federal University. They focus on three main principles, the principle of **Data Centered on the Student**, the principle of **Data Continuity** and the principle of **Data Consistency**.

The principle of **Data Centered on the Student** refers to using a student identifier as a key field to connect all the student data across the tables of the database.

The idea of **Continuity** refers to keeping a history of all the student data. No data about the student should be deleted, it should all be kept in the student's historical record for future analysis; data such as the intermediate grades.

The principle of **Consistency** refers to keeping a correct data structure and organization which makes it impossible to enter contradicting information, and minimizes duplications and errors due to human factors.

The authors, created a custom educational database that is compiled from multiple institutional sources already in place at Siberian Federal University such as 1C Document Management, Plans, Moodle, and other custom faculty platforms.

4.2 SmartFeedback

SmartFeedback [23] is an application designed to collect all three kinds of feedback from users about the applications they are using on their device. It is installed locally (on a phone or a tablet) and is configured to present short, targeted questions to users at random or scheduled times while they are using specific apps. The goal is to gather the user's real time perspective, without interrupting the natural usage flow of the application.

4.3 Faculty of Electronics's Feedback Collecting System

In the article [10], the authors present their feedback collecting system that had already been used for 5 years at the Faculty of Electronics, Vilnius, Gediminas Technical University at the time the article was published. The study lasted 10 years, 5 years with the feedback method and 5 years without.

Although the best, spoken feedback during classroom is subjective to the students that participate to the discussion and is rarely a sum of all the students present in the course room. This can be either because of the lack of courage from some students to express their opinions or the overly active behavior of others.

The solution encountered by the authors in this article was the use of **IQPolls**, an online system that provides free, as well as paid versions, that can be used to gather feedback from students. The surveys were used during lectures or laboratory work, by the teachers and even the students, when presenting different assignments. The results were promising, the analysis of the 10 year's statistical data shows an increase of 4–6% in student performance and 86.3% of the students evaluated positively this feedback collecting system.

5 Literature Review Conclusions

The authors of the presented articles understood the importance of collecting feedback from the students, whether it is regarding online means of learning or on-site ones. In order to offer users a proper study environment, their opinion and feedback should be taken into consideration as we can see from other studies. Feedback should not only be collected but also used to improve the quality of the learning environment and the experience of the learner, to provide the most appropriate learning facilities.

6 Technologies Used in the Implementation of the Application

As of this writing, HTML5 is the most recent form of HTML. It has more features and is better than earlier versions. New semantic tags like canvas, section, main, footer, and header are available and helped design and implement the resources offered by our application better. It also had better support for video and advanced graphics. This new form of HTML along with JavaScript and CSS provided a solid foundation for the resources we provide.

6.1 Design Enhancements

Adaptive Web Design (AWD) [11] creates multiple fixed layouts for different devices based on the detected screen size. The look and even the content of the website might differ depending on the device used. These kinds of website provide tailored websites for each device, with the details that are relevant for each type of user depending on the device they are using.

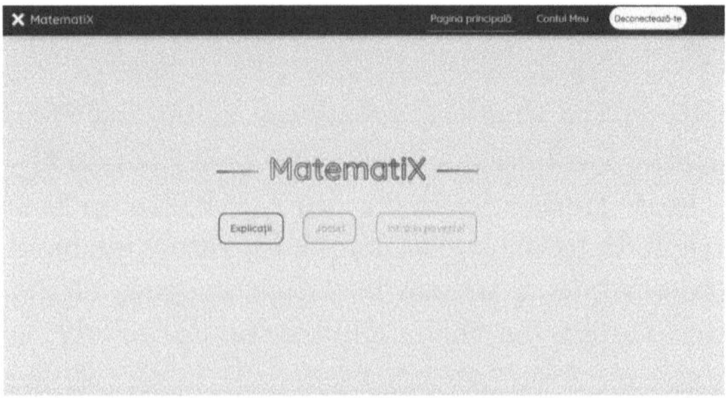

Fig. 1. Main page.

Responsive Web Design (RWD) [24] refers to giving websites the ability to adapt their layout, structure, and content based on the device being used, while ensuing the consistency of the information. It relies on a single flexible layout

Table 1. Responsive vs Adaptive design.

Property	Responsive Design	Adaptive Design
Layout	Fluid and flexible	Fixed for each screen size
Number of Design files	One file	Multiple files
Content	Usually the same across devices	Can be customized based on device
Performance	Slightly heavier due to fluidity	Potentially faster as layouts are optimized
Loading speed	Slower (can be optimized)	Faster
Usage	Easier and less complex	Medium to low
Flexibility	High	Low

that adjusts fluidly to any screen size using CSS media queries and relative units i.e. percentages.

The comparison (see Table 1) concludes that the Adaptive design's performance is better in therms of the speed of content loading because adaptive website load only the content and layout meant for the specific device.

However, in terms of ease of use and maintenance, the responsive websites perform better because they use only a single layout file to adjust the style of the page across screen sizes.

Overall, even if both these approaches are efficient in different contexts, for creating the best website the two need to be combined in order to meet the technological advancements [35].

Considering that a well designed application has to combine responsiveness and adaptiveness concepts, bootstrap was integrated in the application to provide responsive enhancements to our application.

Bootstrap is a Front-end framework for user interfaces and themes used for building web applications and websites that are responsive. It uses HTML, CSS and Java Script.

Bootstrap is based on a grid system made of rows and a maximum of 12 columns. The rows are created by adding to the corresponding div the "row" class and for the columns there are multiple classes of columns that represent different screen sizes: col-, col-sm-, col-md-, col-lg-, and col-xl to which is added the number of columns occupied by that HTML element.

In order to apply the responsive and adaptive concepts in our application, for the games, the score table uses bootstrap responsive display classes. On large screens, the table is shown on the left side of the page alongside the game. On smaller screens, the score table is hidden by default, there is a button above the game that toggles that score table as an overlay on top of the game.

The menu (see Fig. 1) dynamically injected into each page, having a fixed structure. Using JavaScriot, it conditionally displays either the `Log In` button and the link to the `Main Page` for the users who are not logged in or the link to the `Main Page`, the link to the `My Account Page` and the `Log Out` button for authenticated users.

Although the responsive and adaptive qualities of the application were improved, there need to be some more enhancements made to ensure a better usability of the application on mobile devices.

6.2 Application Architecture

The application architecture remained consistent with the previous versions, MatematiX is a client-server web application with a RESTful architecture divided in two tiers, the client side (UI) implemented using HTML, JavaScript and CSS and the server side (API logic) implemented with C# (Fig. 2).

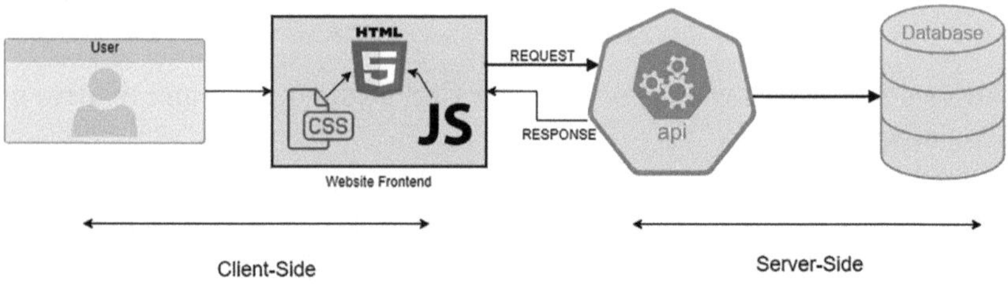

Fig. 2. Application architecture [21].

The database layer has been preserved as a relational SQL system, ensuring continuity in data management across application versions, however, to ensure the persistence of scores records and to enable the tracking of each student's progress over time, the database structure was extended to include the corresponding tables, while the backend was enhanced to correctly manage transactions and maintain data consistency. Additionally, the structure was modified to facilitate the retention of feedback and a record of the feedback received from the users.

6.3 Session Handling and Progress Motorization

The application did not dispose of any user roles, all the resources were previously accessible to any account owner. The application disposes now of two user roles, managed using the Asp.Net provided features, with the possibility of expansion in the future. The user roles are ADMIN and STUDENT.

The previous version of our application did not allow access to the resources of our application unless the users had an account. For this new version we created a few JavaScript functions to help with the handling of sessions for the users that do not have an account.

If a user wants to access the application with no account, they can play the games or interact with the explanations but they will not have a record of the score obtained to the games, or access to the my account page and implicitly the feedback form.

7 The MathematiX Set of New Features

This section of the article presents the enhanced features of the application `Matematix` [22]. In order to comply with the standard design requirements mentioned in the previous section, the interface of the application was modified with a new design.

7.1 The Main Page

The color palette of the main page has been updated to create a more child-friendly aspect while effectively showcasing all the available features of the application. He main page now presents two primary categories of resources: the explanations, organized by grade level and the serious games(see Figure 3). The logo was redesigned as well (see Figure 1).

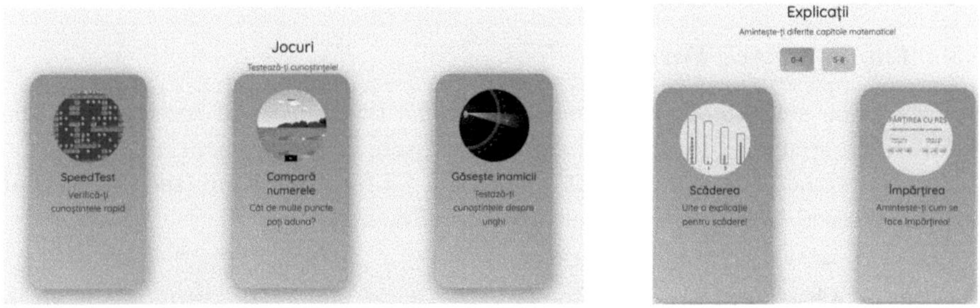

Fig. 3. Features layout.

Another notable design enhancement is the usage of a consistent, universal font across all pages of the application. To ensure a more professional and cohesive user experience, it is essential that the fonts used belong to a single category, as this contributes to visual consistency and helps build user trust. [4].

7.2 The Application's Story

On the main page, the users can also discover the story of the application, the meaning of all the games and explanations found on our website (see Fig. 4).

The main idea of the story presented in our application is that the vegetables are fighting the bugs in order to regain their freedom and the users can help them achieve that by solving the exercises in the story or playing different games.

Two stories—one for the division and one for the subtraction—were used to illustrate the storytelling concept that was incorporated into the app. In order for the children to discover the whole story, they have to correctly solve the exercises given in the story.

Fig. 4. Storytelling integration.

7.3 The Feedback Form

Following the success of the application in the two phases of testing with the children, we created a feedback form for the users of the application.

We redesigned the "my account" page linked a feedback form (see Fig. 6) that can be accessed by anyone with an account (Fig. 5).

7.4 The Angle Game

The "Find the enemies" game is a game designed for children to practice their angle measurement skills. The purpose of the game is to kill the monsters situated

Fig. 5. My account page.

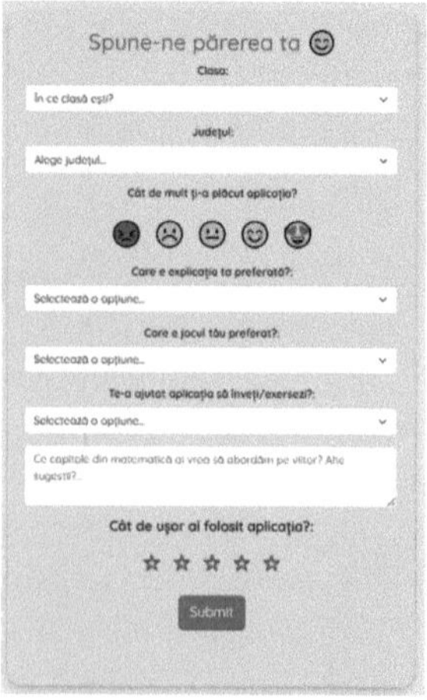

Fig. 6. Feedback Form.

at a certain angle by reading from the protractor. There are two types of levels, for the odd levels the user must position the aim at the given angle and press enter to kill the bug. For the even levels, the user must make use of the aim to find the monster and write it's correct angle in order to kill it. The game is lost when the monsters have reached the center.

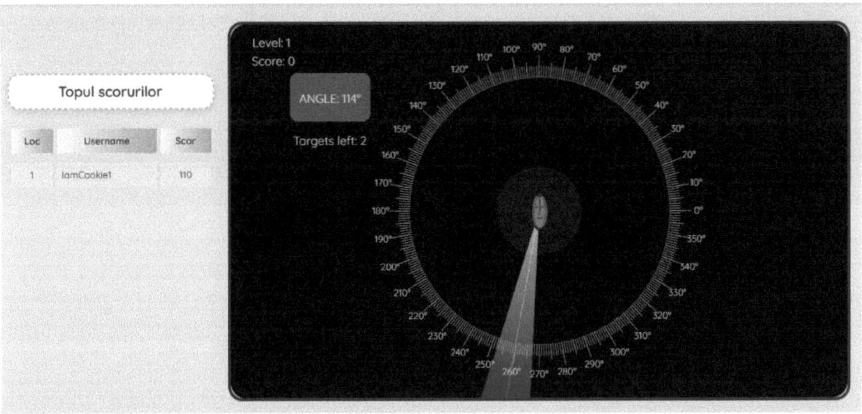

Fig. 7. Angle game with score table.

To ensure the engagement of the children, a table with the top 5 scores is available on the page (see Fig. 7). The score is saved only for the users that have an account in the application, but even if the user does not possess an account, they can see the score they obtained at the game

Furthermore, as mentioned before, for the registered users, a history of the evolution of the scores acquired for each game is kept inside the database ensuring the monitoring of the student's progress.

8 Results and Conclusions

8.1 Application Validation

Since the development of the application, the application was tested two times once with first-to-fourth graders (as presented in the article [21]) and once with fifth-to-eight graders (as presented in the article [22]). Overall, there have been around 140 children that tested the application.

We investigated if there is any correlation between the gender or the age of the children and how much they liked the application. For this, we used Pearson correlation test with the rating given to the application and the gender or age of the participant.

For the Pearson correlation test there are two values that give us the results of the test. The correlation coefficient, $r \in [-1, 1]$ and the p-value, $p \in [0, 1]$.

The correlation coefficient, r, measures strength and direction of a linear relationship between two variables. It is compared to 0 and it's significance can be seen in Table 2.

Table 2. The interpretation of r's values.

r's value	Corelation type	Meaning
$r > 0$	Positive correlation	as one variable increases, so does the other
$r < 0$	Negative correlation	as one variable increases, the other decreases
r=0	No linear correlation	a nonlinear relationship might exist

The p value tests the null hypothesis that r = 0. For it's interpretation, a significance threshold (α) is chosen (in general α=0.05). If the p value id less than the threshold, the correlation is statistically significant, otherwise we cannot conclude that the correlation is real.

In the first correlation test between the age and the rating of the application, r = 0.15 and p = 0.077 which denotes a week correlation, the children in higher grades might be more inclined towards this kind of software but it is not certain.

For the correlation test between the gender and the rating of the application, r-0.044 and p = 0.607 which denotes no significative correlation, the p value is too high, the gender of the children does not influence the success of the application.

8.2 Contributions and Educational Value

Given the obtained results in the testing process and the positive feedback received, an application of this kind would be beneficial for children in the Romanian learning system not in order to replace the role of the teacher but to assist the teachers in the teaching process and the students in the process of practising different mathematical concepts.

An encouraging aspect was the positive feedback of the teachers and some of the parents. Usually nowadays children spend a lot of their free time on the computer and an application like this one could be an alternative that combines the time spent doing homework with the time spent playing on the computer.

As we mentioned before, for the testing process in the future, in order to obtain clearer results regardless of the level of knowledge that the children can gain by using this kind of application, a test should be taken by the children before and after using the application to assist the level of knowledge gained through using the application.

This kind of software is not as available as it should be in Romania, our application is one of the first to provide visual explanations and mainly serious games. An important aspect that we mention regarding our games is that our games are not games that you get to play after learning or if the user has solved a number of exercises. Our games have the purpose to teach the children while playing such that the fun element of the game like the competition factor motivate them to play multiple times the games consequently practicing mathematical concepts.

8.3 Conclusions

The research goal of this paper is to analyse and present studies on the development of e-learning platforms, the resources they offer, and the efficacy of proposed solutions, with a primary focus on the impact of learning various subjects through the integration of serious games, storytelling, and gamification. Additionally, this paper, presents an enhancement of the previous version of the MatematiX application by including new geometrical concepts that have been proven useful and interacting for our previous users. The game and explanation developed targeted the mathematical unit presenting the angle and it's properties. The presented concepts can be further explored and other resources can be provided for a variety of different topics.

The kind of resources that our application provides would be best used and made for punctual subjects in collaboration with the teachers of different grades. The teachers could also benefit from the score records kept for each student to gain insight on the progress of each child.

Moreover, the software, security and database enhancements provide accessibility to our resources and efficient methods for monitoring children's progress and their feedback in our application. The software can be used regardless of the financial aspect or the location of the user, the only requirements are a laptop/computer and connection to the internet.

8.4 Future Development

The application is subject to constant improvement. There are several parts that could be improved and developed more, such as the existing resources for the angle notion.

Following the interest shown from older children (5th, 6th, 7th grade), the aiming is to create more resources for them, centered on the needs that they brought up while testing the application.

Providing that the amount of data collected from the feedback form increases, the data could be processed and used for further improvement. Furthermore, right tools to process the data from the history tables for further development and data analysis need to be determined in order to broaden our knowledge about the children's learning process. The application should be extended to include teacher roles, with extended features and access to the children's evolution and monitoring rights of other aspects of their progress.

Moreover, we want to improve our current resources based on the feedback received so far. One of the improvements would be to add sounds in the games and more visual animations.

Considering the continually expanding artificial intelligence domain, we will conduct a research focusing on it's integration in our application. Object detection could be used to create a real-life geometric description of different geometric shapes detected.

Last but not least, we want to research more thoughtfully how the application can improve the educational progress of the children through a series of tests that should be taken before and after using the application. These tests could provide us with the necessary information regarding the level of difficulty that our software should have and if our application does help the children understand the addressed educational aspects.

References

1. Abdan Syakuran, R., Afrianto, I.: Implementation of gamification in mathematics m-learning application to creating student engagement. Int. J. Adv. Comput. Sci. Appl. **13**(7) (2022)
2. Alvarez, J., Djaouti, D.: An introduction to serious game definitions and concepts. Serious games & simulation for risks management (2011)
3. Barros, C., Carvalho, A.A., Salgueiro, A.: The effect of the serious game tempoly on learning arithmetic polynomial operations. Educ. Inf. Technol. **25**(3), 1497–1509 (2020)
4. Beaird, J., Walker, A., George, J.: The principles of beautiful web design. SitePoint Pty Ltd (2020)
5. Clairet, A.L., et al.: Design, programming, and evaluation of a serious game web application to memorise drug classification and properties. Curr. Pharm. Teach. Learn. **17**(6), 102335 (2025)
6. Del-Moral-Pérez, M.E., Villalustre-Martínez, L., Neira-Piñeiro, M.D.R.: Teachers' perception about the contribution of collaborative creation of digital storytelling to the communicative and digital competence in primary education schoolchildren. Comput. Assist. Lang. Learn. **32**(4), 342–365 (2019)
7. Fraga-Varela, F., Vila-Couñago, E., Martínez-Piñeiro, E.: The impact of serious games in mathematics fluency: a study in primary education. Comunicar: Media Educ. Res. J. **29**(69), 115–125 (2021)
8. Gaggi, O., Ciraulo, F., Casagrande, M.: Eating pizza to learn fractions. In: Proceedings of the 4th EAI International Conference on Smart Objects and Technologies for Social Good, pp. 220–225 (2018)
9. Gaggi, O., Petenazzi, G.: A digital platform for teaching mathematics. In: Proceedings of the 5th EAI International Conference on Smart Objects and Technologies for Social Good, pp. 37–42 (2019)
10. Grazulevicius, G., Barzdenas, V., Vasjanov, A., Liobe, J.: Applying smart devices for gathering real-time feedback from students. Comput. Appl. Eng. Educ. **29**(3), 613–623 (2021)
11. Gustafson, A.: Adaptive web design: crafting rich experiences with progressive enhancement. New Riders (2015)
12. Irmayanti, M., Chou, L.F., Anuar, N.N.B.Z.: Storytelling and math anxiety: a review of storytelling methods in mathematics learning in Asian countries. Eur. J. Psychol. Educ. **40**(1), 24 (2025)

13. Kardefelt-Winther, D.: How does the time children spend using digital technology impact their mental well-being, social relationships and physical activity?: an evidence-focused literature review (2017)
14. Kim, D., Park, H.R., Vorobel, O.: Enriching middle school students' learning through digital storytelling: a multimodal analytical framework. ECNU Rev. Educ. **7**(2), 357–383 (2024)
15. Kustitskaya, T.A., Esin, R.V., Kytmanov, A.A., Zykova, T.V.: Designing an education database in a higher education institution for the data-driven management of the educational process. Educ. Sci. **13**(9), 947 (2023)
16. Lopez, J.Y.A., Huaycho, R.N.N., Santos, F.I.Y., Talavera-Mendoza, F.: The impact of serious games on learning in primary education: a systematic literature. Int. J. Learn. Teach. Educ. Res. **22**(3), 379–395 (2023)
17. Malvasi, V., Gil-Quintana, J., Bocciolesi, E.: The projection of gamification and serious games in the learning of mathematics multi-case study of secondary schools in Italy. Mathematics **10**(3), 336 (2022)
18. Maskeliūnas, R., Kulikajevas, A., Blažauskas, T., Damaševičius, R., Swacha, J.: An interactive serious mobile game for supporting the learning of programming in Javascript in the context of eco-friendly city management. Computers **9**(4), 102 (2020)
19. Nand, K., Baghaei, N., Casey, J., Barmada, B., Mehdipour, F., Liang, H.N.: Engaging children with educational content via gamification. Smart Learn. Environ. **6**, 1–15 (2019)
20. PIE Framework Team: PIE: Portable Interactions and Elements. PIE Labs (2025). https://pielabs.github.io/pie-docs/. Accessed 08 May 2025
21. Popita, D., Coroiu, A.M.: Interactive math explorations using the game-based application matematiX. In: CSEDU (1), pp. 91–102 (2024)
22. Popita, D., Coroiu, A.M.: Upgrading matematiX: a modern approach to learning geometry for middle school students. In: CSEDU (2), pp. 800–807 (2025)
23. Radeck, L.: Collecting feedback and deriving requirements, Heidelberg University, Faculty of Mathematics, Engineering, and Natural Sciences (2025). Ph.D. thesis
24. Rathore, D., Singhal, N.: Web design dilemma: a comprehensive guide to adaptive and responsive design. In: 2024 IEEE International Students' Conference on Electrical, Electronics and Computer Science (SCEECS), pp. 1–5. IEEE (2024)
25. Santos, J., et al.: Developing emotional intelligence with a game: the league of emotions learners approach. Computers **10**(8), 97 (2021)
26. Schoenfeld, A.H.: Why are learning and teaching mathematics so difficult? In: Handbook of Cognitive Mathematics, pp. 763–797. Springer (2022)
27. Scoda, A.D.: The virtual enviroment-a learning environment for our children? In: Conference proceedings of» eLearning and Software for Education «(eLSE), vol. 11, pp. 300–308. Carol I National Defence University Publishing House (2015)
28. Sushkevych, O.: Digital tools and traditional means for storytelling: Balancing in the ESL classroom. German International Journal of Modern Science/Deutsche Internationale Zeitschrift für Zeitgenössische Wissenschaft (73) (2024)
29. Susi, T., Johannesson, M., Backlund, P.: Serious games: An overview (2007)
30. Swerzenski, J.: Why teaching technology must adapt to our teaching. Commun. Educ. **70**(2), 211–213 (2021)
31. Veselinovska, S.S.: Why do children spend less time in the natural environment?/Vospitanie-Journal of Educational Sciences, Theory andPractice **11**(15), 131–143 (2020)

32. Vidakis, N., Barianos, K.A., Xanthopoulos, G., Stamatakis, A.: Cultural inheritance educational environment: the ancient theatre game ThimelEdu. In: European Conference on Games Based Learning, pp. 730–XIII. Academic Conferences International Limited (2018)
33. Walters, L., Green, M., Goldsby, D., Parker, D.: Digital storytelling as a problem-solving strategy in mathematics teacher education: How making a math-eo engages and excites 21st century students. Int. J. Technol. Educ. Sci. **2**(1), 1–16 (2018)
34. Wang, J., Hodgson, R., Cristea, A.I.: Memorable: a multi-player customisable serious game framework for cyber-security learning. In: International Conference on Intelligent Tutoring Systems, pp. 313–322. Springer (2022)
35. Yousaf, N., Butt, W.H., Azam, F., Anwar, M.W.: A systematic review of adaptive and responsive design approaches for world wide web. In: Advances in Information and Communication Networks: Proceedings of the 2018 Future of Information and Communication Conference (FICC), vol. 2, pp. 704–717. Springer (2019)
36. Zazkis, R., Liljedahl, P.: Teaching mathematics as storytelling, Brill (2019)

Enhancing the Data Science Competency Framework for the Era of Generative AI

Maike Holtkemper(✉), Simone Opel, Maria Potanin, Tobias Golz, Johannes Krämer, and Christian Beecks

Department of Data Science, University of Hagen, Universitätsstrasse 11, 58097 Hagen, Germany
maike.holtkemper@fernuni-hagen.de

Abstract. The data scientist profession, described as the "sexiest job of the 21st century," continues to attract intense demand, now further fueled by the rapid rise of generative AI (GenAI). However, the competencies required to develop, implement, and manage large language model (LLM) solutions are largely missing from existing competence frameworks. Building on our previous synthesis of 12 curricula and frameworks, we extend the modified EDISON Data Science Competence Framework with a focused review of GenAI competencies. Following the PRISMA 2020 guidelines, we screened 579 records and identified 41 distinct GenAI competencies. We organized these competencies into seven groups: (1) technical foundations of AI and LLMs, (2) prompt engineering and interaction, (3) evaluation, validation, and critical assessment, (4) integration and application of LLMs, (5) ethical, responsible, and legal AI use, (6) data management and model training, and (7) explainability and transparency. We compared these GenAI groups to the existing framework structure to assess coverage and identify competency gaps. The analysis revealed substantial alignment with current groups but also exposed missing competencies in three key areas: prompt engineering, LLM-specific evaluation and benchmarking, and AI governance. To address these gaps, we introduce three additional competence groups: *GenAI Interaction and Prompt Engineering*, *GenAI Evaluation and Governance*, and *GenAI Integration and Model Operations*. These extensions preserve the framework's evidence-based foundation while ensuring its relevance for GenAI-enabled workflows in education and industry. The updated framework is available through an interactive web application to support instructors, curriculum developers, and practitioners in aligning training and job profiles with the evolving demands of GenAI.

Keywords: Data Science · Competence · Framework · Curricula · Generative AI

C. Meinel et al. (Eds.): CSEDU 2025, CCIS 3148, pp. 443–479, 2027.
https://doi.org/10.1007/978-3-032-39103-2_21

1 Introduction

Over the preceding decade, the profession of data scientist has gained considerable prominence, both in industry and academic discourse. Davenport and Patil famously described it as the *"Sexiest Job of the 21st Century"* [25], a phrase that not only captured public imagination but also signaled the emergence of a new professional identity at the intersection of technology, mathematics, and business. At the time, the role was still taking shape, yet demand was already accelerating, particularly within technology firms and innovative start-ups that sought to capitalize on the growing availability of digital data [25,26].

Ten years later, the same authors revisited their claim in the follow-up article *"Is Data Scientist Still the Sexiest Job of the 21st Century?"*. Their conclusion was unambiguous: far from declining, the appetite for skilled data scientists had intensified, as organizations across sectors recognized the strategic importance of data-driven decision-making [26]. The continued fascination with the profession stems from its unique promise: the ability to apply advanced analytical and computational methods to extract knowledge from heterogeneous, large-scale, and often messy data sources [112].

During this period, technological advances and the expansion of the field have also reshaped the expectations placed on data scientists. Whereas early practitioners often worked as generalists covering a broad range of tasks, the increasing complexity of tools, methods, and applications has prompted a shift toward greater specialization [26]. This transition reflects not only the maturity of the profession but also the growing diversity of contexts in which data science is applied, from scientific research to industry innovation and public sector initiatives.

Despite the growing visibility and recognition of the profession, the demand for data scientists continues to outpace the supply of qualified professionals. Several factors contribute to this persistent shortage. Demographic change has been identified as one explanation, as an aging workforce and shifting labor market dynamics create pressure on the availability of skilled employees [50]. In addition, the role of a data scientist is associated with high entry barriers. These barriers arise from the breadth of expertise required, which spans mathematics, statistics, computer science, and domain-specific knowledge, making it difficult for individuals to acquire and maintain the full spectrum of competencies needed for professional practice [43].

Another key challenge lies in the absence of universally accepted standards for data science education and professional practice. Although numerous frameworks and curricula have been proposed, they often differ in terminology, structure, and scope, leading to inconsistencies in the way competencies are taught, assessed, and recognized across institutions [80,87]. This lack of alignment complicates both curriculum design and workforce planning, leaving organizations uncertain about which competence profiles are most appropriate for their specific projects. Moreover, it hinders mobility and comparability in the labor market, as qualifications may not easily transfer between academic programs, industries, or regions.

The combined effect of these challenges is a professional landscape that remains fragmented [52]. On the one hand, demand for skilled data scientists grows rapidly as organizations pursue data-driven strategies. On the other hand, the absence of common standards and the difficulty of meeting extensive skill requirements contribute to a sustained shortage of talent. Addressing these issues requires not only educational innovation but also consensus on the competencies that should define the profession, thereby enabling clearer role definitions and more effective workforce development [52].

Building on these challenges, our previous research sought to provide greater clarity by systematically analyzing existing curricula and competence frameworks. In that study, we conducted a structured literature review following the guidelines of Webster and Watson [115], which resulted in the identification of 209 relevant publications. After removing duplicates and applying quality criteria, 32 documents were retained for detailed analysis. From this pool, 12 frameworks were selected and examined using qualitative content analysis as described by Kuckartz [67].

The outcome of this synthesis was a modified version of the EDISON Data Science Competence Framework (CF-DS), which served as the foundation for an integrated competence model [88]. By consolidating competencies drawn from diverse sources, the revised framework aimed to address inconsistencies in terminology and coverage across existing approaches. It also highlighted previously unnamed or underrepresented elements of the competence space, including knowledge and skills that had not been explicitly articulated in earlier frameworks.

This work provided a unified structure that aligned academic curricula with professional practice, thereby offering a reference point for both educational institutions and industry stakeholders. In particular, the modified framework contributed to a more systematic understanding of how competencies are acquired and applied in data science projects. It also underscored the importance of competence order, that is, the logical sequence in which knowledge, skills, and abilities are built during training and professional development, an aspect that had often been overlooked in previous studies. By addressing these issues, the framework laid the groundwork for more consistent curriculum design, clearer role definitions, and better workforce planning in data science.

While our earlier study, the modified framework by Potanin et al. [88] represented an important step toward standardization, it did not yet capture the disruptive changes brought about by recent advances in Generative AI (GenAI) and large language models (LLMs). Since 2023, these technologies have become integral to data science workflows, ranging from code generation and automated analysis to new forms of humanAI collaboration. Their rapid diffusion has created demand for competencies that are largely absent from established frameworks and curricula, raising the risk of a widening gap between academic training and industry practice.

To address this gap, the present study extends our earlier work by incorporating a systematic review of GenAI-related competencies. Following the PRISMA 2020 guidelines [85], we conducted searches in the ACM Digital Library and IEEE Xplore, which yielded 579 unique records. After screening and evaluation, 87 full-text articles were examined in detail, and from these, 41 distinct competencies relevant to GenAI were identified. These competencies were organized into seven thematic groups, covering technical foundations, prompt engineering and interaction, evaluation and validation, integration and application, ethical and legal considerations, data management and training, and explainability and transparency.

Beyond mapping these competencies, we introduce three entirely new competence groups to the existing structure: *GenAI Interaction and Prompt Engineering*, *GenAI Evaluation and Governance*, and *GenAI Integration and Model Operations*. These groups capture skill demands that extend beyond traditional data science practice, reflecting novel tasks such as prompt formulation, LLM-specific benchmarking, alignment training, and AI governance. By embedding these additions into the modified EDISON framework [58], we ensure both continuity with established competence areas and adaptability to emerging technological realities.

The resulting framework thus not only consolidates existing knowledge but also expands the competence space to reflect the requirements of GenAI-enabled data science. In doing so, it offers a comprehensive resource for curriculum developers, instructors, and industry practitioners who seek to align training, education, and workforce planning with the evolving demands of the profession [88]. Therefore, this extended version of the study moves beyond a static literature synthesis and positions the competence framework as a dynamic, forward-looking tool for navigating the GenAI era.

This article is structured as follows. Section 3 reviews theoretical foundations of competence frameworks and the implications of GenAI for data science roles. Section 4 outlines our two-step methodology, combining qualitative coding with a systematic review. Section 5 introduces the modified competence framework based on the EDISON CF-DS. Section 6 validates the framework by comparing it against the 41 extracted GenAI competencies and discusses the need for additional GenAI-specific competence groups. Section 7 concludes with implications for curriculum design and outlines directions for future work.

2 Background

In the domain of knowledge acquisition, considerable uncertainty remains regarding the precise skill set required of data scientists. This ambiguity has led to inconsistencies in how data science curricula are designed and how competence frameworks are structured [100]. As a result, academic programs often differ markedly in their emphasis and coverage, producing substantial variation in the knowledge and skills that students acquire [111]. Such disparities complicate both the development of targeted curricula and the comparison of educational outcomes across institutions.

A central reason for this fragmentation is the absence of a modern, adaptable framework that clearly defines the competencies relevant to data science. Without such a framework, it is difficult to establish consensus on which capabilities constitute the foundation of the profession and how they should be sequenced in the learning process. The lack of standardization also creates challenges for the uniform training of data scientists, as institutions interpret the competence space differently and prioritize distinct elements [80]. Consequently, while the demand for data science expertise continues to grow steadily, the pathways for acquiring that expertise remain uneven, highlighting the need for a framework that provides both structure and adaptability in defining professional competencies.

2.1 Competence Framework Terminology

Competence frameworks have become increasingly prominent across many domains over the last decades. Originally developed to guide education and training in professional contexts, they are now also widely used by organizations to define job roles, support workforce planning, and establish criteria for recruitment and career progression [79]. Their central purpose is to establish consensus on what constitutes relevant expertise, promote standardization, and provide a common reference point for both educators and practitioners.

Despite these shared objectives, the terminology surrounding competence frameworks is far from uniform. A significant source of ambiguity stems from the use of the terms *competence* and *competency*. Mills et al. [79] highlight that two dominant conceptual traditions have shaped the field: the *behavioural* approach, which emerged primarily from educational research, and the later *functional* approach, driven by employers' needs. In the behavioural tradition, competencies are understood as cumulative attributes that reflect a learner's evolving performance capabilities [19,84]. By contrast, functional frameworks describe explicit performance expectations for specific professions, defining competencies as discrete states that are either present or absent [17,96].

Over time, hybrid approaches have emerged, combining behavioural and functional perspectives to account for both long-term skill development and the immediate performance standards expected in the workplace [15,70,79,104]. Nevertheless, the inconsistent use of terminology continues to complicate the design of frameworks across domains. In many cases, the term *competency* is used to describe how performance occurs (emphasizing behaviour), while *competence* refers to the state of being able to perform specific tasks effectively (emphasizing function) [27,109].

For the purposes of this study, we adopt the terminology of the EDISON Competence Framework, which uses the term *competence* (and its plural *competencies*) as the overarching category [58]. This choice reflects the functional orientation of our work: competencies are defined as requirements that must be met for successful participation in data science projects. At the same time, we acknowledge that curricula remain essential for developing these competencies incrementally, since they structure the learning process by sequencing knowledge acquisition, skills training, and opportunities for application. In other words, while competence frameworks define the target state of expertise, curricula provide the pathways to reach it.

2.2 The EDISON Data Science Framework

The EDISON Data Science Framework (EDSF) was developed as part of the European Commission's EDISON project, which ran from 2015 to 2017. Its primary goal was to establish the relatively new profession of "data scientist" by defining required competencies, formulating a skills profile, and creating supporting structures such as a body of knowledge and a model curriculum [38,41]. Beyond its educational orientation, the initiative also aimed to secure a sustainable business model for the continuous training of data scientists in Europe, ensuring that both universities and professional education providers could contribute to workforce development [41].

Central to the EDSF is the *Competence Framework for Data Science (CF-DS)*, which identifies the competencies relevant for the profession and links them to associated knowledge and skills [58]. Competence in this context is defined according to the European e-Competence Framework as the demonstrated ability to apply knowledge, skills, and attitudes to achieve observable results [42, p. 5]. Within the CF-DS, this definition is operationalized by systematically associating each competence with the knowledge areas and skills needed to enact it [30].

The CF-DS is structured along four dimensions. First, competencies are grouped into five major areas: *Data Analytics (DSDA), Data Engineering (DSENG), Data Management and Governance (DSDM), Research Methods and Project Management (DSRMP)*, and *Domain-specific Knowledge (DSDK)*. These groups provide a thematic organization that covers both technical and organizational aspects of data science. Second, a *generic description* further contextualizes each competence group by emphasizing domain-specific requirements and challenges, thus adapting the framework to particular industries or application areas. Third, a *proficiency level* dimension links competencies to different roles and responsibilities within data science teams, thereby clarifying expectations across junior, intermediate, and senior levels. Finally, the framework distinguishes between three types of skills: methodological, technological, and soft skills, which complement the knowledge base and enable the practical implementation of competencies.

Taken together, these four dimensions provide a multi-layered perspective that reflects both the breadth and the depth of the data science profession. They highlight not only the technical capabilities required for tasks such as analytics and engineering, but also the methodological and organizational competencies necessary to manage projects and integrate results into business or scientific workflows. By explicitly combining knowledge, skills, and attitudes, the CF-DS represents a comprehensive reference model for data science education and workforce development. At the same time, its flexibility allows for adaptation to evolving technological and professional requirements, making it a living framework that can accommodate emerging fields such as Generative AI.

2.3 The Role of Generative AI

Since ChatGPT was released to the general public in 2022, applications incorporating elements of GenAI have become widespread. GenAI is credited with the potential not only to trigger an evolution in learning and working, but also to unleash disruptive forces, particularly in computer science education, as well as in many other areas of computer science [55]. As a result, an increasing number of papers are focusing on the competencies required to develop and, in particular, to utilize GenAI systems (so-called *AI literacy*) [57,76,120]. However, GenAI is now used not only in business software development, but also albeit not universally in university programming courses. [91].

Particularly in university teaching, GenAI is utilized in various ways, promoting different competencies among students. That means that GenAI systems are often not used as simple chatbots, but rather complex tutor systems are developed to support students better. For example, Pădrean et al. [92] describe a system that promotes novices in acquiring computational thinking in combination with programming, while Osorio et al. [94] discuss support options for students in database courses.

However, Daniel et al. [23] point out that various prerequisites must be met for successful use in higher education and that interaction with students must be structured constructively so that they see these tools as an enrichment rather than a threat. These include approaches that guide students in using GenAI to discover and reflect on stereotypes and bias [7], that investigate how GenAI can be used to promote collaboration among students [63], and that consider where support from GenAI is helpful [90].

These competencies must not only be promoted among students, but they are also needed in professional contexts. As a result, there are now a large number of software engineering courses at universities that prepare students for working with GenAI in professional software development [75,78], because, as Martini [77] has also noted, the rise of GenAI has dramatically changed the software development process and the competencies required for working with data.

The consideration of GenAI and the handling of data also raises various questions regarding the *ethical use* of multiple systems and GenAI. However, in the field of data science in particular, the focus is primarily on privacy and data protection as well as copyright and intellectual property rights [1,49,60].

However, universities also implement other approaches that consider moral theories, dilemmas, and similar issues, in addition to privacy [10], or integrate ethical considerations into software development processes [16].

To combine these concepts and to comprehensively prepare students for professional life and the ethical issues that arise from it, Kiesler et al. [62] recommend that such competencies should be implemented in curricula, especially in data science degree programs, to create a basis for competent and ethical handling in later professional life.

2.4 Curricula and Competence Frameworks in Data Science

Over the past decade, the field of data science has been accompanied by the emergence of numerous competence frameworks that aim to guide the design of educational programs and training initiatives [13,24,87,93,95,97,113]. These frameworks are part of a rapidly evolving research landscape, in which institutions, professional associations, and international organizations are actively engaged in shaping the skill sets required for the profession. Following the introduction of the EDISON Data Science Framework (EDSF) as a landmark initiative of the European Commission, a variety of additional frameworks have been developed. Notable contributions include reports from the National Academies of Sciences, Engineering, and Medicine [80], articles in the *Harvard Data Science Review* [43], and guidelines from the United Nations Global Working Group on Big Data [110]. A particularly influential reference point is the Association for Computing Machinery (ACM) Data Science Curriculum [24], which provides a detailed treatment of the discipline. Unlike the ACM Computer Science Curriculum [20], the ACM's data science curriculum is dedicated exclusively to data science and deliberately omits the broader scope of computer science as a whole.

Comparative studies have sought to evaluate the consistency and coverage of these different approaches. For example, Schmitt et al. [100] examined the CF-DS alongside five alternative competence frameworks. Their analysis included not only framework-level comparisons but also evaluations of several introductory data science courses. The study revealed substantial variation in how competencies are prioritized and taught, underscoring differences in both emphasis and depth across institutions. While the authors provided valuable insights into the diversity of existing approaches, they did not propose a revised or unified framework for addressing these issues. Furthermore, their work did not address the sequencing of competencies, leaving open the vital question of how learning content should be logically structured and built up over time.

Other research has focused more directly on course content and curricular practices. Urs and Minhaj [111], for instance, analyzed a wide range of data science programs to identify the topics most frequently taught. Their analysis clustered course titles into thematic groups and measured their prevalence across programs. Results showed that certain subjects, such as machine learning and database systems, were nearly universal, whereas others, including software development or domain-specific applications, appeared much less often. By mapping these topics to the knowledge areas defined in the ACM Computer Science Curricula of 2013 [108], the authors highlighted both pervasive and missing elements in the educational landscape. This work confirmed that significant disparities exist across institutions, reflecting diverse interpretations of which competencies are most essential for data science education.

Taken together, these studies point to an ongoing fragmentation of the competence landscape. Institutions and organizations continue to define and teach data science in markedly different ways, leading to a lack of alignment not only in academic curricula but also in how competencies are communicated to the labor market, for example, through job advertisements [106]. The absence of a harmonized framework thus remains a significant obstacle to building a consistent professional identity for data scientists.

This fragmentation has become even more pronounced with the rapid rise of large language models (LLMs) and Generative AI (GenAI), which have begun to reshape both academic practice and industry applications. Traditional frameworks often fail to capture the technical, ethical, and organizational skills required to work responsibly with these new technologies. Recent contributions attempt to address this gap by developing competence models tailored to GenAI. Annapureddy et al. [6], for instance, proposed twelve core competencies for GenAI literacy, ranging from foundational knowledge and prompt engineering to programming and ethical awareness. Their work provides a roadmap for integrating GenAI-related skills into formal education and policy.

Other initiatives have moved from theoretical definitions to applied training. Burneo-Arteaga et al. [18] introduced a capability-based framework comprising sixteen competencies distributed across pedagogical, technical, and ethical domains. This structure guided the design of training environments that encourage humanAI collaboration in teaching. Building on this, Elshall and Badir [39] proposed the FACT assessment model, which balances AI-assisted learning with traditional evaluation methods, thereby fostering critical thinking and reducing risks of overreliance on automated systems.

Academic institutions have also started to examine GenAI trends more broadly. Întorsureanu et al. [59] conducted bibliometric and sentiment analyses to track the growing optimism and diversification of GenAI applications in education, identifying roles such as AI tutors, co-teachers, and tools for personalized learning. Complementing this, Ayyoub et al. [8] investigated faculty readiness for GenAI adoption. Their findings underscored the importance of professional development, prior experience, and supportive communities in building AI literacy among educators.

Overall, the literature highlights both the opportunities and challenges of integrating GenAI competencies into data science curricula. While new frameworks and training strategies are emerging, they have yet to converge into a common standard. This highlights the pressing need for competence models that integrate traditional data science skills with the novel demands of GenAI, providing guidance not only for educators and students but also for institutions and policymakers tasked with preparing the future workforce.

3 Methodology

The methodological approach of this study combines elements of systematic literature review and qualitative content analysis. This design was chosen to ensure both breadth and depth: the systematic review enabled a comprehensive mapping of the existing competence frameworks, while the content analysis allowed for detailed coding and integration of competencies into a revised structure.

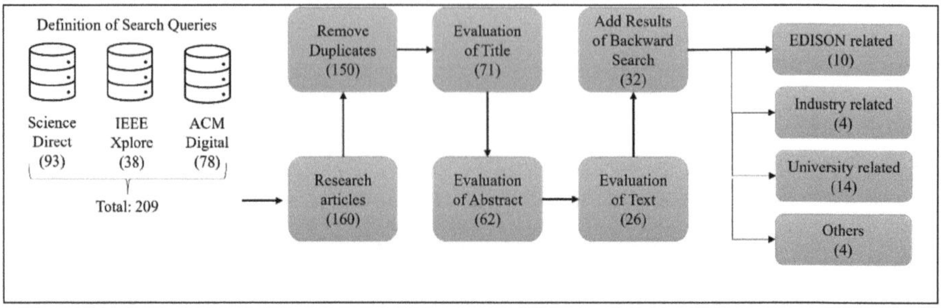

Fig. 1. Literature Review Process [88].

3.1 Literature Review of Competence Frameworks

The present literature review was conducted in accordance with the guidelines established by Webster and Watson [115] and was undertaken in two major scientific databases: the ACM Digital Library and IEEE Xplore. An initial search yielded 209 potentially relevant records, of which 160 were journal articles and the remainder conference proceedings, reports, or white papers. Following the elimination of duplicate entries, a total of 71 unique documents were obtained. The selection process involved the application of inclusion criteria, with particular emphasis on the alignment with competence development in data science, the clarity of the framework description, and the presence of curricular elements (Table 1).

Conducting this screening, 62 documents were selected for full-text examination. Following a thorough evaluation, 32 publications were deemed to have fulfilled all the necessary criteria and were thus chosen for inclusion in the final analysis. Of these, 10 were directly connected to the EDISON project, 4 presented industry-oriented competence models, 14 addressed university programs, and 4 fell into other categories. This distribution provided a balanced overview of academic, industrial, and institutional perspectives on data science education and competence development (see Fig. 1; Table 5).

3.2 Quality Appraisal

Following the literature review process, the identified publications were subjected to a structured quality appraisal to ensure the integrity and reliability of the evidence base. This step followed the critical appraisal framework outlined by Kitchenham [66] and applied predefined checklists adapted from Nidhra et al. [82]. Each publication was assessed against four key questions:

1. Does the topical domain of the research paper align with the objectives of this study?
2. Has a complete competence framework or curriculum been developed?
3. Does the study address a formal education or further training program for data scientists?

Table 1. Findings of Keyword Terms [88].

Database	Keyword	Total Results	Articles	Relevant
ACM	Data Science Curriculum	61	38	20
	Data Science Framework	15	15	13
	Data Science Competency	2	2	2
Total	ACM	78	55	35
IEEE Xplore	Data Science Curriculum	10	9	6
	Data Science Framework	25	25	16
	Data Science Competency	3	3	2
Total	IEEE Xplore	38	37	24
Science Direct	Data Science Curriculum	13	10	5
	Data Science Framework	69	48	4
	Data Science Competency	11	10	3
Total	Science Direct	93	68	12
Total		**209**	**160**	**71**

4. Are the reported results relevant to the research objectives of this analysis?

Responses were scored according to their degree of compliance with the criteria: papers meeting a criterion received a weight of 1, those partially fulfilling it received a weight of 0.5, and those failing to meet it were assigned a weight of 0. The total score determined the quality classification of each study. Publications with a score above 4 were considered *high quality*, those between 1 and 3 were classified as *medium quality*, and those scoring below 1 were rated as *low quality*.

Based on this appraisal, 12 publications were classified as high-quality and 21 as medium-quality. These studies formed the empirical foundation for the subsequent qualitative content analysis. By applying this systematic appraisal, the study ensured that only methodologically sound and contextually relevant contributions informed the construction of the extended competence framework.

3.3 Qualitative Content Analysis

In the next step, twelve research papers (summarized in Appendix, Table 6) were examined using a structured qualitative content analysis, following the approach outlined by Kuckartz [68]. The purpose of this analysis was to identify both commonalities and differences across the selected publications and to systematically map them into a coherent competence framework. Since the frameworks and curricula presented in the literature used heterogeneous formats, ranging from narrative descriptions to structured tables, a consistent coding strategy was required to harmonize the information.

The coding was carried out in several stages. First, a deductive coding frame was developed on the basis of the EDISON Competence Framework for Data

Science (CF-DS), which was chosen because it was the most frequently cited model in the reviewed literature and has been continuously updated since its introduction [58]. Using the CF-DS categories as anchors, relevant text passages were assigned to competence groups, individual competencies, and descriptions. These descriptions included statements about specific skills, required knowledge, or contextual information about how competencies are applied.

In the second stage, inductive coding was applied to capture aspects not sufficiently represented in the CF-DS. This process led to the introduction of new categories, including *Application Development*, *Business Analytics*, *Theoretical Foundations*, and *Soft Skills*, along with further subcategories and sub-subcategories as necessary. The iterative integration of deductive and inductive coding ensured that both established competence areas and emerging themes were systematically represented.

Finally, all codes were consolidated into a refined coding scheme. To ensure methodological rigor, two authors independently coded the documents, and discrepancies were resolved in discussion with a third author. The overall level of agreement between coders was high; in cases of divergence, the final assignment was made based on a majority consensus. An illustration of the coding scheme, including the example of the *DSAD Application Development* category, is presented in Table 2.

This multi-stage coding process provided a robust foundation for synthesizing a consolidated competence framework. By combining deductive alignment with the CF-DS and inductive incorporation of new categories, the analysis not only validated the relevance of existing competence groups but also expanded them to reflect dimensions that had previously been underrepresented in the literature.

Table 2. Final coding scheme for category "Application Development" [88].

Competence Group (Category)	Competence (Sub-category)	Description (Sub-sub-category)
DSAD - Application Development	DSAD01 - Programming	Programming skills, Development issues
	DSAD02 - Libraries and tools	Programming libraries & tools, Development environment
	DSAD03 - Software Engineering	Software Engineering principles
	DSAD04 - Development pipelines	Version control, Development pipelines (automation)

3.4 Literature Review of Generative AI Competencies

This review follows the PRISMA 2020 guidelines for systematic reviews [85] to identify competencies relevant to the development and application of large language models (LLMs) within the context of data science education. A systematic search was conducted, using two scholarly databases: ACM Digital Library and IEEE Xplore. The following queries were used:

1. "Data Science" AND ("Generative AI" OR "Gen AI"),
2. "Data Science" AND ("Curriculum" OR "Curricula" OR "Competency" OR "Education" OR "Teaching" OR "Skill") AND ("Large Language Models" OR "LLM" OR "Generative AI").

In the ACM Digital Library, results were filtered to include only research articles, with no restrictions applied to publication date in either database.

Articles were included if they explicitly addressed competencies relevant to the development or application of LLMs, or if such competencies could reasonably be inferred from the content. No formal exclusion criteria were defined. The selection process was conducted in two stages. First, titles and abstracts were screened for relevance. Second, potentially relevant full texts were assessed based on the inclusion criteria. All screening and selection steps were carried out manually by a single reviewer, without the use of automation or AI-based assistance.

From the 786 initial records (677 from ACM and 109 from IEEE), 207 duplicates were removed, leaving 579 unique entries. After title and abstract screening, 492 were excluded. Of the remaining 87 full-text articles, 30 met the inclusion criteria and were selected for retention. An additional 14 records were identified through other sources, with 2 of them included in the final dataset. A PRISMA flow diagram illustrating the screening process is shown in Fig. 2.

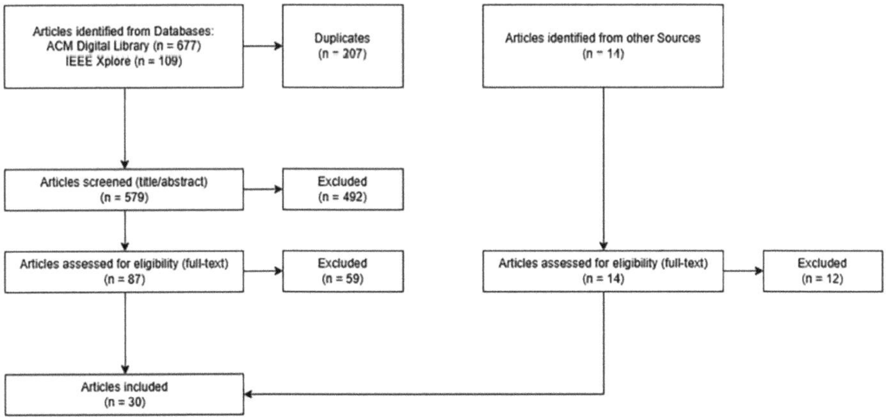

Fig. 2. PRISMA Flow Diagram.

Competence extraction was performed manually, based on inductive analysis of the full texts. Relevant competence statements were identified, merged if thematically overlapping, and then grouped into broader thematic categories. This resulted in the identification of 41 distinct competencies, grouped into seven competence areas:

1. Technical Foundations of AI and LLMs
2. Prompt Engineering and Interaction
3. Evaluation, Validation, and Critical Assessment
4. Integration and Application of LLMs
5. Ethical, Responsible, and Legal AI Use
6. Data Management and Model Training
7. Explainability and Transparency

Each competency was further mapped to the number of articles that referenced it. The most frequently mentioned competencies were *Prompt Engineering* (18 articles), *Validation and Evaluation of Generated Content* (14 articles), and *LLM Capabilities and Limitations* (7 articles). These figures emphasize the central role of prompt formulation and critical assessment of outputs in working with generative models.

To evaluate which areas are most emphasized in the current literature, article frequencies were aggregated at the competence group level (see Table 3).

The most commonly addressed groups were: Prompt Engineering and Interaction (20 mentions), Evaluation, Validation, and Critical Assessment (17 mentions), Technical Foundations of AI and LLMs (13 mentions). This suggests a strong focus on applied interaction techniques and fundamental understanding as essential skill areas for LLM-related education and development. The complete list of identified competencies, along with their group assignments and supporting sources, is presented in Table 7 (Appendix).

Table 3. Article Counts by Extracted Competence Group.

Competence Group	Articles
Technical Foundations of AI and LLMs	13
Prompt Engineering and Interaction	20
Evaluation, Validation, and Critical Assessment	17
Integration and Application of LLMs	7
Ethical, Responsible, and Legal AI Use	10
Data Management and Model Training	8
Explainability and Transparency	2

The identified competencies reflect a comprehensive spectrum of knowledge, skills, and judgment necessary to develop, apply, and critically assess LLMs within data science contexts. Each competence group represents a key capability domain. The first group, *Technical Foundations of AI and LLMs*, emphasizes conceptual understanding of model architectures, capabilities, and limitations, forming the theoretical basis for responsible application. The second group, *Prompt Engineering and Interaction*, encompasses core operational skills for instructing and guiding LLMs effectively, including prompt formulation, problem decomposition, and goal refinement. The third group, *Evaluation, Validation, and Critical Assessment*, captures competencies essential for assessing generated outputs, ensuring quality, and engaging critically with the technology.

The fourth group, *Integration and Application of LLMs*, addresses the embedding of GenAI tools into workflows and projects, highlighting interdisciplinary coordination, tool selection, and domain adaptation. Group five, *Ethical, Responsible, and Legal AI Use*, focuses on the responsible governance of GenAI systems—covering topics such as fairness, transparency, regulatory compliance, and academic integrity. The sixth group, *Data Management and Model Training*, outlines competencies needed to collect, curate, and govern large-scale datasets, manage model biases, and ensure effective training and alignment. Finally, *Explainability and Transparency* addresses the need to make generative systems more interpretable and accountable, particularly in regulated or high-stakes environments. Together, these competencies provide a structured foundation for curriculum development, professional training, and capability assessment in LLM-enabled data science.

4 Findings

4.1 Descriptive Results

Table 6 in Appendix presents the competence frameworks identified through a structured literature review and analysis. The reviewed documents span from 2017 to 2022, with at least one new framework or version released each year. This consistent output underlines the ongoing relevance of developing a framework that remains up-to-date and adaptable to various domains. A majority of the studies (66%) originate from academic contexts, although several also address practical applications. For instance, the EDISON CF-DS framework was validated by expert panels involving stakeholders from both academia and industry. Additionally, practice-oriented works such as the study by Hattingh et al. [53] aim to define industry-relevant skill sets. Thus, the selection of sources strikes a balance between theoretical and practical perspectives. Most of the contributions are grounded in qualitative methodologies, particularly literature reviews, with only one notable exception relying on empirical data collection [47].

4.2 Framework Analysis and Modification

Following the coding procedure outlined in the methodology section, 12 documents were analyzed, resulting in the identification of 8 overarching competence groups. These groups comprise 46 unique competencies, which in turn cover 269 individual elements, including knowledge areas, methodological and technological capabilities, as well as soft skills. The resulting structure forms a key component of the proposed extension to the EDISON CF-DS framework. Of the original five competence groups in EDISON, four were retained. Notably, three of these groups are based on the data scientist definition developed by NIST [83].

- **Data Analytics (DSDA):** Involves selecting and applying suitable statistical and analytical techniques to extract insights, identify patterns, and support data-driven decisions.
- **Data Engineering (DSENG):** Focuses on utilizing engineering methods and modern computing tools to build data analytics solutions, including the development of systems, tools, and infrastructure for managing data across its lifecycle.
- **Data Management and Governance (DSDM):** Encompasses defining and executing strategies for the organized handling of data—covering collection, storage, maintenance, and accessibility to enable further analysis.
- **Research Methods and Project Management (DSRMP):** Entails generating new insights or knowledge by employing scientific and engineering approaches, often aligned with achieving specific research or organizational objectives.

The fifth competence group in the original EDISON CF-DS, *Domain-specific knowledge and expertise*, was revised to reflect the increased focus on practical application introduced through the inclusion of industry-oriented literature. Accordingly, this group was renamed **Business Analytics (DSBA)**.

During the comparative analysis, it became evident that additional groups were necessary to organize all identified competencies in a logical manner. Notably, the original EDISON CF-DS omits personal competencies, which are explicitly included in several other sources [13,44,53,95]. Similarly, competencies related to software engineering and application development [53], theoretical foundations such as mathematics, algorithms, data structures, computational principles, and complexity theory [13,24,44,53,95], as well as personal and interpersonal skills including communication, leadership, and problem-solving [13,24,53,87,113], required the introduction of three new competence groups:

- **Application Development (DSAD):** Focuses on designing and implementing software systems using appropriate technologies and programming languages, including the development of deployment pipelines.
- **Theoretical Fundamentals (DSTF):** Covers foundational theoretical knowledge necessary for applying data science techniques effectively.
- **Personal competencies:** Encompasses key personal and social attributes essential for effective performance in data science roles.

These additions result in a comprehensive set of eight competence groups:

- *Data Analytics (DSDA)*,
- *Data Engineering (DSENG)*,
- *Data Management and Governance (DSDM)*,
- *Research Methods and Project Management (DSRMP)*,

- *Business Analytics (DSBA)*,
- *Application Development (DSAD)*,
- *Theoretical Fundamentals (DSTF)*, and
- *Personal competencies.*

In the next step, the EDISON CF-DS was adapted to align with this extended structure. New competencies were introduced, such as *Business and Organization* or *Information Needs* within the Business Analytics group, and existing ones were reassigned to more suitable categories. Where needed, competencies were also broken down into subcomponents to improve clarity and usability[1].

The structure and logic behind the modified framework are illustrated in Fig. 3 using the DSAD group as an example.

Competence group	Elements (literature synthesis)				Competence	Framework Comparison (literature analysis)												Total	
	Knowledge	Skill-Method	Skill-Technology	Skill-Personal		EDSF	Park City (De Veaux et al.)	IADSS (Fayyad & Hamutcu)	Wu	ACM (Danyluk & Leidig)	APEC (Pompa et al.)	National Academies	Suryan & Gupta	Hassan et al	Fekete et al.	Rosenthal & Chung	Hattingh et al.		%
Application Development					DSAD01 - Programming														
	KDSAD01	SDSAD03	DSDALANG06 DSDALANG09 DSDEV01		Programming	x	x	x	x	x	x	x	x	x	x	x	x	12	100
	KDSAD08	SDSDM15 SDSAD09	x		Development issues	x	x	x	x	x		x						6	50
					DSAD02 - Libraries and tools														
	x	SDSAD04	DSDEV02 DSDEV08		Programming libraries & tools	x	x		x	x		x		x	x	x		8	67
	x	SDSAD08	DSDEV03		Development environment	x		x		x		x				x		5	42
					DSAD03 - Software Engineering														
	KDSAD03 KDSAD05 KDSAD07 KDSTF04	SDSAD01 SDSAD06	DSDEV07		Software Engineering principles	x		x	x	x	x		x	x			x	8	67
					DSAD04 - Development pipelines (DevOps)														0
	KDSAD02	SDSAD05	DSDEV04		Version control	x	x			x		x			x			5	42
	KDSAD04	SDSAD07	DSDEV05		Development pipelines (automation)	x			x			x			x			4	33

Fig. 3. Framework modification and comparison for *DSAD - Application Development* [88].

The Application Development competence group includes the following core competencies: *Programming*, *Libraries and Tools*, *Software Engineering*, and *Development Pipelines*. Consistent with the structuring principles of the e-Competence Framework [42], each competence is assigned a unique identifier, represented here by acronyms. For example, the competence *DSAD01 - Programming* is further broken down into two subcomponents: *Programming* and *Development issues* (Fig. 3). The individual elements derived from the literature synthesis reflect the standard definition of a competence, comprising both knowledge and skill components. Skills are further categorized into methodological, technological, and personal types, although only the first two are assigned acronyms for consistency[2].

The *Application Development (DSAD)* competence group includes four defined competencies. Among them, Programming stands out as universally recognized, appearing with identical naming in all frameworks reviewed (100% agreement), underscoring its relevance across both academic and industry contexts. In contrast, *Development pipelines* were less frequently referenced. The *Data Science Analytics (DSDA)* group, consisting of five competencies with

[1] A detailed overview of the current version of the revised framework and the literature comparison is available under https://e.feu.de/dscompoverview.

[2] The current version of the full catalogue of these elements and their corresponding identifiers is available under https://e.feu.de/dscompcatalogue.

detailed subcategories, also shows strong consistency. Four key areas, *Machine Learning Fundamentals*, *Visualize Results*, *Basic Data Analytics*, and *Statistics*, were identified in every document analyzed. More specialized topics such as *Outlier Identification* [24] or *Descriptive Data Analysis* [30] were mentioned only once.

Within *Data Science Engineering*, seven competencies were identified, many with up to six associated subgroups. Significant overlap was observed in *Data Collection* (75%) and *Data Preparation* (92%) under the *DSENG02* competence. Similarly, *Relational and Non-relational Databases* appeared in 75% of the sources. Overall, the main competence groups show strong coverage in the literature, with agreement rates reaching up to 100%.

By contrast, the groups *Data Management, Research Methods, Project Management*, and *Business Analytics* appeared less frequently. *Data Management* encompasses six competencies, each with up to six subgroups. *Data Management Policy* was cited in nine documents, while other subgroups show less frequent mentions, ranging from 8% to 67%. More detailed elements such as *Identify Data Sources* [24] or *Data Interoperability* [30] were each found in only one source. *Data Quality* was discussed in seven documents (58%).

The *Research Methods and Project Management* group shows its highest agreement in *Research Methods* (58%), *Data Life Cycle* (58%) and *Project Management* (67%). The redefined *Business Analytics (DSBA)* group contains the largest number of competencies, eight in total, but with relatively low overlap across documents 8% to 42%. For instance, *DSBA02 (Fuzzy Concepts)* and *DSBA04 (Process Optimization)* were only mentioned by Demchenko et al. [30] and, in the case of process optimization, by Hassan et al. [13]. Broader topics like *Business Analytics* and *Business Intelligence*, *Domain Knowledge* and (agile) *Decision Making* were more common, each appearing in 42% of sources.

The *Theoretical Fundamentals (DSTF)* group primarily consists of knowledge-
oriented competencies: *Algorithms & Data structures (DSTF01)*, *Mathematics (DSTF02)*, *Computational Fundamentals (DSTF03)* and *Complexity Theory (DSTF04)*. Strong overlap was found especially in *DSTF01* (92%) and *DSTF02* (83%).

Lastly, the *Personal competencies* group was not subdivided using the structure outlined in Table 2. It includes competencies such as *Personal Improvement, Communication, Collaboration, Leadership, Problem Solving*, and *Ethical Thinking*, all categorized as personal skills. Most of these were identified in at least eight of the reviewed documents.

4.3 Web Application

The modified competence framework is designed for broad use and has been tailored to accommodate the diverse needs of various target audiences. As a first step, the framework has been made available for evaluation through a web application[3]. The platform offers a user-friendly, detailed, and accessible presentation format, enabling stakeholders from both academia and industry to engage with the content effectively. Users can explore the framework through three distinct viewing modes, each tailored to support different perspectives and use cases.

1. Competence List: Displays competencies in a tabular format, offering a concise overview. Each table focuses on a specific competence group and lists all related competencies. A filtering option allows users to view either all groups or a selected subset.
2. Competence Grid: Visualizes competence groups as colored tiles. Selecting a group reveals the corresponding competencies, which appear as tiles in the next layer. Further selection opens a detailed view of the chosen competence, including descriptive information along with the associated knowledge and skills.
3. Competence Graph: Illustrates the relationships and dependencies among competencies using a visual network layout, enabling users to explore interconnections more intuitively.

One objective of the proposed modification to the framework is to provide a logical and efficient sequence for acquiring the identified competencies. Some competencies are logically interdependent, suggesting that an efficient sequence could enhance the learning process. These findings could be integrated into the curriculum development process to reduce the workload for both academic institutions during the development phase and for students when gaining the skills [54]. For instance, it is advised that a data scientist initially gain proficiency in programming before delving into the intricacies of specific programming libraries. In the absence of any sequences in the examined frameworks, the authors have formulated an initial proposal based on direct dependencies. A prerequisite for the correctness of the dependencies was that they could be represented in an acyclic graph. It is possible to apply analysis methods without prior experience in collecting and processing data, provided that a corresponding data set is already available. In contrast, it is not possible to use programming libraries without knowledge of the underlying programming language. The arrangement of the competencies according to the defined sequence can be found in the **Competence Graph**[4].

5 Validation

To ensure the future applicability of the modified competence framework in light of rapidly evolving GenAI technologies, we conducted a comparative analysis between the 41 GenAI-specific competencies (see Table 7) and the existing framework structure. While several foundational elements, such as software

[3] Link to current version: https://www.fernuni-hagen.de/static/competence_landscape/.

[4] Link to current version: https://www.fernuni-hagen.de/static/competence_landscape/graph.

development, data management, or theoretical fundamentals, remain relevant, the comparison revealed substantial conceptual gaps in three core areas: prompt-based interaction, AI evaluation and transparency, and legal and ethical challenges related to generative models.

In response, three additional competence groups are proposed to address these emerging requirements:

1. **LLM Interaction and Prompt Engineering:** This group encompasses competencies that reflect the shift from traditional programming paradigms to prompt-based interaction with LLMs. Skills such as prompt engineering, contextualization, goal articulation, and problem decomposition are essential for effectively guiding LLM behavior in applied settings. These competencies are largely absent from existing frameworks and cannot be subsumed under traditional programming or communication skills, necessitating a dedicated category.
2. **Evaluation and Validation of Generative AI:** The second group includes critical assessment skills such as benchmarking LLMs, validating AI-generated content, reviewing code, and ensuring transparency in AI decision-making. With generative models often exhibiting unpredictable behavior (e.g., hallucinations, biased outputs), the ability to critically evaluate outputs and underlying systems becomes essential for responsible deployment. This group encompasses a set of evaluation-oriented competencies that transcend technical, methodological, and ethical boundaries and are not adequately addressed in the original EDISON categories.
3. **AI Ethics, Risk, and Compliance**: This competence group addresses the increasing legal and ethical complexity of GenAI applications. It includes competencies such as responsible AI use, risk management, legal compliance, data privacy, and academic integrity. Unlike the Personal Competencies group, which focuses on soft skills such as leadership and communication, this new category targets domain-specific knowledge of regulatory frameworks and ethical principles. It reflects the need for structured competence development in areas such as AI governance, societal impact assessment, and regulatory alignment, which are essential for the adoption of trustworthy AI.

Together, these three additions ensure that the extended competence framework remains compatible with current and future demands of GenAI development and use. They fill essential gaps that neither the existing technical nor the personal and managerial groups sufficiently address. Their integration supports both curriculum development and team capability assessment in data science projects involving LLMs and other GenAI systems.

6 Discussion and Limitations

Comparing different competence frameworks reveals some limitations that arise from several aspects. On the one hand, the frameworks have different objectives, such as Suryan's focus on the skills of a data scientist in industry [106] versus

Rosenthal's focus on the university education of a data scientist [95]. In addition, the length of the individual research articles varies considerably, leading to differences in the scope and depth of detail of the competence descriptions, as in the case of EDISON CF-DS (176 pages) compared to Rosenthal's Data Science Major (6 pages). Table 4 shows the comparison of the different data sources.

Table 4. Document comparison on finding frequencies [88].

	EDSF	Park City	IADSS	Wu	ACM	APEC	National A.	Suryan	Hassan	Fekete	Rosenthal	Hattingh
Total	118	48	40	56	87	31	72	32	38	46	40	38
in %	87	36	30	41	64	23	53	24	28	34	30	28

A total of 135 possible competence subgroups were recorded. The EDISON CF-DS (87%) and the ACM (64%) achieved the most findings. The fact that EDISON was used as the basis for coding the documents may also explain the high degree of overlap. Concise frameworks typically address broad topics, such as statistics, while expansive frameworks delve into specific topics with greater detail, like decision trees. Additionally, many frameworks use literature analyses or qualitative content analyses as research methods. There is a lack of comprehensive, practical research, such as case studies or quantitative surveys, that examines the core elements of practice.

The discourse can be particularly focused on in the context of new technologies and the flexibility of skills frameworks. The literature examined does not explicitly utilize certain key technologies, such as GenAI or LLMs. In various areas with an industry focus, such as business process management, GenAI can be used to support automated routine tasks or the discovery of process innovations [12]. The question, therefore, also arises as to how this technology can be used in data science projects [46,123] and, associated with this, which competencies are required for the various roles in such a project. For example, the gap between modeling experts and domain users could be closed [123].

To investigate this further, an additional literature review was conducted using the PRISMA 2020 protocol [85], focusing on competencies related to the use and development of large language models in data science education. This resulted in 41 specific GenAI-related competencies grouped into seven overarching competence areas. The most frequently mentioned competencies included *Prompt Engineering*, *Validation and Evaluation of Generated Content*, and *LLM Capabilities and Limitations*, highlighting a shift toward applied interaction, critical assessment, and foundational model understanding as central to future data science skillsets.

These findings reveal a significant limitation in the current frameworks: they are not yet equipped to reflect the requirements introduced by GenAI technologies. Many of the GenAI-related competencies cannot be clearly mapped to existing groups in the modified EDISON framework. Therefore, three additional competence groups were proposed to close this gap:

- **GenAI Interaction and Prompt Engineering:** Capturing competencies related to effective LLM use, interaction design, and task formulation.
- **GenAI Evaluation and Governance:** Including critical assessment, validation, benchmarking, and ethical-legal considerations.
- **GenAI Integration and Model Operations:** Covering model deployment, resource cost awareness, bias mitigation, and model alignment.

The need to introduce new groups instead of mapping the findings to existing ones underscores the inflexibility of traditional frameworks when facing emerging technologies. Without mechanisms for continuous updating, existing frameworks risk becoming obsolete in fast-evolving fields such as AI. This also highlights the necessity of developing modular and adaptable frameworks that can dynamically integrate new domains, such as GenAI.

As a consequence, there is a broader limitation in the current landscape: rather than updating or evolving established frameworks, new frameworks are frequently created from scratch, resulting in fragmentation and a lack of standardization. This hampers their applicability in education and practice. The expanded framework presented here offers a snapshot of current requirements and serves as a baseline for further discourse. However, ongoing feedback from practice and education is essential to maintain its relevance.

As an initial evaluation approach, two expert interviews were conducted with data scientists in practice, and a group discussion was held with three university lecturers. In summary, both the expert interviews and the group discussion highlighted the relevance of a standardized data science competence framework. There was general agreement on the content of the framework, and no significant gaps in the listed competencies were identified. Respondents from both sides gave positive feedback on the overlap with current educational programs and the daily work of a data scientist. Future iterations of the framework should, however, explicitly incorporate GenAI-related skillsets to ensure alignment with ongoing technological shifts.

7 Conclusion

This paper extends the integrated framework from previous work [88] by incorporating competencies reflecting the disruptive influence of GenAI and LLMs. This development lays the groundwork for a standardized framework that promotes adaptability.

The framework was expanded with three new competence groups that address prompt engineering, LLM-specific evaluation, and AI governance. These additions were aligned with existing areas to ensure continuity while addressing emerging gaps. These groups were derived from a systematic review of GenAI-related competencies. This review revealed that, while traditional frameworks remain relevant, they are insufficient for guiding data science practice under GenAI-enabled conditions.

The inadequacy of existing structures emphasizes the need for competencies that evolve in tandem with technological progress. This need is met by competence groups that operationalize interaction, evaluation, and governance in GenAI contexts. Operationalizing these competencies enables curriculum developers to define learning outcomes that reflect current demands. These outcomes provide instructors with guidance for balancing technical proficiency with ethical reflection. Teaching programs designed around these outcomes prepare graduates for roles that are well-suited to GenAI-enabled workflows. These roles allow organizations to plan their workforce more effectively in response to emerging technologies. The organizational alignment resulting from such planning reduces uncertainty when defining project roles and clarifies how competencies interact with automation frameworks.

The reference point also establishes a basis for empirical validation through case studies. These studies are necessary to confirm the practical value of the new competence groups and refine their integration into curricula and professional practice. Once competencies are validated, further research directions will emerge, examining their interaction with automation frameworks, their role in decision-support systems, and their contribution to lifelong learning strategies for professionals who must continuously adapt to evolving technologies.

APPENDIX

Table 5. Findings from Keyword (K) and Backward (B) Search; Categories from the (E)DISON Project, (I)ndustry-relevant competencies, (U)niversity Programs, and (O)ther Categories [88]

Title	Year	Cat.	Type
Model Curricula for Data Science EDISON Data Science [116]	2017	E	K
Customisable Data Science Educational Environment: From competencies Management and Curriculum Design to Virtual Labs On-Demand [32]	2017	E	K
Data Science Model Curriculum Implementation for Various Types of Big Data Infrastructure Courses [117]	2019	E	K
EDISON Data Science Framework (EDSF) Extension to Address Transversal Skills Required by Emerging Industry 4.0 Transformation [36]	2019	E	K
Designing Customisable Data Science Curriculum Using Ontology for Data Science competencies and Body of Knowledge [33]	2019	E	K
Big Data Platforms and Tools for Data Analytics in the Data Science Engineering Curriculum [31]	2019	E	K
EDISON Data Science Competence Framework (CF-DS, Release 4) [30]	2022	E	K
EDISON Data Science Framework (EDSF): Addressing Demand for Data Science and Analytics competencies for the Data Driven Digital Economy [34]	2021	E	K
Data Scientist Professional Revisited: competencies Definition and Assessment, Curriculum and Education Path Design [35]	2021	E	K
Data science in the business environment: Insight management for an Executive MBA [73]	2022	E	K
A Practical and Sustainable Model for Learning and Teaching Data Science [93]	2016	U	K
Systematic Study of Big Data Science and Analytics Programs [119]	2017	U	B
Curriculum Guidelines for Undergraduate Programs in Data Science [113]	2017	U	B
Data Science for Undergraduates Opportunities and Options [80]	2018	U	B
A Functional Approach to Data Science in CS1 [22]	2018	U	K
A Data Science Major: Building Skills and Confidence [95]	2020	U	K
Creating a Balanced Data Science Program [2]	2020	U	K
A CDIO Oriented Curriculum for Division of Data Science and Big Data Technologies: The Content, Process of Derivation, and Levels of Proficiency [122]	2020	U	K
Data Science Curriculum Design: A Case Study [13]	2021	U	K
Developing an Interdisciplinary Data Science Program [97]	2021	U	K
A Data-centric Computing Curriculum for a Data Science Major [44]	2021	U	K
Exploring potential roles of academic libraries in undergraduate data science education curriculum development [101]	2021	U	K
Computing Competencies for Undergraduate Data Science Curricula [47]	2021	U	B
Rankings vs Realities Exploring Competency Differences in Graduate Data Science Programs [72]	2023	U	K
Data Science and Analytics Skills Shortage: Equipping the APEC Workforce with the Competencies Demanded by Employers [87]	2017	I	B
Data Science Competency in Organisations: A Systematic Review and Unified Model [53]	2019	I	K
Toward Foundations for Data Science and Analytics: A Knowledge Framework for Professional Standards [43]	2020	I	B
Investigating Academia-Industry Gap for Data Science Jobs and Curriculum [106]	2021	I	K
Teaching Computational Modeling in the Data Science Era [48]	2016	O	K
Cloud Computing Curriculum: Developing Exemplar Modules for General Course Inclusion [2]	2020	O	K
Establishing ABET Accreditation Criteria for Data Science [14]	2021	O	K
Integrated Data Science for Secondary Schools: Design and Assessment Course Inclusion [99]	2022	O	K
			Total: 32

Table 6. Identified Frameworks for Qualitative Content Analysis [88]

ID	Title	Research Method	Data
1	EDISON Data Science Competence Framework (CF-DS) [29]	Content analysis	Six existing frameworks;evaluated by expert groups (academia & industry)
2	Curriculum Guidelines for Undergraduate Programs in data science [113]	Literature analysis	NSF Workshop on Data Science Education, guidelines for undergraduate majors in Mathematics, Statistics and Computer Science
3	Data Science and Analytics Skills Shortage [87]	Literature review; Project DARE (Data Analytics Raising Employment)	Academic literature, research and technical papers, government reports, working papers, industry publications and surveys
4	Systematic Study of Big Data Science and Analytics Programs [119]	Literature review	DSA programs in the U.S.
5	National Academies of Sciences, Engineering, and Medicine [80]	Content analysis	Information-gathering activities and community conversations
6	Data Science Competency in Organisations: A Systematic Review and Unified Model [53]	literature review	Literature on essential data science workforce competencies
7	Toward Foundations for Data Science and Analytics: A Knowledge Framework for Professional Standards [43]	Literature review	Literature on analytics and data science skills
8	Computing Competencies for Undergraduate Data Science Curricula (ACM) [24]	2 Surveys for Academia and Industry	Results of the surveys
9	Investigating Academia-Industry Gap for Data Science Jobs and Curriculum [106]	Literature review	28 curricula from Indian and Internat. institutions
10	A Data Science Major: Building Skills and Confidence [95]	Following Jolly et al.'s trilogy	Based on data science guidelines such as EDISON, ACM, BHEF, NIST
11	Data Science Curriculum Design: A Case Study Bile [13]	Literature review	122 Data Science degrees in the U.S.
12	A Data-centric Computing Curriculum for a Data Science Major [44]	Standardized structure of majors (University of Sydney)	ACM guideline

Table 7. Identified Competencies for GenAI.

No.	Competence Group	Competence	Description	Source
No.	Competence Group	Competence	Description	Source
Continued on next page				
1	Technical Foundations of AI and LLMs	Foundational Understanding of LLMs	Understanding how LLMs operate, including their features, benefits, and how they process and use information in generative AI applications.	[9, 11, 21, 65, 81, 89]
		Understanding Generative AI Model Types	Knowledge of different generative AI models, such as GANs and transformers, and the principles behind machine learning and neural networks.	[86, 98]
		LLM Capabilities and Limitations	Awareness of what LLMs can and cannot do, including risks like hallucinations.	[4, 9, 65, 103, 105, 118, 121]
		Confidence in Using Generative AI	Confidence in using generative AI tools effectively, including overcoming uncertainty and leveraging their strengths.	[98]
2	Prompt Engineering and Interaction	Generating, Modifying and Transforming Content using Generative AI	Ability to generate, adapt, or transform content across formats using generative AI tools while considering their strengths and limitations.	[98]
		Natural Language Programming	Using natural language to describe desired functionality for programming tasks and communicating with LLMs.	[45, 81]
		Requirement Articulation	Clearly expressing input/output expectations to guide LLMs toward user-specific goals.	[74]
		Prompt Engineering	The ability to design and structure prompts to improve LLM responses. Includes techniques like providing examples and refining prompts to ensure performance and reliability for specific tasks.	[3, 4, 9, 21, 37, 45, 56, 61, 65, 71, 74, 86, 89, 91, 102, 105, 107, 118]
		Contextualization	Crafting prompts by specifying relevant context, constraints, or desired styles. Providing sufficient detail and explicit cues helps generative AI produce more accurate, relevant, and styled output.	[86]
		Problem Decomposition	Breaking complex tasks into smaller steps to improve clarity and effectiveness of prompts. Helps LLMs generate more precise and manageable responses.	[91, 102, 107]
		Goal Definition and Refinement	Defining unclear initial goals and refining them for use with LLMs. Supports clearer task guidance and improves generative output alignment with user intent.	[86, 89, 105, 107]
3	Evaluation, Validation, and Critical Assessment	Evaluating Generative AI Use	Ability to assess whether generative AI is suitable for a task, how much to use it, and where it may improve efficiency, accuracy, or productivity over traditional methods.	[91]
		Critical Interaction with AI	Engaging critically with generative AI by questioning assumptions, limitations, and output quality. Helps mitigate risks and ensures transparency and accountability in use.	[4, 21, 89, 98, 105]
		Validating and Evaluating Generated Content	Assessing the quality, accuracy, and reliability of generated content. Requires cross-checking outputs, identifying hallucinations, and ensuring human review for critical use cases.	[3, 4, 37, 51, 71, 81, 89, 91, 98, 105, 107, 114, 118, 121]
		Code Review and Interpretation	Ability to read, understand, and debug LLM-generated code. Emphasizes evaluating functionality and improving reliability over simply writing code from scratch.	[102]
		LLM Benchmarking	Skill in testing and comparing LLMs using established benchmarks to evaluate task-specific or domain-specific performance.	[3]
		Referencing Generated Content	TUnderstanding when and how to cite AI-generated material. Important for transparency in academic and professional settings.	[98]

(*continued*)

Table 7. (*continued*)

No.	Competence Group	Competence	Description	Source
4	Integration and Application of LLMs	Tool Selection	Ability to choose suitable generative AI tools for a task by understanding model types, evaluating capabilities, and aligning them with specific content or application needs.	[98, 105]
		Project Orchestration	Managing tasks and coordinating multiple generative AI tools in a project. Involves planning, defining goals, and organizing project phases effectively.	[86]
		Application of Domain Knowledge in LLMs	Using specialized domain knowledge to guide or fine-tune LLMs for domain-specific tasks. Helps narrow the problem space and improves relevance of outputs.	[3]
		Integration of LLMs in Software Systems and Workflows	Embedding LLMs into broader systems and workflows. Requires understanding how LLMs interact with different process stages.	[9, 65, 107]
		Integrating LLMs with Software Engineering Practices	Merging LLMs with existing software engineering methods to create scalable and robust solutions for general or domain-specific applications.	[3]
5	AI Ethics, Risk, and Compliance	Understanding LLM Efficiency and Resource Costs	Awareness of LLMs' computational demands, energy use, and ecological impact. Includes recognizing sustainability challenges related to AI infrastructure.	[3, 21]
		LLM Security Awareness	Understanding security risks in AI-generated content and implementing safeguards against vulnerabilities in LLM use and development.	[3, 21, 65]
		Data Privacy Risks from Large Training Datasets	Understanding legal and ethical risks of using sensitive data in training sets due to potential misuse or lack of clarity in data handling.	[21, 65]
		Assessing Generative AI Implications (Social, Ethical, Privacy)	Evaluating ethical, legal, and societal impacts of LLM use in contexts lacking regulation or clear standards.	[98]
		Ethical and Responsible Use of AI	Applying responsible AI practices regarding bias, transparency, legality, and societal outcomes. Focuses on aligning with ethical principles.	[3, 21, 28, 65]
		Copyright Laws	Recognizing copyright risks in training and generating AI content, including ownership and authorship issues.	[3, 65]
		Compliance in Regulated Domains	Interpreting legal frameworks in regulated sectors (e.g., finance) and aligning AI systems with these regulatory requirements.	[11, 105]
		Compliance with AI Laws and Regulations	Ensuring compliance with laws governing AI, such as data protection, IP, and algorithmic decision-making.	[21, 40, 65, 98]
		Academic Integrity	Understanding ethical risks of using LLMs in academia, such as plagiarism and misrepresentation of AI-generated work.	[121]
		AI Risk Management	Identifying and mitigating risks of generative AI, including bias, misinformation, security, and compliance concerns.	[9, 40, 65]
6	Data Management and Model Training	Natural Language Processing	Understanding and processing natural language data, a core requirement for working with LLMs.	[64]
		Data Acquisition	Gathering diverse, large-scale datasets for training LLMs, while respecting licensing and quality standards.	[5]
		Synthetic Data Generation	Creating artificial datasets for model training when real-world data is limited, while monitoring for bias.	[5]
		Data Management and Data Curation	Ensuring LLM training data is high-quality, unbiased, and relevant through careful collection and cleaning.	[3]
		Identifying and Addressing Bias in LLMs	Detecting and mitigating biases in LLM training and output to reduce discriminatory or skewed behavior.	[65, 69, 89, 118, 121]
		Defining and Enforcing Data Governance Processes	Establishing policies for ethical, legal, and secure data usage across the LLM development life cycle.	[5]
		Model Alignment	Training LLMs to behave according to specific values and goals by curating aligned training examples.	[5]
7	Explainability and Transparency	Explainable Generative AI	Making LLM decisions transparent and understandable through techniques that reveal system behavior.	[3]
		Justification Generation	Enabling LLMs to generate legal and logical explanations that support their outputs and decisions.	[11]

References

1. Abdrabou, Y., Özdel, S., Maquiling, V., Bozkir, E., Kasneci, E.: From gaze to data: privacy and societal challenges of using eye-tracking data to inform genai models. In: Proceedings of the 2025 Symposium on Eye Tracking Research and Applications. ETRA '25. Association for Computing Machinery, New York, NY, USA (2025). https://doi.org/10.1145/3715669.3726788
2. Adams, J.C., Zhang, J., Sherriff, M., Heckman, S., Cutter, P.: Creating a balanced data science program. In: Monge, A. (ed.) Proceedings of the 51st ACM Technical Symposium on Computer Science Education, pp. 185–191. ACM, New York, NY, USA (2020). https://doi.org/10.1145/3328778.3366800
3. Ahmed, I., et al.: Artificial intelligence for software engineering: the journey so far and the road ahead. ACM Trans. Softw. Eng. Methodol. **34**(5) (2025). https://doi.org/10.1145/3719006
4. AlOmar, E.A.: Nurturing code quality: leveraging static analysis and large language models for software quality in education. ACM Trans. Comput. Educ. **25**(2) (2025). https://doi.org/10.1145/3722229
5. Alvarado Garcia, A., Candello, H., Badillo-Urquiola, K., Wong-Villacres, M.: Emerging data practices: data work in the era of large language models. In: Proceedings of the 2025 CHI Conference on Human Factors in Computing Systems. CHI '25. Association for Computing Machinery, New York, NY, USA (2025). https://doi.org/10.1145/3706598.3714069
6. Annapureddy, R., Fornaroli, A., Gatica-Perez, D.: Generative AI literacy: twelve defining competencies. Digit. Gov.: Res. Pract. **6**(1), 1–21 (2025). https://doi.org/10.1145/3685680, http://arxiv.org/pdf/2412.12107
7. Apiola, M., Vartiainen, H., Tedre, M.: First year cs students exploring and identifying biases and social injustices in text-to-image generative AI. In: Proceedings of the 2024 on Innovation and Technology in Computer Science Education V. 1. ITiCSE 2024, pp. 485–491. Association for Computing Machinery, New York, NY, USA (2024). https://doi.org/10.1145/3649217.3653596
8. Ayyoub, A.M., et al.: Advancing higher education with genAI: factors influencing educator AI literacy. Front. Educ. **10**, 1530721 (2025). https://doi.org/10.3389/feduc.2025.1530721, https://www.frontiersin.org/journals/education/articles/10.3389/feduc.2025.1530721/full
9. Bakharia, A., Abdi, S.: Shaping programming and data science education: insights from genAI technical book trends. In: 2024 IEEE International Conference on Advanced Learning Technologies (ICALT), pp. 116–120 (2024). https://doi.org/10.1109/ICALT61570.2024.00040
10. Barfield, V., Wallace, C.: Refinement or disruption: patterns of critical inquiry in computing ethics assignments. In: Proceedings of the 30th ACM Conference on Innovation and Technology in Computer Science Education V. 1. ITiCSE 2025, pp. 590–596. Association for Computing Machinery, New York, NY, USA (2025). https://doi.org/10.1145/3724363.3729099
11. Bertrand, A., Eagan, J.R., Maxwell, W., Brand, J.: AI is entering regulated territory: understanding the supervisors' perspective for model justifiability in financial crime detection. In: Proceedings of the 2024 CHI Conference on Human Factors in Computing Systems. CHI '24. Association for Computing Machinery, New York, NY, USA (2024). https://doi.org/10.1145/3613904.3642326
12. Beverungen, D., Buijs, J., Becker, J., et al.: Seven paradoxes of business process management in a hyper-connected world. Bus. Inf. Syst. Eng. **63**, 145–156 (2021). https://doi.org/10.1007/s12599-020-00646-z

13. Bile Hassan, I., et al.: Data science curriculum design: a case study. In: Sheard, J. (ed.) Proceedings of the 52nd ACM Technical Symposium on Computer Science Education, pp. 529–534. ACM, New York, NY, USA (2021). https://doi.org/10.1145/3408877.3432443
14. Blair, J.R.S., et al.: Establishing abet accreditation criteria for data science. In: Sheard, J. (ed.) Proceedings of the 52nd ACM Technical Symposium on Computer Science Education, pp. 535–540. ACM, New York, NY, USA (2021). https://doi.org/10.1145/3408877.3432445
15. Boritz, E.C.C.: Competency-based education and assessment for the accounting profession: a critical review. Acc. Perspect. **2**(1), 7–42 (2003). https://doi.org/10.1506/5K7C-YT1H-0G32-90K0
16. Brooks, A.: Agile ethics: a low stakes, skills-based framework for teaching cs ethics. In: Proceedings of the 2024 on Innovation and Technology in Computer Science Education V. 1. ITiCSE 2024, pp. 492–498. Association for Computing Machinery, New York, NY, USA (2024). https://doi.org/10.1145/3649217.3653539
17. Bruno, A., Bates, I., Brock, T., Anderson, C.: Towards a global competency framework. Am. J. Pharm. Educ. **74**(3) (2010). https://doi.org/10.5688/aj740356
18. Burneo-Arteaga, P., Lira, Y., Murzi, H., Balula, A., Costa, A.P.: Capability-based training framework for generative AI in higher education. Front. Educ. **10**, 1594199 (2025). https://doi.org/10.3389/feduc.2025.1594199, https://www.frontiersin.org/journals/education/articles/10.3389/feduc.2025.1594199/full
19. Chen, H.M., Chang, W.Y.: The essence of the competence concept: adopting an organization's sustained competitive advantage viewpoint. J. Manag. Organ. **16**(05), 677–699 (2010). https://doi.org/10.1017/S1833367200001802
20. Clear, A., Parrish, A.: Computing Curricula 2020 - Paradigms for Global Computing Education. Association for Computing Machinery (2020)
21. Clear, T., et al.: AI integration in the it professional workplace: a scoping review and interview study with implications for education and professional competencies. In: 2024 Working Group Reports on Innovation and Technology in Computer Science Education. ITiCSE 2024, pp. 34–67. Association for Computing Machinery, New York, NY, USA (2025). https://doi.org/10.1145/3689187.3709607
22. Albright, D., Klinge, S., Rebelsky, T.H., S.A.: A functional approach to data science in cs1. In: Barnes, T., Garcia, D., Hawthorne, E.K., Pérez-Quiñones, M.A. (eds.) Proceedings of the 49th ACM Technical Symposium on Computer Science Education, pp. 1035–1040. ACM, New York, NY, USA (2018). https://doi.org/10.1145/3159450.3159550
23. Daniel, S., et al.: Engineering assessment in the age of generative artificial intelligence: a critical analysis. In: 2024 World Engineering Education Forum - Global Engineering Deans Council (WEEF-GEDC), pp. 1–6 (2024). https://doi.org/10.1109/WEEF-GEDC63419.2024.10854936
24. Danyluk, A., Leidig, P.: Computing competencies for undergraduate data science curricula (2021)
25. Davenport, T.H., Patril, D.J.: Data scientist: the sexiest job of the 21st century. Harv. Bus. Rep. (2012). https://hbr.org/2012/10/data-scientist-the-sexiest-job-of-the-21st-century
26. Davenport, T.H., Patril, D.J.: Is data scientist still the sexiest job of the 21st century? Harv. Bus. Rep. (2022). https://hbr.org/2022/07/is-data-scientist-still-the-sexiest-job-of-the-21st-century
27. Davis, R., Turner, E., Hicks, D., Tipson, M.: Developing an integrated career and competency framework for diabetes nursing. J. Clin. Nurs. **17**(2), 168–174 (2008). https://doi.org/10.1111/j.1365-2702.2007.01964.x

28. Deb, D., et al.: Enhancing university curricula with integrated AI ethics education: a comprehensive approach. In: Proceedings of the 56th ACM Technical Symposium on Computer Science Education V. 1. SIGCSETS 2025, pp. 248–254. Association for Computing Machinery, New York, NY, USA (2025). https://doi.org/10.1145/3641554.3701953
29. Demchenko, Y., Belloum, A.: Data Science Body of Knowledge (DS-BoK). EDISON Community Initiative (2022)
30. Demchenko, Y., Belloum, A.: Data Science Competence Framework (CF-DS, Release 4). EDISON Community Initiative (2022)
31. Demchenko, Y.: Big data platforms and tools for data analytics in the data science engineering curriculum. In: Proceedings of the 2019 3rd International Conference on Cloud and Big Data Computing, pp. 60–64. ACM, New York, NY, USA (2019). https://doi.org/10.1145/3358505.3358512
32. Demchenko, Y., Belloum, A., de Laat, C., Loomis, C., Wiktorski, T., Spekschoor, E.: Customisable data science educational environment: from competences management and curriculum design to virtual labs on-demand. In: 2017 IEEE International Conference on Cloud Computing Technology and Science (CloudCom), pp. 363–368. IEEE (2017). https://doi.org/10.1109/CloudCom.2017.59
33. Demchenko, Y., Comminiello, L., Reali, G.: Designing customisable data science curriculum using ontology for data science competences and body of knowledge. In: Proceedings of the 2019 International Conference on Big Data and Education, pp. 124–128. ACM, New York, NY, USA (2019). https://doi.org/10.1145/3322134.3322143
34. Demchenko, Y., José, C.G.J.: Edison data science framework (EDSF): addressing demand for data science and analytics competences for the data driven digital economy. In: IEEE Global Engineering Education Conference (EDUCON), pp. 1682–1687. IEEE (2021)
35. Demchenko, Y., Maijer, M., Comminiello, L.: Data scientist professional revisited: competences definition and assessment, curriculum and education path design. In: 2021 4th International Conference on Big Data and Education, pp. 52–62. ACM, New York, NY, USA (2021). https://doi.org/10.1145/3451400.3451409
36. Demchenko, Y., Wiktorski, T., Cuadrado Gallego, J., Brewer, S.: Edison data science framework (EDSF) extension to address transversal skills required by emerging industry 4.0 transformation. In: 2019 15th International Conference on eScience (eScience), pp. 553–559. IEEE (2019). https://doi.org/10.1109/eScience.2019.00076
37. Drosos, I., Sarkar, A., Xu, X., Negreanu, C., Rintel, S., Tankelevitch, L.: "it's like a rubber duck that talks back": understanding generative ai-assisted data analysis workflows through a participatory prompting study. In: Proceedings of the 3rd Annual Meeting of the Symposium on Human-Computer Interaction for Work. CHIWORK '24. Association for Computing Machinery, New York, NY, USA (2024). https://doi.org/10.1145/3663384.3663389
38. EDISON Initiative: Edison project (2023). https://edison-project.eu/edison/edison-project/
39. Elshall, A.S., Badir, A.: Balancing AI-assisted learning and traditional assessment: the fact assessment in environmental data science education. Front. Educ. **10**, 1596462 (2025). https://doi.org/10.3389/feduc.2025.1596462, https://www.frontiersin.org/journals/education/articles/10.3389/feduc.2025.1596462/full
40. Esposito, M., Tse, T.: Mitigating the risks of generative ai in government through algorithmic governance. In: Proceedings of the 25th Annual International Confer-

ence on Digital Government Research. dg.o '24, pp. 605–609. Association for Computing Machinery, New York, NY, USA (2024). https://doi.org/10.1145/3657054.3657124
41. Commission, E.: Education for data intensive science to open new science frontiers (2017). https://doi.org/10.3030/675419, https://cordis.europa.eu/project/id/675419
42. European Committee for Standardization: European e-Competence Framework (2014)
43. Fayyad, U., Hamutcu, H.: Toward foundations for data science and analytics: a knowledge framework for professional standards. Harv. Data Sci. Rev. **2**(2) (2020)
44. Fekete, A., Kay, J., Röhm, U.: A data-centric computing curriculum for a data science major. In: Sherriff, M., Merkle, L.D., Cutter, P., Monge, A., Sheard, J. (eds.) Proceedings of the 52nd ACM Technical Symposium on Computer Science Education, pp. 865–871. ACM, New York, NY, USA (2021). https://doi.org/10.1145/3408877.3432457
45. Feng, L., Yen, R., You, Y., Fan, M., Zhao, J., Lu, Z.: Coprompt: supporting prompt sharing and referring in collaborative natural language programming. In: Proceedings of the 2024 CHI Conference on Human Factors in Computing Systems. CHI '24, Association for Computing Machinery, New York, NY, USA (2024). https://doi.org/10.1145/3613904.3642212
46. Feuerriegel, S., Hartmann, J., Janiesch, C., Zschech, P.: Generative AI. Bus. Inf. Syst. Eng. **66**, 1–16 (2023). https://doi.org/10.1007/s12599-023-00834-7
47. Force, A.D.S.T.: Computing competencies for undergraduate data science curricula. ACM (2021). https://doi.org/10.1145/3453538
48. Giabbanelli, P.J., Mago, V.K.: Teaching computational modeling in the data science era. Procedia Comput. Sci. **80**, 1968–1977 (2016). https://doi.org/10.1016/j.procs.2016.05.517
49. Ginde, G.: "so what if i used genai?" - Legal implications of using cloud-based genAI in software engineering research. In: 2025 IEEE/ACM Second International Conference on AI Foundation Models and Software Engineering (Forge), pp. 241–245 (2025). https://doi.org/10.1109/Forge66646.2025.00034
50. Grenčíková, A., Habánik, J., Španková, J., Húzevka, M., Šrámka, M.: Current labour market challenges in the light of future economic and demographic developments. Eur. J. Interdisc. Stud. **14**(1) (2022)
51. Gu, K., Shang, R., Althoff, T., Wang, C., Drucker, S.M.: How do analysts understand and verify AI-assisted data analyses? In: Proceedings of the 2024 CHI Conference on Human Factors in Computing Systems. CHI '24. Association for Computing Machinery, New York, NY, USA (2024). https://doi.org/10.1145/3613904.3642497
52. Haertel, C., Holtkemper, M., Staegemann, D., Beecks, C., Turowski, K.: Unveiling data science team roles and competencies: a literature-based analysis (2025)
53. Hattingh, M., Marshall, L., Holmner, M., Naidoo, R.: Data science competency in organisations. In: de Villiers, C., Smuts, H. (eds.) Proceedings of the South African Institute of Computer Scientists and Information Technologists 2019, pp. 1–8. ACM, New York, NY, USA (2019). https://doi.org/10.1145/3351108.3351110
54. Hazzan, O., Mike, K.: Guide to Teaching Data Science - An Interdisciplinary Approach. Springer, Cham (2023). https://doi.org/10.1007/978-3-031-24758-3
55. Hazzan, O., Erez, Y.: Rethinking computer science education in the age of genAI. ACM Trans. Comput. Educ. **25**(3) (2025). https://doi.org/10.1145/3732792, https://doi.org/10.1145/3732792

56. Ho, K.H., Georgiades, M., Fan, T.K.J., Hou, Y., Fong, K.C.K., Chan, T.T.: Work in progress: unlocking code generation through synergistic prompt engineering. In: 2025 IEEE Engineering Education World Conference (EDUNINE), pp. 1–4 (2025). https://doi.org/10.1109/EDUNINE62377.2025.10980842
57. Hornberger, M., Bewersdorff, A., Nerdel, C.: What do university students know about artificial intelligence? Development and validation of an AI literacy test. Comput. Educ.: Artif. Intell. **5**, 100165 (2023). https://doi.org/10.1016/j.caeai.2023.100165, https://www.sciencedirect.com/science/article/pii/S2666920X23000449
58. IEEE (ed.): IEEE Global Engineering Education Conference (EDUCON) (2021)
59. Întorsureanu, I., Oprea, S.V., Bâra, A., Vespan, D.: Generative AI in education: perspectives through an academic lens. Electronics **14**(5), 1053 (2025). https://doi.org/10.3390/electronics14051053
60. Islam, M.R.: Ethical DecisionMaking in GenAI Cybersecurity, pp. 225–254. Wiley, IEEE (2025). https://doi.org/10.1002/9781394279326.ch9
61. Kazemitabaar, M., et al.: Improving steering and verification in AI-assisted data analysis with interactive task decomposition. In: Proceedings of the 37th Annual ACM Symposium on User Interface Software and Technology. UIST '24. Association for Computing Machinery, New York, NY, USA (2024). https://doi.org/10.1145/3654777.3676345
62. Kiesler, N., Opel, S., Thorbrügge, C.: With great power comes great responsibility - integrating data ethics into computing education. In: Proceedings of the 2024 on Innovation and Technology in Computer Science Education V. 1. ITiCSE 2024, pp. 471–477. Association for Computing Machinery, New York, NY, USA (2024). https://doi.org/10.1145/3649217.3653637
63. Kiesler, N., Smith, J., Leinonen, J., Fox, A., MacNeil, S., Ihantola, P.: The role of generative AI in software student collaboraition. In: Proceedings of the 30th ACM Conference on Innovation and Technology in Computer Science Education V. 1. ITiCSE 2025, pp. 72–78. Association for Computing Machinery, New York, NY, USA (2025). https://doi.org/10.1145/3724363.3729040
64. Kim, J.: On transdisciplinary research through data science and engineering education. In: Proceedings of the 2024 16th International Conference on Education Technology and Computers. ICETC '24, pp. 523–528. Association for Computing Machinery, New York, NY, USA (2025). https://doi.org/10.1145/3702163.3702465
65. Kirova, V.D., Ku, C.S., Laracy, J.R., Marlowe, T.J.: Software engineering education must adapt and evolve for an LLM environment. In: Proceedings of the 55th ACM Technical Symposium on Computer Science Education V. 1. SIGCSE 2024, pp. 666–672. Association for Computing Machinery, New York, NY, USA (2024). https://doi.org/10.1145/3626252.3630927
66. Kitchenham, B.: Procedures for performing systematic reviews (2004). https://citeseerx.ist.psu.edu/document?repid=rep1&type=pdf&doi=29890a936639862f45cb9a987dd599dce9759bf5
67. Kuckartz, U.: Qualitative Inhaltsanalyse: Methoden, Praxis. Computerunterstützung. Beltz Juventa, Weinheim and Basel (2012)
68. Kuckartz, U., Rädiker, S.: Qualitative Inhaltsanalyse. Methoden, Praxis, Computerunterstützung: Grundlagentexte Methoden. Grundlagentexte Methoden, Beltz Juventa, Weinheim and Basel, 5. auflage edn. (2022). http://www.content-select.com/index.php?id=bib_view&ean=9783779955337

69. Kumar, A., Devi, M.L., Saltz, J.S.: GenAI tools to improve data science project outcomes. In: 2024 IEEE International Conference on Big Data (BigData), pp. 3143–3152 (2024). https://doi.org/10.1109/BigData62323.2024.10825326
70. Lambert, B., Plank, R.E., Reid, D.A., Fleming, D.: A competency model for entry level business-to-business services salespeople. Serv. Mark. Q. **35**(1), 84–103 (2014). https://doi.org/10.1080/15332969.2014.856737
71. Leung, J., Shen, Z.: Prompt engineering for curriculum design. In: 2024 4th International Conference on Educational Technology (ICET), pp. 97–101 (2024). https://doi.org/10.1109/ICET62460.2024.10869091
72. Li, D., Milonas, E., Zhang, Q.: Rankings vs realities: exploring competency differences in graduate data science programs. In: 2023 IEEE Frontiers in Education Conference (FIE), pp. 1–4. IEEE (2023). https://doi.org/10.1109/FIE58773.2023.10343290
73. Lu, J.: Data science in the business environment: insight management for an executive MBA. Int. J. Manag. Educ. **20**(1), 100588 (2022). https://doi.org/10.1016/j.ijme.2021.100588
74. Ma, Q., Peng, W., Yang, C., Shen, H., Koedinger, K., Wu, T.: What should we engineer in prompts? Training humans in requirement-driven LLM use. ACM Trans. Comput.-Hum. Interact. (2025). https://doi.org/10.1145/3731756, just Accepted
75. MacNeil, S., et al.: Fostering responsible AI use through negative expertise: a contextualized autocompletion quiz. In: Proceedings of the 30th ACM Conference on Innovation and Technology in Computer Science Education V. 1. ITiCSE 2025, pp. 326–332. Association for Computing Machinery, New York, NY, USA (2025). https://doi.org/10.1145/3724363.3729067
76. Mannila, L., et al.: Developing an AI concept inventory for non-experts. In: Proceedings of the 30th ACM Conference on Innovation and Technology in Computer Science Education V. 2. ITiCSE 2025, pp. 705–706. Association for Computing Machinery, New York, NY, USA (2025). https://doi.org/10.1145/3724389.3731283
77. Martini, S.: Teaching programming in the age of generative AI. In: Proceedings of the 2024 on Innovation and Technology in Computer Science Education V. 1. ITiCSE 2024, pp. 1–2. Association for Computing Machinery, New York, NY, USA (2024). https://doi.org/10.1145/3649217.3653527
78. Mejia, D., Holmes, E.D., Marroquin, J., Gorson Benario, J.: Bridging academia and industry: Leveraging generative AI in a software engineering course for practical industry experiences. In: Proceedings of the 30th ACM Conference on Innovation and Technology in Computer Science Education V. 1. ITiCSE 2025, pp. 507–513. Association for Computing Machinery, New York, NY, USA (2025). https://doi.org/10.1145/3724363.3729036
79. Mills, J.A., Middleton, J.W., Schafer, A., Fitzpatrick, S., Short, S., Cieza, A.: Proposing a re-conceptualisation of competency framework terminology for health: a scoping review. Hum. Resour. Health **18**(1), 15 (2020). https://doi.org/10.1186/s12960-019-0443-8
80. Engineering, and Medicine: Data science for undergraduates: opportunities and options. National Academies of Sciences. National Academies Press (2018)
81. Nguyen, S., Babe, H.M., Zi, Y., Guha, A., Anderson, C.J., Feldman, M.Q.: How beginning programmers and code LLMs (mis)read each other. In: Proceedings of the 2024 CHI Conference on Human Factors in Computing Systems. CHI '24. Association for Computing Machinery, New York, NY, USA (2024). https://doi.org/10.1145/3613904.3642706

82. Nidhra, S., Yanamadala, M., Afzal, W., Torkar, R.: Knowledge transfer challenges and mitigation strategies in global software development–a systematic literature review and industrial validation. Int. J. Inf. Manag. **33**(2), 333–355 (2013). https://doi.org/10.1016/j.ijinfomgt.2012.11.004
83. NIST Big Data Public Working Group: Definitions. Taxonomies Subgroup: NIST big data interoperability framework (2019). https://doi.org/10.6028/NIST.SP.1500-1r2
84. Olusegun, J.: The role of continuous learning and development in sustaining employee competence and high performance (2024)
85. Page, M.J., et al.: The PRISMA 2020 statement: an updated guideline for reporting systematic reviews. BMJ **372** (2021)
86. Palani, S., Ramos, G.: Evolving roles and workflows of creative practitioners in the age of generative AI. In: Proceedings of the 16th Conference on Creativity and Cognition. C&C '24, pp. 170–184. Association for Computing Machinery, New York, NY, USA (2024). https://doi.org/10.1145/3635636.3656190
87. Pompa, C., Burke, T.: Data science and analytics skills shortage: equipping the APEC workforce with the competencies demanded by employers (2017)
88. Potanin, M., Holtkemper, M., Golz, T., Beecks, C.: Towards a standardized data science competence framework: a literature review approach. In: Proceedings of the 17th International Conference on Computer Supported Education (CSEDU 2025), vol. 2, pp. 569–581 (2025). https://doi.org/10.5220/0013364200003932
89. Prabhudesai, S., Kasi, A.P., Mansingh, A., Das Antar, A., Shen, H., Banovic, N.: "here the GPT made a choice, and every choice can be biased": How students critically engage with LLMs through end-user auditing activity. In: Proceedings of the 2025 CHI Conference on Human Factors in Computing Systems. CHI '25. Association for Computing Machinery, New York, NY, USA (2025). https://doi.org/10.1145/3706598.3713714
90. Prasad, P., Sane, A.: A self-regulated learning framework using generative AI and its application in CS educational intervention design. In: Proceedings of the 55th ACM Technical Symposium on Computer Science Education V. 1. SIGCSE 2024, pp. 1070–1076. Association for Computing Machinery, New York, NY, USA (2024). https://doi.org/10.1145/3626252.3630828
91. Prather, J., et al.: Beyond the hype: a comprehensive review of current trends in generative ai research, teaching practices, and tools. In: 2024 Working Group Reports on Innovation and Technology in Computer Science Education. ITiCSE 2024, pp. 300–338. Association for Computing Machinery, New York, NY, USA (2025). https://doi.org/10.1145/3689187.3709614
92. Pădurean, V.A., Denny, P., Gotovos, A., Singla, A.: Prompt programming: a platform for dialogue-based computational problem solving with generative AI models. In: Proceedings of the 30th ACM Conference on Innovation and Technology in Computer Science Education V. 1. ITiCSE 2025, pp. 458–464. Association for Computing Machinery, New York, NY, USA (2025). https://doi.org/10.1145/3724363.3729094
93. Ramamurthy, B.: A practical and sustainable model for learning and teaching data science. In: Alphonce, C., Tims, J., Caspersen, M., Edwards, S. (eds.) Proceedings of the 47th ACM Technical Symposium on Computing Science Education, pp. 169–174. ACM, New York, NY, USA (2016). https://doi.org/10.1145/2839509.2844603
94. Ramirez Osorio, V., Zavaleta Bernuy, A., Simion, B., Liut, M.: Understanding the impact of using generative ai tools in a database course. In: Proceedings

of the 56th ACM Technical Symposium on Computer Science Education V. 1. SIGCSETS 2025, pp. 959–965. Association for Computing Machinery, New York, NY, USA (2025). https://doi.org/10.1145/3641554.3701785
95. Rosenthal, S., Chung, T., Zhang, J., Sherriff, M., Heckman, S., Cutter, P.: A data science major. In: Monge, A. (ed.) Proceedings of the 51st ACM Technical Symposium on Computer Science Education, pp. 178–184. ACM, New York, NY, USA (2020). https://doi.org/10.1145/3328778.3366791
96. Rowe, C.J.: Clarifying the use of competence and competency models in recruitment, assessment and staff development. Ind. Commer. Train. **27**, 12–17 (1995)
97. Salloum, M., et al.: Developing an interdisciplinary data science program. In: Sheard, J. (ed.) Proceedings of the 52nd ACM Technical Symposium on Computer Science Education, pp. 509–515. ACM, New York, NY, USA (2021). https://doi.org/10.1145/3408877.3432454
98. Sattelmaier, L., Pawlowski, J.M.: Towards a generative artificial intelligence competence framework for schools. In: Proceedings of the International Conference on Enterprise and Industrial Systems (ICOEINS 2023), vol. 270, p. 291. Springer, Cham (2023). https://doi.org/10.2991/978-94-6463-340-5_26
99. Schanzer, E., et al.: Integrated data science for secondary schools. In: Dorn, B. (ed.) Proceedings of the 53rd ACM Technical Symposium on Computer Science Education, pp. 22–28. ACM, New York, NY, USA (2022). https://doi.org/10.1145/3478431.3499311
100. Schmitt, K.R.B., Clark, L., Kinnaird, K.M., Wertz, R.E.H., Sandstede, B.: Evaluation of Edison's data science competency framework through a comparative literature analysis. Found. Data Sci. **5**(2), 177–198 (2023). https://doi.org/10.3934/fods.2021031
101. Shao, G., Quintana, J.P., Zakharov, W., Purzer, S., Kim, E.: Exploring potential roles of academic libraries in undergraduate data science education curriculum development. J. Acad. Librariansh. **47**(2), 102320 (2021). https://doi.org/10.1016/j.acalib.2021.102320
102. Shen, Y., Ai, X., Soosai Raj, A.G., Leo John, R.J., Syamkumar, M.: Implications of ChatGPT for data science education. In: Proceedings of the 55th ACM Technical Symposium on Computer Science Education V. 1. SIGCSE 2024, pp. 1230–1236. Association for Computing Machinery, New York, NY, USA (2024).https://doi.org/10.1145/3626252.3630874
103. Shibani, A., Knight, S., Kitto, K., Karunanayake, A., Buckingham Shum, S.: Untangling critical interaction with AI in students' written assessment. In: Extended Abstracts of the CHI Conference on Human Factors in Computing Systems. CHI EA '24, Association for Computing Machinery, New York, NY, USA (2024). https://doi.org/10.1145/3613905.3651083
104. Shippmann, J., et al.: The practice of competency modeling. Person. Psychol. **53**, 703–740 (2000). https://doi.org/10.1111/j.1744-6570.2000.tb00220.x
105. Sun, Y., Jang, E., Ma, F., Wang, T.: Generative AI in the wild: prospects, challenges, and strategies. In: Proceedings of the 2024 CHI Conference on Human Factors in Computing Systems. CHI '24, Association for Computing Machinery, New York, NY, USA (2024). https://doi.org/10.1145/3613904.3642160
106. Suryan, K., Gupta, R.: Investigating academia-industry gap for data science jobs and curriculum. In: 2021 International Conference on Data Analytics for Business and Industry (ICDABI), pp. 453–458. IEEE (2021). https://doi.org/10.1109/ICDABI53623.2021.9655894

107. Tankelevitch, L., et al.: The metacognitive demands and opportunities of generative AI. In: Proceedings of the 2024 CHI Conference on Human Factors in Computing Systems. CHI '24. Association for Computing Machinery, New York, NY, USA (2024). https://doi.org/10.1145/3613904.3642902
108. The Joint Task Force on Computing Curricula: Computer science curricula 2013 - curriculum guidelines for undergraduate degree programs in computer science (2013)
109. Thistlethwaite, J.E., Forman, D., Matthews, L.R., Rogers, G.D., Steketee, C., Yassine, T.: Competencies and frameworks in interprofessional education: a comparative analysis. Acad. Med. **89**(6), 869–875 (2014). https://doi.org/10.1097/ACM.0000000000000249
110. UN Global Working Group: Competency framework for big data acquisition and processing (2020)
111. Urs, S.R., Minhaj, M.: Evolution of data science and its education in ischools: an impressionistic study using curriculum analysis. J. Am. Soc. Inf. Sci. (2023)
112. Vaast, E., Pinsonneault, A.: When digital technologies enable and threaten occupational identity: the delicate balancing act of data scientists. MIS Q. **45**(3), 1087–1112 (2021). https://doi.org/10.25300/MISQ/2021/16024
113. Veaux, R.D., et al.: Curriculum guidelines for undergraduate programs in data science. Annu. Rev. Stat. Appl. **4**(1), 15–30 (2017). https://doi.org/10.1146/annurev-statistics-060116-053930, http://arxiv.org/pdf/1801.06814v1
114. Waldo, J., Boussard, S.: GPTs and hallucination. Commun. ACM **68**(1), 40–45 (2024). https://doi.org/10.1145/3703757
115. Webster, J., Watson, R.: Analyzing the past to prepare for the future: writing a literature review. MIS Q. **26**(2) (2002)
116. Wiktorski, T., Demchenko, Y., Belloum, A.: Model curricula for data science Edison data science framework. In: 2017 IEEE International Conference on Cloud Computing Technology and Science (CloudCom), pp. 369–374. IEEE (2017). https://doi.org/10.1109/CloudCom.2017.60
117. Wiktorski, T., Demchenko, Y., Chertov, O.: Data science model curriculum implementation for various types of big data infrastructure courses. In: 15th International Conference on eScience (eScience), pp. 541–547. IEEE (2019). https://doi.org/10.1109/eScience.2019.00074
118. Wolfe, R., Mitra, T.: The impact and opportunities of generative AI in fact-checking. In: Proceedings of the 2024 ACM Conference on Fairness, Accountability, and Transparency. FAccT '24, pp. 1531–1543. Association for Computing Machinery, New York, NY, USA (2024). https://doi.org/10.1145/3630106.3658987
119. Wu, H.: Systematic study of big data science and analytics programs. In: 2017 ASEE Annual Conference and Exposition (2017)
120. Yim, I.H.Y.: A critical review of teaching and learning artificial intelligence (AI) literacy: developing an intelligence-based AI literacy framework for primary school education. Comput. Educ. Artif. Intell., 100319 (2024)
121. Zhou, K.Z., et al.: Ethics, governance, and user mental models for large language models in computing education. XRDS **31**(1), 46–51 (2024). https://doi.org/10.1145/3688089

122. Zhou, T., Jiang, D., Wang, F., Li, X., Zheng, L.: A cdio oriented curriculum for division of data science and big data technologies: the content, process of derivation, and levels of proficiency. In: 2020 8th International Conference on Digital Home (ICDH), pp. 172–177. IEEE (2020). https://doi.org/10.1109/ICDH51081.2020.00037
123. Zschech, P., Horn, R., Hoeschele, D., Janiesch, C., Heinrich, K.: Intelligent user assistance for automated data mining method selection. Bus. Inf. Syst. Eng. **62**, 227–247 (2020). https://doi.org/10.1007/s12599-020-00642-3

Author Index

C. Meinel et al. (Eds.): CSEDU 2025, CCIS 3148, pp. 481–482, 2027.
https://doi.org/10.1007/978-3-032-39103-2

MIX
Papier aus verantwortungsvollen Quellen
Paper from responsible sources
FSC® C105338
FSC
www.fsc.org

If you have any concerns about our products,
you can contact us on
ProductSafety@springernature.com

In case Publisher is established outside the EU,
the EU authorized representative is:
Springer Nature Customer Service Center GmbH
Europaplatz 3, 69115 Heidelberg, Germany

Printed by Libri Plureos GmbH
in Hamburg, Germany